MW00824715

"Why is there evil in the world? Scott Christensen shows that this difficult question is bound up with two larger questions: 'Why did God make the world?' and 'Why did God the Son become a man and suffer evil?' Scripture gives the ultimate answer: to manifest the glory of God. Christensen's articulate, inspiring, and gospel-driven presentation of the 'greater-glory' theodicy explores a significant way that God's Word addresses the problem of evil to strengthen our faith and evoke our worship."

—**Joel R. Beeke**, President, Puritan Reformed Theological Seminary, Grand Rapids, Michigan

"The problem of evil is the most important argument against the existence of God. It is said to be all the more difficult to answer when one adopts a Reformed/Calvinist view of human free will and divine providence, according to which God, in his sovereign decree, determines everything that comes to pass. Scott Christensen accepts the challenge and offers a Reformed *tour de force* in response to the multifaceted problem of evil. He argues that evil is not merely, as the French say, a *pétard mouillé* (a 'wet petard/firecracker'); rather, it is one that does explode, but backfires into glorifying God, in the biblical-theological grand narrative of creation, fall, and redemption. Christensen offers a response that is truly Reformed, not just because of his Calvinist view of free will (though it certainly has that), but because of its focus on the glory of God, the centrality of the person of Jesus, and the good news of redemption in Christ."

—**Guillaume Bignon**, author, *Excusing Sinners and Blaming God*; executive committee member, Association Axiome, a society of French-speaking Christian scholars

"This is the most Bible-saturated, 'logic-sensical,' and God-honoring answer to the so-called problem of evil in our generation. Gifted writer and thinker Scott Christensen has produced in *What about Evil?* an invaluable resource for both the inquisitive believer and the inquiring skeptic alike. I heartily recommend it to everyone wrestling with the reality of a good and sovereign God and the fact that evil still remains in this world."

—**Grant R. Castleberry,** Executive Director, Council on Biblical Manhood and Womanhood

"Scott Christensen's book *What about Evil?* deals with the 'problem of evil'—how can evil exist in a world created and ruled by a God who is sovereign and completely good? Many authors (including me) have taken up this challenge, but it remains a powerful objection to the truth of the Christian faith. Christensen gets beyond the more traditional approaches to the problem, by reminding us that God's wisdom pervades everything he ordains so that the very existence of evil serves his purpose of maximizing goodness and glorifying himself. Of course, Romans 8:28 and other verses *say* that this is true. But Christensen shows us *how* it is true, how even in this fallen world we can begin to grasp something of God's light in the midst of the darkness, indeed *especially* there. I commend this book to readers who seek a serious and thoughtful treatment of this issue."

—**John M. Frame,** Professor of Systematic Theology and Philosophy Emeritus, Reformed Theological Seminary, Orlando

"Scott Christensen delivers an unflinching, clear, and honest defense of the Reformed position on the problem of evil. The volume excels at integrating biblical theology with systematics and rightly situates theodicy in the history of redemption, a story that ultimately brings glory to the triune God. I recommend this project to students, pastors, and teachers who want to ponder this difficult problem anew. I suspect that I'll commend this volume for years to come."

—**Benjamin L. Gladd,** Associate Professor of New Testament, Reformed Theological Seminary, Jackson

"Scott Christensen's work on theodicy is well crafted and contributes to this important conversation in a significant and helpful way. Christensen's assertions are clear, tight, and accessible, reaching the intended audience with persuasive clarity. His appeal to the *felix culpa* argument as found in sixteenth- and seventeenth-century Reformed theology is both unusual and helpful as it grounds theodicy in the doctrine of God's eternal glory in Christ, rather than in a series of explanations or excuses that merely appeal to human desire to be satisfied intellectually or emotionally. Christensen's work is solidly argued and well researched; this book deserves a wide audience."

—**Grant Horner,** Professor of Renaissance and Reformation Studies, The Master's University

"Christians take the problem of evil more seriously than anyone else. This book avoids simplistic philosophical solutions. Instead, the author appreciates that the historical fact of Christ's incarnation, life, death, resurrection, and return provides the only hope when we just don't know all the answers."

—**Michael S. Horton,** J. Gresham Machen Professor of Systematic Theology and Apologetics, Westminster Seminary California

"This book covers a lot of ground as it discusses the perennial question, 'What about evil?' Cogent, clear, and convincing, Christensen's book will require some work to refute. There is a delicate balance between awareness of historical and present-day polemics, which will leave readers satisfied that they have a good idea of the issues at stake concerning a Reformed theodicy."

—**Mark Jones,** Senior Minister, Faith Vancouver Presbyterian Church (PCA), British Columbia, Canada

"Scott Christensen has a real gift for answering difficult theological questions plainly, thoroughly, and above all biblically—with colorful, engaging writing that readers at practically any level can easily comprehend and learn from. If you're troubled by the question of why a good and omnipotent God would create a universe that includes evil—or if you are a Christian struggling to explain the problem of evil to someone else—you will greatly benefit from this book."

—**John MacArthur,** Pastor-Teacher, Grace Community Church, Sun Valley, California; Chancellor Emeritus, The Master's University and Seminary

"This is a bold venture. After all, every attempt to explain the 'Why?' of sin faces the prima facie difficulty that sin, as defined by St. John (1 John 3:4), is without law, and thus irreducible to reason and order. This has not, however, deterred the world's greatest minds from trying, and Scott Christensen belongs to a long and honorable succession. In this volume he sets forth a 'greater-glory theodicy' reminiscent of Augustine's *felix culpa*, according to which the fall created a need for redemption, which in turn created the opportunity for God to show the glory of his redeeming love in the person of his Son. In essence, the answer to the question 'What about evil?' lies in the history of redemption: the story itself is God's vindication, but what is striking is the way in which this volume relates this history to modern theories of the 'architectonics of storytelling.' All great stories, Christensen argues, follow this pattern: creation (the good), fall, and redemption. But the pattern's original lies in the biblical narrative, the unique plot of the transcendent Author himself. Behind the story, however, lies the redemptive acts themselves and, supremely, the hero, Jesus Christ the Redeemer. God's design from all eternity was that in him he would give the supreme revelation of his glory. Christ's work, culminating in a new heaven and a new earth, is God's happy ending. These remarks do scant justice to the massive and varied erudition that lies behind this book. The *felix culpa* argument has never had a more thorough or a more accessible presentation."

—**Donald Macleod,** Professor of Systematic Theology, Edinburgh Theological Seminary

"One question that I often get as a pastor is: Why does evil exist? Without realizing it, the churchgoer is asking a theological question pertaining to one of the most challenging doctrines in all of Christianity. Thankfully, my friend Scott Christensen has written what I believe to be the definitive book on theodicy, *What about Evil?* I've grown to expect from Scott nothing less than cogent thinking, thorough examination, engaging writing, and biblical orthodoxy, and this book delivers on all fronts. After surveying the landscape of thinking on theodicy, Scott argues for the solution that gives God the greatest glory. More than just a sit-down-and-read-through book, *What about Evil?* is a resource that will aid the pastor, scholar, and mature believer. I cannot commend this volume highly enough, and I'm thankful for Scott's tireless labors in writing it."

—**Nate Pickowicz,** Pastor, Harvest Bible Church, Gilmanton Iron Works, New Hampshire; author, *How to Eat Your Bible*

"What Scott Christensen has accomplished with *What about Evil?* is truly exceptional. So many Christians experience an onslaught of questions from unbelievers whenever something of a catastrophic nature seemingly upends society. The natural response of unbelievers is: 'Where was God?' Christians need reasonable answers to this question. I am often disappointed when I hear ministers answer it by chalking the evil up to 'bare permission.' *Permission* is neither helpful nor comforting when a sovereign, benevolent God is on the throne. Scott has masterfully demonstrated from Scripture how believers can answer the seeming 'problem of evil' that puzzles believers. I happily commend this work to the thoughtful student of Scripture."

—**Peter Sammons,** Associate Professor of Theology, The Master's Seminary

"Christensen tackles what is perhaps the most difficult question for Christian theology—the problem of evil. No one can answer every question, as Christensen himself admits. Still, the book is a faithful and learned study on the whole matter, reflecting careful research and scholarship. Here we find a combination that is quite rare: the book is biblically grounded, theologically perceptive, and philosophically astute. Explaining evil in the context of the storyline of the Scriptures is particularly helpful."

—**Thomas R. Schreiner**, James Buchanan Harrison Professor
of New Testament Interpretation, The Southern Baptist
Theological Seminary

"The problem of evil is one of the most difficult questions faced by Christians in the proclamation and defense of the gospel as well as in our daily lives. The question of why God has allowed sin and evil to exist in his good world must be answered with biblical and theological fidelity. Unfortunately, many of the answers given to this question by Christians over the years contain parts of the truth but often miss the big picture centered in the glory of God and God's eternal plan of redemption. In this excellent and helpful book, however, Scott Christensen breaks new ground and offers an antidote to subpar ways of answering the problem of evil by returning to Scripture and giving us a robust 'greater-glory theodicy.' In doing so, this book is faithful to Scripture, is true to Reformed theology, interacts with past and present discussions on the problem of evil with care and precision, and most of all helps the church make sense of the riddle of sin and evil in God's eternal plan to bring glory to himself. If you have wrestled with the issues of theodicy and want the best of theological thinking on them, this book is a must-read. It will give you answers to your questions—but more than this, it will lead you to trust and glory in our triune God in the face of our Lord Jesus Christ."

—**Stephen J. Wellum**, Professor of Christian Theology, The Southern
Baptist Theological Seminary; editor, *The Southern Baptist Journal
of Theology*

"Scott Christensen's *What about Evil?* seeks to reconcile the existence of God and evil by appealing to 'the grand storyline of the Bible.' While acknowledging that he is not an analytic philosopher, Christensen displays great facility with what philosophy can bring and has brought to the table on this question, while choosing to focus his considerable exegetical and systematic-theological gifts on unpacking for his readers the implications of specific biblical revelation for this question. The result is a 'cross-centered theodicy of redemptive glory,' a 'greater-glory theodicy' that, while having affinities with greater-good theodicy and best-of-all-possible-worlds theodicy, is more specifically grounded in biblical narrative, rather than sanctified speculation. Christensen's interaction with contemporary literature on this topic is both wide-ranging and charitable, and much profit may be gained in considering how he lays out his case. Of special note is his anticipation of objections from both secular readers and fellow Christians who might take a different point of view. Highly recommended."

—**Greg Welty,** Professor of Philosophy, Southeastern Baptist Theological Seminary; author, *Why Is There Evil in the World?*

"In his *What about Evil?* Scott Christensen makes a genuine contribution to the discussion of the problem of evil. His treatment of the question from the perspective of the Bible's own story of God's glory in human redemption is self-consciously biblical rather than philosophical, as well as being engaging and conceptually clear at every point. A pleasure to commend!"

—**Fred G. Zaspel,** Pastor, Reformed Baptist Church, Franconia, Pennsylvania; Adjunct Professor of Systematic Theology, The Southern Baptist Theological Seminary; executive editor, *Books at a Glance*

WHAT ABOUT
EVIL?

WHAT ABOUT EVIL?

A DEFENSE OF GOD'S SOVEREIGN GLORY

SCOTT CHRISTENSEN

P U B L I S H I N G

P.O. BOX 817 • PHILLIPSBURG • NEW JERSEY 08865-0817

Library of Congress Cataloging-in-Publication Data
Names: Christensen, Scott, 1965- author.
Title: What about evil? : a defense of God's sovereign glory / Scott Christensen.
Description: Phillipsburg : P&R Publishing, 2020. | Includes bibliographical references and index. | Summary: "Christensen's theological response to the problem of evil examines how sin, evil, corruption, and death not only fit into redemptive history but also magnify the glory of a good God"-- Provided by publisher.
Identifiers: LCCN 2020022888 | ISBN 9781629955353 (cloth) | ISBN 9781629955360 (epub) | ISBN 9781629955377 (mobi)
Subjects: LCSH: Theodicy. | God (Christianity) | Good and evil--Religious aspects--Christianity.
Classification: LCC BT160 .C46 2020 | DDC 231/.8--dc23
LC record available at https://lccn.loc.gov/2020022888

To

Eddie Ogier, Joe Rice, and Marty Irons.

Friends for a lifetime. Brothers in Christ forever.

CONTENTS

FOREWORD

Occasionally one comes across a writer who manages to deal with big themes in exemplary ways—i.e., a writer who seems to know the tiny alleyways of the subject, but keeps the reader's attention focused on the big picture. Such a writer, truly gifted, says something fresh and thought-provoking about the far horizons, yet without losing sight of the details—and without demeaning those who uphold other, more traditional positions. But above all, if that writer is dealing with biblical and theological themes, the treatment of Scripture is fresh and compelling.

Such a writer is Scott Christensen, and his "big theme" is the sovereignty of God. We came across him five years ago in his book *What about Free Will? Reconciling Our Choices with God's Sovereignty*. It is one of the ablest defenses I've seen of confessional compatibilism—that is, the kind of compatibilism upheld by confessing Christians, as opposed to the kind of compatibilism largely condemned by analytic philosophers. Christians hold that two fundamental truths commonly assumed and even taught in Scripture are mutually compatible: (1) God is absolutely sovereign, but his sovereignty never mitigates human responsibility; (2) human beings are morally responsible before God (they believe and disbelieve, they obey and disobey, they love and hate, and these and other actions are morally significant actions for which they are rightly held responsible), but such morally significant behavior does not make God absolutely contingent. If you hold both these statements to be true, you are a compatibilist. In his earlier book, Christensen sought to show that such biblical compatibilism is worked into the very fabric of the biblical storyline and, rightly understood, anchors how Christians think about suffering, prayer, providence, faith, freedom, what the cross achieved, and more.

Integrally related to the theme of divine sovereignty is the theme of theodicy: if God is both utterly sovereign and immaculately good, how can he ordain (permit?) evil in this world? Or, alternatively, granted that there is so much evil and suffering, perhaps he is not good; or, if he is good, perhaps he is not sovereign—he's doing the best he can, poor chap. This is the set of conundrums that Christensen sets out to address in this book, *What about Evil? A Defense of God's Sovereign Glory.*

Christensen rightly insists that the challenge of theodicy is not a uniquely *Christian* problem: *every* worldview faces the problem of evil in one fashion or another. The distinctively Christian form of the problem arises from the distinctively Christian understanding of who God is. Oddly enough (as Christensen points out), most arguments that claim to be Christian theodicies are cast in the categories of analytic philosophy, not biblical theology (though, of course, their proponents quote the Bible often enough). For example, the free-will defense, enthusiastically defended in many Christian circles, argues that free will, often understood in a libertarian sense, is a great, necessary, and glorious element of being human. If God wants us to be human, and not merely robotic, he must allow us free will. By opening up that door, however, God takes a risk: his image-bearers might defy him and bring down evil on themselves. There may be an element of truth in the free-will defense, but it is not a distinctively *biblical* argument, and it has its problems. To give but one example: if in the new heaven and the new earth we human beings are so transformed that sin is no longer possible (i.e., free will ceases to exist), does it mean that we will no longer be human? And if one replies that God simply strengthens our wills so that we will no longer want to sin, then why did he not strengthen our wills before the fall so that we would not want to sin then, thus avoiding the sorry and sordid mess in the first place? Not surprisingly, other theodicies have been advanced: the natural-law defense, the greater-good theodicy, and so forth, all of which Christensen respectfully examines, profiting from them where he can, but ultimately finding them unsatisfactory. They are unsatisfactory, he says, not only because of intrinsic weaknesses, but also because they are not biblical enough: their arguments are too heavily indebted to philosophical structures of thought and too little shaped by the narrative of Scripture.

Christensen argues throughout his book that questions surrounding evil and its place in God's universe under God's sovereignty cannot be faithfully reflected on until they are nestled within the storyline of the Bible itself. Christensen is not so much developing a new theodicy as allowing the themes of the Bible's metanarrative to unfold in their own terms. Small wonder that he is quick to indicate how other writers have pointed the way. In any case, "as every story of redemption must have its crisis (evil), so also it must have its hero. Christ is the protagonist in God's plan of redemption, and his death and resurrection are the instruments by which he achieves it. They are the nucleus of redemption and therefore of God's glory. . . . While we shudder at the shamefulness of Adam's sin that thrust our world into a dark place, paradoxically we can cry out, *O felix culpa!* O fortunate fall! that occasioned the need for a great Redeemer to display the riches of God's glorious grace (Eph. 1:6)."

Nor is this a merely cognitive "solution" to the "problem" of evil. The Bible's narrative of redemption is so relentlessly subversive that Christ's followers are called to weakness, to grace, to showing mercy to the wicked. What begins as a theodicy to the praise of God's glorious grace sweeps along and establishes, among other things, a distinctively Christian ethic.

To feel the weight of Christensen's argument demands a careful reading of the whole book, surely not so much a chore as a glimpse of glory.

D. A. Carson
Emeritus Professor of New Testament,
Trinity Evangelical Divinity School

PREFACE

When I wrote my first book, *What about Free Will?*,[1] I knew I would have to deal with the so-called problem of evil. The question of free will intersects the question of the existence of evil in important ways. Yet my treatment of the problem of evil in that book seemed to only touch the tip of the proverbial iceberg. Reconciling the existence of God and evil has been a perennial conundrum in the history of Christian theology, and the vast literature is as daunting to get one's arms around as the topic itself. So why add another book? Why this book?

Well, first of all, I felt a need to explore the matter by dipping a bit deeper below the surface of the icy mass of the problem that *Free Will* was not designed to do. But second, my offering is a bit unusual for this topic. There have been numerous attempts to produce a rational and morally satisfying Christian theodicy[2] that seeks to make sense of why God has allowed evil to pervade his world. Many of these defenses have been helpful, as I hope to show. Most answers, however, tend to get tangled in a thicket of questions that I believe miss the mark.

While popular treatments abound, most rigorous Christian responses to the problem of evil are dominated by strictly philosophical approaches, and I find this unfortunate. That is not because I find them problematic. To the contrary, they are useful; but by themselves they remain inadequate. Comprehensive biblical, theological, and exegetical responses are wanting. Many scholars who engage in systematic and biblical theology have conceded the problem to the philosophers, and this is not helpful to the church at large.

The fact is, the most satisfying answer to the conundrums surrounding God and the existence of evil is not primarily rooted in the discourse of rational and moral logic and its carefully constructed syllogisms, as helpful

---

1. Scott Christensen, *What about Free Will? Reconciling Our Choices with God's Sovereignty* (Phillipsburg, NJ: P&R Publishing, 2016).

2. The term *theodicy* was coined by the eighteenth-century German philosopher Gottfried Leibniz. *Theodicy* combines the Greek words for "God" (*theós*) and "justice" (*dikē*). The theodicist attempts to justify God in the face of evil.

as these have proved to be, including my own investigations here. Instead, it is theological in nature. Furthermore, it is discovered in the grand storyline of the Bible.

In treating this subject, I will not be as rigorously focused on the plethora of apologetic matters that most philosophical books on this topic are concerned to address. This does not mean that the book has no apologetic value. I believe it does. But traditional apologetic approaches are not my immediate objective. Furthermore, I hope to address logical conundrums with some level of competence even though I lack any expertise as an analytical philosopher. My audience is the perplexed believer searching for a scripturally constructed theology for answers. Even so, I hope an unbeliever can begin to understand something of the wonder of the biblical faith, its God, and its central message by looking at Christianity through the lens of theodicy. Consequently, this will be a profoundly biblical and theological exploration. And I believe the answers provided in the pages of Holy Writ will reflect matters that resonate deeply in the soul of every human being.

I should also say that many books address the problem of evil with a view to providing an immediate salve to suffering readers. This is not one of those books—but not because I lack empathy for those who suffer. I pray that troubled souls are encouraged by the truths I hope to point us to, but this work will not pretend to be the first line of defense for bringing practical relief from pain and suffering.[3] My task will be centered on the bigger picture—how sin, evil, corruption, and death fit into the broad outlines of redemptive history.

These caveats demonstrate that probing the problem of evil can quickly swallow one's cognitive (and emotional) resources. It is impossible to be exhaustive. John Feinberg has rightly said that there are many problems of evil.[4] And there are multiple ways in which these many problems have been addressed. Furthermore, a great deal of epistemic humility is necessary here. Some of the thorny problems with evil are impenetrable to our limited minds.

---

3. Among the many excellent books on handling pain and suffering, I recommend the works of Joni Eareckson Tada. See especially *A Place of Healing: Wrestling with the Mysteries of Suffering, Pain, and God's Sovereignty* (Colorado Springs: David C. Cook, 2010); Joni Eareckson Tada with Steve Estes, *When God Weeps* (Grand Rapids: Zondervan, 2000). See also Paul David Tripp, *Suffering: Gospel Hope When Life Doesn't Make Sense* (Wheaton, IL: Crossway, 2018); David Powlison, *God's Grace in Your Suffering* (Wheaton, IL: Crossway, 2018); Dave Furman, *Kiss the Wave: Embracing God in Your Trials* (Wheaton, IL: Crossway, 2018); Elisabeth Elliot, *A Path through Suffering* (Grand Rapids: Revell, 1990); Elisabeth Elliot, *Suffering Is Never for Nothing* (Nashville: B&H Publishing Group, 2019); Jerry Bridges, *Trusting God* (Colorado Springs: NavPress, 2008); Sinclair B. Ferguson, *Deserted by God?* (Carlisle, PA: Banner of Truth, 1993).

4. John S. Feinberg, *The Many Faces of Evil* (Wheaton, IL: Crossway, 2004), 21–27.

I do not mean to say that certain problems have no solutions, but those solutions will remain hidden from us as long as we remain hidden from God's full disclosure. "The secret things belong to the LORD" (Deut. 29:29). There may be a thousand and one lesser reasons for any instance of evil. God may choose to reveal all, one, or none of them to us. And even when the scales on the eyes of the redeemed have been completely removed on the day of resurrection, there is no guarantee that we will be fully relieved of the nagging unanswered questions. Yet we can be assured that if this is the case, we will have no need for redressing such minor quibbles. I believe we can make sense of the most important questions concerning evil now because God has already revealed them to us.

So what has he revealed? Unfortunately, too many have thought he has said little or nothing. But is Scripture so silent? If one searches for explicit proof texts, perhaps so. We don't find such proclamations as: "And the Lord God said, 'Evil hath come into the world in order that . . .'" Nonetheless, there is a certain ubiquity to the answer threaded throughout the pages of Scripture in compelling ways that we will explore. My hope is that this humble offering will begin to open doors to seeing this broken world in a new light—that God's glorious purposes in creating the conditions for the emergence of such a dark world will become clear to the reader and evoke unprecedented wonder. May it lead us all to cry out: "Oh, the depth of the riches and wisdom and knowledge of God! How unsearchable are his judgments and how inscrutable his ways!" (Rom. 11:33).

Sola Deo Gloria

ACKNOWLEDGMENTS

Writing a book of this nature, seeking to tackle such grave and consequential subject matter, was a daunting task, to say the least. But the weight of the burden was lightened by many who came alongside me and offered their assistance in various ways. I begin by thanking my editor John Hughes, who urged me to write on this subject. Not only is he a wonderful editor, but he has become a great friend. His wisdom and expertise have guided me throughout the project. He read the whole manuscript and made many invaluable suggestions for improvement.

Second, I want to thank the elders of my former place of ministry (Summit Lake Community Church), as well as my current place of ministry (Kerrville Bible Church). Both have graciously allowed me times of study leave to finish the book.

This topic is too vast to try to digest every possible line of thought. I am no scholar, and even though I have tried to read widely and thoroughly, some things will elude even the most careful researcher. With that in mind, I want to thank Cory Madsen, Evan May, James Gibson, Grant Horner, Richard Shenk, Nate Shannon, Christopher Watkin, Fred Zaspel, Mike Riccardi, Phil Johnson, Peter Sammons, Marco Barone, Vern Poythress, and Guillaume Bignon, each of whom read early drafts of various sections of the book and made valuable critiques and suggestions based on their varied perspectives and areas of interest or expertise. They saved me from many catastrophes.

I especially want to thank James N. Anderson, Greg Welty, and Stephen Wellum, who spent considerable time reviewing and critiquing critical sections of the book and patiently educating me in matters far beyond my pay grade. I want to add a special note about Steve Hays (1959–2020), the longtime blogger at Triablogue. His prolific and penetrating writing on theodicy and the problem of evil helped to shape much of my thinking on the subject. He will be missed. The contributions of all these scholars and thinkers have been indispensable. Of course, none would agree with everything I've said; thus, any missteps, errors, and omissions are wholly mine.

Once again, I am deeply honored that D. A. Carson, one of the great biblical scholars of our day, was willing to write the Foreword. The folks at P&R Publishing are wonderful to work with, especially copyeditor Karen Magnuson with her expert eye.

Finally, I thank my beloved wife, Jennifer, and my four sons, Daniel, Andrew, Luke, and Matthew, who have had to put up with long hours of reading and researching, thinking aloud, and wearing out keyboards. We have all gained some lessons in long-suffering! Finally, I thank the transcendent Lord of the universe, who condescended to come to this cracked earth, who loved me and gave himself for me. May my humble offering bring him the glory that only he is worthy to receive.

ABBREVIATIONS

CTJ	*Calvin Theological Journal*
ESV	English Standard Version
IJST	*International Journal of Systematic Theology*
JCLT	*Journal of Christian Legal Thought*
JETS	*Journal of the Evangelical Theological Society*
JRT	*Journal of Reformed Theology*
MSJ	*The Master's Seminary Journal*
NASB	New American Standard Bible
NIDOTTE	William A. VanGemeren, ed., *New International Dictionary of Old Testament Theology & Exegesis* (Grand Rapids: Zondervan, 1997)
NIV	New International Version
NLT	New Living Translation
NRSV	New Revised Standard Version
PAP	Principle of Alternative Possibilities
SBJT	*Southern Baptist Journal of Theology*
WCF	Westminster Confession of Faith
WTJ	*Westminster Theological Journal*

1

INTRODUCTION: THE PROBLEM OF EVIL

There is a darkness in this world that inevitably presses hard on us all, leaving an indelible mark of pain and suffering. Consider these familiar occurrences. A mother endures months of a difficult pregnancy and finally gives birth to a beautiful girl. The emergence of a newborn babe produces a kind of euphoria that only a mother can know. But within days, the frail little child succumbs to infection and dies. Compounding matters, it becomes evident that the hospital staff acted carelessly. Her death could have been easily prevented. Or consider a young married couple working fervently for years to buy that picture-perfect property in the Rocky Mountains. They scrimp and save, using their own hands to build their humble little dream home situated in a stand of thick ponderosa. After driving in the final nail, they relax on their charming new porch to enjoy the fruits of their labor. But the pleasant afternoon sunshine gives way to menacing storm clouds. Suddenly, lightning strikes a nearby tree, and the house is soon caught in an inferno. The owners are without insurance.

Nothing can prepare a father who casually enters his daughter's bedroom, only to discover that she has hanged herself with an extension cord. Then there is the beloved and highly decorated soldier who returns home from several tours of duty in hostile lands. He is rightly treated as a hero. Yet he cannot escape having witnessed unspeakable carnage. Nightmares and horrific flashbacks plague his daily existence. He turns to alcohol and violence to relieve his terror, driving his battered and exasperated wife to file for divorce. His young and confused children are left to wonder what has happened to their beloved daddy.

1

These are but minor episodes in the distressed history of human tragedy, of pain, of suffering—of evil. A thousand similar awful tales could be recounted over the course of time, most of which are far worse: tales of systemic oppression, murder, rape, racism, terrorism, genocide, and geophysical decimation. In the last seventy-five years alone, one thinks of the Rape of Nanking, Auschwitz, the Russian gulags, Cambodia's Killing Fields, and the Rwandan genocide. Among the countless tales of moral depravity, other tales of natural disaster fill our minds with equal dismay: stories of the European Black Death (1347–51), Chilean earthquakes (1647), Krakatoan volcanoes (1883), Spanish flu pandemics (1918), Indonesian tsunamis (2004), Chinese coronavirus pandemics (2020), and endless twisters in Tornado Alley—all laying waste to hearth and home, while obliterating tens of millions of unsuspecting souls. Who has ever walked this earth and not cried out: "When I hoped for good, evil came, and when I waited for light, darkness came" (Job 30:26)?

Disturbing questions emerge from such harrowing, yet all-too-common, incidents. Why? Why must we endure such pain in this world? Why so many foolish errors, misjudgments, and purposeful acts of malice that mar our lives? There is certainly plenty of human blame to go around. But this doesn't fully explain why such darkness constantly hovers over us. A more penetrating set of questions emerges: Where is God? Could he not protect us from harm? Could not the Almighty prevent the demise of so many tragic lives? The one who stops the wind and staves off waves with a word (Mark 4:39, 41) could certainly abate all manner of approaching storms with a simple command. His sovereign power could orchestrate small providences here and there, ensuring our safety in the midst of calamity, or at least mitigate the harsher aspects of our daily travails.

Why does he not intervene?

THE QUESTION OF THEODICY

Such appalling incidents of moral wickedness and natural forces of annihilation are unrelenting, and even mind-numbing once the number of atrocities piles up past counting. And here caution comes knocking, for "evil thrives upon indifference—moral negligence, a stupor of uncaring."[1] Nonetheless, the specter of evil is reawakened when it barrels through the deeply personal and sometimes paralyzing tragedies we suffer, things we wish could be forever erased from our memories. Perhaps Thomas Hardy

---

1. Lance Morrow, *Evil: An Investigation* (New York: Basic Books, 2003), 84.

has spoken for the weary world: "Happiness was but the occasional episode in a general drama of pain."[2] Something is not right with the world. This is not the way it is supposed to be.[3] Consequently, these collective ills raise the most troubling quandary that we distraught creatures can possibly face. How can the good and almighty God allow evil to coexist in the created order he crafted with such singular beauty? What has become of his good creation? Why has he allowed evil to corrupt the broad landscape of our planet and its inhabitants?

This is the question of theodicy—how does one seek to justify a good and sovereign God in the face of evil? John Milton states boldly in *Paradise Lost*: "I may assert eternal providence, and justify the ways of God to men."[4] Is such a task even possible? The problem of theodicy in its more formal articulation goes back to the Greek philosopher Epicurus (341–270 B.C.). It forms a trilemma, juxtaposing the following notions with one another: (1) God is good; (2) God is powerful; and (3) yet evil exists, putting one or both of the first two points under suspicion.

Epicurus's concerns with God and evil were succinctly restated by the eighteenth-century Scottish philosopher David Hume: "Is [God] willing to prevent evil but not able? Then he is impotent. Is he able but not willing? Then he is malevolent. Is he both able and willing? From whence then is evil?"[5] C. S. Lewis casts the problem with his familiar wit: "If God were good, He would wish to make His creatures perfectly happy, and if God were almighty, He would be able to do what He wished. But the creatures are not happy. Therefore, God lacks either goodness, or power, or both."[6]

Historic orthodox Christianity has affirmed these two indisputable characteristics of God: his all-encompassing goodness and his sovereign power. Not a single trace of evil can be discerned in his wholly righteous being. It is impossible for his being to entertain some hint of corruption. Furthermore, by virtue of his sole status as Creator of all space, time, matter, and energy *ex nihilo* (out of nothing), he is undeniably omnipotent. He is the source of all power—every minuscule photon of energy residing in every corner of every galaxy. Now, an omnibenevolent God could not entertain evil in

2. Thomas Hardy, *The Mayor of Casterbridge* (New York: Dover, 2004), 243.

3. Cornelius Plantinga Jr., *Not the Way It's Supposed to Be: A Breviary of Sin* (Grand Rapids: Eerdmans, 1995), 7–8.

4. John Milton, *Paradise Lost*, ed. William Kerrigan, John Rumrich, and Stephen M. Fallon (New York: Random House, 2007), 1.25.

5. David Hume, *Dialogues concerning Natural Religion*, ed. Richard H. Popkin (Indianapolis: Hackett Publishing, 1980), 63.

6. C. S. Lewis, *The Problem of Pain* (New York: Macmillan, 1962), 26.

his creation—right? And if by some mysterious plot evil should stealthily slip into the universe, he would have reason to exercise his omnipotence to remove it immediately—yes?

Alas, evil remains.

So what gives? How can this dystopian reality persist in God's good creation?

Although the existence of pain and evil in the world places these two overarching attributes of God under the microscope of human scrutiny, they are not the only divine attributes to suffer the skeptical eye of his creatures. For example, the existence of evil places God's justice on the witness stand. It seems that any evil that God refuses to prevent exposes his injustice. But maybe the problem lies with his faulty omniscience. Does God fail to see bad stuff coming down the pike before he has a chance to respond? Is he simply unaware of the murder and mayhem going on down here? What about his wisdom? Does he need a remedial course on the best strategies to prevent or arrest evil?

Surely there is no good or wise reason for evil to take root in this world if God is truly in charge. Again, consider the beauty of God. Some would say that devious deeds, disease, death, and destruction all mar the orderly and harmonious elegance of the created order and thus reflect an ugly dimension of the Creator. Does God care? Does he lack true compassion for those who suffer? Or is he subject to the same suffering we face, inhabiting our same weaknesses?

Evil certainly tempts God's creatures to impugn his character, and so this is indeed a serious problem, especially for those who are inclined to accept the testimony of God's supreme and flawless character that the Bible attributes to him. If evil exists, how can God escape culpability for being evil himself? Has the Bible pushed a pack of lies? If Scripture represents the self-revelation of God himself, is God deceiving us? Is he the devil in disguise?

One can easily understand how the problem of evil has become the Achilles' heel of Christian apologetics.[7] While some Christian apologists have been moved to redefine or tweak the attributes of the God of classical biblical theism, this is the one thing that cannot bear the burden of the problem. To toy with the clear revelation of God's character when attempting a theodicy is to admit failure. To the contrary, retaining a robust understanding of the divine attributes is the starting point when seeking to bear the load of evil's unrelenting weight. Unfortunately, we live in a time when anemic views

---

7. R.C. Sproul, *The Invisible Hand* (Phillipsburg, NJ: P&R Publishing, 1996), 159.

of God within the church persist and unrealistic views of reality expose a saccharine weakness to our Christian outlook.

John Piper writes:

> Our vision of God in relation to evil and suffering [has been] shown to be frivolous. The church has not been spending its energy to go deep with the unfathomable God of the Bible. Against the overwhelming weight and seriousness of the Bible, much of the church is choosing, at this very moment, to become more light and shallow and entertainment-oriented, and therefore successful in its irrelevance to massive suffering and evil. The popular God of fun-church is simply too small and too affable to hold a hurricane in his hand. The biblical categories of God's sovereignty lie like land mines in the pages of the Bible waiting for someone to seriously open the book. They don't kill, but they do explode trivial notions of the Almighty.[8]

We are long overdue for a supremely muscular theodicy, a reorientation to Scripture's witness to God's purposeful and unyielding engagement with the powers of darkness—of chaos and misery.

MAPPING THEODICIES

The Christian theist who posits a genuine *theodicy* seeks to set forth a clear purpose of God in allowing evil into his good creation. Other theodicists are more modest, calling their theodicies a *defense*, which merely shows that the problem of evil does not disprove God's existence and that he cares about the adversity that marks human existence. Throughout the ages, many theodicies and defenses have been offered. The following represent some of the more common responses to the problem of evil:[9]

(1) *Free-Will Defense.*[10] This is the most prevalent response to the problem of evil. Free will is regarded as a cherished feature of our humanity without which we could not be responsible for our actions. Furthermore, without free will, we would be consigned to a cold and robotic existence. But this means that our freedom of choice results in both good and evil outcomes. So evil is usually regarded as a risk that God had to allow in order to grant humans significant freedom and responsibility.

8. John Piper, "Suffering and the Sovereignty of God: Ten Aspects of God's Sovereignty over Suffering and Satan's Hand in It," in *Suffering and the Sovereignty of God*, ed. John Piper and Justin Taylor (Wheaton, IL: Crossway, 2006), 18.

9. I will examine and assess each of these responses in greater detail in chapters 5 and 6. It should be noted that many combine different aspects of these various theodicies into a more comprehensive response to evil.

10. See Alvin Plantinga, *God, Freedom, and Evil* (Grand Rapids: Eerdmans, 1977).

(2) *Natural-Law Defense.*[11] God designed orderly, repeatable, predictable laws to govern the world, and good and bad consequences can result from the proper or improper use of these laws. For example, gravity helps stabilize our world but can also be utilized in destructive ways. Therefore, it is not God's fault when we misuse such laws.

(3) *Greater-Good Theodicy.*[12] God has multiple good purposes for evil in the world. Out of such evils come greater goods that could not otherwise come. These goods outweigh the evils that they overcome. Some good purposes are ascertainable and some are not. The fact that some purposes remain hidden does not soundly argue against their existence.[13]

(4) *Soul-Making Theodicy.*[14] Humans are born in a state of immaturity and must experience pain and adversity in order to mature. The Bible indicates that suffering resulting from various evil circumstances builds character. Just as the fiery furnace purifies gold, evil and suffering purify and strengthen the human soul.

(5) *Best-of-All-Possible-Worlds Defense.*[15] An omnibenevolent God would create only a world that was the best possible world that could exist. Yet this world is imperfect and full of undeniable evils. Therefore, those evils must be necessary for God to bring about subsequent goods that make this the best possible world.

(6) *Divine-Judgment Defense.*[16] Pain and suffering are the result of God's retributive punishment of evildoers, including the everlasting judgment of hell. Good comes out of judgment in the form of rehabilitation, deterrence, societal protection, and retribution. The hope of ultimate divine justice redresses the suffering of the innocent.

GREATER-GLORY THEODICY

The theodicy that I believe is most faithful to Scripture is a specific version of the *greater-good theodicy* with modified traces of the *best-of-all-possible-*

11. See Lewis, *Problem of Pain.*

12. See Greg Welty, *Why Is There Evil in the World (and So Much of It)?* (Fearn, Ross-shire, Scotland: Christian Focus, 2018).

13. In a sense, every Christian theodicy seeks to advance the greater good. In other words, evil is a reality that we must make theological sense of, and therefore God must have some good reason for it to exist.

14. See John Hick, *Evil and the Love of God* (New York: Harper and Row, 1975).

15. G. W. Leibniz, *Theodicy*, ed. Austin M. Farrar, trans. E. M. Huggard (New York: Cosimo Classics, 2009).

16. This is not so much a stand-alone theodicy or defense championed by any one theologian or theodicist, but a complementary response to evil in the world that seeks to defend the goodness, righteousness, and justice of God.

worlds defense. In offering this theodicy, I do not suggest that it solves every problem connected to evil in this world. That would be presumptuous. Rather, I offer a theodicy that seeks to resolve the broader issue of why evil exists in the first place. I call it the *greater-glory theodicy* because it seeks to resolve the problem by examining what brings God the greatest glory.[17] God's greatest glory is found in Christ's work of redemption. This work of redemption becomes unnecessary, however, unless there is a good world that was ruined by evil—a world that then cries out for restoration. This theodicy can be summarized by the following argument:[18]

1. God's ultimate purpose in freely creating the world is to supremely magnify the riches of his glory to all his creatures, especially human beings, who alone bear his image.
2. God's glory is supremely magnified in the atoning work of Christ, which is the sole means of accomplishing redemption for human beings.
3. Redemption is unnecessary unless human beings have fallen into sin.
4. Therefore, the fall of humanity is necessary to God's ultimate purpose in creating the world.

This theodicy is sometimes referred to by the Latin phrase *felix culpa.* It can be translated as "fortunate fall," indicating that the fall of humanity in the garden of Eden, though terrible in itself, was a good (fortunate) thing.[19] Some who have suggested or shown an affinity for a theodicy along these lines include Augustine (A.D. 354–430), the great English poet John Milton (1608–74), the Puritan divine John Owen (1616–83), the German philosopher Gottfried Wilhelm Leibniz (1646–1716), and more recently the Christian philosophers Alvin Plantinga and Paul Helm.[20]

The idea is simply this: the fall of humanity was no mistake. It did not catch God by surprise. Nor was it the result of Adam and Eve's free will, as most understand the term *free will.* The fall was planned by God because it

---

17. Daniel M. Johnson calls this theodicy a species of a "divine glory defense." He believes that divine-glory defenses approaching the problem of evil are distinctive to Calvinism. See "Calvinism and the Problem of Evil: A Map of the Territory," in *Calvinism and the Problem of Evil,* ed. David E. Alexander and Daniel M. Johnson (Eugene, OR: Pickwick Publications, 2016), 43–48.

18. See chapter 12 for a detailed explanation of each of these points.

19. The phrase can be traced back to the fourth-century liturgical hymn known as the *Exultet.* See David Lyle Jeffrey, ed., *A Dictionary of Biblical Tradition in English Literature* (Grand Rapids: Eerdmans, 1992), 274.

20. Others who show an affinity for a similar theodicy without explicitly endorsing the *felix culpa* argument include Jonathan Edwards (1703–58) and, more recently, John Piper, Jay Adams, Robert Reymond, and Randy Alcorn. See chapter 12 (esp. 299n63).

brings about the greater good of redemption. A fallen-but-being-redeemed world is far better than an unfallen-not-needing-redemption world. Such a world brings greater glory to God. No better world seems possible than one in which Christ's redemptive work brings such supreme glory to God.

The broader picture here is the Bible's grand, dynamic, and dramatic narrative of creation, fall, and redemption. History does not follow an invariant course—a monochromatic vista of flat, endless tedium. It moves in this downward arc from initial goodness to a world wrecked by sin and natural ruin, and then back upward again toward a magnificent plan of redemption. The lowermost point of the arc (the crisis of sin and evil) accentuates the subsequent upward goal of restoration (via the person and work of Christ). And it is precisely this contrast that magnifies God's glory. Redemption could never enter the scene unless evil's devolution of the good creation made it the inevitable and desired response of God.

What is of interest here is how human beings seem to be hardwired for framing history and our place within it precisely in terms that mirror the Bible's storyline. As we will see, the whole history of storytelling as a fundamental human impulse reflects a single ubiquitous storyline, sometimes called the *monomyth*. Every great story, whether historical or fictitious, gravitates toward some crisis that cries out for resolution. Only such stories captivate the human imagination and longing. A story that is worth its salt is always a story about redemption. But I do not wish to trivialize the afflictions of evil by simply comparing it to a good story. The fact is, our lives are living stories racked with unexpected and unwanted pain whereby we long for redemption.

In either case, as every story of redemption must have its crisis (evil), so also it must have its hero. Christ is the protagonist in God's plan of redemption, and his death and resurrection are the instruments by which he achieves it. They are the nucleus of redemption and therefore of God's glory. The cross and empty tomb are the fulcrum on which the hero shifts the weight of victory. Most heroes overcome the crisis of their story by means of conventional power. They generally defeat the villain (antagonist) or evil by summoning great determination or brute force.

But Christ is no conventional hero, and the cross is no conventional weapon. We do not naturally associate a hero's victory with his death. If the hero of a story dies, this is usually tragic. The cross is an especially tragic symbol. It bespeaks shame and defeat, not victory. Yet surprisingly, in the cross, Jesus defeats evil. Jesus defeats death by dying. He crushes evil by laying it on himself and then shows it to be powerless by rising from the dead. He becomes our hero by being treated as a villain. Weakness is power. This subversive storyline defies all human expectations. It appears foolish to the natural mind (1 Cor. 1:18) and thus proves that the narrative of biblical redemption hails exclusively from a divine source.

It should be clear that the theodicy I offer is commensurate with an evangelical and a broadly Reformed understanding of Scripture and theology.[21] It upholds the meticulous sovereignty of God. It is radically theocentric—God is squarely at its center. The problem of evil is resolved by focusing attention not on some ill-directed notion of human freedom and autonomy, but on how God's actions in creation and providence serve to maximize his own glory. While we shudder at the shamefulness of Adam's sin that thrust our world into a dark place, paradoxically we can cry out, *O felix culpa!* O fortunate fall! that occasioned the need for a great Redeemer to display the riches of God's glorious grace (Eph. 1:6).

WHAT TO LOOK FOR

Here is a chapter-by-chapter summary that outlines the flow of the book's argument.

Chapter 2 considers the historical, religious, cultural, social, and personal context for why evil is such a problem. Chapter 3 explains what evil is and how our conception of the moral character of God frames the problem. There is no question that evil is a problem for both theists and atheists, but only biblical theism provides the preconditions for making sense of evil, and so it is also a particularly potent problem that atheism faces, yet without adequate resources to address it. Chapter 4 sets forth the parameters for establishing a faithful defense or theodicy. Chapters 5 and 6 explore the most common solutions to the problem of evil that Christians have offered. I will consider the strengths and weaknesses of each of these solutions and where the theodicy I offer fits among them.

Chapter 7 considers how our view of God's power and transcendent control over the course of history is essential to a proper theodicy. If we do not understand who God is, then we cannot make sense of how he interacts with evil in the world. Chapter 8 considers the issues introduced in chapter 7 and goes deeper. How do the biblical writers portray evil, and what role does the sovereign God play as evil unfolds? The Bible is

---

21. Reformed theology is commonly associated with the Reformer John Calvin (1509–64), but finds its roots in the theology of Augustine (A.D. 354–430) and has had a rich tradition since the sixteenth-century Protestant Reformation and later Puritanism emerging in the late sixteenth and early seventeenth centuries.

unprecedented in history in terms of its multifaceted interface with evil and God's comprehensive control over it.

Chapter 9 explores where moral responsibility lies when evil is committed. How is God exonerated from being culpable for evil? How does the Bible address these issues? Furthermore, the chapter explores the cause of the fall. What are the origins of sin and evil? This will set the stage for a broader understanding of the problem of evil. Throughout Scripture, there is a sharp tension between God's meticulous providence and his absolute goodness, between his decretive (sovereign) will and his preceptive (moral) will. Thus, we can only conclude that God decreed the fall for some morally good reason.

Chapters 10 through 13 are the heart of the book. Chapter 10 begins by looking at the motif of redemption through the history of storytelling. God has hardwired human beings to long for heroes in redemptive roles whereby evil is defeated and good prevails. Literature and other storytelling mediums reflect a *monomyth*—one universal storyline that evokes a human longing for redemption even as pagan myths and secular stories corrupt the source and true meaning that stand behind this unified storyline.

Chapter 11 sets forth the historical and narrative paradigm that Scripture provides for understanding this ubiquitous story. It summarizes what C. S. Lewis calls the *True Myth* embodied in the divinely directed events of creation, fall, and redemption that lesser monomythic stories can only indistinctly mirror. The inspired, inerrant historical narrative of Scripture frames our understanding of reality and helps us see where evil fits into God's providential unfolding of history.

Chapter 12 is the most important chapter of the book. It presents the case for the biblical theodicy that I call the *greater-glory theodicy.* Once the source for monomythic themes in the history of storytelling can be ascertained in the Bible's grand storyline, this theodicy will begin to make greater sense. It shows how God's ultimate end in creation is to maximize the display of his glory to his creatures through the redemptive work of Christ. But redemption is made unnecessary without the fall. Therefore, God purposed the fall to magnify his glory in a way that an unfallen world simply could not do.

Chapter 13 examines important episodes in the biblical canon that not only mirror the metanarrative of Scripture but highlight this theodicy of redemptive glory. In particular, I focus on the exodus of Israel from Egypt as a paradigm for God's redemptive actions. Within this discussion, I draw special attention to Romans 9:22–23, perhaps the most seminal passage in Scripture that provides us with some propositional anchors to ground this theodicy more directly. I then look at some episodes in the Gospel of John culminating in the Passion Week and how these narratives highlight Christ's redemptive glory.

Chapter 14 narrows the focus on the unique and paradoxical features of the incarnation and kenosis (self-emptying) of Christ that make redemption so glorious. Christ as *the* peerless archetypal Redeemer stands above all redemptive motifs in his utterly unique defeat of evil. There is nothing in the history of ideologies and religions with which to compare him, or his work to redeem sinners. Without the unique features of the person and work of Christ, there can be no hope of redemption. Furthermore, the uniqueness of Christ as the one and only Redeemer of this fallen world further serves to magnify God's glory in redemption.

Chapter 15 dives deeper still into the unique nature of Christ and his suffering. How can God, who is impassible (unable to suffer), enter the world as a suffering Savior? And how is this transcendent, impassible God able to sympathize with his suffering creatures and offer them comfort?

Chapter 16 expands the focus of the greater-glory theodicy to encompass the cosmic scope of redemption. God's glory in redemption includes not only the salvation of a people for himself, but the redemption of the whole of his creation from its corrupted state. Christ's work of redemption does not end at his death and resurrection but continues through his exaltation and the future consummation of his kingdom at his return.

This restoration of "all things" culminates in the creation of the new heaven and the new earth. It considers the comprehensive work of Christ in both judgment and salvation via the *Christus Victor* theme carried in the atonement and Christ's broader victory over Satan and the forces of evil. All instances of evil that have not been defeated by the surprising work of the crucified Lamb at his first coming will be defeated by God's expected use of retributive power as the fierce Lion at his second coming. The contrast between judgment and the grace of salvation provides a further layer of magnification for God's redemptive glory.

Finally, chapter 17 explores one of the surprising results of the Bible's subversive model of redemption. Instead of encouraging conventional power to defeat evil, it encourages unconventional displays of the transformative grace by which one has been rescued from sin and judgment. This means extending mercy (compassion) toward victims of evil, bearing up as a victim under the merciful hand of God, and treating perpetrators of evil with mercy.

Extending forgiveness to one's enemies is perhaps the greatest manifestation of what some call the *grace effect*. This mirroring of how Christ defeats evil in our own lives is one of the greatest tangible apologetics for the Christian faith. The appendix examines the so-called lapsarian debate in Reformed theology, and how it has relevance to the theodicy that I am arguing for.

LIGHT POURING OUT OF DARKNESS

How are we to interpret a world where evil, pain, and suffering permeate the ground we stand on and the air we breathe? Can we make sense of a good, wise, and powerful God in such a world? Can Christianity offer a rational and biblical defense of the God it offers as the only hope for humanity and the crisis we face? If one penetrates the black core of even the most horrendous episodes of the crisis, we find something surprising. Within the core we inevitably find a hope that brightly emerges and illumines our understanding of God's powerful redemptive work—a bold plan that transcends the pain and overcomes the crisis.

An illustration may help us see this truth.

Few episodes in the annals of American history compare to the horrific tragedy of the Donner Party expedition during the winter of 1846–47. Thirty-nine out of eighty-seven people died after being trapped in a frozen landscape in the Sierra Nevada mountains of California. Several fast-moving and unusually severe storms prevented the emigrants from making their way to a new life in the Sacramento Valley. They quickly threw together makeshift shelters that were soon buried in as much as twenty-five feet of snow. Over many months, they entered successively desperate stages of starvation, leaving their thinning bodies with little insulation against the howling cold and near-constant blowing snow.

Unabated hunger is a force so primal that it brooks no rivals for the brutish grip it holds on its victims. Joseph Conrad's wandering seaman Marlow describes such hunger in the haunting novel *Heart of Darkness*:

> No fear can stand up to hunger, no patience can wear it out, disgust simply does not exist where hunger is; and to superstition, beliefs, and what you may call principles, they are less than chaff in a breeze. Don't you know the devilry of lingering starvation, its exasperating torment, its black thoughts, its somber and brooding ferocity? Well, I do. It takes a man all his inborn strength to fight hunger properly. It's really easier to face bereavement, dishonor, and the perdition of one's soul—than this kind of prolonged hunger.[22]

---

22. Joseph Conrad, *Heart of Darkness* (New York: Penguin Books, 1999), 76.

The Donner Party knew these dark sentiments all too well. With no way of escape and no source of food, most who perished (including many women and children) were reluctantly at first, and then remorselessly, cannibalized by their fellow trekkers desperate to avoid the same fate.

In the midst of this ghastly ordeal, however, a curious yet unexceptional incident enthralled little three-year-old Eliza Donner. Many gray days made life in the cold, dank dungeons that served as shelters more miserable than most. But on one particular day, Eliza was sitting on the icy floor of her crude home as a shaft of sunlight briefly cast its beam down into the dark hole. Years later she fondly recalled, "I saw it, and sat down under it. Held it on my lap, passed my hand up and down in its brightness, and found that I could break its ray in two."[23] For a person surrounded by death and carnage, this seems an odd thing to remember. Yet it was the one delightful if fleeting moment for the little girl stuck in that awful place. And who does not savor what is delightful over what is dreadful?

This incident reminds me of how John opened his magisterial gospel expounding on the great protagonist of history. He describes Christ with a profound metaphor: "The light shines in the darkness, and the darkness has not overcome it" (John 1:5). Like Eliza Donner's sunbeam, the apostle's description of the incarnation of Christ represents the entrance of that singular shaft of light capable of penetrating a bleak world full of atrocity, pain, and hopelessness. This light dispels the blackness. It is what Christ came to do. It is what highlights the glory of God and secures the greatest possible good for those who are irrepressibly stained by evil.

But the apostle Paul draws on another light-darkness metaphor in 2 Corinthians 4:6: "For God, who said, 'Let light shine out of darkness,' has shone in our hearts to give the light of the knowledge of the glory of God in the face of Jesus Christ." The image of light shining out of darkness alludes to the creation account, which begins as an unlit watery void (Gen. 1:2–3). Suddenly out of the darkness pours forth a mysterious light. The image is subversive. We don't think of light shining out of darkness, but of light shining into darkness—like shafts of sunlight pouring through openings to miserable prisons encased below layers of hardened snow.

Yet the metaphor aptly describes the work of redemption. We are not conditioned to expect good to emerge out of the murky mass of evil. But God designed evil so that something remarkably white and wonderful would emanate from its black depths. As William Cowper penned, "Behind a

23. Ethan Rarick, *Desperate Passage: The Donner Party's Perilous Journey West* (New York: Oxford University Press, 2008), 146.

frowning providence he hides a smiling face."[24] The glory of God penetrates the darkened hearts of sinners bound by a fetid dungeon of wickedness.

This glory is seen in the face of the divine hero of redemption—Jesus Christ, the Son of God. He immersed himself into the heart of evil on a black Friday and emerged from that evil on a bright Sunday three days later. He defeated death by death. Ironically, he crushed evil by loading its monstrous weight on his buckling body. He became a hero by being treated as a villain. He is not only the light that shone in the darkness; he is also the radiance that streams forth from the abyss. The pages that follow will attempt to highlight the wonder of this divine light pouring out of darkness. In the end, I hope we will see that there really is no problem of evil—only an unfathomably glorious God whose wise and wonderful ways should elicit our astonishment and our adoration.

KEY TERMS

defense
greater-glory theodicy
problem of evil
theodicy

STUDY QUESTIONS

1. What is the problem of evil, and why is it such a problem?
2. Why is it important for Christians to develop a theodicy?
3. Has evil in the world or in your personal life caused you to ask questions about God? If so, how did you resolve those questions?

FOR FURTHER READING

C. S. Lewis, *The Problem of Pain* (New York: Macmillan, 1962).
Greg Welty, *Why Is There Evil in the World (and So Much of It)?* (Fearn, Ross-shire, Scotland: Christian Focus, 2018).

---

24. William Cowper, "God Moves in a Mysterious Way" (1774). The hymn was originally titled "Light Shining out of Darkness" under a section entitled "Conflict" in the famous Olney Hymns (written together with John Newton). See Susan Wise Bauer, "Stories and Syllogisms: Protestant Hymns, Narrative Theology, and Heresy," in *Wonderful Words of Life: Hymns in American Protestant History and Theology*, ed. Richard J. Mouw and Mark A. Noll (Grand Rapids: Eerdmans, 2004), 220. On the significance of the afflicted William Cowper and his powerful hymns, see John Piper, *The Hidden Smile of God: The Fruit of Affliction in the Lives of John Bunyan, William Cowper, and David Brainerd* (Wheaton, IL: Crossway, 2001).

2

THEODICY AND THE CRISIS OF OUR SECULAR AGE

All was quiet on a clear blue Saturday morning, November 1, 1755, in Lisbon, the center of the kingdom of Portugal. It was All Saints' Day, and the streets were empty. Throngs of Roman Catholic parishioners among the city's 250,000 citizens packed themselves into one of the many magnificent cathedrals to celebrate the Mass on this high church day. The solemnity of the occasion was interrupted by a rumbling noise. Many assumed it to be the ironclad wheels of decorated coaches rolling through the cobbled streets of the city. Perhaps their occupants were late in attending services.

But the rumble quickly gave way to violent shaking and a terrible roar. The convulsion appeared to subside, only to be followed by two more devastating temblors. Before they had time to escape, thousands of morning worshipers were buried beneath tons of marble blocks and columns, wood beams, church statuary, and shards of stained glass. The infamous Lisbon earthquake produced an enormous amount of energy equivalent to "475 megatons of TNT or 32,000 Hiroshima bombs."[1] Seismologists estimate that it measured anywhere from 8.5 to over 9.1 on the moment magnitude scale, making it one of the most powerful earthquakes in history.[2]

Around ten thousand inhabitants died in the initial hour of the disaster, but this was only the beginning of the day's terrifying events. The thrusting of the continental plates underneath the North Atlantic Ocean floor aroused the waiting waters above. They quickly formed a tsunami with waves thirty to forty-five feet high. Walls of watery destruction rushed

1. Mark Molesky, *This Gulf of Fire* (New York: Alfred A. Knopf, 2015), 6.
2. Molesky, *This Gulf of Fire*, 6.

up the Tagus River, assaulting the already-ravaged city. The waves would crush ships, piers, seawalls, and additional buildings while dragging more helpless souls into the deadly coastal waters. But even this was not the end.

The most devastating terror that day was the fires that the earthquake induced, ripping through the city and incinerating what remained. The conflagration raged for weeks, gutting churches, palatial homes, monasteries, convents, theaters, libraries, and public marketplaces. The city lay in ruins for nearly six years. The devastation extended far beyond the city, affecting some 5.8 million square miles of the earth's surface, making it an unprecedented disaster.[3] All in all, some thirty thousand to forty thousand people perished with little or no warning.

The toll of the Great Lisbon Earthquake could not be limited to the lives it claimed and the material destruction it wrought. It shook the world in far more devastating ways. For the first time since Christianity had transformed the Western world, God came under broad serious public assault for the problem of pain, evil, and suffering. Lisbon put cracks in the West's long-standing confidence in a wise, powerful, and benevolent God. Philosophers, theologians, professors, statesmen, pastors, priests, and men of letters were all asking the same questions.

Parlors all across Europe were a hotbed for debate.[4] Did the Creator care about the deaths of his innocent creatures? Could he hear the cries of desperation when disaster hit? Why did he not prevent this disaster in the first place? Should God even be invoked? Perhaps such disasters are entirely natural. These questions set theological discourse on a trajectory that, over the course of the last two and half centuries, has left belief in the God of the Bible in a state of peril, and people as confused as ever about the nature of good and evil, of pain and its purpose. To make sense of the problem of evil in our contemporary context, we must understand this trajectory of modern thinking about God, man, meaning, and evil, and the crisis that we find ourselves in.

THE ENLIGHTENMENT ATTACK ON BIBLICAL THEISM

The Lisbon earthquake came at a moment in history as the Enlightenment was coming to prominence. The Enlightenment has marked the most momentous shift in Western civilization since the advent of Christianity in the first century. The Protestant Reformation of the sixteenth century, as important as it

---

3. Molesky, *This Gulf of Fire*, 19.

4. Nicholas Shrady, *The Last Day: Wrath, Ruin, and Reason in the Great Lisbon Earthquake of 1755* (New York: Viking, 2008), 117.

was to the recovery of orthodox Christianity, has not been able to compete with the forces of the Enlightenment that eclipsed it 150 years later.[5] The Enlightenment was many things, but at its heart lay a radical alteration in the way that people began to think about God. The predominantly theocentric (God-centered) worldview that had marked the medieval period through the Reformation shifted to a decidedly anthropocentric (man-centered) worldview that continues to the present.[6]

In 1500, classical Christian theism was firmly entrenched in the Western mind. By 1800, deism was a fashionable alternative. And by 1900, it was no longer unacceptable to call oneself an atheist. Enlightenment thinkers were emboldened to begin throwing off the shackles of orthodox Christianity and its supposedly austere deity, hoping that this would emancipate humanity (cf. Ps. 2:1–3). "The Enlightenment's centerpiece was freedom. Indeed, its *demand* was freedom: freedom from the past, freedom from God, and freedom from authority."[7]

The Enlightenment would change how people thought not only about God, but about man, creation, and morality. It would radically alter theology, epistemology, science, and ethics.[8] Its conception of God stripped him of virtually all he has revealed of himself in Scripture. Instead of an equally transcendent and immanent personal God to whom we owe everything, he was regarded merely as "an abstract Supreme Being who dealt with His cosmos and His creatures through impersonal secondary causes."[9]

On the one hand, God lost his mystery, his otherworldliness, his fearful incomprehensibility.[10] The God of classical theism has been domesticated,

5. Thankfully, for over five hundred years now, the Reformation has helped to shape orthodox biblical Christianity. See Ray Van Neste and J. Michael Garrett, eds., *Reformation 500* (Nashville: B&H Academic, 2016); Carl Trueman, *Reformation: Yesterday, Today and Tomorrow* (Fearn, Ross-shire, Scotland: Christian Focus, 2011).

6. W. Andrew Hoffecker, "Enlightenment and Awakenings: The Beginning of the Modern Culture Wars," in *Revolutions in Worldview*, ed. W. Andrew Hoffecker (Phillipsburg, NJ: P&R Publishing, 2007), 241. The Enlightenment was not a monolithic movement. There were many different strands of Enlightenment thinking, some more conservative and others more radical. See Jonathan I. Israel, *Enlightenment Contested: Philosophy, Modernity, and Emancipation of Man 1670–1752* (Oxford: Oxford University Press, 2006).

7. David F. Wells, *Above All Earthly Pow'rs: Christ in a Postmodern World* (Grand Rapids: Eerdmans, 2005), 29.

8. For the Enlightenment's impact on art, music, and literature, see Nancy Pearcey, *Saving Leonardo* (Nashville: B&H Publishing Group, 2010).

9. James Turner, *Without God, Without Creed: The Origins of Unbelief in America* (Baltimore: Johns Hopkins University Press, 1985), 37.

10. William C. Placher, *The Domestication of Transcendence: How Modern Thinking about God Went Wrong* (Louisville, KY: Westminster John Knox Press, 1996), 6.

humanized.[11] On the other hand, however, his providence was no longer direct and specific, but a general sort of passive oversight whereby the laws of nature did the lion's share of the work of maintaining the day-to-day affairs of the universe.[12] Deism suddenly supplanted theism as the defining feature of the god of public discourse.

With the biblical God relegated to the periphery, man became the measure of all things. This finds its nascent roots in Renaissance humanism, in which the greatness of man and his perfections were celebrated. Consider the ideal Platonic proportions of Leonardo da Vinci's *Vitruvian Man* (1490) or Michelangelo's magnificent sculpture *David* (1501–4), towering above all observers in Florence's Accademia Gallery at fourteen feet high.

But the Enlightenment took the idolizing of man to extremes. René Descartes (1596–1650) began to re-envision epistemology that jump-started the modern world whereby human autonomy eventually replaced the self-existent, self-sufficient, authoritative God of the Bible. Descartes said that a rational foundation for knowledge must begin with man's self-awareness (*Cogito, ergo sum*—"I think, therefore I am"), not with God as the source of knowledge.[13] Human reason began to revolt against its place of subservience to divine revelation until it replaced it altogether. Reason was no longer explained and corrected by revelation. Instead, it became hostile to biblical truth, resulting in the rise of the historical-critical method that sought to erode the inspiration, authority, and sufficiency of Scripture.[14]

Thus began the marginalization of Christianity in the modern world. "By the conclusion of the Enlightenment, compartmentalization of religious faith as a matter of private belief separate from philosophical speculation epitomized the modern worldview."[15]

11. In contemporary thought, process theology has done more to domesticate and humanize God than any other theological vision.

12. Turner, *Without God, Without Creed*, 40.

13. Hoffecker, "Enlightenment and Awakenings," 254. Descartes did not completely dispense with the theistic foundations for knowledge (see John Cottingham, "The Desecularization of Descartes," in *The Persistence of the Sacred in Modern Thought*, ed. Nathan Jacobs and Chris Firestone [Notre Dame, IN: Notre Dame University Press, 2012], 15–37), but he certainly marks the shift to human autonomous reason.

14. See Norman L. Geisler, ed., *Biblical Errancy: An Analysis of Its Philosophical Roots* (Grand Rapids: Zondervan, 1981); Gerhard Maier, *The End of the Historical-Critical Method* (St. Louis: Concordia Publishing House, 1977); Mark S. Gignilliat, *A Brief History of Old Testament Criticism* (Grand Rapids: Zondervan, 2012); Gerald Bray, *Biblical Interpretation: Past & Present* (Downers Grove, IL: InterVarsity Press, 1996); Eta Linnemann, *Historical Criticism of the Bible*, trans. Robert W. Yarbrough (Grand Rapids: Baker, 1990).

15. Hoffecker, "Enlightenment and Awakenings," 255.

Immanuel Kant (1724–1804) further radicalized the epistemological project of Descartes. Before Kant, knowledge was still regarded as objective and external, in which "the mind was simply a mirror in which the external world was reflected."[16] Since Kant, the mind itself has now become a vital source of constructing knowledge. Kant made a distinction between the *noumenal* and the *phenomenal* world. The upper world of the noumenal consists of things as they are in themselves apart from our experience. The lower phenomenal world consists of our experience via empirical and rational means. The noumenal world cannot be known, while the phenomenal world can. Religious faith resides in the realm of the noumenal, which leaves us with uncertainty about its truth. Science and reason reside in the realm of the phenomenal, which gives us reliable sources of truth.

As a result, divine revelation took a blow. All truth claims about religious faith are subject no longer to what God might say but to human reason, as indicated in the title of Kant's treatise *Religion within the Bounds of Bare Reason* (1793). While Kant hoped to put knowledge on a surer footing, in the end "meaning has largely been detached from what is objective and as a result has become radically subjective."[17]

The unintended result of Kant's epistemological project provided justification for postmodernism. Postmodern skepticism has revealed that substituting autonomous human reason for divine revelational truth leads to uncertainty not merely for claims of knowledge in the so-called noumenal realm, but for all claims to knowledge. We are now living in an age of epistemological confusion and despair.

Not only did the Enlightenment push the creature to supplant the Creator, but the notion of *nature* has displaced *creation* alongside the Creator. If God's providence has been shrunk and tossed into a dusty box in the attic, then so has the supernatural worldview that has attended classical Christian theism. We no longer live in a "created" world of transcendence, of otherworldly mystery and power. All is now "nature," reduced to matter and mathematics. The cosmos is entirely explainable by naturalistic causes. Isaac Newton (1642–1727) sought to construct a scientific enterprise based on uncovering the secrets of God's intelligent and intricately designed creation.

Unfortunately, the analytical precision of the finely tuned world that he sought to discover gave rise to a strictly mechanistic view of the universe

---

16. David F. Wells, *God in the Wasteland: The Reality of Truth in a World of Fading Dreams* (Grand Rapids: Eerdmans, 1994), 104.

17. Wells, *God in the Wasteland*, 105.

that, ironically, he sought to oppose.[18] Newton indeed saw the cosmos as a mechanism, but one that was continually animated by divine forces at every turn.[19] "For Newton, laws of nature like universal gravitation depended on God's immediate presence and activity as much as the breathing of an organism depends on the life-principle within."[20]

Newton, however, was lost in translation. The emerging "Newtonian" worldview was a picture of reality that was highjacked from Newton by those who did not understand his distinctly theistic worldview.[21] This made it easier for Enlightenment zealots to eliminate God from a universe that was eventually conceived as a wholly natural realm. By the late nineteenth century, Darwin's theory of evolution via natural selection had become naturalism's *fait accompli*.[22]

The highjacking of Newton simply reflected what was happening on a broader scale with the whole scientific enterprise itself. It is common today to assume that science has had a long-standing feud with Christianity in the West.[23] But the reality is far different. It was primarily a Christian the-istic worldview that first gave rise to the scientific revolution. The beauty and intelligibility of the rationally ordered universe point to a supremely imaginative and intelligent Creator whose wondrous ways are worthy of exploration.[24] Unfortunately, the largely a-theistic disposition of the present scientific outlook has no consciousness of its theistic origins.

The dismantling of a Christian theistic foundation for epistemology and science meant the same for ethics. The Enlightenment sought to ground ethics in something other than God. The Lisbon earthquake revealed that

18. Nancy R. Pearcey and Charles B. Thaxton, *The Soul of Science: Christian Faith and Natural Philosophy* (Wheaton, IL: Crossway, 1994), 76, 88–95.

19. Pearcey and Thaxton, *Soul of Science*, 92.

20. Christopher Kaiser, *Creation and the History of Science* (Grand Rapids: Eerdmans, 1991), 189.

21. Pearcey and Thaxton, *Soul of Science*, 93.

22. Turner, *Without God, Without Creed*, 179–87.

23. This can be traced back to the influential and gross misrepresentations perpetrated by Andrew Dickson White's *History of the Warfare of Science with Theology in Christendom* (1876) and John William Draper's *History of the Conflict between Religion and Science* (1874).

24. See Pearcey and Thaxton, *Soul of Science*; Kaiser, *Creation and the History of Science*; R. Hoykass, *Religion and the Rise of Modern Science* (Grand Rapids: Eerdmans, 1964); Stanley L. Jaki, *The Road of Science and the Ways of God* (Chicago: University of Chicago Press, 1978); James Hannam, *The Genesis of Science: How the Christian Middle Ages Launched the Scientific Revolution* (Washington, DC: Regnery Publishing, 2011). Robert K. Merton's *Science, Technology & Society in Seventeenth-Century England* (repr., New York: Howard Fertig Publisher, 2002) argues that the Puritan work ethic was an important impulse that sparked scientific inquiry in the seventeenth century. For an assessment of "The Merton Thesis" with responses by Merton, see I. Bernard Cohen, ed., *Puritanism and the Rise of Modern Science: The Merton Thesis* (New Brunswick, NJ: Rutgers University Press, 1990).

Westerners were becoming increasingly dismayed by God's ways. If God were held at bay and human dignity were severed from its biblical roots, then this would argue for greater personal control over our destiny and a stronger impetus to pursue a goodness that would transform the world into a better place.[25] "The rationalists envisioned man essentially alone, free and responsible only to himself, in a universe governed from afar by an increasingly remote God."[26] Ethics in the so-called Age of Reason began to be rooted in the notion of universal rational principles, not in a sovereign and virtuous God.

In order to move morality away from biblical Christianity, the doctrine of original sin needed to be dismissed.[27] Jean-Jacques Rousseau (1712–78) brought famous disrepute to the doctrine when he wrote *Émile* (1762) to set forth the notion that man is born innocent, a blank slate on which free will acts to shape the moral soul. The ever-present and destructive lure of Pelagianism was unleashed anew. Consequently, Calvinism (revived Augustinianism) came under particular disdain among Enlightenment philosophers and pundits.[28]

No one understood this assault on biblical Christianity as well as Jonathan Edwards (1703–58), the great New England theologian.[29] This explains several of his important works, such as *The Freedom of the Will* (1754) and *Original Sin* (1758). Edwards was alarmed by the "delusive optimism regarding human nature that was sweeping" the whole of the Western world.[30] Much of the morality of the seventeenth and eighteenth centuries resembled that of orthodox Christianity.[31] Yet the new vehicle to which ethics was tethered would veer further and further away from the objective course originally set forth by biblical theism. The wreckage of postmodern subjectivism has attested to the failure of the Enlightenment's moral outlook.

But postmodernism was already preceded by the detrimental impacts of the new moral philosophy. To some Enlightenment thinkers, such as Robert Owen (1771–1858), the idea of innate human corruption was at the heart

25. George M. Marsden, *Jonathan Edwards: A Life* (New Haven, CT: Yale University Press, 2003), 451; Turner, *Without God, Without Creed*, 69.

26. Andrew Delbanco, *The Death of Satan: How Americans Have Lost the Sense of Evil* (New York: Farrar, Straus and Giroux, 1995), 80.

27. Alan Jacobs, *Original Sin: A Cultural History* (New York: HarperCollins, 2008), 149–50.

28. Delbanco, *Death of Satan*, 81.

29. Marsden, *Jonathan Edwards*, 449; Delbanco, *Death of Satan*, 80–82; Paul Helm, "The Great Christian Doctrine (Original Sin)," in *A God Entranced Vision of All Things*, ed. John Piper and Justin Taylor (Wheaton, IL: Crossway, 2004), 179.

30. Marsden, *Jonathan Edwards*, 449.

31. Turner, *Without God, Without Creed*, 69.

of Christianity's harmful grip on Western culture. Owen's *A New View of Society* (1816) gave greater prominence to the idea that institutions foment corruption in society, not individuals.[32] Never mind that institutions consist of collective individuals!

Karl Marx (1818–83) took Owen's rejection of original sin to a unique conclusion. Institutional oppression is primarily economic (specifically capitalist systems), fueled by Western religious fervor.[33] "Religion," Marx famously said, "is the opiate of the masses." In order to bring freedom to the common man (proletariat), economic equality must come about by revolution. Then it must be enforced by state (institutional!) control of the means of production. Ironically, the atheistic Communist regimes of Marxism have brought about more oppression and death of the common people than any other ideology, political or otherwise, in the history of the world.[34] And it has done so with brutal efficiency. As Randall Jarrell wrote: "Most of us know, now, that Rousseau was wrong: that man, when you knock his chains off, sets up death camps."[35]

LISBON IGNITES THE MODERN CRISIS OF THEODICY

The trail of the Enlightenment to the present post-Christian era in the West is littered with tragic attempts to find meaning without the true God. Its desire to free humanity from the transcendent order and values of biblical Christianity has instead led to skepticism and despair. David Wells observes:

> The autonomous, unaided reason of the Enlightenment has not produced the promised emancipation in our social and political life. Quite the reverse. It has produced the ponderous bureaucratic societies of the West, massive in their structures and weight, unfeeling in their workings, and not infrequently unfriendly to human well-being. Postmodern thinkers are the vanguard of a profound reaction to the failure of the Enlightenment project, giving expression to a deeply held suspicion that modernity is, in fact, the enemy of human life.[36]

Most people are unaware of the forces that have made the contemporary world so empty. We no longer know how to think about meaning and

---

32. Jacobs, *Original Sin*, 178.

33. Richard Lint, "The Age of Intellectual Iconoclasm," in *Revolutions in Worldview*, ed. W. Andrew Hoffecker (Phillipsburg, NJ: P&R Publishing, 2007), 293.

34. See Stéphane Courtois et al., *The Black Book of Communism: Crimes, Terror, Repression*, trans. Jonathan Murphy and Mark Kramer (Cambridge, MA: Harvard University Press, 1999).

35. Quoted in Jacobs, *Original Sin*, xvi.

36. Wells, *God in the Wasteland*, 47.

purpose. And trying to make sense of good and evil has become obtuse, rendering the pain of evil all the more disorienting and unbearable.

It is not as though the problem of evil were unique to us moderns. The ancients queried the problem, including the ancient Hebrews. Job is arguably the oldest book of the Hebrew canon; its chronological milieu precedes that of the patriarchs.[37] The Greeks wrestled with it, as did many of the patristic and medieval theological luminaries of the church: Irenaeus (c. A.D. 130–202), Augustine (A.D. 354–430), Anselm (1033–1109), and Aquinas (1225–74), to name a few. If Susan Neiman is right, the whole history of Western philosophy is merely a postscript to life reflecting on the problem of evil.[38]

But the Enlightenment brought newfound doubts about the old answers that set the stage for an emerging avalanche of unbelief. The Great Lisbon Earthquake rattled loose this avalanche, setting forth the modern crisis of theodicy.[39] Perhaps no one highlighted the mounting doubts about the power and goodness of God in the face of evil as much as Voltaire (1694–1778). In the wake of the Lisbon earthquake, Voltaire questioned the optimism especially promoted by Gottfried Wilhelm Leibniz (1646–1716) and his best-of-all-possible-worlds theodicy.[40] According to Leibniz, an all-wise God would create only that world that he would deem best. Thus, any imperfections (i.e., moral and natural evils) contained in such a world would have to have some optimally good purpose that outweighed any apparent ill effects. Therefore, Leibniz argued that for the best of all possible worlds to come about, evil is necessary. Alexander Pope (1688–1744) popularized this view in his *Essay on Man* (1732–34).

Leibnizian optimism, however, was interpreted with satirical disdain. So . . . Lisbon has been utterly destroyed for no apparent reason? No matter:

> Whatever happens is for the best; the heirs of the dead will benefit financially; the building-trade will enjoy a boom; animals will grow fat on meals

---

37. Other than ancient Israel, most ancient Near Eastern cultures had virtually no concept of moral evil and the personal suffering it creates. Evil in the pagan myths was part of a cosmic struggle with the forces of chaos. Two exceptions are the fragmentary text called the "Babylonian Theodicy" and the Akkadian "Poem of the Righteous Sufferer," both written in the period from 1400 to 800 B.C. See Ronald J. Williams, "Theodicy in the Ancient Near East," in *Theodicy in the Old Testament*, ed. James L. Crenshaw (Philadelphia: Fortress Press, 1983), 42–48; Joseph F. Kelly, *The Problem of Evil in the Western Tradition* (Collegeville, MN: Liturgical Press, 2002), 8–10.

38. Susan Neiman, *Evil in Modern Thought: An Alternative History of Philosophy* (Princeton, NJ: Princeton University Press, 2002), 2–10.

39. Turner, *Without God, Without Creed*, 207.

40. G. W. Leibniz, *Theodicy*, ed. Austin M. Farrar, trans. E. M. Huggard (New York: Cosimo Classics, 2009).

provided by corpses trapped in the debris; an earthquake is a necessary effect of a necessary cause; private misfortune must not be overrated; an individual who is unlucky is contributing to the general good.[41]

Such sentiments reflected Voltaire's unsparing attack on the perceived buoyance of Leibniz's theodicy, which swept across Europe with great popularity.[42] His initial reaction to the disaster was conveyed in *Poème sur le désastre de Lisbonne* ("Poem on the Lisbon Disaster").[43] His pen drips with the bitterest of sarcasm:

> "All's well," ye say, "and all is necessary,"
> Think ye this universe had been the worse
> Without this hellish gulf in Portugal?
> Are ye so sure the great eternal cause,
> That knows all things, and for itself creates,
> Could not have placed us in this dreary clime
> Without volcanoes seething 'neath our feet?[44]

Later he says:

> But how conceive a God supremely good,
> Who heaps his favours on the sons he loves,
> Yet scatters evil with as large a hand?
> What eye can pierce the depth of his designs?
> From that all-perfect Being came not ill:
> And came it from no other, for he's lord:
> Yet it exists. O stern and numbing truth!
> O wondrous mingling of diversities!
> A God came down to lift our stricken race:
> He visited the earth, and changed it not!
>
> . . . The human race demands a word of God.
> 'T is his alone to illustrate his work,
> Console the weary, and illume the wise.[45]

---

41. T. D. Kendrick, *The Lisbon Earthquake* (Philadelphia: J. B. Lippincott, 1955), 180–81.

42. Matthew Stewart argues that Voltaire's caricature of Leibniz as a "metaphysical Pollyanna," though the common perception of Leibniz, is "entirely superficial" (*The Courtier and the Heretic: Leibniz, Spinoza, and the Fate of God in the Modern World* [New York: W. W. Norton, 2006], 328).

43. The *Poème* was written in 1756. But Voltaire's most famous response to Leibnizian optimism came three years later in the satirical novel *Candide* (1759).

44. Paul Hyland, Olga Gomez, and Francesca Greensides, eds., *The Enlightenment: A Source-book and Reader* (New York: Routledge, 2003), 78. This last line reflects the common belief in the mid-eighteenth century that earthquakes were caused by underground volcanoes.

45. Hyland, Gomez, and Greensides, *The Enlightenment*, 80–81.

Voltaire's audacity to question God reveals the sort of pessimism and skepticism that catapulted the Enlightenment's rejection of classical Christian theism in favor of the limp-limbed god of deism that eventually gave way to full-blown atheism.

Voltaire was not alone. Others used the Lisbon earthquake to advance skepticism about the traditional God of the Bible as well, including David Hume (1711–76) and Immanuel Kant. While Hume never mentioned Lisbon in his writings, no doubt his skepticism about theodicy was influenced by the widespread discussion of the earthquake while working on his *Dialogues concerning Natural Religion*, written between 1750 and his death in 1776. He famously states, "Epicurus' old questions are yet unanswered. Is [God] willing to prevent evil but not able? Then he is impotent. Is he able but not willing? Then he is malevolent. Is he both able *and* willing? From whence then is evil?"[46]

On the other hand, Kant wrote three short essays on the earthquake, focusing on the scientific aspects of the disaster. He dismisses God's involvement in the earthquake as pure speculation. He argues that God has no more special regard for man in such disasters than he does for the rest of nature.[47] Divine providence was beginning to slip from the Western conscience.

Or was it?

THE CRISIS OF SECULARIZATION

We have now come to the place where skepticism about God—and especially any attempt at constructing a theodicy—rules the day. The Christian narrative of creation and fall (let alone redemption) is a fantastic myth perpetrated by deluded religionists refusing to adapt to the cold, hard reality of the impersonal, godless, brutal, materialist zeitgeist of modernity. As David Bentley Hart writes:

> Perhaps no doctrine strikes non-Christians as insufferably fabulous than the claim that we exist in the long melancholy aftermath of a primordial catastrophe: that is a broken and wounded world, that cosmic time is a phantom of true time, that we live in an umbratile interval between creation in its fulness and the nothingness from which it was called, that the universe languishes in bondage to the "powers" and "principalities" of this age, which never cease in their enmity toward the kingdom of God.[48]

46. David Hume, *Dialogues concerning Natural Religion*, ed. Richard H. Popkin (Indianapolis: Hackett Publishing, 1980), 63.

47. Kendrick, *Lisbon Earthquake*, 198–200.

48. David Bentley Hart, *The Doors of the Sea: Where Was God in the Tsunami?* (Grand Rapids: Eerdmans, 2005), 61–62.

Yet while our public intellectual climate was progressively and radically altered by the Enlightenment—proscribing God—it has never completely shut out the vexatious thoughts that he is never silent. The twentieth century has been marked by two world wars and a whole host of unprecedented atrocities.[49] The Holocaust, representing all that is horrifying about the modern world, has become the new Lisbon. Ever since, the world has witnessed more discussion of theodicy than perhaps the rest of recorded history. The literature is vast, continually pouring off the presses (let alone the Internet), with no end in sight.[50]

As modernity has tried to push God from our minds, the emerging darkness filling the void has made one thing clear. Persistent reminders of the Almighty always remain lodged in the conscience, however deep. God can be suppressed only so far (Rom. 1:18–19). An unintended crisis was fomented by the Enlightenment. Lisbon supposedly caused fractures in the belief structures of biblical theism. But in reality, modern man's attempt to suppress God has produced the real fractures in Western society.

Charles Taylor in his monumental and influential tome *A Secular Age* chronicles some of the more deeply embedded forces that gave rise to modern secularization in the West.[51] According to Taylor, the process of secularization is the setting forth of the conditions for believability in God. "Why was it virtually impossible not to believe in God in, say, 1500 in our Western society, while in 2000 many of us find this not only easy but even inescapable?"[52] Describing our contemporary world, Taylor remarks, "For

49. According to the research of Lewis M. Simons, the twentieth century witnessed a staggering number of mass murders, totaling around 90,829,000 people. See "Genocide Unearthed," *National Geographic*, January 2006, 28–35. This number comes from the chart on page 30.

50. Between 1960 and 1990 alone, no less than 4,200 philosophical and theological writings appeared in books and journals (Daniel Howard-Synder, ed., *The Evidential Argument from Evil* [Bloomington, IN: Indiana University Press, 1996], ix). Since 1990, the literature has increased exponentially.

51. Charles Taylor, *A Secular Age* (Cambridge, MA: Belknap Press, 2007). Two important works from a Christian perspective that clarify Taylor's cumbersome work are James K. A. Smith, *How (Not) to Be Secular: Reading Charles Taylor* (Grand Rapids: Eerdmans, 2014), and Colin Hansen, ed., *Our Secular Age: Ten Years of Reading and Applying Charles Taylor* (Deerfield, IL: Gospel Coalition, 2017). Carl Trueman and Michael Horton's chapters in *Our Secular Age* provide some correctives to Taylor's analysis. See also Matthew Rose's critique in "Tayloring Christianity," *First Things* (December 2014): 25–30.

52. Taylor, *Secular Age*, 25. See also Turner, *Without God, Without Creed*, xii. Turner declares that the possibility of atheism or even agnosticism during the Middle Ages was virtually a "cultural impossibility" (2). Religious observance of some sort was fully integrated into the social fabric of Europe. "Without some sort of God, the world disintegrated into incomprehensibility. . . . Giving up God meant abandoning any coherent world picture" (3). The very fabric and structure of the cosmos, as well as personal and social meaning, depended on belief in God (4).

the first time in history a purely self-sufficient humanism came to be a widely available option. I mean by this a humanism accepting no final goals beyond human flourishing, nor any allegiance to anything else beyond this flourishing. Of no previous society was this true."[53]

In the old world, God was essential to one's self-understanding. He sat atop the pyramid establishing truth and meaning, and we creatures stood subservient to his claims.[54] "God used to function as a central explanatory concept. As cause and purpose, the idea of God shaped" a whole host of disciplines into a more comprehensive and coherent worldview.[55] Now that the creature has been severed from the Creator, we live in a "Nova Effect," in which an explosion of bewildering options for ascertaining meaning and purpose confronts us.[56] In each case, the self replaces God atop the pyramid while sorting through all claims to truth and meaning, and then determining what one prefers most. God might be one option—and, for many people, an unlikely one.

James Turner notes that belief in God remained steady over the nineteenth century and into the twentieth, "but belief [now] no longer functions as a unifying and defining element of [the] entire culture; it no longer provides a common heritage that underlies our diverse world views."[57] Religion had become privatized by the late twentieth century.[58] Furthermore, what remains of orthodox Christian theistic belief has been profoundly transformed by the forces of secularization. The nova of pluralism and multiculturalism has been called on to fill the emptiness that Christian theism used to fill almost exclusively. The result has produced a profound "modern angst."[59]

But between the Middle Ages and the late nineteenth century, unbelief became a completely viable option (5). He states that by the end of the eighteenth century, there were probably fewer than a dozen atheist intellectuals in Europe and none in America (44).

53. Taylor, *Secular Age*, 18.

54. Even the ancient Greeks saw the need for humans to submit to the gods, except for Epicureanism, which had no use for gods, but this philosophical outlook was rare (Taylor, *Secular Age*, 18–19).

55. Turner, *Without God, Without Creed*, 263–64.

56. Taylor, *Secular Age*, 302–4.

57. Turner, *Without God, Without Creed*, 263. It is important to note, as both Taylor and Turner point out, that unbelief did not drive out belief. To the contrary, Christianity flourished in the nineteenth and twentieth centuries (particularly in America). Rather, unbelief has come alongside belief as being much more plausible and acceptable to Western culture. Secularism, however, has replaced Christian theism as the defining force shaping public discourse and cultural values at large.

58. The exception to this rule is the politicization of evangelicalism in the United States and its desire to return to a mythical Christian America. See John Fea, *Was America Founded as a Christian Nation?* (Louisville, KY: Westminster John Knox Press, 2016); Gregg L. Frazer, *The Religious Beliefs of America's Founders: Reason, Revelation and Revolution* (Lawrence, KS: University Press of Kansas, 2012).

59. Turner, *Without God, Without Creed*, 264.

This is true even for evangelicalism, which has had to constantly guard itself against secularization as well as syncretization due to the relentless influence of so many competing and bewildering worldviews (e.g., naturalism, pragmatism, consumerism, hedonism, secular psychology, narcissism, emotionalism, feminism, and cultural Marxism).

Christian Smith has accurately characterized modern mainstream evangelical belief as "moralistic therapeutic deism."[60] He characterizes the beliefs of this quasi-religious outlook as follows:

1. God who created and orders the world and watches over human life on earth.
2. Wants people to be good, nice, and fair to each other, as taught in the Bible and by most world religions.
3. Central goal of life is to be happy and to feel good about oneself.
4. Does not need to be particularly involved in one's life except when God is needed to resolve a problem.
5. People go to heaven when they die.[61]

According to Taylor, our secular age has imbibed a process of immanentization whereby the world has moved from a pervasive sense of transcendence to one of pervasive immanence. A transcendent world is marked by things beyond the present temporal, material realm. It speaks of the eternal, the supernatural: of disembodied spirits, of heaven and hell, and of God's ubiquitous and weighty presence. We now live in an unconscious "immanent frame" marked by nothing more than what can be found in the temporal and material realm.[62] All human flourishing is confined to

---

60. See Christian Smith, *Soul Searching: The Religious and Spiritual Lives of American Teenagers* (New York: Oxford University Press, 2005); Christian Smith, *Souls in Transition: The Religious and Spiritual Lives of Emerging Adults* (New York: Oxford University Press, 2009).

61. Smith, *Soul Searching*, 162–63.

62. Taylor, *Secular Age*, 542–49. Taylor's distinction between "transcendence" and the "immanent frame" is similar to Peter Berger's observation involving the modern distinction (dichotomy) between private and public spheres of knowledge. Modernity has sharply divided the private sphere, which consists of personal and especially religious preferences, from the public sphere, which consists of scientific knowledge. It represents a values-facts split. Values (part of the private sphere) are a matter of individual taste (i.e., they are both relative and relatively unimportant). Facts (part of the public sphere) are nonnegotiable truths binding on everyone. This reflects Immanuel Kant's distinction between the noumenal world and the phenomenal world. The distinction is also similar to Francis Schaeffer's observation about the two-realm theory of truth. The upper story (private sphere/values) is regarded as the realm of the nonrational or noncognitive. The lower story (public sphere/facts) is regarded as the realm of the rational or verifiable truth. See the summary in Nancy Pearcey, *Total Truth: Liberating Christianity from Its Cultural Captivity* (Wheaton, IL: Crossway, 2004), 20–22.

the here and now, and what can be obtained via self-sufficient means. We are no longer regarded as strangers and aliens in this world, but this world is our home—our only home. There is no more mystery, nothing yonder to look forward to, no future transformation of our weak, corrupted, finite frames. The beatific vision has dissipated into thin air.

Friedrich Nietzsche (1844–1900) represents the unintended apex of the Enlightenment's project to strip the Western world of supernaturalism and its God-consciousness. While many theists excoriate Nietzsche for being blasphemously insolent in his statement that "God is dead," few realize the context in which he made this claim. Nietzsche came to the disconcerting position that a godless world is not the utopian landscape that modern man hoped it would be, but a lonely and terrifying place to live.

In his work *The Gay Science* (1882), he tells the parable of a madman running into a crowd, crying incessantly, "I'm looking for God! I'm looking for God!"[63] The crowd derided him with laughter.[64] But the forlorn prophet would not be silenced. He leaped amid the scoffers and cried:

> "Where is God?" "I will tell you! *We have killed him*—you and I! We are all his murderers. But how did we do this? How were we able to drink up the sea? Who gave us the sponge to wipe away the entire horizon? What were we doing when we unchained this earth from its sun? . . . Are we not continually falling? And backwards, sideways, forwards, in all directions? Is there still an up and a down? Are we not straying as though through an infinite nothing? Isn't empty space breathing at us? Hasn't it got colder? Isn't night and more night coming again and again? Don't lanterns have to be lit in the morning? Do we still hear nothing of the noise of the grave-diggers who are burying God? Do we still smell nothing of the divine decomposition?—Gods, too, decompose! God is dead! God remains dead! And we have killed him!"[65]

For Nietzsche, embracing atheism required a high price to be paid. "After Nietzsche, easy belief and easy unbelief proved impossible."[66] He regarded moral freedom as paramount and felt that Christian morality was repressive. If God exists, then humans cannot be morally free. But if humans are free and

---

63. Friedrich Nietzsche, *The Gay Science*, ed. Bernard Williams, trans. Josefine Nauckhoff (New York: Cambridge University Press, 2001), 125.

64. The crowd consists of both atheists and theists, but it is easy to imagine Nietzsche as targeting the theists instead of the atheists. He says that the churches (of his own day) have become "the tombs and sepulchres of God."

65. Nietzsche, *Gay Science*, 125.

66. Lint, "Age of Intellectual Iconoclasm," 301.

God does not exist, then we face a terrifying loneliness.[67] Humanity can no longer depend on some greater transcendent authority. We must now create our own meaning, what he called "the will to power." This became an "awful responsibility." Given the hopeless plight of man in the absence of God's death, the frightful reality of creating significance is too daunting for most.

The rare person who has the courage to face this challenge Nietzsche called "Superman." And no—this is not the hero of comic-book lore! He is a lonely and desperate figure. Nietzsche shattered the illusion of many Enlightenment savants who saw a different kind of optimism from that of Leibniz once the theistic God was eliminated from the scene. Nietzsche saw the stark reality that without God, there is no goodness left in the world, no discernible purpose to life.[68] Nihilism is the only true heir of atheism.

THE PRESENT CRISIS OF MEANING AND EVIL

Nietzsche's nihilism anticipated the present crisis of meaning more than any could have imagined. While many moderns blithely saunter through their secularized lives, not all is well. Taylor chronicles the "haunted world" that Nietzsche saw lurking beneath the pretentiousness and smugness of this emerging secularism. It is a world full of "cross-pressures" and tensions that leaves secularized man in a state of unease. There is a "wide sense of malaise at the disenchanted world, a sense of it as flat, empty, a multiform search for something within, or beyond it, which could compensate for the meaning lost with transcendence."[69]

Below the surface of our superficial and sanguine outlook lies a nervousness about life, an undercurrent of angst that is most acutely felt when facing the problem of suffering and evil. Nothing highlights the crisis of our age more than the problem of evil.[70] It exposes the "cross-pressures" that Taylor speaks of, the tendency to vacillate from enthusiastically embracing uncertainty to longing for a deeper anchor. "We are unprotected [in this disenchanted world] . . . from suffering and evil as we sense it raging in the world. There are unguarded moments when we can feel the immense weight of suffering, when we are dragged down by it, or pulled down into despair."[71]

Unfortunately, modern man has developed built-in defenses to keep thoughts of transcendence at bay, exacerbating our angst. Taylor calls this the "buffered self"—the impulse to insulate oneself from what lies beyond

67. Lint, "Age of Intellectual Iconoclasm," 302.
68. Lint, "Age of Intellectual Iconoclasm," 305.
69. Taylor, *Secular Age*, 302.
70. Taylor, *Secular Age*, 680–81.
71. Taylor, *Secular Age*, 681.

the natural realm. But there is a profound struggle as postmodernists wrestle with being uncertain of their (pretended) uncertainty. What if the secular postmodern ethos is all wrong? What if unbelief is unsustainable? This world has never stopped being haunted by what Machen called "the awful transcendence of God."[72] Calvin called it the *sensus divinitatis* (sense of the divine).[73] Or as Francis Schaeffer would say, "The God Who Is There."

Atheist Thomas Nagel captures this angst:

> I speak from experience, being strongly subject to this fear myself: I want atheism to be true and am made uneasy by the fact that some of the most intelligent and well-informed people I know are religious believers. It isn't just that I don't believe in God and, naturally, hope that I'm right in my belief. It's that I hope there is no God! I don't want there to be a God; I don't want the universe to be like that.[74]

God cannot be escaped. James K. A. Smith also points to this conflict in contemporary writers such as Julian Barnes.[75] In 2008, Barnes wrote a memoir on the fear of mortality called *Nothing to Be Frightened Of.* He wants to alleviate the fear of death for his fellow secularists, but the opening lines of his book already begin to betray him: "I don't believe in God, but I miss Him."[76]

As Peter Berger has pointed out, "There seems to be a death-refusing hope at the very core of our humanitas."[77] We can't stand the thought of our lives' being terminated. We want to live forever. But this points to something—or *Someone*—that is far bigger than we want to imagine. These uneasy sentiments encapsulate the crisis of secularism, of modernity, of postmodernity. They expose the polarizing tensions that mark the present spiritual and intellectual climate in the West.

One can never think seriously about life or death for long without entertaining questions about transcendence, of deeper objective meaning, of eternal realities that press into the here and now, of an infinite personal Being. But is *he* really there? Wait . . . this is not what science has taught us. We have no souls. There is no immaterial realm. No heaven above. No hell below. No God to tell us what to do. We live, we die, and then it all ends.

Or does it?

72. J. Gresham Machen, *Christianity and Liberalism* (1923; repr., Grand Rapids: Eerdmans, 2009), 54.

73. John Calvin, *Institutes of the Christian Religion*, ed. John T. McNeill, trans. Ford Lewis Battles (Philadelphia: Westminster, 1960), 1.3.1.

74. Thomas Nagel, *The Last Word* (Oxford: Oxford University Press, 1997), 130.

75. Smith, *How (Not) to Be Secular*, 4–5.

76. Julian Barnes, *Nothing to Be Frightened Of* (New York: Alfred A. Knopf, 2008), 1.

77. Peter L. Berger, *A Rumor of Angels* (New York: Doubleday, 1969), 81.

The philosopher Bryan Magee speaks of the fear of what he calls the void of "eternal nothingness" that awaits those who die:

> If the void is the permanent destination of all of us, all value and all significance are merely pretended for purposes of carrying on our little game, like children dressing up. It is, of course, a willing pretense: we cannot bring ourselves to face eternal nothingness, so we busy ourselves with our little lives and all their vacuous pursuits, surrounded by institutions that we ourselves have created yet which we pretend are important, and which help us shut out the black and endless night that surrounds us. It is all, in the end, nothing—nothing whatsoever.[78]

Magee's fear of disintegrating into the void at death is the cause of another fear—the meaninglessness attached to life. "If I was about to be swallowed up by an everlasting void, nothing I did was of the slightest significance . . . . It could therefore make no difference *when* I died, and would have made no difference if I had never been born; that I was in any event going to be for all eternity what I would have been if I had never been born; that there was no meaning in any of it, no point in any of it; and that in the end everything was nothing."[79]

This ever-nagging fear tends to lead people straight back to the God that the West has desperately tried to erase. Death is the most poignant reminder of the ever-present specter of evil in the world. It is "arguably the most fearsome of all evils."[80] And evil, no matter how much we wish to suppress its implications, drives us to God for answers—a God that we instinctively know looms larger than the pain that this world seeks to crush us with.

In an article for the *New Statesman* entitled "Why I Believe Again," A. N. Wilson writes about his conversion and subsequent deconversion to atheism:

> I can remember almost yelling that reading C S Lewis's *Mere Christianity* made me a non-believer—not just in Lewis's version of Christianity, but in Christianity itself. On that occasion, I realised that after a lifetime of churchgoing, the whole house of cards had collapsed for me—the sense of God's presence in life, and the notion that there was any kind of God, let alone a merciful God, in this brutal, nasty world. . . . It was a nonsense, together with the idea of a personal God, or a loving God in a suffering universe. Nonsense, nonsense, nonsense.[81]

78. Bryan Magee, *Confessions of a Philosopher* (New York: Random House, 1997), 229.

79. Magee, *Confessions of a Philosopher*, 252.

80. Michael L. Peterson, *God and Evil: An Introduction to the Issues* (Boulder, CO: Westview Press, 1998), 5.

81. https://www.newstatesman.com/religion/2009/04/conversion-experience-atheism.

The problem of evil is what drove Wilson away from God, the way it has for many in the grip of secularization. But he was dogged with doubts that could not be alleviated by reading his skeptical hero David Hume. He was continually reminded "of all the human qualities that have to be denied if you embrace the bleak, muddled creed of a materialist atheist. It is a bit like trying to assert that music is an aberration, and that although Bach and Beethoven are very impressive, one is better off without a musical sense."[82] Yet Wilson's return to theistic belief was not easy. "My departure from the Faith was like a conversion on the road to Damascus. My return was slow, hesitant, doubting. So it will always be; but I know I shall never make the same mistake again."[83]

The crisis of secularization with all its muddiness and uncertainty about meaning, ethics, and values has magnified the problem of evil so that even confident believers in God face unprecedented struggles. We live in an age of doubt punctuated by brief moments of belief. As Smith has observed, "We don't believe instead of doubting; we believe *while* doubting. We're all Thomas now."[84]

As a result, contemporary Western society appears to have more difficulty facing pain and suffering than any other culture in history.[85] Moderns have lost the capacity for grappling with evil. Andrew Delbanco writes, "A gulf has opened up in our culture between the visibility of evil and the intellectual resources available for coping with it. Never before have images of horror been so widely disseminated and so appalling . . . . The repertoire of evil has never been richer. Yet never have our responses been so weak. We have no language for connecting our inner lives with the horrors that pass before our eyes in the outer world."[86]

82. https://www.newstatesman.com/religion/2009/04/conversion-experience-atheism.

83. https://www.newstatesman.com/religion/2009/04/conversion-experience-atheism. Larry Taunton has given a convincing testimony that even the impenetrable cloak of unbelief that made Christopher Hitchens the hero of many atheists was far more porous than many suppose. See *The Faith of Christopher Hitchens: The Restless Soul of the World's Most Notorious Atheist* (Nashville: Thomas Nelson, 2016).

84. Smith, *How (Not) to Be Secular*, 4.

85. Timothy Keller, *Walking with God through Pain and Suffering* (New York: Dutton, 2013), 14.

86. Delbanco, *Death of Satan*, 3. Elsewhere Delbanco says, "Our culture is now in crisis because evil remains an inescapable experience for all of us, while we no longer have a symbolic language for describing it" (224). Delbanco is thinking of words such as *Satan*, as the title of his book suggests. Jeffrey Burton Russell has also chronicled this demise in understanding evil in his four-volume set of studies: *The Devil: Perceptions of Evil from Antiquity to Primitive Christianity* (1977), *Satan: The Early Christian Tradition* (1981), *Lucifer: The Devil in the Middle Ages* (1984), and *Mephistopheles: The Devil in the Modern World* (1986), each published by Cornell University Press. See also the summary volume: *The Prince of Darkness: Radical Evil and the Power of Good in History* (Ithaca, NY: Cornell University Press, 1988).

Charles Matthewes concurs with this assessment:

> We know neither how to resist nor how to suffer evil, to a significant
> degree because we do not understand it: it bewilders us, and our typical
> response to it is merely a theatricalization, a histrionic which reveals
> no real horror at the reality and danger of evil but rather our fear of
> admitting our incomprehension of what we confront, what it is we are
> called to respond to, when we encounter evil. We oscillate between what
> Mark Edmundson calls a glib optimism of "facile transcendence" and a
> frightened, pessimistic, "gothic" foreboding; this oscillation exhibits the
> guilty conscience of modernity.[87]

The conditions for coping with suffering and evil in our modern era are
only exacerbated by other factors. Historical increases in modern wealth,
technology, and medical care have made life relatively pain-free for most.
We live longer, more comfortably, and healthier. People in the past faced
far greater daily tragedies than we do today, yet they had better mental
resources to handle them. Loss, pain, suffering, violence, and death were
far more common in their direct experiences, yet created far less anxiety.
Evil and suffering were accepted as a normal part of life. Today, suffering
is a strange intrusion and to be avoided at all costs.[88] "We are more shocked
and undone by suffering than were our ancestors."[89] We are more connected
than ever through the Internet, social media, and "smart" devices, yet we
face an epidemic of loneliness.[90] Interminable bouts of stress, anxiety, and
acute panic attacks are increasing and increasingly the norm.[91]

Sigmund Freud (1886–1939) opened wide the door for our modern fragile therapeutic ethos whereby we must escape reality, eschew all moral
responsibility, and shift blame for all that troubles us. Emotional suffering
is on par with physiological ailments caused by foreign pathogens. We
now call depression and sorrow mental disorders that are to be cured by

---

87. Charles T. Matthewes, *Evil and the Augustinian Tradition* (Cambridge: Cambridge University Press, 2001), 4.

88. Keller, *Walking with God*, 23.

89. Keller, *Walking with God*, 16.

90. See presentation from the 125th annual convention of the American Psychological Association (2017) by Julianne Holt-Lunstad, "Loneliness: A Growing Public Health Threat," found at: https://www.apa.org/convention/2017/loneliness.aspx. See also Julianne Holt-Lunstad, "The Potential Public Health Relevance of Social Isolation and Loneliness: Prevalence, Epidemiology, and Risk Factors," *Public Policy & Aging Report* 27.4 (2017): 127–30, found at: https://academic.oup.com/ppar/article/27/4/127/4782506.

91. Alex Williams, "An Anxious Nation," *New York Times*, June 10, 2017, ST1. See https://www.nytimes.com/2017/06/10/style/anxiety-is-the-new-depression-xanax.html.

professionals—psychiatrists and psychologists—the priests of this new cult of self-worship.[92]

Secularization has shifted the focus to personal esteem, affluence, comfort, health, pleasure, and satisfaction, all to be showered on us instantly. Placing these values at a premium has made it increasingly difficult to face adversity. Yet ironically, we have never been more exposed to evil and suffering—copious amounts of it are daily set forth on television, computer, and phone screens. Yet these atrocities are viewed vicariously at a comfortable distance. We remain safely removed from their immediate impact. The sheer number of casual encounters with such walls of stupefying images dismantles our moral sensibilities. Our outrage is short-lived. Our sympathies are fleeting, trivializing the real face of evil. Unfortunately, all the mechanisms with which our secular age has provided us for surviving the onslaught of pain and suffering are failing. Once catastrophe comes knocking on our own doors, we don't know how to answer. Venturing outside our "safe spaces," we are paralyzed. What's more, we are paralyzed *inside* our safe spaces.

IS THEODICY POSSIBLE?

In a post-Christian and post-Enlightenment era, many have supposed that attempting to address the problem of evil with theodicy—justifying God's ways—is futile. Our disenchanted world has rendered such efforts meaningless. Smith suggests that secularists facing horrific loss and tragedy are not usually "tempted by faith or toying with reenchantment; it's that ruthless disenchantment seems more than we can bear."[93] We must stumble under the weight of evil all alone.

Even some theologians lament over the lack of any answers to the problem. Fleming Rutledge writes: "*There has never been a satisfactory account of the origin of evil, and there will be none on this side of the consummation of the kingdom of God. Evil is a vast excrescence, a monstrous contradiction that cannot be explained but can only be denounced and resisted wherever it appears.*"[94]

But the reason why suffering seems acutely more miserable today than ever before has precisely to do with the marginalization of God and the resources

---

92. See Philip Rieff, *Triumph of the Therapeutic: Uses of Faith after Freud* (Chicago: University of Chicago Press, 1987); Christopher Lasch, *The Culture of Narcissism: American Life in an Age of Diminishing Expectations* (New York: W. W. Norton, 1979); William Kirk Kilpatrick, *Psychological Seduction: The Failure of Modern Psychology* (Nashville: Thomas Nelson, 1983); Paul C. Vitz, *Psychology as Religion: The Cult of Self-Worship* (Grand Rapids: Eerdmans, 1994).

93. Smith, *How (Not) to Be Secular*, 67.

94. Fleming Rutledge, *The Crucifixion: Understanding the Death of Jesus Christ* (Grand Rapids: Eerdmans, 2015), 419.

that biblical Christianity provides to face evil. Furthermore, the modern conception of God as monumentally less robust than the God of the Bible makes it impossible to face adversity coherently. It is easy to turn away from God for answers when he has been domesticated, emasculated, and shorn of his transcendence, full power, sovereignty, and holiness. In a cosmic construct in which humanity lies at the gravitational center, God's goodness is reduced to having human tranquility as his highest goal.[95] When that goal seems unachievable, disillusionment quickly sets in. We used to understand that we were limited and vulnerable, and this made it easier to see God through the fog of pain.[96]

Ironically, once we conceive of ourselves as being without limits and able to escape our acute vulnerability, it makes the unavoidable suffering we experience in this world all the more excruciating. Our secular age deludes itself that violence and suffering can be eliminated by human progress.[97] We live under the false pretenses of a tattered COEXIST bumper sticker.

But "as religion goes away, evil does not."[98] Thus, "our age is very far from settling into a comfortable unbelief."[99] Contrary to the zeitgeist of Western secularism, human beings cannot bear to accept that life is meaningless.[100] We are consummate seekers of transcendent purpose, which again leads us to a God greater than the ones we have so feebly constructed over the last three hundred years. This means that not only is a theodicy possible, it has been made urgent by the forces that have brought us to the present crisis of secularization. So while many think that a theodicy is futile in our seemingly godless and horrific world, it is a pathway back to sanity.

To establish a coherent and satisfying theodicy, however, we must return to a countercultural theology grounded in Scripture that strips away the accretions of modern and postmodern speculation about the nature of God. The revisionist god will not do. And nowhere has this revisionist god flourished more greatly than in evangelicalism, which David Wells has chronicled so painfully and thoroughly.[101] He laments, "The fundamental

95. Taylor, *Secular Age*, 650.
96. Taylor, *Secular Age*, 651.
97. Taylor, *Secular Age*, 651.
98. Hansen, *Our Secular Age*, 9.
99. Taylor, *Secular Age*, 727.
100. Reading chapters 14 and 15 ("The Search for Meaning" and "Mid-life Crisis," respectively) in Magee's *Confessions of a Philosopher* (228–75) makes this clear.
101. See Wells's four-volume project: *No Place for Truth; or, Whatever Happened to Evangelical Theology?* (1993), *God in the Wasteland: The Reality of Truth in a World of Fading Dreams* (1994), *Losing Our Virtue: Why the Church Must Recover Its Moral Vision* (1998), and *Above All Earthly Pow'rs: Christ in a Postmodern World* (2005), each published by Eerdmans. The four volumes are summarized in *The Courage to Be Protestant* (Grand Rapids: Eerdmans, 2008).

problem in the evangelical world today is that God rests too inconsequentially upon the church. His truth is too distant, his grace is too ordinary, his judgment is too benign, his gospel is too easy, and his Christ is too common."[102]

God suffers from being weightless, not merely in the culture at large, but in the church—and not in the fading churches of the mainstream denominations, but in the evangelical church.[103] "The traditional doctrine of God remains entirely intact while its saliency vanishes. The doctrine is believed, defended, affirmed liturgically, and in every other way held to be inviolable—but it no longer has the power to shape and to summon that it has had in previous ages." God is "like a child that has been abandoned within a family, still accorded a place in the house, but not in the home."[104]

The church, under pressure from a culture infatuated with self-absorption, has managed to fashion God as an extension of purely humanlike characteristics, only slightly more robust than ourselves. James Turner warns that if belief in God "is to remain plausible over the long haul, [we] cannot regard God as if human, sharing human interests and purposes, accessible to human comprehension."[105] Likewise, Wells says, "A God with whom we are on such easy terms and whose reality is little different from our own—a God who is merely there to satisfy our needs—has no real authority to compel and will soon begin to bore us."[106]

One area in which the classical view of God has succumbed to the spirit of our therapeutically driven age is the notion of a vulnerable, suffering God, a supersensitive deity who is a fellow sufferer with his creatures. The traditional doctrine of God's impassibility (i.e., his inability to suffer as we do) has been all but abandoned by contemporary theologians.[107] How we understand the inner life of God in relation to human suffering has a profound impact on theodicy.[108]

Such anemic views of God in the church are extended into every area of belief and practice, with devastating effects. Ligonier Ministries has commissioned Lifeway Research to conduct biennial studies (starting in 2014) that demonstrate a woeful lack of orthodox beliefs among professing

---

102. Wells, *God in the Wasteland*, 30.
103. Wells, *God in the Wasteland*, 88.
104. Wells, *God in the Wasteland*, 89.
105. Turner, *Without God, Without Creed*, 269.
106. Wells, *God in the Wasteland*, 93.
107. See Ronald Goetz, "The Suffering God: The Rise of a New Orthodoxy," *Christian Century* 103.13 (1986): 385–89; Thomas G. Weinandy, *Does God Suffer?* (Notre Dame, IN: University of Notre Dame Press, 2000), 1–26. God's impassibility is addressed in chapter 15.
108. See chapter 15.

evangelical Christians. Sadly, each successive study has chronicled significant and ever-growing declines in orthodox belief.[109]

Given the sorry state of theological soundness where it is most expected to thrive, no wonder popular culture at large abounds with confusion over questions of God, morality, and the problem of evil.[110] Even C. S. Lewis's way of framing the problem of evil betrays (I'd like to assume unintentionally) the man-centered shift that evangelicals have so easily absorbed into our distorted brand of modern theism. Recall that he said, "If God were good, He would wish to make His creatures perfectly happy, and if God were almighty, He would be able to do what He wished. But the creatures are not happy. Therefore, God lacks either goodness, or power, or both."[111]

This assumes that God exists for us instead of our existing for him. Does God stand at our beck and call? Is it his responsibility to prevent or remove evil to restore our personal tranquility? If so, he has failed. I do not wish to somehow minimalize or trivialize suffering. But as long as the problem of evil is viewed from this anthropocentric perspective, we will pursue answers that do not satisfy—answers that will cast us deeper into the pit, answers that will restrict where our gaze should be drawn.

If evil coexists with a God of unfathomable glory, it can in no way diminish that glory. It must serve in some way to highlight it. If evil can somehow manage to dull the refulgence of the incomparable God, then we are undone. If it renders him a hapless deity, shaking his head in disbelief ("How could this happen to my pristine creation!"), then we are indeed to be pitied as a people.

Jesus was neither dumbstruck nor distraught when he predicted plainly, "In the world you will have tribulation" (John 16:33). He does not see

---

109. See http://thestateoftheology.com/. Another indicator of the dearth of orthodoxy in popular evangelicalism is reflected in the best-selling books listed by the Evangelical Christian Publishers Association (ECPA). Records from 2008 onward indicate an overwhelming number of books sold that are far removed from the beliefs represented in the historic creeds and confessions of orthodox Christianity. See http://christianbookexpo.com/bestseller/archives.php.

110. In a typical Facebook thread regarding an article on the problem of evil, virtually all the 200+ comments evidenced a woeful lack of understanding basic issues of the problem. Many responses promoted shallow platitudes (usually something about free will or sappy pseudo-Christian therapeutic jargon), uninformed rants against Christian theism, denials of objective moral standards (often denying the existence of good and evil altogether), and incoherent thoughts concerning personal pet theories or theories laced with convoluted references to Eastern/New Age mysticism. Basic reasoning skills were almost entirely absent. If someone did put forth a relatively rational argument, it was usually ignored, misunderstood, mocked, or dismissed without coherent reasons.

111. C. S. Lewis, *The Problem of Pain* (New York: Macmillan, 1962), 26.

evil as a remote possibility or even a strong probability. He sees it as an absolute reality in a world over which God perfectly presides. He does not countenance the notion that evil is an unfortunate intrusion on God's good design for history or our lives. But what he does say is marked with a commanding resolve: "Take heart; I have overcome the world."

Jesus has not offered a full-orbed theodicy here, but he hints at evil's resolution—a plan that is centered on himself. We think of evil as crashing down on our heads to destroy us. And indeed, it often does so. But we will see that evil as it is pictured in the Scriptures also comes crashing into the God of the universe in the person of Jesus Christ. Yet when all the nuclear-charged powers of malevolence hit the Son of God, it is not he who is destroyed.

KEY TERMS

deism
Enlightenment
epistemology
nihilism
postmodernism
secularism
secularization
theism
transcendence (general)

STUDY QUESTIONS

1. What is the Enlightenment, and how did it change the Western world?
2. How have views about God changed over time in the Western world?
3. Why have science and reason been pitted against theism and divine revelation as sources of truth? Should they be pitted against each other? Why or why not?
4. What is nihilism, and why is it the logical result of the direction in which Western thinking has gone since the Enlightenment?
5. How has evangelicalism been affected by secularization?
6. Why do people seem to have a harder time facing evil in the world today than previous generations did?
7. Have you seen the influence of secularism in your own life? If so, how has it affected the way in which you view God and the world?

FOR FURTHER READING

W. Andrew Hoffecker, ed., *Revolutions in Worldview* (Phillipsburg, NJ: P&R Publishing, 2007).

James K. A. Smith, *How (Not) to Be Secular: Reading Charles Taylor* (Grand Rapids: Eerdmans, 2014).

James Turner, *Without God, Without Creed: The Origins of Unbelief in America* (Baltimore: Johns Hopkins University Press, 1985).

Advanced

Charles Taylor, *A Secular Age* (Cambridge, MA: Belknap Press, 2007).

David F. Wells, *God in the Wasteland: The Reality of Truth in a World of Fading Dreams* (Grand Rapids: Eerdmans, 1994).

3

PROBING THE DARKNESS

October 24, 1994, seemed like an ordinary day for three-year-old Michael Smith and his fourteen-month-old brother, Alex. They were carefully strapped into the car seats of their mother Susan's bright-red Mazda. But something terrible happened. Susan called the police in a panic, claiming that the car had been hijacked by a stranger, and then spent nine days on national television, pleading for their abductor to return her precious children. The nation was transfixed, sympathizing with a grieving mother. But detectives suspected that she was lying, and soon after she made her confession.

Susan Smith had driven the car with her two little boys to the boat ramp of John D. Long Lake not far from their home in Union, South Carolina. Then she suddenly exited the vehicle and let the car slip down the ramp and into the bottom of the lake, drowning Michael and Alex. It turns out that she was estranged from her husband, David, the father of her boys. And now the man she longed to spend her life with had written her a devastating letter to break things off. He never desired children of his own. And he could never see himself caring for *her* children. Maybe without them he might reconsider his relationship with Susan.

Shortly after Susan was sentenced to thirty years in prison for her crime, Rod Rosenbaum penned an article on the problem of evil for the *New York Times Magazine* entitled "Staring into the Heart of the Heart of Darkness."[1] He wonders how our modern world should think about the sorts of deeds that a Susan Smith commits. He asks about her "state of mind that night, the degree of actual responsibility she bore for her act. Was it an 'evil deed,'

---

1. See http://www.nytimes.com/1995/06/04/magazine/staring-into-the-heart-of-the-heart -of-darkness.html.

or the product of dysfunction disorder, past abuse, mental disease? Since no one 'in her right mind' could have committed the evil deed, she must have been 'out of her mind,' she must have 'lost her mind': she wasn't really responsible."[2] Rational modern "minds" don't act this way.

He continues:

> And so there were already whispers of sexual abuse, of "a suicide by proxy syndrome," even of Prozac use. She was beginning to look less like the perpetrator than the victim: she was the victim of an "irresistible impulse," she had no choice, it really wasn't her act, it really wasn't her. . . . Yet something about the act, some primal, mythic, Medea-like aura emanating from the fact of a mother killing her young seemed to summon up the stark language of evil, the search for some Satanic cause.[3]

Was this mother morally responsible for an act that seems fundamentally and objectively reprehensible? Rosenbaum has trouble accepting this explanation. As one apparently infected by the poison of postmodernism, he cannot abide by any explanation. On the one hand, something undeniably sinister was transpiring in those disturbed lake waters. On the other hand, evil seems so remote, so archaic, so draconian, in a world shorn of transcendence. We're as appalled at evil as we ever were, yet we're constantly trying to suppress its naked reality. We live in a haunted, confused world where pinning down the nature of evil eludes us.

This is one of the problems that confront us when trying to think about a theodicy. Peter Geach captures our modern angst: "What we cannot hope to understand in this life is sin. Sin is the surd or absurd element in the universe."[4] Yet without understanding the "element" of sin—of evil—our secularized age has no way to justify moral outrage or to make sense of pain and suffering.

In the wake of biblical theism's demise, good and evil are foreign concepts. In its place, secularization has produced a mesmerizing array of ill-informed assertions. If evil exists, certainly God cannot. Yet on the other hand, if evil persists, then God must be refusing to do his job to make the world a safe place for us. We have a right to be angry—at him. Yes—the phantom God is to blame for the mess we are in. Some boldly assert that God and evil are one and the same. But—to even talk about evil is to use categories that no

---

2. http://www.nytimes.com/1995/06/04/magazine/staring-into-the-heart-of-the-heart-of-darkness.html.

3. http://www.nytimes.com/1995/06/04/magazine/staring-into-the-heart-of-the-heart-of-darkness.html.

4. Peter Geach, *Providence and Evil: The Stanton Lectures 1971–2* (Cambridge: Cambridge University Press, 1977), 63.

longer exist. It is offensive to dredge them up. It might even be hate speech. But what is hate speech? What is moral outrage? What is anger, whether justifiable or not, without some notion that there is a thing called *evil*? Like it or not, evil is a thing, and we are stuck trying to make sense of it.

Here is the secularist's quandary. If a tangled Darwinian, Nietzschean, Marxist, Freudian cosmos exists, then what is evil? Can evil exist in a purely materialist, naturalistic framework infected with a strange brew of nihilism and therapeutic narcissism? Those caught in this nexus want desperately to challenge believers with hard questions about God and evil. Yet the secularists have trouble being able to make enough sense of reality to pose the two as a problem.

In the end, theodicy is as much a problem for atheists as it is for theists. The honest and careful theist must admit that evil is a problem because he has a clear view of who God is and what evil is. But the atheist and his cousin the agnostic have the deeper problem. They must suffer the ill effects of evil while having no way to explain it. The secularist cannot justify its existence if God does not exist. In other words, the only reason why evil is a problem at all is that God *does* exist. The existence and nature of good and evil demand God's existence, indeed his superintendence, and this explains why theodicy will never go away.

So before we can address the matter of theodicy, we must first probe the darkness. We must come to terms with the nature of evil before considering why God intends for it to exist.

THE REAL FACE OF A GODLESS WORLD

Many secularists want to salvage meaning and morals in a godless world. But that is not possible without embracing serious contradictions in the fundamental premises of such a worldview. Nietzsche clearly demonstrated that a world without transcendence—without God—is a place where *"there are altogether no moral facts."* Morality amounts to "absurdity."[5]

Bertrand Russell is among the few honest atheists who openly recognized this. A world where God is dead is a realm where meaning and morals escape us. In a famous essay entitled "A Free Man's Worship" (1903), Russell writes:

> Man is the product of causes which had no prevision of the end they were achieving; that his origin, his growth, his hopes and fears, his loves and his beliefs, are but the outcome of accidental collocations of atoms; that no fire, no heroism, no intensity of thought and feeling, can preserve

5. Friedrich Nietzsche, *Twilight of the Idols*, in *The Portable Nietzsche*, ed. and trans. Walter Kaufman (New York: Penguin Books, 1982), 501.

an individual life beyond the grave; that all the labors of the ages, all the devotion, all the inspiration, all the noonday brightness of human genius, are destined to extinction in the vast death of the solar system, and that the whole temple of man's achievement must inevitably be buried beneath the debris of a universe in ruins—all these things, if not quite beyond dispute, are yet so nearly certain, that no philosophy which rejects them can hope to stand. Only within the scaffolding of these truths, only on the firm foundation of unyielding despair, can the soul's habitation henceforth be safely built.[6]

Russell sounds like Albert Camus. In the midst of World War II (1942), Camus lamented that in this new nihilistic climate that we have crafted for ourselves in the modern world, "there is but one truly serious philosophical problem, and that is suicide. Judging whether life is or is not worth living amounts to answering the fundamental question of all philosophy."[7]

Little has changed from Russell in 1903 and Camus in 1942 to Richard Dawkins in 1995, who said:

In a universe of blind physical forces and genetic replication, some people are going to get hurt, other people are going to get lucky, and you won't find any rhyme or reason in it, nor any justice. The universe we observe has precisely the properties we should expect if there is, at bottom, no design, no purpose, no evil and no good, nothing but blind, pitiless indifference. As that unhappy poet A. E. Housman put it:

For Nature, heartless, witless Nature
Will neither know nor care.[8]

For all the bluster that Dawkins exhibits in his militant stance against God and religion, he at least admits with his Nietzschean forebears to where the logic of atheism leads. In a purely materialist, naturalist world, morals and values become unanchored subjective local constructs that constantly change with the shifting of the cultural sands. Given the honest trajectory of the nihilism that obtains in a godless cosmos, it is difficult to talk meaningfully about the existence of good and evil. Confusion abounds. As Lance Morrow admits, "Evil is the most powerful word in the language, and the most elusive."[9]

6. Bertrand Russell, *Mysticism and Logic* (New York: Barnes & Noble, 1917), 47–48.

7. Albert Camus, *The Myth of Sisyphus and Other Essays* (New York: Vintage Books, 1991), 3.

8. Richard Dawkins, *River out of Eden: A Darwinian View of Life* (New York: Basic Books, 1995), 133.

9. Lance Morrow, *Evil: An Investigation* (New York: Basic Books, 2003), 7.

SECULAR CONFUSION ABOUT EVIL

Here is the problem. "The old language of evil has become a collection of what George Orwell called 'dead' metaphors . . . . It is at most a dormant language, of the sort one recognizes when using common words like 'awful,' which once expressed the fear and trembling of the puny creature full of awe before the majesty of God, but now more usually denotes a taste like spoiled milk or the irritation of sitting through a dull movie."[10]

This is what secularism has done. It has de-Godded God and domesticated our age in order to magnify every mundane and ignoble feature of our creatureliness above the Creator. We have gerrymandered the world as if designed for our own insipid gratification and no longer for God's glory. It is inconceivable that any kind of god would create a world whereby our personal happiness is not his highest goal. It shocks us, especially in the Western world, more than any previous generation that such conditions could exist to strip us of our self-defined bliss.

We chafe against Carl Henry's assessment: "The Creator has not arranged the universe for maximal creaturely happiness, least of all if happiness means unruffled ease and self-satisfied contentment."[11] This creates an existential nightmare once pain and suffering crash our party of illusions. Consequently, many secular definitions of evil blithely conceive it apart from any moral considerations. Moral and natural evil collapse into anything that causes human discomfort and suffering.[12]

Jeffrey Burton Russell, who has studied the history of Western conceptions of evil, has himself succumbed to this egregious error: "The essence of evil is abuse of a sentient being, a being that can feel pain. It is the pain that matters. Evil is grasped by the mind immediately and immediately felt by the emotions; it is sensed as hurt deliberately inflicted."[13] There is no question that evil (both moral and natural) causes pain and suffering. But while Burton may not realize it, he has reduced and defined evil in terms of self-referential *feelings*. The primary concept of evil—that is, moral evil—is not seen as violating a universally consistent and objective set of ethical standards to which all humans have obligations. But it is that which deliberately strips away our personal subjective feelings of happiness.[14]

---

10. Andrew Delbanco, *The Death of Satan: How Americans Have Lost the Sense of Evil* (New York: Farrar, Straus and Giroux, 1995), 11.

11. Carl F. H. Henry, *God, Revelation and Authority*, vol. 6, *God Who Stands and Stays*, pt. 2 (Wheaton, IL: Crossway, 1999), 296.

12. Careful distinctions between moral and natural evil will be made later (see pages 51–59).

13. Jeffrey Burton Russell, *The Devil: Perceptions of Evil from Antiquity to Primitive Christianity* (Ithaca, NY: Cornell University Press, 1977), 17.

14. David F. Wells, *Above All Earthly Pow'rs: Christ in a Postmodern World* (Grand Rapids: Eerdmans, 2005), 119.

We are not talking about normal egregious acts of mistreatment, hatred, oppression, and violence. In the absence of a transcendent standard, the threshold for what is regarded as malevolence is lowered and distorted by our narrowly defined frame of reference, marked as it is by radical self-absorption and self-inflated perceptions of our own importance. Evil is what makes us feel bad, violating our preferential whims. When unpredictable fate replaces divine providence, evil merely becomes a matter of "bad luck."[15]

The modern and postmodern outlook also tends to look at evil in an atomistic manner: occasional and isolated disturbances of individuals that can be remedied through education, social and political reforms, psychological therapy, or psychotropic medications.[16] Trying to pin down evil to an objective moral standard that demands personal culpability is largely disappearing. Words such as *sin* and *evil* are toned down to more palpable terms such as "disorders" and, in extreme cases, "acts of aggression."[17] These are unfortunate episodes of normal, though perhaps antisocial, behavior that are the result of environmental factors, genetics, or our psychological past over which we have no control.[18]

We no longer have willful sinners. We have victims instead of criminals. We have psychopathic and sociopathic sicknesses needing therapeutic and medical treatment.[19] We don't blame people for being sick; we pity them. So what used to be called acts of wickedness "have no moral lesson for us; the guilt or remorse points to no real wrong. We strive to understand them in order to reduce their force, to become able to live with them," but not to castigate them with biblical reprimands.[20] "On the therapeutic register," the old Christian ethical system "is itself pathological, part of the problem that represses our nature."[21]

But how is sterilizing evil with clinical terminology from the ever-expanding editions of the *Diagnostic and Statistical Manual of Mental Disorders* supposed to comfort us that a Susan Smith or an Adolf Eichmann is no cause for worry? Yes, the inconceivable specimens of pure evil in a Cormac McCarthy novel really do exist, but the white-clad clinicians

---

15. Delbanco, *Death of Satan*, 153.

16. Morrow, *Evil*, 12–13.

17. Delbanco, *Death of Satan*, 4; Jeffrey Burton Russell, *The Prince of Darkness: Radical Evil and the Power of Good in History* (Ithaca, NY: Cornell University Press, 1988), 248.

18. Russell, *Prince of Darkness*, 274.

19. Charles Taylor, *A Secular Age* (Cambridge, MA: Belknap Press, 2007), 618.

20. Taylor, *Secular Age*, 621.

21. James K. A. Smith, *How (Not) to Be Secular: Reading Charles Taylor* (Grand Rapids: Eerdmans, 2014), 107.

who pretend that they have solved all the disconcerting features of every abnormal behavior are suddenly at a loss for words.

Hannah Arendt spoke of the pencil-pushing Eichmann and the banality of evil and was severely criticized for it.[22] But why should we be surprised? A godless world is a nihilistic world, and a nihilistic world is permeated with a banality that the Holocaust should not be able to shatter. Some forget how much Hitler imbibed the poison of Nietzsche and drenched his vision of Nazism with its dreadful but numbing consequences.[23]

This ubiquitous denial of personal culpability is also expressed in the identity politics that dominates modern moral and political discourse. "Evil tends to be seen as exogenous, as brought on by society, history, patriarchy, capitalism, the 'system' in one form or another."[24] Here we see the influence of Karl Marx (1818–83) (and Sigmund Freud [1886–1939] as well) and his neo-Marxist progeny, such as Antonio Gramsci (1891–1937), György Lukács (1885–1971), Theodor Adorno (1903–71), and Herbert Marcuse (1898–1979).[25] Evil resides not within individuals but with oppressive institutions and systems such as the patriarchal family and the conservative sexual ethics of Christianity.

No longer does Aleksandr Solzhenitsyn's biblical form of *mea culpa* come in view. The Russian dissident spent eight years (1945–53) in the gulag after being accused of spreading anti-Soviet propaganda. One day, after witnessing a prison guard's unusual cruelty, Solzhenitsyn came to realize that given the same circumstances, he would have behaved in the same way. He said that the gulag taught him that everyone had the heart of Stalin. "The line separating good and evil passes not through states, nor between classes, nor between political parties either—but right through every human heart."[26]

Solzhenitsyn is repudiating the Marxist maxim that evil is what divides oppressive classes from oppressed classes. For example, in the contemporary debate over racism in America, a neo-Marxist view of evil is prominent in leftist thinking. The problem of race, according to Marxist-driven "Critical Theory," is a problem of parasitical "white privilege" whereby one class

22. Hannah Arendt, *Eichmann in Jerusalem: A Report on the Banality of Evil* (1963; repr., New York: Penguin Books, 2006).

23. Richard Weikart, *Hitler's Religion: The Twisted Beliefs That Drove the Third Reich* (Washington, DC: Regnery Publishing, 2016), 22–28.

24. Taylor, *Secular Age*, 618.

25. See Roger Scruton, *Fools, Frauds and Firebrands: Thinkers of the New Left* (New York: Bloomsbury, 2015).

26. Aleksandr I. Solzhenitsyn, *The Gulag Archipelago Part III–IV*, trans. Thomas P. Whitney (New York: Harper & Row, 1975), 615.

of people makes the other its victim. In this case, it is "whiteness," not the individual, that is fundamentally evil. It is no wonder that addressing racial problems has taken an unfortunate step backward.[27]

Yet for others, evil has become positively mysterious, a kind of nefarious electromagnetic force, a toxic gas that passes through the air unseen and somehow infects people with its ethereal power.[28] Morrow supposes that evil is a "body-snatcher" that "steals the soul." The soul in his materialist conception is nothing more than the space between neurons in the brain where synapses fire. He claims, "Evil brings on a falsifying transformation, the sudden substitution of a wicked shadow self, of Mr. Hyde. Evil is your horrid alternate suddenly emerging. Evil is the wicked twin, your negative, your Cain that kills the better self."[29]

Once you eliminate creatures who are made in the image of a holy and righteous God, and who stagger willfully and terribly under the weight of original sin, evil must be consigned to such mysterious outside forces, to psychological disorders or the realm of the incomprehensible.

Ironically, in this muddled framework, the emotional, fragile self dramatically defines the subjective experience of evil, but the acting self is far removed from the emanation of evil. Evil becomes a kind of foreign intruder that besets our natural benign function. It suddenly emerges to surprise us like a disease, an invasive pathogen. It is merely an unexpected evolutionary development that happens to form a bit of a bad aftertaste.

From a biblical perspective, these various strains of moral confusion are nothing more than the inevitable sinful human tendency to suppress the reality of God that deludes the creature into thinking that he will be freed from moral constraints to experience human flourishing. Instead, this stubborn suppression only increases one's capacity for descending deeper into darkness and self-deception (Rom. 1:18–23). "The heart is deceitful above all things, and desperately sick; who can understand it?" (Jer. 17:9).

We humans have a limited capacity for determining what constitutes human flourishing. Apart from divine revelation, we will replace the right-

---

27. Scott Allen, "A Tale of Two Worldviews," *WORLD*, February 10, 2018, found at: https://world.wng.org/content/a_tale_of_two_worldviews. See also P. Andrew Sandlin, "A Primer on Cultural Marxism," *JCLT* 8.2 (2019): 10–16. For an assessment of critical theory, see Helen Pluckrose and James Lindsay, *Critical Theories: How Activist Scholarship Made Everything about Race, Gender, and Identity—and Why This Harms Everybody* (Durham, NC: Pitchstone Publishing, 2020). For a biblical and gospel-centered approach to racial unity, see H. B. Charles Jr. et al., *A Biblical Answer for Racial Unity* (The Woodlands, TX: Kress Biblical Resources, 2017).

28. Morrow, *Evil*, 29.

29. Morrow, *Evil*, 29.

ful model for flourishing with cheap, degrading, and devastating substitutes. Those substitutes distort any vision of the good life and leave people stumbling in the blackness, trying to sort out what constitutes the good. Man without God will abandon any keen moral sense. He will rename acts of wickedness as "errors" in judgment. He will even swap moral truth for moral falsehood. "Woe to those who call evil good and good evil, who put darkness for light and light for darkness, who put bitter for sweet and sweet for bitter!" (Isa. 5:20).

Linda Bird Francke provides us with a stark reminder that one cannot repress moral truth for long before it exposes the weak foundations on which we seek to deny the obvious. In 1976, a few short years after *Roe v. Wade* legalized abortion in the United States, Francke penned one of the most striking yet ironic testaments to the sanctity of human life.

In an article for the *New York Times*, the famous pro-abortion journalist, using the pseudonym Jane Doe, recalls her experience in the waiting room of an abortion clinic before the tragic operation to end her baby's life:

> Though I would march myself into blisters for a woman's right to exercise the option of motherhood, I discovered there in the waiting room that I was not the modern woman I thought I was.
>
> When my name was called, my body felt so heavy the nurse had to help me into the examining room. I waited for my husband to burst through the door and yell "Stop," but of course he didn't. I concentrated on three black spots in the acoustic ceiling until they grew in size to the shape of saucers, while the doctor swabbed my insides with antiseptic.
>
> "You're going to feel a burning sensation now," he said, injecting Novocain into the neck of the womb. The pain was swift and severe, and I twisted to get away from him. He was hurting my baby, I reasoned, and the black saucers quivered in the air. "Stop," I cried, "Please stop." He shook his head, busy with his equipment. "It's too late to stop now," he said. "It'll just take a few more seconds."
>
> What good sports we women are. And how obedient. Physically the pain passed even before the hum of the machine signals that the vacuuming of my uterus was completed, my baby sucked up like ashes after a cocktail party. Ten minutes start to finish. And I was back on the arm of the nurse.
>
> There were 12 beds in the recovery room. Each one had a gaily flowered draw sheet and soft green or blue thermal blanket. It was all very feminine. Lying on these beds for an hour or more were the shocked victims of their sex life, their full wombs now stripped clean, their futures less encumbered.

Finally, then, it was time for me to leave. . . . My husband was slumped in the waiting room, clutching a single yellow rose wrapped in a wet paper towel and stuffed into a Baggie.

We didn't talk all the way home . . . .

My husband and I are back to planning our summer vacation now and his career switch.

It certainly does make more sense not to be having a baby right now—we say that to each other all the time. But I have this ghost now. A very little ghost that only appears when I'm seeing something beautiful, like the full moon on the ocean last weekend. And the baby waves at me. And I wave at the baby. "Of course, we have room," I cry to the ghost. "Of course, we do."[30]

Immersing oneself in the mire of moral bewilderment only serves to increase misery. When the light dawns on the darkened lies you've slept with, waking up to drink the cup of regret is unbearable. When evil strikes hard from the outside or emerges willingly or unwittingly from within, the person living in a de-Godded world is left to wonder, like Camus, whether life is worth living. All you have left in this muddled milieu is an "inarticulate dread."[31]

Linda Francke shows us that most people under the spell of our secular age still have trouble escaping the fact that evil is much more concrete than we are led to believe by the reigning cultural elites. It points to transcendence, to deeper meaning.

Even hardcore moral skeptics return to the language of evil when probing the frozen bloody tundra around one of Siberia's gulags, crushed skulls in Cambodia's Killing Fields, the hollow gas chambers at Auschwitz, or the smoldering base of the Twin Towers in the aftermath of 9/11. Tim Keller writes:

One of the things that distinguishes us from animals is that we do not simply squeal under suffering and seek to flee it. We search to find some point in the pain and thereby to transcend it, rather than seeing ourselves as helpless cogs in a cruel machine. And this drive to find meaning in suffering is not only dignifying, it is indelible. . . . Without meaning, we die.[32]

---

30. Linda Bird Francke, "There Just Wasn't Room in Our Lives Now for Another Baby," in *Contemporary Moral Issues: Diversity and Consensus*, ed. Lawrence M. Hinman (Upper Saddle River, NJ: Prentice Hall, 1996), 20–22. The original article can be found at http://www.nytimes.com/1976/05/14/archives/there-just-wasnt-room-in-our-lives-now-for-another-baby.html.

31. Delbanco, *Death of Satan*, 9.

32. Timothy Keller, *Walking with God through Pain and Suffering* (New York: Dutton, 2013), 22.

While our post-Christian era may have trouble defining evil, we never lose our intuitive ability to recognize it all around us. So the time is ripe for discovering a satisfying theodicy. The vast constellation of all the cultural currents over the last three centuries has led us to a moment rich with opportunity. But entering the theodical maze cannot happen unless we define evil on God's terms, not on godless terms.

THE BIBLICAL CONCEPT OF EVIL

As we venture forward, let us now draw forth some definitions and distinctions regarding the nature of good and evil from a divine (biblical) perspective.

Distinguishing Moral and Natural Evil

When discussing the problem of evil, philosophers and theologians make a distinction between moral and natural evil. *Moral evil* is that which proceeds from personal (i.e., human and angelic) beings as sentient creatures with moral agency—the ability and desire to make moral decisions. Such evil is perpetrated by intentional actions or by neglect of acting in a way that people ought to act. One can intentionally toss an infant into a swimming pool to watch her drown. Without a shadow of doubt, that is evil. But one could watch an infant accidentally fall into a swimming pool and then neglect to save her, having the ability to do so. That, too, is evil.

Natural evil is some adverse condition in the world that does not necessarily proceed from specific moral choices of human beings but causes pain and suffering nonetheless.[33] The link between moral and natural evil is that both cause various kinds of pain and suffering for us.

Natural evil can fall into different categories—for example: (1) *natural disasters* such as earthquakes, tsunamis, tornadoes, famine, or pestilence; (2) *accidents* such as a blown tire while driving a car, or tripping and falling down the stairs; (3) *illness and disease* such as pneumonia, cancer, or leprosy; (4) *physical and mental handicaps* such as malformed limbs or Down syndrome; (5) *physical toil* due to the physiological weaknesses of the human body combined with the hard (and sometimes harsh) conditions of the natural environment we live in (Gen. 3:17–19).

Some would include *animal pain* in the category of natural evil, such

---

33. Alvin Plantinga, *God, Freedom, and Evil* (Grand Rapids: Eerdmans, 1977), 30; John Hick, *Evil and the Love of God* (New York: Harper and Row, 1975), 12. We could categorize some natural evil under the influence of Satan or demonic entities (see Plantinga, *God, Freedom, and Evil*, 58). See, for example, Matt. 9:32–33; 12:22–23; 17:14–18; Luke 13:10–13.

as when a male grizzly bear kills its cubs, or the ichneumon wasp paralyzes a caterpillar and then lays its eggs on it so that the emerging larvae slowly eat it alive.[34] Another dimension of natural evil concerns the seemingly indifferent circumstances that transpire such that immoral people prosper and moral or innocent people experience adversity (Job 12:4–6; Ps. 73:2–9). The world seems consigned to impersonal, dispassionate fate that favors no one.

From a biblical perspective, natural evil is ultimately a consequence of moral evil. In other words, we live in a world cursed by the disobedience of our parents, Adam and Eve (Gen. 3:13–19; Rom. 8:19–22). All manner of natural evils are simply a reflection of a cursed creation. Often the standard Hebrew word for "evil" (*raʿ/raʿaʾ*) in the Old Testament is translated as "disaster" (ESV) or "calamity" (NASB) in contexts that speak of natural catastrophes (cf. Isa. 45:7).[35]

Generally speaking, natural evil (and good) befalls the moral and immoral alike; it afflicts the believer as much as the unbeliever (Matt. 5:45; Acts 14:17). A massive boulder tumbling down the cliff above a winding mountain road can as easily crush the car of a theist as that of an atheist. This does not mean that indifferent fate replaces divine providence; it simply means that God is not automatically predisposed to suspend creation's curse for some but not others (Eccl. 9:2). Nor does this mean that God might have reason at various times to protect some people from the consequences of evil, natural or otherwise. It is the task of theodicy to try to understand some of those reasons—why the God who has the requisite power to overrule *any* instance of evil at any given time doesn't do so *all* the time.

This perspective also disabuses us of an unfortunate distortion. The Enlightenment reacted to a misplaced theodicy that suggested that every instance of natural evil was divine retribution for some specific infraction of God's moral law (just as Job's three thoughtless friends did!).[36] While in some cases this direct line of causation is true, it is the exception to the

---

34. Charles Darwin, in a letter to Asa Gray, said, "I cannot persuade myself that a beneficent and omnipotent God" would design such a wasp. See Darwin Correspondence Project, Letter 2814, "To Asa Gray, 22 May [1860]," found at: www.darwinproject.ac.uk/letter/DCP-LETT-2814.xml.

35. William A. VanGemeren, ed., *New International Dictionary of Old Testament Theology & Exegesis* (Grand Rapids: Zondervan, 1997), 3:1155–56. In addition to "disaster," the ESV also translates *raʿaʾ* as "evil," "calamity," "trouble," or "harm" in similar contexts. See Job 21:30; Prov. 24:16; 28:14; Jer. 18:8, 11; 23:12; 26:3; 29:11; 36:3; 42:10, 17; 44:2; 51:60, 64; Ezek. 14:22; Dan. 9:12–14; Amos 3:6; 6:3; 9:10; Obad. 13; Jonah 1:7–8; 3:10; 4:2; Mic. 1:12; 3:11; Hab. 2:9. In many of these passages, disaster is related to the devastation of war and not necessarily natural catastrophes.

36. Susan Neiman, *Evil in Modern Thought: An Alternative History of Philosophy* (Princeton, NJ: Princeton University Press, 2002), 242–43.

rule. Natural evil is the universal and indiscriminate consequence of the curse of Adam's sin.[37]

Respected Christians such as John Wesley expressed unreserved confidence that the Lisbon earthquake (1755) was God's punishment on a city rife with immorality and Roman Catholic apostasy.[38] The answer to Amos's rhetorical question is certainly correct: "Does disaster come to a city, unless the LORD has done it?" (Amos 3:6; cf. Ps. 46:8). Yet by no means does any particular natural disaster occur as a direct consequence of moral rebellion, nor could we peer into the mind of God to know unless he directly revealed that information to us.

Pain and suffering are not always or even usually "the immediate consequence of a particular sin. That is a hideous piece of heresy, capable of inflicting untold mental anguish. It would mean that the people who suffer the most in this world must be those who have sinned the most in this world; and that is demonstrably untrue, both in the Bible and in experience."[39] The righteous and the wicked suffer alike (Eccl. 2:14).

Jesus makes it clear that when the tower in Siloam collapsed and killed eighteen people, it wasn't because these people had committed some particular crime warranting this particular outcome. It is not obvious that the incident was to be interpreted as a punitive response of God. The dead were no worse sinners than anyone else in Jerusalem at the time (Luke 13:4).

The man born blind in John 9:1–3 didn't suffer this condition because he or his parents had sinned. Quite the opposite. God brought about this "natural evil" in order to display his glory through healing the man's blindness. That is not exactly a form of retributive justice. Of course, Job is the consummate example of a righteous man who suffers evil.

A few qualifications should be noted here. Natural evil is evil only inasmuch as it causes seemingly unjustified pain and suffering to humans. You must be in the wrong place at the wrong time when a tornado hits and destroys your home while your neighbor's is left untouched. Also, there is nothing intrinsically evil (moral or otherwise) about some things designated

37. See, for example, the exceptions in Ps. 78:44–48; Isa. 13:11–13; 24:17–21; Jer. 18:11; 19:3, 15; Nah. 1:5–6.

38. See John Wesley, "Serious Thoughts Occasioned by the Late Earthquake at Lisbon," in *The Works of Rev. John Wesley*, vol. 8 (New York: J & J Harper, 1827), 165–74. According to Kendrick, this was one of the fastest-selling pamphlets in England in the aftermath of the earthquake, undergoing six editions. See T. D. Kendrick, *The Lisbon Earthquake* (Philadelphia: J. B. Lippincott, 1955), 239.

39. D. A. Carson, *How Long, O Lord? Reflections on Suffering and Evil*, 2nd ed. (Grand Rapids: Baker Academic, 2006), 44.

as natural evil. A hurricane that never reaches land, destroying people and property, is not regarded as evil.

Furthermore, some naturally occurring "destructive" events have a good function. For example, forest fires clear the forest of dead trees and bring about conditions for renewal and greater forest health. Hurricanes break up the harmful bacterial toxins of algal blooms in ocean waters, sometimes called red tides. The fierce winds also reoxygenate the waters, improving the conditions for marine life where the red tides previously existed.

Examples such as these indicate why some theologians dispute whether natural disasters are a result of the fall or whether the fall made humans susceptible to the harm that comes from processes already embedded in the natural created order. It is not important to resolve what apparently "destructive" aspects of the creation were inherent in prefall conditions and what were not.[40] It is sufficient to know that in the aftermath of the fall, any adverse conditions in the natural world that cause undue pain and suffering to God's creatures can be constituted as instances of natural evil.

Defining Moral Evil

No philosophy, religious tradition, or ideological framework has provided such a deeply penetrating and robust grounding for the understanding of good and evil as biblical Christianity. Ironically, most religions outside the Judeo-Christian tradition would concur with the broad consensus of our secular age that the emanation of evil is far removed from persons themselves. There is a consistent denial that evil resides within human nature, and therefore personal culpability is a moot point. Evil is consigned to external impersonal malevolent forces.[41]

Christianity also provides a unique grounding for moral imperatives in the personhood of God. It sees humans as creatures with the same personhood, created in the image of God. This means that our sense of good and

---

40. I would argue that human and animal death, illness, disease, and so forth did not exist before the fall (Rom. 5:12, 17). See James Stambaugh, "Whence Cometh Death? A Biblical Theology of Physical Death and Natural Evil," in *Coming to Grips with Genesis: Biblical Authority and the Age of the Earth*, ed. Terry Mortenson and Thane H. Ury (Green Forest, AR: Master Books, 2008), 373–97.

41. Win Corduan, "Evil in Non-Christian Religions," in *God and Evil: The Case for God in a World Filled with Pain*, ed. Chad Meister and James K. Dew Jr. (Downers Grove, IL: InterVarsity Press, 2013), 195. Corduan provides a good introduction to other religious conceptions of good and evil in this essay. See also the summary in Keller, *Walking with God*, 13–31. For a fuller treatment, see John Bowker, *Problems of Suffering in Religions of the World* (Cambridge: Cambridge University Press, 1970).

evil "situates humans, not in relation to their fellow humans, society, and the state, but in relation to God, the heavenly Judge."[42]

The Westminster Standards are a good starting place to define moral evil, which is equivalent to the biblical concept of sin. "Sin is any want of conformity unto, or transgression of, any law of God, given as a rule to the reasonable [rational] creature [1 John 3:4]."[43] Note that sin is tied to a sense of obligation. There is an *oughtness* connected to moral reasoning and acting, to things required of us and things forbidden. This assumes a prior innate knowledge of good and evil.

Jeffrey Burton Russell, who is by no means speaking from Christian presuppositions, notes: "When we observe an act of cruelty, we do not engage in a complicated process of subjecting data to values analysis or the criteria of an abstract ethical system. We react with certain intuitive knowledge that the act is evil."[44] Russell assumes that our ability to quickly recognize evil, even in an age of radical moral relativism, speaks of some immovable anchor of internal moral knowledge.

The biblical name for that internal anchor is the *conscience*. It is like an "independent third party" who has set up shop inside our souls to alert us when something is morally right or morally awry.[45] Paul says:

> For when Gentiles, who do not have the law, by nature do what the law requires, they are a law to themselves, even though they do not have the law. They show that the work of the law is written on their hearts, while their conscience also bears witness, and their conflicting thoughts accuse or even excuse them. (Rom. 2:14–15)

In other words, one does not need to be of pure Jewish stock standing at the base of Mount Sinai watching the divine stylus chisel the Ten Commandments onto Moses' stone tablets. That stylus has already chiseled the moral law of God onto the fleshly tablets of every human heart. And the conscience acts as an arbitrator pronouncing our guilt or innocence.[46]

Notice that Paul's assertion here depends on a previous assertion that he made in Romans 1. The foundation for our universally intuitive recognition of good and evil is not rooted in some abstract law of nature—something

---

42. Herman Bavinck, *Reformed Dogmatics*, ed. John Bolt, trans. John Vriend, 4 vols. (Grand Rapids: Baker Academic, 2003–8), 3:130.

43. Westminster Larger Catechism Q24 (cf. Westminster Shorter Catechism Q14).

44. Russell, *Prince of Darkness*, 257.

45. Andrew David Naselli and J. D. Crowley, *Conscience: What It Is, How to Train It, and Loving Those Who Differ* (Wheaton, IL: Crossway, 2016), 23.

46. Naselli and Crowley, *Conscience*, 25.

akin to "moral gravity." It is rooted in a "law" given by a supreme personal moral Being to whom we are accountable. Paul says of the human race:

> For what can be known about God is plain to them, because God has shown it to them. For his invisible attributes, namely, his eternal power and divine nature, have been clearly perceived, ever since the creation of the world, in the things that have been made. So they are without excuse. (Rom. 1:19–20)

Thus, we are not talking simply about innate knowledge of moral laws. We are talking about innate knowledge of a moral Lawgiver. The ever-present sense of obligation connected to our moral awareness indicates an obligation to the divine Lawgiver and Judge (Lev. 19:2; 1 Peter 1:16). Why is there such an obligation to an unseen arbiter communicating through the conscience (John 16:8–11)? Because God is also our Creator (Ps. 100:3), our de facto Owner—the rightful Possessor of our person. We are not our own. We belong to the all-powerful, all-knowing Lord and Master of the universe (Ps. 24:1).

It follows that if God is the source of objective moral standards, then he himself must be characterized by moral perfection. "God is light, and in him is no darkness at all" (1 John 1:5). He is "the unchanging norm of what is true and right in all places, times, and cultures, a God whose reality is unaltered by the ebb and flow, the relativity, of life, unaffected by private perceptions or internal psychology."[47]

This explains why Paul, after detailing the catalogue of human depravity in Romans 3:9–20, describes our fundamental condition this way: "For all have sinned and fall short of the glory of God" (v. 23). The glory of God represents the fullness of God's magnificent and immaculate attributes with an emphasis on his unbridled holiness (otherness). Such a God deserves honor and our full allegiance. It is his rightful due.[48] To not offer this honor and allegiance is an attempt to strip him of glory and seek glory for ourselves.

Furthermore, to fall short of the glory of God is to bare a shattered *imago Dei*. The reflection of the moral image of God within the fallen creature is irreparably broken apart from divine intervention. "Sin is a radical disruption in the core of our being."[49]

---

47. David F. Wells, *God in the Wasteland: The Reality of Truth in a World of Fading Dreams* (Grand Rapids: Eerdmans, 1994), 91.

48. Anselm, *Why God Became Man [Cur Deus Homo]*, in *Anselm of Canterbury: The Major Works*, ed. Brian Davies and G. R. Evans (Oxford: Oxford University Press, 1998), 283.

49. John M. Frame, *Systematic Theology: An Introduction to Christian Belief* (Phillipsburg, NJ: P&R Publishing, 2013), 850.

Furthermore, as Paul seeks to establish the moral corruption of humanity in Romans 1–3, he indicates a fundamental aversion to God as our righteous Creator and Lawgiver. As Bavinck states, "Though sin is appallingly many-sided, with untold moral dimensions, at its heart it is a religious revolt against God."[50]

Quoting John Owen, J. I. Packer observes that the biblical concept of sin is fundamentally oriented against God and is thus characterized by "disgrace, fraud, blasphemy, enmity, hatred, contempt, rebellion and injury, poison, stench, dung, vomit, polluted blood, plague, pestilence, abominable, and detestable."[51] Packer goes on to state, "Sin is essentially the resolve—the mad, utterly blameworthy, but nonetheless, utterly firm resolve—to play God and fight the real God. Sinners resolve to treat themselves as the center of the universe and so they keep God at bay on the outer circumference of their lives."[52]

Even though sinful humans know the true God, they wish they did not. In Romans 1, Paul declares, "For the wrath of God is revealed from heaven against all ungodliness and unrighteousness of men, who by their unrighteousness suppress the truth" (v. 18). At the core of the human soul you will never find an atheist or a moral relativist. Moral truth as implanted by the divine source remains deep inside and is constantly seeking to make itself more openly known, but humans under the curse of original sin are constantly suppressing that truth to one degree or another. Even though "they knew God" (v. 21) and his "righteous decree" (v. 32), "they did not honor him as God or give thanks to him, but they became futile in their thinking, and their foolish hearts were darkened" (v. 21).

Humans have a tacit knowledge[53] of a personal God who stands as their Possessor and holy Judge. He demands that they be holy as he is holy (Lev. 11:44–45; 19:2; 20:7; 1 Peter 1:16). And yet they reject this clear, reasonable, and unimpeachable revelation. As a result, there is an irrationality to human sinfulness.[54] "Claiming to be wise," humans "became fools" (Rom. 1:22), "and exchanged the glory of the immortal God" for dumb idols of their own making (v. 23).

---

50. Bavinck, *Reformed Dogmatics*, 3:126.

51. J. I. Packer, "The Necessity of the Atonement," in *Atonement*, ed. Gabriel N. E. Fluhrer (Phillipsburg, NJ: P&R Publishing, 2013), 11.

52. Packer, "Necessity of the Atonement," 11.

53. The notion of *tacit knowledge* comes from Michael Polanyi. See his *Personal Knowledge*, enlarged ed. (Chicago: University of Chicago Press, 2015); Michael Polanyi, *The Tacit Dimension* (1966; repr., Chicago: University of Chicago Press, 2009). He uses it to indicate that "*we can know more than we can tell*" (Polanyi, *Tacit Dimension*, 4).

54. Frame, *Systematic Theology*, 851.

"Man's nature," according to Calvin, is "a perpetual factory of idols."[55] Denying the one true God does not mean abandoning the impulse to worship. Rather, there is a never-ending drive to replace the triune God with infinitely inferior and more palpable gods along with a set of degenerate moral precepts as a further means of suppressing the truth. The unregenerate host of humanity hate the light of divine moral truth. They cannot bear to allow it to shine on them lest it expose the blackness of their shame, their dishonor, their guilt and rebellion (John 3:20).

This leaves people in a place where they lament evil in the world but misjudge its true nature because they misjudge its impact within themselves. The desensitized offspring of our secular age do not know how to handle fleeting moments of their own shame. "Having displaced God, sinners can no longer gauge the depths of their sin, even if they do experience a tormented conscience."[56]

This doesn't mean that we are as bad as we can be. That is not what the classical doctrine of total depravity teaches. But we must grapple with these questions: "Is sin a superficial aberration? Deep down, is there a core to us that remains unscathed by sin, that remains unsullied, neutral and pure? Or is sin something that is now in the very roots of a sinner, in the heart, affecting the very grain of our being?"[57] The consistent witness of Scripture and experience affirms the latter.

In the end, the proclivity for personal moral evil in the world stems from "a false standard . . . , a false goal . . . , and a false motive."[58] The divine standard is replaced with a dubious human standard. The goal is human autonomy aided by whatever gods we invent. The motive is not to glorify the triune God but to glorify ourselves—to steal a false and feeble glory that corrupts all that is good and right and true.

> The heart wants what it wants. That's as far as we get. That's the conversation stopper. The imperial self rules all. Inquiring into the causes of sin takes us back, again and again, to the intractable human will and the heart's desire that stiffens the will against all competing considerations. Like a neurotic and therapeutically shelf-worn little god, the human heart keeps ending discussions by insisting it wants what it wants.[59]

55. John Calvin, *Institutes of the Christian Religion*, ed. John T. McNeill, trans. Ford Lewis Battles (Philadelphia: Westminster, 1960), 1.11.8.

56. Wells, *God in the Wasteland*, 53.

57. Michael Reeves and Hans Madueme, "Threads in a Seamless Garment: Original Sin in Systematic Theology," in *Adam, the Fall, and Original Sin: Theological, Biblical, and Scientific Perspectives*, ed. Hans Madueme and Michael Reeves (Grand Rapids: Baker Academic, 2014), 218.

58. Frame, *Systematic Theology*, 849.

59. Cornelius Plantinga Jr., *Not the Way It's Supposed to Be: A Breviary of Sin* (Grand Rapids: Eerdmans, 1995), 62.

Biblical Christianity stands alone in making such an unapologetic, trenchant, and sober assessment of the heart of evil. It is one that the world cannot bear to abide by, for reasons evidenced by the nature of evil that we have just described.

Evil as the Antithesis of Human Flourishing

Biblical morality has pervasive implications for our well-being both as individuals and as collective societies. We rarely isolate evil merely as a personal problem. We see it as a social phenomenon that always exacerbates the problem of evil. Pervasive evil is never far from each one of us because each of us expresses it in our relationships to everyone around us.

Thus, evil permeates the full spectrum of human-to-human relations, from two people at enmity with each other to societies that imbibe an entire ethos of moral corruption. Mankind is captive to an evil world system. The Gospel of John often characterizes the "world" (*kosmos*) in this way.[60] "The world as a whole organized system of spiritual force is a fact. It is the very embodiment of evil. It is a pervasive entity that exists quite apart from particular evil individuals; it is the structure of all reality apart from God. It is a mind-set and frame of reference totally different from and opposed to that of Christ and his disciples."[61] This means that the further we distance ourselves from God, the greater potential for evil to proliferate in the world and increase our misery while at the same time eradicating our ability to understand it and cope with it.

Therefore, one way to frame the problem of moral evil is how it disrupts peace (Rom. 3:17). Peace is not merely the absence of conflict and war between persons, but the positive attribute of *"universal flourishing, wholeness, delight"* that binds us to God and one another.[62] Moral evil first disrupts the peace that we were designed to have with God (Gen. 3:8). As sinners, we are foremost a people at enmity with the Creator (Rom. 5:10).

Second, our enmity with God disturbs the peace we have with others (Gen. 3:16; 4:8). It then disturbs the peace we have with creation (vv. 17–19). This hints at the solution to the problem of evil. A biblical theodicy will be one that restores peace. It will highlight reconciliation and redemption. It will restore *shalom* between God and man, between man and man, and between man and creation.[63]

---

60. See John 7:7; 8:23; 14:17; 15:18–19; 17:14, 25 (cf. 1 John 2:15–17). See also D. A. Carson, *The Gospel according to John* (Grand Rapids: Eerdmans, 1991), 122–23. Paul also puts forth this conception in 1 Corinthians 1:20–21, 27; 2:12; 3:19 (cf. 1 Cor. 2:14).

61. Millard J. Erickson, *Christian Theology*, 2nd ed. (Grand Rapids: Baker, 1998), 664.

62. Plantinga, *Not the Way It's Supposed to Be*, 10.

63. Plantinga, *Not the Way It's Supposed to Be*, 16. For a fuller exploration of this theme, see Graham A. Cole, *God the Peacemaker: How Atonement Brings Shalom* (Downers Grove, IL: InterVarsity Press, 2009).

Evil as Privation of Good

As Augustine (A.D. 354–430), and later Anselm (1033–1109) and Aquinas (1225–74), wrestled with the nature of evil in a world created by a God of pristine goodness, a question arose concerning the metaphysical nature of evil. They argued that evil does not have the properties of *being*. It is without substance, *nonbeing*.[64] It is a privation (corruption) of good that is characteristic of *being*. Goodness was necessarily present in all things at the moment of creation (Gen. 1:31).[65] All that God created was good (1 Tim. 4:4).

Thus, God cannot be the Creator—that is, the efficient cause—of evil.[66] Augustine also proposed the idea of privation to combat the dualism of both Manicheanism and Pelagianism, which erroneously supposed that humans had an intrinsic capacity for acting equally good or evil. In these heresies, evil is as natural as good.

When Augustine posited evil as *nonbeing*, however, he was not saying that evil is *nothing*, as many have misinterpreted him.[67] It is certainly not an illusion, as some Eastern religions propose. In particularly dark moments, evil obviously overshadows good in ominous ways. Furthermore, privation is not conceived as the *absence* or *negation* of good per se. Nor is it strictly that which is *contrary* to good.[68]

Evil conceived as privation refers to a deficiency, corruption, decay, distortion, disorder, or deprivation of some good feature that God created a thing to naturally possess.[69] It is something that has gone wrong with the way things ought to be. It is deprivation of the supreme goodness and

---

64. Augustine, *Confessions*, 7.11–13; Anselm, *On the Fall of the Devil*, 9–11; Aquinas, *Summa Theologica*, 1.49.

65. Bavinck, *Reformed Dogmatics*, 3:136.

66. This is contrary to some Calvinists, such as R.C. Sproul Jr., who contend that God created evil, albeit doing so without sinning. See R.C. Sproul Jr., *Almighty over All: Understanding the Sovereignty of God* (Grand Rapids: Baker, 1999), 54.

67. John Frame questions the language of nonbeing. How can something go from being (good) to nonbeing (evil) without ceasing to exist? This seems to be Platonic nonsense. He points out that Scripture never describes sin in metaphysical terms; therefore, we should not reduce ethics to metaphysics. "Such reduction depersonalizes sin. In such reduction, sin becomes a defect in creation itself . . . rather than the rebellion of created persons against their personal Creator" (Frame, *Systematic Theology*, 288–89). He suggests that if there is any trace of truth in the privation theory (and I think there is), then we should speak of good as "created being" and evil as "uncreated being" (299n40). Yet that seems problematic, too. Perhaps the best way to resolve the tension is to say that evil is "corrupted being" due to the fall (this was suggested to me by Marco Barone).

68. Phillip Cary, "A Classic View," in *God and the Problem of Evil: Five Views*, ed. Chad Meister and James K. Dew Jr. (Downers Grove, IL: InterVarsity Press, 2017), 16–17.

69. Cary, "Classic View," 14–16; Eleonore Stump, *Wandering in Darkness: Narrative and the Problem of Suffering* (Oxford: Oxford University Press, 2010), 384.

beauty of God himself. "There is no such thing as cold, only lower degrees of heat (or the complete lack of it). . . . Death is not the opposite of life, but its privation. A cloth can exist without a hole, but the hole cannot exist without the cloth. . . . A shadow is nothing but the obstruction of light—no light, no shadow."[70]

Sin is parasitic. "Evil takes the form of real defects with real effects, but it gets its power to do anything at all from the reality of the good things it deforms."[71] Biblical descriptions equate it to the undoing of good—*un*righteousness, *un*godliness, *in*justice, law*less*ness, and the like.[72] As Herman Bavinck says, "Sin cannot have its own principle and its own independent existence; it only originated *after* and exists only *by* and in connection *with* the good. While evil does depend on the good, the reverse is not true."[73]

This is why evil often mimics good (2 Cor. 11:14). It "is always doomed to borrow, despite itself, from the treasury of virtue."[74] Cornelius Plantinga points out, "To do its worst, evil needs to look its best. Evil needs to spend a lot on makeup. . . . Vices have to masquerade as virtues—lust as love, thinly veiled sadism as military discipline, envy as righteous indignation, domestic tyranny as parental concern."[75]

The forces of iniquity that we inflict on our souls tamper with our moral sanity. They thrive on self-beguiling charms; behind a thin veil of truth lurk desperate lies.[76] Evil turns everything on its head, disrupting the order, beauty, and harmony of the created order. Os Guinness speaks of evil as something altogether alien to our fundamental design as God's image-bearing creatures: "A human being whose heart is filled with the intent to harm rather than to seek another's good is disordered and decisively less of a human being. Evil is therefore in essence that which was not supposed to be, a rupture in the cosmic order of things, a cancer whose malignancy has spread to every part of life, a form of red-handed mutiny against life as it was supposed to be."[77]

70. Randy Alcorn, *If God Is Good: Faith in the Midst of Suffering and Evil* (Colorado Springs: Multnomah Books, 2009), 25.

71. Cary, "Classic View," 20.

72. Many of these terms in New Testament Greek use the alpha privative prefix (*a-*) before the principal terms they negate.

73. Bavinck, *Reformed Dogmatics*, 3:138.

74. Bavinck, *Reformed Dogmatics*, 3:139.

75. Plantinga, *Not the Way It's Supposed to Be*, 98.

76. See Prov. 12:20; Rom. 3:13; Col. 2:8; 2 Thess. 2:10; 2 Tim. 3:5; Heb. 3:13; Rev. 12:9.

77. Os Guinness, *Unspeakable: Facing Up to Evil in an Age of Genocide and Terror* (New York: HarperSanFrancisco, 2005), 140.

WHO BEARS THE PROBLEM OF EVIL?

Given this robust view of good, evil, and the God that biblical Christianity promotes, one is tempted to suppose that Christianity bears the greatest burden for making sense of the apparent dilemma that this presents. Purposely juxtaposing the intractable horror of evil with an equally intractable God of supreme goodness and power seems to be a self-inflicted lethal wound that the Christian must be laughably pitied for. The religious skeptic, the confident secularist, the aloof agnostic, and the defiant atheist all seem to rest on firmer ground. They don't have to make strong claims for objective morals, nor do they have to try to exonerate God for permitting so much earthly pandemonium. But is there reason for smugness among the non-Christian cognoscenti?

Moral Nihilism or Moral Realism?

The so-called religious nones have basically two paths to tread for grounding morals. The most obvious route is Nietzsche's *moral nihilism.* Any objective morals and obligations are denied altogether. We have here full-on moral subjectivism; no moral choice is to be preferred over another.[78] In other words, there is no discernible ground for morals. The notorious serial killer Ted Bundy clearly expresses the logic of embracing such a view, one in which he assumes the "courageous" role of Nietzsche's Superman while maintaining Darwin's lack of distinction between humans and animals. There is no inherent (God-given) dignity in the human species.

A tape recording was made with one of his victims in which he states bluntly:

> Then I learned that all moral judgments are "value judgments," that all value judgments are subjective, and that none can be proved to be either "right" or "wrong." . . . [There is no] "reason" to obey the law for anyone, like myself who has the boldness and daring—the strength of character— to throw off its shackles. . . . I discovered that to become truly free, truly unfettered, I had to become truly uninhibited. And I quickly discovered that the greatest obstacle to my freedom, the great block and limitation to it, consists in the insupportable "value judgment" that I was bound to respect the rights of others. I asked myself, who were these "others"? Other human beings, with human rights? Why is it more wrong to kill a human animal than any other animals, a pig or a sheep or a steer? Is your life more to you than a hog's life to a hog? Why should I be willing to sacrifice more pleasure for the one than for the other? Surely, you would not, in this age of scientific enlightenment, declare that God or nature has

---

78. One of the most serious cases for moral subjectivism is J. L. Mackie, *Ethics: Inventing Right and Wrong* (New York: Penguin Books, 1977).

marked some pleasures as "moral" or "good" and others as "immoral" or "bad"? In any case, let me assure you, my dear young lady, that there is absolutely no comparison between the pleasure I might take in eating ham and the pleasure I anticipate raping and murdering you. That is the honest conclusion to which my education has led me—after the most conscientious examination of my spontaneous and uninhibited self.[79]

The vast majority of self-conscious non-Christian, nontheistic thinkers would be appalled by the impeccable argument for moral nihilism that Bundy makes here.[80] Few people, no matter how opposed they are to biblical morality, would affirm that a Ted Bundy or a Jeffrey Dahmer's actions are morally inconsequential. "Could it really be true that there's nothing wrong with skinning someone alive? Is it plausible that my revulsion toward this kind of horror differs only in degree from my revulsion toward cold, slimy asparagus?"[81]

In other words, some moral skeptics, following in the footsteps of David Hume (1711–76), have argued that making *imperatival* ethical statements such as "Hitler should not kill Jews" is little different from making *preferential* statements such as "I hate asparagus."[82] There is no difference between moral obligation and personal feelings.

This explains why most secularists insist on traveling down some path of *moral realism*, the idea that moral judgments are grounded in objective truth values or standards that are independent of the person making such value judgments. But such objective moral standards must be transcendent: timeless, invariant, and universal—and herein lies the dilemma. How do you ground such moral judgments if God does not exist?

The nontheist has trouble escaping what Dostoevsky's character Mitya Karamazov boldly declares to his brother Alyosha in *The Brothers Karamazov*: "Without God and the future life? It means everything is permitted now, one can do anything."[83] So: "No God? No transcendent realm

---

79. James Fieser and Louis P. Pojman, *Ethics: Discovering Right and Wrong*, 6th ed. (Belmont, CA: Wadsworth, 2009), 17.

80. Though shocking, Marquis de Sade (1740–1814) anticipated Bundy's moral perversion two centuries earlier. *Sadism* is derived from his name.

81. Mitch Stokes, *How to Be an Atheist: Why Many Skeptics Aren't Skeptical Enough* (Wheaton, IL: Crossway, 2016), 228–29.

82. Norman L. Geisler and Paul D. Feinberg, *Introduction to Philosophy* (Grand Rapids: Baker, 1980), 356; cf. Steven B. Cowan and James S. Spiegel, *The Love of Wisdom: A Christian Introduction to Philosophy* (Nashville: B&H Academic, 2009), 331–32.

83. Fyodor Dostoevsky, *The Brothers Karamazov*, trans. Richard Pevear and Larissa Volokhonsky (New York: Farrar, Straus and Giroux, 1990), 589. The existentialist Jean-Paul Sartre also affirms this point in *Existentialism Is a Humanism*, ed. John Kulka, trans. Carol Macomber (New Haven, CT: Yale University Press, 2007), 29.

(heaven or hell) beyond the here and now? Well, then . . . no restraints on our immoral actions. Let's cast off these illusory chains of morality and live free!"

To avoid this conclusion, secularist moral philosophy has tried to ground objective morals in other sources, namely, naturalistic science. But such attempts are shaky, to say the least. Many Darwinians, such as Steven Pinker, believe that natural selection has hardwired our brains for certain moral distinctions in the same way we are wired to distinguish between colors such as red and green. In other words, our brain chemistry has developed over time such that we regard certain things as morally acceptable and others as morally reprehensible. In this account, evolution could have wired us differently. Just as green might be red in an alternate world, so Auschwitz would be wholly acceptable in an alternate world.[84]

Michael Ruse believes that the maxim "Love thy neighbor as thyself" as it stands by itself has no foundation. Any deeper transcendent meaning it might contain is illusory. According to evolutionary psychology, ethics is merely a biological adaptation within the human species that serves as "an aid to survival and reproduction" and nothing more.[85] Richard Dawkins thinks our "Good Samaritan urges" are evolutionary "misfirings." Though they might sometimes be good misfirings, nonetheless they are "Darwinian mistakes: blessed, precious mistakes."[86] Of course, one wonders where Dawkins grounds his apparently transcendent definition of *good, blessed,* and *precious.*

At best, Pinker, Ruse, Dawkins, and others hold to a diluted version of moral realism. The fact is, many atheist thinkers are flummoxed by the tension that exists between the logical bent toward moral nihilism that atheism leads to and the desire to retain some reasonable moral standards.[87] Many waffle between moral realism and moral subjectivism.

For example, Jerry Coyne affirms the intuitive rightness of giving to charities, eradicating disease and poverty, and seeking to improve justice generally in the world.[88] Yet in the same breath he says: "Although evolution operates in a purposeless, materialistic way, that doesn't mean that our lives have no purpose. Whether through religious or secular thought,

---

84. Steven Pinker, "The Moral Instinct," *New York Times Magazine,* January 13, 2008.
85. Michael Ruse, "Evolutionary Theory and Christian Ethics," in *The Darwinian Paradigm* (London: Routledge, 1989), 262, 268–69.
86. Richard Dawkins, *The God Delusion* (New York: Houghton Mifflin, 2008), 252–53.
87. The atheist Alex Rosenberg acknowledges the tensions here in *The Atheist's Guide to Reality: Enjoying Life without Illusions* (New York: W. W. Norton, 2011), 96–98, 143.
88. Jerry A. Coyne, *Why Evolution Is True* (New York: Penguin Books, 2009), 231.

we make our own purposes, meaning, and morality."[89] Thus, meaning and morals are personally or socially constructed within a broader meaningless cosmos. We are not told how such a bifurcated reality can possibly cohere.

Likewise, Greg Epstein, humanist chaplain at Harvard University, tries to show that secular humanism basically adopts the essential timeless moral features of the Ten Commandments,[90] yet he also says, "Not only do we not need 'objective' values to condemn heinous crimes and uphold ethical standards, we cannot ever be confident that objective values exist."[91] He seems unaware that condemning heinous crimes is impossible without objective moral standards. What makes a crime "heinous" without an objective standard of heinousness?

In the end, all nontheistic worldviews must borrow from biblical theism to make any sense of objective moral standards. The atheist doesn't have to believe in God to be moral, but to be moral God must exist, whether he believes in him or not. John Lennon can claim that "All You Need Is Love,"[92] but not while imagining that "above us" there is "only sky."[93]

Grounding Morality in the Personal-Relational God

Nontheistic attempts to ground morality apart from God fail on a different level as well. Our moral sensibilities (or what remains after secularism has dulled them) are fundamentally connected to personhood and personal relationships. Furthermore, morality makes sense only when it is grounded in the personhood of the triune God and the subsequent relationship that his image-bearing creatures have with him. Adam's sin drove a wedge first and foremost between God and man. Then it severed the harmony between man and man, as well as man and creation.[94]

Thus, sin is a "fundamental reversal of all relationships, a revolution by which the creature detached himself from and positioned himself against God, an uprising, a fall in the true sense, which was decisive for the whole world and took it in a direction and on a road away from God."[95] This

---

89. Coyne, *Why Evolution Is True*, 231.

90. Greg M. Epstein, *Good without God* (New York: HarperCollins, 2009), 118–19, 135–40. Epstein reframes many of the commandments by using modern leftist categories that essentially negate their moral force.

91. Epstein, *Good without God*, 35.

92. Barry Miles, *Paul McCartney: Many Years from Now* (New York: Henry Holt and Company, 1997), 354.

93. http://www.johnlennon.com/music/singles/imagine/.

94. Eugene H. Merrill, *Everlasting Dominion: A Theology of the Old Testament* (Nashville: B&H Publishing Group, 2006), 208–9; Frame, *Systematic Theology*, 852.

95. Bavinck, *Reformed Dogmatics*, 3:129.

personal-relational dynamic is precisely what secularization has sought to reject so vehemently. But this hopelessly muddles the way in which moral imperatives are expressed in our actual experience as human beings.

Regardless of ideological and religious commitments, when people think of concrete examples of moral good, it is nearly impossible not to think of universally accepted virtues such as compassion, mercy, patience, kindness, fairness, and truthfulness, as Jerry Coyne and Greg Epstein have admitted. In place of these virtues, evil is understood to be actions that promote malice, greed, cruelty, dishonesty, bitterness, rancor, and so forth. In a word, moral virtue bespeaks love, and evil bespeaks hatred.

This explains why the Beatles want to sing, "All You Need Is Love." In spite of all manner of cultural distortions of the nature of love, the seed of the concept expressing the second greatest commandment, "Love thy neighbor as thyself" (Mark 12:31; Rom. 13:9; Gal. 5:14), is deeply embedded in the moral conscience of every human being, as atheist Michael Ruse has acknowledged. But all these virtues and vices presuppose interpersonal relationships. Good and evil are meaningless apart from how persons treat other persons. Thus, moral imperatives are grounded in a source that is itself personal. This rules out naturalistic sources, which are impersonal and nonrelational.

Now, some might argue that certain virtues and vices are cultivated privately and have no bearing on how we relate to others. How can what we read, fantasize about, or watch on television affect our neighbor? But private conduct eventually has public ramifications. All moral habits, regardless of when and where they are cultivated, shape personal character. And personal character ultimately bears on personal relationships. If a man spends countless hours viewing pornography on the Internet, it is certain that he will begin to view sex in a way that degrades others and dispassionately objectifies them for the gratification of his perverted desires. He may not become a serial rapist, but his heart gravitates toward such moral degeneracy (Matt. 5:28).

This brings us back to moral obligations and to the source of such obligations—our relationship to the triune God. Objective moral standards imply moral obligations. And moral obligations are fundamentally relational. They cannot be grounded in nature, natural selection, or Platonic ideals, as some modernists, such as Steven Pinker, have suggested.[96]

For example, how can the idea of justice exist as an abstract idea without consideration of how *persons* are treated by other *persons*? Furthermore,

96. Pinker, "Moral Instinct."

how does the existence of some independent moral idea place burdens of moral duties, imperatives, and obligations on such persons?[97] Nature is a nonintelligent, nonrelational, nonpersonal entity.

Morals are not propositions of fact about the way things *are*; they are facts about the way things *ought* to be. Abstract propositions such as 2 + 2 = 4 do not impose obligations on us. They don't *want* us to do something. Abstract propositions don't have intentions. They do not move our consciences to consider how we *ought* to act. Moral intuitions, however, press us to act in one way or to refrain from acting in other ways. Thus, morals do not have an abstract naturalistic source. This is a category mistake. Only personal, intelligent beings demand moral obligations from us.

Furthermore, in order for moral obligations to make any sense, there must be a personal-relational Lawgiver (a permitter, forbidder, obligator), and there must be one who is being "permitted, forbidden, or obligated."[98] "Right, wrong, and obligation are concepts related to the actions that people perform in relation to some standard set by another person or persons. . . . Right, wrong, and obligation are *person relative*."[99]

But can we look to a human lawgiver for the sorts of virtues and moral imperatives that we universally accept? What human or humans could serve as an objective standard for moral duties that we *ought* to abide by? What candidate can we look to who represents complete moral objectivity and perfection? After all, every human effort to form a just society has failed miserably.

The standard for moral imperatives must be a personal lawgiver who is unequivocally free of the potential for moral corruption; otherwise, such a lawgiver would forfeit the sort of trust that is required for any equitable moral imperatives that he would impose on others. In other words, we must turn to the Christian God. "Only in biblical religion is there an absolute principle that is personal."[100] Only the personal Lawgiver and Judge of the universe and of human hearts qualifies as the supreme exemplar of righteousness, justice, truthfulness, and love.

God "is Goodness and all that is good flows from him" (cf. Luke 18:19; 1 John 1:5).[101] Thus, when we act with moral duty, it is because we *ought* to

97. William Lane Craig, *On Guard: Defending Your Faith with Reason and Precision* (Colorado Springs: David C. Cook, 2010), 136–38.

98. Stokes, *How to Be an Atheist*, 205.

99. Stokes, *How to Be an Atheist*, 205–6.

100. John M. Frame, *The Doctrine of God* (Phillipsburg, NJ: P&R Publishing, 2002), 26.

101. Richard A. Shenk, *The Wonder of the Cross: The God Who Uses Evil and Suffering to Destroy Evil and Suffering* (Eugene, OR: Pickwick Publications, 2013), 185. This dispenses with

act in obedience specifically to the Supreme Lawgiver and Judge. We owe our ethical allegiance to him. This is otherwise known as the moral argument for God's existence.[102]

But there is another unique requirement for such a lawgiver. Morality is clearly tied to personhood, but not singular personhood. Moral actions are necessarily tied to a plurality of persons. Without a plurality of persons in relation to one another, love as an overarching moral principle would make no sense. Love makes sense only when there is a dispenser of love (a lover) and a recipient of love (the loved). Augustine writes, "Now love means someone loving and something loved with love. There you are with three, the lover, what is being loved, and love."[103] When the Scripture speaks of God as love (1 John 4:8, 16), this is an attribute that speaks to his self-existence (aseity) and simplicity (i.e., all the attributes of God being identified with the essence of God). The love of God stands apart from his creation and any relationship that he chooses to establish with his image-bearing creatures.

Thus, love must, first and foremost, exist not as an expression of a *unitarian* god but as the relationships that occur *ad intra* (internally) among the members of the *Trinitarian* God of the Bible.[104] Such moral relationships exist within the Trinity entirely independent of God's creation of people.[105] This is why Jesus speaks of the Father's love for him "before the foundation of the world" (John 17:24). Christ is the eternally "beloved" Son of God (Matt. 3:17; 12:18; 17:5). The love that God then displays to his creatures flows from his own Trinitarian being (John 17:22–26).

This means that other non-Christian theistic religions are ruled out when it comes to grounding objective morals. The triune God alone is the

---

the so-called Euthyphro dilemma: Is something morally good because God wills it, or does God will it because it is morally good? If the first statement is true, then what prevents God from willing things that are repugnant? His commands become arbitrary. If the second statement is true, then God is subject to a standard that exists outside himself (e.g., some Platonic ideal). This is a false dilemma with a simple response. God commands what is morally good as a necessary consequence of his nature, which itself is unequivocally and immutably good.

102. See C. Stephen Evans, "Moral Arguments for the Existence of God," in *The Stanford Encyclopedia of Philosophy*, ed. Edward N. Zalta (Fall 2018), found at: https://plato.stanford.edu/archives/fall2018/entries/moral-arguments-god/.

103. Augustine, *The Trinity*, in *The Works of Saint Augustine: A Translation for the 21st Century*, ed. John E. Rotelle, trans. Edmund Hill (New York: New City Press, 1991), 6.14 (255).

104. This argument has been made persuasively by Richard of St. Victor (1110–73) in *De Trinitate*, bk. 3. See Ruben Angelici, *Richard of Saint Victor, On the Trinity: English Translation and Commentary* (Eugene, OR: Cascade Books, 2011). For an assessment of Richard's rationalist argument for the Trinity, see Robert Letham, *The Holy Trinity: In Scripture, History, Theology, and Worship*, rev. ed. (Phillipsburg, NJ: P&R Publishing, 2019), 259–64.

105. Stokes, *How to Be an Atheist*, 241.

paradigm for the moral expectations that govern the relationship between God and his creatures, as well as the expectations between us creaturely *neighbors*. The only difference is that the moral actions that exist in intra-Trinitarian relationships are governed by the perfectly righteous nature of the members of the Godhead. Thus, *obligation* is not a word to be used in describing the love between the Father and the Son. They love inexorably and perfectly due to the intrinsic immutable divine nature they share.

But *obligation* enters the vocabulary of man-to-God relations and man-to-man relations because humans are burdened by a corrupt moral nature. We must be compelled by a duty to act in a way that militates against the tendencies of our sinful nature. This is not merely the moral argument for God. It is the moral argument for the *triune* God of Scripture. It is an argument from the problem of evil itself.[106]

Our collective human consciences share a revulsion for evils such as rape, torture, and pedophilia. We know that we must refrain from engaging in these horrific acts. And knowing that we cannot ground objective moral standards and unequivocal moral duties apart from God tells us how extremely hard it is to escape the fact that he has hated these things long before we did.

CHRISTIANITY'S GOOD PROBLEM

This doesn't make the problem of evil go away, but it clears the field of debris and charges of Christian hubris. Yes, Christianity has this problem squarely dropped in its own lap, but that is not the terrible burden that so many have said it is. Nontheistic accounts of good and evil are bankrupt, and that is a far more serious problem. Christianity has a problem, but it is a good problem to have because nobody else has the resources to address it.

Non-Christians can only feign outrage over injustices without giving an account for why they *ought* to be outraged. Humans cannot explain why we suffer from injustices unless there is a way to objectively quantify that something *ought not* to have happened as it did. Can we justify sympathizing with starving children if we have no way of saying that real evil has befallen them? Biblical Christianity has a way to answer these questions that no other religion or ideology can match. Evil is possible only in a Christian worldview. But this

---

106. Alvin Plantinga makes this argument in his essay "A Christian Life Partly Lived," in *Philosophers Who Believe*, ed. Kelly James Clark (Downers Grove, IL: InterVarsity Press, 1993), 73; and Gregory E. Ganssle makes a more detailed case in "Evil as Evidence for Christianity," in *God and Evil: The Case for God in a World Filled with Pain*, ed. Chad Meister and James K. Dew Jr. (Downers Grove, IL: InterVarsity Press, 2013), 214–23.

means that it now bears the burden of answering the deeper question—why? What theodicy can it offer? How can it defend God from the charge of being himself evil? It is to these questions that we now turn.

KEY TERMS

moral evil
moral nihilism
moral realism
moral relativism
natural evil

STUDY QUESTIONS

1. Why does the modern Western world have such trouble with defining evil?
2. How does the Bible define moral evil?
3. What is the difference between moral and natural evil? What are some different examples of natural evil?
4. Can the concepts of good and evil exist without God? Why or why not?
5. Why are intra-Trinitarian relationships important for grounding ethics (i.e., notions of good and evil)?
6. Is the problem of evil more of a problem for atheists or Christians? Explain your answer.
7. Do you see yourself as a good person who occasionally sins, or do you see yourself as a sinner who nonetheless does some good things? What are the implications of your answer to this question for understanding who you are as a human being, especially in light of who God is?

FOR FURTHER READING

Andrew Delbanco, *The Death of Satan: How Americans Have Lost the Sense of Evil* (New York: Farrar, Straus and Giroux, 1995).
Cornelius Plantinga Jr., *Not the Way It's Supposed to Be: A Breviary of Sin* (Grand Rapids: Eerdmans, 1995).
Jeffrey Burton Russell, *The Prince of Darkness: Radical Evil and the Power of Good in History* (Ithaca, NY: Cornell University Press, 1988).
Mitch Stokes, *How to Be an Atheist: Why Many Skeptics Aren't Skeptical Enough* (Wheaton, IL: Crossway, 2016).

4

JUSTIFYING THE WAYS OF GOD

One of Arthur Conan Doyle's short masterpieces of murder, mystery, and intrigue to be solved by the venerable Sherlock Holmes is the tale entitled "The Adventure of the Cardboard Box." A curious parcel arrives at the home of one Miss Susan Cushing that contains two severed ears. It turns out that the ears belong to her sister Mary and her illicit lover, both of whom were murdered by Mary's husband, Jim Browner. But the package has come to Susan mistakenly. The real recipient was intended to be her other sister, Sarah.

Mr. Browner meant to terrify Sarah with the severed ears, blaming her for his crime of passion. You see, she once tried to seduce him. When he resisted Sarah's advances, she convinced his wife, Mary, that he was a scoundrel and compelled her to invest her affections in another man. The tortured Browner regrets his crime. The story treats him as a victim of Sarah's sinister plot to ruin him. She is portrayed as the real villain.

At the end of the sordid tale, the ever-quizzical detective ponders the problem of evil:

> "What is the meaning of it, Watson?" said Holmes solemnly . . . . "What object is served by this circle of misery and violence and fear? It must tend to some end, or else our universe is ruled by chance, which is unthinkable. But what end? There is the great standing perennial problem to which human reason is as far from an answer as ever."[1]

When the fogs of cultural confusion clear over the reality and meaning of evil, people still grope for answers. Having a clear vision of the evilness of

---

1. Sir Arthur Conan Doyle, *The Complete Sherlock Holmes* (New York: Doubleday, 1960), 901. I first heard this quote from a lecture by apologist David Wood.

evil does not relieve us of the relentless drive to understand why it pervades our world and our lives. A palpable tension is revealed in Holmes's statement. On the one hand, we cannot imagine a universe ruled by chance despite our modern Darwinian penchant to think otherwise. On the other hand, evil seems so random, so pointless—so utterly unanswerable.

Yet in the last half-century, we have seen unprecedented interest among the most astute thinkers in the world, clamoring to provide answers to this nagging quandary. We know that if God exists, descending into the deeper portals of his ways in this wicked world must be reckoned with. Is there a definitive answer to why God created a wonderful world, only for it to be sullied by such dastardly deeds and dismal catastrophes? While skepticism abounds, many Christians believe we can answer that question in the affirmative.

This chapter will examine some of the primary issues involved when seeking to provide answers to the problem of evil. How has the contemporary debate unfolded? What is meant by the problem of evil? What is the difference between the logical, evidential, and existential (personal or religious) problems that critics, skeptics, doubters, and sufferers pose? What must a theodicy do in its attempt to solve the problem? Is a theodicy even possible? Can we positively say that God has a specific reason for evil's existence?

Some say that the best we can do is merely to defend God's honor against claims that he is the author of evil. Can we do more than that? Answering these preliminary questions will set the context for examining the most prominent theodicies on offer among Christian thinkers. In the two chapters that follow, I will evaluate their strengths and weaknesses. These theodicies coalesce around two basic approaches: the *free-will defense* and the *greater-good defense*. Afterward, I will begin laying out a distinctive theodicy in the following chapters—one that I believe is most faithful to the contours of orthodox Reformed and evangelical theology, and the witness of Scripture.

The topic is vast, the issues complex, the questions myriad, and the responses as varied as the multihued colors of the rainbow. It is hoped that some clarity and appropriate perspectives can be provided, some anchors we can drop to prevent us from drifting in this vast sea of bewildering questions. At the end of this journey, may we come face to face with a majestic God who is not flummoxed by evil. He is not unconcerned about the pall of suffering that smothers the world or the vale of tears that each of us must personally face.

Even the faithful believer in Christ is inevitably buffeted on every side with trials and tribulation (1 Peter 1:6). When first confronting adversity, we may cry out with David in Psalm 13: "How long, O Lord? Will you forget me forever? How long will you hide your face from me?" (v. 1). But in the end, we should be able to rejoice with Israel's hopeful king: "I will sing to the LORD, because he has dealt bountifully with me" (v. 6).

THE CONTEMPORARY DEBATE OVER GOD AND EVIL

Since 1955 and the publication of the seminal article entitled "Evil and Omnipotence" by the respected philosopher J. L. Mackie, the problem of evil has been a mainstay of philosophical discourse.[2] Mackie maintained that the presence of evil in the world demonstrates a direct contradiction in beliefs held by orthodox Christians concerning the nature of God. He appealed to the classic trilemma of God and evil first raised by Epicurus (341–270 B.C.) and famously restated by David Hume (1711–76). It is known today as the *logical* problem of evil.

The argument can be presented most succinctly in the following way:

1. God is omnipotent (all-powerful).
2. God is omnibenevolent (all-good).
3. Evil exists.
4. Therefore, God does not exist.

Historically, there has been little dispute that premise 3 is true.[3] The focus is on a supposed contradiction between premise 1 or premise 2 (or both premises) and premise 3. If such a contradiction exists, then this would presumably rule out God's existence (4)—at least the God of the Bible.

Now, some hidden assumptions in the first two premises need to be made clear. They can be restated such that two conclusions now follow:

1'. An omnipotent God *can* prevent evil.
2'. An omnibenevolent God *wants* to prevent evil.
3'. Evil exists.

This leads to the following conclusion:

4'. Therefore, either God is not omnipotent (*cannot* prevent evil) or he is not omnibenevolent (*will not* prevent evil).

And this leads to the same conclusion as before:

5. Therefore, God does not exist.

2. J. L. Mackie, "Evil and Omnipotence," *Mind*, n.s., 64.254 (1955): 200–212.
3. Postmodernism, however, has left many people wondering whether there is such a thing as evil. See chapters 2 and 3.

Maybe premise 2′ is true and premise 1′ is false. In that case, God sincerely desires to prevent evil in the world, but he is simply unable to do so. He lacks the power to prevent or stop evil's progress.

This is essentially what the famed Rabbi Kushner argued in his bestselling book *When Bad Things Happen to Good People*. Kushner says, "I can worship a God who hates suffering but cannot eliminate it, more easily than I can worship a God who chooses to make children suffer and die, for whatever exalted reason."[4] If this is true, then it would contradict the Christian belief that God has the requisite power to do all that is logically possible for him to do, and there seems to be no logical reason why such a God could not prevent evil.[5]

But perhaps premise 1′ is true while premise 2′ is false. There are two ways to read this. First, perhaps God is not omnibenevolent. If that is true, then it renders the God of the Bible nonexistent. The second way to read this is to reject the assumption expressed in the second part of premise 2′. Although God is all-good and abhors all evil, we have to ask: is it true that he *wants* to prevent every instance of evil?

The Christian philosopher Alvin Plantinga has shown that this must be not merely *possibly* true, but *necessarily* true, in order for the argument to hold; and so far, no one has shown that to be the case.[6] In other words, there is an internal inconsistency in how the premise is stated. God, being all-good, may have good reasons for permitting the evil we see. And this is where the heart of the response to Hume, Mackie, and others has resided. Ronald Nash clarifies the matter: "Most attempts to answer the problem of evil are variations of a basic theme, namely, that God permits evil either to make possible some greater good or to avoid some greater evil."[7]

As is obvious, the logical argument against God from evil seeks to explicitly torpedo two critical attributes of God, namely, his omnipotence and omnibenevolence. The argument, however, implicitly puts other attributes of God

4. Harold S. Kushner, *When Bad Things Happen to Good People* (New York: HarperCollins, 1989), 134.

5. God's omnipotence cannot contradict that which is logical, for both characteristics mark the immutable being of God. For example, God cannot make square circles or married bachelors. That would deny his being.

6. Alvin Plantinga, *God, Freedom, and Evil* (Grand Rapids: Eerdmans, 1977), 24–29.

7. Ronald H. Nash, *Faith and Reason: Searching for a Rational Faith* (Grand Rapids: Zondervan, 1988), 198. We should not confuse Nash's statement as an endorsement of what is known as the greater-good defense. There is a sense in which any theodicy is an attempt to show that God has some greater good that outweighs his permitting evil. For some, God is pursuing general goods, such as maintaining human free will or natural laws (see chapter 5). For others, God is pursuing particular goods, such as soul-building (see chapter 6).

under fire as well. For example, if God is omniscient (all-knowing), he would be fully aware of every evil that came down the pike long before it arrived. He cannot claim ignorance. So why doesn't he devise some preemptive strategies before evil makes its appearance?

Furthermore, his exhaustive knowledge would make him aware of what those strategies are. This leads to another attribute that comes under fire. God is not only all-knowing, but also all-wise. He has the wisdom to ascertain the best—the perfect—strategies for preventing evil.

What about his justice? What God, being perfectly just, would allow evil to desecrate the good, to defile the innocent, and to allow innumerable wicked perpetrators to go unpunished? Furthermore, some find it hard to believe that if God is the quintessence of beauty, he would not prevent his creation from being spoiled by global disasters, destroying natural resources and marring the design and artistry of the created order.

In short, the unity, purity, excellence, perfection, and unrivaled supremacy of God's attributes make his coexistence with evil a mystery of the highest imaginable order. How do we untangle this mystery without jettisoning the Bible's clear picture of a supreme God?

DIFFERENT PROBLEMS OF EVIL

It is important to note that there is more than one problem of evil. The classical argument against God from evil, resurrected by Mackie and others, is known as the *logical* problem of evil. Alvin Plantinga, who is one of the most highly regarded Christian philosophers in modern times, sought to answer Mackie's challenge in 1967 in his book *God and Other Minds*.[8] He reintroduced the argument, represented in the earlier thought of the seminal Christian thinker Augustine (A.D. 354–430), called the *free-will defense*.[9]

8. See chapters 5 and 6 in *God and Other Minds* (Ithaca, NY: Cornell University Press, 1967). Plantinga repeated his argument in chapter 9 of his book *The Nature of Necessity* (New York: Oxford University Press, 1974) and then in his more popular work *God, Freedom, and Evil*.

9. See chapter 5. There is some debate over whether Augustine, who is associated with strong views of God's meticulous providence over all things, held to libertarian free will (which denies meticulous providence) or compatibilistic notions of free will (which embraces meticulous providence). It appears that early on, he held to at least a limited form of libertarianism when utilizing the free-will defense for the problem of evil. This is indicated in his work *On the Free Choice of the Will*, which was written in stages between A.D. 387 and 395. But by the time he wrote *On Grace and Free Will* (A.D. 426–27), he appears to have embraced a compatibilistic view of free agency. Augustine abandoned the free-will defense and became its greatest critic in his later years. In its place he embraced the greater-good defense (see chapter 6). These points are persuasively argued by Jesse Couenhoven, "Augustine's Rejection of the Free-Will Defence: An Overview of the Late Augustine's Theodicy," *Religious Studies* 43.3 (2007): 279–98. See also Eric L. Jenkins, *Free to Say No? Free Will and Augustine's Evolving Doctrine of Grace and Election* (Eugene, OR: Wipf and Stock,

Plantinga's argument has proved so influential and successful that most philosophers no longer seek to use the logical problem of evil in seeking to disprove the existence of God. As Feinberg notes: "The confident assertion so common 'on the street,' that suffering and evil simply disproves the existence of God, has been almost entirely abandoned in professional and academic circles."[10] Instead, skeptics have moved to more modest nuanced arguments that question the *probability* of God's existence based on other aspects of the problem. These largely fall under what is called the *evidential* problem of evil. Philosophers who argue against God in this fashion no longer question the coexistence of God and evil per se, conceding the arguments of Plantinga and others. Instead, they suggest that (1) the tremendous *quantity* of evil in the world or (2) the *horrendous* (and therefore *gratuitous*) nature of some evils indicates the improbability of God's existence.

In the case of vast amounts of evil, it is suggested that there may be legitimate reasons for some evil, but pervasive evil everywhere we turn? We can't tune in to the news without being accosted by countless acts of greed, avarice, corruption, and murder. This seems to count against the Christian God. In the case of horrendous evil, the suggestion is that some acts of wickedness are so bad that evil must be considered gratuitous. In other words, it appears to be utterly pointless, without any remotely or discernibly good reason for existing. They are dehumanizing, soul-destroying, life-ruining evils that strip meaning and purpose from our existence.[11] They represent sadistic, monstrous moments in which evil itself degenerates into the inexplicable, the unintelligible, the utterly irrational.

2012). Note the compatibilistic language in *On Grace and Free Will*: "The Almighty accomplishes in human hearts even the movement of their will, to accomplish through them what He wills to accomplish through them . . . . God works in human hearts to incline their wills to whatever He wills, either to good due to His mercy or to evil due to their deserts" (*On the Free Choice of the Will, On Grace and Free Choice, and Other Writings*, ed. and trans. Peter King [Cambridge: Cambridge University Press, 2010], 179–80). The following statement in the *Enchiridion* (A.D. 420) indicates his later affinity for the greater-good defense: "The Omnipotent God . . . would not allow any evil in his works, unless in his omnipotence and goodness, as the Supreme Good, he is able to bring forth good out of evil" (*Enchiridion*, ed. and trans. Albert C. Outler [Philadelphia: Westminster Press, 1955], 3.11). For arguments that Augustine maintained consistency and continuity between early and later views, see Peter Brown, *Augustine of Hippo: A Biography*, rev. ed. (Berkeley, CA: University of California Press, 2000), 441–520. Among those who argue that Augustine's views of free will never changed, see Eleonore Stump, "Augustine on Free Will," in *The Cambridge Companion to Augustine*, ed. Eleonore Stump and Norman Kretzmann (Cambridge: Cambridge University Press, 2001); Carol Harrison, *Rethinking Augustine's Early Theology: An Argument for Continuity* (Oxford: Oxford University Press, 2006), 198–237.

10. John S. Feinberg, *The Many Faces of Evil* (Wheaton, IL: Crossway, 2004), 89.

11. Marilyn McCord Adams, *Horrendous Evils and the Goodness of God* (Ithaca, NY: Cornell University Press, 1999), 26–29.

Who can justify God's permitting the rape, slow torture, and murder of an innocent little girl? The ubiquitous bloodbaths of worldwide war? The Holocaust? Elie Wiesel captures the force of gratuitous evil in his haunting Holocaust memoir *Night*. Wiesel managed to survive Auschwitz-Birkenau and Monowitz concentration camps during World War II. Upon arriving at Auschwitz, the teenage Elie immediately witnessed little babies' being unloaded from the back of a truck and summarily tossed into a fire for extermination.

> NEVER SHALL I FORGET that night, the first night in camp, which turned my life into one long night seven times sealed.
> Never shall I forget that smoke.
> Never shall I forget the small faces of the children whose bodies I saw transformed into smoke under a silent sky.
> Never shall I forget those flames that consumed my faith forever.
> Never shall I forget the nocturnal silence that deprived me for all eternity of the desire to live.
> Never shall I forget those moments that murdered my God and my soul and turned my dreams to ashes.
> Never shall I forget these things, even were I condemned to live as long as God Himself.
> Never.[12]

Later Wiesel and thousands of others looked on as two men and a boy were sent to the gallows for apparent acts of sabotage in the encampment.

> The three condemned prisoners together stepped onto the chairs. In unison, the nooses were placed around their necks.
> "Long live liberty!" shouted the two men.
> But the boy was silent.
> "Where is merciful God, where is He?" someone behind me was asking.
> At the signal, the three chairs were tipped over.
> Total silence in the camp. On the horizon, the sun was setting. . . .
> Then came the march past the victims. The two men were no longer alive. Their tongues were hanging out, swollen and bluish. But the third rope was still moving: the child, too light, was still breathing . . . .
> And so he remained for more than half an hour, lingering between life and death, writhing before our eyes. And we were forced to look at him at close range. He was still alive when I passed him. His tongue was still red, his eyes not yet extinguished.
> Behind me, I heard the same man asking:
> "For God's sake, where is God?"

12. Elie Wiesel, *Night* (New York: Hill and Wang, 2006), 34.

And from within me, I heard a voice answer:
"Where is He? This is where—hanging here from this gallows . . . ."[13]

Perhaps we can understand why God permits moderate amounts of evil, maybe some indecorous acts that don't rock our moral sensibilities to the core. But that is not the atmosphere we breathe. There are one too many Adolf Hitlers and Heinrich Himmlers in the world. Too many Hurricane Katrinas wiping out whole cities. Too many societal poisons that ruin everything. How do we handle the *quantity* and horrendous *quality* of so much evil? Surely, we think, God could achieve any good he has in mind apart from so much pain and suffering.

Finally, there is the *existential* or *emotional* problem of evil (sometimes called the *personal* or *religious* problem). This is not the perspective of the furrow-browed professor in the classroom, urging his students to think rationally about the ethical dilemma facing the defender of the Christian faith. It is the personal dimension, the spiritual battle that rages hard within.

This is where evil directly intersects our own lives, where it claws at our tender hearts and leaves wounds that never seem to heal. It is where we all become like a destitute Job or a desperate David fleeing from his mortal enemy, Saul. It is where we wonder together with Elie Wiesel: "Where is He?" Is God hanging from the gallows? Or has he retreated into eternal silence to leave our tormented souls to hang and writhe in mortal agony alone?

David wasn't the last person to cry, "How long, O Lord? Will you forget me forever? How long will you hide your face from me?" (Ps. 13:1). Rational answers here do not satisfy. Even when a certain logical resolution of the broader problem has been recognized, we are rarely if ever entirely satisfied. The soul still stings, wonders, and wallows in bewilderment, questioning the divine wisdom of it all. The silence of God *is* palpable, painful—and we must wait and ache and wait some more and beat our breast and fight despair.

WHAT MUST A THEODICY DO?

A thoroughgoing theodicy must somehow address both these cognitive (logical) and deeply existential questions or risk falling on deaf ears. Most of the time, Christians who face an existential crisis of faith due to some severe trial are not comforted by an argument. We need a transcendent level of assurance that God's steadfast love is never going to fail us

---

13. Wiesel, *Night*, 64–65.

(Lam. 3:22–23). In either case, a theodicy must meet a certain threshold of credibility in order to satisfy our pangs of doubt.

Greg Welty defines the task of theodicy and gives us a handle on some essential criteria that should frame a faithful attempt to justify the ways of God in the face of evil: "A theodicy has the following structure: there are goods that God is aiming at in his universe, but because of the kinds of goods God is aiming at, he cannot get them without permitting various evils."[14] Welty indicates two criteria that a faithful theodicy must meet if it is to genuinely uphold the character of God. Where a theodicy fails is where it compromises the character of God.[15]

Goods Dependent on Evil

The first criterion must demonstrate that the goods that a faithful theodicy promotes are *dependent* on the existence of evil. Generally, good things in this world (and likely most other good things) are not dependent on evil. But there appear to be unique goods God seeks that are dependent on the presence of evil. These goods cannot come about unless God gives the go-ahead for evil to take place. For example, the wonder of forgiveness is a remarkable good that could not exist unless some moral infraction preceded the extension of a forgiving spirit to the perpetrator of the wrongdoing. If God can get certain goods without evil, then he will.[16]

This means that there can be no gratuitous evil, no matter how dreadful—evil that exists for no good and necessary reason. But not all theodicists agree on this point. Those who see God as pursuing general goods (usually free-will theists), such as human freedom of choice (i.e., libertarian free will), will say that God's pursuit of good is dependent on the *possibility* of evil, which unfortunately also risks the *possibility* of gratuitous evil. But those who see God as pursuing *particular* goods (usually those espousing the greater-good theodicy), such as building the character of human beings, will say that God's pursuit of those goods is dependent on the *actuality* of the occurrence of certain evils. For many of these theodicists, there can be no gratuitous evil.[17] I hope to demonstrate that this latter position is correct.

While this may seem hard to reconcile, it is the conclusion we must draw

14. Greg Welty, *Why Is There Evil in the World (and So Much of It)?* (Fearn, Ross-shire, Scotland: Christian Focus, 2018), 42–43.

15. Welty, *Why Is There Evil?*, 43–46. It should be noted that Welty presents these as criteria for what is called the *greater-good theodicy* and not necessarily other types of theodicies. Still, I think that if any theodicy fails to meet these two criteria, then it is suspect.

16. Welty, *Why Is There Evil?*, 43–45.

17. Welty, *Why Is There Evil?*, 168–77.

from the fact that God is the all-powerful, all-good, all-wise sovereign God that the Bible reveals. He stands fast at guard, permitting absolutely no evils in the world that do not contribute to his good purposes. For example, the world came to a place during Noah's day at which evil had strained the limits set by God. "The LORD saw that the wickedness of man was great in the earth, and that every intention of the thoughts of his heart was only evil continually" (Gen. 6:5). God determined that things could not go on like this, and so he destroyed the world by a global flood.

The same situation happened in Sodom and Gomorrah. We might say that the level of evil that poured from these depraved cities reached a point of no return, a stark line in the sand that God deemed nothing should cross. He determined that no good could outweigh continuing to allow these dens of wickedness to continue existing, and so he brought fire and brimstone down on their heads.

Likewise, God permitted the Israelites to be enslaved for four hundred years before they came to the promised land. Why precisely this long? Because the Canaanites had not yet reached their quota of iniquity, so to speak. Once they had reached that threshold at which the net moral value of their continued injustices would become negative, then they would come under judgment. In other words, the bad situation they created with their sin approached the point of gratuitousness—of outweighing any good reason for it to continue—and so God said, "No more" (Gen. 15:13–16).[18]

We see something similar with those saints who will be martyred during the great tribulation. The martyrs "cried out with a loud voice, 'O Sovereign Lord, holy and true, how long before you will judge and avenge our blood on those who dwell on the earth?'" (Rev. 6:10). They were "told to rest a little longer, until the number of their fellow servants and their brothers should be complete, who were to be killed as they themselves had been" (v. 11). Only then would their blood be avenged. Only God knows when the net moral value of any situation reaches that threshold at which judgment must put a decisive end to the horrendous evil that is transpiring.

Goods That Are Weighty Enough

The second matter that a theodicy must demonstrate, according to Welty, is that the goods that justify the existence of evil need to be worth it. They need to be *weighty* and important enough goods worth pursuing. Such

---

18. See Kirk Durston, "The Destruction of the Canaanites: Why God Must Sometimes Destroy Civilizations and Cultures," *Thoughts about God, Truth, and Beauty* (blog), https://kirkdurston.com/blog/canaandestruction.

goods must outweigh the evils that are necessitated in order to bring about those goods. "Getting a pathetically trivial good by way of an enormous evil will have made the universe worse than it was before, since things would be better off with neither of those things than with them both."[19]

Welty illustrates the point this way: "Imagine if someone asserted that unless the Holocaust happened, the inventor of his favorite flavor of ice cream would not have existed (and he tells some crazy story that allegedly links the two things)."[20] Such a link would be absurd. Whatever goods God intended by purposing the Holocaust to take place must far outweigh the enormous pain, suffering, and opprobrium of his glorious name that first resulted from that massive horror. Elie Wiesel was understandably tempted to think that the Holocaust defeated the God of the Bible, consigning him to the gallows along with that young boy. But if a theodicy is worth its salt, that simply cannot be true. Yes, the Holocaust was beyond horrendous and leaves us with many unanswered questions, but in the end, it cannot be considered gratuitous. The task of a theodicy carries the enormous burden of explaining why.

DEFENSE OR THEODICY?

Before we consider common responses to the problem of God and evil, it should be noted that not all Christians take the same strategy in answering the looming questions that arise. Some Christian philosophers make a distinction between a *theodicy* and a *defense*.[21] In the parlance of philosophical discussion, a theodicy, technically speaking, is a positive case explaining why God allows (i.e., does not prevent) or decrees evil in the world. It outlines precisely what good and sufficient reasons God has for doing so.

On the other hand, a defense seeks to answer charges brought against God in light of evil, namely, how God can be exonerated from the charges that he is less than God in the face of evil, or that he is culpable for evil in some way. A defense may indicate *possible* reasons why God permits (i.e., does not prevent) evil to transpire, but it doesn't seek to give a *definite* solution to the problem. It merely seeks to show that, broadly speaking, there is no logical inconsistency between the existence of God and the existence of evil.

In other words, it says that the one who has raised the charges against God based on evil has not made his case. K. Scott Oliphint likens a defense to staving off an attack on one's castle in medieval times. One may not gain

---

19. Welty, *Why Is There Evil?*, 45.
20. Welty, *Why Is There Evil?*, 45.
21. Philosophers differ on the use of this terminology.

any new territory in such a defense, but he has not given up the territory he holds to the enemy and has kept the castle strong.[22]

Many believe that a defense therefore carries a lighter burden than a theodicy. But that is not always satisfying. The problem with a mere defense is that it seems to weasel out of the hard questions people face. Nobody wrestling with the problem wants to be told, "Well, this might be a possible reason why God allows evil. Certainly, there is no sound argument against it, but we don't want to be too dogmatic."

Now, it could be that some uncertainty exists about God's reasons for purposing or permitting evil. Perhaps the Bible is altogether silent on the question. I hope to argue later that the Bible is not silent. But we should not be presumptuous. I believe that the Bible makes the case for a broad, all-encompassing theodicy, but this doesn't mean that such a theodicy answers every question that arises, especially when it comes to specific instances of evil and what that fully means for those directly affected by it.

It is hubris to suppose that we have tidy, exhaustive answers to the questions that plague everyone caught in a morass of malevolence. We cannot pretend to know all the reasons why a young mother has had her third miscarriage or why the members of a church viciously maligned and then fired their faithful pastor who had lovingly, though imperfectly, served them for thirty-five years. Nonetheless, I think there are reasons to embrace a theodicy and not merely a defense.

In either case, in the responses to evil to be explored in the coming chapters, the terms *theodicy* and *defense* will be used somewhat loosely and interchangeably. Furthermore, few theodicists look to a single defense or theodicy to address the problem of evil. Some responses target particular aspects of the problem that others seem inadequate to deal with. A theodicy is not required to answer every question in order to be true or useful.[23] This means that not all responses are mutually exclusive. Many apologists champion a cumulative approach, and there is nothing wrong with this as long as one theodicy does not contradict what another says. Yet some theodicies do make conflicting claims, and that must be addressed. We will now turn to the most common responses to evil made by Christian theism.

KEY TERMS

defense
evidential problem of evil

---

22. K. Scott Oliphint, *Covenantal Apologetics* (Wheaton, IL: Crossway, 2013), 169.
23. Feinberg, *Many Faces of Evil*, 26.

existential problem of evil
gratuitous evil
horrendous evil
logical problem of evil
theodicy

STUDY QUESTIONS

1. What are the three different ways of framing the problem of evil?
2. What is the difference between horrendous evil and gratuitous evil? Give examples of what might be categorized as gratuitous evil even if you don't think such a category of evil exists.
3. According to Greg Welty, what are the two criteria that a theodicy must meet if it is to be faithful in upholding the character of God?
4. What is the technical difference between a theodicy and a defense? Do you think Christians should bear the burden of providing a full-on theodicy or merely a defense when addressing the problem of evil?
5. What do you see as the biggest problem of evil for yourself, either intellectually or emotionally and spiritually?

FOR FURTHER READING

Alvin Plantinga, *God, Freedom, and Evil* (Grand Rapids: Eerdmans, 1977).

Greg Welty, *Why Is There Evil in the World (and So Much of It)?* (Fearn, Ross-shire, Scotland: Christian Focus, 2018).

Elie Wiesel, *Night* (New York: Hill and Wang, 2006).

Advanced

John S. Feinberg, *The Many Faces of Evil* (Wheaton, IL: Crossway, 2004).

5

GUARDING THE SACRED TREASURE OF FREE WILL

Comfortably lying in his golden lair, the old dragon snorted, "My armour is like tenfold shields, my teeth are swords, my claws spears, the shock of my tail is a thunderbolt, my wings a hurricane, and my breath death!" So declared Lord Smaug the Impenetrable to the terrified little creature Bilbo Baggins in Tolkien's classic tale *The Hobbit*.[1] Smaug had long overtaken the Dwarf kingdom of Erebor known as the Lonely Mountain. Within the heart of the mountain, for some 171 years, the dragon had fiercely guarded mounds of treasure—gold, silver, pearls, gems of every variety.

But the greatest treasure of the hoard was the Arkenstone, a family heirloom sought by Thorin Oakenshield, the exiled Dwarf King of Durin's Folk. The venerable warrior and his Company came to reclaim the gem along with the mountain kingdom from the feared dragon. It was under Thorin's employ that the hobbit Bilbo penetrated the dragon's lair, arousing him from a deep sleep.

Thorin later described the coveted Arkenstone to Bilbo: "It was a globe with a thousand facets; it shone like silver in the firelight, like water in the sun, like snow under the stars, like rain upon the Moon!"[2] Unbeknownst to Thorin or the dragon, however, Bilbo had already discovered the piece and secretly slipped it into his pocket as it lay near Smaug during their colorful confrontation. Upon realizing his misfortune, the dragon's fiery wrath was incited. Smaug would now search out the wretched thieves who had stolen

1. J. R. R. Tolkien, *The Hobbit* (1966; repr., New York: Houghton Mifflin, 1997), 203.
2. Tolkien, *The Hobbit*, 207–8.

his treasure and make good on his earlier claims to Bilbo: "I kill where I wish and none dare resist. I laid low the warriors of old and their like is not in the world today."[3]

The fire-breathing creature proceeded to lay waste to the nearby community of Lake-town until he was slain by the courageous Bard the Bowman. Thorin eventually acquired his precious gemstone, but only after he himself had been slain in the Battle of the Five Armies. It was placed on his chest as he was laid to rest in a tomb deep in the heart of Lonely Mountain.

Many Christians look upon the possession of free will as a sacred treasure from God above. For theodicists known as *free-will theists,* free will resembles the Arkenstone—and it must be guarded at great cost. Their God is not unlike the infamous Smaug, but their characters and aims are diametrically opposed. The God of free-will theism is an infinitely benevolent and undefeatable God who fiercely guards this treasure not merely for himself but for the good of his moral creatures—especially his image-bearing ones. He is the cherished sentinel of free will.

First, he knows that free will is an indispensable master key that alone can unlock meaningful and loving relationships. Second, he understands that freedom of choice is a properly basic feature of our humanity, ensuring our ability to act in morally responsible ways. Moreover, this treasure of free will also ensures that God himself cannot be blamed for the irresponsible use of it by his morally responsible creatures.

Free-will theists employ free will for the problem of evil in what is known as the *free-will defense.* This response to the problem sees the preservation of free will as vital. Without it, good is not possible. But with it comes a great risk—by its abuse, the unfortunate reality of evil is introduced into our experience. The free-will defense views God's providence as a noble model of self-restraint and noninterference, affording humanity a remarkable degree of autonomy.

Furthermore, it is often coupled with the *natural-law defense.* Free creatures must have a world governed by predictable stable laws in which to operate. Thus, God cannot be frequently interfering with those laws (or human freedom); otherwise, it would tamper with the environment in which free decisions are most maximized. But how are we to assess these popular theodicies? Do they hold up to the scrutiny of the Bible's testimony about God, human nature, and moral responsibility? Is free will a rational and biblical response to the problem of evil? Let us examine the arguments.

3. Tolkien, *The Hobbit,* 203.

THE FREE-WILL DEFENSE

There is no question that the free-will defense is the most common response to the problem of evil. It employs a version of human free agency that philosophers and theologians refer to as *libertarian* free will (which has no relationship to the political philosophy). Among those free-will theists who adopt libertarianism are Arminians, open theists, and Molinists. Most Calvinist (Reformed) theologians adopt a version of free agency known as *compatibilism*, and thus they reject libertarianism and the free-will defense.

The central issue here is whether God ultimately determines the choices that humans make. Libertarians say that human freedom of choice is not compatible with divine determinism, whereas compatibilists say that it is.[4] This may explain why so many Christians—scholars and laypeople alike— embrace the free-will defense. Embracing the all-encompassing meticulous providence of classic Reformed and Calvinist theology is a far harder pill than most are willing to swallow.[5]

But it remains to be seen which view accords best with Scripture and reason. I will argue in the course of these pages that the free-will defense fails the test and that the Reformed view overcomes any perceived deficiencies it has. It offers a superior theodicy that is biblically and philosophically satisfying while magnifying the glory of God as no other theodicy does.

Libertarian free will can be defined as follows: "Each of us, when we act, is a prime mover unmoved. In doing what we do, we cause certain events to happen, and nothing—or no one—causes us to cause those events to happen."[6] The two important ideas here are that God cannot be the originator (determiner) of our choices, and that truly free acts are uncaused outside our own choosing. Only we can be the sufficient cause of our own choices— what philosophers call *agent causation*. Our choices are not determined by

4. I explore this debate in greater depth in my book *What about Free Will? Reconciling Our Choices with God's Sovereignty* (Phillipsburg, NJ: P&R Publishing, 2016), which defends a biblical model for compatibilism while critiquing libertarianism. For a much more philosophically rigorous defense of compatibilism, see Guillaume Bignon, *Excusing Sinners and Blaming God: A Calvinist Assessment of Determinism, Moral Responsibility, and Divine Involvement in Evil* (Eugene, OR: Pickwick Publications, 2018).

5. For a classic statement on God's decree and meticulous providence, see WCF chapter 3 ("Of God's Eternal Decree"), and chapter 5 ("Of Providence").

6. Roderick M. Chisholm, "Human Freedom and the Self," in *The Elements of Philosophy: Readings from Past and Present*, ed. Tamar Szabo Gendler et al. (New York: Oxford University Press, 2008), 485. Note that among philosophers there is a dizzying array of different beliefs about human freedom and the causes of our choices, although they tend to coalesce around libertarianism or compatibilism. I am focusing my attention only on those views most commonly held among Christian thinkers.

anyone (especially God) or anything outside our own will to choose. Thus, libertarianism is *indeterministic*.

Most libertarians embrace a second plank in their definition of free will that philosophers call the *Principle of Alternative Possibilities* (*PAP* for short). This is fancy language for the idea of *contrary choice*: if Mary chooses one course of action (*A*), her freedom of will gives her the power to equally choose a contrary (alternative) course of action (*not A*) in exactly the same set of circumstances.[7]

When Mary came to the fork in the road, she chose to turn right. But if we could rewind the clock, as soon as Mary came to the fork, she could as easily have chosen to turn left. Alvin Plantinga's definition of free will employs both ideas (*indeterminism* plus *contrary choice*): "If a person is free with respect to a given action, then he is free to perform that action and free to refrain from performing it; no antecedent conditions and/or causal laws determine that he will perform the action, or that he won't. It is within his power, at the time in question, to take or perform the action and within his power to refrain from it."[8]

This notion of human freedom is the essential component of the free-will defense. Plantinga summarizes the defense this way:

> A world containing creatures who are significantly free [i.e., having libertarian freedom] . . . is more valuable, all else being equal, than a world

7. Most free-will theists hold that the PAP (contrary choice) is essential to the definition of libertarian freedom. For example, see Roger E. Olson, "The Classical Free Will Theist Model of God," in *Perspectives on the Doctrine of God: 4 Views*, ed. Bruce A. Ware (Nashville: B&H Academic, 2008), 150. Some libertarians, however, see problems with it. For example, the Molinist William Lane Craig accepts libertarian free will as indeterministic but rejects the PAP. See "Response to Gregory A. Boyd," in *Four Views on Divine Providence*, ed. Stanley N. Gundry and Dennis W. Jowers (Grand Rapids: Zondervan, 2011), 225. In either case, Guillaume Bignon has persuasively demonstrated that it is incoherent for libertarianism to be indeterministic while denying the ability to choose otherwise (i.e., PAP). Determinism by its nature indicates that only one possible outcome can result from the antecedent factors that effectively generate the choices of moral agents; therefore, indeterminism necessarily entails the idea of contrary choice. See *Excusing Sinners and Blaming God*, 124–28.

8. Alvin Plantinga, *God, Freedom, and Evil* (Grand Rapids: Eerdmans, 1977), 29. Bruce Reichenbach's comprehensive definition of libertarian free will is helpful: "To say that a person is free means that, given a certain set of circumstances, the person (to put it in the past tense) could have done otherwise than he did. He was not compelled by causes either internal to himself (genetic structure or irresistible drives) or external (other persons, God) to act as he did. Though certain causal conditions are present and indeed are necessary for persons to choose or act, if they are free these causal conditions are not sufficient to cause them to choose or act. The individual is the sufficient condition for the course of action chosen" ("God Limits His Power," in *Predestination and Free Will: Four Views of Divine Sovereignty and Human Freedom*, ed. David Basinger and Randall Basinger [Downers Grove, IL: InterVarsity Press, 1986], 102).

containing no free creatures at all. Now God can create free creatures, but He can't *cause* or *determine* them to do only what is right. For if He does so, then they aren't significantly free after all; they do not do what is right *freely*. To create creatures capable of *moral good*, therefore, He must create creatures capable of moral evil; and He can't give these creatures the freedom to perform evil and at the same time prevent them from doing so. As it turned out, sadly enough, some of the free creatures went wrong in the exercise of their freedom; this is the source of moral evil. The fact that free creatures sometimes go wrong, however, counts neither against God's omnipotence nor against His goodness; for He could have forestalled the occurrence of moral evil only by removing the possibility of moral good.[9]

The free-will defense is offered for three principal reasons. First, it is meant to ground moral responsibility in the powers of free choice granted to humans. Walls and Dongell write:

> We believe that libertarian free will is intrinsic to the very notion of moral responsibility. That is, a person cannot be held morally responsible for an act unless he or she was free to perform that act and free to refrain from it. This is a basic moral intuition, and we do not believe there are any relevant moral convictions more basic than this one that could serve as premises to prove it.[10]

In other words, Walls and Dongell would agree with Plantinga that for God "to create creatures capable of *moral good*, therefore, He must create creatures capable of moral evil; and He can't give these creatures the freedom to perform evil and at the same time prevent them from doing so."[11]

Second, the defense seeks to exonerate God from culpability for the evil that human beings freely choose. If God does not determine our choices, then he cannot be called the author of sin. Moral responsibility is confined to the freedom of the creature, who acts independently of the Creator.

Third, many argue that without libertarian freedom, loving relationships are eviscerated. Gregory Boyd states that humans "must possess the capacity and opportunity to reject love if they are to possess the genuine capacity and ability to engage in love."[12] For example, if our choice to love

9. Plantinga, *God, Freedom, and Evil*, 30.

10. Jerry L. Walls and Joseph R. Dongell, *Why I Am Not a Calvinist* (Downers Grove, IL: InterVarsity Press, 2004), 105.

11. Plantinga, *God, Freedom, and Evil*, 30.

12. Gregory A. Boyd, *Satan and the Problem of Evil* (Downers Grove, IL: InterVarsity Press, 2001), 52.

God is determined by God, then it seems to follow that our love for him is coerced, and coerced love is no love at all. We would be unwilling prisoners of a tyrannical deity.

Thus, if meaningful moral good is to obtain in this world, God must risk the unfortunate possibility of evil. The Arminian John Wesley (1703–91) said, "Were human liberty taken away, men would be as incapable of virtue as stones."[13] Moral good necessitates the moral freedom afforded by libertarian free will, but moral evil is the unfortunate side effect of abusing such freedom.

According to most free-will theists (e.g., Arminians and open theists), this means that God must restrict what sovereign powers he does possess. He must guard himself from desiring to tamper with our moral freedom or to intervene too quickly or frequently when things don't go as planned. This is to be expected in a theological construct in which God exercises a loose kind of give-and-take *general* providence, not the *meticulous* providence that Calvinism embraces. The plan he ordains (i.e., his decree) is a general plan, not a detailed blueprint for history.[14]

This general providence means that intervening in a world in which people have such moral freedom, preventing them from acting wickedly, is to undermine the value of moral good—a value that is directly tied to the ability to choose equally between good and evil. If God were to abuse his sovereign powers, he would abuse man's freedom and prevent all meaningful good from taking place. Thus, he must self-limit his power.[15] The Arminian theologian Roger Olson states the matter clearly: "God is sufficiently powerful to stop anything from happening, but he does not always exercise that power, because to do so would be to rob his free and rational creatures, created in his image, of their distinct reality and liberty."[16]

PROBLEMS WITH THE FREE-WILL DEFENSE

How are we to assess the free-will defense? Tim Keller is right when he notes, "The free will theodicy has become very popular, but it may be so partially because our culture inclines us to find it appealing. It sounds plausible to people in Western civilization, where we have been taught to

13. John Wesley, "On Divine Providence," in *The Works of Reverend John Wesley*, vol. 2 (New York: J. Emory and B. Waugh, 1831), 102.

14. See Jack W. Cottrell, "The Nature of the Divine Sovereignty," in *The Grace of God, the Will of Man*, ed. Clark H. Pinnock (Minneapolis: Bethany House, 1989), 97–119.

15. Cottrell, "Nature of the Divine Sovereignty," 107–11.

16. Roger E. Olson, *Arminian Theology: Myths and Realities* (Downers Grove, IL: InterVarsity Press, 2006), 132.

think of freedom of choice as something also sacred."[17] For some, this sort of freedom is no small matter. It is suggested that God must *necessarily* grant his image-bearing creatures libertarian free will and *never* tamper with its exercise.

Open theist Thomas Oord says, "God *must* give freedom and cannot override the gift given."[18] The nature of human freedom necessitates that God refrain from tampering with it. If so, God's powers are not self-restricted; they are necessarily restricted by the existence of libertarian freedom. This undermines the robust doctrine of omnipotence that Christian orthodoxy has usually attributed to God.[19]

It is doubtful that most free-will theists would agree with Oord, but this seems to be a reasonable conclusion from the critical importance that libertarian freedom bears in free-will theism. In either case, Oord's obsession with the Arkenstone of libertarian freedom is indicative of free-will theism in general. Without this conception of freedom, "the raison d'etre of free will theism disappears."[20] Therefore, the fundamental problems with the free-will defense as a response to God and evil center on the viability of libertarian free will. Here are nine critical problems that it faces.

Libertarian Free Will Lacks Biblical Support

Most libertarians assume that their brand of free will is a given, and that the Bible operates on this assumption.[21] For example, the "whosoever will" passages (e.g., John 3:16) seem to suggest libertarian free will whereby one has an innate ability to heed or resist the gospel call.[22] Yet these passages (and others appealed to) can be explained in terms of God's preceptive (moral or instructive) will, which can be resisted, whereas his decretive

17. Timothy Keller, *Walking with God through Pain and Suffering* (New York: Dutton, 2013), 91.

18. Thomas Jay Oord, "An Essential Kenosis View," in *God and the Problem of Evil: Five Views*, ed. Chad Meister and James K. Dew Jr. (Downers Grove, IL: InterVarsity Press, 2017), 89; see also Gregory A. Boyd, "God Limits His Control," in *Four Views on Divine Providence*, ed. Stanley N. Gundry and Dennis W. Jowers (Grand Rapids: Zondervan, 2011), 191–92.

19. In this regard, Oord's view of God is not far removed from that of Rabbi Harold Kushner (see p. 74).

20. Paul Helm, "Response to John Sanders," in *Perspectives on the Doctrine of God: 4 Views*, ed. Bruce A. Ware (Nashville: B&H Academic, 2008), 244.

21. Olson, "Classical Free Will Theist Model of God," 157–61.

22. Steve W. Lemke, "A Biblical and Theological Critique of Irresistible Grace," in *Whosoever Will: A Biblical-Theological Critique of Five-Point Calvinism*, ed. David L. Allen and Steve W. Lemke (Nashville: B&H Publishing Group, 2010), 122–27. Other passages that libertarians often appeal to include Josh. 24:15; Isa. 55:1; Jer. 33:3; Mark 16:15–16; Acts 8:36–37; 2 Cor. 9:7; Rev. 3:20; 22:17.

(sovereign) will cannot be resisted.[23] The "whosoever will" passages also fit the Reformed distinction known as the *general call* to salvation, which is extended to all sinners, as distinguished from the *effectual call* to salvation whereby God effectually draws elect sinners to himself (John 6:44).[24]

Now, it must be admitted that the Bible contains no explicit teaching on the precise nature of free agency, but what it does say appears to support compatibilism, not libertarianism (see chapter 7). Alister McGrath argues that libertarian free will as a tool to explain certain issues in theology arose under the influence of Greek thought: "By the end of the fourth century, the Greek fathers had formulated a teaching on human free will based upon philosophical rather than biblical foundations. Standing in the great Platonic tradition, heavily influenced by Philo, and reacting against the fatalism of their day, they taught that man was utterly free in his choice of good or evil."[25]

Libertarian Free Will Denies Meticulous Providence

The plain reading of Scripture indicates that God meticulously decrees and presides over every event that unfolds within his creation, including the choices that his creatures make (see detailed arguments in chapters 7 and 8). As the humbled ruler Nebuchadnezzar declared, "I blessed the Most High, and praised and honored him who lives forever, for his dominion is an everlasting dominion, and his kingdom endures from generation to generation; all the inhabitants of the earth are accounted as nothing, and he does according to his will among the host of heaven and among the inhabitants of the earth; and none can stay his hand or say to him, 'What have you done?'" (Dan. 4:34–35).

God's "will" here is his sovereign or decretive will. Furthermore, Scripture indicates that we are wholly dependent on God for every aspect of our being, having been created out of nothing (*ex nihilo*) (Acts 17:24–25, 28). Libertarianism, however, presupposes that we are "sources of primary causality" and thus largely independent of God.[26]

---

23. See 161n30. For a fuller discussion on the distinction between the decretive and preceptive wills of God, see John Piper, "Are There Two Wills in God?," in *Still Sovereign*, ed. Thomas R. Schreiner and Bruce A. Ware (Grand Rapids: Baker, 2000), 107–31, also available at http://www.desiringgod.org/resource-library/articles/are-there-two-wills-in-god; Christensen, *What about Free Will?*, 85–88, 203–4.

24. See Matthew Barrett, *Salvation by Grace: The Case for Effectual Calling and Regeneration* (Phillipsburg, NJ: P&R Publishing, 2013).

25. Alister McGrath, *Justitia Dei: A History of the Christian Doctrine of Justification*, 2 vols. (Cambridge: Cambridge University Press, 1986), 1:19.

26. Paul Kjoss Helseth, "God Causes All Things," in *Four Views on Divine Providence*, ed. Stanley N. Gundry and Dennis W. Jowers (Grand Rapids: Zondervan, 2011), 42.

The apostle Paul is unequivocal in his affirmation of meticulous providence. The divine predestination of humans to salvation is part of the broader scope of the ordering of history "according to the purpose of him who works all things according to the counsel of his will" (Eph. 1:11). Again, God's "will" here can be none other than his sovereign decretive will. In this regard, libertarians hold that if God interferes in the affairs of humans, then their freedom and responsibility is stripped, even when they do evil. But Scripture indicates that God intervenes to stop evil all the time.[27]

God kept Abimelech from violating Sarah (Gen. 20:6). He arrested the raging armies of Egypt by the waves of the Red Sea (Ex. 14:21–29). God stopped the abuse of so-called free will when Nadab and Abihu were struck down by fire (Lev. 10:1–2). Likewise, he put to death the sons of Eli for similar evil deeds (1 Sam. 2:25). God warned the magi and Joseph of Herod's sinister plots (Matt. 2:12–15; cf. v. 20). Christ halted Paul on the road to Damascus before he could do more damage to the Christian cause (Acts 9:1–6). Such examples could be multiplied.

The libertarian, however, faces a different conundrum. Since the Bible clearly indicates God's sovereign intervention—and some libertarians agree that he occasionally intervenes—then why doesn't God intervene in all cases of evil? If he does not intervene, then he is obviously, at the very least, permitting evil to happen when he knows full well that he could intervene and stop it.

God warned the magi and Joseph of Herod's murderous designs, yet he did not spare the baby boys from the wicked ruler's slaughter in Bethlehem (Matt. 2:16–18).[28] God's preventing such evil in one case and permitting it in another is a decision he makes that allows evil to proceed, uninterrupted by his providential interventions. Thus, we can draw no other conclusion: God sovereignly intends all evil to happen that he does not prevent. God in his inscrutable wisdom "judges that the good effects of permission *outweigh* the bad effects of intervention"; otherwise, he would intervene.[29] "His permissions are *willing* permissions, done for particular reasons" that we may rarely understand.[30]

---

27. The language of divine intervention can be misleading because it suggests that God suddenly learned something that he didn't know before and then decided to interrupt a process that he does not normally manage. It only appears from the human perspective that God intervenes. God is constantly sustaining every aspect of creation and his creatures' actions. His "intervention" is part of his preordained plan. But God accommodates his activity in Creator-creature relations that resemble creature-creature relations. See chapter 7 for more on God's providence.

28. See Léon Cogniet's haunting depiction of this episode from Matthew's Gospel in his 1824 painting *Scène du Massacre des Innocents* (*Scene of the Massacre of the Innocents*).

29. Greg Welty, *Why Is There Evil in the World (and So Much of It)?* (Fearn, Ross-shire, Scotland: Christian Focus, 2018), 174.

30. Welty, *Why Is There Evil?*, 175.

Libertarian Free Will Undermines the Doctrine of Depravity

The consistent testimony of Scripture is that we are morally corrupted and enslaved to sin. Our wills are in spiritual bondage to evil. Calvinism calls this problem *total depravity* (the *T* in the acronym *TULIP*).[31] Every aspect of the unregenerate person is corrupted—our mind, will, emotions, desires, motivations, and so on. Jesus tells us, "Everyone who practices sin is a slave to sin" (John 8:34). Since all humans have sinned (Rom. 3:23), all are enslaved.

According to Romans 8:7, the fundamental orientation of the person who lives in the "flesh," indicating the absence of the Holy Spirit within, is hostility toward God. The unbelieving, unregenerate mind "does not submit to God's law; indeed, it cannot. Those who are in the flesh cannot please God" (vv. 7–8). Thus, unbelievers are both *unwilling* and *morally unable* to please God by their choices (cf. vv. 9–18). They suffer from a total inability to effect any aspect of salvation. This doctrine is also called in broadly Christian orthodoxy *original sin*, which includes *original guilt* from Adam, as well as *original inclination* to sin due to our depraved nature.

Only the doctrine of irresistible and efficacious grace (*irresistible grace* is the *I* in *TULIP*) is sufficient to overcome the bondage of the will and enable it to please God as part of the divine work of redemption.[32] During the Reformation, Martin Luther debated the Roman Catholic humanist Erasmus. Erasmus defined free will as one's ability to apply himself to acting morally good so as to lead to salvation.[33]

Luther responded: "If there were enough good in 'free-will' for it to apply itself to good, it would have no need of grace!"[34] Likewise, Erasmus said that the "motions of the mind to evil can be overcome." He attributes an inherent goodness to humanity that is far above our pay grade. Luther responded, "What need is there of the Spirit, or Christ, or God, if 'free-will' can overcome the motions of the mind to evil?"[35] He stated, "It is . . . apparent from their very works and experience that man without grace can will nothing but evil."[36] If free will has such power in one instance of good, why can it not always do good?

---

31. See David N. Steele, Curtis C. Thomas, and S. Lance Quinn, *The Five Points of Calvinism* (Phillipsburg, NJ: P&R Publishing, 2004).

32. See Barrett, *Salvation by Grace*.

33. Martin Luther, *The Bondage of the Will*, trans. J. I. Packer & O. R. Johnston (Grand Rapids: Fleming H. Revell, 1957), 137.

34. Luther, *Bondage of the Will*, 145.

35. Luther, *Bondage of the Will*, 157.

36. Luther, *Bondage of the Will*, 318.

Guillaume Bignon argues that it does not help the Arminian to say that "humans *can* avoid sinning but merely *don't*, or just *happen* not to." The Bible does not support the idea "that fallen humans have the categorical ability to be perfectly righteous and simply happen not to be; we are told that they lack the ability altogether."[37]

Arminianism responds to the problem of original sin or total depravity by introducing the doctrine of prevenient grace. The Arminian theologian Roger Olson asserts:

> This common (not universal) Arminian doctrine of universal prevenient grace means that because of Jesus Christ and the Holy Spirit no human being is actually in a state of absolute darkness and depravity. Because of original sin, helplessness to do good is the natural state of humanity, but because of the work of Christ and the operation of the Holy Spirit universally no human being actually exists in that natural state.[38]

Thus, prevenient grace supposedly mitigates the effects of moral depravity and restores libertarian free will in the sinner. God supplies further effusions of grace before conversion. A sinner may avail himself of this extra grace if he so chooses. But he can equally reject it as well. In other words, no grace of God is wholly effective (sufficient) for salvation. The sinner must cooperate with it. God must respect the sinner's choice.

But this eviscerates the biblical doctrine of grace enshrined in the Reformation principle of grace alone (*sola gratia*).[39] It leaves salvation ultimately in the hands of the sinner, giving him room to boast, contrary to the testimony of Scripture.[40] If two sinners are equal recipients of saving grace and one rejects it, disbelieving the gospel, while the other accepts it and believes, what distinguishes the two responses? No matter how you cut it, you must conclude that the one who cooperated with the grace, using his free will to believe, must have been the better, smarter, more righteous person.

Unless salvation is *all* of grace, we invite room for boasting in our personal contribution, and this smacks of works-righteousness. The *all-sufficient* grace of God is the only power unto salvation (Rom. 1:16; Eph. 2:8–9). Thus, the Bible denies that we have libertarian free will.

---

37. Bignon, *Excusing Sinners and Blaming God*, 151.
38. Olson, *Arminian Theology*, 154.
39. See Carl R. Trueman, *Grace Alone: Salvation as a Gift of God* (Grand Rapids: Zondervan, 2017).
40. See, for example, Rom. 3:27; 4:2; 1 Cor. 1:26–31; Gal. 6:14; Eph. 2:8–9.

Libertarian Free Will Renders Decision-Making Arbitrary

Free will according to libertarianism means that one can equally choose *A* or *not A* under the same precise circumstances. In other words, all things being equal right up until the point of choosing, the options of *A* and *not A* are freely available. So if Mary walks into her local diner and has reasons for ordering the pancakes (maybe she loves their scrumptious fluffiness!), those reasons cannot be sufficient for her to choose the pancakes. She could overcome those reasons and choose the omelet instead, having no sufficient reasons for doing so. Thus, all the factors that might influence Mary's choice of breakfast can be exactly the same, and there is absolutely no guarantee of what she will end up choosing. If the combination of those factors inclines her to *only one* choice, then her freedom is thwarted.

This is why the brand of free agency underlying the PAP (contrary choice) is sometimes called the *liberty of indifference*. This suggests that to be free, people must have an indifference about the choices they make such that they could have equally made alternative choices, being under no compulsion to choose one way or another. Whatever choices are made cannot have a sufficient explanation, and this leads to the serious charge that our decision-making becomes arbitrary.

But people do not perceive their choices to be arbitrary. There are generally perceivable reasons that sufficiently explain why one choice was made and not another. This is the case in compatibilist models of human freedom. In compatibilism, alternative choices are certainly presented to the free agent, but those choices are made *only* because there are alternative reasons for them that did not apply to the other options. In other words, different factors—various influences, circumstances, desires, and so forth—generate particular motives that lead to particular choices. A factors always lead to choice A, and B factors always lead to choice B.

This all contends for compatibilist freedom—a freedom of inclination, not indifference. Compatibilist freedom argues that we always choose according to our strongest inclination (desire)—the combination of various decisive factors that lead to the strongest motive for choosing in one and *only* one direction.[41]

God Does Not Have Libertarian Free Will

If unlimited libertarian free will is the extremely valuable commodity that so many think it is, then we would expect God to have this same freedom.

41. For a fuller explanation of how compatibilist freedom works, see chapters 7 and 8 in my book *What about Free Will?*

After all, the libertarian argument is that in order to generate genuine moral good, one must risk generating moral evil. Yet when it comes to God, nothing could be further from the truth. God does not have this unhindered power of contrary choice. His choices are limited to only good choices, because absolute righteousness is essential to his being. He is pure light, devoid of darkness (1 John 1:5). And God cannot deny himself (2 Tim. 2:13). Thus, "God's sinlessness is broadly logically necessary."[42] This truth hinders neither his freedom nor the goods that come with it.[43]

Likewise, Jesus could not have acted sinfully during his earthly ministry, yet that did not stop him from freely loving people in ways that are more significant and meaningful than what is afforded by our supposedly unhindered freedom.

Furthermore, free-will theists assume that libertarian freedom "is a necessary condition for a loving relationship."[44] But does the freedom to hate enhance or give significance to our freedom to love?[45] The most beautiful bond of love that exists is that between members of the Trinity. Yet there is no possibility that the Father and the Son could act contrary to their singularly focused love for each other. They willingly, unreservedly, and necessarily love each other perfectly and can do no other. Furthermore, we praise God for his inability to act other than according to his righteous character. Thus, praise and blame are not dependent on the power of contrary choice. Libertarian free will is not necessary for moral responsibility.

Calvin extends the point about God's necessarily righteous nature and actions to include Satan's inability to act other than unrighteously: "If the fact that [God] must do good does not hinder [his] free will in doing good; if the devil, who can only do evil, yet sins with his will—who shall say that

42. Bignon, *Excusing Sinners and Blaming God*, 106. In other words, God's sinlessness is an ontological necessity of his very being.

43. God's freedom is unique (*sui generis*) in that it is inextricably tied to his divine independence or self-sufficiency. For example, he is free to create or not create, depending on what purposes he chooses to pursue. Yet God can never act against his essential nature and character. In contrast, whatever freedom humans possess is a dependent freedom—dependent on God's meticulous providential sustaining power and purposes. In either case, neither God nor humans can act against their respective natures (see chapter 7). Note that this argues for a kind of limited PAP. But again, alternative choices (always good ones in God's case) always have sufficient reasons behind those choices.

44. John Sanders, *The God Who Risks: A Theology of Providence* (Downers Grove, IL: InterVarsity Press, 1999), 223. See also Olson, "Classical Free Will Theist Model of God," 148; Boyd, "God Limits His Control," 190.

45. For a thorough critique of the notion that genuine love necessitates libertarian free will, see Thaddeus J. Williams, *Love, Freedom, and Evil: Does Authentic Love Require Free Will?* (New York: Rodopi, 2011).

man therefore sins less willingly because he is subject to the necessity of sinning?"[46] Calvin here refers to the bondage of humanity's will due to original sin (Rom. 3:9–18).

If God and Satan are restricted to their natures with regard to righteousness and wickedness (respectively) and yet act willingly, freely, voluntarily, then it follows that humans in their unredeemed, unregenerated state of corruption can act only corruptly and not otherwise, and yet still act freely and with no harm done to their moral responsibility. The specific argument regarding angels could be framed another way. No biblical evidence suggests that once Satan and his host of demonic followers fell from their pristine state of innocence, they were given any opportunity to repent or that they had the power and inclination to do so.

Likewise, after the fall of these angelic creatures, we are given no evidence that the *unfallen* angels had an ability or desire to henceforth rebel against God. Each set of angels (i.e., those who fell from original perfection and those who remained in unfallen perfection) appear to exist in unchanging confirmed states of unrighteousness in the case of fallen angels and righteousness in the case of unfallen angels. Their respective blameworthy and praiseworthy actions are neither denied nor to be viewed as their willful desires to remain in these states of guilt and innocence. This begins to suggest that God had a sovereignly decreed purpose for the fall of angels (see chapter 16). Furthermore, it suggests that moral responsibility is grounded in something other than libertarian free will (see chapter 9).

God Could Design Us to Choose Only Good

Many libertarians (namely, Arminians) believe that God voluntarily limits his providential control in order to secure his creatures' free will. But why couldn't God maintain a significant and uncompromised degree of free will (i.e., alternative choice) among his creatures and simply limit those choices to a host of different good options? After all, God is limited in his own actions by only good choices, and we find nothing that diminishes his freedom and praiseworthiness by that fact.[47]

Free will in this case would be limited, but it is not clear that unhindered free will (the ability to make both good and evil choices) is preferable to

---

46. John Calvin, *Institutes of the Christian Religion*, ed. John T. McNeill, trans. Ford Lewis Battles (Philadelphia: Westminster, 1960), 2.3.5.

47. Again, this argues for a limited model of the PAP in which only good choices are possible. This certainly applies to heavenly freedom for believers, but such freedom is best understood as compatibilistic, not libertarian. See the next point.

one that limits our choices to only good ones. In other words, is the risk of evil worth the other goods that unlimited free will supposedly preserves? Does God value the rapist's freedom to rape above the prevention of rape?

Libertarian Free Will Does Not Exist in Heaven

All orthodox Christians agree that there will be no ability to sin in heaven (i.e., the eternal state). In other words, all the glorified believers' choices will be good choices with no possibility of acting evil or even thinking an evil thought.[48] We will be fully conformed to the same unhindered moral perfection that Christ has (Rom. 8:29; 1 John 3:2). "God will guarantee that we will not sin in heaven."[49] Thus, the greatest plane of existence contains no hint of the unhindered libertarian free will that free-will theists argue for in this world. Nonetheless, it will be a place of perfect freedom and bliss, full of perfect love between God and the redeemed. Its unfallen condition will far outstrip every state of affairs that marks our present fallen condition.

Thus, if libertarian free will is such a valuable, even necessary, treasure—indispensable for generating moral good—then how do we explain that heaven will have no such treasure, no Arkenstone? How is it that neither God himself nor the angels possess such freedom of contrary choice? If libertarian free will is not necessary for freedom to exist in the greatest Being (God) or in the greatest place (heaven), then how could it be necessary for human freedom and responsibility in the here and now?

Libertarian Free Will Has Trouble with Divine Foreknowledge

God knows exhaustively and infallibly all past, present, and future events that transpire in his creation. This is known as the *doctrine of foreknowledge*.[50] But according to libertarianism, our free will is indeterministic, and one could have always chosen differently than he did, so then how can God know what his creatures will choose?

How, for example, could Jesus know with certainty that Peter would deny him precisely three times within a brief period (Matt. 26:34) if it were

48. Conversely, the same could be said for unbelievers in hell. There is no evidence that they have the ability or desire to repent and thus reverse their condition (i.e., postmortem salvation). See J. I. Packer, "Universalism: Will Everyone Be Ultimately Saved?," in *Hell under Fire*, ed. Christopher W. Morgan and Robert A. Peterson (Grand Rapids: Zondervan, 2004), 170–94.

49. James S. Spiegel, *The Benefits of Providence: A New Look at Divine Sovereignty* (Wheaton, IL: Crossway, 2005), 192.

50. For an able defense of Scripture's teaching on God's exhaustive, infallible foreknowledge, see Steven C. Roy, *How Much Does God Foreknow? A Comprehensive Biblical Study* (Downers Grove, IL: InterVarsity Press, 2006).

possible for him to choose otherwise in the precise situations in which Peter found himself? What gives us reason to think that Jesus knew that the denials would happen three times? Why not two out of three times? Why didn't one of the denials come *after* the rooster crowed? If libertarian freedom holds true, then God could always be fooled by the decisions that we choose to make. We can fool ourselves. Libertarian freedom risks having our choices become unpredictable and arbitrary.

When Mary heads to the local diner for breakfast, she may be firmly resolved to get the pancakes, but then at the last minute she could change her mind and get the omelet instead for no sufficient reason. If Mary is truly free in the libertarian sense, then neither God nor even Mary herself can know what choice she will make until *after* she makes it. And herein lies the problem. The future cannot change the fixity of God's past knowledge. Therefore, the future itself is fixed, not merely because God foreknows it, but because he has foreordained it (Eph. 1:11). And what God foreordained, he foreknows. The New Testament terminology confirms this understanding.[51] The matter speaks to the supreme sovereign authority and wisdom of God. As Calvin remarks, "If God foresaw what he did not will to be, then he does not have the highest authority."[52]

There are serious theological problems here. If libertarian freedom is true, then it undermines not only God's omniscience and authority, but his transcendent timelessness and aseity (self-existence and self-sufficiency). The only way that God could know for certain the future choices of his creatures would be to wait for people to make their choices. Thus, he would have to exist *in time* instead of existing as the timelessly eternal God.[53] He would be limited by the constraints of time, which is a construct he created for the sake of his finite creation.

51. Walter Bauer, William F. Arndt, F. Wilbur Gingrich, and F. W. Danker, *A Greek-English Lexicon of the New Testament*, 2nd ed. (Chicago: University of Chicago Press, 1979), 703–4; Colin Brown, ed., *The New International Dictionary of New Testament Theology* (Grand Rapids: Zondervan, 1986), 1:693. The verb *proginosko* ("foreknow") is found five times in the New Testament (Acts 26:5; Rom. 8:29; 11:2; 1 Peter 1:20; 2 Peter 3:17). The noun *prognosis* ("foreknowledge") is found two times (Acts 2:23; 1 Peter 1:2). In both cases, the terms are generally used to speak of God's actions toward others in the sense of "choosing beforehand." Old Testament passages that indicate divine foreknowledge include 1 Chron. 28:9; Job 28:24; Pss. 139:1–4; 147:5; Isa. 41:21–23; 42:9; 44:7; 45:21; 46:9–11; 48:3–7; Jer. 1:5 (cf. Heb. 4:13).

52. John Calvin, *The Secret Providence of God*, ed. Paul Helm, trans. Keith Goad (Wheaton, IL: Crossway, 2010), 75.

53. For a careful defense that God is timelessly eternal, see Paul Helm, *Eternal God: A Study of God without Time*, 2nd ed. (Oxford: Oxford University Press, 2010); Paul Helm, "Divine Timeless Eternity," in *God and Time: Four Views*, ed. Gregory E. Ganssle (Downers Grove, IL: InterVarsity Press, 2001), 28–62.

He would also be held hostage by the future choices of his creatures. His plans could be scuttled as he waited nervously for those creatures to do what he hoped they would do. Thus, libertarianism makes the Creator dependent on the creation. Libertarians respond to the divine-foreknowledge problem differently, depending on their other theological commitments.[54]

Simple Foreknowledge (Arminianism)

Most free-will theists of the classical Arminian variety hold to the *simple foreknowledge* position.[55] This view says that after God chooses to create a particular kind of world (i.e., one with creatures containing libertarian free will), then the knowledge he gains from what will happen in that world affords him a prevision of the choices that people *will definitely* make in that world, an exhaustive trailer of all coming attractions.

Jack Cottrell states, "Even before the creation God foreknew every free-will act, even every *planned* free-will act, since he knows human hearts, plans, and intentions. These are not uncertainties for God; he does not have to wait for them to occur before he can know them with certainty."[56] In classical Arminianism, God's sovereign purposes for creation and humanity are largely construed as broad and general, not narrow and particular. His decree is largely conditional—conditioned on human freedom and the knowledge he gains from future human choices.[57]

For example, in regard to the election of believers to salvation, the classical Arminian Roger Olson writes, "God foreknows every person's ultimate

---

54. Not all views on the foreknowledge problem are treated here. Other positions include the Ockhamism, Boethianism (divine timelessness), and antinomy views. For accessible treatments of the views and their problems, see John S. Feinberg, *The Many Faces of Evil* (Wheaton, IL: Crossway, 2004), 104–18; Thomas V. Morris, *Our Idea of God* (Downers Grove, IL: InterVarsity Press, 1991), 86–102; Linda Zagzebski, "Foreknowledge and Free Will," in *The Stanford Encyclopedia of Philosophy*, ed. Edward N. Zalta (Summer 2017), found at: https://plato.stanford.edu/entries/free-will-foreknowledge/. For more rigorous treatments of this issue, see *Divine Foreknowledge: Four Views*, ed. James K. Beilby and Paul R. Eddy (Downers Grove, IL: InterVarsity Press, 2001); William Hasker, *God, Time, and Knowledge* (Ithaca, NY: Cornell University Press, 1989); Linda Zagzebski, *The Dilemma of Freedom and Foreknowledge* (New York: Oxford University Press, 1991).

55. The views presented here are common among most classical Arminians (as influenced by Jacob Arminius [1560–1609]), such as John Wesley (1703–91), Richard Watson (1781–1833), Thomas Summer (1812–82), John Miley (1813–95), Orton Wiley (1877–1961), and, more recently, Jack Cottrell, Thomas Oden, F. Leroy Forlines, Robert Picirilli, and Roger Olson. A more sophisticated and philosophically rigorous view of simple foreknowledge is defended by Dave Hunt, "The Simple-Foreknowledge View," in *Divine Foreknowledge: Four Views*, ed. James K. Beilby and Paul R. Eddy (Downers Grove, IL: InterVarsity Press, 2001), 65–103. See especially Paul Helm's response to Hunt (*Divine Foreknowledge*, 114–18).

56. Cottrell, "Nature of the Divine Sovereignty," 112.

57. Cottrell, "Nature of the Divine Sovereignty," 111.

and final decision regarding Jesus Christ, and on that basis God predestines people to salvation or damnation." Furthermore, God never "predetermines or preselects people for either heaven or hell apart from their free acts of accepting or resisting the grace of God."[58] Thus, for Arminians, election is conditional, based on the foreseen and freely exercised faith of the sinner, not unconditional (as in Calvinism).[59]

This view says that our independent power of choosing determines what God can and can't know about our future. Olson declares, "God simply knows the future because it will happen; his knowing future free decisions and actions of creatures does not determine them. Rather that they will happen determines God's knowing them because God has decided to open himself up to be affected by the world."[60] But as we have already noted, this wreaks havoc on God's aseity (independence and self-sufficiency) and the Creator-creature distinction. God is not dependent on his creatures in any way. The opposite is the case (Job 41:11; Ps. 50:12; Acts 17:24–25).

Furthermore, Olson attributes backward causation to human choices. As Feinberg notes, "If we are really to have power over what God believed in the past, then we must be able to do something to bring about God's having a different belief than he had. But we agree that this is absurd."[61] Because the future is indeterministic in a world with libertarian freedom, by its nature the future course of that world would be uncertain. This means that God simply cannot know what his creatures would choose in such a world. This is why many Arminians acknowledge that how God can know the indeterminate choices of free creatures is a mystery.[62]

Supposing that God did know the future libertarianly free choices of his creatures, however, this would make any idea of divine predestination or foreordination a useless redundancy. Since the future is what it is, all that God can say is: "Oh, this is what is going to happen in the future? Okay, I will ordain it to happen."

The simple-foreknowledge position makes a mockery of God's decree, since it wholly depends on his foreknowledge. God would not be able to

---

58. Olson, *Arminian Theology*, 180.

59. For Arminian defenses of conditional election, see Jack W. Cottrell, "Conditional Election," in *Grace Unlimited*, ed. Clark H. Pinnock (Minneapolis: Bethany House, 1975), 51–73; Robert E. Picirilli, *Grace, Faith, Free Will* (Nashville: Randall House, 2002), 48–64. For Calvinistic defenses of unconditional election, see R.C. Sproul, *Chosen by God* (Wheaton, IL: Tyndale House, 1986); C. Sam Storms, *Chosen for Life* (Wheaton, IL: Crossway, 2007).

60. Olson, "Classical Free Will Theist Model of God," 156.

61. John S. Feinberg, *No One like Him: The Doctrine of God* (Wheaton, IL: Crossway, 2001), 757.

62. F. Leroy Forlines, *Classical Arminianism: A Theology of Salvation* (Nashville: Randall House, 2011), 74–76.

decree any plan in this case. Furthermore, since the knowledge of the future would include his own actions, he couldn't change them without changing the responses of his creatures. His own actions would be what they would be. Any freedom he would have would be hamstrung by his foreknowledge. This is absurd. God's knowledge of the future must be predicated on what he has already freely ordained, not the other way around.

Open Theism

A second way to handle the foreknowledge problem is found in the *open theist* position.[63] Open theism may be the most consistent position holding to libertarian freedom, but that is no consolation to the orthodox Christian wishing to preserve the fullness of God's attributes. Open theism solves the problem by denying that God has exhaustive infallible foreknowledge of the future.

William Hasker clarifies: "Much (not all) of the future is known by God as what *might happen*, and as what *will probably happen*, but not as what *will definitely* take place."[64] John Sanders adds, "Future actions of genuine free creatures can only be known as probabilities, not certainties."[65] Furthermore, there is the real "possibility that [people] will not respond in the way [God] intended and desired for them to do."[66] In other words, open theism rightly acknowledges the logic that if libertarian freedom is true, then God can be fooled. He cannot know the future with any certainty. Open theism, ironically, *openly* embraces a heterodox theology.[67]

Aside from denying the obvious orthodox testimony of Scripture regarding God's omniscience, open theism also becomes a high-stakes gamble. God has no idea whether more evil might occur than good. And the evil could be so horrendous as to shock God himself. He risks becoming a Dr. Frankenstein, regretting the monster he has created. The God of open theism does not resemble the almighty, all-wise, loving God of Scripture at all. James Anderson says, "In the field of human affairs, we think poorly of those who

---

63. William Hasker, "The Open Theist View," in *God and the Problem of Evil: Five Views*, ed. Chad Meister and James K. Dew Jr. (Downers Grove, IL: InterVarsity Press, 2017), 57–76; Boyd, "God Limits His Control," 183–208; Gregory A. Boyd, "The Open-Theism View," in *Divine Foreknowledge: Four Views*, ed. James K. Beilby and Paul R. Eddy (Downers Grove, IL: InterVarsity Press, 2001), 13–47.

64. Hasker, "Open Theist View," 60.

65. John Sanders, "God, Evil, and Relational Risk," in *The Problem of Evil: Selected Readings*, ed. Michael L. Peterson, 2nd ed. (Notre Dame, IN: University of Notre Dame Press, 2017), 330.

66. Hasker, "Open Theist View," 60.

67. For a detailed critique of open theism and its view of foreknowledge, see John M. Frame, *The Doctrine of God* (Phillipsburg, NJ: P&R Publishing, 2002), 488–500; John M. Frame, *No Other God: A Response to Open Theism* (Phillipsburg, NJ: P&R Publishing, 2001).

take high risks not only at their own expense but at the expense of others who never consented to those risks. Why should we think well of a God who plays a cosmic-scale game of roulette with the lives of his creatures?"[68]

Molinism[69]

A third way of handling the foreknowledge problem is found in the *Molinist* position derived from the sixteenth-century Jesuit priest Luis de Molina (1535–1600).[70] Molinism seeks to reconcile a more robust view of divine providence with libertarian free will while embracing a unique view of divine foreknowledge. It divides divine knowledge into three categories. First, *natural knowledge* refers to all necessarily factual truths and possibilities known to God immediately and intuitively (e.g., 2 + 2 = 4; bachelors are unmarried men). This is knowledge of all that *is* or *could be*. It is prevolitional in the sense that it is independent of (logically prior to) what God decrees to happen.

Second, *free knowledge* refers to God's knowledge of all that *will* certainly be. Such knowledge is based on God's decree (his sovereign will) whereby he freely and unchangeably decrees (wills) all events in history that come to pass. Because it is dependent on his decree, free knowledge is postvolitional and thus contingent.[71] All orthodox Christians hold to natural knowledge. Calvinism and Molinism hold to free knowledge.[72]

Third, unique to Molinism is the belief in *middle knowledge*, which is claimed to lie somewhere (in a logical progression) between natural and free knowledge. Middle knowledge means that God knows *counterfactuals*

---

68. James N. Anderson, "Calvinism and the First Sin," in *Calvinism and the Problem of Evil*, ed. David E. Alexander and Daniel M. Johnson (Eugene, OR: Pickwick Publications, 2016), 227.

69. I am indebted to Greg Welty for his help in clarifying this section.

70. See William Lane Craig, "God Directs All Things," in *Four Views on Divine Providence*, ed. Stanley N. Gundry and Dennis W. Jowers (Grand Rapids: Zondervan, 2011), 79–100; William Lane Craig, "The Molinist View," in *God and the Problem of Evil: Five Views*, ed. Chad Meister and James K. Dew Jr. (Downers Grove, IL: InterVarsity Press, 2017), 37–55; William Lane Craig, *The Only Wise God* (Grand Rapids: Baker, 1987); Kenneth Keathley, *Salvation and Sovereignty: A Molinist Approach* (Nashville: B&H Academic, 2010).

71. *Prevolitional* and *postvolitional* are not meant to suggest that God knows or chooses in time (as open theists believe). Being timelessly eternal, all of God's knowledge and willing is immediate to him. Rather, these terms are used to indicate the logical relationship of God to different kinds of knowledge.

72. Molinists typically deny the sort of meticulous *causal determinism* that marks most Reformed (Calvinist) views of providence even though they affirm God's meticulous decree. God meticulously decrees the outcome of all things but does not meticulously cause those outcomes. See Craig, "God Directs All Things"; Keathley, *Salvation and Sovereignty*, 20–27. See also James N. Anderson, "How Biblical Is Molinism? (Part 2)," found at: http://www.proginosko.com/2015/11/how-biblical-is-molinism-part-2/.

of creaturely freedom—what people *would* freely choose (in a libertarian sense) under any possible scenario in any possible world (state of affairs) that might exist.[73] This knowledge is like free knowledge in that it is contingent (because it is dependent on what others would freely choose), and it is like natural knowledge in that it is prevolitional (because it is independent of or logically prior to God's eternal decree).

Thus, God doesn't determine the range of possibilities; they arise strictly from what free creatures *would* do in each situation. For example, in the actual world we live in, God knew that Islamic terrorists would crash airplanes into the World Trade Center towers in New York on September 11, 2001. According to standard accounts of libertarian free will, however, given the same set of circumstances leading up to the critical point of decision, the terrorists *could* have crashed into the Empire State Building instead of the Twin Towers. But according to Molinism, God's knowledge of true counterfactuals (prior to choosing what world he would decree) suggests that they *would* not do that.

After a panoply of possible worlds are set before God along with the total matrix of what each person would freely choose in those worlds, he then sovereignly selects (decrees) one particular feasible world that best serves his purposes.[74] This gives him genuine foreknowledge of all that will certainly occur in that world, and he then providentially ensures that all its details take place in real time and history. Molinists claim that their view preserves God's meticulous providence, his exhaustive foreknowledge, and human

73. Craig, *Only Wise God*, 135. Supposed instances of middle knowledge in Scripture include Ex. 13:17; 1 Sam. 23:8–14; Jer. 23:21–22; Matt. 11:21–24; 1 Cor. 2:8. Yet these passages can be easily explained on the basis of God's natural and free knowledge. God knows all possible outcomes of the normal (and abnormal) means he employs to achieve what he decrees (note that the providential outworking of God's decree is not fatalistic but uses secondary causes). These passages indicate that if God had decreed something contrary to what took place, then he would have also decreed the different means (and circumstances) by which those alternative outcomes would have come about. See Paul Helm, "Response to Bruce A. Ware," in *Perspectives on the Doctrine of God: 4 Views*, ed. Bruce A. Ware (Nashville: B&H Academic, 2008), 128–29; Paul Helm and Terrance L. Tiessen, "Does Calvinism Have Room for Middle Knowledge? A Conversation," *WTJ* 71.2 (2009): 437–38. The Molinist William Lane Craig acknowledges that these passages cannot be used to prove that God has middle knowledge, just hypothetical knowledge, which in and of itself is not controversial among different theologians. See Craig, "God Directs All Things," 84.

74. Craig, "God Directs All Things," 83. Note the Molinist distinction between "feasible" and "possible" worlds. A possible world may be logically possible, but it may not be feasible. A feasible world is one of the possible worlds that God can actualize, because its actualization is consistent with the truth of counterfactuals of creaturely freedom. God can't actualize "infeasible" worlds, because to do so would contradict the counterfactuals, and the truth of those doesn't depend on him.

libertarian freedom while excusing God from moral culpability for human beings' misuse of their freedom to choose evil.

It is not clear, however, how Molinism escapes the same problems of the simple-foreknowledge view by introducing middle knowledge. No matter what the circumstances are, is it possible for God to infallibly know the indeterminate counterfactual choices of his creatures without violating their freedom? For example, what prevented God from knowing that one of the terrorists would not decide to fly into the Empire State Building instead of one of the World Trade Center towers? As Hasker points out, "With regard to a possible free choice that is never actually made, there are truths about what the creature *might possibly do* in that situation, and perhaps truths about what the creature *would probably do*, but there is no truth stating what [one] *would definitely do*."[75]

Furthermore, since the counterfactuals of creaturely freedom are relevant only prior to God's decreeing the world that he chooses to actualize (create), once that world was decreed, nothing could prevent the 9/11 terrorists from using libertarian freedom in the actual here and now to renege on the whole plan and plunge their planes into the Upper Bay near the Statue of Liberty at the last moment. It seems that their libertarian freedom in the actual world is an illusion. The only freedom that people appear to have is confined to the mind of God (i.e., via his middle knowledge) prior to his deciding which world to make. They have no freedom to change what he has already decreed, rendering libertarian free will moot in the real world.

Thus, it is hard to see how there can be real knowledge of counterfactuals of creaturely freedom.[76] Sometimes this glaring weakness in the Molinist position is framed in terms of something called the *grounding objection*.[77] James Anderson lays out this issue via a critical event in human history. God's so-called middle knowledge of a counterfactual of freedom would include the following scenario: "If Adam were placed in the Garden of Eden and tempted by Satan, he would sin."[78]

According to Molinism, this truth must be contingent—dependent on what the person called *Adam* would do. It must be known beforehand and thus independent of (logically prior to) God's decree to create the world that this happened in. But how can God know that this statement is true?

---

75. William Hasker, "The Open Theist Response," in *God and the Problem of Evil: Five Views*, ed. Chad Meister and James K. Dew Jr. (Downers Grove, IL: InterVarsity Press, 2017), 154.

76. Hasker, *God, Time, and Knowledge*, 52.

77. See Steven B. Cowan, "The Grounding Objection to Middle Knowledge Revisited," *Religious Studies* 39 (2003): 93–102.

78. Anderson, "Calvinism and the First Sin," 223.

On what factual basis can he know it to be a legitimate truth claim? It can't be grounded in God's nature (i.e., his *natural knowledge*) because God's nature is necessarily what it is, and so it cannot ground contingent truths, which depend on the future acts of free agents. And it cannot be grounded in his decree (i.e., his *free knowledge*) because that would imply that Adam's choice was divinely determined, and Molinism denies that free choices are determined by God.

Furthermore, it cannot be grounded in Adam's nature or any other creature either (e.g., Satan), since the essence of this statement must be true prior to God's decree to create such creatures.[79] Therefore, middle knowledge lacks any grounds whatsoever, and this is absurd, since we ordinarily assume that contingent truths about creatures have grounds, unless we are given a *very* good reason to think otherwise. Middle knowledge appears to be a kind of knowledge that exists independently of creation and independently of God himself, who must be the source of all knowledge (Col. 2:3).

So it is not clear that middle knowledge can be a legitimate form of divine knowledge, or knowledge at all. Many Molinists sidestep this problem by saying that we don't know how God knows such counterfactuals of freedom to be true. They are unexplainable brute facts, and so apparently *nothing* makes them true.[80]

This is an ironic outcome, for the entire Molinist project ostensibly seeks to ground God's *free knowledge* (i.e., his decree) in his supposed *middle knowledge*, and yet middle knowledge has no grounding. They must appeal to mystery at the most critical point, and this scuttles their whole scheme.[81] The fact remains that libertarian freedom by its nature must limit the omniscience of God. God could foreknow the choices that anyone would make only if he had determined them beforehand by his sovereign decree.[82]

Molinism has other problems.[83] But even if it offered a coherent account of human freedom, divine foreknowledge, and providence, it would not escape the problem of divine culpability for Adam's sin and the whole introduction of evil into the world. Molinists must say that God considered all feasible worlds among possible worlds, including that world in which Adam would

---

79. Molinists believe that there are many true counterfactuals about creatures who are never created, so how can their truth depend on these creatures who never exist?

80. Cowan, "Grounding Objection," 99.

81. Anderson, "Calvinism and the First Sin," 224.

82. Paul Helm, review of *Molinism: The Contemporary Debate*, ed. Ken Perszyk, *Themelios* 37.3 (2012): 569.

83. See responses to William Lane Craig in *Four Views on Divine Providence*, ed. Stanley N. Gundry and Dennis W. Jowers (Grand Rapids: Zondervan, 2011), 101–39.

freely sin, and that he decreed that world anyway. Since God acted in a way that would ensure Adam's sin, Molinism has the same trouble that Calvinism does in escaping the charge that God *caused* Adam (and all other human beings) to sin and is thus culpable for it.[84]

Finally, Molinism limits God's choices in terms of feasible worlds that he can create. He has to "play with the hand he has been dealt, that is to say, actualize a world that is feasible for him given the counterfactuals that are true."[85] Unfortunately, he appears to have been stuck with only feasible worlds that contain all the insufferable permutations of evil. Evil enslaves God, dictating to him what he can and cannot create. But in another way, God has to be extremely lucky—the luckiest being who exists. Craig writes, "In some possible worlds he might have been dealt a very lousy hand indeed."[86]

Molinism suggests that God could have been faced with a situation in which *every* possible person he had available to him to place in a feasible world would *always* choose evil in *every* circumstance, and he would have no alternatives.[87] In that case, there would have been no world that he could redeem through the sending of his Son. He would be stuck with a world that had "*inherent irredeemability*."[88] But luckily, that didn't happen! We can't be sure *who* Molinists have to thank that God was not faced with this terrible prospect!

Molinism tries to preserve the robust character of God revealed in the pages of Scripture, but ends up maligning that God. It leads to the same problem of the simple-foreknowledge view (the open theist has it, too), which is a failure to preserve God's aseity (self-existence, independence, and self-sufficiency), timelessness, authority, and freedom. It eviscerates the Creator-creature distinction and strips God of his Godness.

Anderson explains:

> Scripture clearly depicts God's independence as a *great-making prop-erty*. To put it in Anselmian terms: if God is that being than which no greater can be conceived, then the Molinist view of God falls short, for it's easy to conceive of a being greater than the God of Molinism, namely, a

---

84. See Greg Welty's important article in this regard: "Molinist Gunslingers: God and the Authorship of Sin," in *Calvinism and Middle Knowledge,* ed. John D. Laing, Kirk R. MacGregor, and Greg Welty (Eugene, OR: Pickwick Publications, 2019), 51–68.

85. Craig, "Molinist View," 38.

86. Craig, "Molinist View," 38.

87. Thanks to Greg Welty for drawing this point to my attention. On the *sheer luck* problem, see Steven B. Cowan, "Molinism, Meticulous Providence, and Luck," *Philosophia Christi* 11.1 (2009): 156–69.

88. Cowan, "Molinism, Meticulous Providence, and Luck," 168.

God whose decisions don't depend on contingencies beyond his control. An *absolutely* great being must be *absolutely* independent of any external constraints or conditioning factors.[89]

Free-will theism offers many other solutions to reconciling infallible divine foreknowledge with libertarian free will, and I have canvassed only some of the more prominent views.[90] But suppose that free-will theism has found ways that satisfy the problem—this does not help to solve the problem of evil. The doctrine of divine foreknowledge best fits within the classic view of theism as propounded by the likes of Augustine, Anselm, and Aquinas, and subsequently championed since the sixteenth century by the Reformed and Calvinist tradition.

Libertarian Free Will Allows Gratuitous Evil

Libertarian free will has trouble explaining so-called gratuitous evils: various evils that appear to be pointless, having no necessary connection to greater goods. What possible good can come from the rape of a little girl? The atheist William Rowe highlights this particular problem: "The idea that none of these instances of [gratuitous] suffering could have been prevented by an omnipotent being without the loss of greater good seems an extraordinary, absurd idea, quite beyond our belief."[91] What prevents God from striking down the rapist before or during his vile act or keeping him from repeating it? Every theodicist has the burden of addressing Rowe's challenge. For the free-will theist, resorting to God's desire to retain the libertarian freedom of evil perpetrators becomes an obvious problem.

Michael Peterson simply dismisses the problem. He argues that we should accept gratuitous evil on the face of it. If evil seems senseless, then it probably is.[92] Elsewhere he explains, "The kind of freedom which is basic to the

---

89. Anderson, "How Biblical Is Molinism? (Part 5)," found at: http://www.proginosko.com/2018/02/how-biblical-is-molinism-part-5/.

90. Of course, open theism rejects the need for reconciliation because it rejects infallible divine foreknowledge altogether, but this unorthodox response must be rejected.

91. William L. Rowe, *Philosophy of Religion: An Introduction* (Encino, CA: Dickenson, 1978), 89.

92. Michael L. Peterson, "Christian Theism and the Evidential Argument from Evil," in *The Problem of Evil: Selected Readings*, ed. Michael L. Peterson, 2nd ed. (Notre Dame, IN: University of Notre Dame Press, 2017), 180. Not all libertarians accept the existence of gratuitous evil. See, for example, Jeremy A. Evans, *The Problem of Evil: The Challenge to Essential Christian Beliefs* (Nashville: B&H Academic, 2013), 34. Yet gratuitous evil appears to be an inevitable consequence of God's consistent noninterference with libertarian freedom.

accomplishment of great and noble actions is the kind of freedom which allows the most atrocious deeds. In creating man and giving him free will, God thereby created an astonishing range of possibilities for both the creation and destruction of value."[93] Thomas Oord, an open theist, argues that God's steadfast, self-giving love *necessarily* constrains him to give us the freedom that allows rape and murder.[94]

But is preserving libertarian free will worth the price of such horrendous evil? To return to one of Welty's criteria for a faithful theodicy, the supposed goods that libertarianism secures do not seem weighty enough to justify the terrible evils that it risks generating. Horrendous evil presents three possible scenarios for the free-will theist's model of divine providence. The first two scenarios appear to hamstring God. First, he sits in heaven, wringing his hands in utter dismay, lamenting, "Oh! How I wish I could do something to stop this horrific atrocity! But alas, free will is an intrinsic feature of my gift to humanity, and I am powerless to stop its exercise" (Oord). In this case, God *could not* prevent evil.[95]

Or second, he says, "Sorry, my dear, unfortunate victims of senseless violence. The only way I could stop this from happening would be to violate the greater good of human freedom I have given to the perpetrators of this violence" (Peterson). In this case, God could prevent evil but simply *would not*.[96]

But some free-will theists (e.g., classical Arminians) acknowledge a third scenario. They agree that God could and does intervene in many cases of horrendous evil. Arminian Roger Olson states, "Occasionally God suspends free will with a dramatic intervention that virtually forces a person to decide or act in some way. But in general God steps back and allows human beings a limited range of choices."[97] Nonetheless, God obviously does not intervene in many cases.

93. Michael L. Peterson, *Evil and the Christian God* (Grand Rapids: Baker, 1982), 103.

94. Oord, "Essential Kenosis View," 90.

95. Walter J. Schultz, "'No-Risk' Libertarian Freedom: A Refutation of the Free-Will Defense," *Philosophia Christi* 10.1 (2008): 165.

96. Schultz, "'No-Risk' Libertarian Freedom," 165.

97. Olson, "Classical Free Will Theist Model of God," 151. Olson's position has other problems of its own. If God suspends libertarian free will, then he must also suspend moral responsibility. One of the reasons for promoting libertarian freedom is that it is regarded as the only ground for moral responsibility. Furthermore, seeing that God could intervene in cases of evil, it is hard to see how God himself does not bear at least some moral culpability in Olson's model of divine providence. Seemingly the only way in which God could escape culpability would be if it were impossible for him to intervene, in which case God would have truly created a monster. But few libertarians (Thomas Oord apparently being one of those exceptions) hold that God is wholly incapable of sovereign intervention.

This reality is unfortunately compounded by the fact that Arminianism holds to God's exhaustive foreknowledge. He knows precisely every evil choice that every person will make and does nothing to stop it. It is hard to see how he does not become an accessory to evil on that count. In such accounts, God is like the policeman who passively stands by, watching a thug steal a feeble old woman's purse. When asked why he didn't intervene, he says, "I didn't want to violate the thug's free will." Libertarian free will is a more valuable commodity than criminal intervention to such Arminians. But if God were to occasionally intervene, then he would be violating one's free will and thus eviscerating the moral freedom and responsibility of that person.

Each of these positions faces the same intractable problem whereby God stands by, watching innumerable gratuitous acts of evil unfold while doing nothing about it. But can we imagine God's standing by idly while the powerful and evil Hutu systematically slaughtered the Tutsi in the Rwandan genocide? Not at all . . . unless there is some greater intended divine design here that we cannot readily see. But the free-will theist must break from his reliance on the free-will defense to go down this road. Many do, adding some variation of the greater-good defense (see next chapter) to their arsenal of arguments, but not without risking several of the supposed goods of libertarian free will.

Other problems remain. We have already seen that God routinely intervenes, either stopping or preventing evil from happening, nonetheless allowing all sorts of other evils to persist.[98] This means that God stands inescapably behind evil that free-will theists otherwise consider senseless, contributing to no real good whatsoever. In other words, the logic of libertarianism says that God invites gratuitous evil—evil that cannot possibly have any good reason for transpiring.[99] But if this is true, then it robs God of one of the essential attributes that come under attack in the problem of evil—his all-encompassing and perfect goodness.

Free-will theism debases the fullness of God's omnipotence as well as his omnibenevolence. A theodicy having any worth whatsoever can never in any case compromise the perfections of God's attributes. This is anathema!

In either case, we cannot be smug. Christians (including Calvinists) must admit that horrendous evil is a disconcerting problem for all theodicists.[100]

---

98. See page 92.

99. Calvinism says that God purposes evil that is horrendous (hard to swallow), but never evil that is gratuitous (without meaning or purpose). It is best to call it *inscrutable evil* because we do not have the resources to make full sense of it.

100. Arminians seem to think that this is a problem only for Calvinists. See Walls and Dongell, *Why I Am Not a Calvinist*, 208; Roger E. Olson, *Against Calvinism* (Grand Rapids: Zondervan, 2011), 90–91.

The Reformed theologian Paul Helm sums up the position we should hold. The creation does not contain a single irrational or senseless reality, lest it reflect an irrational and senseless Creator. Nonetheless:

> Why God should allow the fact, extent and power of evil is a mystery to us at present. The Christian can be assured that even evil is subsumed under the divine purposes, and plays an integral part in them. Does this take away the force of evil, does it flatten it, or remove the tragedy and waste that are its products? Not at all! The Christian has only to glance at the cross to be convinced this is not so.[101]

I will argue later that this position must extend further. Although we cannot ascertain all the multiple facets of good that God extracts from evil, I believe we can be certain that *all* evil contributes to a broad theodicy that leaves no mystery for us in the present. Ironically, that theodicy, as Helm begins to allude to, is centered on the cross of Christ.

Libertarian free will figures prominently in most Christian responses to evil. This is unfortunate because it shifts our focus away from Scripture's testimony of God's glorious character and ends up compromising it in favor of preserving the all-consuming good of the gemstone called *free will*. Preserving this sort of creaturely freedom as the solution to the problem of evil is unashamedly man-centered. Free will becomes a convenient escape hatch. The valuable good that so many think it is turns out to be an illusion forfeiting all its trumped-up explanatory power.

Free-will theists suppose that God's hands-off approach to our freedom is a great blessing, though at times risky. While many think that God's love motivates his preservation of our freedom, this falls flat once we experience horrific tragedy. Why? Because when tragedy strikes, God can only be regarded as inattentive to our suffering. There is no guarantee that the evil befalling us has any divine purpose. God may offer sympathy, but his respect for our freedom means that he can offer no hope of intervention. He cannot say that there is some transcendent good for this evil that has invaded our lives.

This is no consolation to the suffering soul. What hope can we attach to our prayers? Petitionary prayer in the face of evil seems futile if God's way of escaping the problem of evil is to say that he cannot interfere with the free exercise of people's wills. There must be a better answer.

---

101. Paul Helm, *The Providence of God* (Downers Grove, IL: InterVarsity Press, 1994), 222–23.

THE NATURAL-LAW DEFENSE

The free-will defense is often coupled with the *natural-law defense*. While the free-will defense seeks to resolve questions about moral evil, the natural-law defense seeks to resolve questions about natural evil, those unfortunate sources of suffering that stem from how the laws of nature work in the world.[102] Putting these two defenses together is supposed to be a great advantage over other defenses and theodicies (see chapter 6).

Greg Welty explains: "First, they don't involve in any way God's *intending* that evils come to pass, much less the idea that evils are *required means* to any goods that God intends to come to pass. Rather, the evils of the world are the *unintended* by-products of God's aiming to provide us two great goods: the good of free choice, and the good of having a stable environment in which to exercise that free choice."[103]

The natural-law defense states that God created the world with a natural order that can't be violated willy-nilly, operating one way at one moment and a different way at another. If our actions are to have reliability that includes predictable consequences, then we need a stable, predictable environment in which those actions take place. If our choices lacked predictability, they would spawn unwanted and unnecessary fear. Only when universal, regular, predictable, repeatable laws of nature govern the results of our actions can we have confidence in making the choices we do.

Unfortunately, we must contend with the inflexibility of these laws that often causes unintended consequences that result in pain and suffering. Thus, nature can at once be beautiful, orderly, beneficial, eliciting our wonder and praise, and yet be brutal, pitiless, indifferent. The same gravity that prevents us from hurtling off the planet can cause us to be crushed to death if a boulder comes tumbling down the mountainside. The same fire that warms our frigid bodies and heats our food can incinerate our homes. The same forces that create innumerable pleasures exact excruciating pains. "Can there be conscious, volitional, sentient beings that are also unable to feel pain but still appreciate those experiences that are pleasurable and produce happiness?"[104]

The laws of nature can be utilized for good or ill. If we make deliberately foolish choices or inadvertent mistakes, the laws will not be suddenly bent or suspended so that we can avoid unpleasant consequences. If God intervened every time matters went awry, then we would never learn to rely on

---

102. Well-known defenses for the natural-law defense are found in C. S. Lewis, *The Problem of Pain* (New York: Macmillan, 1962), and Richard Swinburne, *Providence and the Problem of Evil* (Oxford: Oxford University Press, 1998).

103. Welty, *Why Is There Evil?*, 156.

104. Evans, *Problem of Evil*, 12.

the laws he created to govern the creation. They might as well not exist. Thus, natural evil is the hard cost that God pays to maintain a stable world in which our choices matter.

The natural-law defense has some merit, but its limitations and other problems rule it out as a comprehensive explanation for natural evil. Does the structure of the laws governing the natural world provide a necessary or sufficient explanation for the pain and suffering that often result from them? Some natural-law theodicists can't envision a world in which natural laws exist without risking ill effects along with the good. Michael Peterson observes,

> "Even the slightest modification may produce manifold and intricate differences between this natural order and the envisioned one.
>
> The whole matter becomes so complex that no finite mind can conceive of precisely what modifications the envisioned natural world would have to incorporate in order both to preserve the good natural effects and to avoid the . . . evil ones."[105]

Peterson seems to think that God is imprisoned by his own laws, unable to escape their inevitable structure as well as hindered by his inability to intervene. God in this scenario is pictured more as the distant god of deism than as the Lord of the universe who sustains his creation at every moment (Acts 17:24–28).[106]

Furthermore, Peterson suffers from a failure of imagination. The Bible describes two other worlds with perfectly stable environments in which no pain or suffering results from the laws that govern those worlds—the prelapsarian (prefall) state of Eden and the new heaven and the new earth. How the laws in those two worlds differ from the present world may be hard (if not impossible) to discern, but that does not rule out their existence. It is simply enough to know that before the fall, Adam enjoyed a painless world with no interruption of the laws that governed it. The same will be true for the future world.

Thus, the present structure of the laws of nature that produce both good and ill effects is by no means a necessary state of affairs. God could have easily structured those laws with pain-free, Edenic bliss. And this poses a different kind of problem for those who espouse the natural-law defense as a complementary response to evil with the free-will defense.

105. Peterson, *Evil and the Christian God*, 115–16.
106. In this regard, using the terminology *laws of nature* can be misleading. Though sometimes useful, it is not biblical language. *Laws of nature* is a crude and misapplied designation for God's uninterrupted, active, ordinary work of providence.

Some Arminians think that natural evil is a problem for the Calvinist doctrine of divine providence.[107] But nothing about the Arminian view of divine providence says that God is unable to intervene in natural disasters or disease in order to prevent, stop, or minimize suffering. After all, hurricanes and cancer cells have no libertarian free will; therefore, God has no freedom to violate by preventing the occurrence of natural evils.[108]

Natural evil needs to be understood as the result of the modification of Eden's laws, and is part of the curse under which God thrust his creation due to Adam's disobedience (Rom. 5:12; 8:19–22). Before the fall, creation's laws cooperated with humans, making the work that God gave us to do much easier. But something in the nature and function of those laws appears to have been radically altered after the fall (Gen. 3:17–19).[109] The ill effects of the present laws of nature therefore reflect a decidedly broken world whereby pain, suffering, and death are endemic to our fallen existence.[110] In many ways, it is an *unnatural* world, a place that is not supposed to be this way. It becomes a world in which we are forced to recognize our weakness, our helplessness, our acute vulnerability.

Thus, natural evil serves a more transcendent purpose. First, it produces an inner angst that ought to engender a longing for Eden, a longing for restoration, renewal, redemption—a grand rebirth in which the "old order of things" will have "passed away" (Rev. 21:4 NIV) while all things will be made new (Rev. 21:5), that is, "imperishable, undefiled, and unfading" (1 Peter 1:4), and the curse has been forever removed (Rev. 22:3).[111]

Second, the fallen world compels us to see our dependence on something greater than ourselves, and greater than the laws of nature. We are dependent on a providential and merciful God. We need him. We are desperate without him, and this points us to the need for a theodicy that drives us far beyond what the more modest and domesticated features of the natural-law defense can offer.

107. See, for example, Walls and Dongell, *Why I Am Not a Calvinist*, 208; Olson, *Against Calvinism*, 89.

108. Bignon, *Excusing Sinners and Blaming God*, 172–73.

109. James Stambaugh, "Whence Cometh Death? A Biblical Theology of Physical Death and Natural Evil," in *Coming to Grips with Genesis: Biblical Authority and the Age of the Earth*, ed. Terry Mortenson and Thane H. Ury (Green Forest, AR: Master Books, 2008), 373–97; John C. Whitcomb and Henry M. Morris, *The Genesis Flood* (Philadelphia: Presbyterian and Reformed, 1961), 468–73.

110. The natural-law defense has a hard time explaining natural disasters, such as earthquakes and tornadoes. First, no one brings devastation on himself by misusing the laws that govern these disasters. They are unrelated to our choices. Second, it is unclear that such disasters are the necessary consequence of the laws of nature. What prevents God from structuring the laws so that devastating disasters never occur?

111. This hints at the theodicy I will offer later.

In summarizing the free-will and natural-law defenses, Welty points out that they represent theodicies promoting *general* goods. God sets up a structured universe in which the principles of free will and natural law govern the world. In this scenario, God does not specifically or directly intend evil to take place; it is an unfortunate by-product of these general goods. In this kind of universe, God does not "plan" for any particular evil to occur or for any particular pain to result.[112] "Rather, it is the *value* of such an environment, and the *value* of the goods that could arise in such an environment, which God intends. . . . Moral and natural evils are in the world due to *general* policies God pursues, rather than because of *particular* choices he has made which ensures their occurrence."[113] God doesn't intend for evil to occur, but these general policies are necessary for *any* good at all to occur, and thus the risk of evil from the unfortunate misuse of these policies is the price he must pay to get those goods.[114]

But one wonders whether there is any benefit here, general or otherwise. If this is the universe we live in, then God is hamstrung by evil in order to arrive at any possible good. It also means that many evils occur for no good reason at all. They are gratuitous. It is easy to see how many scoff at the power and goodness of such a God. How are these and other divine attributes faithfully upheld, let alone magnified? They render God as significantly less robust than the picture that Scripture paints.

There must be a better way. Let's us consider such possibilities.

KEY TERMS

Arminianism
Calvinism
foreknowledge (of God)
free will
free-will defense
free-will theism
libertarianism
meticulous providence
Molinism
moral responsibility
natural-law defense
open theism

112. Welty, *Why Is There Evil?*, 168–69.
113. Welty, *Why Is There Evil?*, 170.
114. Welty, *Why Is There Evil?*, 170.

STUDY QUESTIONS

1. What two main ideas define the libertarian conception of free will?
2. What is the free-will defense, and how does it seek to resolve the problem of evil?
3. The problems with the free-will defense largely center on its problematic view of free will. The author lists nine critical problems with libertarian free will. What do you think are the three most critical problems of the nine listed? Explain why.
4. What are the three ways in which free-will theists address the foreknowledge problem? Which of the three ways do you think is most problematic?
5. What are the strengths and weaknesses of the natural-law defense?
6. Has this chapter challenged your own thinking about free will? If so, how?

FOR FURTHER READING

Scott Christensen, *What about Free Will? Reconciling Our Choices with God's Sovereignty* (Phillipsburg, NJ: P&R Publishing, 2016).

Stanley N. Gundry and Dennis W. Jowers, eds., *Four Views on Divine Providence* (Grand Rapids: Zondervan, 2011).

C. S. Lewis, *The Problem of Pain* (New York: Macmillan, 1962).

Chad Meister and James K. Dew Jr., eds., *God and the Problem of Evil: Five Views* (Downers Grove, IL: InterVarsity Press, 2017).

Alvin Plantinga, *God, Freedom, and Evil* (Grand Rapids: Eerdmans, 1977).

Bruce A. Ware, ed., *Perspectives on the Doctrine of God: 4 Views* (Nashville: B&H Academic, 2008).

Advanced

James N. Anderson, "How Biblical Is Molinism? (Parts 1–5)," found at: http://www.proginosko.com.

Guillaume Bignon, *Excusing Sinners and Blaming God: A Calvinist Assessment of Determinism, Moral Responsibility, and Divine Involvement in Evil* (Eugene, OR: Pickwick Publications, 2018).

John D. Laing, Kirk R. MacGregor, and Greg Welty, eds., *Calvinism and Middle Knowledge* (Eugene, OR: Pickwick Publications, 2019).

6

WORKING FOR THE GREATER GOOD

The story is well known. Five young missionaries dedicate their lives to reach one of the most violent tribal peoples in the twentieth century—the fierce Waodani of Ecuador.[1] Their rate of intertribal homicide at 60 percent was the worst that anthropologists had ever studied.[2] Most Waodani living today have a story of how one of their family members was murdered by a fellow Waodani. One of the missionaries, Nate Saint, made repeated flights in his bright-yellow Piper Cruiser over the thick Ecuadorian jungles to drop friendly gifts to the Waodani.

Eventually, he found a suitable sandbar along the Curaray River to land his plane, so that he and the other four missionaries could make their first face-to-face contact with the tribe. After four days of waiting on what they called Palm Beach, two young women and a man emerged from the jungle to meet the strangers. The initial contact seemed promising, but two days later tragedy struck hard.

On January 8, 1956, Nate Saint, Jim Elliot, Pete Fleming, Ed McCully, and Roger Youderian were speared to death by six tribal warriors, their bodies hacked by machetes and then unceremoniously tossed into the river to be eaten by fish and turtles. A few weeks later, *LIFE* magazine published the story with extensive photos of the tragedy.[3] The shocking news reached the whole world.[4]

1. In original reports of the story, the tribe was referred to as "Aucas," a derogatory term meaning "naked savages" used by their enemies.
2. Stephen F. Saint, "Sovereignty, Suffering, and the Work of Missions," in *Suffering and the Sovereignty of God*, ed. John Piper and Justin Taylor (Wheaton, IL: Crossway, 2006), 115.
3. "'Go Ye and Preach the Gospel': Five Do and Die," *LIFE* 40.5, January 30, 1956, 10–19.
4. The *LIFE* story was followed by Jim Elliot's wife Elisabeth's books *Through Gates of*

Credibility was strained to see any sense in it, unless you were Rachel Saint or Elisabeth Elliot. Rachel was the sister of Nate Saint, and Elisabeth the wife of Jim Elliot. These women forged ahead, making inroads with the perpetrators of these brutal murders. Within a few years, the warriors who had killed their family members were transformed by the gospel and gave their lives to Christ.

Later in life, Nate's son Steve came to learn the horrifying details of his father's death. But Steve harbors no bitterness. He does not suffer disillusionment at God's ways. Instead, he is uncharacteristically grateful for someone whose father was so callously slaughtered. He dismisses the common view of tragedy among Christians, namely, that God cannot be invoked as standing behind it. "I don't think God merely tolerated my dad's death. I don't think he turned away when it was happening." Then Steve makes this radical admission: "I think he planned it. Otherwise I don't think it would have happened."[5]

Who says such things?

When Steve was five years old, the year of his father's murder, he was waiting for him to make good on his promise to teach him to fly. The Missionary Aviation Fellowship pilot was not only his dad, but his hero. Nonetheless, Steve would never change the course of history even if he could. He says unashamedly, "God planned my dad's death." A man who would come to be one of Steve's dearest friends was a man whom he would call "Grandfather." His name was Mincaye, and he was among the six warriors who had killed Steve's father.

Mincaye was a killer without mercy in 1956. Fifty years later, Steve knew him as the eternal object of mercy, that of his Lord and Savior, Jesus Christ.[6] Mincaye adopted Steve as his own son, and the love between them grew as deep as human affections can extend. Only the secret mysteries of God's providence could plan such strange good to emerge from evil.

Steve Saint's approach to the problem of evil and suffering is clearly not the mainstream. Historically and broadly speaking, Christianity has addressed the problem of moral evil in two primary ways. First, the most prominent response is some variation of the *free-will defense*, which says that God has no specific purpose for evil, that it is the unfortunate

---

Splendor (New York: Harper, 1957) and then *Shadow of the Almighty* (New York: Harper, 1958). Many other books appeared as well. More recently, Steve Saint, the son of Nate Saint, published *End of the Spear* (Carol Stream, IL: Tyndale House, 2005) to tell his continuing story about the Waodani tribe.

 5. Saint, "Sovereignty, Suffering," 117.

 6. Mincaye died on April 28, 2020.

consequence of granting his creatures the valuable gift of libertarian free will. The murder of five missionaries is sad but unavoidable. It is the necessary risk that God takes to create people who make meaningful choices. This unhindered freedom to choose supposedly avoids the coercion that would result if God ultimately determined the direction that our choices take.

The second solution, that of the Saints and Elliots, is some variation of the *greater-good theodicy* (*greater-good defense* is used interchangeably here), which we will explore in this chapter.[7] In contrast to the *general* goods of the free-will defense, this theodicy indicates that God decrees evil because it accomplishes some *particular* greater good (or in some cases prevents a worse evil) that would not be possible unless evil were part of the equation.

As Augustine asserts, "The Omnipotent God . . . would not allow any evil in his works, unless in his omnipotence and goodness, as the Supreme Good, he is able to bring forth good out of evil. . . . For God judged it better to bring good out of evil than to allow no evil to exist."[8] If God could achieve the particular good in question without evil or in some other "lower-cost way," then he would.[9] Most Calvinists tend to embrace some kind of greater-good argument, even though it has not received much sustained attention among recent Reformed theologians and philosophers.[10]

In this chapter, we will explore several other defenses/theodicies that are akin to the greater-good defense or correlate to it in some way. These are the *soul-making theodicy*, the *best-of-all-possible-worlds defense*, and the *divine-judgment defense*.

THE GREATER-GOOD THEODICY

Many passages of Scripture indicate that second-order goods come forth from first-order evils. For example, James exhorts, "Count it all

---

7. See pages 81–82 for the distinction between a theodicy and a defense.

8. Augustine, *Enchiridion*, ed. and trans. Albert C. Outler (Philadelphia: Westminster Press, 1955), 3.11; 8.27. Thomas Aquinas, appealing to Augustine, says, "This is part of the infinite goodness of God, that He should allow evil to exist, and out of it produce good" (*Summa Theologica*, 1.2.3).

9. Stephen Wykstra, "The Skeptical Theist Response," in *God and the Problem of Evil: Five Views*, ed. Chad Meister and James K. Dew Jr. (Downers Grove, IL: InterVarsity Press, 2017), 175. See also Paul Helm, *The Providence of God* (Downers Grove, IL: InterVarsity Press, 1994), 197.

10. That appears to be changing. The best contemporary argument for the greater-good theodicy is from the Calvinist philosopher Greg Welty, *Why Is There Evil in the World (and So Much of It)?* (Fearn, Ross-shire, Scotland: Christian Focus, 2018). See also essays in David E. Alexander and Daniel M. Johnson, eds., *Calvinism and the Problem of Evil* (Eugene, OR: Pickwick Publications, 2016). It should be noted that many theodicists combine the greater-good theodicy with libertarian free will, but it seems to accord best with Calvinist/Reformed accounts of the problem of evil.

joy, my brothers, when you meet trials of various kinds [i.e., first-order evils], for you know that the testing of your faith produces steadfastness [i.e., second-order good]. And let steadfastness have its full effect, that you may be perfect and complete, lacking in nothing" (James 1:2–4). Such a good could be achieved by God in no other way.

Some people intend their actions for nefarious purposes, and this is all that we might see. But God intends those same actions for a greater good (Gen. 50:20), and we don't always see what that good is. God has a specific *telos* to evil—an end, a goal, a design. It has a teleological function.[11] This presupposes God's providential control over evil (Ps. 103:19). God especially causes "all things"—that is, every good *and* evil moment, every bright *and* blackened molecule—to work for the greater good of his chosen ones (Rom. 8:28). The believer's present sufferings are indeed bitter, yet their foul taste is contrasted with the polarizing sweetness of our future glory (Rom. 8:18), which points to our greatest good—the beatific vision whereby we long to come face to face with the God of all wonders (Ps. 16:11).

Paul states this truth magnificently in 2 Corinthians 4:17: "For this light momentary affliction is preparing for us an eternal weight of glory beyond all comparison." This present affliction will not last forever; it is merely "momentary." It seems like a burden too great to bear, but in reality, it is "light" as a feather compared to the "eternal weight of glory" that will soon be ours—a glory simply "beyond all comparison" to anything that we can currently ponder with our limited imaginations.

James teaches that the trials that test our faith are intended to produce within us "perfect and complete" character, so that we are lacking no good thing within (James 1:2–4).[12] When we step back from our suffering and glimpse it from a cosmic perspective, it ought to produce a transcendent joy that no one can steal (v. 2).

Such evil becomes "necessary" in order to forge a faith "more precious than gold" (1 Peter 1:6–7).[13] Christians are not promised a path of carefree ease and tranquility in this life. Rather, they are required to endure "many tribulations" before they "enter the kingdom of God" (Acts 14:22). Nonetheless, God promises that our blood, sweat, and toil are not in vain because he is working mightily within us to complete the good and glorious work of redemption he began (Phil. 1:6; 2:12–13).

---

11. G. C. Berkouwer, *The Providence of God* (Grand Rapids: Eerdmans, 1952), 258.

12. See also Rom. 5:3–5.

13. Thomas R. Schreiner notes that the phrase "if necessary" (1 Peter 1:6) indicates "that the sufferings believers experience are not the result of fate or impersonal forces of nature. They are the will of God for believers" (*1, 2 Peter, Jude*, New American Commentary 37 [Nashville: Broadman & Holman, 2003], 67).

Initially, no one had reason to suppose that the slaughter of five innocent men in a remote South American jungle could generate any good. But looking in retrospect, the good of the 1956 Palm Beach massacre is easily calculated. Not only have the Waodani people repudiated their violent past and embraced the gospel, but the striking deaths of these men served to inspire countless missionaries ever since to risk their comfortable lives to spread the gospel across the globe. History may well look on this tragic incident as the pivotal moment that propelled modern missions into hyperdrive. The five men's experience of *physical death* has resulted in vast multitudes of people experiencing *spiritual life*.

But is calculating the good from *every* instance of evil such an easy task? No, it is not.

OBJECTIONS TO THE GREATER-GOOD THEODICY

The primary and most serious objection to the greater-good theodicy is that no matter what good arises from God's decree to permit evil, it makes him the author of evil—that is, God becomes morally culpable for its existence. This charge will be addressed in chapter 9. But a related concern suggests that if this theodicy has some merit on the face of it, nonetheless it cannot account for the supposed greater goods that come from most evils.[14] Do the ends justify the means? Are the goods weighty enough to justify the evil necessitated by them?

Perhaps the example of the Waodani incident is the rare exception. Most evil does not appear to have such a tidy justification. Do all tragic deaths serve such palpably good purposes? Can any ultimate good accrue to the unbeliever who faces eternal damnation? After all, Romans 8:28 applies only to those "who love God" and "who are called according to his purpose."[15] Can we know enough to say that a particular good justifies the evil that produced it? In many (perhaps most) cases, we would have to humbly answer no. Can we even know what goods a particular evil might produce? Perhaps rarely.

Gratuitous Evil

The problem is exacerbated when we consider horrendous incidents of evil that many would regard as gratuitous. Note that a distinction between *horrendous* and *gratuitous* evil should be made. Horrendous evil is evil that is undeniably

---

14. J. Richard Middleton, "Why the 'Greater Good' Isn't a Defense: Classical Theodicy in Light of the Biblical Genre of Lament," *Koinonia* 9.1, 2 (1997): 81–113.

15. See how this question is addressed on pages 123–27.

heinous but not pointless. Gratuitous evil is any evil (usually horrendous evil) that seems pointless, having no apparently good reasons for existing. Any act of horrendous evil elicits a psychological force to the objection that renders a calm and coherent response nearly impossible to offer. And this is not simply a problem of the greater-good defense. It is a problem for all theodicies.

No one captures the existential wrenching that certain heinous evils produce as powerfully as the objections of Ivan in Dostoyevsky's *The Brothers Karamazov*. He zeroes in on the problem by focusing on the most vulnerable victims of evil—the children.[16] Ivan, speaking to his Christian brother Alyosha, remarks that humans are the worst of creatures. Worse than animals. "No animal could ever be so cruel as a man, so artfully, so artistically cruel."[17] He details how Turkish soldiers cut infants out of their mothers' wombs. Others tossed nursing babes into the air to catch them on their bayonets as their mothers looked on.

Then Ivan unveils darker deeds:

> Imagine a nursing infant in the arms of its trembling mother, surrounded by the Turks. They've thought up an amusing trick: they fondle the baby, they laugh to make it laugh, and they succeed—the baby laughs. At that moment a Turk aims a pistol at it, four inches from its face. The baby laughs gleefully, reaches out its little hands to grab the pistol, and suddenly the artist pulls the trigger right in its face and shatters its little head . . . Artistic, isn't it? By the way, they say the Turks are very fond of sweets.[18]

And if one might dismiss this as an aberration of foreign infidels and uneducated brutes, Ivan turns to examples of their own Russian kinsmen. They, too, have a sadistic lust to torture children. "It is precisely the defenselessness of these creatures that tempts the torturers, the angelic trustfulness of the child, who has nowhere to turn and no one to turn to—that is what enflames the vile blood of the torturer."

Ivan speaks of "educated parents" who subjected their "poor five-year-old girl to every possible torture":

> They beat her, flogged her, kicked her, not knowing why themselves, until her whole body was nothing but bruises; finally they attained the height

16. The examples that Ivan recounts are drawn from actual accounts that Dostoevsky discovered from the news of his day.

17. Fyodor Dostoevsky, *The Brothers Karamazov*, trans. Richard Pevear and Larissa Volokhonsky (New York: Farrar, Straus and Giroux, 1990), 238.

18. Dostoevsky, *Brothers Karamazov*, 238–39.

of finesse: in the freezing cold, they locked her all night in the outhouse, because she wouldn't ask to get up and go in the middle of the night (as if a five-year-old child sleeping its sound angelic sleep could have learned to ask by that age)—for that they smeared her face with excrement and made her eat the excrement, and it was her mother, her mother who made her![19]

After raising the temperature of our blood, Ivan then proceeds to drive the point home to Alyosha in a way that cannot fail to confound us all:

> Can you understand that a small creature, who cannot even comprehend what is being done to her, in a vile place, in the dark and cold, beats herself on her strained little chest with her tiny fist and weeps with her anguished, gentle, meek tears for "dear God" to protect her—can you understand such nonsense, my friend and my brother, my godly and humble novice, can you understand why this nonsense is needed and created? Without it, they say, man could not even have lived on earth, for he would not have known good and evil. Who wants to know this damned good and evil at such a price? The whole world of knowledge is not worth the tears of that little child to "dear God."[20]

Ivan then appears to set the greater-good defense in his sights:

> Imagine that you yourself are building the edifice of human destiny with the object of making people happy in the finale, of giving them peace and rest at last, but for that you must inevitably and unavoidably torture just one tiny creature, that same child who was beating her chest with her little fist, and raise your edifice on the foundation of her unrequited tears—would you agree to be the architect on such conditions? Tell me the truth.[21]

Alyosha could only reply sheepishly, "No, I would not agree." All such evil seems undeniably gratuitous.

The Answer to Gratuitous Evil: Skeptical Theism

Let us not delude ourselves. A thousand other similar tales of real and confounding horror put a strain on the greater-good defense and, for that matter, any other attempt at justifying the ways of God. Can such *apparently* gratuitous evils ever justify any good that God would seek to achieve?

19. Dostoevsky, *Brothers Karamazov*, 242.
20. Dostoevsky, *Brothers Karamazov*, 242.
21. Dostoevsky, *Brothers Karamazov*, 245.

It would seem utterly presumptuous to speak in the affirmative with any ounce of confidence. Furthermore, fishing for a tidy answer is pastorally disastrous when seeking to comfort the afflicted. Silence is often the better part of wisdom.[22]

What lessons can we learn from the Nazi death camps? Some would say, "None." It is impertinent to even ask the question. Yet there is an important response to the charge that the greater-good defense cannot escape gratuitous evil. It is known as the *skeptical-theism defense*, which is an unfortunate designation.[23] It should be called *"sensibly humble* theism," as the following will make clear.[24] The sensibly humble (skeptical) theist says that we do not know enough (thus the skepticism) to make definite pronouncements about the goods that God may have in permitting particular evils, especially those that are horrendous. As risky and smug as it may appear, the charge regarding gratuitous evil cannot be a defeat for the greater-good theodicy because its driving question can be easily turned around.

We may be undeniably uncertain what goods a particular evil might produce, but can we rest secure in the opposite position? Being severely limited in our knowledge and wisdom, can we say that absolutely *no* goods can be justified by the evils that might produce them? "The critic has to prove a universal negative: *there is no reason* that would justify God in permitting whatever difficult case of evil" we wish to dredge up from the pit of horrors.[25]

To embrace this claim is at least equally presumptuous. One would have to pretend to know the furthest recesses of the infinite mind of God, ferreting out his incomprehensible knowledge and wisdom (Isa. 40:13–14; 55:9; Rom. 11:34). There are uncharted expanses of the mind of God that he has chosen not to reveal to us, intricacies of his vast plans that we could not pretend to untangle even if we had access to them. "If the complexities of an infinite God's divine plan for the unfolding of the universe [*do*] involve God's recognizing either deep goods, or necessary connections between various evils and the realization of those goods, or both of these things,

---

22. For a modern account of horrific child abuse and how God nonetheless used it to bring about redemptive good, see Mez McConnell, *Is There Anybody Out There? A Journey from Despair to Hope* (Fearn, Ross-shire, Scotland: Christian Focus, 2015); Mez McConnell, *The Creaking on the Stairs: Finding Faith in God through Childhood Abuse* (Fearn, Ross-shire, Scotland: Christian Focus, 2019).

23. Stephen Wykstra, "The Skeptical Theist View," in *God and the Problem of Evil: Five Views*, ed. Chad Meister and James K. Dew Jr. (Downers Grove, IL: InterVarsity Press, 2017), 173–84.

24. Wykstra, "Skeptical Theist View," 111. Wykstra terms the objector's view "*insanely hubristic* theism."

25. Welty, *Why Is There Evil?*, 139.

would our inability to discern these goods or connections give us a reason for thinking they aren't there? What would be the basis of such confidence?"[26] We must confess with James Henley Thornwell:

> God is at once known and unknown. In His transcendent Being, as absolute and infinite, though a necessary object of faith, He cannot be an object of thought. We cannot represent Him to the understanding, nor think Him as He is in Himself. But in and through the finite He had given manifestations of His incomprehensible reality, which, though not sufficient to satisfy the demands of speculation, are amply adequate for all the ends of religion.[27]

A simple illustration may suffice. If a nurse drops a hypodermic needle and says, "I see no dog hairs on the needle," we can draw a strong inference: "It doesn't appear that there are dog hairs on the needle." But it is an "absurdly weak" inference to move from saying, "I see no viruses on the needle" to saying, "It doesn't appear that there are viruses on the needle."[28] If there were viruses on the needle, we would not expect to see them. We are quite certain that we *could not* see them.[29]

Our comprehension of divine knowledge, wisdom, and purposes—especially concerning particular instances of evil—is limited at best. And what we *do* know is emphatically infantile compared to God.[30] Welty points out that medieval scientists had no reason to think that quantum mechanics was true, but that doesn't mean that it wasn't as true then as it is now. There are many truths in specialized disciplines and areas of knowledge that most people have little or no expertise in (e.g., mathematics, physics, medicine, jurisprudence, linguistics).[31] This doesn't mean that these areas of knowledge are riddled with falsehood. It means that we don't always understand the truths they contain.

Evil, no matter how horrendous, can never be regarded as gratuitous—without any meaningful purpose. Can evil descend into the depths of the inscrutable? Absolutely! We would be foolish to believe anything less. But it never descends into the dark and dispiriting pit of the gratuitous. To hold

---

26. Welty, *Why Is There Evil?*, 147.
27. James Henley Thornwell, *The Collected Writings of James Henley Thornwell*, ed. John B. Adger (Richmond, VA: Presbyterian Committee of Publication, 1871), 1:107, quoted in Mark Jones, *God Is: A Devotional Guide to the Attributes of God* (Wheaton, IL: Crossway, 2017), 15.
28. Wykstra, "Skeptical Theist View," 114.
29. Wykstra, "Skeptical Theist View," 115–16.
30. Wykstra, "Skeptical Theist View," 116.
31. Welty, *Why Is There Evil?*, 143.

to gratuitous evil is to grant that God is capricious or perhaps out of his league—that somehow the Hitlers, the Stalins, the Maos, and the Pol Pots slipped past his notice. If this were true, then God would be rendered powerless before the forces of evil. Evil would pose as an autonomous entity standing outside of God's self-sufficient, independent, transcendent existence. His all-encompassing lordship over creation would be impugned. Instead, he would be wringing his hands in despair—perhaps greater despair than ours. And what's more, we would lose all confidence and trust in such a God. He would rightfully inspire a grand exodus of all who believed in him. If evil were ultimately senseless, then God could not be God.

When reading the prologue to the book of Job, we soon realize that Job had no idea what God was doing, namely, proving to Satan that Job's faith would survive the devil's diabolical attacks. Lack of understanding, however, is not an insurmountable barrier to having confidence in God's wisdom and good purposes, as mysterious as they may be (Phil. 4:6–7). Furthermore, we are in no position to demand that God give us answers.

When Job was at his best, he was prepared to accept whatever the hand of God laid on him, which his innocence in the matter could not fathom. His wife wanted him to "'curse God and die.' But he said to her, 'You speak as one of the foolish women would speak. Shall we receive good from God, and shall we not receive evil?'" (Job 2:9–10). In the affirmation of this truth, "Job did not sin with his lips" (v. 10). He did not speak with impertinence, nor did he assign moral culpability to God. Job did not run from the inscrutable tension between God's ways: "Though he slay me, I will hope in him" (13:15). "The book of Job may assure us that *there is* an illuminating prologue for our lives, involving a divine pursuit of weighty, dependent goods."[32]

As the spouse of the great pastor-theologian Jonathan Edwards (1703–58), Sarah Edwards (1710–58) was a far different wife from Job's. She understood what it means to love and worship a sovereign God. When her husband unexpectedly died of a smallpox inoculation, she wrote to console and counsel her daughter Esther:

> My very dear Child,
>   What shall I say? A holy and good God has covered us with a very dark cloud. O that we may kiss the rod, and lay our hands on our mouths! The Lord has done it. He has made me adore his goodness, that we had him so long. But my God lives; and he has my heart. O what a legacy my

---

32. Welty, *Why Is There Evil?*, 150.

husband, and your father, has left us! We are all given to God; and there I am, and love to be.

Your ever affectionate mother,
Sarah Edwards[33]

Sarah does not deny the pain of her husband's loss. And like Job, she does not lay blame on God. Yes, his rod was heavy, but he is holy and good. Her husband was seen as a gift from his hand. "The LORD gave, and the LORD has taken away; blessed be the name of the LORD" (Job 1:21). She can turn to no other. Her heart belongs to the grand Possessor of her soul. She loves to find her solace in his company, though she might be unacquainted with his deeply wise and mysterious ways.

We do not always know why God takes away what seems to be of such great benefit to us, leaving us to stumble into a vale of tears (Ps. 84:6). Yet this need not dumbfound us. Not having the requisite knowledge to make sense of every vestige of our suffering doesn't mean that we are consigned to total darkness. Stephen Wykstra strikes the appropriate balance: "Conditional theistic humility about *how much* or how *often* we humans should expect to see or grasp the purposes of any God capable of creating and sustaining our universe is entirely *compatible* with holding that we are nevertheless *capable* of seeing and grasping many truths about God and God's purposes."[34]

This softens the concern that a theodicy has to answer every last question about evil. Certainly it is desirable for a theodicy to be as comprehensive as possible, but an exhaustive theodicy (at least in this world) is impossible. Yet entrusting our suffering souls to a supremely holy, wise, and benevolent God in seemingly impossible circumstances is precisely what he wants us to do. There is more to glean from a lowly Sarah Edwards than from many learned philosophers and theologians, trying to ferret out the ways of God that are "past finding out!" (Rom. 11:33 KJV).

No Incentive to Fight Evil

Another objection to the greater-good theodicy suggests that we have no incentive to refrain from, to pray against, or to fight evil if God always has some greater purpose for it.[35] We should stand by and let evil take its

---

33. Jonathan Edwards, "C146. Sarah Pierpont Edwards to Esther Edwards Burr," in *Correspondence by, to, and about Edwards and His Family* (*JWE Online*, vol. 32), quoted in Dane C. Ortlund, *Edwards on the Christian Life* (Wheaton, IL: Crossway, 2014), 35.

34. Wykstra, "Skeptical Theist View," 121.

35. Middleton, "Why the 'Greater Good' Isn't a Defense," 91.

course, or even push it along, so that God will achieve his greater good.[36] But this objection fails to see what strikingly different ground we stand on from God. Given our radically limited wisdom, knowledge, and power, we cannot presume the prerogatives of God. We have no ability to ensure that good can emanate from evil or entertain knowledge of what sort of second-order goods could be generated by a particular evil.[37]

How do we know that evils won't lead to greater evils that God does not intend instead of greater goods?[38] Therefore, we are *never* to pursue evil so that good may come (Rom. 3:8). Rather, we are *always* called to "overcome evil with good" (12:21). Paul warns us, "See that no one repays anyone evil for evil, but always seek to do good to one another and to everyone" (1 Thess. 5:15; cf. Rom. 12:17). Our finite and corrupted condition constrains us in ways that utterly separate us from the transcendently sovereign, wise, and holy ends of God.

Thus, while God hates evil with a purer hatred than we can ever muster (Hab. 1:13), he also has an utterly unique providential relation to evil's existence. Greg Welty observes:

> It is not evil to ordain that evil be, especially if one has the requisite knowledge and power to ensure the greater good (having knowledge to consider relevant alternatives, and having power to assure that evils will not be in vain with respect to providential purposes). . . . If God has the right to impose suffering, and the requisite knowledge and power to ensure greater goods out of it, it would not only *not be evil* for God to so ordain suffering, it would be *positively good* for him to do so.[39]

This is an astounding point for Welty to make. It is enormously difficult for us to fathom how God could ordain horrendous evil and suffering, but we are the ones who are out of our league, not God. God would never ordain evil unless weightier second-order goods would emerge from it. Furthermore, some goods cannot be achieved in any other way. Even an omnipotent God cannot achieve certain goods without certain prior evils.[40] It would be wrong for him not to ordain certain evils.

For example, in order for the greatest good ever—the plan of redemption— to be brought about, the Son of God had to be unjustly tried and crucified (Acts 2:22–23; 4:27–28).[41] Without knowing this plan, we would be appalled

---

36. William Hasker, "The Open Theist Response," in *God and the Problem of Evil: Five Views*, ed. Chad Meister and James K. Dew Jr. (Downers Grove, IL: InterVarsity Press, 2017), 160.

37. Welty, *Why Is There Evil?*, 118.

38. Welty, *Why Is There Evil?*, 196.

39. Welty, *Why Is There Evil?*, 118.

40. This point has been made by Steve Hays.

41. This point will be elaborated on in the theodicy I offer in chapter 12.

by the fact that it pleased the Father to "crush" his own Son (Isa. 53:10). When Christ was tried and crucified, God ordained the greatest injustice ever perpetrated. Yet it was precisely designed to achieve the greatest good that the world has ever known. God gladly ordains those evils he utterly hates. But he never ensures that any evil transpires if it would not achieve a far weightier good than the evil itself. God most certainly hates it when a child is tortured. He hates it when an innocent man is tried and killed, yet this happened to his own Son by his "definite plan and foreknowledge" (Acts 2:23).

Sometimes the only response to our unflagging dismay at the mystery of God's providential ways is to cover our mouths and to bow in worship before such a God (Job 40:1–5). "For who has known the mind of the Lord, or who has been his counselor? Or who has given a gift to him that he might be repaid? For from him and through him and to him are all things. To him be glory forever. Amen" (Rom. 11:34–36).

THE SOUL-MAKING THEODICY

A particular brand of the greater-good defense is the *soul-making theodicy*. It was first articulated by the early church father Irenaeus (c. A.D. 130–202) and more recently promoted by John Hick.[42] The soul-making theodicy says that humans are born in a state of immaturity and must undergo adversity as part of the process of becoming mature. How can moral virtues be cultivated in a world created in perpetual innocence with no trace of suffering, a place where only hedonistic pleasures and happiness abound?

Only in a world full of suffering and adversity do you see traits such as perseverance, courage, forgiveness, patience, mercy, sympathy, and self-sacrificial love.[43] These virtues "logically require the presence of evil or suffering for their cultivation."[44] The definition of such virtues is otherwise meaningless. Scripture consistently commends suffering for the character it produces.[45]

Furthermore, a world with adverse consequences for evil behavior is better than one in which God mitigated those consequences.[46] Imagine if there

42. See John Hick, *Evil and the Love of God* (New York: Harper and Row, 1975). Hick's brand of soul-making embraces universal salvation and libertarian free will, but the soul-making theodicy requires neither to make sense.
43. John Hick, "Soul-Making and Suffering," in *The Problem of Evil*, ed. Marilyn McCord Adams and Robert Merrihew Adams (Oxford: Oxford University Press, 1990), 168–69.
44. Jeremy A. Evans, *The Problem of Evil: The Challenge to Essential Christian Beliefs* (Nashville: B&H Academic, 2013), 51.
45. See, for example, Rom. 5:3–4; 8:17–18; Phil. 3:10–11; Heb. 2:10; 5:8; James 1:2–4; 1 Peter 1:6–7; 4:13.
46. Hick, "Soul-Making," 186.

were no repercussions for drinking too much alcohol—no negative alteration of behavior and no hangovers. Or imagine that after a bank was robbed, its money vaults were somehow magically replenished. Suppose running down a pedestrian while recklessly driving your car left him unharmed.

Without consequences for such incidents, there would be no moral lessons learned to strengthen moral character. One would act carelessly, with utter abandon, and with impunity. There would be no need to build character through self-control, honesty, perseverance, alertness, common sense and wisdom, and the like. We would be less inclined to deem certain things sinful because they would cause no ill effects. The greatest displays of moral character are those that are forged in the fires of adversity.[47]

The soul-making theodicy certainly dispels the notion that God created the world for our unmitigated pain-free bliss. The price required to obtain the sorts of virtues that only the crucible of suffering can produce makes those virtues far more valuable and cherished than those obtained with greater ease or those that are native to humanity's prefallen condition. Ironically, suffering has all the components to produce a deep joy in the life of a believer obtainable no other way. It exceeds the undifferentiated bliss that finite creatures subsisting in a perpetual state of prefall innocence could experience. All the maturing fruits of the Spirit (Gal. 5:22–23) seem to require at least some adversity to establish their full potential.

Many do not know that the great prince of preachers, Charles Spurgeon, was the subject of lifelong fits of depression that often brought him to the brink of despair.[48] Yet he embraced his trials and sufferings just as Christ embraced the cross:

> I can bear my personal testimony that the best piece of furniture that I ever had in the house was a cross. I do not mean a material cross; I mean, the cross of affliction and trouble. I am sure, that I have run more swiftly with a lame leg than I ever did with a sound one. I am certain that I have seen more in the dark than ever I saw in the light,—more stars, most certainly,—more things in heaven if fewer things on earth. The anvil, the fire, and the hammer, are the making of us; we do not get fashioned much by anything else. That heavy hammer falling on us helps to shape us; therefore, let affliction and trouble and trial come.[49]

47. Hick, "Soul-Making," 178–79.
48. See Zack Eswine, *Spurgeon's Sorrows* (Fearn, Ross-shire, Scotland: Christian Focus, 2014).
49. Charles H. Spurgeon, "Christ's Yoke and Burden," *Metropolitan Tabernacle Pulpit*, vol. 49, Sermon 2,832 (September 2, 1886), found at: https://www.spurgeon.org/resource-library/sermons/christs-yoke-and-burden#flipbook/.

Alistair Begg would agree. In grieving the premature death of his mother, he writes, "More spiritual progress is made through failure and tears than success and laughter."[50] A love that is not tested cannot be seen for what it's worth. Where does love reside when your wife takes to unexpected illness such as dementia and every simple task that most people take for granted suddenly becomes a monumental feat of reasoning and concentration? What does a husband do? Will his love rise to the occasion with persistent self-sacrifice, or will it crumble because it was never strong in the first place?[51]

There is no question—adversity tests the mettle of our souls. According to 1 Peter 1:6–7, the crucible of suffering forges a faith purer than gold in the life of the believer. Peter emphasizes that such "trials" are "necessary" (1 Peter 1:6; cf. Acts 14:22). In other words, God ordains only those trials that are critical for the forging of greater faith (1 Peter 1:7). Such supremely valuable faith can come no other way.

What are we to make of the soul-making theodicy?

The principles behind this theodicy are certainly biblical and have tremendous value for the believer, but the theodicy is not without problems. Many have criticized it, employing the same objections that the greater-good defense garners (see above). But it suffers from other concerns as well. For example, we must admit that while evil has a soul-building effect on Christians, it does not have that effect on others. Countless incidents of adversity appear to have a soul-destroying effect. The experience of our cursed world causes many people to become embittered, hateful, distrustful, and even violent. They turn to vices that wreck their marriages, careers, and friendships. Cain was encouraged to build his soul under relatively mild adversity (Gen. 4:6–7); instead, he chose to establish an unfortunate legacy of violence and murder for the future of humanity (v. 8).

William Dembski wonders, "How many flunk out of Hick's school of soul-making? How many do not merely flunk out but end up in the gutter, addicted to sensuality, money, fame, or power? How many cannot be said to have enrolled in any school whatsoever, whose days are consumed simply in the struggle to survive?"[52] Cain never recovered from the bitter fruit of his

---

50. Alistair Begg, *Made for His Pleasure: Ten Benchmarks of a Vital Faith* (Chicago: Moody Publishers, 1996), 102.

51. See how Douglas Groothuis handled his own wife's dementia in *Walking through Twilight: A Wife's Illness—A Philosopher's Lament* (Downers Grove, IL: InterVarsity Press, 2017).

52. William A. Dembski, *The End of Christianity: Finding a Good God in an Evil World* (Nashville: B&H Academic, 2009), 31.

choices. If the *only* reason evil existed was to mature all the souls impacted by it, then such a strategy would have failed miserably.[53]

Tim Keller makes another interesting point: "Many people with bad souls get very little of the adversity they apparently need, and many with great souls get an amount that seems to go far beyond what is necessary for spiritual growth."[54] The Psalms abundantly testify to this dilemma.[55] Many wicked people seem to prosper while the righteous suffer inordinately.

As noted already, however, we must recognize that we cannot know whether adversity has a soul-building effect or not.[56] In the case of Cain? Perhaps no. But in the lives of Abraham, Joseph, Moses, Ruth, David, Daniel, Esther, Mary, Peter, Paul, and countless others? Yes. We must argue that suffering that targets many sinners leads them to the God of the universe. Furthermore, no matter the time, the place, or the circumstances, suffering in the life of every believer—past, present, or future—never proves to be in vain. It is never wasted. God does not purpose any suffering in those he redeems that does not have some greater soul-building good attached to it. He causes *all* things—whether good *or* ill—to work together for our temporal and eternal benefit (Rom. 8:28), even if we do not always fully grasp what that benefit is.

Nonetheless, the soul-making theodicy has limited value and can never be the basis for a comprehensive theodicy. Is the building of the souls of the faithful through adversity the sole reason for allowing evil to wreck the beauty and tranquility of the whole created order? As important as such soul-building is, there must be reasons that penetrate the enigma of ubiquitous sin and corruption, of universal death and decay, and of all manner of catastrophe with greater depth than the soul-making theodicy does.

THE BEST-OF-ALL-POSSIBLE-WORLDS DEFENSE

The brilliant German (Lutheran) philosopher Gottfried Wilhelm Leibniz (1646–1716) first propounded the idea that a God of unbridled perfection would create the best world possible, and that such a world must contain evil. Although Leibniz had worked on this idea for some fifty years, his most famous and thorough articulation of it came in a piece originally entitled

---

53. This explains why John Hick has endorsed universalism, believing that no soul will be damned after death, but will undergo sufficient soul-building in the afterlife in order to get to heaven. Unfortunately, he has turned his theodicy into a gospel of works-righteousness.

54. Timothy Keller, *Walking with God through Pain and Suffering* (New York: Dutton, 2013), 90.

55. See Pss. 34; 35; 36; 37; 73; 74; 77; 79; 82; 83; 88.

56. See Wykstra, "Skeptical Theist Response."

Essays of Theodicy, on the Goodness of God, the Freedom of Man and the Origin of Evil, published anonymously in 1710 (known mostly today simply as *Theodicy*).

The *best-of-all-possible-worlds defense* is another variation of the greater-good defense. For example, Leibniz says, "God cooperates morally in moral evil, that is, in sin, without being the originator of sin, and even without being accessory thereto. He does this by permitting it justly, and by directing it wisely toward the good."[57] In this he concurs with Augustine: God "would not allow any evil in his works, unless in his omnipotence and goodness, as the Supreme Good, he is able to bring forth good out of evil."[58] God *must* and *will* do his best. If God did not do his best, would this not undermine the worship that he supremely deserves?[59] Everything Leibniz says indicates that the two theodicies are complementary.

The best-of-all-possible-worlds defense proceeds from a consideration of the essential attributes that God would necessarily have. Anselm (1033–1109) argued persuasively that God is a being "than-which-a-greater-cannot-be thought."[60] He is supreme in every way and in the fullest sense possible. He is maximally great. He has nothing but the "greatest possible array" of "great-making properties" that such a God could have.[61] However great God truly is—and we have no capacity to know those limits—no greater conception of God is possible.

This means that God, being infinite and omniscient, knows every possible good world (state of affairs). Upon surveying all these worlds, God knows which one is superior to all others. And because God is supremely wise and good, he chooses to create that single world that he deems perfect

57. G. W. Leibniz, *Theodicy*, ed. Austin M. Farrar, trans. E. M. Huggard (New York: Cosimo Classics, 2009), 182.

58. Augustine, *Enchiridion*, 11.

59. Philip L. Quinn, "God, Moral Perfection, and Possible Worlds," in *The Problem of Evil: Selected Readings*, ed. Michael L. Peterson, 2nd ed. (Notre Dame, IN: University of Notre Dame Press, 2017), 443.

60. Anselm, *Proslogion*, 2–3, in *Anselm of Canterbury: The Major Works*, ed. Brian Davies and G. R. Evans (Oxford: Oxford University Press, 1998), 87–88. In philosophical theology, this is known as *perfect-being theism*. See Thomas V. Morris, *Our Idea of God* (Downers Grove, IL: InterVarsity Press, 1991), 35–40. For an accessible treatment of God as the perfect being, see Matthew Barrett, *None Greater: The Undomesticated Attributes of God* (Grand Rapids: Baker, 2019). For a more philosophical defense of perfect-being theism, see Katherin A. Rogers, *Perfect Being Theology* (Edinburgh: Edinburgh University Press, 2000).

61. Morris, *Our Idea of God*, 37. Some of those properties are God's aseity (self-existence/self-sufficiency), independence, transcendence, infinity, immutability, simplicity (unity and indivisibility of his attributes), timeless eternality, impassibility (being unaffected by external realities), omnipresence, omnipotence, omniscience, omnibenevolence, omnisapience (being all-wise), meticulous providence, and, of course, incomprehensibility.

even though, ironically, it contains imperfections.[62] If such a supremely good world could not be conceived in the divine mind, then God would not be compelled to create it. If God has not created such a world, then is it not conceivable that another morally superior God has done so? Leibniz says no because that would refute the classic God of biblical theism.[63]

Voltaire's famed objection to Leibnizian optimism in his virulent satire *Candide* (1759) misinterprets Leibniz's theodicy as saying that this is the best possible world that any particular *individual* could live in. But Leibniz never said this. He contended that when all things are considered as a whole, this world is best *overall* compared to any other conceivable world. In other words, some people will suffer terribly, but this suffering contributes to other goods that accrue to a greater overall good that mitigates the bad effects of the suffering that any one person might experience.

While one can imagine worlds with far less evil or no evil at all, those worlds overall cannot be construed as better; otherwise, God would have considered them as superior to the world he made. If a better world is possible and God did not create such a world, then his supreme goodness is maligned.

Leibniz suggests that the black backdrop of evil accentuates the brightness of the good by contrast and that this is better than if there were no contrasting evil.[64] Augustine likewise saw God's ordering of evil as part of the broader beauty of the universe. The creation has "touches of black in appropriate places" that enhance the brighter colors elsewhere.[65] The lack of evil would domesticate the good, rendering the world as bland, undistinctive, monochromatic. But if you focus on only one dissonant portion of the canvas, you miss how it contributes to the magnificence of the whole painting.[66]

One of the primary objections to the best-of-all-possible-worlds defense is that no explanation is given as to how evil specifically contributes to this world's being the best world. How do we know for sure that it is the best there is? Leibniz argues that we have no obligation to provide an explanation because we are not in a position to know.

---

62. Jill Hernandez, "Leibniz and the Best of All Possible Worlds," in *God and Evil: The Case for God in a World Filled with Pain*, ed. Chad Meister and James K. Dew Jr. (Downers Grove, IL: InterVarsity Press, 2013), 96.

63. Quinn, "God, Moral Perfection, and Possible Worlds," 442.

64. Leibniz, *Theodicy*, 130.

65. Augustine, *City of God*, trans. Henry Bettenson (New York: Penguin Books, 1984), 40.23.

66. Augustine, *City of God*, 11.18; Steven Nadler, *The Best of All Possible Worlds: A Story of Philosophers, God, and Evil* (New York: Farrar, Straus and Giroux, 2008), 101.

This is the same broad objection and response made with respect to the greater-good defense answered by the skeptical-theism response.[67] Again, we cannot pretend to know in every instance how the all-wise, all-good, infinitely knowledgeable God uses evil to generate greater goods or to make this the best possible world. Therefore, we cannot dictate to God what the best world would look like. We must "rescue ourselves as judges" of the Almighty and his plans.[68] It is sufficient to rest in God's knowledge of what is best. Our finite, corrupted capacities are unable to plumb the inscrutable depths of his reasoning (Rom. 11:33–36).

Others object that we can clearly conceive of a better world than the one we live in. For example, we already know the new earth (2 Peter 3:13) to be such a world, one where evil will be absent, and the Bible makes it clear that that world is far more glorious than this fallen one. As I will argue later (in chapter 12), however, the reason that the future world is so glorious is that it represents the culmination of God's redemptive plan. But redemption is one of those greater goods that emerge from the morass of this present malevolent world.

Redemption necessitates the prior presence of evil from which it emerges. Moreover, redemption is the supreme good that flows from the presence of a corrupted creation and corrupted creatures clamoring for some kind of restoration of this painfully disordered place. Paul makes this clear in Romans 8:18–23:

> For I consider that the sufferings of this present time are not worth comparing with the glory that is to be revealed to us. For the creation waits with eager longing for the revealing of the sons of God. For the creation was subjected to futility, not willingly, but because of him who subjected it, in hope that the creation itself will be set free from its bondage to corruption and obtain the freedom of the glory of the children of God. For we know that the whole creation has been groaning together in the pains of childbirth until now. And not only the creation, but we ourselves, who have the firstfruits of the Spirit, groan inwardly as we wait eagerly for adoption as sons, the redemption of our bodies.

Another serious objection to Leibniz's view is that he saw both moral and natural evil as built into the natural structure of the world, ignoring original sin (the spread of Adam's sin to subsequent humanity) and the Edenic curse (the curse on the creation due to Adam's sin), which Paul explains in Romans 5 and 8, respectively. Leibniz saw evil as integral to the balance and harmony of the created order, but this cannot be. Moral and natural evil cannot be inherent properties of the "very good" creation that the impeccably good God established (Gen. 1:31).[69]

Nonetheless, a paradox is at work here. In one sense, it must be affirmed that God intended the world to experience the curse of sin as a foil for the greater good of its redemption. Yet we must also affirm that there is a palpable sense in which this world is *decidedly not* the way it is supposed to be. Original sin and the Edenic curse have caused an unnatural disruption in the moral fabric of the world and in the natural laws that govern it.[70] This is why we long for the Edenic world to be restored along with the idyllic laws that made it such a wonderful place to be. The "old order of things" must pass away (Rev. 21:4 NIV). A time will come when Eden will be restored. But this great and future restoration will be far more magnificent than the old Eden.

How so?

We may imagine an unfallen world (Eden before the fall) that required no redemption, and we might even say that such a world would be better than this present one, all things being equal. But that could never compare to the future world described in Scripture, because its supreme glory is made glorious only by the fact that it will be re-formed (2 Peter 3:10–13) out of this fallen world of "futility" to which God "subjected it" (Rom. 8:20).

The new heaven and the new earth will have unsurpassed value precisely because God in his grace will raise it up from such a wretched condition. We all know the joy of seeing the sun coming out after a foreboding black storm has pounded the fragile landscape. The wonder of the coming world is like a vibrant rainbow emerging from a perilous storm. It cuts through silver-tinged clouds, parting their curtains to reveal deep blue skies, with the whole scene punctuated by streaks of the sun's effulgent beams. What makes this picture all the more wondrous is that only moments before, rolling black thunderheads along with driving wind and rain had assaulted all semblance of tranquility. Without this emergence from threatened disaster, the glory of the peaceful aftermath is diminished.

What do we know of peace without war? It is true that no earthly peace *appears* to justify the wars that precede it. But the peace on offer in the future heavenly kingdom is no ordinary peace. It is certainly no earthly peace with which we are familiar. It is marked by utterly transcendent qualities—an

---

69. G. C. Berkouwer rightly criticizes this notion. See *Providence of God*, 257–58.

70. See pages 54–59. For a defense of original sin in light of contemporary objections to the doctrine, see the relevant contributions in Hans Madueme and Michael Reeves, eds., *Adam, the Fall, and Original Sin: Theological, Biblical, and Scientific Perspectives* (Grand Rapids: Baker Academic, 2014).

unprecedented form of tranquility unmarred by earthly imperfections, curses, evils, and hostilities. But the value of its peace is made exponentially more peaceable by pondering the brutal warfare out of which it materialized (see Ps. 46).

Heaven's joy is made brightest only when preceded by the most tenebrous tears soaking the earth. What can we make of the sprightly beauty of its music without the songs of this present darkness being carried forth in minor keys, especially the haunting notes of those lonely elegies that faintly whisper in the wind against the backdrop of a gray and brooding landscape? The fact that earthly peace is imperfect, fleeting, and even sometimes altogether illusory has a unique good attached to it. It causes a deep-seated longing for a heavenly peace that is perfect, eternal, and fuller than we can imagine. This is why Scripture repeatedly calls us to long—to ache deeply—for the hope of this eternal *shalom*.[71]

Having said this, we still cannot advance the best-of-all-possible-worlds defense as a satisfying theodicy for another important reason. It undermines the freedom of God in creation. Leibniz suggests that God's "supreme wisdom, united to a goodness that is no less infinite, cannot but have chosen the best. For as a lesser evil is a kind of good, even so a lesser good is a kind of evil if it stands in the way of a greater good; and there would be something to correct in the actions of God if it were possible to do better."[72] Leibniz appears to be saying that *only one* world could qualify as the best of all possible worlds. If that is true, however, then it follows that if this is indeed the best of all possible worlds, then it must be a *logically necessary* world.[73] God had no freedom to exercise about which world to create.

Furthermore, this would make God's *act of creation itself* logically necessary. It is important to note that the notion of *possible world* in Leibniz's theodicy does not simply mean the "possible planet Earth" or the "possible creation" as a whole, but the "possible state of affairs," that is, the way that things *could be* or *could have been*. Thus, there is a possible state of affairs in which God decides not to create at all and he alone exists, but Leibniz's theodicy appears to preclude this possibility.

A more faithful way to ponder a perfect Creator who has perfect freedom is to consider the following two claims about the world:

71. 1 Thess. 1:10; 4:17–18; Titus 2:13; Heb. 11:10; 1 Peter 1:13; 1 John 3:2–3; Rev. 3:10–12; 22:20.
72. Leibniz, *Theodicy*, 128.
73. I am indebted to James Anderson for drawing the arguments here and in the following paragraph to my attention. See also Terrance L. Tiessen, "A Response to John Laing's Criticisms of Hypothetical-Knowledge Calvinism," in *Calvinism and Middle Knowledge*, ed. John D. Laing, Kirk R. MacGregor, and Greg Welty (Eugene, OR: Pickwick Publications, 2019), 173.

1. "This is the best of all possible worlds."
2. "There is no possible world better than this world."

Claim 1 (which Leibniz makes) certainly entails claim 2. But the converse is not true. Claim 2 does not entail claim 1. Claim 1 is a stronger claim, but it commits Leibniz to far more than the evidence can sustain. Claim 2 is more modest and defensible. Why?

Because it preserves God's freedom as well as the optimally great God that Leibniz rightfully affirms. Both claim 1 and claim 2 indicate that there are innumerable worlds worse than this one. Claim 2, however, says that there may be other worlds *equal* to this world, but that there is no possible world *better* than this world. In other words, it leaves open how one might judge what an optimally good world *must* look like.

There is no single criterion of *goodness* by which to judge such a world. One world with more goodness may be better in some respects, whereas one with less goodness may be better in other respects. The point is, there may be any number of possible equal and optimal worlds exemplifying the highest goods that an optimally good God could have chosen to create that do not deny his freedom. I will argue later that this is indeed the case.[74]

THE DIVINE-JUDGMENT DEFENSE

There is a nagging question about the greater-good defense and its forego-ing kin thus far explored. It is easy to see that much of the greater good that proceeds from evil has benefit for the believer. But what about those who do not know God, those whom God has not chosen to be recipients of any apparently greater goods, especially the extremely valuable good of redemption? If Scripture is true, the vast majority of the earth's inhabit-ants will not partake of the beatific vision—that glorious moment when the heavenly Father's children will shed mortality and finally gaze on his unbridled majesty for the fullness of their joy.[75] What greater good could there be for such mean creatures?

But sadly, most will tread a darkened path to eternal destruction (Matt. 7:13–14). Where is the good in this? Well . . . if we are talking about the good for damned souls suffering eternal conscious torment in hell, then it is hard to see any benefit for them. It would have been better if they had never been born (26:24). But that which is good must be defined by wider parameters than those set by distorted expectations that place a premium

74. See pages 301–6.
75. See Num. 6:24–26; Pss. 16:11; 17:15; 27:4; Matt. 5:8; 1 Cor. 13:12; 1 John 3:1–3; Rev. 22:3–5; cf. 1 Peter 1:8–9.

on universal, maximum bliss for the human race at all costs. Many live with the fatal belief that God's love obliges him to overlook our supposed peccadilloes and human foibles.

This common perception works especially hard to avoid an important response to evil: the retributive justice of God. We might call this response the *divine-judgment defense.*[76] Its premise is simple: the prevailing evil in the world along with its consequent suffering is divine punishment extended to perpetrators of evil. The good that emerges here is focused not on human happiness but on the vindication of divine righteousness. It speaks to the display of God's righteous response to evil—his unflagging justice, his dogged determination to track down violators of all that is good, honorable, and true and to make certain that all wrongs are redressed, that no evil goes unpunished.

The world must know that the supremacy of his moral integrity will not be pushed into perpetual silence, that no wicked scheme will finally escape. Not only will God's justice be vindicated, but he will vindicate all those who have ever been oppressed, maligned, and mistreated.[77] Earthly justice is less than perfect. The world is often rife with complete travesties of justice. But God will never allow any injustice to ultimately prevail.

God manifests temporal punishments for sin that encompass natural evils such as earthquakes and hurricanes (cf. Isa. 29:5; Ezek. 38:19; Amos 3:6), as well as moral evils that plague sinful people and societies. Romans 1:24–32 indicates that God tolerates evil only so much before he gives especially rebellious people over to their nefarious deeds. He removes all his restraints to their vileness so that it increases in excess, coming back down on their heads as judgment.

76. Historically, this has not been regarded as a specific defense or theodicy championed by theologians and theodicists; nonetheless, it represents an important matter that Christians have faced concerning the problem of evil. Scripture often portrays God's response to evil via retributive judgment. See James L. Crenshaw, ed., *Theodicy in the Old Testament* (Philadelphia: Fortress Press, 1983); Antii Laato and Johannes C. de Moor, eds., *Theodicy in the World of the Bible: The Goodness of God and the Problem of Evil* (Leiden: Brill, 2003); Elizabeth Boase, "Constructing Meaning in the Face of Suffering: Theodicy in Lamentation," *Vetus Testamentum* 58.4–5 (2008): 449–68. Taken in a different sense, we might call this the *problem of hell* (see below). See John S. Feinberg, *The Many Faces of Evil* (Wheaton, IL: Crossway, 2004), 395–444; Evans, *The Problem of Evil*, 81–112; Marilyn McCord Adams, "The Problem of Hell: A Problem of Christians," in *God and the Problem of Evil*, ed. William L. Rowe (Malden, MA: Blackwell Publishing, 2001), 282–309.

77. Scripture is replete with cries for and promises of vindication for the righteous (innocent) against the machinations of the wicked. See, for example, 2 Chron. 6:22–23; Job 6:29; Pss. 13; 35; 43; 54; 74; 79; 82; 94; Isa. 50:8; Jer. 15:21; Mic. 7:7–10; Luke 18:7–8; 2 Thess. 1:5–8; Rev. 6:10; 16:5–7; 18:20; 19:2.

God's ultimate hand of retribution is visited on unrepentant sinners at the day of judgment, when they will incur everlasting punishment.[78] God is glorified not only in salvation but in damnation as well.[79] Salvation serves to exemplify his grace and mercy as a particular manifestation of his love. Damnation exemplifies his justice as a unique manifestation of his white-hot righteousness. The two sets of attributes stand in stark tension, magnifying the fullness of his being. Incidentally, neither grace nor justice has occasion to be displayed unless God intended evil to interrupt the innocence of Eden.

But can the divine-judgment defense give a comprehensive answer to why evil exists in the first place, and why it persists at every turn in so many ways? No, it cannot. First, while it is true that the *general* presence of moral and natural evil forms part of the curse resulting from Adam's disobedience (Gen. 3:14–20; Rom. 5:12; 8:20–31), not all manifestations of evil are the result of specific infractions of God's moral law.

Job was exemplary for his righteousness, yet he experienced both natural and moral evil for reasons that have no correspondence to his moral actions. When the disciples asked whether the man born blind in John 9 had experienced this malady because of his own sin or that of his parents (v. 2), Jesus responded, "It was not that this man sinned, or his parents, but that the works of God might be displayed in him" (v. 3). In the case of Job, God intended to bring himself glory through Job's steadfast faith in the face of his many afflictions. And in the case of the blind man, God intended to bring himself glory by granting miraculous sight to this cast-off of society. The trials of both men magnified God's glory as well as the joy that only the redemption from those trials could have brought them.

Second, while the divine-judgment defense certainly explains why evil should be punished once it occurs, it cannot justify the existence of evil in the first place. How does it explain Adam's initial disobedience, since Adam had not sinned before? If the first sin is a form of punishment, who exactly was God seeking to punish?[80]

Furthermore, we must concur with Paul Helm, who states that it is "perfectly consistent with [God's] justice that no moral evil at all be permitted" in this world.[81] Nothing demands that God permit evil just so that he can

---

78. See Isa. 66:22–24; Dan. 12:2–3; Matt. 18:6–9; 25:31–46; Mark 9:42–48; 2 Thess. 1:6–10; Jude 7, 13; Rev. 14:9–11; 20:10, 14–15.

79. John Calvin, *Institutes of the Christian Religion*, ed. John T. McNeill, trans. Ford Lewis Battles (Philadelphia: Westminster, 1960), 3.24.14.

80. Welty, *Why Is There Evil?*, 125. The same could be said for Satan's initial sin as well (Welty, *Why Is There Evil?*, 125).

81. Helm, *Providence of God*, 209–10.

display his justice. The fact that he has permitted, even ordained, evil and responds justly to it is more about displaying his glory than about responding justly to evil per se. (I will explore this later in the theodicy I will offer.)

Objections to Divine Retribution

Yet there are those who object to or reject altogether the divine retribution associated with the divine-judgment defense. One objection is that it undermines the love and goodness of God. It charges God with failing to be an equal-opportunity employer, extending love and mercy to some but not others. But God is not obligated to love all people equally and in the same way. Scripture makes some important distinctions in the nature of God's love.

D. A. Carson indicates at least five ways in which it does so:[82] (1) the peculiar love between the Father and the Son (John 3:35; 5:20; 14:31); (2) God's providential love over creation; (3) God's salvific love for the fallen world (John 3:16; 1 John 2:2); (4) God's particular, electing love toward the saints (Eph. 1:3–6); and (5) God's conditional love toward the saints, conditioned on their obedience (John 15:9–10; Jude 21). The sentimental notion that God loves all people equally and unconditionally is not sustained by the Bible's testimony.[83]

God's love is a discriminating love, and there is nothing unjust about this.[84] We expect discriminating love in our own relationships. Husbands are to love their wives in ways in which they would never love other women.[85] Parents are to love their children in special ways in which they would not be expected to love other children. To neglect one's responsibilities to family for the sake of extending love to others would be immoral.[86] By nature, familial love is deeper, fuller, and greater than other kinds of love—as it should be. So for God to show discriminating love does not impugn his moral character.

Furthermore, he is free to be discriminating. He chose Abraham to be the recipient of his promises, and with him a narrowly designated progeny.

82. See D. A. Carson, *The Difficult Doctrine of the Love of God* (Wheaton, IL: Crossway, 2000), 16–21.

83. Carson, *Difficult Doctrine of the Love of God*, 24.

84. See Paul Helm, "Discrimination: Aspects of God's Causal Activity," in *Calvinism and the Problem of Evil*, ed. David E. Alexander and Daniel M. Johnson (Eugene, OR: Pickwick Publications, 2016), 145–67.

85. Helm, "Discrimination," 152–53.

86. Matthew J. Hart, "Calvinism and the Problem of Hell," in *Calvinism and the Problem of Evil*, ed. David E. Alexander and Daniel M. Johnson (Eugene, OR: Pickwick Publications, 2016), 262–67.

He chose Isaac, not Ishmael. He loved Jacob and hated Esau (Mal. 1:2; Rom. 9:13). Joseph found special favor in his eyes over his eleven brothers. And so this pattern continues throughout history.

God's discriminating love formed the basis of electing some to salvation but not others (Eph. 1:4–5). "I will have mercy on whom I have mercy, and I will have compassion on whom I have compassion" (Rom. 9:15; cf. v. 18; Ex. 33:19). God is not required to show mercy; otherwise, it would not be mercy—rather, it would become a matter of justice. Justice involves obligations to the demands of righteousness. God is obligated by his own righteousness to be just. Mercy, however, is that which is freely chosen. Though mercy is part of the intrinsic character of God, he is under no moral obligation to extend it to anyone. He does so freely, only at his own discretion.

And this brings us to the primary objection that divine retribution faces. Many encounter horrendous evil, excruciating pain, untimely disasters, and unjustified acts of cruelty. Is not God unjust in allowing such evils to afflict the innocent? We know that Job endured great injustice, but in the end, God blessed him, restoring double his fortunes and allowing him to die satisfied (Job 42:10–17). He died with a future hope expressed in this prophetic insight: "For I know that my Redeemer lives, and at the last he will stand upon the earth" (19:25). Job had a nascent view of the Messiah's establishing his kingdom in a world that Job saw himself participating in.

Yet non-Christians suffer without such hope, some horribly so. Was the Holocaust a judgment on the Jews? If not, then how can Christians claim that thousands upon thousands of Holocaust victims will be consigned to an eternity in hell simply because they did not acknowledge Christ for salvation? Have not these already suffered enough hell on earth? Is this the God we find in Scripture? Does this not make him as cruel as the Nazis? Does this not make him a devil?

These are painfully difficult questions, but they must be faced by any honest theodicist. They are the sorts of questions that Abraham contemplated when God told him of his plan to destroy Sodom and Gomorrah: "Will you indeed sweep away the righteous with the wicked? . . . Far be it from you to do such a thing, to put the righteous to death with the wicked, so that the righteous fare as the wicked! Far be that from you! Shall not the Judge of all the earth do what is just?" (Gen. 18:23, 25).

God always does what is just. "Righteousness and justice are the foundation of your throne" (Ps. 89:14; cf. 97:2). God's justice is both remunerative (rewarding the righteous, Isa. 35:4) and retributive (punishing the wicked, Ex. 34:7). In all cases, God is careful to make certain that his justice will "grant every person his or her due."[87] God will mete out rewards and punishments in precise proportion to the praiseworthy or blameworthy actions of all his morally responsible creatures.

But herein lies the problem. No image-bearing creature of God is truly righteous (Rom. 3:10–18). All without exception have fallen short of the standard of righteousness marked by the glory of God (v. 23; Rev. 16:9). Those who attain a righteous standing before God do so because of his discriminating and justifying grace (Rom. 3:24). The verdict on all others is clear and sobering: "it is appointed for man to die once, and after that comes judgment" (Heb. 9:27). That judgment is justified because throughout history humankind has always leaned hard in one determined direction.

That direction was established early on. Barely do we turn past the first few pages of history when we read, "The LORD saw that the wickedness of man was great in the earth, and that every intention of the thoughts of his heart was only evil continually" (Gen. 6:5). Mankind's unchecked evil demanded that God respond justly. He did so with a cataclysmic flood. This means that even though we are often the unfortunate victims of evil intentions, we can never escape those intentions ourselves.

We cannot forget the candid confession of Aleksandr Solzhenitsyn. Even though he suffered as an innocent prisoner of the unspeakably cruel Russian gulags, he saw his own evil heart reflected in the heart of his tormentors. "The line separating good and evil passes . . . right through *every* human heart."[88] Solzhenitsyn saw that we embody the potential extremes of the cursed human condition. We are all, in one degree or another, both Holocaust victims and Nazi victimizers.

This sobering truth is reflected in one of the hardest lessons that Jesus ever taught. He was asked to respond to a horrific act of injustice, one that displays the unusual cruelty of the first-century Roman authorities and their disdain for the Jews. Luke records:

> There were some present at that very time who told him about the Galileans whose blood Pilate had mingled with their sacrifices. And he answered them, "Do you think that these Galileans were worse sinners than all the other Galileans, because they suffered in this way? No, I tell you; but unless you repent, you will all likewise perish." (Luke 13:1–3)

87. Herman Bavinck, *Reformed Dogmatics*, ed. John Bolt, trans. John Vriend, 4 vols. (Grand Rapids: Baker Academic, 2003–8), 2:226.

88. Aleksandr I. Solzhenitsyn, *The Gulag Archipelago Part III–IV*, trans. Thomas P. Whitney (New York: Harper & Row, 1975), 615 (emphasis mine).

In case his audience has missed the point, Jesus continues, "Or those eighteen on whom the tower in Siloam fell and killed them: do you think that they were worse offenders than all the others who lived in Jerusalem? No, I tell you; but unless you repent, you will all likewise perish" (Luke 13:4–5). We do not know any other facts about these two incidents, but they are clearly tragic. A group of Galilean worshipers somehow occasioned the Judean governor Pilate's act of tyrannical violence. Such unjustified violence was commonly perpetrated against the first-century Jews (and ever since, we might add).[89] Jesus' answer seems callous. The implication behind the question seems to be that maybe the Galileans deserved this fate. Perhaps it is an example of the divine-judgment defense. Jesus dismisses that notion, but this is no consolation. In one sense—the sense that we naturally focus on—the Galileans were innocent. They happened to catch Pilate in an unusual moment of unjustified fury.

Yet Jesus' point is not their specific innocence in this particular incident, but the fact that these victims bear a broader burden of guilt for sin that is no more and no less than that of their fellow Galileans. By implication, *all* people, regardless of the tragic circumstances they face, are equally guilty as sinners before a holy God.

If people do not repent, they will die in their sins and face eternal judgment. In other words, you can live to a ripe old age and die peacefully in your bed or you can be cut down prematurely, violently, your blood mingled with sacrifices, defiling the sacred worship of God. In either case, unless you repent, you will perish eternally.[90] The manner of one's death is irrelevant. You may die young or old. You may die justly or unjustly. You may die accidentally, a tower of stones crushing your fragile body (Luke 13:4), or you may die naturally, the normal course of life coming to its end after many fruitful years. But all face the same destiny. All are appointed to die, and then comes judgment (Heb. 9:27).

Suffering a tragic fate does nothing to mitigate one's culpability before God. Holocaust victims will not receive lighter treatment for their sins because they did not deserve their criminal treatment by detestable Nazis. They will be treated fairly by the God of perfect justice, bearing no greater

---

89. Darrell L. Bock, *Luke 9:51–24:53*, Baker Exegetical Commentary on the New Testament (Grand Rapids: Baker, 1996), 1205.

90. The word "perish" (*apollymi*) used in Luke 13:3, 5 does not mean merely "to die," but "to suffer loss via eternal perdition." This is often how the term is used in salvific contexts (cf. John 3:16; 10:28; 1 Cor. 1:18; 15:18). See Hans-Cristoph Hahn, "Destroy, Perish, Ruin," in *The New International Dictionary of New Testament Theology*, ed. Colin Brown (Grand Rapids: Zondervan, 1986), 1:464.

punishment than they incur by their own moral shortcomings. This means that they can also be assured that their oppressors will be treated as their deeds deserve (Rev. 20:13).

All sinners will be judged, and all sinners will be judged justly. Some, because of the heinous nature of their sins, will suffer far more than others (Luke 10:10–15). Therefore, we must conclude that one notably powerful purpose served by tragedy is this: it is a sobering call to repentance. It is an awakening moment whereby God's supreme holiness is on display. His transcendent righteousness *will be* vindicated. Tragedy is a loud siren blaring its warning to all people everywhere that death is imminent and that far greater disaster awaits you if you do not consider your helpless, wretched condition . . . *now*! It is a severe mercy, and we dare not miss its power to wreck our spiritual slumber and our callous disregard for what is truly important.

You do not know when death will come knocking at your door. Therefore, the threat of tragedy is a call to get your house in order before you stand at the foot of the supreme Judge.

The Problem of Hell

One last objection to divine retributive justice must be addressed. Throughout church history, there has been resistance to the doctrine of hell. That resistance has increased dramatically since the latter part of the twentieth century.[91] Albert Mohler writes:

> There are particular doctrines that are especially odious and repulsive to the modern and postmodern mind. The traditional doctrine of hell as a place of everlasting punishment bears that scandal in a particular way. The doctrine is offensive to modern sensibilities and an embarrassment to many who consider themselves to be Christians. Those Friedrich Schleiermacher called the "cultured despisers of religion" especially despise the doctrine of hell.[92]

91. Many evangelicals have abandoned the idea of hell as eternal conscious torment for more palpable positions regarding punishment for sin. The primary alternative has been annihilationism (sometimes called *conditionalism* or *conditional mortality*). Well-known evangelicals who have embraced this position include John W. Wenham, John R. W. Stott, W. Graham Scroggie, Michael Green, Philip E. Hughes, Clark H. Pinnock, Dale Moody, Edward W. Fudge, E. Earl Ellis, Anthony C. Thiselton, Ben Witherington, Roger E. Olson, and John Stackhouse. Others have tried to embrace some form of universalism or a Protestant version of purgatory.

92. R. Albert Mohler Jr., "Modern Theology: The Disappearance of Hell," in *Hell under Fire*, ed. Christopher W. Morgan and Robert A. Peterson (Grand Rapids: Zondervan, 2004), 37.

As we have already seen (in chapters 2 and 3), the Enlightenment has changed everything, starting with the nature of God. Many have protested that the Bible's clear teaching on hell, described as eternal conscious torment, makes God unjust and reflects a religion of fear. The God of such punishment is compared to "vindictive deities who delight in tormenting their victims."[93] It is said to fundamentally violate his love and goodness. Nonetheless, Scripture is clear that the unredeemed will go "into eternal punishment," while the redeemed will go "into eternal life" (Matt. 25:46).[94]

Is everlasting punishment unjust? *Finite* sins such as committing adultery, stealing a car, or killing a neighbor are serious moral infractions. But do they demand *infinite* punishment? Some earthly evils may demand a long sentence from the civil magistrate, maybe even capital punishment, but do all our collected earthly transgressions warrant a divine sentence that will never end? Do they warrant the unending infliction of torment that the Bible describes?

Annihilationism clearly has an emotional appeal. Serving a limited time in hell until one's crimes have been atoned for appears to make more sense. Once the sentence is complete, why not terminate the body and soul altogether—or, better yet, release the criminal and allow him a second chance? This question must not be dismissed. Why does eventual annihilation or postmortem opportunities for repentance as responses to temporal sins appear to be more just?

There are several ways to answer this perplexing matter. First, we fallen, finite creatures are in no position to determine for God what is just in punishing our own sin. Postmodern man is plagued with exalted views of our own goodness. There is a concerted refusal to consider that our definitions

93. Edward Fudge writing in Edward William Fudge and Robert A. Peterson, *Two Views of Hell: A Biblical & Theological Dialogue* (Downers Grove, IL: InterVarsity Press, 2000), 82.

94. Note the parallel between these two phrases indicating parallel eternal destinies. Both "eternal punishment" (*kolasin aionion*) and "eternal life" (*zoen aionion*) are preceded by the same accusative preposition "into" (*eis*). This means that both parties enter into a place that lasts eternally: the unredeemed "into" a place of eternal punishment and the redeemed "into" a place of eternal life. See also Daniel 12:2, where the same parallel exists. Jesus is most likely alluding to Daniel's statement (Joyce G. Baldwin, *Daniel*, Tyndale Old Testament Commentaries [Downers Grove, IL: InterVarsity Press, 1987], 204). See also Matt. 18:6–9; 25:31–46; Mark 9:42–48; 2 Thess. 1:6–10; Jude 7, 13; Rev. 14:9–11; 20:10, 14–15. For defenses of the orthodox doctrine of hell, see essays in Christopher W. Morgan and Robert A. Peterson, eds., *Hell under Fire* (Grand Rapids: Zondervan, 2004); Robert A. Peterson, "The Case for Traditionalism," in *Two Views of Hell: A Biblical & Theological Dialogue* (Downers Grove, IL: InterVarsity Press, 2000), 117–81; Robert A. Peterson, *Hell on Trial: The Case for Eternal Punishment* (Phillipsburg, NJ: P&R Publishing, 1995); Denny Burk, "Eternal Conscious Torment," in *Four Views on Hell*, ed. Preston Sprinkle, 2nd ed. (Grand Rapids: Zondervan, 2016), 17–43; W. G. T. Shedd, *The Doctrine of Endless Punishment* (1885; repr., Carlisle, PA: Banner of Truth, 1986).

of sin and evil not only downplay the divine revelation on these matters, but purposely subvert them.[95] We think that sin is not nearly as bad as the Bible asserts it to be.

Second, we delude ourselves about what constitutes the right response to the incorrigible depths of our own sin. D. A. Carson writes, "I doubt any of us is equipped to assess what is 'appropriate' punishment for defiance of the holy and sovereign God, save God himself."[96] Corresponding to our inflated self-worth, there is a tendency to domesticate God, to "de-god" him, as Carson says elsewhere.[97] The supremacy of God's holiness, righteousness, justice, and honor is severely underplayed even in our best moments. We dare not venture anywhere near the refulgence of his infinite and unbridled glory while bearing any taint of sin.

This is what Anselm had in mind (long before the self-absorption of postmodernism) when he indicated that sin offends the infinite honor of the Almighty, and for that reason alone demands everlasting punishment.[98] This truth is illustrated by considering the magnitude of the offense of killing Jesus, the Son of the living God. We must affirm that this is the greatest earthly crime ever committed, the only time in history that a truly innocent man was murdered—brutally so.

R.C. Sproul illustrates the point further:

> We can easily recall the name of the person who shot John Fitzgerald Kennedy on November 22, 1963, but can we recall as easily the name J. D. Tippet, the police officer the assassin allegedly shot on the same day? We remember details of the death of John Kennedy, but we forget the name of the other man who was killed by the same assassin on the same day in the same city. Why is murdering a policeman such a terrible crime? It is a crime to commit homicide at all, but the higher the office of the one killed, the greater the significance it holds for us. When a president is murdered, it is an assassination. It becomes an unforgettable moment in a nation's history. Yet the assassination of a president is nothing compared to the murder of the Prince of life Himself.[99]

95. D. A. Carson, *How Long, O Lord? Reflections on Suffering and Evil*, 2nd ed. (Grand Rapids: Baker Academic, 2006), 85–86.

96. Carson, *How Long, O Lord?*, 92.

97. D. A. Carson, *The God Who Is There: Finding Your Place in God's Story* (Grand Rapids: Baker, 2010), 33.

98. Anselm spells this out in *Proslogium*, chapters 8–11; and in *Cur Deus Homo* in book 1, chapters 11–15.

99. R.C. Sproul, *Acts*, St. Andrew's Expositional Commentary (Wheaton, IL: Crossway, 2010), 82.

This principle holds true in everyday life. It is worse to mistreat your elderly grandmother than it is to mistreat the stranger you just cut off on the freeway. Now, one may argue that a crime against one human is just as serious as it is against another, considering that all humans are equally made in God's image. But the murder of Jesus Christ is qualitatively different. He is the incarnate Son of God and therefore has a value that is infinitely greater than that of any ordinary human. Consequently, any sin against the infinite honor of God is an immeasurable offense requiring an immeasurable length of time to repay. Our obligations to God far exceed any obligations we have to ordinary persons.

Randy Alcorn brings further clarity to the matter: "Scripture nowhere teaches infinite punishment; rather, it teaches punishment proportionate to the evil committed. The confusion comes in mistaking *eternal* for *infinite*. No one will bear in Hell an infinite number of offenses; they will bear only the sins they have committed (see Revelation 20:12–13)." Alcorn continues, "It may take five seconds to murder a child, but five seconds of punishment would hardly bring appropriate justice. Crimes committed against an infinitely holy God cannot be paid for in finite measures of time."[100]

Conversely, Robert Peterson makes this point about Christ's bearing the punishment of sinners: "Because of the infinite dignity of Christ's person, his sufferings, though finite in duration, were of infinite weight on the scales of divine justice . . . . As God incarnate, Jesus was capable of suffering in six hours on the cross what we can suffer only over an infinite period of time."[101]

It is also important to consider that we have every reason to think that hell affords no opportunity for repentance. This is true not only because the damned are *incapable* of repentance, but more importantly because they are emphatically *undesirous* of repentance (Rom. 8:6–8). Jesus repeatedly described hell as a place of "weeping and gnashing of teeth."[102] The idiom "gnashing of teeth" expresses extreme suffering, anger, and, in particular, rage (Acts 7:54 NIV).[103]

The severe divine judgments connected to the tribulation as described by John in the book of Revelation produce not repentance, but rather blasphemy against God (Rev. 9:20–21; 16:9, 11, 21). If temporal judgments bring about rebellion and blasphemy against God, we can only imagine what rage will seethe within those suffering eternal torments.

100. Alcorn, *If God Is Good*, 317.
101. Peterson, "Case for Traditionalism," 175.
102. See Matt. 8:12; 13:42, 50; 22:13; 24:51; 25:30; Luke 13:28; cf. Acts 7:54.
103. Bock, *Luke 9:51–24:53*, 1238; R. C. H. Lenski, *The Interpretation of St. Luke's Gospel* (Minneapolis: Augsburg Publishing House, 1946), 752; Leon Morris, *Luke*, Tyndale New Testament Commentaries (Downers Grove, IL: InterVarsity Press, 1988), 248.

As Jeremy Evans notes, "Scripture indicates [that] . . . the effects of transgression on a person is that as we persist in these choices we forge a character toward a particular destiny, the culmination of which (in the negative sense) is a completely hardened heart against God."[104] Unchecked, sin deforms our character until it reaches the uncharted depths of perversity (Isa. 59:12–13).[105] Since the denizens of hell do not enjoy the calming, stabilizing, restraining presence of God (2 Thess. 1:9), they will rage against the Almighty in an unbridled frenzy. Their fulminations will never cease, nor will they stop storing up further divine wrath (cf. Rom. 2:5). Their perpetual recurring judgments will be fully justified.

Yes, this is a grievous state of affairs. And just as God finds no delight in the death and judgment of the wicked, neither should we (Ezek. 18:23; 33:11). Yet God must be just. His righteous justice must forever remain the foundation of his throne (Ps. 89:14).

TOWARD A MORE FAITHFUL THEODICY

After surveying these theodicies and defenses, where do we stand? While there is much to commend in the greater-good species of arguments, something is missing. It is difficult to conclude that the staggering ubiquity of evil in the world justifies whatever earthly temporal goods result, even if those goods are substantial. There must be some overarching transcendent purpose, some deeply rooted reason for evil's primordial existence, its infiltration and subversion of creation's pristine foundations.

Nothing prepared us for this strange and dissonant aberration. There must be a weight of goodness so great, bounding outward from evil's black core, that this sinister disruption of creation not only is justified but also pales in comparison to the other this-worldly goods that emanate from it. I hope to put forth an argument in the coming pages that highlights such a theodicy marked by a deep gravitas—an unearthly weightiness. It is a theodicy that stems from a grander view of God than is usually proffered by those who feel he is overshadowed by evil.

Many theodicists speak as though God were flummoxed by evil, that he knew it to be a possibility but couldn't imagine the force by which it overtook his creation. They speak as though God faced an insurmountable dilemma when confronted by this reality, that perhaps his scrutinized attributes were not up to the task. Maybe evil has caused his throne to falter a bit.

Nothing could be further from the truth.

104. Evans, *Problem of Evil*, 101.
105. Evans, *Problem of Evil*, 100.

There happens to be a theodicy that sees evil as no surprise, not even a possible surprise, but instead as that which meticulously follows a well-thought-out plan devised by the triune God long before he laid the foundations of the cosmos. Many of the theodicies and defenses set forth in this chapter are compatible with a broad spectrum of theological orientations. The theodicy that I will explore in the coming pages, however, takes the best advantage of their strengths in a way that is not always recognized, largely because they often fail in coming to grips with the greatness of God vis-à-vis the problem of evil that they are ostensibly explicating.

The theodicy that I will present is rooted in a self-consciously robust view of God that has been most thoroughly defended by classic Reformed (Calvinistic) theology. It is best described as a specific species of the greater-good argument combined with qualified aspects of the best-of-all-possible-worlds argument.

Many have dismissed Reformed efforts at defending a theodicy because of purportedly glaring weaknesses. Because the successors of Augustine and Calvin have a strong view of the sovereignty of God, the assumption is that they have a correspondingly weak view of his moral culpability for evil. Furthermore, divine culpability is one issue that has been conspicuously absent from the survey of the positions in this chapter. How do greater-good arguments address this thorny question?

The free-will defense boasts of its ability to deflect the matter altogether. Evil is an *unintended* by-product of God's granting his image-bearing creatures libertarian free will. Free will supposedly shifts moral responsibility from the Creator to the creature. In the greater-good brands of theodicy, evil is *intended* by God, and this appears to pose a greater liability for these positions, especially if they are tethered to Reformed theology, since it espouses God's meticulous providence over *all* the affairs of humanity, good and evil.

Yet Reformed theology is not disadvantaged at all. It has the resources to make better sense of moral responsibility than any other theological tradition. It has the resources to construct a more faithful theodicy. As I attempt to construct this theodicy in the chapters that follow, I will explore how it addresses these and many other issues.

KEY TERMS

best-of-all-possible-worlds defense
divine-judgment defense
gratuitous evil
greater-good theodicy

horrendous evil
skeptical-theism defense
soul-making theodicy

STUDY QUESTIONS

1. What is the basic idea behind the greater-good theodicy?
2. What are some examples in Scripture in which God brings good out of evil?
3. How does the greater-good theodicy respond to the charge that it has no way to justify any good that God might bring about from so-called gratuitous evils?
4. What are the strengths and weaknesses of the soul-making theodicy?
5. What are the strengths and weaknesses of the best-of-all-possible-worlds defense?
6. Why do people object to divine retribution and hell? How does the Christian respond to these objections?
7. Do you think the types of greater-good defenses represented in this chapter do a better job of answering the problem of evil than the free-will defense does? Why or why not?

FOR FURTHER READING

Christopher W. Morgan and Robert A. Peterson, eds., *Hell under Fire* (Grand Rapids: Zondervan, 2004).
Greg Welty, *Why Is There Evil in the World (and So Much of It)?* (Fearn, Ross-shire, Scotland: Christian Focus, 2018).
Stephen Wykstra, "The Skeptical Theist Response," in *God and the Problem of Evil: Five Views*, ed. Chad Meister and James K. Dew Jr. (Downers Grove, IL: InterVarsity Press, 2017), 173–84.

Advanced

David E. Alexander and Daniel M. Johnson, eds., *Calvinism and the Problem of Evil* (Eugene, OR: Pickwick Publications, 2016).

7

THE TRANSCENDENT
AUTHOR OF HISTORY

Nearly a thousand years before Christ's birth, the inquisitive king of the Hebrews—David, son of Jesse—gazed into a thick black, starry sky and then penned these words:

> When I look at your heavens, the work of your fingers,
>   the moon and the stars, which you have set in place,
> what is man that you are mindful of him,
>   and the son of man that you care for him?
> Yet you have made him a little lower than the heavenly beings
>   and crowned him with glory and honor. (Ps. 8:3–5)

If you live at least seventy-five miles from any city of more than a hundred thousand people, then you cannot look out into a clear summer sky without being amazed at the starry host, especially the densely pixelated cloud streaking across the expanse of the heavens that we call the Milky Way. If you spend enough time contemplating this wonder, you can't help but place yourself in David's state of mind, pondering your existence, your smallness, your fragility, your mortality—and then wonder why the majestic God who made all this should extend the least bit of thought toward you, let alone consider you and your kind the apex of all that he has created.

If David had taken the time to count, he might have numbered anywhere from twenty-five hundred to three thousand stars. If he had a telescope, he might have seen as many as a hundred thousand stars. Even at that rate, it would have been only the tiniest fraction of the 150 *billion* stars that make up our galaxy, and that is a modest estimate because we simply don't know. Yet ours is one of billions of other galaxies that we are only beginning to discover.

Consider the immensity of what David was looking at. If the Milky Way galaxy were the size of the North American continent, our minuscule solar system occupying a backwater portion of the galaxy would be the size of a cup of tea located somewhere in the barren desert of Nevada. If you searched inside that teacup for our humble little abode that we call planet Earth, you couldn't see it with your naked eye. You would need a powerful microscope to identify the poor little speck. And remember, ours is a modest galaxy.

In the vast expanse of our solar system, of our galaxy, of the unfathomable reaches of the universe, what is this earth? Who are these living, breathing, thinking creatures that inhabit this desperate outlier of the cosmos? Who are we that we'd even have the capacity to ponder such questions? It has been an ageless puzzle. It puzzled David millennia ago—and today with all our advances, our technology, our sophistication, it still puzzles us. But this quest for self-discovery is so alluring only because we instinctively know that our lives and this world are marked by a pervasive transcendence, or what Rudolf Otto called the *mysterium tremendum* ("fearful mystery").[1]

Slowing down to ponder the anatomy of the heavens has a way of bringing on this strange and awful sense that sweeps over us, making the hair on our arms stand on end, sometimes making us tremble. Suddenly the world—with its pleasures and pains, its trifles and troubles, its simple wonders and sinister affairs—seems to morph into a vague and distant dream. Our minds get swallowed up into something utterly other, something foreign and massive. We get transported from reality, and suddenly *everything* we are familiar with turns trivial. Our pretended place of importance in the world dissipates. The fearful mystery of something far, far bigger envelops our soul, and we gain a genuine, if fleeting, glimpse of our insignificance and of a deeper meaning to it all. And strangely, it feels right. It feels *true*.

What is this interruption? This brief transporting to transcendence? David knew.

It is what Moses encountered on the top of Sinai. What Isaiah saw in his vision of *the* temple. What Peter, James, and John witnessed at the Mount of Transfiguration.

It is the *holy*. It is a partial unveiling of the glory of the Most High. The reason why David is perplexed that humans should garner some small praise and that they retain an unexpected dignity is that the heavens reveal to

---

1. Rudolf Otto, *The Idea of the Holy* (Oxford: Oxford University Press, 1958).

us the transcendent Lord of the universe. Our value pales immensely, not within the scope of the vast cosmos and all its starry host, but in view of the one who created, sustains, and directs the entire expanse of time, space, matter, and existence. David frames his question about man in Psalm 8 with an exclamation about this God who dwells in unapproachable light: "O LORD, our Lord, how majestic is your name in all the earth! You have set your glory above the heavens" (v. 1; cf. v. 9). "Heaven, even highest heaven, cannot contain him" (2 Chron. 2:6).

Before we can make sense of where God intersects the presence of evil in this world, we must gain a glimpse of his transcendent character. Scripture uncovers a magnificent vision of God that is overwhelming. It makes small-souled people nervous. It is anchored in several unmistakable and fundamental truths. First, God's transcendence means that he is the eternal, infinite, wholly self-sufficient I AM. He is the uncreated Creator, Possessor, and Sustainer of all things.

Second, from this lofty position emerges God's supreme lordship. He is completely sovereign in decreeing all that transpires in the course of history. Then he providentially ensures that everything unfolds according to the divine plan. Third, this all-encompassing divine determinism is compatible with human freedom and responsibility. God does not operate as an impersonal fatalistic force. His sovereignty does not undermine or bypass human willing and choosing. He coerces no one to do what they do.

Having established these truths, we find that a second set of truths emerges. First, God is unassailable in his perfect righteousness and goodness, and could never entertain evil thoughts or plans. But second, we see that God's sovereignty *must* extend to evil. Evil cannot escape God's plans or his providential power. It has no independent power or designs that could undermine the transcendent Author of history. Thus, all the evil that transpires must conform to the goodness of his plans that can proceed from none other than the goodness of his character. Yes, there is profound tension here. God is wholly sovereign over evil and God is wholly good. But this is what we should expect from the incomprehensible holiness (otherness) of God.

So these twin truths render God free from all culpability for sin and evil. Responsibility for moral evil must be rooted in creaturely actions and their ill motives. Finally, this sets forth the criteria for making sense of the mysterious fact of the fall of our human parents, Adam and Eve. More importantly, it sets the stage for a more detailed theodicy that explains the reason for the fall. I will attempt to sketch this vision of God in this and the following two chapters.

A MAGNIFICENT VISION OF GOD

Humans are persistently inclined to paint their view of God with decidedly anthropomorphic hues. While the Bible often accommodates our understanding of God with such familiar language, we must never forget that he is infinitely more magnificent than anything or anyone that we can remotely imagine (Isa. 46:5).

Too many people desire to domesticate him. They want to fashion him into something more like us and not enough like the God he is. If we are ever to make sense of God's relationship to the world, to history, to human action, and particularly to evil, then we must grapple with a magnificent vision of God that rises above the paltry conceptions of mortal men. Such a vision arises only within the robust theistic worldview best expressed by the Reformed understanding of God's revelation of himself in Scripture.

B. B. Warfield explains this unique vision of God: "It lies in a profound apprehension of God in his majesty, with the inevitably accompanying poignant realization of the exact nature of the relation sustained to him by the creature as such, and particularly by the sinful creature."[2] He continues at length:

> [Calvinistic] theism comes to its rights only in a teleological conception of the universe, which perceives in the entire course of events the orderly outworking of the plan of God, who is the author, preserver, and governor of all things, whose will is consequently the ultimate cause of all.... [It is] the product of an overwhelming vision of God, born from the reflection in the heart of man of the majesty of a God who will not give his glory to another; can not pause until it places the scheme of salvation itself in relation to a complete world-view, in which it becomes subsidiary to the glory of the Lord God Almighty.... It begins, it centers, it ends with the vision of God in his glory: and it sets itself before all things to render to God his rights in every sphere of life-activity.[3]

The Incomprehensible, Holy, Transcendent Lord of All

While there exists a bridge between Creator and creature, an overlapping identity—especially between God and humans as his image-bearing creatures—the more proper starting place for understanding God is his incomprehensible holiness: his transcendence. That is, God is utterly *sui generis*—in a fundamental category of *otherness* whose alien depths simply

2. Benjamin B. Warfield, "Calvinism," in *The New Schaff-Herzog Encyclopedia of Religious Knowledge*, ed. Samuel Macauley Jackson (New York: Funk and Wagnalls, 1908), 2:359.
3. Warfield, "Calvinism," 2:360–61.

cannot be penetrated by finite minds. "God belongs to a different order of being to ourselves."[4]

> Can you find out the deep things of God?
> Can you find out the limit of the Almighty?
> It is higher than heaven—what can you do?
> Deeper than Sheol—what can you know?
> Its measure is longer than the earth
> and broader than the sea. (Job 11:7–9)

To speak of the "deep things of God" is to venture into subject matter incomparable to anything in the created universe.[5]

Bavinck observes, "The distance between God and us is the gulf between the Infinite and the finite, between eternity and time, between being and becoming, between the All and the nothing. However little we know of God, even the faintest notion implies that he is a being who is infinitely exalted above every creature."[6] Later Bavinck states, "There is no knowledge of God as he is in himself. We are human and he is the Lord our God. There is no name that fully expresses his being, no definition that captures him. He infinitely transcends our picture of him, our ideas of him, our language concerning him. He is not comparable to any creature."[7]

David Bentley Hart notes, "Much of the language used of [God] is negative in form and has been reached only by logical process of abstraction from those qualities of finite reality that make it sufficient to account for its own existence."[8] This is also why Scripture often resorts to anthropomorphic (humanlike) terminology to describe God.

We have no language to understand him as he is in himself. In fact, Bavinck says that when Scripture speaks of the nature, actions, and words of God, it "does not just contain a few scattered anthropomorphisms but is anthropomorphic through and through. . . . If God were to speak to us in a divine language, not a creature would understand him."[9] God is ineffable—words crumble to the ground when they try to wrap themselves around his essence.[10]

4. Graham A. Cole, *The God Who Became Human: A Biblical Theology of Incarnation* (Downers Grove, IL: InterVarsity Press, 2013), 37.

5. See also Ex. 8:10; 15:11; 1 Sam. 2:2; Pss. 8:1; 57:5, 11; 89:6–8; Isa. 40:18, 25; 46:5, 9.

6. Herman Bavinck, *Reformed Dogmatics*, ed. John Bolt, trans. John Vriend, 4 vols. (Grand Rapids: Baker Academic, 2003–8), 2:30.

7. Bavinck, *Reformed Dogmatics*, 2:47.

8. David Bentley Hart, *The Experience of God: Being, Consciousness, Bliss* (New Haven, CT: Yale University Press, 2013), 31.

9. Bavinck, *Reformed Dogmatics*, 2:99–100.

10. Matthew Barrett, *None Greater: The Undomesticated Attributes of God* (Grand Rapids: Baker, 2019), 23.

This does not mean that God is unknowable, but that "his greatness is unsearchable" (Ps. 145:3), given that he "dwells in unapproachable light" (1 Tim. 6:16). Bavinck sums it up: "God's self-consciousness is archetypal; our knowledge of God, drawn from his Word, is ectypal."[11] Archetypal knowledge is God's perfect knowledge of himself. Ectypal knowledge is derivative knowledge that comes from archetypal knowledge but is accommodated to our finite understanding.[12]

God always condescends to us, speaking to us, as Calvin puts it, in baby-talk.[13] Yes, we possess some rudimentary knowledge that is sufficient and true for the purposes of God's self-disclosure in both nature (Rom. 1:18–21) and Scripture (2 Peter 1:2–3), but such knowledge can never be exhaustive or exacting, let alone venture into the inscrutable heights of the Most High (Pss. 47:2; 97:9; Acts 7:48). There will always be mystery, a vagueness, an obliqueness whereby we view him as through "a mirror dimly" (1 Cor. 13:12).[14]

Thus, God's otherness, the unique holiness of divinity—"his transcendently august and venerable majesty"[15]—can be oriented around two poles. First, there are God's incommunicable attributes. In other words, whatever is true of God that is not true of us as his creatures speaks to his holiness.[16] Second, there are his communicable attributes. Whatever overlapping features exist between God and his image-bearing creatures (human beings) are incomprehensibly greater in God than in us, and this, too, speaks of his holiness.

George Swinnock says, "Even in these properties wherein man resembleth his Maker, he is exceedingly unlike him, and falls infinitely short of him."[17] We are vaguely *like* as well as utterly *unlike* God at the same time. Thus, when thinking of God, we stand at a precipice, trying to gaze across

11. Bavinck, *Reformed Dogmatics*, 2:107.

12. J. Todd Billings, *Union with Christ: Reframing Theology and Ministry for the Church* (Grand Rapids: Baker Academic, 2011), 86.

13. John Calvin, *Institutes of the Christian Religion*, ed. John T. McNeill, trans. Ford Lewis Battles (Philadelphia: Westminster, 1960), 1.13.1.

14. Barrett points out that our knowledge of God is neither univocal (identical to God's knowledge of himself) nor equivocal (uncertain); rather, it is analogical (sharing similarities but not identical to God's knowledge of himself). See *None Greater*, 33.

15. Archibald Alexander Hodge, *Outlines of Theology* (New York: Robert Carter and Brothers, 1879), 163.

16. Joel R. Beeke and Paul M. Smalley write: "Incommunicable pertains to [divine] attributes for which no analogy exists in human beings, such as God's eternity and omnipresence." Nonetheless, they write, "Many, if not all, of the incommunicable attributes find some resemblance in the created image of God. . . . There must be some creaturely analogy to these attributes for us to contemplate them" (*Reformed Systematic Theology*, vol. 1, *Revelation and God* [Wheaton, IL: Crossway, 2019], 543).

17. Quoted in Beeke and Smalley, *Revelation and God*, 543.

a vast chasm into a thousand suns searing black holes into our eyes. We must affirm with Augustine that the moment we begin to think we have fully comprehended God, we have comprehended something entirely other than God.[18]

To say that God is God is to say that he "is an unbounded sea of being."[19] The great I AM (Ex. 3:14) is Being itself—the infinite, all-encompassing wellspring of life and existence: of matter, spirit, time, motion, power, thought, order, design, beauty, virtue, purpose, and mystery formed together in all its wonderful complexity. Thus, he alone is uncreated, the ever-active uncaused cause of all (Aquinas's unmoved mover).[20] God is *a se* (having aseity)—that is, eternally independent, self-existent, self-sufficient, self-satisfied, having no need of anything outside himself (Acts 17:25).[21] This can be said of no one and nothing else. God is absolute. His existence, attributes, and actions have no antecedent causes; they are eternally self-determined. In this way, he is necessary, infinite, and transcendent.

By contrast, we are contingent, are finite, and exist in a narrow frame of immanence (this alone constricts our thoughts about God). The whole of creation, and especially God's image-bearing creatures, is *becoming*—that is, all created things come into existence out of nothing (*ex nihilo*) by God and for God (Rom. 11:36).[22] Furthermore, "he upholds the universe by the word of his power" (Heb. 1:3).[23] This means that we lowly creatures are wholly dependent on the one Creator for the continuous sustaining of every movement of every fiber of body, mind, and soul. "In him we live and move and have our being" (Acts 17:28).

We do not get to define what or who we are. We do not belong to ourselves. Since God created us, we belong to him together with all else

---

18. In seeking to formulate a faithful biblical model of God, theologians throughout church history have always encountered a tension between emphasizing his otherness (his transcendence) versus his relatedness (i.e., his immanence or nearness) in relation to his image-bearing creatures. See David Wells's discussion in *God in the Wasteland: The Reality of Truth in a World of Fading Dreams* (Grand Rapids: Eerdmans, 1994), 125–33.

19. Stephen Charnock, *The Existence and Attributes of God* (repr., Grand Rapids: Baker, 1996), 1:287, quoted in Barrett, *None Greater,* 148.

20. Aquinas borrowed the phrase *unmoved mover* from Aristotle but poured a whole different meaning into it, commensurate with the long-standing patristic tradition known as *classical theism.*

21. For a fuller treatment of God's aseity, see Barrett, *None Greater,* 55–69.

22. Passages that teach absolute creation *ex nihilo* include Isa. 44:24; 48:13; John 1:3; Rom. 4:17; Heb. 11:3. See also Gen. 1:1; Ex. 20:11; Neh. 9:6; Ps. 102:25; Eccl. 11:5; Isa. 45:12, 18; Acts 4:24; 14:15; 17:23–26; Col. 1:15–17; Rev. 4:11.

23. The Greek term translated "upholds" (*theron*) is a present active participle indicating continuous action. See also Col. 1:17. Nehemiah 9:6 says that God "preserves" (Heb. *hayyeh*) or "gives life" to his creation/creatures.

that he has created (Ps. 24:1).[24] We stand thoroughly accountable to his authority in all dimensions of our being. "For the LORD is our judge; the LORD is our lawgiver; the LORD is our king; he will save us" (Isa. 33:22). "All authority in heaven and on earth" rests with the divine Son of God (Matt. 28:18).

Therefore, it is not wise to chafe against the living God or his authoritative control. The Almighty owes us nothing (Job 41:11), and we owe him everything. As the humbled ruler Nebuchadnezzar was compelled to acknowledge, "All the inhabitants of the earth are accounted as nothing, and he does according to his will among the host of heaven and among the inhabitants of the earth; and none can stay his hand or say to him, 'What have you done?'" (Dan. 4:35). "Behold, the nations are like a drop from a bucket, and are accounted as the dust on the scales" (Isa. 40:15). All the material and immaterial forces of creation down to the tiniest particle and unit of energy are subject to his transcendent lordship.

And yet, in all this, God has come down to us. He is not *absolute* transcendence; otherwise, he would be completely unknowable. He has graciously condescended to our plain of existence. Every feature of his design and purpose for us serves in one way or another to drive our frail frames to *coram Deo*—to humbly live before the face of God, to flourish under his gracious gaze. "For thus says the One who is high and lifted up, who inhabits eternity, whose name is Holy: 'I dwell in the high and holy place, and also with him who is of a contrite and lowly spirit, to revive the spirit of the lowly, and to revive the heart of the contrite'" (Isa. 57:15).

The epitome of the immanence of God is wrapped up in the mystery of the incarnation, of Immanuel, God with us—the Son of God's emptying himself by assuming a human nature and submitting himself to the cruelest of humanly devised tortures, strangely enough, in order to rescue the same such cruel creatures (Phil. 2:6–7). Jesus Christ represents the paradoxical wonder of the transcendent and immanent God. And his life and work as the enfleshed God-man are so unexpected, so alien, that they serve to enhance the mystery of divine transcendence.

The Sovereign Author of All

So we see a logical progression in this understanding of God. We move from the matrix of his aseity, transcendent holiness, and incomprehensibility

---

24. God as Possessor of all things proceeds from God as Creator of all things. The heavens and earth belong to him (see Ex. 19:5; Deut. 10:14; Pss. 50:10–12; 95:3–7; 1 Cor. 10:26). The nations belong to him (see Pss. 22:28; 47:8–9; 96:10; Jer. 10:7; Mal. 1:11, 14).

to his status as Creator, Sustainer, and authoritative Lord of creation, and even as the God who condescends to and directly interacts with his creation. After apprehending the critical importance of this peculiar Creator-creature distinction, we can come to the distinctive outlines of his direct sovereignty. J. A. Crabtree argues that the sort of meticulous providence (i.e., comprehensive deterministic sovereignty) embraced by the biblical witness (as understood in the Reformed tradition) entails the primacy of God's transcendence.[25] He writes, *"To reject divine determinism is to deny the transcendence of God."*[26]

Likewise, Calvin understood the primacy of seeing God as transcendent Creator before considering him as the sovereign Lord over every meticulous and mundane aspect of creation: "Faith ought to penetrate more deeply, namely, having found him Creator of all, forthwith to conclude he is also everlasting Governor and Preserver—not only in that he drives the celestial frame as well as its several parts by a universal motion, but also in that he sustains, nourishes, and cares for, everything he has made."[27]

God alone is Creator and Sustainer of all, therefore Possessor of all, and therefore Lord of all. Without this vision of the incomprehensible, holy, transcendent Lord of the universe that frames our fundamental thoughts about God, we will go painfully wrong in trying to ascertain the nature of his sovereignty. We will end up domesticating it, making it more palatable for our narrow, anthropocentric (man-centered) tastes.

Some theologians think Scripture is unclear on what it means for God to be sovereign.[28] Nothing could be further from the truth. The question is whether we are prepared to accept its scathing verdict on our pretended autonomy and the desire to shield the Almighty from charges that he is a moral monster or the devil in disguise, all because our shortsightedness can't envision evil as falling within the bounds of his control and cosmic purposes. But this is precisely why God's sovereignty must always be seen in the light of these fundamental characteristics of his distinct Godness.

---

25. J. A. Crabtree, *The Most Real Being: A Biblical and Philosophical Defense of Divine Determinism* (Eugene, OR: Gutenberg College Press, 2004), 65–66.

26. Crabtree, *Most Real Being*, 66 (emphasis in the original).

27. Calvin, *Institutes*, 1.16.1. Crabtree affirms the same. See *Most Real Being*, 97–110. God's sovereignty entails not only the primacy of his transcendence but also his creation of all things *ex nihilo*. Crabtree writes, *"If it is true that the Bible teaches absolute divine creation* ex nihilo, *then the Bible necessarily teaches divine determinism"* (Crabtree, *Most Real Being*, 109 [emphasis in the original]). Note that the Westminster Confession places its chapter on "Creation" (chapter 4) before its chapter on "Providence" (chapter 5).

28. Thomas Jay Oord, *The Uncontrolling Love of God: An Open and Relational Account of Providence* (Downers Grove, IL: InterVarsity Press, 2015), 189.

Now, then, the sovereignty of God is an all-encompassing way to speak of his lordship over all that he has created. As David declares, "The Lord has established His throne in the heavens, and His sovereignty rules over all" (Ps. 103:19 NASB). Loraine Boettner places the sovereignty of God in its transcendent context: "The world as a whole and in all its parts and movements and changes was brought about into unity by the governing, all-pervading, all-harmonizing activity of the divine will, and its purpose was to manifest the divine glory."[29] God's sovereignty entails (1) his eternal decree, (2) his providence, and (3) his omnipotence. Let us consider each of these facets of divine sovereignty.

God's Decree

Scripture speaks of the decretive (sovereign) will of God whereby, as the Westminster Confession of Faith declares, "God, from all eternity, did, by the most wise and holy counsel of his own will, freely, and unchangeably ordain whatsoever comes to pass."[30] Before the onset of material and chronological reality, God ordained everything that "comes to pass," establishing the course of time and history, from the beginning of creation to the eternal kingdom that he will establish in the future.

His decree is eternal ("from all eternity") in that it was established before the foundation of the world (Eph. 3:11).[31] It is "unchangeable," meaning that God planned a fixed course for all things. No one and nothing can change what he determines to take place: "For the Lord of hosts has purposed, and who will annul it? His hand is stretched out, and who will turn it back?" (Isa. 14:27; cf. v. 24).[32] No plan of God's can fail; it is set in stone forever (Hab. 2:3).[33]

29. Loraine Boettner, *The Reformed Doctrine of Predestination* (Philadelphia: Presbyterian and Reformed, 1932), 14.

30. WCF 3.1 (on "God's Eternal Decree"). Passages indicating God's decretive will include Pss. 33:8–11; 103:19; Prov. 21:1; Isa. 14:24, 27; 46:10; Jer. 50:45; Lam. 3:37–38; Dan. 4:17; Acts 2:23; 4:27–28; Rom. 1:10; 9:19; 1 Cor. 1:1; Eph. 1:5, 9, 11; Phil. 2:13 (cf. Ezek. 36:27); Col. 1:19—James 1:18; 1 Peter 3:17; Rev. 4:11. God's decretive will is distinguished from his preceptive will—what God establishes as good, right, wise, and true—sometimes called God's *moral will* or *instructive will*. Passages indicating God's preceptive will include Ezra 10:11; Ps. 103:21; Isa. 65:12; Ezek. 18:23; Matt. 7:21; John 7:17; Acts 17:30; Rom. 12:2; Eph. 6:6; 1 Thess. 4:3; 5:18; Heb. 10:36; 1 Peter 4:2; 1 John 2:17. For further discussion, see John Piper, "Are There Two Wills in God?," in *Still Sovereign*, ed. Thomas R. Schreiner and Bruce A. Ware (Grand Rapids: Baker, 2000), 107–31, also available at http://www.desiringgod.org/resource-library/articles/are-there-two-wills-in-god; John M. Frame, *The Doctrine of God* (Phillipsburg, NJ: P&R Publishing, 2002), 531–42.

31. See also Pss. 33:11; 139:16; Isa. 37:26; Jer. 31:3; Matt. 25:34; Acts 15:18; 2 Tim. 1:9; 2 Thess. 2:13; 1 Peter 1:20.

32. See also Num. 23:19; 1 Sam. 15:29; Job 12:13–16; 42:2; Prov. 19:21; 21:30; Isa. 43:13; Dan. 4:35; Mal. 3:6; James 1:17.

33. See also Gen. 41:32; Job 14:5; Isa. 55:10–11; Jer. 15:2; 27:7; Hab. 2:3; Matt. 24:36; Luke 21:24; 22:22; John 8:20; 14:1–3.

Furthermore, God was not compelled to create the world or to order it in any particular manner except as proceeding from his "most wise and holy counsel." God will not author a story that reflects anything less than what his holy and perfect nature prescribes. He consulted no one (Isa. 40:13–14). He orders all things "freely" and self-determinedly, doing "all that he pleases" (Ps. 115:3; cf. 135:6).

He chooses some and not others (Rom. 9:15). Like a potter, he fashions each vessel for whatever purpose he has determined (vv. 20–21). And the products of his hands are in no position to question him:

> Woe to him who strives with him who formed him,
>   a pot among earthen pots!
> Does the clay say to him who forms it, "What are you making?"
>   or "Your work has no handles"?
> Woe to him who says to a father, "What are you begetting?"
>   or to a woman, "With what are you in labor?" (Isa. 45:9–10)

Note how God establishes his sovereign decree based on his transcendent nature as the one and only God. Speaking through Isaiah, he proclaims:

> Remember the former things of old;
> for I am God, and there is no other;
>   I am God, and there is none like me,
> declaring the end from the beginning
>   and from ancient times things not yet done,
> saying, "My counsel shall stand,
>   and I will accomplish all my purpose,"
> calling a bird of prey from the east,
>   the man of my counsel from a far country.
> I have spoken, and I will bring it to pass;
>   I have purposed, and I will do it. (Isa. 46:9–11)

The language here indicates a comprehensive view of time and events. The "end from the beginning" is a merism that implies everything in between. God's "declaring" (expressing his foreknowledge) what is yet to happen ("things not yet done") in the course of history is coterminous with his "counsel" that "shall stand."

Indeed, as the psalmist declares, "The counsel of the Lord stands forever, the plans of his heart to all generations" (Ps. 33:11; cf. Prov. 19:21). He will sovereignly ensure that absolutely everything, having declared it all beforehand as part of his eternal "purpose," will be accomplished.

Predictive prophecy is simply a rare instance of God's choosing to reveal to us beforehand what he plans to do in the future (Gen. 18:17–18). His plan includes the actions of his creatures, whether a lowly "bird of prey" or "the man of my counsel." God simply speaks forth what he plans to do, and then he brings it to pass: "I have purposed, and I will do it."

Paul paints a similar comprehensive picture of God's sovereign decree. In Ephesians 1, the apostle places the divine election of the "saints who . . . are faithful" (v. 1) that occurred "before the foundation of the world" (v. 4) within the broader context of God's "plan for the fullness of time" that includes "things in heaven and things on earth" (v. 10). This is clearly a cosmic perspective, encompassing the full gamut of events in the universe. This plan is the unveiling of the "mystery" of God's decretive "will" that is established "according to his purpose" (v. 9).[34]

The fulfillment of this plan is centered on the central figure of history, Jesus Christ. It is he who will "unite all things" (v. 10), bringing together all the seemingly loose ends of history (as seen from our perspective). Paul is primarily concerned with how the "predestined" church figures in this plan of God (v. 11). Predestination here "is but an instance or example of a more general activity—God's choice of all things."[35]

In other words, this small, albeit critical, part of history's broader narrative plot is "according to the purpose of him who works all things [i.e., 'things in heaven and things on earth'] according to the counsel of his will" (v. 11). There is no indication here that anything is left out. God ordains absolutely everything that comes to pass.[36]

God's Providence

God is not only the Architect of history, but also its executor. He ensures that his plans are carried out per his designs. What he has purposed, he will do (Isa. 46:11). This is what Paul means when he tells us that God "works all things according to the counsel of his will" (Eph. 1:11). The moment God acts, things happen (Isa. 48:3). God's providence is not a general guidance, as free-will theists propose,[37] but a meticulous providence—a finely detailed

---

34. Note that Ephesians 1:5 also indicates that divine predestination (adoption) is part of God's decretive "will."

35. John S. Feinberg, *No One like Him: The Doctrine of God* (Wheaton, IL: Crossway, 2001), 514.

36. For a thorough defense that Ephesians 1:11 teaches meticulous providence against objections by those espousing general providence and libertarian free will (i.e., free-will theists), see Feinberg, *No One like Him*, 680–93.

37. Jack W. Cottrell, "The Nature of the Divine Sovereignty," in *The Grace of God, the Will of Man*, ed. Clark H. Pinnock (Minneapolis: Bethany House, 1989), 106–13; Gregory A. Boyd, "God Limits His Control," in *Four Views on Divine Providence*, ed. Stanley N. Gundry and Dennis W. Jowers (Grand Rapids: Zondervan, 2011), 183–208.

outworking (execution) of his decree in the temporal unfolding of history whereby he superintends every event, action, and creaturely decision.[38] Calvin stresses that divine providence is "not an idle observation by God in heaven of what goes on in earth, but His rule of the world which He made; for He is not the creator of a moment, but the perpetual governor. Thus the providence we ascribe to God belongs not only to His eyes but to His hands."[39] The Heidelberg Catechism defines divine "providence" as "the almighty and ever present power of God by which God upholds, as with his hand, heaven and earth and all creatures, and so rules them that leaf and blade, rain and drought, fruitful and lean years, food and drink, health and sickness, prosperity and poverty—all things, in fact, come to us not by chance but by his fatherly hand."[40] Nothing happens independent of his sustaining and governing power. There is not a single errant atom drifting about in the cosmos.

Historically, divine providence has been understood by Reformed theologians to contain three dimensions.[41] First, *government* refers to God's specific guidance of history to achieve his desired ends (i.e., what he decrees). Second, *preservation* refers to God's sustaining power that lies behind the laws of nature. Such laws are simply a way for us to accurately quantify the fact that "he upholds the universe by the word of his power" (Heb. 1:3; cf. Col. 1:17). Third, *concurrence* indicates God's normative manner of working through secondary causes to accomplish his designs, including the laws of nature and the compatibilistically determined choices of human beings.[42]

This indicates the *ordinary* means of his providence. At other times, God acts directly and immediately to accomplish his purpose, bypassing secondary causes. This indicates his *extraordinary* providence. Such rare providential actions include what we call *miracles*—that which cannot be

---

38. Numerous passages indicate a sweeping range of God's sovereign/providential activity. Bruce Ware calls these "spectrum texts" in "A Modified Calvinist Doctrine of God," in *Perspectives on the Doctrine of God: 4 Views*, ed. Bruce A. Ware (Nashville: B&H Academic, 2008), 94. See, for example, Num. 24:23; Deut. 32:39; Josh. 21:44; 1 Sam. 2:6–7; 1 Chron. 16:31; Job 42:2; Pss. 2:4; 10:16; 24:7–10; 29:10; 33:8–11; 47:7; 75:6–7; 106:2; 115:3; 127:1; 135:6; 145:1–3, 21; Prov. 21:1; Eccl. 7:13–14; Isa. 14:24, 27; 29:15–16 (potter-clay image; cf. Isa. 45:9–10; 55:10–11; 64:8; Jer. 18:1–10; Rom. 9:20–21); 33:22; 40:15, 17; 43:11–13; 44:6–8, 24–28; 45:5–7, 23; 46:9–11; 48:12–13; 55:11; Lam. 3:37–38; Dan. 2:21; 4:17, 34–35; Matt. 28:18; 1 Cor. 15:28; Eph. 1:22; Phil. 3:20–21; Rev. 19:16 (cf. 1 Tim. 6:15; Rev. 17:14). Note especially that Isaiah 40–48 is a comprehensive apology of Yahweh's power and sovereignty.

39. John Calvin, *Concerning the Eternal Predestination of God*, trans. J. K. S. Reid (Louisville, KY: Westminster John Knox Press, 1961), 162.

40. Lord's Day 10: Q&A 27.

41. Louis Berkhof, *Systematic Theology* (1941; repr., Grand Rapids: Eerdmans, 1996), 169–76; WCF 5.1–3 (on "Providence").

42. See discussion on compatibilism below (pages 170–76).

explained by any quantifiable, natural, normal, repeatable process (i.e., laws of nature). How do you explain a woman's being created from a rib (Gen. 2:22), the sun's standing still (Josh. 10:12–14), a floating axe head (2 Kings 6:5–7), a child's being born of a virgin (Luke 1:34–35), wine's emerging from water (John 2:7–11), thousands' being fed from a boy's lunch (John 6:1–14), or the resurrection of the dead (Luke 24:1–12)?[43]

Paul indicates this cosmic, comprehensive, and meticulous providence of God, saying that there is "one God and Father of all, who is over all and through all and in all" (Eph. 4:6). Scripture speaks repeatedly and abundantly of God's "causing" or "bringing" about events, thoughts, responses, and actions covering the full gamut of reality.[44]

The providential actions of God include the forest as well as the trees. He sets forth times, seasons, and sweeping epochs, determining the status of the nations, places where men will live, and where kings will rule.[45] He determines the time and place of all who are born, when and how they will die, and what their station in life will be.[46] "The LORD kills and brings to life; he brings down to Sheol and raises up. The LORD makes poor and makes rich; he brings low and he exalts" (1 Sam. 2:6–7).

But he also acts in the insignificant and mundane realities of his creation. He feeds the birds and cares for the lilies of the field (Matt. 6:26, 28–30). Not one sparrow falls to the ground unless God so determines (Matt. 10:29). His hand causes lightning to strike its mark precisely (Job 36:32). As Calvin comments, "It is certain that not one drop of rain falls without God's sure command."[47] When people cast lots and their dice are thrown, he alone ensures the results (Prov. 16:33). There are no random arrows flying about (1 Kings 22:28, 34). God's universe contains no chance events.[48] Chance is an illusion, an ill-conceived notion of a godless worldview.[49]

---

43. These miraculous incidents assume the literal and historical veracity of the narrative accounts from which they come. See pages 254–58.

44. For example, many Hebrew verbs in the Old Testament are expressed in the hiphil stem, which indicates active causation. In innumerable instances, God is the subject of such verbs in relation to what transpires in natural and human events. See Bruce K. Waltke and M. O'Connor, *An Introduction to Biblical Hebrew Syntax* (Winona Lake, IN: Eisenbrauns, 1990), 433–46.

45. Isa. 40:15; Dan. 2:21; Acts 1:7; 14:16–17; 17:26.

46. Gen. 21:2; Ex. 4:11; Job 14:5; Pss. 31:15; 139:16; Isa. 45:7; James 4:14–15. Note passages indicating that God opens and closes wombs (e.g., Gen. 16:2; 20:18; 30:2; Pss. 113:9; 127:3).

47. Calvin, *Institutes*, 1.16.5.

48. Gen. 37:28; 45:5; 1 Sam. 9:5–10, 15–16; Job 5:6; Jonah 1:7; Mark 14:30; Acts 1:24, 26.

49. Calvin, *Institutes*, 1.16.2. See also R.C. Sproul and Keith Mathison, *Not a Chance: God, Science, and the Revolt against Reason* (Grand Rapids: Baker, 2014); Vern S. Poythress, *Chance and the Sovereignty of God: A God-Centered Approach to Probability and Random Events* (Wheaton, IL: Crossway, 2014).

God's Omnipotence

God's sovereign decree and his providential execution of it would mean nothing unless he possessed the requisite power necessary to make it all happen. As King Jehoshaphat declared: "O LORD, God of our fathers, are you not God in heaven? You rule over all the kingdoms of the nations. In your hand are power and might, so that none is able to withstand you" (2 Chron. 20:6).

All orthodox Christians (including most free-will theists) agree that God is omnipotent—possessing the power to do anything that (1) is logically possible and (2) does not contradict his other attributes.[50] For example, God cannot perform pseudo-actions such as making square circles or irresistible forces colliding with immovable forces.[51] He cannot do anything unrighteous or unjust. God has no power to sin. John Frame clarifies what all this means:

> We cannot define precisely what God is able to do. But we are confident that he can do everything Scripture describes him as doing, and much more. And we know that the only preventers are his own truth, righteousness, faithfulness, and so on. That fact should assure us that God is entirely competent to accomplish all his righteous, loving purposes.[52]

While God's possession of such power is largely uncontroversial in orthodox theology, what most free-will theists deny is God's unrestricted use of such power. They suppose that God respects the libertarian free will of humans above his own unrestricted free and sovereign manifestation of power.[53] Furthermore, love is regarded as his supreme attribute, exalted above all others. As a result, his love proscribes the extent to which he can rightfully exercise his power.

---

50. Anthony Kenny, "The Definition of Omnipotence," in *The Concept of God*, ed. Thomas V. Morris (Oxford: Oxford University Press, 1987), 132; Frame, *Doctrine of God*, 518–21.

51. George I. Mavrodes, "Some Puzzles concerning Omnipotence," in *The Power of God*, ed. Linwood Urban and Douglas N. Walton (New York: Oxford University Press, 1978), 131–34.

52. Frame, *Doctrine of God*, 523. So we must deny that God has absolute power whereby he could do absolutely everything infinitely conceivable, as William of Occam (1285–1347) proposed. If true, God's nature would be entirely eviscerated. One could not distinguish him as righteous or unrighteous, just or unjust, loving or hating, wise or foolish, good or evil. He would be nothing but unqualified raw power with an unfettered brand of libertarian freedom. Frame indicates that defining omnipotence apart from the fullness and unity of God's revealed attributes (i.e., his simplicity) would be to have no God at all (523–24). See also Barrett, *None Greater*, 190–95.

53. Roger E. Olson, *Arminian Theology: Myths and Realities* (Downers Grove, IL: InterVarsity Press, 2006), 131.

For example, Greg Boyd thinks that God "rules by love, not control."[54] But this does not accord with the testimony of Scripture that we have seen thus far. Job understood the immensity and incomprehensibility of God's power when describing his cosmic actions in the heavens and on earth (Job 26:5–13), and then he goes on to declare: "These are just the beginning of all that he does, merely a whisper of his power. Who, then, can comprehend the thunder of his power?" (26:14 NLT).

Isaiah picks up where Job left off:

> Do you not know? Do you not hear?
>   Has it not been told you from the beginning?
>   Have you not understood from the foundations of the earth?
> It is he who sits above the circle of the earth,
>   and its inhabitants are like grasshoppers;
> who stretches out the heavens like a curtain,
>   and spreads them like a tent to dwell in;
> who brings princes to nothing,
>   and makes the rulers of the earth as emptiness.
>
> Scarcely are they planted, scarcely sown,
>   scarcely has their stem taken root in the earth,
> when he blows on them, and they wither,
>   and the tempest carries them off like stubble.
>
> To whom then will you compare me,
>   that I should be like him? says the Holy One.
> Lift up your eyes on high and see:
>   who created these?
> He who brings out their host by number,
>   calling them all by name;
> by the greatness of his might
>   and because he is strong in power,
>   not one is missing. (Isa. 40:21–26)[55]

History's Transcendent Author

This picture of an unfathomable and transcendent Lord presiding over the wondrous works of his hands lends itself to a particular model of divine

---

54. Gregory A. Boyd, *God of the Possible* (Grand Rapids: Baker, 2000), 69.

55. Cf. Isa. 40:28–31. Other passages indicating the mighty power of God include Gen. 18:14; Ex. 15:6; Num. 11:23; Job 38–41 (see esp. 38:31–33); 42:2; Pss. 62:11 (cf. Job 40:9); 147:4–5; Isa. 40:3–5, 10, 12–17; 44:24–28; 45:9–10; 50:2; 59:1; Jer. 10:12; 32:17; Matt. 19:26; 26:53; Mark 14:36; Luke 1:37, 51–52; Eph. 1:19–21; 3:20; Phil. 3:21; Heb. 1:3; Rev. 4:11; 11:17; 19:1.

sovereignty and providence. God doesn't set forth a chain reaction of events in time and space that follow a crass form of cause and effect. History is not an elaborate maze of dominoes set in motion by the Primordial First Cause.[56] The determinism that the Bible ascribes to God is not mechanistic, as though humans were just cogs in a grand machine.[57]

To be sure, we must not pretend that we can know the precise manner of how God causally determines the course of events in history.[58] There is a dynamic mystery to the divine outworking of God's decree. In either case, the model that best suits God's providence evokes the image of a *transcendent author.*[59]

Yet God is not like a Shakespeare, a Milton, a Tolstoy, or a Tolkien. He is not to be likened to some prolific playwright or scripter of grand epics. Quite the opposite. It is the perennial earthly storyteller who mirrors God. The Most High is not *like* an author. He is *the* Author. The human author is like him. God is the paradigmatic Narrator. He is the composer of an epic oratorio, pulling every instrument, every voice, every disparate movement into a harmonious and triumphant crescendo.

History—excuse the triteness of the muddled etymology—is indeed *his story.* The plotline of history is but an extension and expansion of the narrative arc that marks the pages of divine Scripture, beginning in Genesis and ending in the Revelation of John the Apostle.

The classical theist David Bentley Hart, strangely enough, rejects this model of providence: "God will not unite all of history's many strands in one great synthesis, but will judge much of history false and damnable."[60]

56. James N. Anderson, "Calvinism and the First Sin," in *Calvinism and the Problem of Evil,* ed. David E. Alexander and Daniel M. Johnson (Eugene, OR: Pickwick Publications, 2016), 207–8.

57. Greg Welty, "Molinist Gun Control: A Flawed Proposal? A Reply to Kenneth Keathley's 'Friendly Reply,'" in *Calvinism and Middle Knowledge,* ed. John D. Laing, Kirk R. MacGregor, and Greg Welty (Eugene, OR: Pickwick Publications, 2019), 85.

58. For a discussion of the difficulties behind specifying the precise nature of divine determinism and causality, see James N. Anderson's article "Calvinism and Determinism," at https://www.proginosko.com/2014/07/calvinism-and-determinism/. See also comments by Paul Helm in "Response to John Sanders," in *Perspectives on the Doctrine of God: 4 Views,* ed. Bruce A. Ware (Nashville: B&H Academic, 2008), 243; and Welty, "Molinist Gun Control," 83–86.

59. Crabtree, *Most Real Being,* 110–41, 225–44; Anderson, "Calvinism and the First Sin," 208–10.

60. David Bentley Hart, *The Doors of the Sea: Where Was God in the Tsunami?* (Grand Rapids: Eerdmans, 2005), 104. Hart distorts the Reformed view of divine sovereignty, using the derisive moniker "dread sovereignty" (89). He ponders, "One wonders, indeed, if a kind of reverse Prometheanism does not lurk somewhere within such a theology, a refusal on the part of the theologian to be a creature, a desire rather to be dissolved into the infinite fiery flood of God's solitary and arbitrary act of will. In any event, such a God, being nothing but will willing itself, would be no more than an infinite tautology—the sovereignty of glory displaying itself in the

If this is true, then some of God's enemies can claim victory because he was unable to utilize his goodness, wisdom, power, and foreknowledge to overcome some of the actors he created. And it is this notion that is false and damnable. Hart has failed to grapple with the testimony of Scripture. In contrast, Loraine Boettner writes:

> From the divine viewpoint there is unbroken order and progress from the first beginnings of the creation to the end of the world and the ushering in of the kingdom of heaven in all its glory. The divine purpose and plan is nowhere defeated nor interrupted; that which in many cases appears to us to be defeat is really not such but only appears to be, because our finite and imperfect nature does not permit us to see all the parts in the whole nor the whole in all its parts. If at one glance we could take in "the mighty spectacle of the natural world and the complex drama of human history," we should see the world as one harmonious unit manifesting the glorious perfections of God.[61]

Thus, history is not a chess match whereby God merely anticipates the moves of his creatures like a grand master.[62] Such a model of providence places God in the position of acting and reacting in relation to the semiautonomous plans of others seeking to wrest control of history for themselves. It suggests that his plans operate on the fly, contingent and dependent on each disparate direction his creatures take.

Furthermore, if they have libertarian free will, then he can never have certainty of what their choices may be. There is always the possibility that his plans can be foiled. Perhaps he can ensure some things here or there, but we would have no guarantee of a cohesive purposeful outcome.

Such a God would not evoke our confidence or deserve our worship. In contrast, the God that the psalmist declares is a bulwark for our trust in him: "Let all the earth fear the LORD; let all the inhabitants of the world stand in awe of Him. For He spoke, and it was done; He commanded, and it stood fast" (Ps. 33:8–9 NASB). Such a God gives us confidence that when tragedy strikes, when we "hoped for good" and "evil came," and when we "waited for light" and "darkness came" (Job 30:26), there is no need to fret.

---

glory of sovereignty—and so an infinite banality" (91). Hart acts as though Reformed theology extracted God's sovereignty from the totality of his other attributes (love, goodness, mercy, wisdom, justice, etc.) and thus denied the simplicity and unity of God's being and attributes. Nothing could be further from the truth.

61. Boettner, *Reformed Doctrine of Predestination*, 15.

62. Peter Geach, *Providence and Evil: The Stanton Lectures 1971–2* (Cambridge: Cambridge University Press, 1977), 58–59.

God is firmly in control. He "is our refuge and strength, a very present help in trouble" (Ps. 46:1).

THE COMPATIBILITY OF DIVINE AND HUMAN ACTIONS

When we consider God's sovereignty over the forest, few people object. But when we consider his sovereign control over individual trees, people start to squirm in their seats, especially if those trees include the leaves, branches, trunks, and roots of their own personal lives. The fact is, human actions are not exempt from the providence of God but represent the particular emphasis of Scripture. God's fixed decree includes the future actions of specific individuals.[63] Human choices are determined by God.

But this does not entail some notion of Christian fatalism—an oxymoron if there ever was one. Fatalism is a distinctive pagan brand of mindless and impersonal determinism. The Bible nowhere portrays such an idea. Loraine Boettner gives a good definition of *fatalism*:

> All events come to pass through the working of a blind, unintelligent, impersonal, non-moral force which cannot be distinguished from physical necessity, and which carries us helplessly within its grasp as a mighty river carries a piece of wood.... It snatches the reins of universal empire from the hands of infinite wisdom and love, and gives them into the hands of a blind necessity. It attributes the course of nature and the experiences of mankind to an unknown, irresistible force, against which it is vain to struggle and childish to repine.[64]

God is not the grand puppet master, and we are not dangling marionettes devoid of active minds, emotions, desires, and wills. We make real choices, with real consequences that proceed from real deliberations, motives, and circumstances that shape the outcomes of those choices. Nonetheless, those choices dovetail perfectly with the sovereign determinations of God. This is known in today's philosophical parlance as *compatibilism*.

Defining Compatibilism

The Westminster Confession's statement on "God's Eternal Decree" (3.1) begins by saying, "God, from all eternity, did, by the most wise and holy counsel of his own will, freely, and unchangeably ordain whatsoever comes to pass." But then the statement makes this important qualification: "yet

---

63. See, for example, Gen. 18:17–19; Jer. 1:5, 9–10; Dan. 2:28; Matt. 20:18–19; Luke 22:34 (cf. v. 61); John 6:64; James 4:13–16.
64. Boettner, *Reformed Doctrine of Predestination*, 205.

so, as thereby neither is God the author of sin, nor is violence offered to the will of the creatures; nor is the liberty or contingency of second causes taken away, but rather established."

We will consider the statement about God's being the author of sin in chapter 9, but for the moment let us focus on the last two clauses: "nor is violence offered to the will of the creatures; nor is the liberty or contingency of second causes taken away, but rather established." The Confession affirms compatibilism. Biblical compatibilism states that God's meticulous sovereignty (determinism) is compatible with human freedom and responsibility.[65]

Thus, there is a dual explanation for every choice that we human beings make. God's sovereign determination serves as the sufficient *primary* (ultimate) but *remote* cause of our choices, while we serve as the *secondary* but *proximate* (the near or immediate) cause of our choices. While there is some degree of mystery in acknowledging this "double agency" (dual causation), there is nothing contradictory in affirming it. Paul Helm brings some clarity here: "The primary cause [God] is an enabling and sustaining cause, making possible secondary causes and setting bounds to them." Furthermore, the primary (divine) cause is not an event in time, whereas the secondary (human) cause is. Rather, it is "an eternal cause which has the whole of the creation as its effect."[66] Secondary causes have no independent power. Everything we say and do is dependent on God.[67]

Yet God's causal power is rarely if ever directly experienced. Most people are unaware that he stands behind the choices they make. In this regard, God's fixed providential direction is never coercive. He never moves people to act against their will. This is in spite of the protestations of those like Paul's interlocutor in Romans 9:19 who say, "Why does [God] still find fault? For who can resist his will?"

The implication is that God is morally culpable for people's actions, even their sinful ones. But James 1:13 is emphatic: "Let no one say when he is tempted, 'I am being tempted by God,' for God cannot be tempted with evil, and he himself tempts no one." One of the implications here is that God does not infuse an evil will into the one who sins. Satan does not coerce people either. The evil one's temptations are powerful and debilitating (2 Cor. 4:4), but sinners willfully abide by the "desires" of the devil (John 8:44) of their own accord.

---

65. For a fuller treatment and biblical defense of compatibilism, see my book *What about Free Will? Reconciling Our Choices with God's Sovereignty* (Phillipsburg, NJ: P&R Publishing, 2016).
66. Paul Helm, *The Providence of God* (Downers Grove, IL: InterVarsity Press, 1994), 86.
67. Helm, *Providence of God*, 87.

Ultimately, the sinful inclinations of the heart instrumentally determine whether temptation is given into (James 1:14). When Yahweh hardened Pharaoh's heart (Ex. 14:4), the Egyptian despot did not struggle against God's providential determination. Pharaoh's "stubborn" will was in full accord with the sovereign will of God (7:13–14 NASB). Pharaoh acted voluntarily without coercion, and thus was fully responsible for his actions (9:34) even as they necessarily followed God's deliberate determination. Exodus 10:27 tells us that Yahweh "hardened Pharaoh's heart," yet Pharaoh "was not willing" to let God's people go (NASB).

Now, from the human side of the equation, tangible factors serve as complementary explanations for the choices we make. Namely, we always choose according to the matrix of *internal* dispositions and *external* temporal influences that direct us to the path that we are most inclined to take. We always choose what we most *want* to choose, and what we most want to choose corresponds to our *strongest* motives, desires, and internal inclinations as influenced by a variety of external factors, such as our immediate circumstances, our interpersonal interactions, our upbringing, our education, the influence of authority figures, the sources of media we consume, and so forth. To the extent that any given external factor forms a coercive influence such that our choices are constrained by them, then we are less free, and thus correspondingly less responsible for our actions. If little Johnny is threatened with violence by big Billy the bully if he doesn't pull Sally's hair, then he is less morally culpable than he would be if he did the dastardly deed without Billy's bullying.

When all is said and done, as Jonathan Edwards says, "a man never, in any instance, wills anything contrary to his desires, or desires anything contrary to his will."[68] Another way to put the matter is that we act in a way that seeks to preserve our self-interest. Jesus declares, "For where your treasure is, there your heart will be also" (Matt. 6:21).

The seventeenth-century French scholar Blaise Pascal agrees:

> All men seek happiness. This is without exception. Whatever different means they employ, they all tend to this end. . . . The will never takes the least step but to this object. This is the motive of every action of every man.[69]

We will make a contrary choice only if the antecedent factors lead to a *sufficient* motive that appeals to our self-interested inclinations.

---

68. Jonathan Edwards, *The Freedom of the Will*, vol. 1 of *The Works of Jonathan Edwards*, ed. Paul Ramsey (New Haven, CT: Yale University Press, 1957), 139.

69. Blaise Pascal, *Pascal's Pensées*, trans. W. F. Trotter (New York: E. P. Dutton, 1958), 113 (thought #425).

Remember Mary and her pancakes?[70] When she walks into the diner, she is inclined to order those fluffy stacks of scrumptiousness that she loves, not the bland omelet. But if the diner has run out of her prized blueberry syrup, Mary is suddenly dejected because she hates all other syrups, and that becomes for her the *sufficient* reason to choose the omelet instead.

Choosing based on this natural self-love is reflected in the Golden Rule. Again, Jesus teaches, "So whatever you wish that others would do to you, do also to them, for this is the Law and the Prophets" (Matt. 7:12). We are to look not merely to our own interests, as is naturally expected, but to the interests of others (Phil. 2:3–4). In either case, self-interested love is a built-in preservation mechanism that drives our decision-making, and Jesus and Paul acknowledge this. We often struggle with *competing* motives within. Ted has fallen for both the Firebird and the Thunderbird. He likes both so much that it is hard to distinguish which car he prefers most, but he has the money to purchase only one. So sooner or later, the attractive features of one of the vehicles will draw out the strongest motive, and he will make his choice.

On the other hand, our sense of self-preservation is often caught between *conflicting* motives, and we are compelled to choose the lesser of two evils. "I don't *want* to give this thug all my money, but then I *really* don't *want* that .45 caliber he is pointing at my head to expel all my brain matter on the sidewalk. So . . . I will (reluctantly) give the man the money." Decisions are eventually made once a clear, even if slight, winner emerges out of the matrix of *conflicting* and *competing* motives that battle within.[71]

But another matter that takes us further into the inner chambers of our decision-making nucleus is critical to the biblical model of free agency. It brings us face to face with the most important choices we make—those of a moral and spiritual nature.

Let us summarize. First, we choose what we *most want* to choose. Second, what we most want to choose stems from our *strongest motives* as influenced by various internal and external factors. But third, all moral and spiritual decisions are circumscribed by the spiritual condition of our hearts.

The language of the "heart" in the anthropology of the Bible speaks to our basic spiritual and moral nature as human beings. The default position of every person is to be enslaved to a fundamentally corrupt nature at the core of our souls. Jesus warns, "Everyone who practices sin is a slave to sin" (John 8:34). We are spiritually "dead in trespasses and sins" (Eph. 2:1,

70. See pages 95 and 99.
71. See Christensen, *What about Free Will?*, 156–62.

5). According to Romans 8:7, because the "flesh"-bound sinner is "hostile" toward the things of God, the sinner has neither any *moral ability* ("cannot") to submit to God's righteous laws nor any *desire* ("does not") to submit to them. Thus, we are ironically free and enslaved at the same time so long as we are tethered to this corrupted nature.

In order for us to make choices that have any kind of genuine moral and spiritual value, a radical change must take place within. Our corrupted natures must undergo a metamorphosis. We must be born again—regenerated by the power of the Holy Spirit (John 3:4–8). We must be "made alive together with Christ" (Eph. 2:5) before we are able to make decisions that are truly God-pleasing and God-glorifying in nature. This transformation is not self-generated. It must result from the electing love of God (Eph. 1:4–5), who calls us and draws us out of "the pit of destruction, out of the miry bog," and then sets our "feet upon a rock" of unshakable, unbreakable salvation (Ps. 40:2).

This means that salvation is not *synergistic*, meaning "two [*syn-*] agents working [*ergon*]," but *monergistic*, meaning "one [*mono-*] agent working [*ergon*]." We do not cooperate with the grace of God, as Arminianism teaches. The Reformed principle of *sola gratia* ("grace alone") means that God's gracious action is sufficient to bring about the conversion of sinners.

In free-will theism (particularly Arminianism), grace is necessary but not sufficient. The self-generated faith of the unbelieving sinner must cooperate with divine grace, either accepting or rejecting it via libertarian free will, before salvation accrues to the sinner.[72] This makes salvation ultimately dependent on the sinner and not the grace of God. But Scripture (Calvinism) slays all boasting in ourselves (1 Cor. 1:26–31). We have no inherent capacity for faith or repentance. Divine grace must radically renew our corrupted natures so that our hearts are effectually and irresistibly enabled to choose Christ for salvation (Eph. 2:8–9). Thus, regeneration of necessity must precede faith, making salvation truly and wholly a work of grace.[73]

Biblical Evidence for Compatibilism

The evidence for the dual agency marking biblical compatibilism is pervasive in Scripture.[74] The book of Proverbs contains general statements to this effect: "The heart of man plans his way, but the LORD establishes his steps"

---

72. In classical Arminianism, this is known as *prevenient grace*. See Olson, *Arminian Theology*, 154.

73. For a fuller treatment of these issues, see Matthew Barrett, *Salvation by Grace: The Case for Effectual Calling and Regeneration* (Phillipsburg, NJ: P&R Publishing, 2013).

74. For a more detailed look at the biblical evidence for compatibilism, see Christensen, *What about Free Will?*, 93–133.

(16:9). "Many are the plans in the mind of a man, but it is the purpose of the LORD that will stand" (19:21). "The king's heart is a stream of water in the hand of the LORD; he turns it wherever he will" (21:1).[75]

Revelation 17 indicates that a coalition of peoples ("ten horns") will give their allegiance to the Antichrist ("the beast"), yet in their doing so, God will "put it into their hearts to carry out his purpose by being of one mind" (v. 17). James instructs his readers not to be presumptuous about their future plans, for they cannot know what God has planned for them (James 4:15; cf. 1 Cor. 4:7). Isaiah declares, "O LORD, you are our Father; we are the clay, and you are our potter; we are all the work of your hand" (Isa. 64:8).[76] Many similar passages indicate that people serve as God's providential instruments. Such texts never convey a sense of divine coercion or that somehow people's choices are made mindlessly or unwillingly.[77]

Some striking examples of compatibilism are indicated by complementary texts in which one passage (or statement) speaks of human actors' standing behind a particular action, while the corresponding passage (or statement) attributes the same action to God.

For example, Genesis 45:4 indicates that Joseph's brothers are the culprits for selling him into slavery. Joseph tries to calm them: "Now do not be distressed or angry with yourselves because you sold me here." But then he turns around and states that it was God who did this act (vv. 5, 7). Joseph does not shy away from the paradoxical tension in the juxtaposition of these notions when he says moments later, "So it was not you who sent me here, but God" (v. 8). This does not deny his brothers' part in the incident; it indicates that God is the primary actor.

Likewise, when Jonah disobeys God's call to preach to the Ninevites, God "hurled" a great storm into the sea (Jonah 1:4). As a result, the frightened sailors "picked up Jonah and *hurled* him into the sea" as well, after which God caused the sea to "cease from its raging" (v. 15).[78] Yet in chapter 2, we learn that it is not merely the sailors who hurled the wayward prophet "into the heart of the seas," but also God who did (2:3).

Acts 2 records Peter's momentous sermon on the day of Pentecost. In the climax of his message, he zeroes in on the central matter of importance to

---

75. See also Prov. 16:1; 20:24; cf. Ezra 6:22 (cf. 7:6); Ps. 37:23; Jer. 10:23.

76. Again, take note of similar potter-clay passages: Isa. 29:15–16; 45:9–10; Jer. 18:1–10; Rom. 9:20–21.

77. See, for example, Isa. 10:15; 13:5; 44:28; 46:11; Jer. 1:5; 50:25; Hab. 1:5–13; Acts 9:15; Rom. 9:20–23.

78. As a side note, God's providence is clearly at work in directing the weather here.

the proclamation of the gospel: the cross of Christ. The apostle does not shrink from confronting his Jewish audience, declaring, "You crucified and killed" Jesus "by the hands of lawless men" (v. 23). Later, in Acts 4, the gathered church prays to the "sovereign Lord" (v. 24) and acknowledges specific culprits in this incident: "For truly in this city there were gathered together against your holy servant Jesus, whom you anointed, both Herod and Pontius Pilate, along with the Gentiles and the peoples of Israel" (v. 27).

In both records of the incident, deliberate actions are attributed to human agents, who acted voluntarily and without coercion. But this does not paint the full picture. Peter adds to his charge a critical piece of information: "This Jesus" was simultaneously "delivered up according to the definite plan and foreknowledge of God" (2:23). In the same way, the praying church adds that Pilate, Herod, the Gentiles, and the Jews simply colluded with one another "to do whatever your hand and your plan [i.e., the 'sovereign Lord'] had predestined to take place" (4:28; cf. v. 24).

The work of salvation and of the sanctification that accompanies it is wholly of God and his grace. But this does not leave its recipients in a state of passivity. Jesus states that the "Father gives" a people to him to be redeemed. And of these that the Father gives, he says, "All . . . will come to me, and whoever comes to me I will never cast out" (John 6:37). The Father first "gives," and then inevitably those whom he gives "will come"—not forcibly, not robotically, but of their own accord.

Paul and Barnabas obediently and boldly preached to Galatian Gentiles, "And as many as were appointed to eternal life" by the sovereign decree of the Lord responded appropriately and "believed" (Acts 13:48; cf. 18:9–10). Lydia acted in faith in response to the preaching of Paul only because "the Lord opened her heart to respond" (16:14 NASB). God's people have a moral obligation to be holy, to be sanctified; yet it is God who ultimately sanctifies (Lev. 20:7–8).

Paul calls believers in Philippians 2:12 to "work out" the sanctifying dimension of their "salvation with fear and trembling," suggesting the sorts of humble motives that they are to cultivate as they actively seek to grow in Christ. And yet it is not their own work, but "God who works in you, both to will and to work for his good pleasure" (v. 13; cf. 2 Thess. 2:13). Paul acknowledges that he has "worked harder" than any of the other apostles to proclaim the gospel of the risen Lord, "though it was not I, but the grace of God that is with me" (1 Cor. 15:10).[79]

---

79. See also Gal. 2:20; Eph. 1:19; 3:20; Phil. 1:16; 4:13; Col. 1:22–23, 29; Heb. 13:20–21.

THE GOD OF EVIL?

We have provided a biblical vision of God's sovereign and meticulous decree in which he ensures that its blueprint for history will providentially come to fruition. We have also shown that God's sovereignty is not at odds with the voluntary choices of responsible and willing agents. Scripture clearly affirms both facts. But how do these facts bear on the ubiquitous presence of evil in the world? Does God's sovereign will encompass that which violates his moral precepts—indeed, his own moral character? Does God merely *allow* evil, or is it part of his eternal decree for history? And if it is part of his eternal decree, then how can he escape the charge that he is to be ultimately blamed for a plan that includes what we know is destructive to human flourishing? It appears to violate his impeccable goodness. This is the most difficult question that Reformed theology faces. How does it address this charge? We will explore some answers in the next two chapters.

KEY TERMS

Calvinism
compatibilism
decretive will (of God)
fatalism
immanence (of God)
meticulous providence
omnipotence (of God)
transcendence (of God)
transcendent Author (God as)

STUDY QUESTIONS

1. What attribute or set of attributes is the proper starting place when thinking about who God is? Explain why.
2. What are the three ideas that entail the Reformed (Calvinistic) view of divine sovereignty? Explain each of these ideas.
3. How does viewing God as a "transcendent Author" help us to understand the biblical model of his sovereignty and providence?
4. What is the compatibilistic view of human freedom and responsibility?
5. What are some biblical examples of compatibilism?
6. How has your own view of God changed over time? How have these changes affected the way in which you live your life?

FOR FURTHER READING

Matthew Barrett, *None Greater: The Undomesticated Attributes of God* (Grand Rapids: Baker, 2019).

Scott Christensen, *What about Free Will? Reconciling Our Choices with God's Sovereignty* (Phillipsburg, NJ: P&R Publishing, 2016).

John M. Frame, *The Doctrine of God* (Phillipsburg, NJ: P&R Publishing, 2002).

Paul Helm, *The Providence of God* (Downers Grove, IL: InterVarsity Press, 1994).

Advanced

Herman Bavinck, *Reformed Dogmatics*, ed. John Bolt, trans. John Vriend, 4 vols. (Grand Rapids: Baker Academic, 2003–8).

J. A. Crabtree, *The Most Real Being: A Biblical and Philosophical Defense of Divine Determinism* (Eugene, OR: Gutenberg College Press, 2004).

Jonathan Edwards, *The Freedom of the Will*, vol. 1 of *The Works of Jonathan Edwards*, ed. Paul Ramsey (New Haven, CT: Yale University Press, 1957).

John S. Feinberg, *No One like Him: The Doctrine of God* (Wheaton, IL: Crossway, 2001).

8

WALKING THROUGH THE
BIBLE'S DARK FOREST

When you tread through the landscape of the Bible, it doesn't take long before you encounter shadowy corners, unnerving places that disturb the unsuspecting and faint of heart. It is like walking into parts of Fangorn Forest from Tolkien's Middle-earth where the Great Darkness still lingers. In other words, the Bible is not a sanguine book. It is not a placid child's tale. It has hard edges, dangerous themes, and raw footage of sinister episodes. The divine revelation does not shrink back from evil in all its feral and inglorious realism.

Since the dawn of writing, no book, no writer, no chronicler of history, no crafter of literary arts has painted evil with starker colors or tones. The unvarnished ugliness of evil points to the Bible's historicity and veracity. No other ancient writing lays bare the violence of its villains and the weaknesses of its heroes as Scripture does. Furthermore, the Bible's God does not hide behind comfortable platitudes. His white-hot holiness is not disturbed or in any way dimmed in the slightest by the cold-black presence of wickedness as it wafts into his pristine order.

Many Christian philosophers and theologians are quick to shield God's providence from evil, supposing that he might become contaminated by exposure to it. But the God of the Bible shows no such concern. He gladly declares both his full control over and his intricate plans for the same evil he hates with a holy hatred and thus condemns in no uncertain terms. This paradoxical feature of the biblical witness—God's holy sovereignty walking alongside repulsive wickedness—is foundational for grasping a scriptural theodicy. And there is no question, this paradox is perplexing.[1] How can

1. The word *paradox* here is used in the sense of two or more disparate realities that appear

God decree and ensure (in his meticulous providence) the happening of things that he otherwise vehemently opposes? Does this not make him some kind of cosmic schizophrenic? A psychopathic deity?

As I hope to show, the tensions in this paradox are clearly displayed in the teaching of Scripture. And this leaves theologians with a dilemma. It has resulted in two fundamental but opposing visions concerning God, man, and evil. One vision is to downplay or reinterpret the biblical data. It seeks to exonerate God at all costs, putting forth a picture of reality in which his providence is curtailed in one degree or another at the expense of granting humanity an unwarranted level of autonomy via free will (defined in libertarian terms). This more anthropocentric (man-centered) vision is promoted by the free-will theists associated with Arminianism, Molinism, and open theism. It is reflected in the free-will defense.

We have already explored the opposing vision, which sees God in his unbridled glory. It is decidedly theocentric (God-centered). This is the God as explicated in the classical and Reformed tradition—the God of Augustine, Anselm, Calvin, Luther, Owen, Edwards, Warfield, Sproul, and Packer. It is reflected in the greater-good brands of theodicy. Humanity's role is not denigrated here; it is shown to give way to a God of a far grander and more all-encompassing nature than many of his timid apologists are wont to afford him.

These opposing visions can be seen in two respected theologians who see God at work in tragedy with far different spectacles. Both men lost their precious daughters to premature deaths. Both reflected on God's role in those deaths, but their conclusions differ profoundly. The New Testament scholar Ben Witherington's thirty-two-year-old daughter Christy died of a pulmonary embolism in 2012. Witherington writes, "God did not do this to my daughter. . . . God does not terminate sweet lives."[2] This is a powerful statement that resonates with many who grieve. We cannot conceive of a good God's taking our loved ones in the prime of their lives.

Witherington goes on to say, "I do not believe in God's detailed control of all events." He references the words of Job, who lost not one but all of his daughters—*and* his sons. Job responds, "The LORD gave, and the LORD

---

to pose a contradiction when no real contradiction exists. The doctrine of the Trinity and the hypostatic union of Christ the God-man are examples of such biblical paradoxes. Joshua Rasmussen makes a helpful distinction: "A paradox is something we do not see how to put together, whereas a contradiction is something we do see cannot go together" (*How Reason Can Lead to God: A Philosopher's Bridge to Faith* [Downers Grove, IL: InterVarsity Press, 2019], 15).

2. See http://unitedmethodistreporter.com/2012/04/06/death-of-a-daughter-our-experience-of-grief-begins-with-a-good-god/.

has taken away; blessed be the name of the LORD" (Job 1:21). Witherington suggests, "This is not good theology." He believes that to utter such words is to venture into blasphemy. He asserts that it was the devil, not God, who took his daughter Christy away.

We can only wish, however, that Witherington had taken the time to contemplate the divinely inspired commentary offered by the author immediately after the afflicted Job claims that God took his children: "In all this Job did not sin or charge God with wrong" (v. 22). Job rightly assigns *responsibility* to God for this calamity, but the infallible words of his biographer carefully note that Job does not assign *moral culpability* to God. There is a vast difference here. While we must not turn cold and unsympathetic, after the dust of grief and death settles, we must note something amiss in Witherington's understanding of God.

Contrast this with the words of theologian Fred Zaspel, writing about his daughter Gina, who died at age twenty-nine after battling a great illness for twelve years. She died about a year after Ben Witherington's daughter did.

> Through the years of her suffering we reminded ourselves often that the God who in grace had rescued her in Christ from sin loves her even more than we do. And so we trust his providence. He is too wise ever to make a mistake, and too good ever to do us wrong. And we acknowledge that just as he was free and sovereign in giving Gina to us 29 years ago, so now he is free and sovereign—and good and just—in taking her. He has not wronged us. Indeed, not only do we affirm this great truth—we rest in it. This God is himself our Father, a Father who knows what is best for his children and faithfully directs our lives accordingly. Moreover, he is the Father who in love one day gave up his own Son to bear our curse in order to redeem us to himself. Yes, there are many "Why?" questions that we cannot answer, but we lack no proof of God's love or his goodness. And we bless him today with deeper passion than ever.[3]

Zaspel would concur with the theological vision of Steve Saint, who says of his missionary father's being murdered by Waodani warriors in 1956, "God planned my dad's death."[4] Job is even more stark in his appraisal of God's sovereign but mysterious ways: "Though he slay me, I will hope in him" (Job 13:15; cf. Hab. 3:17–18).

There is no question that this way of thinking about divine providence transports us to some of the more incomprehensible dimensions of the

---

3. https://credomag.com/2013/11/reflections-on-the-loss-of-our-daughter-fred-zaspel/.
4. See pages 117–19.

transcendent God that we canvassed in the previous chapter. Only the Augustinian-Calvinist-Reformed tradition penetrates the darkened mysteries of the fall, of evil, of all the cursed movements of natural calamity and human ill-will. No other theological orientation can adequately handle the weight of theodicy without cringing or collapsing underneath its terrifying demands.

Yet what should be surprising to skeptics is how such a God has sustained an equally transcendent hope in many who have traveled the darkest portals of pain, malice, and atrocity. Consequently, this theological vision does not result in a crass, unfeeling triumphalist perspective, as some accuse it of. It rests in a supremely confident, purposeful victory that satisfies the deep-seated longing we all have to see evil summarily defeated and some sense made of its existence. But most of all, it casts a brilliant light on a God of such unfathomable wonder and glory as to leave us dumbfounded and ready to fall on our knees in a trembling, self-effacing, yet gratifying posture of sweet adoration.

GOD'S ABSOLUTE GOODNESS

Before we can adequately consider God's sovereign relationship to evil, it is important to affirm the doctrine of God's absolute goodness. This is the one premise concerning the nature of God in the traditional trilemma forming the problem of evil that remains uncontestable and uncontroversial. Recall again these three propositions about reality:

1. God is omnipotent (all-powerful).
2. God is omnibenevolent (all-good).
3. Evil exists.

Premise 3 is a given unless one holds the untenable position that evil in this world does not exist or is simply an illusion (such as some Eastern religions teach).

The crucial question for Christians concerns the relationship between premises 1 and 2. The question is not whether there is a conflict between the two premises, but how their meanings complement each other in light of premise 3. Premise 1 is generally where the problem lies. How do we construe the omnipotence of God? More precisely, how does the exercise of his power relate to the broader question of his sovereignty in relation to evil? Does God's sovereign power extend over the forces of evil? Does he permit evil? Or does he positively decree each instance of it? If the latter is the case, then does this not undermine his goodness? Does it not make him morally responsible for evil?

We will address these questions shortly. But the answers given by the Augustinian-Calvinist-Reformed position quickly come under fire as if they somehow denied premise 2 altogether, that God is not all-good. Jerry Walls suggests, "The Calvinist must sacrifice a clear notion of God's goodness for the sake of maintaining his view of God's sovereign decrees."[5] But nothing could be further from the truth.

All orthodox Christians agree on the general outlines of how to construe God's goodness. Nonetheless, we must see that God's goodness and his power as the sovereign God necessarily go together. They must never in any circumstances be separated. God's sovereignty never trumps his goodness, as some accuse Calvinism of teaching. And let's be honest—some unthinking Calvinists have led many to suppose that this is the Reformed position. On the other hand, God's goodness never trumps his sovereignty.

Many free-will theists emphasize God's love and goodness as the controlling paradigm for solving the problem of evil. But the unity and simplicity of God's being mean that we cannot single out one of his attributes and place it above another. "All the attributes are equally God's being. In him there is no higher and lower, no greater and smaller."[6] The God of mercy is equally the God of justice. The God of love is equally the God of wrath. Wrath cannot be understood apart from God's love, and vice versa.[7]

Now, when we come to speak of God's goodness, it is a way of encompassing the perfections of what makes him supremely attractive, especially to the faithful worshiper of God. God's goodness speaks of his unbridled beauty (Ps. 27:4). When Moses sought to see the divine glory—the full refulgence of Yahweh's unveiled being—God responded by saying that "all my goodness" would pass before the prophet (Ex. 33:19). He is *absolute* goodness in the sense that he alone is marked by the beauty and perfections of all that is good (Matt. 5:48; Mark 10:18). He is the "overflowing fountain of all good."[8]

David declares, "Oh, taste and see that the Lord is good! Blessed is the man who takes refuge in him!" (Ps. 34:8). In this regard, God's goodness

5. Jerry Walls, "The Free Will Defense, Calvinism, Wesley, and the Goodness of God," *Christian Scholar's Review* 13.1 (1983): 29.

6. Herman Bavinck, *Reformed Dogmatics*, ed. John Bolt, trans. John Vriend, 4 vols. (Grand Rapids: Baker Academic, 2003–8), 2:216.

7. Joel R. Beeke and Paul M. Smalley, *Reformed Systematic Theology*, vol. 1, *Revelation and God* (Wheaton, IL: Crossway, 2019), 628.

8. Belgic Confession, art. 1.

is simply his benevolence. God does that which is to the benefit of his creation. He is the source of all natural, moral, and spiritual good.[9] "The LORD is good to all, and his mercy is over all that he has made" (Ps. 145:9; cf. vv. 13–16).[10] The well-being of creation and its creatures is owed to the blessings of a supremely good God. He is love (1 John 4:8). He is kindness (Ps. 145:17). He is faithfulness (Ps. 36:5). He is eternally merciful and gracious (Lam. 3:22). He is marked by long-suffering, steadfast loyalty, and forgiveness toward ill-deserving sinners (Ex. 34:6–7). Nothing impedes his "abundant goodness" (Ps. 145:7).

God's goodness is also closely connected to his holiness, especially as that rich term refers to his distinctly exalted moral purity.[11] God is wholly righteous and free of any taint of evil, of any moral defilement. God is called "The Rock, his work is perfect, for all his ways are justice. A God of faithfulness and without iniquity, just and upright is he" (Deut. 32:4). The apostle John declares, "God is light, and in him is no darkness at all" (1 John 1:5). God "dwells in unapproachable light" (1 Tim. 6:16), meaning that he subsists as a God of white-hot righteousness. All his moral actions are circumscribed by his righteous character.[12]

Thus, it is impossible for him to entertain an evil thought or intention. There is no possible scenario in which God could contemplate an evil thought, utter an evil word, or commit an evil deed: "Hear me, you men of understanding: far be it from God that he should do wickedness, and from the Almighty that he should do wrong" (Job 34:10).

The prophet Habakkuk extols the unparalleled outlook of his righteous God: "You . . . are of purer eyes than to see evil and cannot look at wrong" (Hab. 1:13). David is even more emphatic: "For you are not a God who delights in wickedness; evil may not dwell with you" (Ps. 5:4). There is no place in the being of God where evil can enter and make itself a home. All manner of wickedness is repugnant to such a holy God (Prov. 6:16–19).

God's righteousness means that he demands obedience of his image-bearing creatures. Every human being is under a divinely mandated obligation to abide by the moral law that God has inscribed on our hearts (Rom. 2:14–15). When he issues his commands, they are never contrary to his own righteous character. Six times in the book of Leviticus, Yahweh demands of

---

9. Bavinck, *Reformed Dogmatics*, 2:213.

10. See also Ps. 16:2; Matt. 5:45; Acts 14:17; James 1:17.

11. Beeke and Smalley write: "We may speak of God's moral holiness not as a separate attribute from God's majestic holiness [his transcendence], but as another dimension of the one divine holiness" (*Revelation and God*, 575).

12. John M. Frame, *The Doctrine of God* (Phillipsburg, NJ: P&R Publishing, 2002), 446.

his people, "Be holy, for I the Lord your God am holy."[13] As God is morally perfect, he calls all to emulate his perfection (Matt. 5:48).

Furthermore, the demands of an impeccably righteous God also indicate that he is wholly just. He rewards righteousness equitably and punishes all wickedness impartially (Ex. 34:7; 1 Sam. 26:23; Rev. 20:12–13). He will never leave righteousness to fail nor evil to ultimately triumph. All wrongs will be righted. Once he hands down his perfectly just verdicts, they will prevail.

The Almighty is also "the great and dreadful God" (Dan. 9:4 kjv); he "is a consuming fire" (Heb. 12:29). Rebellion against him is folly. Evildoers will tremble before his bar of perfect justice. "It is a fearful thing to fall into the hands of the living God" (Heb. 10:31). According to the oracle of doom in Isaiah 13:6–13, "every human heart will melt" one day before the "fierce anger" of God Almighty. "Pangs and agony will seize" those who have not repented of their pomp and arrogance. The supreme Judge will come on "the day of the Lord" to "destroy sinners" and bring "desolation" to their habitation. No creatures will escape his evaluation of their moral status and the reception of their just recompense.

Since all have sinned and fallen short of the glory of his moral perfection (Rom. 3:23), each person faces one of two destinies. Some will be justified by his grace through the redemption of his Son (Rom. 3:24), and the "fullness of joy" that proceeds from God's presence and goodness is their inheritance forevermore (Ps. 16:11). All others will face the terrifying prospect of having to "suffer the punishment of eternal destruction, away from the presence of the Lord and from the glory of his might" (2 Thess. 1:9), because of their disbelief in and dishonor of him, and their unrepentant rebellion against him.

Having sketched this portrait of God's goodness, how can we say that it coheres with his sovereignty over evil? Making sense of the matrix of divine goodness and divinely sovereign power at the intersection where evil makes itself known is central to the task of theodicy. Free-will theism has been found wanting. What about Reformed theology and its greater-good proposals?

GOD'S SOVEREIGNTY OVER EVIL

The default orientation of most Christians, including some Reformed theologians, is to construe God's sovereignty with a great degree of caution to preserve his perfect goodness and unblemished righteousness. There is no

13. See Lev. 11:44–45; 19:2; 20:7, 26; 21:8.

reason to fault this impulse, as we will see. No Christian, including the Calvinist, wants to implicate God in evil. Yet to say that God is sovereign over *all* things cannot admit exceptions without equivocating on terms.

If God's sovereign decree is all-encompassing and his providence is meticulously administered (as we have shown), then there is no shrinking away from the obvious—God must determine all evil to take place. And this is not something to be embarrassed about. As Jonathan Edwards has said, it is far better that "the good and evil which happens in God's world, should be ordered, regulated, bounded and determined by the good pleasure of an infinitely wise Being" than by impersonal chance or the unpredictable and futile machinations of men's free will.[14]

But it is one thing to cite passages of Scripture that make broad affirmations of meticulous sovereignty; what about specific affirmations of the causal connection between God and evil?

The Transcendent Lord of All Calamity

To see this connection, we must return to Scripture's declaration of God's transcendent lordship as clearly seen in passages such as Isaiah 46:9–11 (see comments in chapter 7). Such far-reaching, all-encompassing, and mind-boggling views of the enormousness of God are extended to include a darker reality in a parallel passage a few pages earlier. God speaks to the great Medo-Persian king, Cyrus, "his anointed" (Isa. 45:1):

> I am the LORD, and there is no other,
>> besides me there is no God;
>> I equip you, though you do not know me,
> that people may know, from the rising of the sun
>> and from the west, that there is none besides me;
>> I am the LORD, and there is no other.
> I form light and create darkness;
>> I make well-being and create calamity;
>> I am the LORD, who does all these things. (Isa. 45:5–7)

Again, Yahweh sets himself apart from other so-called gods, and from every creature. He subsists in a class by himself. In other words, Yahweh "is *categorically different in nature and existence* from everything he has made."[15] Thus, he seeks to magnify his utter uniqueness, his otherness, his

14. Jonathan Edwards, *The Freedom of the Will*, vol. 1 of *The Works of Jonathan Edwards*, ed. Paul Ramsey (New Haven, CT: Yale University Press, 1957), 405.

15. Peter J. Gentry and Stephen J. Wellum, *Kingdom through Covenant: A Biblical-Theological Understanding of the Covenants*, 2nd ed. (Wheaton, IL: Crossway, 2018), 649.

transcendence, his supreme holiness, and his incomprehensible glory as the infinite, everlasting God.

Corresponding to this emphatic claim, he makes a stunning declaration regarding his sovereignty over evil through the mouth of his prophet Isaiah. The repeated merisms of "light" and "darkness" along with "well-being" and "calamity" indicate two poles that include everything in between. The term "calamity" (v. 7) is the standard Hebrew term for "evil" (*ra'*).[16] Not only that, but the passage uses a special word for "create" (*bara'*) twice (v. 7) in connection to "darkness" and "calamity" (evil). This term is reserved in the Old Testament for God's creative activity alone (e.g., Gen. 1:1; Ps. 51:10; Isa. 42:5; 43:1).[17] God is therefore affirming that he alone is the ultimate source of the transpiring of all evil, moral as well as natural, in an "all-inclusive sense."[18]

The context here is important. It is difficult to conceive that God could retain his absolute goodness while being the untainted ordainer of evil unless it has first been established that God exists *sui generis*—as the uniquely exalted Lord of heaven and earth, of space and time, of the visible and invisible, of all rulers and authorities—indeed, of good *and* evil.

A similar exalted view of God's sole transcendent rule and authority is affirmed by Jeremiah: "Who has spoken and it came to pass, unless the Lord has commanded it? Is it not from the mouth of the Most High that good and bad come?" (Lam. 3:37–38; cf. Eccl. 7:14). First, God is acknowledged as the ultimate source for all that comes to pass (v. 37). He commands, and it is accomplished (cf. Isa. 48:3). In similar fashion to Isaiah 45:7, "good and bad" (Lam. 3:38) indicates a comprehensive scope to what God determines to transpire. The term "bad" (like "calamity" in Isaiah 45:7) is yet again the standard Hebrew term for "evil." Yet notice that it is not some lowly entity that is the source for these occurrences, but the "Most High."

The broader context for Jeremiah's pronouncement is the affliction that the weeping prophet has experienced by watching his beloved city of Jeru-

---

16. William A. VanGemeren, *New International Dictionary of Old Testament Theology & Exegesis* [*NIDOTTE*] (Grand Rapids: Zondervan, 1997), 3:1155–56. See also Amos 3:6 for a similar usage of *ra'/ra'a'*. Similar merisms occur in Exodus 4:11, where God tells Moses that he makes men "mute, or deaf, or seeing, or blind." In Deuteronomy 32:39, he says, "See now that I, even I, am he, and there is no god beside me; I kill and I make alive; I wound and I heal; and there is none that can deliver out of my hand" (cf. 1 Sam. 2:6–7; 2 Kings 5:7; Ps. 75:7).

17. *NIDOTTE*, 1:731–32. This point is qualified when the verb is used in the qal and niphal stems. When the verb occurs in the piel stem, it means "to cut." Only then is it used of human agents.

18. Edward J. Young, *The Book of Isaiah*, vol. 3, *Chapters 40–66* (Grand Rapids: Eerdmans, 1972), 200. This is not to suggest that evil was part of God's original creation; it simply means that it was part of his eternal decree.

salem succumb to Babylonian invaders (587 B.C.). He acknowledges God's sovereignty over this calamity, and that does not leave him in a state of hopelessness. A few verses earlier, he speaks of his compassionate God: "But, though he cause grief, he will have compassion according to the abundance of his steadfast love; for he does not afflict from his heart or grieve the children of men" (Lam. 3:32–33).

In other words, even though God is the determining force behind the "grief" that humans suffer, it is not the intention of his heart to "afflict" them simply for the sake of affliction. He does not purpose evil for evil's sake. Instead, it has some broader purpose, always designed for a greater good (cf. vv. 19–26).[19]

Scripture does not affirm a distant, austere, uncaring deity. Only a God of transcendent power and purpose can offer his suffering creatures genuine and meaningful compassion (James 5:11). He never has to throw his hands up in dismay, trying to deflect blame while seeking to garner some modicum of sympathy. "No, really! I didn't have anything to do with it! I was just as surprised as you are that this terrible thing happened!" We must dispense with anemic deities. We serve a robust and sovereign God whose mercies are equal to his providential powers.

Only the transcendent Lord is qualified to decree good *and* evil without his comprehensive, unbridled holiness being contaminated by the latter (Deut. 32:39; 1 Sam. 2:6). While the Almighty does not *do* evil, he ordains even its worst manifestations to take place. One reason why this fact is so hard to swallow is that we tend to evaluate the nature and actions of God as though he were confined to the finite realm of the creature and not the transcendent realm of deity. As the sole Creator, Possessor, and sovereign Lord of all, he is not comparable to any mortal sovereign. He is no cosmic mafioso boss. He is no divine Don Corleone.

This completely defangs the viciousness of Ivan Karamazov's disturbing challenge to his timid Christian brother:

> Imagine that you yourself are building the edifice of human destiny with the object of making people happy in the finale, of giving them peace and rest at last, but for that you must inevitably and unavoidably torture just one tiny creature, that same child who was beating her chest with her little fist, and raise your edifice on the foundation of her unrequited tears—would you agree to be the architect on such conditions? Tell me the truth.[20]

19. Paul Helm, *The Providence of God* (Downers Grove, IL: InterVarsity Press, 1994), 190.
20. Fyodor Dostoevsky, *The Brothers Karamazov*, trans. Richard Pevear and Larissa Volokhonsky (New York: Farrar, Straus and Giroux, 1990), 245.

Alyosha's reply, "No, I would not agree," is the only sane (and compassionate) reply that any of us could offer. Yet it is not even a legitimate question to ask of a God who subsists in his own transcendent order of reality from which we are denied access. This is where we come face to face with the incomprehensible and unbridgeable Creator-creature barrier.

No human being could dare suppose that he could think or act as God does. We cannot pretend to transgress the Creator-creature distinction. "For my thoughts are not your thoughts, neither are your ways my ways, declares the Lord. For as the heavens are higher than the earth, so are my ways higher than your ways and my thoughts than your thoughts" (Isa. 55:8–9).

At the end of surveying the vast sweep of God's sovereignty in Romans 9–11, the apostle Paul is overwhelmed at the exalted theology that he has sought to unfold. He declares, "Oh, the depth of the riches and wisdom and knowledge of God! How unsearchable are his judgments and how inscrutable his ways!" (Rom. 11:33). Only such an ineffable God of wonder could be the source ("from him"), the sustaining power ("through him"), and the glorious goal ("to him") of "all things" (v. 36).

Specific Instances of God's Sovereign Hand over Evil

Scripture is not content to express God's sovereignty over evil in broad generalities, but indicates specific instances of it.

Job's Suffering
Job is the most well-known example. Before the unfolding tragedy of the book of Job, the curtains of heaven are pulled back for us to see something that not even Job was aware of—an exchange between God and Satan over the poor man's destiny. In the first chapter, God, the primary agent of all that transpires in the book, draws Satan's attention to this "blameless and upright man, who fears God and turns away from evil" (Job 1:8). God then presents him as a test case for how a righteous man can endure the destruction of his livelihood.

This is important to see because many focus on the prominent role Satan plays as he instigates Job's innocent suffering. But clearly, his role is secondary. As Martin Luther used to say, the devil is "God's devil."[21] Satan is merely a pawn in this storyline, a secondary agent taking up God's challenge of seeing whether Job's integrity would stand up under severe assaults. The devil oversees the sending of thieves, murderers, various natural calamities, even

---

21. Martin Luther, *Luther's Works*, vol. 26, *Lectures on Galatians 1535, Chapters 1–4*, trans. and ed. Jaroslav Pelikan (St. Louis: Concordia Publishing House, 1963), 190.

"fire from God" that destroys Job's children and his property (vv. 13–19). But in the end, Satan can do nothing that God does not first determine (v. 12).[22]

The devastated Job acknowledges the sovereignty of God in giving him all that he has and then summarily taking it away: "Naked I came from my mother's womb, and naked shall I return. The LORD gave, and the LORD has taken away; blessed be the name of the LORD" (Job 1:21). He does not charge the Almighty with wrongdoing (v. 22) but blesses his name in an act of simple worship.

Where in history do we find such remarkable and faithful resolve on the part of such a traumatized father? "A man may stand before God stripped of everything that life has given him, and still lack nothing."[23] Even Satan is compelled to acknowledge God's control over the situation (1:11; 2:5). But here is where many are befuddled. How does God respond? Is he dismayed by the tragic deaths of Job's sons and daughters? Does he think that things got out of hand? Has Satan gone too far? Should he have put a tighter leash on him? If any of this is true, then why does he instigate a second wave of calamity (2:3)?

Note how God frames this second challenge to Satan: Job "still holds fast his integrity, although you *incited me* against him to destroy him without reason" (2:3). God puts forth the challenge, yet it is Satan who "incites" God against the innocent man. God accepts broad responsibility for Job's calamity, but deftly distances himself from moral liability.[24] Nothing is left to chance. God knows full well that Job will retain his moral integrity and refuse to curse him in the face of murder and mayhem (Job 1:11; 2:5) because he has predetermined the outcome. Job passes the test, but his wife does not. She says, "Do you still hold fast your integrity? Curse God and die" (2:9). Notice that she doesn't say, "Curse Satan and die."

Humans intuitively turn to God when calamity strikes because they understand in their heart of hearts that he controls the events of history. Job remains unmoved by the seething anger building up in her heart: "You

22. Satan supposed that he could tempt Jesus to sin. But being the father of lies (John 8:44), he is ironically self-deceived. Satan's temptation of Christ was instigated by the Holy Spirit (Matt. 4:1) so that Christ could be tempted in all things as we are, and yet remain free of sin as our High Priest and Advocate before the Father (Heb. 4:14–16; 1 John 2:1). The Son of God needed to be tested and to learn obedience as our human representative (Heb. 5:8). See pages 368–71.

23. Francis I. Andersen, *Job*, Tyndale Old Testament Commentaries (Downers Grove, IL: InterVarsity Press, 1976), 88.

24. According to 2 Samuel 24:1, God (the primary agent) "incited" David to number Israel. In verse 10, David (a secondary agent) takes responsibility for this, telling God that he has "sinned greatly." First Chronicles 21:1, however, indicates that it was Satan (another secondary agent) who "incited" David to do this.

speak as one of the foolish women would speak. Shall we receive good from God, and shall we not receive evil?" (v. 10).[25]

Once again, we might expect many readers to think that Job has uttered something impertinent, even blasphemous. Yet the inspired author says, "In all this Job did not sin with his lips."[26] In other words, he believes God to be *responsible* for the evil that transpires, but not morally *culpable* for it.

In the aftermath of Job's calamity, his fortunes are restored, including the births of more sons and daughters (Job 42:10–16). But it is no impersonal fate that restores his livelihood; it is Yahweh (vv. 10, 12). The Lord gives and the Lord takes away, and then he gives again.

Even Job's brothers and sisters understand this robust theology of providence. The inspired writer records their faithful theodical thoughts: "they showed him sympathy and comforted him for all the *evil* that the LORD had brought upon him" (v. 11).[27] In all that unfolds in the book of Job, Satan is never mentioned on the lips of the human participants. Yahweh alone is regarded as the author of Job's calamity, yet he remains free of moral culpability.

Divine Hardening

The Bible consistently indicates that human decision-making proceeds from the thoughts and intentions of the heart (see chapter 9). Furthermore, many passages speak of God's looking at the heart when judging a person's character.[28] This indicates that a person retains a significant kind of personal control over his or her inner thoughts and dispositions, and thus responsibility for what is generated in the heart.

Many might suppose that this is evidence of libertarian free will. But not so fast. Many other—complementary—passages indicate that the heart is controlled by God.[29] For example, compare what Solomon writes. In Proverbs 21:2, he states, "Every way of a man is right in his own eyes, but the LORD weighs the heart." In the previous verse, however, he asserts, "The king's heart is a stream of water in the hand of the LORD; he turns it wherever he will" (Prov. 21:1; cf. Ezra 6:22; 7:27).[30]

25. Note the use of the Hebrew *ra'/ra'a'* again, translated here straightforwardly as "evil."
26. In Job 12:16, Job says that "the deceived and the deceiver are his [i.e., God's]."
27. Again, *ra'/ra'a'* for "evil" is used here.
28. Gen. 6:5; 1 Sam. 16:7; 1 Kings 8:39; 1 Chron. 28:9; Luke 16:15; John 2:24–25; Acts 1:24; Rom. 8:27.
29. See Deut. 29:4; Ezra 1:1; Neh. 2:12; Ps. 105:25; Jer. 32:40; Ezek. 36:26; Rev. 17:17.
30. Proverbs 16:1–2 draws a similar comparison to 21:1–2, using the more general term "man" instead of "king." See also Gen. 20:5–6.

There is no contradiction here. It merely affirms compatibilism. We are constantly conscious that our hearts belong to us—we have ownership of our inner being, our person. Yet our hearts rest first and foremost in the hands of the ultimate Owner of human souls. God acknowledged the personal integrity (innocence) of Abimelech's heart when he had every opportunity to sin with Abraham's wife, Sarah, yet he did not. At the same time, however, the Lord indicates that he himself directed Abimelech's heart away from sin (Gen. 20:5–6).

Now, what is striking is how many times Scripture indicates that God freely hardens the hearts of his creatures. "He has mercy on whomever he wills, and he hardens whomever he wills" (Rom. 9:18). Pharaoh is a prime example of this divine heart-hardening.[31] Exodus 4–14 records the episodes surrounding the plagues of judgment on the Egyptians and the exodus of the Israelites from enslavement to them. Throughout the ordeal, numerous times Pharaoh is said to have hardened his heart.[32] Yet prominently interspersed in the same episodes, we read that God hardened his heart.[33]

Paul Copan gives what appears to be a reasonable explanation for this contrast: "*Self*-hardening may lead to *divine* hardening—namely, God's withdrawal of particular graces, giving people over to the stubbornness of their hearts."[34] But this fails to acknowledge that God informed Moses long before the intrepid leader encountered Pharaoh that the Lord intended to harden the Egyptian ruler's heart (Ex. 4:21).

There is no disparity between Pharaoh's hardening and God's hardening. Pharaoh is the secondary but immediate cause of the hardening. He consciously, willingly, freely generated the stubbornness in his refusals to let God's people go. At the same time, God is the primary but remote cause of Pharaoh's hardening.[35] Scripture is merely affirming a dual (compatibilistic) explanation for what is transpiring in the stubborn ruler's heart.

This hardening is extended to the Egyptian citizens. Psalm 105:25 tells us that God "turned their hearts to hate his people, to deal craftily with

---

31. See also Deut. 2:30; Josh. 11:19–20; Ps. 81:12; Isa. 6:9–10 (cf. Mark 4:12; John 12:40; Acts 28:26–27); 63:17; Rom. 11:7–10, 25. Similar passages include 1 Kings 12:15; 2 Chron. 25:20; Isa. 29:9–10; Ezek. 14:9; Matt. 13:13. Jonathan Edwards amasses other passages in which God hardens hearts and otherwise sends forth individuals to act wickedly. See *Freedom of the Will*, 400–403.

32. See Ex. 7:13, 22; 8:15, 19, 32; 9:7, 34–35.

33. See Ex. 4:21; 7:3; 9:12; 10:1, 20, 27; 11:10; 14:4, 8.

34. Paul Copan, "Evil and Primeval Sin," in *God and Evil: The Case for God in a World Filled with Pain*, ed. Chad Meister and James K. Dew Jr. (Downers Grove, IL: InterVarsity Press, 2013), 111.

35. John Calvin, *The Secret Providence of God*, ed. Paul Helm, trans. Keith Goad (Wheaton, IL: Crossway, 2010), 101.

his servants." The fact that he "turned" the course of their hearts indicates that initial circumstances had inclined them otherwise. Perhaps the general populace was sympathetic to the plight of the Jews, yet God reoriented them. Their favorable inclinations soon morphed into hatred. Consequently, they were glad to see them depart (see v. 38).

God indicates that all this hardening had a greater good. He communicates to Pharaoh, "But for this purpose I have raised you up, to show you my power, so that my name may be proclaimed in *all the earth*" (Ex. 9:16; cf. Rom. 9:17). The supernatural power invested in the devastating plagues and the glorious exit of the Israelites through the midst of the Red Sea left an indelible impact not only on all who witnessed these things (Ex. 7:3), but on subsequent history.

The glory of God's powerful hand of deliverance is heightened by the inconceivable and repeated refusals of Pharaoh to let the Israelites go. Who would normally persist in such stubbornness in the face of unprecedented devastation unless God had designed it? Thus, the exodus has become a universal paradigm, synonymous with divine deliverance from oppression, salvation from one's enemies, and rescue from an impossible predicament.

The manner in which God hardens human hearts remains a mystery. The fact of divine hardening must be understood in the light of the truth of James 1:13: "Let no one say when he is tempted, 'I am being tempted by God,' for God cannot be tempted with evil, and he himself tempts no one." God in his unbridled holiness is unable to be touched with evil. He has no evil thoughts, commits no evil actions, and therefore cannot even be tempted by evil, let alone possess the capacity to tempt others.

God never actively moves the will of the sinner. He never infuses evil thoughts into the mind of anyone. Thus, God's manner of hardening at times may be a withdrawal of his common graces, as Paul Copan suggests. He may remove his restraints to human evil, as Paul indicates in Romans 1:24–32. Three times Paul uses the phrase "God gave them up" (vv. 24, 26, 28) to indicate that he allows a breach in the dam that holds back the wicked from carrying out their evil desires. At times he has "allowed all the nations to walk in their own ways" (Acts 14:16). He allows victims to fall prey to killers (Ex. 21:12–13).

At other times, Scripture indicates that Satan or other evil spirits become his instruments to incite evil, as in the case of Job.[36] In this sense, we might say that God *permits* sin and evil—yet this is not a passive or "bare permission,"[37]

---

36. See, for example, Judg. 9:23; 1 Sam. 16:14; 1 Kings 22:2–23; 2 Chron. 18:19–22; 2 Thess. 2:11.
37. WCF 5.4.

but rather a deliberate, active, or "willing permission."[38] Scripture uses a range of language to indicate that all evil is ultimately part of God's purposeful decree. We must not avoid the language of divine causation or determinism.

D. A. Carson disabuses us of the tendency of many theologians to employ the guarded language of divine permission: "The biblical writers are rather bolder in their use of language than the timid theologians!"[39] He continues:

> Little is gained by being more "pious" in our use of language than the Bible is, and much may be lost. By being too protective of God, we are in fact building a grid out of only a subset of the biblical materials, and filtering out some of what is revealed in the Bible about the God who has so graciously disclosed himself. The result, rather sadly, is a god who is either less than sovereign or less than personal, either incompetent and frustrated or impassive and stoical. But the God and Father of our Lord Jesus Christ is utterly transcendent and passionately personal. These are among the "givens" of Scripture, and we sacrifice them to our peril.[40]

In whatever manner the mystery of God's providence is construed, Scripture distances him from being the *direct* cause of evil. Thus, while God's *decree* is exercised monolithically and unilaterally, encompassing both good and evil, his *providential control* over what he has decreed operates in more nuanced fashion.

God's providence as it stands behind good and evil as its primary causal agent is asymmetrical. He stands behind good in a direct way and behind evil indirectly.[41] God is to be praised for all the good he causes, but moral culpability for evil is always attributed to secondary agents alone.[42] Bruce Ware notes,

---

38. Helm, *Providence of God*, 101. Frame calls it an "efficacious permission" (*Doctrine of God*, 178).

39. D. A. Carson, *How Long, O Lord? Reflections on Suffering and Evil*, 2nd ed. (Grand Rapids: Baker Academic, 2006), 199.

40. Carson, *How Long, O Lord?*, 200. Carson's statement about God's not being "impassive" but rather "passionate" should not be construed as denying the doctrine of divine impassibility. See chapter 15.

41. Helm, *Providence of God*, 190–91; Carson, *How Long, O Lord?*, 189; Matthew Barrett, *None Greater: The Undomesticated Attributes of God* (Grand Rapids: Baker, 2019), 200–203. For the relationship between how God stands asymmetrically behind good and evil and his permission of evil, see Guillaume Bignon, "'Lord Willing and God Forbid': Divine Permission, Asymmetry, and Counterfactuals," in *Calvinism and Middle Knowledge*, ed. John D. Laing, Kirk R. MacGregor, and Greg Welty (Eugene, OR: Pickwick Publications, 2019), 221–40; Guillaume Bignon, *Excusing Sinners and Blaming God: A Calvinist Assessment of Determinism, Moral Responsibility, and Divine Involvement in Evil* (Eugene, OR: Pickwick Publications, 2018), 210–27.

42. Again, compare verse 1 of 2 Samuel 24 with verse 10.

"When God controls *good*, he is controlling what *extends from his own nature*; yet when he controls *evil*, he controls what is *antithetical to his nature*."[43] Evil qua evil can never proceed from the character of a perfectly good God.

When God decrees evil, however, it must always have some good purpose, some extraordinarily constructive and weighty end. Consequently, it must proceed in some mysterious way from an aspect of God's all-good nature.[44] Somehow he is able to ordain evil and providentially ensure that it take place, and yet he emphatically commits no evil whatsoever. He can do only good.

In ordaining and ensuring that evil take place, God does something utterly unique that always ensures what is ultimately good; and this is something that *only he can do*, and we can never fully grasp it, precisely because it is he who does it.

And herein lies the tension between the incomprehensible transcendence of a God whose ways are far past finding out and his sovereign, infinitely wise plan and purposes for the unfolding of evil. In the end, while evil is infinitely abhorrent to God, its existence must have some supremely good purpose because God would decree absolutely nothing that would detract from his infinite wisdom, goodness, and holiness.[45]

So we must affirm with E. W. Smith:

> Did we believe that so potent and fearful a thing as sin had broken into the original holy order of the universe in defiance of God's purpose, and is rioting in defiance of His power, we might well surrender ourselves to terror and despair. Unspeakably comforting and strengthening is the Scriptural assurance . . . that beneath all this wild tossing and lashing of evil purposes and agencies there lies, in mighty and controlling embrace, a Divine purpose that governs them all.[46]

It remains to be seen where the primary locus of God's wise and holy purpose lies, but we will explore this in due course.

The Greatest Evil

When we survey the history of evil in the world, it is difficult to pinpoint the most egregious examples. In the mid-eighteenth century, many would

43. Bruce Ware, "A Modified Calvinist Doctrine of God," in *Perspectives on the Doctrine of God: 4 Views*, ed. Bruce A. Ware (Nashville: B&H Academic, 2008), 103.
44. This differs from what Ware says later ("Modified Calvinist Doctrine of God," 105–6).
45. This is commensurate with perfect-being theology or what some regard as classical theism.
46. Egbert Watson Smith, *The Creed of the Presbyterians* (New York: Baker & Taylor Co., 1901), 176–77, quoted in Loraine Boettner, *The Reformed Doctrine of Predestination* (Philadelphia: Presbyterian and Reformed, 1932), 240–41.

have pointed to the Lisbon earthquake. In the mid-twentieth century, many would have pointed to the Nazi Holocaust of the Jews. Dostoevsky's heart-rending examples of tortured children in the nineteenth century are drawn from actual news stories in the haunting discourses of Ivan Karamazov in *The Brothers Karamazov*. It makes for painful reading.

Everyone has excruciating examples that often come far closer to home. But there is only one example that we can categorize as the greatest evil ever perpetrated. It is the one example that strains injustice to its limits. It is the one example in which suffering itself strains the limits of comprehension. It also demonstrates that God himself does not remain aloof from the pain that evil produces, because he entered that pain via the incarnation.

We are talking about the crucifixion of the Son of God. It should not escape our notice that God meticulously planned and executed the greatest evil perpetrated in history, and that evil involved God himself entering its dark portals.

We learn from Isaiah's prophecy of the Suffering Servant (Isa. 52:13–53:12) that God planned that the divine Messiah would undergo horrendous suffering: "As many were astonished at you—his appearance was so marred, beyond human semblance, and his form beyond that of the children of mankind" (52:14). His preincarnate majesty and beauty would be set aside (53:2). He would become a forsaken man: "He was despised and rejected by men, a man of sorrows and acquainted with grief; and as one from whom men hide their faces he was despised, and we esteemed him not" (53:3).

But this was not the worst of it. He was the object not merely of human forsakenness but of God-forsakenness (cf. Ps. 22:1; Matt. 27:46). He was "stricken, smitten by God, and afflicted" (Isa. 53:4). He was "wound[ed]" and "crushed." God caused "chastisement" to fall upon him (v. 5). He was as a "lamb that is led to the slaughter" (v. 7). "By oppression and judgment he was taken away" (v. 8). All this happened to one who had "done no violence, and there was no deceit in his mouth" (v. 9). He underwent an "anguish of his soul" that no other man has ever undergone (v. 11), while being "poured out" to a death that only the worst "transgressors" experience (v. 12). And here is the hard part to come to grips with: "It was the will of the LORD to crush him; he has put him to grief" (v. 10).

To understand what took place in the crucifixion of Christ is to touch on the heart of evil and God's response to it. And this hints at where a biblical theodicy must be located—in a cosmically oriented work of redemption via the substitutionary atonement of Christ. But it suffices for the time being to say that Christ bore the enormous weight of evil on his shoulders and that this was by God's design. God ensured that his decretive "will . . . to crush him" was carried out in providentially meticulous detail. Nothing would circumvent the divine decree (John 18:11). And in order to accomplish it, God determined it to take place at the hands of evildoers.

Peter understood this when speaking to the very evildoers who had perpetrated this crime: "Men of Israel, hear these words: Jesus of Nazareth, a man attested to you by God with mighty works and wonders and signs that God did through him in your midst, as you yourselves know—this Jesus, delivered up according to the definite plan and foreknowledge of God, you crucified and killed by the hands of lawless men" (Acts 2:22–23). Christ was crucified by "lawless" and unjust people only because God had planned it that way.[47]

The early church made this same point when praying to her sovereign God: "For truly in this city there were gathered together against your holy servant Jesus, whom you anointed, both Herod and Pontius Pilate, along with the Gentiles and the peoples of Israel, to do whatever your hand and your plan had predestined to take place" (Acts 4:27–28). Herod and Pilate, along with the Gentiles and Jews who willingly participated in Christ's death, are simply among those in a long line of evil instruments that God uses to accomplish his purposes.[48]

Pilate in particular was a key instrument in this unfolding plan. He thought he had all the imperial authority at his disposal to easily release or crucify Jesus (John 19:10). But Jesus corrects this faulty understanding of his authority and will: "You would have no authority over me at all unless it had been given you from above" (v. 11). From the earthly perspective, temporal circumstances conspired so that Pilate was compelled by threats of the Jewish religious leaders to turn him over to Caesar for failing to punish a supposed pretender to the imperial throne (v. 12).

Pilate thought he had authority over Jesus, but he didn't even appear to have an adequate handle on the Jews. He certainly didn't have greater authority than Caesar. But we know that it was only by a heavenly authority that he was able to do anything. Pilate was thwarted from pursuing his intention to release Jesus (v. 12) because nothing would thwart the plan of God.[49]

47. See also Luke 24:26; Acts 3:18; 13:27–29.

48. See, for example, 2 Sam. 16:10–11; Isa. 10:5–6, 15; Hab. 1:6, 11. God obviously appoints good instruments as well. See 1 Sam. 12:6; Jer. 1:5; Acts 9:15; 13:2; Rom. 1:1; Gal. 1:15.

49. The case of Pilate is similar to that of Eli's sons. When their father sought to rebuke and encourage them to repent of their evil ways, they would not listen (1 Sam. 2:25). There is no question that they acted willingly, but the primary impetus for their refusal to repent was that "it was the will of the LORD to put them to death." In 2 Samuel 17, Absalom was seeking the best counsel to defeat his father, David, but he and his advisers would be blinded to that good counsel. We read: "And Absalom and all the men of Israel said, 'The counsel of Hushai the Archite is

Part of that plan dictated that long before Jesus was born, he had been "appointed for the fall and rising of many" (Luke 2:34).[50] Jesus was appointed to be "a stone of stumbling, and a rock of offense." Peter says that many would "stumble" because they would "disobey the word." But they also stumbled because "they were destined to" (1 Peter 2:8; cf. Isa. 8:14).

Among those destined to stumble and fall was Judas Iscariot. During the Last Supper, Jesus reveals that one of his disciples would betray him: "For the Son of Man goes as it has been determined, but woe to that man by whom he is betrayed!" (Luke 22:22). Jesus has been divinely "determined" to meet death, but not apart from the pitiable instrument that conspires to turn him over to his executors.

Matthew and Mark add that "it would have been better for that man if he had not been born" (Matt. 26:24; cf. Mark 14:21). That is a chilling announcement. God did not have to create Judas for this task and then appoint him to it. Nonetheless, he is the "son of perdition"—the man whom God has destined to fulfill Scripture (John 17:12 NASB).[51] Judas is a prime evidence of Proverbs 16:4: "The LORD has made everything for its purpose, even the wicked for the day of trouble."

Although Judas's actions were predetermined by the divine decree, this did not relieve him of moral responsibility; otherwise, Jesus would not have pronounced a "woe" upon him. Contemplating his birth would not generate any alarm. Judas's own self-focused remorse and suicide indicated his struggle with culpable blame. Unfortunately, he could never bring himself to repentance. He was blinded to the fact that the one he had a hand in condemning is full of mercy and pardon.

The free-will theist might complain that Judas's divine destiny meant that he *could not* repent. This is a fair-minded concern, but it fails to grapple with the fact that in either case, he *would not* repent. Judas was never coerced to act as he did. He did so willingly, freely, and with evil intent.

WHAT ABOUT MORAL CULPABILITY?

So God's self-revelation recorded in the pages of Scripture includes these two indisputable truths: First, God's being is characterized by impeccable goodness. He is wholly righteous and free of any taint of evil in his nature, and

---

better than the counsel of Ahithophel.' For the LORD had ordained to defeat the good counsel of Ahithophel, so that the LORD might bring harm upon Absalom" (v. 14). See also 1 Kings 12:15.

50. See also Matt. 26:31; John 3:19; 9:39; 12:37–40; 2 Cor. 2:15–16.

51. "Son of perdition" is best understood as one who is "destined for destruction." See Craig S. Keener, *The Gospel of John: A Commentary*, vol. 2 (Peabody, MA: Hendrickson, 2003), 1058–59. The same phrase is used in 2 Thessalonians 2:3 to describe "the man of lawlessness" (i.e., the Antichrist).

therefore in his thoughts, his words, and his actions. Second, God sovereignly decrees and providentially ensures all the evil that transpires in this world.

Even though many non-Calvinistic Christians have denied the second claim, a sense embedded within the *imago Dei* of our humanity knows that if God is truly who he has revealed himself to be, then he must be the all-encompassing Sovereign of both good *and* evil, as Job clearly understood (Job 1:21–22; 2:10). Only Reformed theology has had the unabashed fortitude to admit this and the consistent scriptural hermeneutic to demonstrate it.

But doesn't this leave us stuck with an irresolvable conundrum? It is still hard to escape the charge that it makes God the "author of evil." His moral culpability does not appear to be mitigated by these facts. How can God charge his secondary agents with guilt for that which he has already determined they will do? William Lane Craig states the problem this way: "The deterministic view holds that even the movement of the human will is caused by God. God moves people to choose evil, and they cannot do otherwise. God determines their choices and makes them do wrong. If it is evil to make another person do wrong, then in this view God not only is the cause of sin and evil, but he becomes evil himself, which is absurd."[52]

How does the Calvinist answer this charge? Is there any possibility of reconciling God's goodness with his sovereignty over evil while freeing God from all charges of acting sinfully, of being indistinguishable from the devil himself? We will explore that question in the next chapter.

KEY TERMS

decretive will (of God)
meticulous providence
omnipotence (of God)
transcendence (of God)

---

52. William Lane Craig, "Response to Paul Kjoss Helseth," in *Four Views on Divine Providence*, ed. Stanley N. Gundry and Dennis W. Jowers (Grand Rapids: Zondervan, 2011), 60–61. Craig here implies that the Calvinistic view of providence entails divine coercion because people could not "do otherwise" and God "makes them do wrong." They are forced against their will to act in ways in which they don't want to act. This is a distortion of the Calvinistic view of divine determinism. One could do and would want to do otherwise if and only if the choosing agent had a sufficient motive based on alternative circumstances and thus reasons for acting otherwise. This helps distinguish compatibilism from libertarianism. Under libertarian free will, one may choose an alternative course of action even when all the circumstances are the same. Under compatibilism, an alternative course of action can come about only if the circumstances are different, producing a different set of reasons that inform a differing motive for what one chooses. God does not bypass the choosing agent's own desires and motives for choosing as he does.

STUDY QUESTIONS

1. What does the Bible say about God's goodness? Why is the all-encompassing goodness of God so important when thinking about the problem of evil?
2. How does the Bible speak of God's sovereignty over evil? What would be concluded about God if he had no control or no plan for the evil that transpires in the world?
3. Why is it important to focus on God's transcendence when thinking about his sovereignty over evil?
4. How does compatibilism explain the hardening of Pharaoh's heart?
5. How does compatibilism explain the arrest, trial, and crucifixion of Jesus by evil men?
6. Can you think of instances in which God's sovereign goodness has worked in your own life during times of adversity or tragedy?

FOR FURTHER READING

D. A. Carson, *How Long, O Lord? Reflections on Suffering and Evil*, 2nd ed. (Grand Rapids: Baker Academic, 2006).

John M. Frame, *The Doctrine of God* (Phillipsburg, NJ: P&R Publishing, 2002).

Paul Helm, *The Providence of God* (Downers Grove, IL: InterVarsity Press, 1994).

9

THE CHALLENGE OF
MORAL RESPONSIBILITY

In Mario Puzo's gripping novel *The Godfather*, Vito Corleone (powerfully portrayed by Marlon Brando in the film version) is the don of the most powerful crime family in America during the 1940s and '50s. The mafioso boss is the sovereign dictator of his family's villainous conduct without himself lifting a finger to directly carry out any of their misdeeds.

One is struck with his rise from the mean streets of Manhattan's Lower East Side to the fashionable *nobile* of his manicured Long Island estate. He prizes honor, respect, tradition. He is the protector of the downtrodden and avenger of their mistreatment. He sacrificially and passionately contends for the well-being of his family, upholding high ideals and a tight moral code of loyalty.

Yet when an upstart rival dares to disrupt his illegal gambling or racketeering schemes, he surrenders no qualms in ordering his brutal murder. And he does so while sipping a glass of the finest imported Sicilian wine, calmly resting in his leather-upholstered throne in his smartly decorated den.

Many accuse the Calvinist God of being a divine Don Corleone. Freewill theists charge Reformed theology with depicting God in exceptionally dignified tones even though at the same time he dictates who is and who isn't viciously rubbed out. Perhaps he refrains from bloodying his own hands, but how does that distinguish him from an ordinary crime boss? How can he be exonerated from being the blameworthy instigator of evil?

The analogy has an initial compelling force, but it bears no resemblance to how the Creator relates to actions carried out in the plane of creation.

There is a radical dissimilarity between the way in which highly circumscribed, fallen, finite creatures carry out evil designs and the way in which
an utterly holy, wise, and infinite God ordains and providentially ensures
the same evil. While some earthly analogies may capture certain aspects of
God's relationship to evil, his nature occupies a class by itself and derails all
attempts to penetrate the deeper portals of understanding on this matter.

Nonetheless, sufficient indicators demonstrate that God can sovereignly
order the course of evil in this world without being culpable for wrongdoing. Sinister charges of malevolence concerning the divine character utterly
fail. God bears no fault whatsoever. He is meticulously sovereign over every
instance of evil but remains emphatically free from being charged with
guilt for it.

Let us examine the case for this bold assertion.

THE TRANSCENDENT AUTHOR OF EVIL

We have already offered one answer to this question by pointing to God's
transcendence, which sets him apart from the standards of any human
tribunal. We finite mortals cannot assail the immortal and infinite God for
mysteries that cannot possibly be comprehended. But there is less mystery
here than many suppose. The providential model of God as the *transcendent
Author* of history (see chapter 7) presents an analogy by which God can
easily be sovereign over evil without being morally culpable for it.

We must first dispense with the pejorative connotation that the word
author has assumed when discussing God and the problem of evil. While
the Westminster Confession of Faith has antipathy toward the term, saying that God is not "the author of sin,"[1] we should note the reasonableness
of this assertion given the historical context of mid-seventeenth-century
theology. Unfortunately, it can be misunderstood today. The Westminster
divines meant to indicate that God is not to be justifiably *blamed* for sin.
He bears no *moral responsibility* for evil. He is not the *doer* of evil.[2]

---

1. WCF 3.1. See also WCF 5.4 and Canons of Dort, Article 15: "Reprobation."

2. Jonathan Edwards writes: "If by 'the author of sin,' be meant the sinner, the agent, or actor
of sin, or the doer of a wicked thing; so it would be a reproach and blasphemy, to suppose God
to be the author of sin. In this sense, I utterly deny God to be the author of sin . . . . But if by 'the
author of sin,' is meant the permitter, or not a hinderer of sin; and at the same time, a disposer
of the state of events, in such a manner, for wise, holy and most excellent ends and purposes,
that sin, if it be permitted or not hindered, will most certainly and infallibly follow: I say, if this
be all that is meant, by being the author of sin, I don't deny that God is the author of sin (though
I dislike and reject the phrase . . .)." *The Freedom of the Will*, vol. 1 of *The Works of Jonathan
Edwards*, ed. Paul Ramsey (New Haven, CT: Yale University Press, 1957), 399.

When considering the exalted and incomparable otherness of God as standing independent of his creation, however, we must say that in a sense, God is the Author of all things, including evil (which the Confession affirms using different language).

John Frame draws out the analogy by pointing to Shakespeare. When the famous playwright authors *Macbeth*, he stands outside the story as "the ultimate cause of everything" taking place inside the story, and this includes the unsavory portions.[3] Frame continues:

> Although Duncan's death can be explained by causes within the drama, the author is not just the "primary cause" who sets in motion a chain of causes and effects that unfold without his further involvement. Rather, he writes every detail of the narrative and dialog; as author, he is involved in everything that happens. So there are two complete causal chains. Every event in Macbeth has two causes, two sets of necessary and sufficient conditions: the causes within the play itself, and the intentions of Shakespeare.[4]

This dual causation involving primary and secondary agents is an allusion to classic compatibilism, which helps to frame the model of providence that best exonerates God from moral blame. In one sense, Shakespeare "made" Macbeth kill Duncan.[5] But we don't attribute moral culpability to Shakespeare for Duncan's death.[6] That belongs to Macbeth. The primary agent (author) is not liable for the crime; rather, the secondary agent (actor) is.

Furthermore, Shakespeare, as the transcendent author, frames the fictional world that Macbeth and Duncan live in, and this sets forth the moral conditions by which Macbeth's crime is evaluated and judged as wicked.[7] Without the author's establishing a world where murder is understood to be evil, the author's crafting of a plot with murder would not evoke the reader's moral indignation. It is the righteous presuppositions of the author that determine good and evil.[8]

3. John M. Frame, *The Doctrine of God* (Phillipsburg, NJ: P&R Publishing, 2002), 156. Frame borrows this analogy from Wayne Grudem, *Systematic Theology* (Grand Rapids: Zondervan, 1994), 321–22.

4. Frame, *Doctrine of God*, 157.

5. Frame, *Doctrine of God*, 157.

6. Frame, *Doctrine of God*, 179–80; J. A. Crabtree, *The Most Real Being: A Biblical and Philosophical Defense of Divine Determinism* (Eugene, OR: Gutenberg College Press, 2004), 252; James N. Anderson, "Calvinism and the First Sin," in *Calvinism and the Problem of Evil*, ed. David E. Alexander and Daniel M. Johnson (Eugene, OR: Pickwick Publications, 2016), 208.

7. Frame, *Doctrine of God*, 157.

8. Note that these righteous presuppositions have to resonate with the reader as well.

In evaluating the overall storyline, however (not just the characters' individual actions), if the plot has a morally satisfying resolution whereby righteousness, justice, and goodness are upheld in the face of all the various strands of evil, then we don't merely praise the upstanding protagonists; we praise the author for creating a virtuous story.[9]

If evil appears to triumph over good, the author is to be blamed. But if good is portrayed as benevolent, valiant, beautiful, steadfast, and ultimately triumphant, then the author is to be praised—all the more so when good faces insurmountable odds against horrendous evil. The greater the crisis of evil, the greater the triumph for the good that prevails over it. The greater the triumph, the greater praise the author garners for crafting a *good* and compelling story.

This is why we make distinctions in novels, movies, and so on that contain evil or sinful deeds. Some storylines are crafted from a worldview that is morally ambiguous at best or that deliberately celebrates sin and evil at worst. But others are crafted to show the sinfulness of sin and to celebrate the goodness of good.

The 1991 Academy Award–winning film *The Silence of the Lambs* subtly aggrandizes the ambiguous heroics of Hannibal Lecter, the brilliant, chianti-drinking, cannibalistic serial killer. His gratuitous evil is moderated by his high culture and sophisticated charms. Compare this to the 1993 Academy Award–winning film *Schindler's List*. Here we see equal displays of horrendous evil, yet the film is wholly redemptive in showing how the evil of the Holocaust was overcome by one man who had the means to save multitudes from destruction. The film does not shy away from graphic violence, but it is recruited into service for good.

Shakespeare's plays and Dostoevsky's novels fit into this latter category. The former kinds of stories are unedifying and destructive of good. The latter, although they contain evil, are edifying and reinforce what is good. God's plan for history is the paradigm for this latter category (see chapters 10 and 11). Thus, seeing God's transcendence as analogous to the transcendence of an author considerably loosens the tension that Scripture presents between his meticulous sovereignty and his impeccable goodness.

We should note the shortcomings of this analogy. Shakespeare is *absolutely* transcendent with respect to his literary creations. None of the characters in his plays have any idea that they are creations of a transcendent author. Shakespeare stands completely outside his stories. This is not true of God. God is not marked by *absolute* transcendence. He is both transcendent

---

9. This is the case whether the story is a comedy or tragedy. See chapter 10.

and immanent. He is independent of his creation, yet at the same time he is part of the story he has crafted.[10] In fact, he is its primary Actor. Every creature lives its life in reference to the Creator, the Author, the Director, the lead Actor. In this sense, the actors in God's story are not unaware of his transcendent authority and presence. Furthermore, his immanent place in the unfolding plot is highlighted in the incarnation, whereby the Son of God truly is the story's primary hero—poised to achieve triumph and bring victory over the forces of evil.

But this does not detract from the significant implications of God's also being the transcendent Author. There is no reason to think that because God necessarily participates in the historical plot he has authored, somehow he is automatically implicated in its evil. That would be the case only if he had evil intentions for the evil he writes into the plot or if he himself acted evilly in the course of his actions in the unfolding of the plot. God never decrees evil for the sake of evil, nor can he do any evil.[11]

GOD AS THE DEFICIENT CAUSE OF EVIL

The point has been made that God's relationship to good and evil is asymmetrical, not symmetrical. He stands behind good in a more direct way and behind evil in an indirect way (and in some senses a passive way). God can never be the efficient cause of evil. Augustine states, "The truth is that one should not try to find an efficient cause for a wrong choice. It is not a matter of efficiency, but of deficiency; the evil will itself is not effective but defective. . . . To try to discover the causes of such defection—deficient, not efficient causes—is like trying to see darkness or to hear silence."[12]

Jonathan Edwards makes a similar point with a powerful analogy whereby he compares the nature and action of God to that of the sun. The sun is not the efficient cause of cold and darkness, but the deficient cause. So it is with God and evil.

> As there is a vast difference between the sun's being the cause of the lightsomeness and warmth of the atmosphere, and brightness of gold and diamonds, by its presence and positive influence; and its being the occasion of darkness and frost, in the night, by its motion whereby it descends below the horizon. The motion of the sun is the occasion of the

10. C. S. Lewis, *Surprised by Joy: The Shape of My Early Life* (New York: Harcourt Brace & Company, 1956), 227.
11. Paul Helm, *The Providence of God* (Downers Grove, IL: InterVarsity Press, 1994), 190.
12. Augustine, *City of God*, trans. Henry Bettenson (New York: Penguin Books, 1984), 12.7.

latter kind of events; but it is not the proper cause, efficient or producer of them; though they are necessarily consequent on that motion, under such circumstances: no more is any action of the Divine Being the cause of the evil of men's wills. If the sun were the proper *cause* of cold and darkness, it would be the *fountain* of these things, as it is the fountain of light and heat: and then something might be argued from the nature of cold and darkness, to a likeness of nature in the sun; and it might be justly inferred, that the sun itself is dark and cold, and that his beams are black and frosty. But from its being the cause no otherwise than by its departure, no such thing can be inferred, but the contrary; it may justly be argued, that the sun is a bright and hot body, if cold and darkness are found to be the consequence of its withdrawment; and the more constantly and necessarily these effects are connected with, and confined to its absence, the more strongly does it argue the sun to be the fountain of light and heat. So, inasmuch as sin is not the fruit of any positive agency or influence of the Most High, but on the contrary, arises from the withholding of his action and energy, and under certain circumstances, necessarily follows on the want of his influence; this is no argument that he is sinful, or his operation evil, or has anything of the nature of evil; but on the contrary, that he, and his agency, are altogether good and holy, and that he is the fountain of all holiness.[13]

MORAL RESPONSIBILITY TIED TO INTENTIONS

One of the most important considerations shedding light on why God cannot be charged with evil concerns the moral *intentions* that stand behind evil. Scripture never connects moral responsibility to free-will theism's notion of contrary choice as enshrined in libertarian views of free will. Instead, it uniformly ties moral responsibility to two criteria. The first criterion is the knowledge of good and evil. Romans 1–2 decisively argues that humans intuitively know the moral law of God written on their hearts while their consciences alert them to whether their actions violate or uphold that law (Rom. 2:12–13). Thus, they also intuitively know that they stand accountable to God, who is their just and holy Judge (Rom. 1:32).

Second, and crucially, moral culpability is tied to the intentions of the heart. The heart, in biblical language, is Mission Control Central of the human soul: "Keep your heart with all vigilance, for from it flow the springs of life" (Prov. 4:23). Every issue of life comes gushing forth from the wellsprings of the heart. Jesus declares, "For where your treasure is, there your

---

13. Edwards, *Freedom of the Will*, 404. See also Herman Bavinck, *Reformed Dogmatics*, ed. John Bolt, trans. John Vriend, 4 vols. (Grand Rapids: Baker Academic, 2003–8), 3:63.

heart will be also" (Matt. 6:21). The heart is where we form those fundamental desires that determine the choices we make. A corrupt heart produces corrupt desires that transgress the knowledge of good, which is borne witness to by our consciences. As a result, corrupt desires lead to corrupt fruit. Jesus warns, "For out of the heart come evil thoughts, murder, adultery, sexual immorality, theft, false witness, slander" (Matt. 15:19; cf. Mark 7:21–23).

Jesus extends this principle when speaking to the corrupt religious leaders:

> Either make the tree good and its fruit good, or make the tree bad and its fruit bad, for the tree is known by its fruit. You brood of vipers! How can you speak good, when you are evil? For out of the abundance of the heart the mouth speaks. The good person out of his good treasure brings forth good, and the evil person out of his evil treasure brings forth evil. (Matt. 12:33–35; cf. 7:17–20; Luke 6:43–45)

Good and bad trees represent good and bad people. They represent the internal nature of the person and the orientation of his or her heart.[14] Good (regenerate) hearts produce good fruit in the form of words and deeds. Evil (unregenerate) hearts can produce only evil fruit (James 3:11–12; cf. Jer. 13:23).

We are not sinners because we sin; we sin because at the core of our being we are sinners. This means that a good heart must be made—or, more precisely, remade. It must undergo a radical retransformation before it can produce the good fruit that our unsullied parents Adam and Eve had before the fall. This speaks to the need of spiritual and supernatural regeneration (John 3:3–8; cf. Ezek. 36:26).[15]

Thus, when it comes to evaluating people's good or bad deeds (fruit), we must first look at the heart. Jeremiah 17 is concerned about those who trust in anything other than Yahweh, those "whose heart turns away from the Lord" (v. 5). The evaluation of the situation is grim: "The heart is deceitful above all things, and desperately sick; who can understand it?" (v. 9). God's judgment on such recalcitrant sinners in the next verse goes straight to the source of humanity's moral machinery: "I the Lord search the heart and test the mind, to give every man according to his ways, according to the fruit of his deeds" (v. 10; cf. 11:20; 20:12).[16] A man's "ways" and the "fruit

---

14. R. T. France, *Matthew*, Tyndale New Testament Commentaries (Downers Grove, IL: InterVarsity Press, 1985), 211.

15. See Matthew Barrett, *Salvation by Grace: The Case for Effectual Calling and Regeneration* (Phillipsburg, NJ: P&R Publishing, 2013); John Piper, *Finally Alive* (Fearn, Ross-shire, Scotland: Christian Focus, 2009).

16. See also 1 Sam. 16:7; 1 Kings 8:39; 1 Chron. 28:9; Pss. 7:9; 26:2; Dan. 11:27; Luke 16:15; Acts 1:24; 8:20–23; 15:8–9; Rom. 8:27; Rev. 2:23.

of his deeds" proceed from the heart and mind. Each one of these people, God says, "follows his stubborn, evil will, refusing to listen to me" (16:12; cf. 18:12).

Thus, when God considers one's morally responsible actions, he looks at the intentions, the motives, the fundamental desires and affections of the heart that drive our words and actions, which in turn defy the holy God to whom we will give account. "All the ways of a man are clean in his own sight, but the LORD weighs the motives" (Prov. 16:2 NASB).[17] Divine judgment uses no other criterion. When the whole ancient world turned to intractable wickedness and God destroyed it by a flood, this divine judgment was based on the fact that "the LORD saw that the wickedness of man was great in the earth, and that every intention of the thoughts of his heart was only evil continually" (Gen. 6:5; cf. 8:21).

Likewise, when Paul speaks of the final judgment, he tells us, "Therefore do not pronounce judgment before the time, before the Lord comes, who will bring to light the things now hidden in darkness and will disclose the purposes of the heart. Then each one will receive his commendation from God" (1 Cor. 4:5). This "commendation" may result in praise or blame. How aligned are one's thoughts to the standard of righteousness as reflected in the perfect character of God? How pure are one's motives (Phil. 1:17; cf. James 2:4; 4:3)? This will determine the course of God's just and righteous evaluation.

This also explains the penetrating power of God's inspired revelation. "For the word of God is living and active, sharper than any two-edged sword, piercing to the division of soul and of spirit, of joints and of marrow, and discerning the thoughts and intentions of the heart" (Heb. 4:12). The veracity of God's Word is not confined to pious externals that can always belie inward corruption (Luke 16:15). Shiny cups and whitewashed tombs are no match for the divine Word of truth (Matt. 23:25–28).[18]

OUGHT IMPLIES CAN?

One objection to the scenario painted here concerns human beings' moral ability. Free-will theists frequently suggest that if God places moral obligations on us, then we must have the freedom and power to meet those obligations; otherwise, our moral responsibility is eviscerated. Thus, *ought*

---

17. See also Prov. 17:3; 21:2; 24:12.

18. Conversely, on occasion one's external actions may violate an express moral command when the intentions of the heart are good. For example, the midwives lied about the births of Hebrew babies to save their lives, and Rahab lied about the Israelite spies to aid the just invasion of Jericho, and both are given divine praise (Ex. 1:15–21; Heb. 11:31).

implies *can*. If we *ought* to obey the moral commands of God, then it is only fair that we be constituted so that we *can* obey them.[19] This perspective implies that freedom to obey or disobey (i.e., to exercise libertarian freedom) is necessary for moral responsibility.

This also helps explain why some free-will theists (e.g., Arminians) introduce prevenient grace, that special grace that God extends to all people whereby the effects of original sin are mitigated so that our wills are not entirely enslaved to sin. We must have an ability to choose against sin or we could not be held responsible for not obeying the call of the gospel.

How does the Calvinist respond?[20] Moral obligations do not require moral ability. Nor does an inability to redress moral wrongs exempt one from the just demands and penalties of the law. Suppose someone breaks into the Musée du Louvre in Paris, steals Leonardo da Vinci's masterpiece the *Mona Lisa*, and then lights it on fire in front of the Eiffel Tower. Who knows how to calculate the loss of such a priceless piece of historical art? Hundreds of millions of dollars? A billion dollars?

In either case, it is unlikely that the perpetrator would have the means to repay the loss. In fact, no matter how much money the perpetrator might have, the loss itself would be permanently detrimental to the aesthetic enjoyment of the whole world because the artwork could never be replaced. And so, regardless of the monetary value it represents, the penalty for destroying it would be incalculable.

Since the perpetrator would have no ability to repay or redress the loss of the masterpiece, does this exempt him from being liable for the crime? Of course not. His liability is tied to the vile intentions he had in stealing and destroying the *Mona Lisa*, not to whether he had the ability to redress his crime or even to whatever ability he had to refrain from committing the crime in the first place.

The principles here hold true in biblical models of justice. Our moral responsibility is not tied to whether we can obey the law of God. The fact is, we cannot. Even our best deeds as unregenerate sinners are like "filthy rags" (Isa. 64:6 NIV). Furthermore, the obedience that God demands from us is comprehensive and perfect obedience to his moral law (Matt. 5:48; James

---

19. Paul Copan, "Evil and Primeval Sin," in *God and Evil: The Case for God in a World Filled with Pain*, ed. Chad Meister and James K. Dew Jr. (Downers Grove, IL: InterVarsity Press, 2013), 110.

20. See the fuller discussion in Guillaume Bignon, *Excusing Sinners and Blaming God: A Calvinist Assessment of Determinism, Moral Responsibility, and Divine Involvement in Evil* (Eugene, OR: Pickwick Publications, 2018), 75–77.

2:10). No one is capable of meeting these demands, which is why Christ's vicarious obedience is essential to our hope of salvation.[21]

THE GOOD INTENTIONS OF GOD

The moral intentions of human beings created in the image of God are merely a reflection of the framework by which God himself is morally constituted. In other words, all of God's actions proceed from thoughts, motives, purposes, and desires of his heart.[22] But what is the orientation of his heart?

When Moses prayed that God would relent from his anger toward his rebellious people, he sought to protect Yahweh from accusations by Israel's enemies that their God had evil intentions (Ex. 32:12). Moses understood that God's intentions are always good—impeccably good without even a hint of corruption—and thus he appealed to God on that basis.

Note the connection between God's good purpose and his overarching sovereignty, as indicated by Isaiah 46:9–11:

> Remember the former things long past,
> For I am God, and there is no other;
> I am God, and there is no one like Me,
> Declaring the end from the beginning,
> And from ancient times things which have not been done,
> Saying, "My purpose will be established,
> And I will accomplish all My good pleasure";
> Calling a bird of prey from the east,
> The man of My purpose from a far country.
> Truly I have spoken; truly I will bring it to pass.
> I have planned it, surely I will do it. (NASB)

The term translated in verse 10 as "good pleasure" (Heb. *hepes*) speaks of willing something in which one finds delight or pleasure.[23]

This must be understood in light of Psalm 5:4: "For You are not a God who takes pleasure in wickedness; no evil dwells with You" (NASB).[24] It is

21. Reformed theology makes a distinction between the passive and active obedience of Christ. Christ's active obedience is expressed in fulfilling the positive demands of the law of God on behalf of the believer. His passive obedience is expressed in bearing the penalty of the believer's having transgressed the law of God. See Louis Berkhof, *Systematic Theology* (1941; repr., Grand Rapids: Eerdmans, 1996), 379–82.

22. Passages that indicate the motives, desires, or purposes of God's heart include Gen. 6:6; Ps. 33:11; Jer. 23:20; 30:24; cf. Isa. 44:28; 55:11; 63:4; Jer. 15:1; 31:20; Hos. 10:10.

23. *NIDOTTE*, 2:231–34. Near-equivalents would be "good purpose," "good plan," "good intention."

24. "Pleasure" (*hapes*) here is the verbal form of "good pleasure" (noun) in Isaiah 46:10.

not remotely possible for God to take delight in wickedness for the sake of wickedness. Therefore, if God takes no pleasure in wickedness, then it stands to reason that any wickedness brought to pass by the Sovereign of the universe must have some transcendently good intention standing behind it.

For example, this divine "good pleasure" saw fit to bring about the greatest injustice that the world has ever known. It "pleased" (Heb. *hapes*) Yahweh "to crush" the messianic Servant, "putting Him to grief" (Isa. 53:10 NASB).[25] We must not miss the shocking nature of Isaiah's language. But in what sense could God possibly take delight in subjecting his innocent Son to the murderous designs of evil men? This seems preposterous and blasphemous. It certainly *cannot* mean that God's delight was a *sinister* delight.

God did not and could not delight in his Son's demise as one delights in evil for the sake of evil. That would impute evil motives to God. God cannot have the "malevolent wishes of a sinner."[26] Rather, the delight stems from the unsearchable riches of good that necessarily came from this disposition of the Father toward his beloved Son. Those riches are found in the wondrous work of redemption of both a chosen people and the whole of the cursed cosmos!

This is indicated by the play on words in Isaiah 53:10. While "[Yahweh] was *pleased* [*hapes*, verb] to crush Him, putting Him to grief" as the Messiah came to "render Himself as a guilt offering," this was done so that Yahweh would see the Messiah's "offspring, He will prolong His days, and the *good pleasure* [*hepes*, noun] of [Yahweh] will prosper in His hand" (NASB). Paradoxically, the Father was pleased to crush the Son so that the Son would prosper.[27]

Even the Son took delight in his own demise, though it was a most unpleasant affair. The author of Hebrews calls us to gaze on "Jesus, the founder and perfecter of our faith, who for the joy that was set before him endured the cross, despising the shame, and is seated at the right hand of the throne of God" (Heb. 12:2). The "joy" (Gr. *charas*) that Jesus derived from enduring the shame of an unjust crucifixion, imposed on him by the divine will, was in knowing that the price it exacted from him, though unfathomably steep, was the means by which the redemption of the world was purchased. The triune God's delight in the necessary evil of the cross

25. Some translate "pleased" as "will" (ESV, NIV) in the sense of God's sovereign or decretive will, but this misses the sense of the Hebrew term.
26. Paul Helm in debate with William Lane Craig, "Calvinism vs. Molinism," in *Calvinism and Middle Knowledge*, ed. John D. Laing, Kirk R. MacGregor, and Greg Welty (Eugene, OR: Pickwick Publications, 2019), 251.
27. *NIDOTTE*, 2:230.

is not a focused delight in the cross itself, but a delight in the supreme glory and good that it produced.

It is here that we find the conundrum of God's moral culpability for evil most clearly resolved. It is impossible for God to have evil intentions for the evil that he sovereignly ensures will transpire. There is no contradiction in saying that he decrees that which he otherwise vehemently hates.[28] He retains the unique prerogative to sovereignly will the death of Christ even as it came at the hands of those who violated his moral will (Acts 2:23; cf. 4:27–28).

Nonetheless, he decrees evil *only if* he can establish some good and weighty reason for its occurrence that could come no other way.[29] If there were absolutely no morally justifiable reasons for any particular evil to transpire, then God would absolutely refrain from decreeing its existence. If God has sufficiently good and excellent reasons for the evil he decrees that outweigh any adverse effects that the evil might produce—and those goods could not come about apart from the evils connected to them such that the outcome would be better had the evil not taken place—then God cannot be charged as blameworthy for the evil.[30]

Some might protest, "Is this not an instance of the ends justifying the means?" This concern may have traction when assessing faulty, sinful humans with mixed and uncertain motives and less-than-adequate wisdom to construct their feeble and tainted plans. But the "sensibly humble theist"[31] knows that it is not possible to apply such reasoning to God, whose transcendent and infinitely vast knowledge, wisdom, and power perfectly draw together countless threads of an amazing tapestry in which each instance of good and evil plays its part in his unfolding plan for history and redemption.[32]

God is uniquely situated to ordain evil for the sake of good, something that no human is situated to do (Rom. 3:8). Furthermore, God's incomprehensibility invariably cuts us off from being able to assess his inscrutable counsels. In many (perhaps most) cases, we cannot pretend to know what God might be doing with all the vast strands of good and evil he decrees for his good and wise purposes.

---

28. Edwards, *Freedom of the Will*, 407–9.
29. Greg Welty, *Why Is There Evil in the World (and So Much of It)?* (Fearn, Ross-shire, Scotland: Christian Focus, 2018), 45.
30. Welty, *Why Is There Evil?*, 43–45; Crabtree, *Most Real Being*, 254; Bavinck, *Reformed Dogmatics*, 3:64–65.
31. Stephen Wykstra, "The Skeptical Theist View," in *God and the Problem of Evil: Five Views*, ed. Chad Meister and James K. Dew Jr. (Downers Grove, IL: InterVarsity Press, 2017), 111.
32. See pages 123–27 on the skeptical-theism defense.

Job's miserable comforters made many true statements about sin, righteousness, justice, and God; yet they were painfully wrong when they tried to speak on God's behalf, presuming to understand why he was bringing such affliction on their suffering friend (Job 42:7–9). Nor can we demand that God explain himself. Job sought for God to explain himself for the evil he providentially oversaw in Job's life, and the answer he got was stark and humbling. The essence of it was this: *I am God and you are not* (see Job 38–41). The insignificant Job (40:4) shrank back from the incomprehensible transcendence of God and said: "I know that you can do all things, and that no purpose of yours can be thwarted. . . . I have uttered what I did not understand, things too wonderful for me, which I did not know. . . . Therefore I despise myself, and repent in dust and ashes" (42:2–3, 6).

COMPATIBILISM AND MORAL RESPONSIBILITY

Biblical compatibilism—the compatibility of divine and human choosing—helps us sort out where moral responsibility lies. While God authors the plot in which evil takes place for his good purposes, it is only secondary agents who bear the moral culpability for the evil he decrees. The manner in which God is the primary causal agent ensuring that evil takes place cannot be equated to the manner in which secondary agents directly cause their own sinful actions.[33]

The Creator-creature distinction must be maintained here.[34] "God has causal powers at his disposal which his creatures do not, and we shouldn't assume that the exercise of those causal powers has the same entailment as that of human causal powers."[35] God's determining a person to sin is a remote and indirect form of causation and bears no resemblance to the person directly and immediately causing his own sin. God does not act on behalf of the choosing agent. The agent deliberately, willingly, voluntarily acts without any divine coercion. Again, we see the transcendence of God here. "Divine causation is *sui generis* [in a class by itself] and is thus related only *analogically* to creaturely causation."[36] God can never be the efficient cause of evil. It is not the transcendent God who sins; it is the creaturely agent who intends evil and then acts on those evil intentions.

David Alexander uses the following illustration to make this point while

---

33. See David E. Alexander, "Orthodoxy, Theological Determinism, and the Problem of Evil," in *Calvinism and the Problem of Evil*, ed. David E. Alexander and Daniel M. Johnson (Eugene, OR: Pickwick Publications, 2016), 134–36; Anderson, "Calvinism and the First Sin," 209, 211–16.

34. Anderson, "Calvinism and the First Sin," 215.

35. Anderson, "Calvinism and the First Sin," 216.

36. Anderson, "Calvinism and the First Sin," 207.

clarifying the difference between divine and human intentions for sin. Suppose that Sam tells a lie about some great personal idea he had in order to deceive others into thinking he is really smart. But this doesn't mean that God is simultaneously telling the same lie that Sam tells in order to deceive others into thinking God is really smart (as if God needed to do that).

Sam has the intention of making others think he is smart. But God's causing Sam to tell this lie has an entirely different intention distinct from Sam's that bears no blame for Sam's lie.[37] Again, moral culpability is tied to one's intentions, and God never intends (wills) sin for the sake of sin. He always intends (wills) it for the sake of some greater good.

The story of Joseph shows how Scripture supports this compatibilistic account of moral responsibility for evil. Joseph's brothers acknowledge their unquestionable guilt in selling their hated sibling into slavery. After being reunited with Joseph, who now has the power to retaliate against them, they are acutely aware of their culpability:

> Then they said to one another, "In truth we are guilty concerning our brother, in that we saw the distress of his soul, when he begged us and we did not listen. That is why this distress has come upon us." And Reuben answered them, "Did I not tell you not to sin against the boy? But you did not listen. So now there comes a reckoning for his blood." (Gen. 42:21–22)[38]

The brothers are not the only ones to acknowledge their guilt. Joseph also indicates that they bear the blame for this evil as he witnesses the shock and dismay in their faces. But he extends mercy to them, saying, "Do not be distressed or angry with yourselves because you sold me here" (Gen. 45:5).

The reason that Joseph makes such a gracious response is revealed in his next statement: "For God sent me before you to preserve life." He recognizes God's hand as standing behind everything that has brought them to this place. He goes even further: "So it was not you who sent me here, but God" (v. 8). This a remarkable admission for someone who has every reason to harbor bitterness and the power to execute revenge. It is a way of saying that God is the ultimate (primary) cause of this event. He dictated the terms whereby Joseph would be sold by his brothers into Egyptian slavery, and as we will see, God had morally justifiable reasons for doing so.

This leads us to Genesis 50:20, a crucial text of Scripture that brings clarity to the matter of moral responsibility. Again, Joseph seeks to ease

---

37. Alexander, "Orthodoxy," 136.
38. See also Gen. 44:32; 50:15, 17.

the guilty consciences of his brothers: "Do not fear, for am I in the place of God?" (v. 19). A good, wise, and powerful God is orchestrating everything; therefore, there is no need to fret. Then Joseph declares, "As for you, you meant evil against me, but God meant it for good, to bring it about that many people should be kept alive, as they are today."

There is a dual explanation for Joseph's being sold into slavery. His brothers did the deed, but God stood behind their actions. God is the primary agent, while they are the secondary agents. Both intended the evil to take place. The difference lies in the internal desires that birthed their intentions. For Joseph's brothers, their actions were born of a hateful motive. They "meant evil." For God, the evil could be born of nothing other than a good motive—to deliver his chosen people from certain doom. He "meant it for good."

In the book of Exodus, as Yahweh prepares to deliver his people from bondage, he informs Moses that he will harden Pharaoh's heart (Ex. 4:21; 7:3), extending his judgments beyond what ordinary people could reasonably bear without breaking under the strain. God's purpose here is to so overwhelm Pharaoh, the Egyptians, and indeed the whole world that a universal terror will prevail (15:14–16). Everyone will know that there is one supreme God and Judge in all the earth (9:14–17; cf. 10:1–2). But God's work of hardening does not exculpate Pharaoh. God hardens him even as he willingly refuses to let the Israelites go (10:27).

Hardness of heart carries with it a willful disregard for God (1 Sam. 6:6; 2 Chron. 36:13), and Pharaoh himself acknowledges this culpability. After the plague of divinely orchestrated hail nearly destroys the nation, we read: "Then Pharaoh sent for Moses and Aaron, and said to them, 'I have sinned this time; the Lord is the righteous one, and I and my people are the wicked ones'" (Ex. 9:27 NASB). Pharaoh is not cognizant that God stands behind the hardening of his heart. All he knows is his own willful pattern of sinful stubbornness.[39] He reluctantly acknowledges that Yahweh is the "righteous one" and that he and his people are the "wicked ones."

This is a shallow confession, since shortly afterward "he sinned yet again and hardened his heart, he and his servants" (9:34). Nonetheless, the ruler of Egypt speaks better than he knows, for indeed God has nothing but "righteous" motives for hardening Pharaoh's heart, whereas Pharaoh has only "wicked" motives springing from his own stone-cold soul.

When moral evil takes place in this world, blame is always assigned to secondary agents who willingly purposed evil in their hearts. Blame for

---

39. See, for example, Ex. 5:2; 7:14, 23; 8:15, 19, 29, 32; 9:34; 10:3, 10, 16, 28.

the same evil can never be assigned to God because he can purpose only that which is good and morally justifiable.[40] He always has good intentions for the evil that he decrees and ensures will take place. We do not always know what those good intentions are, but we can be assured that they exist.

This has tremendous practical importance. It causes us to realize that evil does not occur independently. It has no power of its own. No evil, no demon, no satanically inspired scheme can surprise God, escaping his notice. But furthermore, no evil scheme exists outside his all-powerful hand or his all-wise, all-good purposes.

That stillborn baby is not an accident. That horrific rape, though entirely senseless in one regard, cannot be devoid of any possible good purpose. Any immediate or direct good may not now—or ever—be discernible. The pain it generates may be unbearable. But God will generate deep goods in ways that we may never see.

Another example in which compatibilism sheds light on moral responsibility is found in Isaiah 10. God calls Assyria "the rod of my anger" (v. 5) and his "axe" (v. 15), even though the despotic nation has no sense whatsoever that it is an instrument in God's hands. The Assyrians think they act wholly of their own accord. God sends this rod against "a godless nation" (Judah and Israel) as a form of righteous judgment against them (v. 6). His intention is to uphold his justice. But Assyria "does not so intend, and his heart does not so think; but it is in his heart to destroy, and to cut off nations" (v. 7). Assyria and her king have malevolent intentions, operating from an "arrogant heart" and a "boastful look" in the eye, even as they, as God's secret instruments, complete his righteous "work on Mount Zion and on Jerusalem" (v. 12).

Once Yahweh is finished invisibly wielding Assyria as his weapon of justice, however, then he will punish the nation and its king for their arrogance and self-importance:

> Shall the axe boast over him who hews with it,
>   or the saw magnify itself against him who wields it?
> As if a rod should wield him who lifts it,
>   or as if a staff should lift him who is not wood!
> Therefore the Lord God of hosts
>   will send wasting sickness among his stout warriors,
> and under his glory a burning will be kindled,
>   like the burning of fire. (Isa. 10:15–16)

---

40. Anderson, "Calvinism and the First Sin," 212.

Some will protest. How does this seem fair? (We are back at Romans 9:18–21.) But the sovereign Lord remains free of the evil that his providentially directed instruments commit because he *always* has holy purposes for that evil, while they have only unholy purposes.[41]

Nor can anyone say that God has forced him to act against his will. "God does not determine the actions of humans *against* their wills, but *through* their wills."[42] Calvin writes:

> Satan and evildoers are not so effectively the instruments of God that they do not also act in their own behalf. For we must not suppose that God works in an iniquitous man as if he were a stone or a piece of wood, but He uses him as a thinking creature, according to the quality of his nature, which He has given him. Thus, when we say that God works in evildoers, that does not prevent them from working also in their own behalf.[43]

Thus, the perpetrator of sin can never say, "God made me do this," as though he were being forced against his will. God effectively ensured his sin, but God emphatically did not sin his sin—no more than Shakespeare sins the sins of Macbeth. The only sin that exists is that which exists in the heart of the willful perpetrator. God can have no sin in his heart even as he ensures that others sin as instruments of the often-unsearchable good that the Almighty designs their sin to have.

There is no conflict between human choosing and divine choosing, between human freedom and divine freedom. There is no conflict between primary and secondary causation, between the plot that the divine Author writes and the actors who willingly carry it out. Furthermore, God is free to sovereignly will that which his moral will has commanded us not to do. As Augustine notes, "That which is done against his will is not done without his will."[44] Calvin adds, "There is a great difference between what is fitting for man to will and what is fitting for God, . . . for through the bad wills of evil men God fulfills what He righteously wills."[45]

---

41. Habakkuk 1:5–12 provides a similar case. Yahweh says, "I am raising up the Chaldeans," whom he has "ordained" for "judgment" and "established . . . for reproof" (v. 12). This does not mitigate the fact that they are an "impetuous people" (v. 6 NASB) and come only for the sake of "violence" (v. 9). As a result, "they will be held guilty" (v. 11 NASB) for their "wickedness," which God, being of pure eyes, cannot approve (v. 13) or allow to go unpunished.

42. Bignon, *Excusing Sinners and Blaming God*, 22.

43. John Calvin, *Treatises against Anabaptists and Libertines*, trans. B. W. Farley (Grand Rapids: Baker, 1982), 245, quoted in Bavinck, *Reformed Dogmatics*, 2:614.

44. Augustine, *Enchiridion*, ed. and trans. Albert C. Outler (Philadelphia: Westminster Press, 1955), 26.100.

45. John Calvin, *Institutes of the Christian Religion*, ed. John T. McNeill, trans. Ford Lewis Battles (Philadelphia: Westminster, 1960), 1.18.3.

Therefore, when his creatures willingly transgress his clear moral will written on their hearts (Rom. 2:14–15) in service of his secret and sovereign will, they will bear the demands of his irreproachable justice. In the end, reconciling God's meticulous sovereignty with the matrix of divine and human freedom, and particularly moral responsibility, is not the insurmountable task that so many detractors have suggested.[46]

THE ENIGMA OF THE FALL

Of all the questions concerning the existence of evil, however, none is more perplexing than that of its primeval origins. Who is ultimately responsible for the emergence of evil in the perfectly good world of our freshly created parents, Adam and Eve? Bavinck muses, "The question of the origin of evil, second only to that of existence itself, is the greatest enigma of life and the heaviest cross for the intellect to bear."[47]

This is especially true in the case of Reformed theology. In speaking to this issue, we must unequivocally affirm that God created all things in a state of unalloyed goodness. Everything was "very good" (Gen. 1:31). The design, order, beauty, and moral condition of the creation and God's image-bearing creatures reflected the unalloyed goodness of the Creator. Thus, humans were created with a nature inclined to act good, to pursue a career in righteousness.

Man was not created as a blank slate equally poised between good and evil. This would be a Pelagian error and would undercut the goodness of God's creation. But if humans were created in a state of moral purity, then how could they have so easily fallen into sin?[48]

The standard Christian response to the question of evil's origin is that Adam and Eve possessed libertarian free will before the fall. Reformed thought affirms that the first couple indeed had free will but not necessarily libertarian free will. Most Reformed accounts of prefall freedom are commensurate with compatibilism.

For example, the Westminster Confession on free will states: "Man, in his

---

46. Bignon, *Excusing Sinners and Blaming God*, 61.

47. Bavinck, *Reformed Dogmatics*, 3:53; cf. Francis Turretin, *Institutes of Elenctic Theology*, ed. John T. Dennison Jr., trans. George Musgrave Giger, 3 vols. (Phillipsburg, NJ: P&R Publishing, 1992–97): 1:606.

48. This discussion assumes a literal historical fall along with literal historical persons named Adam and Eve. For a defense of the historical Adam, see William VanDoodewaard, *The Quest for the Historical Adam: Genesis, Hermeneutics, and Human Origins* (Grand Rapids: Reformation Heritage Books, 2015). For various issues on the question of Adam, the fall, and original sin, see the relevant chapters in Hans Madueme and Michael Reeves, eds., *Adam, the Fall, and Original Sin: Theological, Biblical, and Scientific Perspectives* (Grand Rapids: Baker Academic, 2014).

state of innocency, had freedom and power to will and to do that which is good and well-pleasing to God; but yet mutably, so that he might fall from it."[49] This follows Augustine's dictum that prefall Adam was "able to sin" (*posse peccare*) and "able not to sin" (*posse non peccare*).[50] Most Reformed thinkers have affirmed this point.[51]

Turretin held that Adam possessed a "mutability and liberty," meaning that he could somehow depart from his state of holiness.[52] "He could indeed stand if he wished, but could also if he wished become evil.... The proximate and proper cause of sin therefore is to be sought nowhere else than in the free will of man."[53]

Likewise, the contemporary Reformed theologian Donald Macleod states, "Adam's choice was foreordained as a free act, not 'caused' by any prior event or circumstance within the causal nexus (and, of course, the divine decree itself is not part of the causal nexus). He, himself, Adam, was the cause of his own decision, and had any third party been present as an intelligent observer they would have found it impossible to predict what choice Adam would make."[54]

Still, the Reformed compatibilistic account of freedom that we have defended does not automatically solve the problem. Compatibilism indicates that our actions arise from the state of our nature, which in turn gives rise to particular desires and motives that determine the direction of our choices. A perfectly good nature produces perfectly good desires, which produce perfectly good choices. Likewise, a corrupted nature produces corrupted desires and choices (Matt. 7:17–20; Luke 6:43–45). If no defective internal condition could have possibly predisposed Adam and Eve to act contrary to their good nature, then what did?

This seems to point us to the troublesome thought that, given the Reformed doctrine of divine sovereignty, God was the direct cause of Adam and Eve's sin. Note that we cannot simply resort to the notion that they

49. WCF 9.2 (see also WCF 4.2).
50. Augustine's initial thought seemed to have embraced libertarian free will for prefall man, but then he appears to have changed his mind over the course of his life, embracing more of a compatibilistic account of human freedom that applied to his understanding of the fall. See Jesse Couenhoven, "Augustine's Rejection of the Free-Will Defence: An Overview of the Late Augustine's Theodicy," *Religious Studies* 43.3 (2007): 279–98.
51. Donald Macleod, "Original Sin in Reformed Theology," in *Adam, the Fall, and Original Sin: Theological, Biblical, and Scientific Perspectives*, ed. Hans Madueme and Michael Reeves (Grand Rapids: Baker Academic, 2014), 135–36.
52. Turretin, *Institutes of Elenctic Theology*, 1:607.
53. Turretin, *Institutes of Elenctic Theology*, 1:607.
54. Macleod, "Original Sin," 136.

were deceived by the satanically inspired serpent (which is certainly true), for this simply pushes the question back to how Satan, created in a state of goodness himself, could have fallen without an antecedent corrupt nature moving him in that direction.[55]

Reformed thinking cannot revert to libertarian free will as an explanation for Adam and Eve's sinful choice, since libertarianism must entail indeterminism. Libertarianism necessarily rules out God's determination of what Adam chose to do.[56] Such freedom is incompatible with a God who

---

55. There are good reasons to think that Isaiah 14:11–15 and Ezekiel 28:12–19 contain allusions to Satan's fall (cf. Luke 10:18; Rev. 12:9). See Michael Green, *I Believe in Satan's Downfall* (Grand Rapids: Eerdmans, 1981), 36–42; Graham A. Cole, *Against the Darkness: The Doctrine of Angels, Satan, and Demons* (Wheaton, IL: Crossway, 2019), 90–93.

56. Guillaume Bignon has persuasively shown that libertarian free will becomes meaningless unless it embraces an indeterministic orientation (see *Excusing Sinners and Blaming God*). There is some tension and controversy in Reformed theology at this point. Recent debates center on how precisely historic Reformed orthodoxy has defined free will (in both its prefall and postfall conditions). Revisionist views on Reformed thought regarding divine sovereignty and human freedom are found in the work of Willem J. van Asselt, J. Martin Bac, and Roelf T. de Velde, eds., *Reformed Thought on Freedom: The Concept of Free Choice in Early Modern Reformed Theology* (Grand Rapids: Baker Academic, 2010); and Richard A. Muller, *Divine Will and Human Choice: Freedom, Contingency, and Necessity in Early Modern Reformed Thought* (Grand Rapids: Baker Academic, 2017). Many scholars reject (rightly, I believe) these revisionist perspectives. See in particular Paul Helm, "Reformed Thought on Freedom: Some Further Thoughts," *JRT* 4.3 (2010): 185–207; Paul Helm, "'Structural Indifference' and Compatibilism in Reformed Orthodoxy," *JRT* 5.2 (2011): 184–205; Paul Helm, "Necessity, Contingency, and the Freedom of God," *JRT* 8.3 (2014): 243–62. It must be admitted that Jonathan Edwards brought a whole new level of philosophical precision and sophistication in his incisive analysis of divine sovereignty and free will that had previously been unheard of in his seminal work *Freedom of the Will*, published in 1754. Many scholars (such as Richard Muller) think Edwards departed from Reformed orthodoxy on free will, but scholars such as Paul Helm have persuasively argued that his nascent compatibilism fits the views of Calvin and the mainstream of subsequent Reformed orthodoxy. See Helm's rebuttal of Muller's view in Paul Helm, "Jonathan Edwards and the Parting of Ways?," *Jonathan Edwards Studies* 4.1 (2014): 42–60; Paul Helm, "Turretin and Edwards Once More," *Jonathan Edwards Studies* 4.3 (2014): 286–96. These are in response to Muller's articles: Richard A. Muller, "Jonathan Edwards and the Absence of Free Choice: A Parting of Ways in the Reformed Tradition," *Jonathan Edwards Studies* 1.1 (2011): 3–22; Richard A. Muller, "Jonathan Edwards and Francis Turretin on Necessity, Contingency, and Freedom of Will. In Response to Paul Helm," *Jonathan Edwards Studies* 4.3 (2014): 266–85. Some of the difficulty in interpreting the Reformed tradition has to do with the evolution in each successive era of the language used to delineate the position that Reformed theology holds (e.g., the likes of Calvin in the sixteenth century, Turretin in the seventeenth, Edwards in the eighteenth, Hodge in the nineteenth, and Helm in the latter twentieth and early twenty-first centuries). Thus, while the terminology of *compatibilism* and *libertarianism* may describe the historical views of Calvinists and Arminians (and other free-will theists), those terms were coined in modern philosophical debates about determinism and freedom. Contemporary debates over the issues use a different lexicon from those of previous eras, and while the sophistication and complexity of the debate have been exponentially magnified in contemporary discussion (even beyond Edwards), I do not believe the basic positions have changed over the course of history.

decrees and providentially ensures that the fall take place, the latter being indisputably affirmed by every strain of Reformed theology.[57] We have shown other reasons why libertarian free will cannot be reconciled with the biblical view of God, man, sin, and the nature of freedom and responsibility (see chapter 5). Elsewhere, the Westminster Confession on the fall says, "Our first parents, being seduced by the subtilty and temptation of Satan, sinned in eating the forbidden fruit. This their sin, God was pleased, according to His wise and holy counsel, to permit, having purposed to order it to His own glory."[58] This is not a "bare permission" but a deliberate willing that sin not be prevented from occurring.[59]

Bavinck is forthright:

> The possibility of sinning is from God. The idea of sin was first conceived in his mind. God eternally conceived sin as his absolute polar opposite and thus, in that sense, included it in his decree, or else it would never have been able to arise and exist in reality. It was not Satan, nor Adam and Eve, who first conceived the idea of sin: God himself as it were made it visible to their eyes. By means of the tree of the knowledge of good and evil and the probationary command, he clearly showed human beings the two roads they could take. And before the fall he even permitted an evil

57. See, for example, Calvin, *Institutes*, 1.16.8; 1.18.1; 3.23.4, 7–8; Turretin, *Institutes of Elenctic Theology*, 1:516; Bavinck, *Reformed Dogmatics*, 3:29; Berkhof, *Systematic Theology*, 220.

58. WCF 6.1; cf. WCF 5.2.

59. WCF 5.4. Note that the language of "permission" is different in Calvinist and Arminian views of divine providence. Arminianism embraces a general permission whereby God leaves it entirely up to his creatures (via their libertarian free will) whether they will choose "A or B or C and so on *ad infinitum*" (Helm, *Providence of God*, 172). This includes evil options. Given that libertarianism is indeterministic, this means that God permits both the evil and the good. Thus, libertarianism must affirm that God cannot stand positively behind any good that his creatures do, and this creates problems for the libertarian view of his goodness and providence. See Guillaume Bignon, "'Lord Willing and God Forbid': Divine Permission, Asymmetry, and Counterfactuals," in *Calvinism and Middle Knowledge*, ed. John D. Laing, Kirk R. MacGregor, and Greg Welty (Eugene, OR: Pickwick Publications, 2019), 224. In contrast, Calvinism embraces a specific permission (Helm, *Providence of God*, 172). It is not a disengaged permission, but an "efficacious permission" (Frame, *Doctrine of God*, 178; cf. Turretin, *Institutes of Elenctic Theology*, 1:516–17). Thus, God specifically permits his creatures to choose evil that he has ordained by not preventing it and by ensuring the circumstances in which the evil comes about. Nonetheless, this permissive will of God seeks to guard him from being the direct cause of evil. James Bruce has argued that the Arminian brand of divine permission is not commensurate with a loving God. His permission of sin becomes a matter of inactivity or inattention. In contrast, Calvinism holds that a loving God engages in an active, attentive permission of sin with a view toward achieving specific greater goods that could not be obtained unless he permitted the sin in question to take place. See James E. Bruce, "Not the Author of Evil: A Question of Providence, Not a Problem for Calvinism," in *Calvinism and the Problem of Evil*, ed. David E. Alexander and Daniel M. Johnson (Eugene, OR: Pickwick Publications, 2016), 98.

power from without to insinuate itself into Paradise, using the snake as its medium, and to discuss with Eve the meaning of the probationary command. There is therefore no doubt that God willed the possibility of sin.[60]

Bavinck is still being cautious here. God did not merely will the "possibility" of sin; he willed its inevitability. There are several things to note about the conditions that God set forth to ensure that the fall would take place. First, he placed the "tree of the knowledge of good and evil" in the midst of the garden, testing our first parents with the probationary command (Gen. 2:16–17). There is nothing to suggest that the tree was inherently evil; that would defy the goodness of God's creation. But why place the tree there? Why not make *every* tree freely edible without consequence?

Second, God could have easily prevented the serpent from slithering into the garden to tempt Adam and Eve. After all, he later set cherubim in place to prevent the first couple from reentering the garden after they had sinned (Gen. 3:24). Why not cut off temptation at the pass? While we cannot speculate about the secret counsels of God, one wonders whether an undisclosed conversation ensued between God and Satan such as occurred concerning Job (Job 1–2), in which God initiated the calamity that befell the righteous man through the evil machinations of Satan. Nothing we have seen in the scriptural account of God and evil indicates that this would be unlikely as part of what happened in the garden of Eden.[61]

Third, God could have constituted man with a nature that precluded the possibility of sinning, the sort of nature that he will have in his glorified state in heaven.[62] In Augustinian language, we would say that humans will be fully redeemed and glorified creatures who are "not able to sin" (*non posse peccare*) ever again. It would appear from these facts alone that God deliberately intended the fall to take place.

But does this mean that he was the direct cause of the first sin?

How does this answer the conundrum of why good trees produce bad fruit? How can bitter water flow out of sweet springs (cf. James 3:11)?

We must admit that if compatibilistic accounts of how we make choices are true, then indeed we face a seemingly insurmountable conundrum. If Adam and Eve had compatibilistic freedom, then they should not have fallen into sin.[63] There have been several attempts to address this difficulty.

---

60. Bavinck, *Reformed Dogmatics*, 3:66.
61. We should note that once Satan fell, he was not afforded an opportunity to repent. This suggests that he is simply a pawn in God's plans for the fall.
62. See WCF 9.5.
63. Anderson, "Calvinism and the First Sin," 203.

For example, Reformed theology has consistently held that Adam was not impeccable (i.e., incapable of sinning). He was created in a state of moral purity but was nonetheless corruptible.

Some believe that this indicates a defect in Adam's moral constitution. But Reformed theologians have pointed to the fact that human beings, in the nature of the case, are finite creatures wholly dependent on God for breathing, moving, thinking—indeed, their entire existence (Acts 17:28). As finite creatures, we lack any self-sufficient power for anything. It is a matter of God's sustaining power that we exist and subsist in this world.[64] That is not a defect. That is simply the reality for finite creatures. They are not God.

Thus, some suggest that although God provided the *sufficient* grace for Adam and Eve to act in accordance with their good natures—to obey God and resist temptation—God did not supply them with an *efficacious* grace that would positively enable them to persevere in doing so.[65] Or we may say that God withdrew his grace so that the finite Adam would succumb to temptation. In contrast, in the final state, God never withdraws his grace, which will sustain his glorified but finite creatures in an immutable state of righteousness.[66] Furthermore, James Anderson has proposed the notion that Adam and Eve may have been possessed of a "weakness of will" (called "akrasia") whereby one freely acts in a way that is surprisingly pursued against one's better judgment.[67]

These proposals may not fully answer the question of how our primordial parents—having no internal corruption that would incline them toward sin, enjoying unhindered and fully satisfying fellowship with God—would suddenly turn from that Edenic bliss in a spasm of doubt, distrust, and self-exalting pride. But what we can say with confidence is this: what Adam and Eve did, they did of their own accord, willingly and uncompelled by God or Satan, such that they alone are to be blamed for their actions. God did not infuse them with evil thoughts and desires or with an evil will.[68]

And here we must return to Augustine's insight that we should not look

---

64. Edward D. Morris states that when the Westminster Confession speaks of prefall Adam's will as "subject to change" (4.2), "it appears to warrant the inference that such exposure to a lapse into transgression and sin is an inevitable condition of finite existence" (*Theology of the Westminster Symbols* [Columbus, OH: Champlin Press, 1900], 255).

65. Turretin, *Institutes of Elenctic Theology,* 1:611; Bavinck, *Reformed Dogmatics,* 3:66–67; cf. Macleod, "Original Sin," 136. See also Augustine, *City of God,* 12.1, 7; 14.13; *Rebuke and Grace—De Corruptione et Gratia,* 10.26; *The Gift of Perseverance,* 7.13; cf. Couenhoven, "Augustine's Rejection of the Free-Will Defence," 286–87; Bignon, *Excusing Sinners and Blaming God,* 221.

66. See WCF 9.5.

67. Anderson, "Calvinism and the First Sin," 217. Morris makes a similar suggestion. See *Westminster Symbols,* 255.

68. Turretin, *Institutes of Elenctic Theology,* 1:514.

for an efficient cause of evil. It has a deficient cause, and that is "like trying to see darkness or to hear silence."[69] Nonetheless, God determined Adam and Eve to fall. Thus, we cannot avoid crossing over to inscrutable nether regions here. Indeed, no theological persuasion can avoid the inscrutable realities at this point. At its core, sin is inexplicable.

Bavinck points out that the origin of sin was "based on illusion, an untrue picture, an imagined good that was not good. In its origin, therefore, it was folly and an absurdity. It does not have an origin in the true sense of the word, only a beginning."[70] There is indeed a mystery to iniquity (*mysterium iniquitatis*).[71] The alien character of sin—and from our vantage point, its strange senselessness—has a black, impenetrable thickness that only the light of the secret counsels of the triune God can explode.

And herein lies something to cling to.

Nothing as monumental and consequential as the fall could be an accident, a risk, or an unfortunate side effect of some other desirable condition. Most theologians have proposed libertarian free will as a desirable condition of prefall humanity. But knowing the risk of gratuitous evil and its utter devastation is too high a price to pay for such a brand of freedom, especially since it is demonstrably unnecessary for a good world. Such a risk is truly inexplicable.

Why not create the conditions of the good world that the Bible calls *heaven* right from the start—a place where it is impossible for humans to sin and where peace and joy will endure forever? Something that has had such far-reaching consequences as the fall, disrupting the beauty of the created order, disturbing its material peace, and adversely affecting the whole of humankind and history—"a primary catastrophe of cosmic proportions"[72]—could never in any case be so cavalierly treated by God, as though he had no control over it and no design for its occurrence. This would make him reckless at best, and indeed sinister at worst.

This points to the fall as having a grander set of divine goals that would be unrealized if it had never happened. If God deliberately purposed and ensured that the fall would occur—why? Wouldn't the world have been better off without it? What possible good could outweigh the devastating disease with which evil has infected the world?

Let us begin exploring a remarkable answer to that question.

---

69. Augustine, *City of God*, 12.7.

70. Bavinck, *Reformed Dogmatics*, 3:69.

71. See G. C. Berkouwer, *Sin* (Grand Rapids: Eerdmans, 1971), 130–48.

72. Colin E. Gunton, *The Triune Creator: A Historical and Systematic Study* (Grand Rapids: Eerdmans, 1998), 172.

KEY TERMS

compatibilism
moral responsibility
transcendence (of God)
transcendent Author (God as)

STUDY QUESTIONS

1. How does the model of divine providence whereby God is pictured as a "transcendent Author" help us understand why he is not culpable for evil?
2. Is God the efficient cause of evil? Why or why not?
3. What is the primary basis for determining moral responsibility, according to Scripture? Why do you think Scripture emphasizes this?
4. How can God be responsible for ordaining evil without being morally responsible for it at the same time?
5. How does compatibilism help us understand who is morally responsible for evil?
6. What is the best explanation for the origins of the fall?
7. Have you ever blamed God for some evil that occurred? If so, how did you resolve the tension that this created for you?

FOR FURTHER READING

Scott Christensen, *What about Free Will? Reconciling Our Choices with God's Sovereignty* (Phillipsburg, NJ: P&R Publishing, 2016).

John M. Frame, *The Doctrine of God* (Phillipsburg, NJ: P&R Publishing, 2002).

Paul Helm, *The Providence of God* (Downers Grove, IL: InterVarsity Press, 1994).

Greg Welty, *Why Is There Evil in the World (and So Much of It)?* (Fearn, Ross-shire, Scotland: Christian Focus, 2018).

Advanced

David E. Alexander and Daniel M. Johnson, eds., *Calvinism and the Problem of Evil* (Eugene, OR: Pickwick Publications, 2016).

Guillaume Bignon, *Excusing Sinners and Blaming God: A Calvinist Assessment of Determinism, Moral Responsibility, and Divine Involvement in Evil* (Eugene, OR: Pickwick Publications, 2018).

Jonathan Edwards, *The Freedom of the Will*, vol. 1 of *The Works of Jonathan Edwards*, ed. Paul Ramsey (New Haven, CT: Yale University Press, 1957).

10

EVERYBODY LOVES
A GOOD ENDING

For generations, children have been reared on fascinating fairy tales from the likes of the Brothers Grimm and Hans Christian Andersen. One of my favorites as a small boy was the English tale recounting the fate of *The Three Little Pigs*. Such a tale must be read to children with pathos, mimicking the little piggies' squealing manner: "Not by the hair of my chinny chin chin!" and the frightful bellowing of the big bad wolf: "I'll huff and I'll puff and I'll blow your house in!" Freshly expelled from their homes, the little pigs each sought to establish their fortunes and began by building their own homes. But the first two pigs lacked the moral resolve to make it in a dangerous world. They were thrifty but not very sensible. Each hastily built his home, one with straw and the other with sticks. They longed for immediate pleasure, not protection.

Neither anticipated the snarling wolf with saliva-drenched fangs, poised to make bacon from these foolish swine. The tremendous blows of the beast quickly decimated the frail little hovels, leaving the pigs defenseless. And by now, every child is wide-eyed in anticipation of the fate of the third poor creature. But the last pig was wise, taking great pains to construct a brick-fortified home exceeding all standards of wind resistance.[1] He was clever, too, positioning a boiling kettle of water to capture the crafty canine when he came tumbling down the chimney. The unlikely hog of a hero shrewdly vanquished his ferocious foe.[2]

---

1. The influence of biblical imagery can be seen in this fairy tale. Building with sticks, straw, and brick is reminiscent of 1 Corinthians 3:10–15. The wolf's blowing alludes to storm winds assaulting the houses in Jesus' parable of the wise and foolish builders in Matthew 7:24–27 (cf. Luke 6:47–49). The image of the wolf as a cunning foe is common in Scripture as well (Ezek. 22:27; Matt. 7:15; 10:16; John 10:12; Acts 20:29).

2. Like many other fairy tales, *The Three Little Pigs* has undergone an evolution. The earliest

Such tales open doors of enchantment in us all. Every child grows up longing for a good yarn. The lure of a fantastic story captivates us from the earliest ages: gripping plots complete with monsters and mysteries, heroes and villains set in whimsical landscapes where dangers lurk about in dark forests and magical swords free fair maidens. These are not silly flights of fancy, gratuitous forms of escapism—they are otherworldly tales that help children frame this-worldly reality as they learn their place in it.[3] And such stories are most certainly not confined to the children. We aged misanthropes need them perhaps more than our little ones, albeit in a little more sophisticated form.

But where are we going with this line of thought in a book about theodicy? In order to make sense of God's design for evil in this world, I begin by directing our attention to this realm of story. The Bible provides few direct clues that allow us to solve the problem of evil in the world. While many aspects of evil and God's purposes for it remain mysterious and inscrutable, the lack of direct propositional statements does not settle the matter. I believe the answer to the broader question of evil's entrance into God's good creation is embedded in the grand storyline of Scripture wherein every truth of the Christian faith, including evil, finds its place.

Furthermore, the broad themes of that storyline in terms of creation, fall, and redemption are surprisingly mirrored in the whole history of storytelling. The architectonics of storytelling demonstrate the universal longing for redemption from the conflict that is called *evil*; and that redemption is ultimately found in only one story—the one that God has directly revealed in the historical plotline of the Bible, and that he is also working out in the rest of history.

WHY WE NEED STORIES

That extraordinary human trait that drives the formation of *words*— sophisticated symbology—put together into a particular order so as to animate interior thoughts, desires, emotions, reasonings, and imaginations

---

printed version of the story seems to be that of James Orchard Halliwell from 1886. In his version, the first two pigs are eaten by the wolf, while the third pig eats the wolf. By the middle of the twentieth century, the demise of the first two pigs has been eliminated. Instead, they escape, making their way to the third pig's home while together they feast on the boiled wolf. By the latter part of the twentieth century, the tale has been completely shorn of any such "distasteful" elements. In the end, no one dies. The wolf falls into the boiling hot kettle but jumps out, screaming, and runs away, never to be seen again. Most of the moral edges are completely softened.

3. See Bruno Bettelheim, *The Uses of Enchantment: The Meaning and Importance of Fairy Tales* (New York: Alfred A. Knopf, 1975); Vigen Guroian, *Tending the Heart of Virtue: How Classic Stories Awaken a Child's Moral Imagination* (New York: Oxford University Press, 1998).

in all their wonderful and comprehensive complexity is a power realized nowhere else in the material cosmos. God has endowed us with a unique gift among his creatures—the gift of language.[4] And the highest art of language is storytelling.

The urge to tell stories is clearly one of the distinguishing marks of human existence. Animals communicate instinctively to one another about approaching danger and about where to find food, water, and other necessities; but they do not regale their companions with tall tales of the grand hunt or romantic rendezvous in the forest.[5] But for humans, stories are primal. Tolkien notes, "To ask what is the origin of stories . . . is to ask what is the origin of language and of the mind."[6] It is to ask what kind of God exists—a master Playwright who infuses storytelling into his creation and into his image-bearing creatures, who tell stories because they themselves act in stories. Elie Wiesel quips: "God made man because he loves stories."[7] It doesn't matter whether the stories we put forth stem from the world of fiction or nonfiction. The best history mirrors the best fiction, and the best fiction returns the favor.[8]

But why are we captivated by stories? Why do we need them?

To make sense of our place in the world, we automatically assemble our fragmented experiences together into a sensible and satisfying narrative. When telling our personal stories, we filter out all the tedious, mundane moments. Knowing whether you sleep on your side or your back makes no difference to anyone. But our curiosity is piqued if you can sleep soundly amid a raging storm that is tearing your little boat to pieces (Mark 4:35–41). That is a story that must be told.

We have a propensity for framing a constellation of the most important, exciting, and even disturbing threads of our lives, each converging, ebbing, and flowing to a clear destination, and attended with various successes and hardships. From the cradle to the casket, we do our best to weave our most significant experiences into a comprehensive and coherent tapestry that we trust will tell us a meaningful life story. Neil Postman observes:

4. See Tom Wolfe, *The Kingdom of Speech* (New York: Little, Brown and Company, 2016). Of course, angels have the gift of language, too (1 Cor. 13:1).

5. Gene C. Fant Jr., *God as Author: A Biblical Approach to Narrative* (Nashville: B&H Publishing Group, 2010), 8.

6. J. R. R. Tolkien, "On Fairy-Stories," in *The Monsters and the Critics and Other Essays*, ed. Christopher Tolkien (London: George Allen and Unwin, 1983), 119.

7. Elie Wiesel, preface to *The Gates of the Forest* (Austin, TX: Holt, Rinehart and Winston, 1966).

8. Carl R. Trueman, *Histories and Fallacies: Problems Faced in the Writing of History* (Wheaton, IL: Crossway, 2010), 13–15.

Without stories as organizing frameworks we are swamped by the volume of our own experience, adrift in a sea of facts. Merely listing them cannot help us, because without some tale to guide us there is no limit to the list. A story gives us direction by providing a kind of theory about how the world works—and how it needs to work if we are to survive. Without such a theory, such a tale, people have no idea what to do with information. They cannot even tell what is information and what is not.[9]

Our personal stories achieve deeper significance only when they fit within a grander communal story. We need to fit into a narrative that is larger than ourselves or we lose sight of who we are as individuals and as collective communities. Flannery O'Connor writes, "A people is known, not by its statements or its statistics, but by the stories it tells."[10] This kind of broader storytelling is the "backbone of civilization," says Brian Godawa. "It has maintained ritual, systematized beliefs and taught dogma. In essence, story incarnates the myths and values of a culture with the intent of perpetuating them."[11]

MYTH AND MYTHMAKING

The sort of *myth* that Godawa is talking about is not the popular perception whereby people maintain confident and persistent beliefs in a distorted reality or an outright fabrication—a pernicious falsehood.[12] Instead, *myth* here is a storytelling impulse that we lean on to frame the identity of the community of people that we belong to. Myths are worldviews constructed through stories, complete with rituals, corporate identity markers, values, and ethics, as well as familiar heroes and the villains that the heroes have conquered to achieve the goals necessary to forge human meaning and purpose.[13]

Myths tell a society what is important.[14] They provide explanations for the origins and destiny of a people and the world they dwell in as they

9. Neil Postman, "Learning by Stories," *Atlantic Monthly*, December 1989, quoted in Daniel Taylor, "In Praise of Stories," in *The Christian Imagination*, ed. Leland Ryken (Colorado Springs: Shaw Books, 2002), 421. See also Rod Dreher, "The Story of Your Life," found at: http://www.theamericanconservative.com/dreher/story-of-your-life-esfahani-smith/.

10. Flannery O'Connor, *Mystery and Manners: Occasional Prose* (New York: Farrar, Straus and Giroux, 1969), 192.

11. Brian Godawa, *Hollywood Worldviews* (Downers Grove, IL: InterVarsity Press, 2009), 61.

12. Robert A. Segal, *Myth: A Very Short Introduction* (New York: Oxford University Press, 2004), 6.

13. The concept of *myth* is notoriously confusing and slippery. This is true in anthropology, religious studies, sociology, psychology, historiography, and literature. There seem to be as many different definitions and uses of the term as there are those who study it. For a helpful introduction to the problem, see Segal, *Myth*; James W. Menzies, *True Myth: C. S. Lewis and Joseph Campbell on the Veracity of Christianity* (Eugene, OR: Pickwick Publications, 2014), 22–41.

14. Northrop Frye, *The Great Code: The Bible and Literature* (New York: Harcourt Books, 1982), 33.

perceive it. The myths that people construct tell them who they are, where they came from, where they are going, and why they exist. In this sense, the mythic stories that define a society or culture are situated in a frame of transcendence, that is, transworldly significance.[15] It moves from the profane to the sacred, from the earthly to the heavenly. It is about something bigger than ourselves. It speaks of spiritual forces, and gods that rule the unseen realm. For Christians, it speaks of the one true God, the sovereign Lord of the universe.

In this mythic tradition, the Sumerians had the *Epic of Gilgamesh* (twenty-first century B.C.), the Greeks had Homer's *Iliad* and *Odyssey* (eighth century B.C.), the Romans had Virgil's *Aeneid* (29–19 B.C.), and the Anglo-Saxons had *Beowulf* (A.D. 1000)—and this is only a small slice of the Western canon that we are most familiar with. History tells us that all humans are myth-makers. No society has survived long without the creation of myths. We are meaning-seekers through stories, historical narratives, legends, and grand epics. Those who have trouble putting the components of their lives into a coherent and satisfactory mythic storyline of epic proportions are at risk of living a disintegrated existence full of anxiety and angst. As Postman puts it, "Without air, our cells die. Without a story, our selves die."[16]

Not every myth that people devise is true. The story-myths that we construct are often full of myths of the other type—untruths, fictitious narratives. Nonetheless, everyone situates his or her life within some kind of myth, whether true or false, historical or fictitious, and sometimes a stew of both fact and fiction. Tolkien observes, "History often resembles 'Myth', because they are both ultimately of the same stuff."[17] Nonetheless, real history—the uninteresting, tedious, and disordered type—is often recast with dramatic distortions, fabrications, and exaggerations so that it will rise to the level of a grand and worthy myth. Such shaping of myth and history discards those inconvenient factual distractions that do not contribute to the desired identity and meaning that a people wish to create for themselves.

Think of a few of the selective events that have arisen as special representatives of America's founding: Paul Revere's midnight ride, the shot heard around the world at Lexington and Concord, Washington's crossing the Potomac, and Patrick Henry's "give me liberty, or give me death!" speech. Each of these historical events has contributed to the shaping of the American identity. But to one degree or another, each event's retelling

15. Brian Godawa has made this point.
16. Taylor, "In Praise of Stories," 408.
17. Tolkien, "On Fairy-Stories," 127.

is usually stretched here, squeezed there, refined, recast, and reshaped into immortal myth. In this sense, all myths that people create are historically inaccurate and deficient at some level even as they attempt to capture something faithful and universal in our desires and experiences. Yet there is only one "True Myth," C. S. Lewis tells us, and that is the story—the veridical history—given to us by the triune God of Scripture.[18] We will come to this story shortly.

LIFE AND LITERATURE

The essence of an epic historical event does not have to sacrifice what is true; it simply needs to carefully distill the essence of the event so that it reflects the powerful shared experiences of our lives. According to Leland Ryken, "If we can see our own experience in the characters and events of a story, it has captured something universal about life. History tells us what happened, while literature tells us what happens."[19] Thus, good history is crafted with the art of good literature. It is why the historical narratives of the Bible are deeply personal and told with literary genius.

The character Lee in John Steinbeck's novel *East of Eden* is discussing the venerable impact of the Cain and Abel narrative with his friends. He remarks, "No story has power, nor will it last, unless we feel in ourselves that it is true and true of us."[20] Later he says, "If a story is not about the hearer he will not listen. And I here make a rule—a great and lasting story is about everyone or it will not last. . . . I think this [i.e., Cain and Abel] is the best-known story in the world because it is everybody's story. I think it is the symbol story of the human soul."[21] Lee was so intrigued by the details of the Cain and Abel narrative that he studied Hebrew for two years just so that he could better understand the sixteen verses it occupies in Genesis 4.[22]

Historiography and fiction must bear a shared frame for reality. Good fiction is meant to mirror the transcendent aspects of broader historical and mythic narratives so that the mundane bits and pieces of our life stories are tethered to an anchor of meaning. Even some of the most implausible

---

18. C. S. Lewis, "Myth Became Fact," in *God in the Dock*, ed. Walter Hooper (Grand Rapids: Eerdmans, 1970), 63–67.

19. Leland Ryken, *Words of Delight: A Literary Introduction to the Bible* (Grand Rapids: Baker, 1992), 83.

20. John Steinbeck, *East of Eden* (New York: Penguin Books, 1952), 266.

21. Steinbeck, *East of Eden*, 268.

22. The tensions between sin, acceptance, alienation, longing, and bondage and freedom contained in the Cain and Abel story form the impetus for the plot in Steinbeck's novel, whose title is a reference to Genesis 4:16.

creations of the literary imagination mirror this-worldly existence. *Alice in Wonderland* is not as far-fetched as we might suppose.

"No matter how unreal some of the conventions of literature may be, the human issues that it concerns are those of actual human experience. That is why a reader's excursion into the imagined world of literature is not an escape from reality but a window *to* reality, not a flight away from what really exists but a flight *to* it."[23]

The novelist Andrew Klavan confesses: "Stories are not just entertainment, not to me. A story records and transmits the experience of being human. It teaches us what it's like to be who we are. Nothing but art can do this. There is no science that can capture the inner life. No words can describe it directly. We can only speak of it in metaphors. We can only say: it's like this—this story."[24]

Storytelling has the capacity to unearth truth in sundry regions where the most articulate propositions might flounder. The art of literature "appeals to our understanding through our imagination. . . . If we *recognize* and *feel* the horror of Cain's behavior in the story of Cain and Abel, we have grasped the truth of the story."[25] Dostoevsky's *Crime and Punishment* does not analyze guilt and shame like a geologist using his scale, his ruler, and his arithmetic to investigate specimens of quartz. Instead, their incorporeal substance must emerge in the tortured path of the depressive, near-insane Raskolnikov—the principal character of Dostoevsky's masterpiece.

Gene Fant recalls how Harriet Beecher Stowe fanned more flames of public outrage with her literary pen over the evils of slavery than did many eloquent diatribes by the respected statesman Frederick Douglass. *Uncle Tom's Cabin* did not seek to *tell* the truth about slavery; it sought to *show* it through a compelling plot. "The powerful truths that undergird the novel communicated in particularly effective ways, precisely because it was a vibrant work of fiction rather than a dry essay on the evils of chattel slavery and man's inhumanity to his fellow man."[26]

Storytelling invigorates our virtues as it equally exposes our vices. It concretizes the abstract and injects knowledge deeper into our mental awareness. Literature is a teacher, an ethicist, a philosopher, a sage, a shaper of worldviews—some for good, some for ill. Savvy storytelling can equally

23. Leland Ryken, *Triumphs of the Imagination: Literature in Christian Perspective* (Downers Grove, IL: InterVarsity Press, 1979), 94.

24. Andrew Klavan, *The Great Good Thing* (Nashville: Thomas Nelson, 2016), 137.

25. Ryken, *Words of Delight*, 15.

26. Fant, *God as Author*, 11; Andrew Delbanco, *The Death of Satan: How Americans Have Lost the Sense of Evil* (New York: Farrar, Straus and Giroux, 1995), 127.

persuade in the service of truth or error. Unfortunately, a vast array of the storytelling impulse is wasted on degenerate, subversive, or purely vapid efforts. In our modern context, we have never been in greater need of discernment.[27] Christians must be wise connoisseurs (2 Cor. 6:14–15). In either case, our literary legacies demonstrate why a fruitful imagination is essential to human flourishing. The narrative thread woven throughout the Bible is itself the paradigm of visceral storytelling as truth. Its power lies in its uncanny ability to diagnose the inner character of human life and history via a divinely infallible microscope (Heb. 4:12).

THE EMERGING MONOMYTH

Literature is as diverse as the disparate peoples and times that mark the boundless world we live in. Our world is saturated with all manner of myths, folk tales, fairy tales, fables, and other works of fantasy. We pen novels, dramatic chronicles, biographical histories, and sweeping epics. And yet, surprisingly, literary critics have uniformly acknowledged a strange phenomenon in the history of literature and of storytelling in general. Thomas Foster puts the matter bluntly: "There is only one story. Ever. One. It's always been going on and it's everywhere around us and every story you've ever read or heard or watched is part of it."[28] Foster may be employing some hyperbole here, but his point should not be overlooked.

Ever since Aristotle, perhaps the world's first literary critic, careful analysis of storytelling has revealed certain universal commonalities.[29] Every well-crafted story devises a poignant *conflict* that piques audience interest, which then demands *resolution* in the unfolding of the plot.[30] The form that such storytelling takes is called the *monomyth*, the "one story."[31] A compelling

27. This is especially true as contemporary storytelling has moved from a largely literary to an audiovisual medium—that is, television, film, and the Internet. Although dated, Neil Postman's *Amusing Ourselves to Death* (New York: Penguin Books, 1985) is still relevant.

28. Thomas C. Foster, *How to Read Literature like a Professor* (New York: HarperCollins, 2014), 27.

29. Aristotle analyzed the Greek tragedies (not comedies) for their common literary features in his work *Poetics*. See the Oxford World's Classics edition translated by Anthony Kenny (Oxford: Oxford University Press, 2013).

30. Ryken, *Words of Delight*, 62–63; Grant Horner, *Meaning at the Movies* (Wheaton, IL: Crossway, 2010), 84.

31. Some confine the term *monomyth* to its use by Joseph Campbell, especially in *The Hero with a Thousand Faces* (Princeton, NJ: Princeton University Press, 1949). Campbell regards the monomyth as equivalent to what is known as the "Hero's Journey," one of many archetypes in storytelling. I use the term in a much broader sense, following Leland Ryken (see *Triumphs of the Imagination*, 77–81), who draws from the work of Northrop Frye, especially *Anatomy of Criticism* (Princeton, NJ: Princeton University Press, 1957); Northrop Frye, *The Educated Imagination* (Bloomington, IN: Indiana University Press, 1964).

narrative needs a compelling crisis, a ruinous set of circumstances that cry out for resolution.

Without this conflict-resolution motif, we lose interest. Our minds wander off into more absorbing pursuits. The more insurmountable the conflict appears, the more compelling the story becomes. What we need is a victory in an unwinnable war against an enormous enemy—a vastly stronger, better equipped, more experienced army of adversaries. A comely princess unaware of her identity living in poverty-stricken obscurity needs to be discovered by a rich and noble prince. An untested nerdy rocket scientist whom everyone mocks must figure out how to rescue a doomed mission to the moon. Heroes need to be forged through fiery furnaces. Villains need to be shown that their sinister plots are no match for moral courage and determination. And some villains need to undergo a moral transformation themselves.

In his seminal essay "On Fairy-Stories," J. R. R. Tolkien summarized the heart of this universal storytelling device in a single word he coined— *eucatastrophe*.[32] The term paradoxically means "good catastrophe." He explains its use in the essay via a letter he wrote to a friend. *Eucatastrophe* is "the sudden happy turn in a story" in which matters otherwise appeared hopeless. In the most gripping stories, such a reversal "pierces you with a joy that brings tears (which I argued it is the highest function of fairy-stories to produce)."[33] The best stories begin and end in joy.[34] The ideal plot is U-shaped.[35] Good is followed by the descending darkness of catastrophe and then followed by the ascending restoration of good again. The stories that leave the most lasting impression are the ones in which "the darkest hour is just before dawn."[36]

Some of the best stories do not end well, but in either case they highlight our insatiable need for good endings. But the happily-ever-after forfeits its glory if that which preceded it has reduced the climax from an impossible ascent of Everest to navigating a speed bump in the Walmart parking lot.

32. Tolkien, "On Fairy-Stories," 155–56. Tolkien prefers the term *fairy-story* to refer to a story that has a transcendent monomythic quality.

33. "Letter 89," in *The Letters of J. R. R. Tolkien*, ed. Humphrey Carpenter (New York: Houghton Mifflin Harcourt, 2000), 101. To see how Tolkien worked out his conception of *eucatastrophe* in *The Lord of the Rings*, see Tom Shippey, *J. R. R. Tolkien: Author of the Century* (New York: Houghton Mifflin Harcourt, 2002), 206–12; Ralph C. Wood, *The Gospel according to Tolkien* (Louisville, KY: Westminster John Knox Press, 2003).

34. Tolkien, "On Fairy-Stories," 156.

35. Ryken, *Triumphs of the Imagination*, 80.

36. Laura Ingalls Wilder, *On the Banks of Plum Creek* (repr., New York: HarperCollins, 1971), 228.

We don't like plots with flat lines. They need indomitable conflicts. They need a eucatastrophe. Although specific storylines differ—whether composed as comedy, tragedy, romance, satire, or epic—the overall arc of the plot undergirds a native impulse to contrast good and evil, success and failure, prosperity and adversity, in such a way that what is perceived to be good and right and true should triumph—if not in the resolution of the story itself, then at least in the minds of the audience.

Heroism must be celebrated and villainy condemned. Virtues must be reinforced while vices are exposed and found wanting. How these realities are defined and employed in the plot arc varies, sometimes widely, depending on the worldview from which they spring. Sometimes what is good is regarded as evil and vice versa; and "woe" if this is so (Isa. 5:20). But every worldview seeks to justify its moral imperatives as that which is *good*, whether it meets the true standard of goodness or not. The point is, without the familiar storytelling architecture by which what is *perceived* as good must be magnified in the face of what is *perceived* as evil, the story itself fails to resonate with the sensibilities of our humanness.[37] If in the end what is perceived as evil is celebrated over what is perceived as good, then the audience is wrecked. Such an outcome is unthinkable.

This unifying, universal storyline is found not only in the long history of literature, but more recently in our present filmmaking and television era.[38] The most basic forms that this monomyth takes are tragedy and comedy.[39] According to the great medieval poet Dante, a tragedy is a story

37. Gene Fant points out that postmodern literature has often sought to subvert this order. But the exception proves the rule. See *God as Author*, 88. Robert Jenson has written an insightful essay in which he mourns the loss of story in the postmodern world. The Enlightenment (read *modernism*) sought to make coherent sense of the world and affirm a universal story, but without a universal storyteller (God). Such a project was bound to fail. Without a universal storyteller, one cannot make sense of the universal story. Thus, in postmodernism we have parts and pieces of a narratable world but no way to put them together in a cohesive dramatic storyline because once you jettison the universal storyteller, the universal story is soon jettisoned as well. See Robert W. Jenson, "How the World Lost Its Story," *First Things* 36 (October 1993): 19–24, found at: https://www.firstthings.com/article/2010/03/how-the-world-lost-its-story. The advent of postmodernism has exposed a seminal crisis in contemporary life in which ethics and aesthetics (the arts) have no grounding. See D. A. Carson, *The Gagging of God: Christianity Confronts Pluralism* (Grand Rapids: Zondervan, 1996); Charles Taylor, *A Secular Age* (Cambridge, MA: Belknap Press, 2007).

38. See Godawa, *Hollywood Worldviews*; Christopher Vogler, *The Writer's Journey: Mythic Structure for Writers*, 3rd ed. (Studio City, CA: Michael Wiese Productions, 2007).

39. I suggest that all other types of fiction are subgenres that fit under tragedy or comedy or some combination of both (i.e., tragicomedy). A recent computer study of some two thousand story arcs revealed six basic types of stories categorized as follows (each is either comedy or tragedy): (1) Rags to Riches (rise); (2) Riches to Rags (fall); (3) Man in a Hole (fall, then rise);

that begins with joy and ends in pain. A comedy begins in pain and ends with joy.[40] Our souls long for the good outcome of a comedy, and we dread the painful outcome of a tragedy.

But even in tragedy, we are encouraged to long even more for the ending of comedy. It is important to note that tragedy is not a celebration of evil's triumph. Few stories consciously seek to celebrate what is *perceived* as evil even if they do so unwittingly or with a consciously distorted ethic.[41] Instead, tragedy produces grieving over the good that ought to have triumphed, yet it fell short because of the story's flawed (tragic) heroes who were overcome by their flaws or the crisis they faced.

When tragedy evokes tears (or even loathing), it highlights the deeper yearning for the joyous resolution that is often so rare in actual life. So even though thoughtful tragedy produces a cathartic effect, comedy is always the ideal to which tragedy points. In either case, both tragedy and comedy reveal that the monomyth always has a deeply embedded moral order that highlights for us the way things *ought* to be, even (and *especially*) when they are not that way. If all stories were tragedy, our spirits would be crushed in a vise of angst. But if all stories were comedy, our spirits would drip with saccharine until all longing was inescapably submerged in its sap. The history of the monomyth tells us that we need both. Life does not always end well, but this creates greater longing for how life ought to end.

THE MONOMYTH AND PLOT STRUCTURE

Literary criticism has been consistent not only in its acknowledgment of the monomyth, but also in its delineation of the specific elements of the plot

(4) Icarus (rise, then fall); (5) Cinderella (rise, then fall, then rise); (6) Oedipus (fall, then rise, then fall). See Adrienne LaFrance, "The Six Main Arcs in Storytelling, as Identified by A.I.," *Atlantic*, July 12, 2016, found at: https://www.theatlantic.com/technology/archive/2016/07/the-six-main-arcs-in-storytelling-identified-by-a-computer/490733/.

40. Gene Edward Veith Jr., *Reading between the Lines* (Wheaton, IL: Crossway, 1990), 102. Comedy here is defined in its classic sense, not the modern sense of a lighthearted story inducing laughs all along the way. Comedy in the classic sense can include most modern dramas and even horror stories (e.g., Stephen King novels).

41. For example, the film *The Cider House Rules* (1999) celebrates abortion, which a biblical ethic regards as evil. The story frames the choice to abort unborn babies as morally courageous (Horner, *Meaning at the Movies*, 57). More recently, a children's book entitled *Promised Land* (2017) by authors Adam Reynolds and Chaz Harris celebrates homosexual relationships. The Huffington Post describes the book as "telling the story of a farm boy and prince who meet, build a friendship and eventually fall in love in the face of adversity.... [It] borrows elements from classic fairy tales and utilizes them in a queer and empowering framework." Note that the title alludes to biblical imagery, which seeks to invest the story with moral and religious credibility. Furthermore, the story draws from the need to frame the story arc around overcoming a conflict using proven monomythic patterns in "classic fairy tales." Yet all this is done to subvert a biblical ethic.

structure around which most stories are built. Aristotle said that a story must have a beginning, a middle, and an end.[42] This is so axiomatic that it seems trivial. But what he meant is that a story must have a plot arc that moves about the central conflict in order to make the story work. Furthermore, the central conflict and its resolution must employ archetypal themes and characters (protagonists and antagonists) that universally resonate with audiences.

In the nineteenth century, the German novelist and playwright Gustav Freytag summarized well what Aristotle and so many others have observed about successful plot structure. He detailed this in his influential work *The Technique of Drama*.[43] His analysis, based on studying Greek and Shakespearean tragedies, is known as *Freytag's Pyramid* and has been ubiquitously adapted to fit most genres of fiction, whether in literature or on the screen.[44] The following is a basic outline:

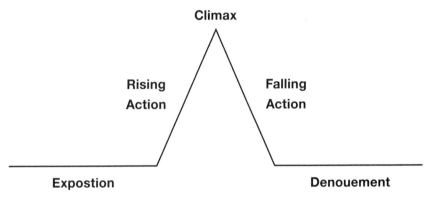

Fig. 10.1. Freytag's Pyramid

(1) *Exposition.* This is where the story is set up, introducing the characters and themes that lead to the emerging conflict. A carefully designed story will develop the characters so that the audience is readily engaged: endeared to its heroes and appalled by its villains.

(2) *Rising action.* As the conflict builds, the plot thickens. Aristotle saw this as an "entanglement" or the tying of a knot.[45] The hero faces an uncertain future, creating anticipation and intrigue.

(3) *Climax.* Here is the critical point, the moment of crisis when the conflict reaches its apex and there appears to be no reasonable way to resolve

---

42. Aristotle, *Poetics*, 2.7 (26).
43. First published in Leipzig, Germany, in 1863 as *Die Technik des Dramas*.
44. Fant, *God as Author*, 91–101. For outlines similar to Freytag's, see Godawa, *Hollywood Worldviews*, 80–86; Ryken, *Triumphs of the Imagination*, 58; Ryken, *Words of Delight*, 104.
45. Aristotle, *Poetics*, 3.18 (39). Kenny translates "entanglement" as "complication."

matters. At this point, the audience is most deeply engaged and feeling the strain of the story's tension. The climax marks the turning point of the plot. In the case of a tragedy, the turning point goes from bad to worse, and in a comedy, from bad to good.

(4) *Falling action.* This moves the conflict toward resolution, whether satisfying (comedy) or unsatisfying (tragedy). In Aristotle's language, it is the "reversal" at which point the knot starts to be untied.[46] In some cases, an unexpected twist in the plot catches the audience off guard. In some cases, a grand epiphany lights on the hero or an all-important revelation is made known that leads to the resolution of the conflict or causes the hero to see matters as they truly are—for better or worse.

(5) *Denouement.* Here comes the final unraveling of the action when the conflict is resolved—the knot finally untied. In the case of a comedy, all is made well; the happily-ever-after can begin. In the case of tragedy, it is the final catastrophe that unfolds, but always with a moral lesson to be learned.[47]

Given these features, it is easy for anyone to analyze a good novel, film, or even TV sitcom such as *I Love Lucy* or episodes of *CSI: Crime Scene Investigation.* Frank Capra was a master at employing the monomyth and its plot structure in his films. Consider the enduring 1946 classic *It's a Wonderful Life* (spoiler alerts ahead!). The hero of the story is George Bailey (James Stewart). Bailey needs some heavenly intervention, so a low-ranking guardian angel named Clarence is briefed on Bailey's situation so that he can be sent down to help him (I can't vouch for Capra's faulty theology!). That leads to the *exposition* of the film, the backstory that sets up the conflict.

We learn that George has been an outstanding citizen from his youth, saving people's lives and well loved by all. This leads to the *rising action* of the film. George is determined to leave the tired old town of Bedford Falls to explore the world and pursue greatness. Instead, he is forced to squander all his potential by taking over the family business, the broken-down Building & Loan; otherwise, it will fall into the hands of the cutthroat banker and oppressive overlord of Bedford Falls, Mr. Potter (Lionel Barrymore). The villain is squarely in place. Things look up when George marries the girl who's always loved him, Mary Hatch (Donna Reed). They have children, and he slowly makes the Building & Loan successful, helping people buy their own homes so that they don't have to grovel at Potter's feet.

---

46. Aristotle, *Poetics*, 2.11 (30).

47. The moral lesson is emphasized in classic Greek tragedies, and especially Shakespearean tragedies. For an analysis of Shakespeare's tragedies, see G. Wilson Knight, *The Wheel of Fire* (New York: Routledge, 2001); Peter J. Leithart, *Brightest Heaven of Invention* (Moscow, ID: Canon Press, 1996), 113–202.

But George is never satisfied. His dreams can never be fulfilled unless he sacrifices his moral scruples and succumbs to Potter's ploy to secure the dogged competitor as his wealthy but traitorous associate. This is the core of the moral conflict that the movie highlights. Now, Bailey is too good a man to pay the high moral price for Potter's lucrative bait, but it drives him to great distraction nonetheless. The plot's tension gets ratcheted up when Bailey's business partner, the absent-minded Uncle Billy, misplaces eight thousand dollars to keep the Building & Loan solvent. Of all places, he has accidentally slipped the envelope of cash into the folds of Potter's newspaper. Potter knowingly keeps the cash as he sees his opportunity to crush George Bailey for good.

George comes completely unglued at the prospect of being charged with fraud and going to jail. He turns out into the snowy night in suicidal desperation. The *climax* comes as George stands on a bridge, ready to throw himself into the icy waters below. But in answer to a desperate prayer, his guardian angel, Clarence, arrives at the bridge and throws himself in first, knowing that George will save him. It is Clarence's move to save George, and this is the turning point of the plot.

But how will the knot be untied—the conflict resolved? George still believes that his family, his friends, and the whole town would be better off if he were dead—or, better yet, if he had never been born. And suddenly, an idea is hatched in Clarence's mind—an epiphany indicating the *falling action* that will lead to the resolution of the plot. Through some heavenly magic, Clarence shows George what Bedford Falls would look like if he had never been born.

In an eerie sequence of encounters in which no one knows who he is, George slowly comes to realize that without his existence, Bedford Falls is not the quaint, happy little town that it really is, but a hellish place under the control of Bailey's evil nemesis—a town known as Pottersville. The many lives that George enriched are miserable wretches without him. But the revelation of the wonderful life George had becomes apparent only when his own wife does not recognize him, running away and shrieking in fear. This is George's own epiphany, the plot's *falling action*. Now he understands.

In distress, George returns to the bridge where he saved Clarence and prays for his real life to be restored. "I want to live again! Please, God, let me live again!" The prayer is answered as the alternative reality dissipates and George is resurrected as a new man, better than he was. Pottersville returns to Bedford Falls, and George is willing to accept whatever dire destiny awaits him. The *denouement* of the plot takes place when he gets back home and sees that all his friends, family, and townspeople have rallied together, scraping up all they have to pay his bank debt. George Bailey finally realizes that his life's dream was not in some lucrative and exotic locale, but had been in the homely Bedford Falls all along. The town didn't need him as much as he needed the town.

THE MONOMYTH AND REDEMPTION

While the characteristic features of the monomyth can be discovered in many shapes and sizes, within its nucleus there resides a single ubiquitous theme. Brian Godawa asserts that all "storytelling is about *redemption*—the recovery of something lost or the attainment of something needed.... Stories are finally, centrally, crucially, primarily, *mostly* about redemption."[48] Flannery O'Connor observes, "There is something in us, as story-tellers, and as listeners to stories, that demands the redemptive act, that demands that what falls at least be offered the chance to be restored."[49] For example, *It's a Wonderful Life* is about the redemption of George Bailey. In this regard, Bailey is a comedic hero.

The classic tragic hero is Sophocles' Oedipus, who seeks to save his city (Thebes) from a plague, but disaster is fated for him instead. When he learns that he has unknowingly killed his father, Laius, and has been married to his mother, Jocasta, all the while seeking to avoid these fated prophecies, he watches his mother-wife kill herself and then seizes two pins from her gown and gouges out his eyes to blind him from the horror he has committed. What makes the story compelling is that the audience is endeared to Oedipus, hoping for his redemption but consigned to grieving over his tragic end. Thus, even when it fails to materialize, every good story taps into the audience's natural longing for redemption.

Like the structure of the monomyth itself, this nearly universal fixation with redemption is curious and defies explanation as a matter of some strange coincidence. Nor can it be explained by a slow accretion of literary and cultural consensus, since the global history of storytelling shows that consistently compatible monomythic tales have existed in various times, places, and cultures in complete isolation from one another. Literary critics have therefore been uniformly puzzled about the origins of the monomyth

---

48. Godawa, *Hollywood Worldviews*, 21.

49. O'Connor, *Mystery and Manners*, 48. We should be careful not to overstate the case here. The fact is, many redemptive motifs are hard to discern or absent altogether, especially in frivolous or poorly crafted stories. And as noted earlier, postmodernism has purposely subverted this impulse. Nonetheless, some redemptive notion is generally present in most stories, if only vaguely so.

and its reflection of redemptive themes—and furthermore, why they have been so universally appealing to audiences.[50]

Christian literary critics, however, have not suffered under such uncertainty.[51] Let me explain. The ideal form of the monomyth is the comedy that reflects a U-shaped plotline. It begins in a state of bliss (how things *ought* to be), and then descends to a point of crisis (how things have gone wrong), and then finally returns to its former state of bliss—somehow getting back to how things ought to be. Yet that final state is attended with a greater sense of appreciation for having been baptized in a fiery conflict that appeared irreversible.

That appreciation for the good outcome is missing without a challenging crisis to forge such satisfaction. After all, who does not cherish life more dearly after narrowly escaping death? Being delivered from the lions' den renews the vigor of one's existence. This undoubtedly points us to the U-shaped storyline reflected in the grand narrative of Scripture—creation, fall, and redemption. Jerram Barrs says, "All great art contains elements of the true story: the story of the good creation, the fallen world, and the longing for redemption."[52]

Leland Ryken has spent a lifetime studying literature and its themes from a biblical worldview. In his important work *Triumphs of the Imagination*, he details many of the archetypal themes and characters that can be found in literature across the world.[53] Archetypes are "images, plot motifs and character types that recur again and again in literature."[54] They represent timeless and universal patterns of responses to various human situations.

Storytelling takes the complexities of real life and strips them away so that these archetypal patterns emerge in a clear and powerful way. Real life is so often fragmented and disordered that it is hard to see these patterns. This explains why stories bring such clarity to our perception by mirroring what is essential in our experiences. And this explains why stories resonate with our humanity.[55]

---

50. Fant, *God as Author*, 96.

51. Fant, *God as Author*, 96–107; see also Ryken, *Triumphs of the Imagination*, 77–81; Ryken, *Words of Delight*, 48–49; Tony Reinke, *Lit! A Christian Guide to Reading Books* (Wheaton, IL: Crossway, 2011), 51–52.

52. Jerram Barrs, *Echoes of Eden* (Wheaton, IL: Crossway, 2013), 67. Gene Fant uses similar triadic metaphors to describe this pattern in literature, art, and even the natural sciences. See *God as Author*, 70, 77–79, 96–101.

53. Ryken's chart contrasting "Ideal" and "Unideal" archetypes is instructive. See *Triumphs of the Imagination*, 86–87.

54. Ryken, *Triumphs of the Imagination*, 83.

55. Ryken, *Triumphs of the Imagination*, 84–85.

Ryken clarifies:

> If we stand back from the list of archetypes, it becomes an index to the two major themes of literature as a whole. They are the things that people long for (wish fulfillment) and the things that people find wrong in the world around them (anxiety). If the world of imaginative literature is a record of what exists within the human mind, we can discern, from the perspective of the Christian faith, two theological truths underlying literature as a whole. They are the fact of sin and the Fall, and the longing for redemption and restoration. The desire to return to the garden—the quest to regain the lost paradise—is a pattern underlying most literature. It can be traced both in literature that laments the way things are [tragedy] and in literature that offers a better alternative to the existing world [comedy].[56]

THE MONOMYTH AND GENERAL REVELATION

How do we make sense of this universal apprehension of monomythic themes? General or natural revelation indicates that God has embedded certain limited truths within creation and within the impulses of his image-bearing creatures who seek meaning for their fractured lives. We read, "The heavens declare the glory of God, and the sky above proclaims his handiwork" (Ps. 19:1). As God's image-bearers, we have what Calvin called the *sensus divinitatis* ("sense of the divine").[57]

Paul teaches, "What can be known about God is plain" to all human beings, "because God has shown it to them. For his invisible attributes, namely, his eternal power and divine nature, have been clearly perceived, ever since the creation of the world, in the things that have been made" (Rom. 1:19–20). While creation reveals a certain divine order, beauty, and purpose, the human conscience serves to alert us to God's moral laws written on the heart (Rom. 2:14–15). God's common grace affords us all equal access to these natural truths apart from direct special revelation (Job 32:8; Acts 14:16–17).

C. S. Lewis writes, "The resemblance between [pagan] myths and the Christian truth is no more accidental than the resemblance between the sun

---

56. Ryken, *Triumphs of the Imagination*, 90.

57. John Calvin, *Institutes of the Christian Religion*, ed. John T. McNeill, trans. Ford Lewis Battles (Philadelphia: Westminster, 1960), 1.3.1. See how Alvin Plantinga explains Calvin's *sensus divinitatis* in *Knowledge and Christian Belief* (Grand Rapids: Eerdmans, 2015), esp. 30–56; Alvin Plantinga, *Warranted Christian Belief* (New York: Oxford University Press, 2000). Plantinga says that belief in God and other Christian beliefs can be rationally warranted apart from argumentation. This apologetic methodology is well known as Reformed epistemology.

and the sun's reflection upon a pond, or between a historical fact and the somewhat garbled version of it which lives in popular report."[58] Elsewhere he says that myths are, at "best, a real though unfocused gleam of divine truth falling on human imagination."[59]

The Dutch theologian Herman Bavinck remarks, "No doubt among the heathen this wisdom has in many respects become corrupted and falsified; they retain only fragments of truth, not the one, entire, full truth. But even the fragments are profitable and good."[60] Unbelieving worldviews are composed of bits and pieces of truth here, falsehoods over there, gleaned from various philosophies and ideologies, and then mixed together into a syncretistic salad.[61] But as Tony Reinke suggests, "Non-Christian worldviews, no matter how faulty, are rarely (if ever) entirely false."[62] Even though the unbeliever is always suppressing divine truth, it is always pushing back and breaking through (Rom. 1:18–19).

Furthermore, even the rankest pagans have the seeds of genuine religion implanted within (*semen religionis*).[63] What humans wrongfully worship in ignorance nonetheless reflects something of the truth more fully disclosed in the revelation of Scripture (Acts 17:22–29). Bavinck writes:

> All the elements and forms that are essential to religion (a concept of God, a sense of guilt, a desire for redemption, sacrifice, priesthood, temple, cult, prayer, etc.), though corrupted, nevertheless do also occur in pagan religions. Here and there even unconscious predictions and striking expectations of a better and purer religion are voiced. Hence Christianity is not only positioned antithetically toward paganism; it is also paganism's fulfillment. Christianity is the true religion, therefore also the highest and purest; it is the truth of all religions. What in paganism is the caricature, the living original is here. What is appearance there is essence here. What is sought there can be found here.[64]

58. C. S. Lewis, *Reflections on the Psalms* (New York: Harcourt, Brace, 1958), 107.

59. C. S. Lewis, *Miracles* (New York: Macmillan, 1960), 134n1.

60. Herman Bavinck, "Calvin and Common Grace," in *Calvin and the Reformation: Four Studies*, ed. Geerhardus Vos (New York: Fleming H. Revell, 1909), 103, quoted in Reinke, *Lit!*, 192n10.

61. Horner, *Meaning at the Movies*, 81–82.

62. Reinke, *Lit!*, 59.

63. Calvin, *Institutes*, 1.4.1.

64. Herman Bavinck, *Reformed Dogmatics*, ed. John Bolt, trans. John Vriend, 4 vols. (Grand Rapids: Baker Academic, 2003–8), 1:319–20. Later Bavinck says, "All that still exists in the way of true religion, true doctrine, or pure morality among pagans, specifically in Greek philosophy, is derived from revelation and therefore belongs to Christianity. Christianity, accordingly, does not first begin in the days of the apostles but was germinally present from the beginning in [divine] revelation. It is as old as the world and therefore receives testimony from all the true and the good that is found in the religions and philosophical systems of paganism, in fact even from every human soul" (Bavinck, *Reformed Dogmatics*, 1:509).

Thus, pagan mythic worldviews have at least some perception of "the original state of reality (creation), what went wrong with that original state (Fall) and [the longing] to recover or return to that original state (redemption)."[65]

Even the nonreligious—atheists, agnostics, skeptics, and nihilists of all stripes—cannot escape this fact. Simon Wiesenthal suffered in the concentration camps of Nazi Germany. He was unsure of his belief in God. He resolutely, though perhaps reluctantly, clung to cold fate—death will come when it comes, and that will be it.[66] Yet he still feared the grave. When his group of Jewish prisoners was marched past a well-kept cemetery of German soldiers, he knew that he would not be treated with such dignity. Above each of their graves was planted a sunflower.

He relates:

> I stared spellbound. The flower heads seemed to absorb the sun's rays like mirrors and draw them down into the darkness of the ground as my gaze wandered from sunflower to grave. It seemed to penetrate the earth and suddenly I saw before me a periscope. It was gaily colored and butterflies fluttered from flower to flower. Were they carrying messages from grave to grave? Were they whispering something to each flower to pass on to the soldier below? Yes, this was just what they were doing; the dead were receiving light and messages.
>
> Suddenly I envied the dead soldiers. Each had a sunflower to connect him with the living world, and butterflies to visit his grave. For me there would be no sunflower. I would be buried in a mass grave, where corpses would be piled on top of me. No sunflower would ever bring light into my darkness, and no butterflies would dance above my dreadful tomb.[67]

Sadly, Wiesenthal expresses no hope of life after death. The only hope he retains is some tenuous connection to this broken world through some of the still-lovely remnants of a better world—sunlight, color, sunflowers, and butterflies. He puts together a sad and feeble story of hope (just barely), but unfortunately focuses it on the same cruel world that was leading him to his demise. Nonetheless, he sees very dimly through a broken mirror pieces of the world as it should be. He naturally and rightly groans for that world without knowing anything about it.

65. Godawa, *Hollywood Worldviews*, 22.
66. Simon Wiesenthal, *The Sunflower: On the Possibilities and Limits of Forgiveness* (New York: Schocken Books, 1998), 15.
67. Wiesenthal, *The Sunflower*, 14.

REDEMPTIVE LONGING THWARTED

Wiesenthal demonstrates that while the monomythic impulse is hardwired within us, unfortunately it short-circuits. General revelation points us to redemptive longing but cannot deliver the knowledge of true redemption. Thomas Howard believes the drive to construct story-myths is a way for humans to "search for perfection," be it "truth, beauty, goodness, wholeness, bliss, repose, order, form, the eternal, and so on."[68] Yet "we find sooner or later all the data of our experience to be faulted . . . . We want tranquility and we find tumult. We want permanence and we find decay. We want order and we find havoc. We want health and we find sickness. We want strength and we find weakness. We want beauty and we find horror."[69] The actual storyline here is fraught with tragedy.

Tony Reinke comments, "The fatal problem with a non-biblical worldview is that fragments of truth, goodness, and beauty that are perceived can never be assembled into a cohesive picture of God's world. The best non-Christian worldviews may include truth, but those random truths will never reveal the scope of God's saving plan."[70] Every attempt to fill up the vacuum that exists in the human heart leads either to blissful ignorance or to frustration, misery, and cynicism, as Solomon knew all too well (read the book of Ecclesiastes).

For some, when repeated attempts to find the good and satisfying ending fail, nihilism is the eventual result: life rooted in meaninglessness and continuous cycles of hopelessness. So many angst-ridden souls mimic the tragic figure Sisyphus, who was mercilessly condemned by the god Zeus to roll a massive boulder up a hill, only to see it roll back down the dreaded embankment. Sisyphus was cursed to repeat this futile task for eternity. Upon examining this sense of purposelessness that permeates such a broken world, Albert Camus concluded that adopting the absurd struggle of Sisyphus is our only option.[71]

Unfortunately, Camus and the rest of humanity are consigned to looking at the world through murky lenses. Indistinct forms move about in the light and retreat into shadow but can never be positively identified. This is where general revelation comes to its limits. It is the point at which the unregenerate cannot perceive what truly matters. Man is blind by nature, unable to see the redemptive truth of the gospel (1 Cor. 2:14). Worse yet,

---

68. Thomas Howard, "Myth: Flight to Reality," in *Christian Imagination*, ed. Leland Ryken (Colorado Springs: Shaw Books, 2002), 336–37.
69. Howard, "Myth: Flight to Reality," 337.
70. Reinke, *Lit!*, 59.
71. Albert Camus, *The Myth of Sisyphus and Other Essays* (New York: Vintage Books, 1991).

he is doubly blind. Satan casts an additional layer of darkness over man's corrupted nature.

The apostle Paul says, "And even if our gospel is veiled, it is veiled only to those who are perishing. In their case the god of this world has blinded the minds of the unbelievers, to keep them from seeing the light of the gospel of the glory of Christ, who is the image of God" (2 Cor. 4:3–4). The light of the gospel blazes with unfathomable glory, yet it is all blackness to the unregenerate.

The search for true redemption requires a different set of lenses that were not supplied to us upon entry into this world. The source of the universal storyline is fully and accurately disclosed only in God's specific and special revelation, and we require a new nature to see it. We must come to Scripture after having been fitted with spectacles that filter reality with lucidity and precision. The history of Western storytelling has been profoundly influenced by the actual data of Scripture in its general delineation of monomythic themes: creation (how things ought to be), fall (how things went wrong), and redemption (the restoration of things to the way they ought to be).

When the precise truths surrounding the gospel are proclaimed in this fallen world, however, they are regarded as foolish and scandalous (1 Cor. 1:18–31). The irony is that the biblical worldview supplies the world with the source of these monomythic themes, but when the true nature of redemption (i.e., the One True Story) is brought to the fore of the world's attention, it is rejected in favor of lesser stories and more palpable ideologies. Whatever general truths are indelibly impressed on unregenerate minds are turned around and used to deny the clearest revelation of truth, particularly the core of redemptive verities deposited in the treasury of the gospel and its hero, Jesus Christ.

The gospel emphasizes that the principal conflict of humanity is not with outside adversaries, but with the corruption of our own hearts. We suffer from an utterly helpless yet culpable moral condition, and the uncompromising justice of God rests hard against our evil. The fact is, these notions touch a raw nerve and thus become abhorrent to the unredeemed (Rom. 1:32). Oh . . . and forbid that the means of redemption should come through the bloody atoning death of God's Son—an abject horror that some call "cosmic child abuse" perpetrated by a bloodthirsty deity, seeking to appease his indignation.[72] After suppressing such uncomfortable truths, the One

---

72. Unfortunately, this language and its serious errors are being perpetrated by professing Christians. See Steve Chalke and Alan Mann, *The Lost Message of Jesus* (Grand Rapids: Zondervan, 2003), 182–83; Wm. Paul Young, *Lies We Believe about God* (New York: Simon & Schuster, 2017), 165–72. For a faithful response, see Steve Jeffery, Michael Ovey, and Andrew Sach, *Pierced for Our Transgressions: Rediscovering the Glory of Penal Substitution* (Wheaton, IL: Crossway, 2007).

True Story and the true God can be replaced only with false stories and false gods (Rom. 1:18–23). Fallen humans are lured by a form of redemption that falls woefully short of the truth.

Nonetheless, the universal plot structure (monomyth) as ascertained in the history of our storytelling gives ample and unassailable testimony to God's revealed truth even if that testimony is insufficient to bring genuine redemption to bear on tragic souls. But in this grim state of affairs, the world's only hope is to fervently pray that God would transform its tragic selves into comedic heroes rescued by the one great hero—Jesus Christ. He is the archetype of all archetypal heroes and yet not like any one of them. He is the incomparable incarnate God who entered our faulted stories and altered the plot as the story's only Redeemer. To adapt an Augustinian phrase, our stories will fill our hearts with restlessness until we find our rest in God's story. And it is in that story that the conflict—the crisis, the fall, the broad problem of evil—finds its only satisfactory resolution. We need to examine that story.

KEY TERMS

comedy
eucatastrophe
Freytag's Pyramid
general revelation
monomyth
myth
tragedy
True Myth

STUDY QUESTIONS

1. What was one of your favorite stories as a child? Why did you like it?
2. Why do people love stories, and why are they so important?
3. What is the monomyth?
4. What is Freytag's Pyramid? Explain each of its elements.
5. Can you give an example of a U-shaped plot (or one using Freytag's Pyramid) from a story, a film, or a television show—one not mentioned in the book?
6. What does redemption have to do with storytelling?
7. How does general revelation explain the monomyth, and what limits does general revelation place on the value or usefulness of the monomyth?

8. What does storytelling, the monomyth, and redemptive longing have to do with the problem of evil? How have you experienced this longing in your own life?

FOR FURTHER READING

Gene C. Fant Jr., *God as Author: A Biblical Approach to Narrative* (Nashville: B&H Publishing Group, 2010).

Brian Godawa, *Hollywood Worldviews* (Downers Grove, IL: InterVarsity Press, 2009).

C. S. Lewis, "Myth Became Fact," in *God in the Dock*, ed. Walter Hooper (Grand Rapids: Eerdmans, 1970), 63–67.

Leland Ryken, *Triumphs of the Imagination: Literature in Christian Perspective* (Downers Grove, IL: InterVarsity Press, 1979).

———, *Words of Delight: A Literary Introduction to the Bible* (Grand Rapids: Baker, 1992).

Advanced

Aristotle, *Poetics*, trans. Anthony Kenny (Oxford: Oxford University Press, 2013).

Herman Bavinck, *Reformed Dogmatics*, ed. John Bolt, trans. John Vriend, 4 vols. (Grand Rapids: Baker Academic, 2003–8).

J. R. R. Tolkien, "On Fairy-Stories," in *The Monsters and the Critics and Other Essays*, ed. Christopher Tolkien (London: George Allen and Unwin, 1983).

11

THE ONE TRUE STORY

Some believers have experienced their conversion to Christ in some strange places. For C. S. Lewis, it was while riding in the sidecar of his brother's motorcycle on the way to Whipsnade Park Zoo in Bedfordshire, England.[1] He writes, "I was driven to Whipsnade one sunny morning. When we set out I did not believe that Jesus Christ is the Son of God, and when we reached the zoo I did."[2] Now, that sounds strange coming from such an intellectual giant as Lewis. Did his conversion result from the exhilarating ride? Did he magically believe out of nowhere?

Well, it's not that simple. Lewis had been an atheist until about a year before this motorcycle ride. At that time, he became convinced of theism but was not yet a convert to the Christian faith. Many things intervened in that long year to bring Lewis to Christ. But one event nine days before the ride was instrumental in his conversion.[3]

A late-night conversation ensued between Lewis and his friends Hugo Dyson and J. R. R. Tolkien. These men spent hours discussing literature as members of the famous literary club the Inklings.[4] Alister McGrath notes, "Lewis' love of literature is not a backdrop to his conversion; it is integral to his discovery of the rational and imaginative appeal of Christianity."[5] The

1. Devin Brown, *A Life Observed: A Spiritual Biography of C. S. Lewis* (Grand Rapids: Brazos Press, 2013), 155–56.

2. C. S. Lewis, *Surprised by Joy: The Shape of My Early Life* (New York: Harcourt Brace & Company, 1956), 237.

3. Concerning the complex chronology of Lewis's conversion, see Alister McGrath, *C. S. Lewis: A Life* (Carol Stream, IL: Tyndale House, 2013), 131–59.

4. Philip Zaleski and Carol Zaleski, *The Fellowship: The Literary Lives of the Inklings: J. R. R. Tolkien, C. S. Lewis, Owen Barfield, Charles Williams* (New York: Farrar, Straus and Giroux, 2015).

5. McGrath, *Lewis*, 133.

men argued over the merits of Christianity. Lewis could see Jesus as a good moral example, but the notion of the Son of God crucified and resurrected was appalling to him.

The critical portion of their discussion centered on the importance of myths and their relationship to Christianity. Lewis believed that various cultural and literary myths, though fascinating, were nothing more than "lies breathed through silver."[6] How could Christianity be any different? Tolkien and Dyson argued that although myths are "misguided" and "contain error," they also "reflect a splintered fragment of the true light"—the light that God has revealed in the One True Story—the paradigm for the monomyth reflected in so many stories, myths, legends, and fairy tales.[7]

Lewis's perceptions were radically altered by this conversation. A month later, he explained what had happened that night in a letter to his friend Arthur Greeves:

> Now what Dyson and Tolkien showed me was this: that if I met the idea of sacrifice in a Pagan story I didn't mind it at all: again, if I met the idea of a god sacrificing himself to himself . . . . I liked it very much and was mysteriously moved by it: again, that the idea of the dying and reviving god (Balder, Adonis, Bacchus) similarly moved me provided I met it anywhere *except* in the Gospels.[8]

After wrestling with the evidence, Lewis explained what he came to believe:

> Now the story of Christ is simply a true myth: a myth working on us in the same way as the others, but with this tremendous difference that *it really happened*. . . . Christianity is God expressing Himself through what we call "real things". Therefore it is *true* . . . . The "doctrines" we get *out* of the true myth . . . are translations into our *concepts* and *ideas* of that [which] God has already expressed in a language more adequate, namely the actual incarnation, crucifixion, and resurrection.[9]

As McGrath notes, "Lewis grasped the reality of Christianity through his imagination, and then began to try and make rational sense of what his imagination had captured and embraced."[10]

6. Humphrey Carpenter, *J. R. R. Tolkien: A Biography* (London: George Allen & Unwin, 1977), 147.

7. Carpenter, *Tolkien*, 147.

8. C. S. Lewis, *The Collected Letters of C. S. Lewis*, vol. 1, *Family Letters 1905–1931*, ed. Walter Hooper (New York: HarperCollins, 2004), 976–77.

9. Lewis, *Family Letters*, 977.

10. McGrath, *Lewis*, 153. C. S. Lewis has long been regarded as an enigma in the Christian

Understanding the greatest story ever told is the starting place for resolving the conflict of evil. While ordinary worldly storylines of redemption pique our interest, the stories themselves will not give us genuine aid in making sense of why they resonate with us so deeply. They are too often foggy, full of corruption and even outright error. As subcreations, they do not have the "supremely convincing tone of Primary Art" that the story coming from the Creator has.[11] They are second-order creations dimly mirroring the first-order narrative.[12]

Furthermore, they cannot help us make sense of the central conflict of humanity—the sin and evil that have corrupted the world. Their fictional usefulness cannot ultimately remedy real-world pain. We need the One True Story of creation to fall, and then fall to new creation, as told by the one transcendent Author of real-world history, to resolve the problem of evil. As John Frame puts it, "The whole Bible addresses the problem of evil, for the whole story turns on the entrance of sin and evil into the world and on God's plan for dealing with it."[13] Let us set the stage for this remarkable story.

THE NARRATIVE CHARACTER OF SCRIPTURE

Leland Ryken writes, "Christianity is the most literary religion in the world. It is the religion in which the word has a special sanctity."[14] This means that the Bible is a profoundly literary book—or shall we say *books*. The sum of its sixty-six books embodies a grand narrative. There are narratives within the larger metanarrative, all contributing to an overarching canonical plot of creation, fall, and redemption.

The importance of the narrative character of Scripture cannot be overestimated. Its story-oriented framework undergirds the truth of Christianity and our impulse as humans to be driven by stories. Because God is the

world. While he is often adored by evangelical Christians, he has also been excoriated for holding decidedly "unevangelical" views, for example, on Scripture and the atonement. For an assessment of his life and theology, see Joe Rigney, *Lewis on the Christian Life* (Wheaton, IL: Crossway, 2018); John Piper and David Mathis, eds., *The Romantic Rationalist: God, Life, and Imagination in the Work of C. S. Lewis* (Wheaton, IL: Crossway, 2014).

11. J. R. R. Tolkien, "On Fairy-Stories," in *The Monsters and the Critics and Other Essays*, ed. Christopher Tolkien (London: George Allen and Unwin, 1983), 156.

12. Tolkien, "On Fairy-Stories," 156; cf. Royce Gordon Gruenler, "Jesus as Author of the Evangelium: J. R. R. Tolkien and the Spell of the Great Story," in *New Approaches to Jesus and the Gospels: A Phenomenological and Exegetical Study of Synoptic Christology* (Grand Rapids: Baker, 1982), 204.

13. John Frame, *Apologetics: A Justification of Christian Belief* (Phillipsburg, NJ: P&R Publishing, 2015), 159.

14. Leland Ryken, *Triumphs of the Imagination: Literature in Christian Perspective* (Downers Grove, IL: InterVarsity Press, 1979), 21.

original storyteller, his inspired Word provides the "precondition for the intelligibility of storytelling.... The biblical notion of linear history, with an author, characters and a purposeful goal, [is] the philosophical foundation of the search for meaning in a narrative of life. Storytelling is meaningless gibberish unless reality itself is narratable. And reality is unnarratable in a universe without a transcendent narrator."[15]

Historically, Christianity has highlighted propositional assertions as the primary vehicle for communicating biblical truth and constructing a careful theology. For example, Pauline logic is crucial for our understanding of many biblical doctrines. Yet the broader canon of Scripture conveys truth through wider genres and modes of thinking.[16] While propositional language brings a particular kind of light—an exacting laser beam of tight reasoning—it must be complemented by the visceral impact of these non-propositional literary forms.

The drama of story (and poetry) adds sound, color, flavor, texture, and aroma to revelational truth that simply cannot be conveyed by theological abstraction. *Drama* and *doctrine* are equally necessary and complementary components to our understanding of the Christian faith. The drama of Scripture informs doctrine, and doctrine digs deeper into the meaning of the drama. Drama grips the heart, while doctrine fortifies the mind.[17]

The pedagogy of Jesus himself is largely centered on more literary discourses. When he wished to arrest his audience, he would tell them a parable. Parables were but one of the many unconventional and literary means by which he conveyed theological truth. "Jesus was a *metaphorical* theologian. That is, his primary method of creating meaning was through metaphor, simile, parable and dramatic action rather than through logic and reasoning. He created meaning like a dramatist and a poet rather than like a philosopher."[18]

This doesn't mean that Jesus was unconcerned with careful rational articulation of truth claims. As God, he is the very source of logic (Col. 2:3). His mind is characterized by the rational order he infused into his creation and his image-bearing creatures. But he also brings truth to bear on the imagination.

Here is where the narrative character of Scripture becomes important to

---

15. Brian Godawa, *Hollywood Worldviews* (Downers Grove, IL: InterVarsity Press, 2009), 70.

16. Only about 30 percent of the Bible contains propositional or didactic language.

17. Berry Belvedere, "What Narrative Can't Say: The Limits of Narrative Theology," found at: https://mereorthodoxy.com/what-narrative-cant-say-limits-narrative-theology/.

18. Kenneth E. Bailey, *Jesus through Middle Eastern Eyes* (Downers Grove, IL: InterVarsity Press, 2008), 279.

our inquiry. Scripture contains little in the way of explicit propositions that might form a basis for constructing a theodicy. I believe the reason why is that the power of a biblical theodicy is better conveyed in the deeply affective nature of the metanarrative of Scripture—the paradigmatic source of the universal storyline that literary critics call the *monomyth*.

While some texts provide important propositional anchors (e.g., Rom. 3; 8; 9; 1 Cor. 15; Eph. 1; Phil. 2),[19] the more poignant way to make sense of God's overarching purpose for evil is to see how it fits into the Bible's storyline as the principal conflict around which God seeks to highlight redemption. In this regard, when it comes to questions of evil, pain, and suffering, the Bible is primarily focused on the forest, not the trees. It looks at the whole and doesn't always bother with the myriad parts. It answers the broad questions but doesn't usually deal with matters such as these: Why this or that evil? Why now and not then? Why her instead of him?[20]

Nonetheless, the visceral impact of Scripture's narrative plot tells us more than many plain expositions might. Its stark penetrations into the depths of evil would not convey its horror if all it said was, "Evil is bad . . . really, really bad." Showing communicates more evocatively than telling.[21] Likewise, if all we knew about redemption were detailed in precise doctrinal statements, it would not elicit the sort of spellbinding wonder and enchantment that comes from seeing redemptive motifs unfold in the drama of the biblically framed story of historical redemption.

For example, the exodus story gives a whole new meaning to the word *redemption*. The dramatic storyline conveyed in the varied and unified narratives of the Old and New Testaments intersects the actual experience of the redeemed because they are part of this story—the continuing history of redemption that the transcendent Author of history is unfolding.

This chapter will summarize the Bible's grand storyline. The following chapters will analyze (using propositional arguments) the meaning of this story in terms of how it frames a biblical theodicy. The central focus of the scriptural plot is its redemptive messianic hero, who turns out to be the Son of God. The conflict of humanity's fall elicits the promise and foreshadowing of the messianic Son of God in the Old Testament plot.

---

19. See treatments of these passages especially in chapters 12, 13, 14, and 16.

20. John Piper, "Why God Doesn't Fully Explain Pain," *Desiring God*, July 14, 2008, https://www.desiringgod.org/articles/why-god-doesnt-fully-explain-pain.

21. Recent studies of Hebrew narrative indicate that showing (communicating the theological message via the characters' words and actions) is often preferred over telling (explaining the characters' words and actions). See Meir Sternberg, *The Poetics of Biblical Narrative: Ideological Literature and the Drama of Reading* (Bloomington, IN: Indiana University Press, 1985).

The incarnation, life, death, resurrection, ascension, and glorious return of the messianic Son of God to establish God's eternal kingdom mark the New Testament plot. The narrative supplies the drama and wonder of what God is doing.

But the bare narrative will not do. It must be accompanied by exposition—exegetical and theological abstraction. As J. Gresham Machen notes, "'Christ died'—that is history; 'Christ died for our sins'—that is doctrine. Without these two elements, joined in an absolutely indissoluble union, there is no Christianity."[22] Both showing (historical narrative) and telling (theology) are necessary complements to each other. Thus, biblical truth does not imbibe postmodernism's disdain for propositional truth claims. The narrative (and poetic) portions of Scripture are always clarified in the broader context by translating its truths into dogma (i.e., theological assertions).

THE BIBLE, HISTORY, AND MYTH

The literary giants Tolkien and Lewis called the biblical narrative the *True Myth*. This designation can be misleading. For evangelicals, the use of the term *myth* in biblical studies does not usually garner praise, and for good reason.[23] It is preferable to identify the grand narrative of Scripture as the *One True Story*. While the biblical storyline is the archetypal source of all meaningful storytelling—the monomyth—it is most certainly not to be equated with the largely fictional and error-ridden character of all lesser stories and myths.[24]

The Bultmannian project of the demythologization of Scripture is bunk. The biblical canon is not myth in the common sense: that is, falsehoods, fictions, fables, and fantasies. Nor does it contain historical exaggerations, distortions, or accretions that conceal some elusive historical core. While it has some features that are often likened to ancient Near Eastern and Hellenistic myths and the like, it is also distinguished from those myths in three important ways.

---

22. J. Gresham Machen, *Christianity and Liberalism* (1923; repr., Grand Rapids: Eerdmans, 2009), 23.

23. See, for example, Gordon J. Wenham, "Genesis 1–11 as Protohistory," in *Genesis: History, Fiction, or Neither? Three Views on the Bible's Earliest Chapters*, ed. Charles Halton and Stanley N. Gundry (Grand Rapids: Zondervan, 2015), 82–85. In spite of his cautions, it is unclear how much Wenham himself affirms the historicity of Scripture. For an appraisal of the way in which *myth* has been used in biblical studies, see John N. Oswalt, *The Bible among the Myths* (Grand Rapids: Zondervan, 2009).

24. In this regard, we must also be careful with identifying the biblical narrative as the paradigmatic *monomyth* in order to avoid the confusing implications of the term *myth*.

First, it does not embrace the pagan worldviews of those myths. It seeks to refute them.[25] Second, it is self-consciously crafted as factual history that has been shown to be reliable, including all its manifestations of the supernatural.[26] Miracles form a crucial dimension of its history lest we become functional atheists.[27]

Furthermore, "redemption must take place *in* this world if it is going to offer any lasting help to people who live *in* this world."[28] A wedge must not be driven between the various literary features of the Bible that highlight its supremely transcendent character and its historical veracity that it self-consciously upholds.[29] To be sure, the transcendent and universally resonating character of Scripture is not merely the narration of interesting historical events. It is the narration of the most *important* historical events in order to penetrate and illuminate *true reality*—reality as God reveals it. Only in this sense could we agree that "myth narrates a sacred history."[30] That sacred history is the historical-redemptive history of the Bible.[31] It is not a vaguely reenacted mythic mirror of some impenetrable sacred pseudo-Platonic reality. This is reality as God directs it in real time and

25. See John D. Currid, *Against the Gods: The Polemical Theology of the Old Testament* (Wheaton, IL: Crossway, 2013).

26. On the importance of the historicity of the Bible, see James K. Hoffmeier and Dennis R. Magary, eds., *Do Historical Matters Matter to Faith?* (Wheaton, IL: Crossway, 2012). For a defense of the historical reliability of the Old Testament, see K. A. Kitchen, *On the Historical Reliability of the Old Testament* (Grand Rapids: Eerdmans, 2003); Eugene H. Merrill, *Kingdom of Priests: A History of Old Testament Israel*, 2nd ed. (Grand Rapids: Baker Academic, 2008); David M. Howard Jr. and Michael A. Grisanti, eds., *Giving the Sense: Understanding and Using Old Testament Historical Texts* (Grand Rapids: Kregel, 2003). For the New Testament, see Craig L. Blomberg, *The Historical Reliability of the Gospels* (Downers Grove, IL: InterVarsity Press, 2007); Craig L. Blomberg, *The Historical Reliability of the New Testament* (Nashville: B&H Academic, 2016); Richard Bauckham, *Jesus and the Eyewitnesses: The Gospels as Eyewitness Testimony*, 2nd ed. (Grand Rapids: Eerdmans, 2017); Craig S. Keener, *Acts: An Exegetical Commentary*, 4 vols. (Grand Rapids: Baker Academic, 2012–15); Colin J. Hemer, *The Book of Acts in the Setting of Hellenistic History* (Winona Lake, IN: Eisenbrauns, 1990). For a critique of evangelical views compromising the historical reliability of the Gospels, see Lydia McGrew, *The Mirror or the Mask: Liberating the Gospel from Literary Devices* (Tampa, FL: DeWard Publishing, 2019). See also Lydia McGrew, *Hidden in Plain View: Undesigned Coincidences in the Gospels and Acts* (Tampa, FL: DeWard Publishing, 2017).

27. Gruenler, "Jesus as Author of the Evangelium," 207–9.

28. William Varner, "The Seed and Schaeffer," in *What Happened in the Garden?*, ed. Abner Chou (Grand Rapids: Kregel, 2016), 168.

29. David M. Howard Jr., "History or Story? The Literary Dimension in Narrative Texts," in *Giving the Sense: Understanding and Using Old Testament Historical Texts*, ed. David M. Howard Jr. and Michael A. Grisanti (Grand Rapids: Kregel, 2003), 54–73.

30. Mircea Eliade, *Myth and Reality*, trans. Willard R. Trask (New York: Harper & Row, 1963), 5.

31. Bryan D. Estelle, *Echoes of Exodus: Tracing a Biblical Motif* (Downers Grove, IL: InterVarsity Press, 2018), 118.

real space in the lives of real people. The whole of Scripture highlights the grand historical-redemptive motifs that God has decreed in the unfolding of this history while framing that history with those elements that are essential to the identity, meaning, and purpose of humanity. This is God through Christ reconciling the world to himself (2 Cor. 5:19).

Third, the Bible stands alone as the divinely breathed (2 Tim. 3:16) inerrant Word of the living God (Heb. 6:18). Therefore, it is the source of all the critical truths we need to make sense of the world we live in (John 17:17; 2 Peter 1:3). The mythopoetic character of Scripture is never to be divorced from its essential truthfulness. Consequently, its historical claims are without error. Its truth claims are factual, wholly rational, and unassailable. No pagan myth can match the Bible's utterly unique divine character.[32]

John Oswalt has persuasively argued that ancient Near Eastern mythologies are radically dissimilar to the biblical worldview even as they may reflect disordered bits and pieces of universal themes in the Bible's storyline that are indistinctly mirrored in the world.[33] The ancient worldviews that were set against the Bible have no concept of history as we know it. Instead, episodes taking place in the real world were conceived as cyclical—everything being in a continual "now" or endlessly repeating the same episodic trap. People were regarded as colorless cogs in a cosmic wheel spinning around and around, yet going nowhere. In seeking to appease their various gods for basic necessities and protections, they lacked any personal connection to those gods. This view of reality is suffused with pessimism.

In contrast, the biblical view of reality sees it as linear. It is moving from one place to another, with a beginning, middle, and end, linking one episode after another toward a purposeful goal.[34] Thus, in the biblical

32. Important recent works on the nature of Scripture include Peter A. Lillback and Richard B. Gaffin Jr., eds., *Thy Word Is Still Truth: Essential Writings on the Doctrine of Scripture from the Reformation to Today* (Phillipsburg, NJ: P&R Publishing, 2013); John MacArthur, ed., *The Inerrant Word: Biblical, Historical, Theological, and Pastoral Perspectives* (Wheaton, IL: Crossway, 2016); D. A. Carson, *Collected Writings on Scripture* (Wheaton, IL: Crossway, 2010); John M. Frame, *The Doctrine of the Word of God* (Phillipsburg, NJ: P&R Publishing, 2010); Gregory K. Beale, *The Erosion of Inerrancy in Evangelicalism: Responding to New Challenges to Biblical Authority* (Wheaton, IL: Crossway, 2008). For a more accessible treatment, see Kevin DeYoung, *Taking God at His Word* (Wheaton, IL: Crossway, 2014).

33. Oswalt, *The Bible among the Myths*, 122–24. Oswalt focuses primarily on the Old Testament, but a similar argument can be made for the New Testament.

34. Oswalt, *The Bible among the Myths*, 111–12, 116–17. See also David Bebbington, *Patterns in History* (Downers Grove, IL: InterVarsity Press, 1979), 43–67; Anthony A. Hoekema, *The Bible and the Future* (Grand Rapids: Eerdmans, 1979), 25, 31–32; T. Maurice Pugh, "Dispensationalism and Views of Redemption History," in *Dispensationalism and the History of Redemption: A Developing and Diverse Tradition*, ed. D. Jeffrey Bingham and Glenn R. Kreider (Chicago: Moody Press, 2015), 221–23.

worldview, "history is teleological: that is, it is goal-oriented; it is designed. This in turn presupposes a goal-setter, a planner, a designer."[35] This is how stories operate. History is a grand story that requires a transcendent Author.[36]

Furthermore, in the biblical concept of history, people are regarded as dignified individuals having a direct personal relationship with the one true God, who directs the flow of history as well as everyone's place in it. And because the divine Author is supremely good and sovereign, the future is optimistic. "Only if the future is in some way guaranteed can human confidence in what lies ahead be sustained."[37] So the good will triumph over evil. Christ, the central protagonist of history, will be victorious.

This linear, purposeful, and personal notion that we call *history* is so axiomatic today that we take its origins for granted. Oswalt quotes Gerhard Von Rad, who says, "[The Old Testament's] ability to deal with extensive complexes of connected history and not just episodes must be regarded as one of the most momentous advances in man's understanding of himself, since its effects upon the spiritual development of the whole West are incalculable."[38]

The Greeks, namely, Herodotus and Thucydides, are routinely acknowledged as the architects of historical writing, but the Hebrews had a more fully worked-out philosophy of history nearly a millennium earlier.[39] As Oswalt indicates, the entire Bible is so rooted in such a self-conscious perception of the veracity of its historical worldview that if its actual historical claims were easily falsified, the recorders of that history would be placed under a suspicion that is wholly implausible.[40] He concludes, "If we look

35. Brent Kinman, *History, Design and the End of Time: God's Plan for the World* (Nashville: Broadman & Holman, 2000), 10. See also Hoekema, *The Bible and the Future*, 26–28.

36. Note how the apostle Paul narrates Old Testament history in his sermon at Pisidian Antioch in Acts 13:16–24. God is the repeated grammatical subject (i.e., Author) of each episodic phase of Israel's history.

37. Bebbington, *Patterns in History*, 90.

38. Oswalt, *The Bible among the Myths*, 143.

39. Yet even the ancient Greeks and classical antiquity in general were strapped to a cyclical view of history. See Oscar Cullmann, *Christ and Time*, trans. Floyd V. Filson (Philadelphia: Westminster, 1950), 52; Bebbington, *Patterns in History*, 29–33. Bebbington indicates that most ancient cultures imbibed some form of this cyclical view of history (*Patterns in History*, 21–42). One of the first extensive studies of this worldview is Mircea Eliade's *The Myth of the Eternal Return: Cosmos and History*, trans. Willard R. Trask (New York: Bollingen Foundation, 1954). Bebbington also notes that modern secular conceptions of history borrowed from the linear and goal-oriented concept of Christian history via the idea of human progress (an Enlightenment idea) while rejecting the concept that history is providentially guided by a sovereign, transcendent God (Eliade, *Myth of the Eternal Return*, 68–69).

40. Oswalt, *The Bible among the Myths*, 151.

at the Bible as a whole, where else is there anything like it in its world, or indeed, in *the* world? There is nothing like it. In its historical narratives covering the sweep of a nation's existence *and* the glories and tragedies of individual life, it is unparalleled."[41]

This points to the utter uniqueness of the Christian faith. As B. B. Warfield has pointed out:

> Precisely what characterizes Christianity . . . among the religions, is that it is a "historical religion," that is, a religion whose facts are its doctrines; which does not consist in a "tone of feeling," a way of looking at things— as for example the perception of a Father's hand in all the chances and changes of life—but has to tell of a series of great redemptive acts in which God the Lord has actually intervened in the complex of nature and the stream of history in a definitely supernatural manner. If these facts are denied as actual occurrences in time and space, Christianity is denied; if they are neglected, Christianity is neglected. Christianity is dismissed from the world of reality, and evaporated into a sentiment— "an iridescent dream."[42]

The comprehensive and sweeping flow of the historical narrative from Genesis to Revelation is the divinely inspired datum from which we can frame the meaning of life and existence—*true reality*. It is the only world-view that adequately situates good and evil in the broader panorama of history and how our own lives are shaped by this God-orchestrated story. When the historical orientation of the biblical revelation is combined with the spectacular quality of its literary genius, it is no wonder that the Bible has cast a long and unprecedented shadow over the subsequent history of Western culture and its literature.[43] It explains why Scripture has "pre-eminently the 'inner consistency of reality'" that is missing from pagan myths.[44]

FRAMING THE PLOTLINE OF SCRIPTURE

So how do we put the pieces of the biblical story together? There are a number of ways in which various scholars with differing theological commitments

---

41. Oswalt, *The Bible among the Myths*, 192.

42. Benjamin B. Warfield, *Critical Reviews*, in *The Works of Benjamin B. Warfield*, vol. 10 (repr., Grand Rapids: Baker, 2000), 479.

43. Northrop Frye, *The Great Code: The Bible and Literature* (New York: Harcourt Books, 1982), xii.

44. Tolkien, "On Fairy-Stories," 156.

have sought to ascertain the overall framework of Scripture's narrative storyline, but they all hang the plot points, more or less, on the following movements of the drama: (1) the initial creation account in Genesis 1–2; (2) the fall of Adam and Eve in Genesis 3 and its cosmic consequences; (3) the initiation of redemption with the seed of Abraham—the nation of Israel; (4) the climax of redemption in the incarnation of the Son of God and his death and resurrection; (5) the progress of redemption after the ascension of Christ in the expansion of the church; and finally (6) the consummation of redemption at the return of Christ.[45] Throughout the successive acts of this grand plan, the Bible "has a unifying plot conflict consisting of the great spiritual struggle between good and evil. Virtually every event that we read about in the Bible shows some movement, whether slight or momentous, toward God or away from him, toward good or evil. The world of the Bible is claimed by God and counterclaimed by evil."[46] Yet this is not a duel between two equal cosmic powers that leaves the reader in suspense. God serves as the grand Author of these two trajectories in such a way that good—the goodness of God—will necessarily triumph over evil.

The conflict is set in motion so that the audience—the human participants in the story—will be awed by the glory of God, the ultimate protagonist and hero of the story. God not only has written and is now directing this unfolding drama, but has also entered the story as its leading actor. Roland M. Frye writes:

45. For example, the following works represent various traditions from covenantal (e.g., Geerhardus Vos's redemptive-historical brand of biblical theology) and dispensational theologians as well as others who cannot be categorized as either (e.g., progressive covenantalists such as Gentry and Wellum), yet all would agree with this basic framework: Geerhardus Vos, *Biblical Theology: Old and New Testaments* (Grand Rapids: Eerdmans, 1948); Bingham and Kreider, *Dispensationalism and the History of Redemption*; D. T. Desmond Alexander, *From Eden to the New Jerusalem* (Downers Grove, IL: InterVarsity Press, 2008); Craig G. Bartholomew and Michael W. Goheen, *The Drama of Scripture: Finding Our Place in the Biblical Story* (Grand Rapids: Baker Academic, 2014); Michael J. Vlach, *He Will Reign Forever: A Biblical Theology of the Kingdom of God* (Silverton, OR: Lampion Press, 2016); Peter J. Gentry and Stephen J. Wellum, *Kingdom through Covenant: A Biblical-Theological Understanding of the Covenants*, 2nd ed. (Wheaton, IL: Crossway, 2018); G. K. Beale, *The Temple and the Church's Mission: A Biblical Theology of the Dwelling Place of God* (Downers Grove, IL: InterVarsity Press, 2004); James M. Hamilton Jr., *God's Glory in Salvation through Judgment: A Biblical Theology* (Wheaton, IL: Crossway, 2010); Thomas R. Schreiner, *The King in His Beauty: A Biblical Theology of the Old and New Testaments* (Grand Rapids: Baker Academic, 2013); Graeme Goldsworthy, *According to Plan: The Unfolding Revelation of God in the Bible* (Downers Grove, IL: InterVarsity Press, 1991); Michael D. Williams, *Far as the Curse Is Found: The Covenant Story of Redemption* (Phillipsburg, NJ: P&R Publishing, 2005).

46. Leland Ryken, *Words of Delight: A Literary Introduction to the Bible* (Grand Rapids: Baker, 1992), 31.

The characterization of God may indeed be said to be the central literary concern of the Bible, and it is pursued from beginning to end.... Not even the most seemingly insignificant action in the Bible can be understood apart from the emerging characterization of the deity. With this great protagonist and his designs, all other characters and events interact, as history becomes the great arena for God's characteristic and characterizing actions.[47]

Randy Alcorn sums up how the biblical plotline addresses the theodical conundrum we face:

The problem of evil lies at the very heart of the biblical account and serves as the crux of the unfolding drama of redemption. The first act of human evil moved God to bring decisive judgment while simultaneously unveiling his master plan. To complete redemption—as well as that of the entire fallen creation—he sets in motion his strategy of incarnation, atoning death, resurrection, and ultimate return.[48]

D. A. Carson sums it up this way: God's redemptive reign and saving actions in the world anticipate "the restoration of goodness, even the transformation to a greater glory, of the universe gone wrong (Rom. 8:21), and arrives finally at the dawning of a new heaven and a new earth (Rev. 21–22; cf. Isa. 65:17), the home of a righteousness (2 Peter 3:13)"—a God-saturated paradise beyond anything that we could ever imagine.[49] The center of the story, which is the center of the Bible, which is the center of theology and therefore the center of all things, is God and his glory. "For from him and through him and to him are all things. To him be glory forever. Amen" (Rom. 11:36).[50]

Thus, the fundamental storyline (overarching theme) of the Bible is how God's glory is magnified in his response to evil through the sending of a Redeemer, his beloved Son, Jesus Christ. The story itself is the theodicy of Scripture. And while this story contains a crisis of stupendous proportions, we do not blame the Author of the story for writing it into the plot, precisely because the wonder of the story is how the crisis gets resolved in

47. Roland M. Frye, *The Bible: Selections from the King James Version for Study as Literature* (Boston: Houghton Mifflin, 1965), xvi, quoted in Ryken, *Words of Delight*, 31.

48. Randy Alcorn, *If God Is Good: Faith in the Midst of Suffering and Evil* (Colorado Springs: Multnomah Books, 2009), 21.

49. D. A. Carson, *The Gagging of God: Christianity Confronts Pluralism* (Grand Rapids: Zondervan, 1996), 202.

50. Hamilton, *God's Glory in Salvation*, 53–56. See pages 287–91 on the centrality of God's glory in Scripture.

due course. Every lie, every murder, every rape, every act of brutality, every form of degrading oppression and violence forms part of the crisis—both in the actual plotline of Scripture and in its microcosmic reflection of the crisis in the broader sweep of history.

As traumatic as the crisis is, however, the glory that attaches to its resolution through the work of Christ far exceeds its crushing weight. Thus, instead of blaming the Author for introducing the crisis, he is praised for authoring a plot whereby sin, evil, pain, suffering, and death are swallowed up in victory (1 Cor. 15:54).[51] The greater the crisis, the more costly its resolution and the more glorious its defeat.

Let us frame the storyline by using the five standard plot points from Freytag's Pyramid: (1) *exposition*; (2) *rising action*; (3) *climax*; (4) *falling action*; and (5) *denouement.*[52]

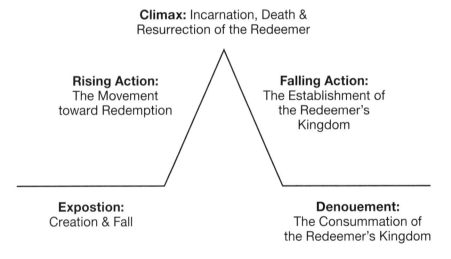

Climax: Incarnation, Death & Resurrection of the Redeemer

Rising Action: The Movement toward Redemption

Falling Action: The Establishment of the Redeemer's Kingdom

Expostion: Creation & Fall

Denouement: The Consummation of the Redeemer's Kingdom

Fig. 11.1. The Biblical Storyline

51. An author would be blamed for evil in a story only if the story glorified evil, treating it as virtuous or allowing evil to defeat good. J. A. Crabtree writes: "The evil of a story must not be judged on the basis of whether it contains evil within it. Rather, it must be judged on the bases of (a) the motive behind the story, (b) the purpose it accomplishes, and (c) the final effect that it has. If the motive behind it is pure, its purpose is righteous, and its final effect is good, then the story is a good creation, not an evil one. It is one that a morally perfect person would be justified in creating, regardless of what particular evils may exist within its pages" (*The Most Real Being: A Biblical and Philosophical Defense of Divine Determinism* [Eugene, OR: Gutenberg College Press, 2004], 253).

52. See pages 236–40 This is not to suggest that God anticipated Freytag's Pyramid when planning the arc of history. It is simply a useful literary tool to help us frame the story of the Bible in the same way it has helped to frame other monomythic stories.

Exposition: Creation and Fall

The Creation

The great historical drama begins with creation. The opening verse of Genesis is ripe with the *exposition* of the story, setting up the conditions under which the conflict will arise. "In the beginning, God created the heavens and the earth" (Gen. 1:1). Notice that the universe does not emerge out of some *thing* but some *One*—a person.[53] Furthermore, the Bible does not introduce God with a defense of his existence. His presence is assumed as the most fundamental precondition of reality.

Umberto Cassuto explains the Bible's unprecedented focus on this Creator-Ruler-God who is distinguished from all other pagan gods of the ancients (who are no gods at all—Ps. 96:5) and their flawed myths:

> Then came the Torah and soared aloft, as on eagles' wings, above all these nations. Not many gods but One God; not theogony, for a god has no family tree; nor wars nor strife nor clash of wills, but only One will, which rules over everything, without the slightest let or hindrance; not a deity associated with nature and identified with it wholly or in part, but a God who stands above nature, and outside of it, and nature and all its constituent elements, even the sun and all other entities, be they never so exalted, are only His creatures, made according to His will.[54]

The "constituent elements" of all created reality, concisely managed in one verse, indicate that God has eternally existed irrespective of the advent of time ("the beginning") as well as space and matter ("the heavens and the earth"). The implication is that while the creation has its beginning in God, God has no beginning. He creates all out of nothing—*ex nihilo*.[55] Notice also the clear dissimilarity between God as Creator and the created. Time, space, matter, and all creaturely life are wholly dependent on him—the one who requires nothing outside himself to exist. He is self-sufficient in himself, but all-sufficient for his creatures (Acts 17:25). Furthermore, he is no idle god of deism, but the living, active, sustaining Lord of all.

The verse already hints at the central place that the earth will play in this story as indicated by the rest of the narrative in Genesis 1 and 2. It is striking that the "heavens" constitute a vast and incomprehensible expanse,

---

53. Gregory Koukl, *The Story of Reality* (Grand Rapids: Zondervan, 2017), 47.
54. Umberto Cassuto, *From Adam to Noah: A Commentary on the Book of Genesis (Part 1)*, trans. Israel Abrahams (Jerusalem: Magnes Press, 1989), 8.
55. See discussion in John M. Frame, *The Doctrine of God* (Phillipsburg, NJ: P&R Publishing, 2002), 298–302.

whereas the earth is but a microscopic particle of dust by comparison. Yet its actual composition is uniquely spectacular; and for this reason, this little hovel will be the primary stage for God to display the riches of his glory.[56] He is its sole Possessor: "The earth is the Lord's and the fullness thereof, the world and those who dwell therein" (Ps. 24:1).

As the narrative progresses, the lens is focused even more narrowly on one particular object of God's creation called *adam* (Heb. for "man"). God creates "man," both "male and female," uniquely in his own image (Gen. 1:26–27). While there is dissimilarity between Creator and creature, there is similarity as well. No other creatures are afforded this special dignity. "What is man that you are mindful of him, and the son of man that you care for him? Yet you have made him a little lower than the heavenly beings and crowned him with glory and honor" (Ps. 8:4–5).

While God is *the* center of the story, man is central to God's unfolding plan. He is a supporting character. Thus, God places the man Adam and his wife Eve in a garden (Gen. 2:8)—a divine sanctuary of delights[57]—in order that his personal presence might be manifested to them (3:8) in a place marked by perfect harmony and fellowship. They are not their own. They, too, belong to God, and Eden is his dwelling place on the earth.[58] As bearers of the divine image, they have been uniquely fitted and mandated to fill and govern the world as God's vice-regents to bring him glory (1:28).[59] That glory is to extend from the garden to the whole earth.[60] They have been commissioned "to Edenize the entire creation."[61] Practically speaking, this means that humanity has been tasked with a cultural mandate to pursue every intellectual, technological, aesthetic, and social discipline to establish a civilization of God-drenched wonder.

Throughout the account, every aspect of this creation is pronounced "good."[62] Everything, material and immaterial, is "very good" (Gen. 1:31)—

---

56. To see what a unique physical place the earth is, see Guillermo Gonzalez and Jay W. Richards, *The Privileged Planet* (Washington, DC: Regnery Publishing, 2004).

57. Alexander, *From Eden to the New Jerusalem*, 21.

58. G. K. Beale and Mitchell Kim, *God Dwells among Us: Expanding Eden to the Ends of the Earth* (Downers Grove, IL: InterVarsity Press, 2014).

59. C. John Collins argues that the image of God should be understood in terms of resemblance (our nature is in some sense like God), representation (we are God's representative rulers on earth), and relation (we were designed for relationship with God and other humans). See *Genesis 1–4: A Linguistic, Literary, and Theological Commentary* (Phillipsburg, NJ: P&R Publishing, 2006), 61–67.

60. Hamilton, *God's Glory in Salvation*, 50, 74.

61. Jeremy R. Treat, *The Crucified King: Atonement and Kingdom in Biblical and Systematic Theology* (Grand Rapids: Zondervan, 2014), 55–56.

62. The Hebrew term for "good" (*tob*) is used seven times in Genesis 1 (i.e., 1:4, 10, 12, 18, 21, 25, 31).

beautiful, without blemish—the way things *ought* to be. God is the sum and substance of goodness (Ps. 100:5); therefore, he cannot make anything bad. In the light of God's glorious goodness, his creatures can bask in fullness of joy with pleasures forevermore flowing from the palm of his hand (16:11). There is no longing, no anxiety, no dissatisfaction. No sin. No death. All is right in the world. No conflict on the horizon. No hint of disorder. Every dream, every utopia, every fleeting tranquil thought that passes through the present afflicted psyche of humanity is found in the untainted paradise of Eden and of its unbroken fellowship with the Creator.[63]

But this paradise is soon to be lost, its glory dissipated.

The Fall

Genesis 3 wastes no time in introducing the central conflict of the story. The sunny warmth of the garden is immediately overshadowed by dark, billowy, fast-churning storm clouds. The order, the beauty, the peace, the harmony described in Genesis 1 and 2 comes quickly crashing down. This all comes by way of meeting the main villain of the story, the "crafty serpent" better known as Satan (Rev. 20:2). Just as the Bible portrays God without a hint of evil, the Bible portrays Satan without a hint of goodness. This "liar and the father of lies" (John 8:44) maligns God, seeking to usurp his authority and to turn Adam and Eve against him.

God has invited Adam to enjoy the fruit of the garden; nonetheless, he has presented him with a critical test: "of the tree of the knowledge of good and evil you shall not eat, for in the day that you eat of it you shall surely die" (Gen. 2:17). The serpent wants the man to fail the test. But instead of targeting Adam, he preys on the vulnerable Eve, thus also usurping the authority of her husband, whom God has directly charged to maintain order in the garden.[64] Satan seeks to subvert the whole order of the creation

---

63. This militates against views of earth history that posit death (either animal or protohuman death) and corruption for millions of years before the creation of man. The paradigm of creation, fall, and redemption is the source of the U-shaped monomythic pattern of uncorrupted goodness followed by corruption and then a return to uncorrupted goodness. In other words, the pattern makes no sense unless we accept the natural reading of Genesis 1–2 as a literal six-day creation event with no deep time somehow secretly embedded in the narrative. See James Stambaugh, "Whence Cometh Death? A Biblical Theology of Physical Death and Natural Evil," in *Coming to Grips with Genesis: Biblical Authority and the Age of the Earth*, ed. Terry Mortenson and Thane H. Ury (Green Forest, AR: Master Books, 2008), 373–97; Trevor Craigen, "Can Deep Time Be Embedded in Genesis?," in *Coming to Grips with Genesis: Biblical Authority and the Age of the Earth*, ed. Terry Mortenson and Thane H. Ury (Green Forest, AR: Master Books, 2008), 193–210.

64. John D. Currid, *A Study Commentary on Genesis*, vol. 1, *Genesis 1:1–25:18* (Darlington, UK: Evangelical Press, 2003), 117.

and derail humanity's task of glorifying God in the establishment of a holy kingdom.[65]

The craftiness of Satan is on display in several ways. His posing of the question to Eve seems innocent enough: "Did God actually say, 'You shall not eat of any tree in the garden'?" (Gen. 3:1). D. A. Carson observes, "In some ways the question is both disturbing and flattering. It smuggles in the assumption that we have the ability, even the right, to stand in judgment of what God said."[66] Already the serpent has planted a seed of doubt in Eve's mind.

What is unbelief? It is to doubt the truthfulness of God's Word, and this is the seedbed of all sin. Satan also insinuates that God's command is too prohibitive. Being restricted from eating from "any" tree of the garden is the opposite of God's words. Only one tree has been forbidden; the rest have been freely given (2:16–17). There is a shell of truth in the serpent's statement, but at its core resides a grotesque lie. Such is the subtlety of all of Satan's deceptions (2 Cor. 11:14). The idea is that God's commands are harsh. He has no concern for the well-being of his creatures.

Eve's heart is captured. Her response shows no enthusiasm for the truth. Well, yes . . . we can eat "of the fruit of the trees of the garden" (Gen. 3:2). Missing from her answer is that *any* tree is to be *freely* eaten from except one (2:16). Is she prepared to think that the magnificent paradise that God has provided to her and Adam is so disenchanting after all? She has everything that she could possibly want or need. How easily temptation provokes one to dismiss the obvious. Now to convince herself that God's command is too restrictive, she adds that they are not even to "touch" the forbidden fruit (3:3). When we dislike God's commands, we often exaggerate their conditions in order to accuse them of being legalistic. God is conceived of as a pleasure-stealing ogre.

Adam and Eve doubt God's goodness and wisdom, and this leads to disbelief in his integrity. They convince themselves that he has lied to them. "You will not surely die," the serpent rejoins (Gen. 3:4). "The first doctrine to be denied, according to the Bible, is the doctrine of judgment. . . . If you can get rid of that one teaching, then rebellion has no adverse consequences, and you are free to do anything."[67] The couple's disbelief will lead to the unthinkable. They will throw off the shackles of this overbearing God

65. Eugene H. Merrill, *Everlasting Dominion: A Theology of the Old Testament* (Nashville: B&H Publishing Group, 2006), 208–9.
66. D. A. Carson, *The God Who Is There: Finding Your Place in God's Story* (Grand Rapids: Baker, 2010), 31.
67. Carson, *The God Who Is There*, 32.

who cares nothing for them. Rebellion is marked by dissatisfaction and resentment of being placed under God's sovereign and moral will. It is a repudiation of his rightful lordship.[68]

To finalize the rebellion, divine lordship must be replaced. Satan's next step is to convince Eve that her "perfect and complete" state of existence is an illusion.[69] God is withholding something vastly beneficial for her, something that rightfully belongs to her. If she eats the fruit, she will be . . . just like God (Gen. 3:5)! Her "eyes will be opened" to new and wonderful worlds of power, pleasure, and freedom! She will have knowledge of good and evil. This is true from an experiential perspective (v. 22). But it is one thing to have the objective and exhaustive understanding of good and evil that God alone has. It is another to gain a knowledge of good and evil by engaging in acts of evil.[70] Again, Satan belies his craftiness. He leads Eve to think that by throwing off God's laws, she will be able to forge her own. She will be autonomous, the captain of her own soul. She will be her own lord, exercising her own sovereignty. She will attempt to "de-god" God.[71]

Now that her cognitive rationalizations for disobedience are complete, she can turn her eyes to the object of her newly conceived desire. What she dares not touch, let alone eat, suddenly has a dark allure. The fruit (Gen. 3:6) is "physically appealing (*good for food*), aesthetically pleasing (*a delight to the eyes*), and sapientially transforming (*desirable in acquiring wisdom*)."[72] And all this time, Adam, "who was with her" (v. 6), is curiously silent. No more. Together they partake, and before the fruit has a chance to slide down their throats, the fall is complete. The conflict of the ages comes raging onto the stage as the audience stares wide-eyed, mouths gaping, hearts surging—all aghast.

And what wonders come into view as "the eyes of both were opened" (Gen. 3:7)? None. No power. No pleasure. No freedom. No feeling-like-God euphoria. Rather, a sudden realization of ugliness, of nakedness, of shame and disillusion. Instead of power, there are vulnerability and helplessness. Instead of pleasure, there are pain and suffering. Instead of freedom, there is bondage. Instead of feeling like God, there is the searing reality of frail creatureliness. Wounded by the guilt of their own moral irresponsibility,

68. Schreiner, *The King in His Beauty*, 9.
69. Grant Horner, "Genesis 3—A Map of Misreadings," in *What Happened in the Garden?*, ed. Abner Chou (Grand Rapids: Kregel, 2016), 112.
70. Carson, *The God Who Is There*, 32; Merrill, *Everlasting Dominion*, 201–2.
71. Carson, *The God Who Is There*, 33.
72. Victor P. Hamilton, *The Book of Genesis: Chapters 1–17*, New International Commentary on the Old Testament (Grand Rapids: Eerdmans, 1990), 190.

Adam and Eve hide themselves from God. Instead of experiencing harmony and fellowship with their God, they feel exposed before his holy justice. Paradise has been lost.

The conflict of the story is sealed by the divine curses that inexorably fall upon the man, his wife, and their progeny. They bring ruin and death on themselves and the creation. Death means separation. Physical death separates one's immaterial soul from the material body. But this isn't the worst of it. In its darkest dimension, "death is alienation from the life of God."[73]

They are banished from the garden and all the benefits of his presence there (Gen. 3:23). All fellowship and harmony with their Creator is broken. An inner angst sets in. And it can never be rectified apart from reconciliation with him. But the man and his wife experience alienation from each other as well (v. 16), and from the creation itself. Before the fall, the creation was a domesticated wonderland. After the fall, it becomes a thorny wilderness that resists our efforts to tame it at every turn (vv. 17–19). "The whole world lies in the power of the evil one" (1 John 5:19), and his grip can be broken by no mortal.

The storyline of the Bible has already unfolded at a dizzying pace. Grant Horner writes, "The first three chapters of Genesis are the most important and momentous words ever written. Everything else one believes about the Bible and Christian theology and practice depends ultimately on this brief, dense, rich packet of profound language. It strikes at the core of everything that matters. . . . Errors are most serious when we are unaware of our entanglement."[74]

And it is here that the historicity of Adam and the fall is critical. Stephen Wellum explains:

> If the early chapters of Genesis are not history, it is not only difficult to take the Bible on its own terms, but also Sin and Death are no longer something "abnormal" that needs to be destroyed but a "normal" part of God's universe. One is no longer able to say that Adam, as the representative of the human race, was once "good" but in history brought sin into the world which has resulted in all of the horrendous effects of sin and injustice . . . . Instead, it seems that Sin and Evil are part of God's created order from the very beginning.[75]

73. Hamilton, *God's Glory in Salvation*, 78.
74. Horner, "Genesis 3—A Map of Misreadings," 101.
75. Stephen J. Wellum, "Getting the God of the Cross Right . . . and Very Wrong: A Response to Fleming Rutledge," *Credo Magazine* 8.1 (April 4, 2018), found at: https://credomag.com /article/getting-the-god-of-the-cross-rightand-very-wrong/.

Without a historical Adam and fall, doubt is also cast on the rest of the biblical storyline's resolution to this central crisis of humanity.

Rising Action: The Movement toward Redemption

What unfolds in the *rising action* of the story is a movement toward redemption. But within that movement are multiple failures. The rise to redemption is a stumbling one. We see two trajectories in the Old Testament. One arc foreshadows divine redemption—that is, God's solution to the conflict. The other arc chronicles Israel's failure to redeem herself. But as central as Israel is to the story, we must not forget to see ourselves in her plight.

This is not merely the story of Israel; it is the story of broken but redeemable humanity. The first glimpse of these two trajectories comes in the immediate aftermath of Adam and Eve's sin. To conceal the shame of their nakedness, the couple fashions crude coverings from fig leaves (Gen. 3:7), but this solution is insufficient. Here we had hoped for Adam to emerge as a comedic hero, but he disappoints. Adam shows that every human attempt to rectify our sin-racked brokenness runs headlong into bankruptcy. Instead, God meets Adam and Eve's failure by supplying them with adequate "garments of skins" (v. 21). This gracious act introduces the notion of atoning blood sacrifices for the first time, prefiguring the means of redemption.[76]

The cryptic promise in Genesis 3:15 indicates another hint at where the redemptive trajectory is going.[77] This primordial prophecy indicates that the divine Author had already conceived a plot for this story before the foundation of the world (Acts 2:23; 1 Peter 1:20; cf. Eph. 1:4). Speaking to the serpent, God says, "I will put enmity between you and the woman, and between your offspring and her offspring; he shall bruise your head, and you shall bruise his heel" (Gen. 3:15).

This verse has been rightly called the *protoevangelium* (the "first gospel"). The "offspring" (lit., "seed") of the serpent refers to those in subsequent history who seek to oppose God's redemptive plan for humanity (John 8:44). The "offspring" of the woman, Eve, refers to the collective "seed of Abraham"[78] from whom will also come a single "Seed" who will "crush to pieces" the head of the serpent, even as the serpent will "crush" the heel of this descendant.[79]

---

76. Schreiner, *The King in His Beauty*, 10.

77. See Varner, "Seed and Schaeffer," 153–72; James Hamilton, "The Skull Crushing Seed of the Woman: Inner-Biblical Interpretation of Genesis 3:15," *SBJT* 10.2 (2006): 30–54.

78. Schreiner, *The King in His Beauty*, 17.

79. Translation is from Walter C. Kaiser Jr., *Toward an Old Testament Theology* (Grand Rapids: Zondervan, 1978), 36. See also Hamilton, "Skull Crushing Seed of the Woman," 32; Varner, "Seed

We have here the first prophetic allusion to the one redemptive (comedic) hero who will defeat Satan, sin, death, and all other evils.[80] The prophecy is full of irony. *Crushing* ("bruising") is a metaphor for death. The death of the Messiah—the crushing of his heel—is the precise means by which the serpent's "skull" (Satan)[81] will be crushed for good. Both crushings are *fatal*, but only one is *final*.[82] The wound to the heel will recover (an allusion to the Messiah's resurrection). The wound to the serpent's head will never recover (Heb. 2:14–15). A price must be paid for redemption. The Messiah will be a wounded Victor.

The failures of mankind continue to plunge as we witness how postfall sin and alienation precipitate the first murder (Gen. 4:1–8). Soon a state of anarchy develops: "The LORD saw that the wickedness of man was great in the earth, and that every intention of the thoughts of his heart was only evil continually" (6:5). The Judge unleashes his just wrath by annihilating the creation through a global flood.[83] But to preserve the "seed of the woman" and the promise of redemption, he graciously spares Noah.

God then establishes the "seed" (descendants) of Abraham through a set of far-reaching promises sealed with a unilaterally binding *unconditional* covenant that God will maintain (12:1–3; 15:1–21).[84] This nation will be God's new vice-regents on the earth to magnify his glory. The land promised to Abraham and his descendants echoes Eden.[85]

---

and Schaeffer," 163–64. Note that the referents are narrowed in the second part of the verse from collective groups to individuals, as the singular masculine pronouns *he* and *his* indicate. The Septuagint (third-century B.C. Greek translation of the Old Testament) here breaks with Greek grammar in that these pronouns do not agree with their antecedents in gender and number. See Walter C. Kaiser Jr., *The Messiah in the Old Testament* (Grand Rapids: Zondervan, 1995), 40.

80. For how the messianic promise is traced out in the Old Testament, see Kaiser, *Messiah in the Old Testament*; Herbert W. Bateman IV, Darrell L. Bock, and Gordon H. Johnston, *Jesus the Messiah: Tracing the Promises, Expectations, and Coming of Israel's King* (Grand Rapids: Kregel, 2012); Gerard Van Groningen, *Messianic Revelation in the Old Testament* (Grand Rapids: Eerdmans, 1990).

81. Hamilton, "Skull Crushing Seed of the Woman," 31.

82. Varner, "Seed and Schaeffer," 166.

83. For a defense of the flood as global, see William D. Barrick, "Noah's Flood and Its Geological Implications," in *Coming to Grips with Genesis: Biblical Authority and the Age of the Earth*, ed. Terry Mortenson and Thane H. Ury (Green Forest, AR: Master Books, 2008), 251–81. For a thorough examination of the geologic evidence of the global flood, see Andrew A. Snelling, *Earth's Catastrophic Past: Geology, Creation & the Flood*, 2 vols. (Dallas: Institute for Creation Research, 2009).

84. Schreiner, *The King in His Beauty*, 18. For the nature of biblical covenants, see Gentry and Wellum, *Kingdom through Covenant*, 129–45; Peter J. Gentry and Stephen J. Wellum, *God's Kingdom through God's Covenants: A Concise Biblical Theology* (Wheaton, IL: Crossway, 2015), 47–55.

85. Hamilton, *God's Glory in Salvation*, 81.

But before the people of God occupy the promised land, he places them in four hundred long years of bondage to the Egyptians so that by the end of that time they would ache deeply for deliverance. God hears the cries of his people (Ex. 3:7) and brings about a miraculous exodus to display his redemptive power (9:16). This mighty act of deliverance forges Israel's identity as a nation. During this time, God raises up Moses as a type of the Messiah to come (Deut. 18:15, 18) to lead his people.[86] He establishes another covenant through the great prophet: a bilateral *conditional* covenant whereby obedience on the part of the human party, Israel, brings blessing from the divine party, the Lord God—Yahweh.[87] Disobedience would bring curses (Deut. 28). Unfortunately, the nation, like her parental predecessors Adam and Eve, repeatedly disobeys the law given to Moses.

As her transgressions pile up, the nation incites her God to deliver her into exile in the lands of her enemies. Through the failures of inept and immoral kings along with the lure of every pagan form of idolatry, Israel abandons Yahweh and comes into bondage once again. Her hopes of being redeemed by mere adherence to the law are a failure. But God knows that Israel needs to come to this place of failure so that he can reinforce to her that salvation always comes by looking to him alone.[88]

When Israel returns to the land of promise, nothing is ever the same. She does not recover her former glory such as graced the land in the days of King David and Solomon. But even these kings are never what they seem. Israel's great heroes, from Abraham to Joseph, from Moses to Joshua, from David to Josiah, are all flawed—in many ways, tragically so. Her prophets, though often faithful in the face of brutal opposition, cannot lead the obstinate nation to lasting salvation.

Yet through all the defections, and occasional bright moments, God is advancing his solution to human depravity and evil. His grace is upon those who place their trust in him (Isa. 12:2). He provides ever-increasing glimpses of the coming Messiah through covenant promises and prophecies, through types and shadows in the sacrificial worship of the temple, and through archetypal events and characters.

Climax: Incarnation, Death, and Resurrection of the Redeemer

When all seems lost, when hope is a rare commodity, when God's people once again come under the oppressive rule of another more powerful nation

---

86. Kaiser, *Messiah in the Old Testament*, 57–61.

87. Gentry and Wellum argue that the biblical covenants cannot be neatly divided into unilateral (unconditional) and bilateral (conditional). Instead, the covenants have aspects of both. Though God is gracious to keep the promises of his covenants, he always demands obedience from the receiving party. See *Kingdom through Covenant*, 608–11.

88. See Ps. 62:1; Isa. 45:22, 25; 55:6–7; cf. Gal. 3:24.

called Rome, a bright and mysterious star appears on the horizon (Matt. 2:1–2). It signals to curious inquirers that a momentous event has occurred. It signals that the *rising action* of the story is giving way to the *climax*. The "wise men from the east" ascertain what lowly shepherds in Bethlehem already knew—the Messiah has been born, occurring through improbable circumstances (Luke 2:8–20).

God's plan of redemption requires a human hero, but not any sort of hero that we have ever seen before.[89] At the most crucial point in the story, a most remarkable and unexpected event unfolds. The Author enters directly into the plot and dons the robes of humanity. Not only is this hero a man like us (Heb. 2:9, 14), but he is already God of very God (Col. 1:15; 2:9), existing from all eternity (John 1:1). The incarnated God is the center of the story—of history itself.

The apostle John introduces the central climax of redemption in his Gospel account by mirroring the opening of the creation account in Genesis 1:1. This puts the story in the "context of cosmic history."[90] John writes, "In the beginning was the Word, and the Word was with God, and the Word was God. He was in the beginning with God. All things were made through him, and without him was not any thing made that was made" (John 1:1–3). Christ ("the Word") is identified as having the same place as *Elohim* (Heb. for "God"), the Creator of "all things." As the "Word," he becomes the fullest revelation of God. He is God come in the flesh (John 1:14), who alone is capable of addressing history's great entanglement, of untying the impossibly tight knot that Adam tied.

The Son of God will return all things as they were at the moment of creation (Acts 3:21), but they will be even better than the uncorrupted state of Eden, having been purchased for such a high price. Jesus comes as the second Adam, who demonstrates perfect obedience to his Father (John 4:34) and is thereby suited to achieve what neither the tragic figure (hero) Adam nor any other human being could achieve (1 Cor. 15:22, 45).

But there is another remarkable twist in this plot.

The Jews of Jesus' day expect the Messiah to be a warrior. After all, he is the "son of David," the greatest warrior-king that Israel ever saw (Matt. 21:9).

---

89. The Gospels were written as first-century biographies intended to present Jesus as a hero or protagonist to be embraced by the reader. See Benjamin Gladd, "Mark," in *A Biblical Theological Introduction to the New Testament*, ed. Michael J. Kruger (Wheaton, IL: Crossway, 2016), 62. See also Richard A. Burridge, *What Are the Gospels? A Comparison with Graeco-Roman Biography* (Waco, TX: Baylor University Press, 2018). For a corrective of views on the Gospels as mirroring Greco-Roman biography, see McGrew, *The Mirror or the Mask*, 67–86.

90. Hamilton, *God's Glory in Salvation*, 381.

They expect a conventional defeat of Israel's enemies, their Roman oppressors. Even though Isaiah prophesied that the Messiah would die an atoning death to bring about the redemption of God's people (Isa. 52:13–53:12), the grand Author blinds them to these realities, which again Isaiah prophesied (John 12:39–40).[91] They fail to realize that their greatest enemy is not outside them—not the Romans, not the culture, not even Satan. The true enemy is something deeply rooted within. No ordinary means of power can defeat the evil that resides in the human heart. That conflict cannot be overcome by a conventional hero.

The defeat of evil will shatter the conceptions of both Jews and Gentiles. Here we have an unusual hero who has been born for a singularly important purpose—to die.[92] Jesus Christ "came to be butchered."[93] In 1 Corinthians 1, Paul states that Christ's heroic act performed on a bloodstained piece of wood was regarded as utter foolishness (v. 18). It causes the Jews to be deeply offended and the Gentiles to mock the Christian faith (v. 23). Strangely, sin and evil will be vanquished by God's weakness, not his power (v. 25). Jesus' victory will be achieved through his voluntary vulnerability before wicked men.[94] Nobody sees this coming. And yet in that moment of utter weakness, the greatest power in history is put on display.

Now, none of this makes sense at the time. When Jesus is arrested, tried, and crucified, it appears that all hope has been lost. His disciples flee (Mark 14:50). Terror and dismay overcome all who have looked to him for salvation. Often the climax of any great story is preceded by a quagmire that envelops the hero (protagonist) and from which there is no seeming escape. The hero's defeat at the hands of the villain (antagonist) appears imminent. It is the moment that has the audience at the farthest edge of their seats in nervous anticipation.

In this case, Satan believes he has defeated Christ just as he defeated the first Adam. He has crushed the Messiah's heel (Gen. 3:15). Yet it seems that Satan himself is blinded to the prophecies of Isaiah. He is blinded to his own crushing defeat (Heb. 2:14; 1 John 3:8). The whole scenario is shocking—scandalous. The Jews could never fathom a cursed Messiah dying the ignoble and humiliating death of crucifixion (Gal. 3:13).[95]

But they haven't even the remotest idea of what is coming next.

Before all this, Jesus has told his fickle interlocutors, "Destroy this temple, and in three days I will raise it up" (John 2:19). Their response (v. 20) shows

---

91. See Darrell L. Bock and Mitch Glaser, eds., *The Gospel according to Isaiah 53: Encountering the Suffering Servant in Jewish and Christian Theology* (Grand Rapids: Kregel, 2012).

92. Carson, *The God Who Is There*, 151.

93. Carson, *The God Who Is There*, 153.

94. D. A. Carson, *Scandalous: The Cross and Resurrection of Jesus* (Wheaton, IL: Crossway, 2010), 20–26.

95. Hamilton, *God's Glory in Salvation*, 419.

that they had no facility for grasping Jesus' metaphors (v. 21). Jesus' death is so unexpected because everyone knows that death is an intrusion on God's good creation.[96] It was God's penalty for the sin of Adam and all his progeny (Rom. 6:23). But it takes death—Jesus' death—to render death, sin, Satan, and all other evil powerless. God "disarmed the rulers and authorities and put them to open shame, by triumphing over them in" his Son (Col. 2:15).

This is no ordinary drama. This is "the strange triumph of a slaughtered lamb."[97] Dorothy Sayers places the plot in perspective: "That God should play the tyrant over man is a dismal story of unrelieved oppression; that man should play the tyrant over man is the usual dreary record of human futility; but that man should play the tyrant over God and find him a better man than himself is an astonishing drama indeed."[98]

But if death is to achieve victory, then the God-man cannot remain long in the tomb in which his crucified body lies. The crucifixion of Christ has been shocking enough—in a way that has brought those who hoped in him down to the abyss of despair. The intervening hours between 3 o'clock on a cold, dark Friday afternoon and the emerging dawn that we now call the Lord's Day are the longest and eeriest silence that the world has ever witnessed.

When several forlorn women approach an empty tomb that morning, there is an equally shocking response, and yet one not of despair but of the rapturous heights of hope and joy. When the reader comes to the passion narratives in the four Gospels where the bright angel attending the open door of the grave declares to the women, "He is not here, for he has risen" (Matt. 28:6), the same stupendous reaction is expected.

> Could neither Seal nor Stone secure,
> Nor Men, nor Devils make it sure?
> The Seal is broke, the Stone cast by,
> And all the Pow'rs of Darkness fly.[99]

Jesus doesn't come into this world just to die. He "comes to die *and rise again.*"[100] C. S. Lewis captures the importance of this remarkable supranatural person and event located at the center of Christianity: "The Christian story is precisely the story of one grand miracle, the Christian assertion being

---

96. Stambaugh, "Whence Cometh Death?," 373–97.
97. Carson, *Scandalous,* 75.
98. Dorothy L. Sayers, "The Greatest Drama Ever Staged," in *The Whimsical Christian* (New York: Macmillan, 1978), 15–16.
99. Charles Wesley, "Hymn I," in *Hymns for Our Lord's Resurrection* (London: W. Strahan, 1746), 2.
100. Carson, *The God Who Is There,* 153.

that what is beyond all space and time, what is uncreated, eternal, came into nature, into human nature, descended into His own universe, and rose again, bringing nature up with Him. It is precisely one great miracle. If you take that away there is nothing specifically Christian left."[101]

The uniqueness of the Christian faith comes in the uniqueness of Christ and what he came to do. Lewis continues:

> The story of the Incarnation is the story of a descent and resurrection. When I say "resurrection" here, I am not referring simply to the first few hours, or the first few weeks of the Resurrection. I am talking of this whole, huge pattern of descent, down, down, and then up again. What we ordinarily call the Resurrection being just, so to speak, the point at which it turns. Think what the descent is. The coming down, not only into humanity, but into those nine months which precede human birth … and going lower still into being a corpse, a thing which, if this ascending movement had not begun, would presently have passed out of the organic altogether, and have gone back into the inorganic, as all corpses do. One has a picture of someone going right down and dredging the sea-bottom. One has a picture of a strong man trying to lift a very big, complicated burden. He stoops down and gets himself right under it so that he himself disappears; and then he straightens his back and moves off with the whole thing swaying on his shoulders.[102]

Christ descends to the sea bottom to disappear into the depths of seeming defeat, all the while defeating evil, and then rising up from the chaos and with him bringing forth the treasure of a new hope: a kingdom over which sin, Satan, and death have no power, a kingdom that will morph into a glorious new creation whose luster exceeds all imagination, having been purchased for an inestimable price. Christ's body cannot turn to dust, moving from organic to inorganic. The success of what the incarnate Lord of the universe achieves on the bloody cross makes sense only when, three days hence, before decay sets in, shocked onlookers gaze into his empty tomb.

Falling Action: The Establishment of the Redeemer's Kingdom

Jesus' death and resurrection represent the *climax* of the story of redemption. His ascension into heaven and exaltation at the right hand of his Father mark the beginning of the *falling action* of the plot wherein his kingdom is beginning to be established and takes root in the broad soils of redemp-

---

101. C. S. Lewis, "The Grand Miracle," in *God in the Dock*, ed. Walter Hooper (Grand Rapids: Eerdmans, 1970), 80.
102. Lewis, "Grand Miracle," 82.

tion. Before his ascension, Jesus has instructed his followers to go into all the world and proclaim the gospel (Matt. 28:18–20)—the message that God in his grace reconciles to himself the sons of Adam through the work achieved by the Son of God (2 Cor. 5:17–21). The impact of Jesus' death and resurrection is incalculable. It has changed and is still changing everything. What starts as 120 persons in a crowded room hidden in the back streets of Jerusalem (Acts 1:15) quickly envelops the Roman world.

This new sect of people, called "Christians" (Acts 11:26), is no longer strictly identified with its Jewish roots. God's plan of redemption will no longer encompass the Jews alone; it will be a transethnic, transnational phenomenon (Acts 10) that will bring a tectonic shift to the world as we know it.[103] Jesus proclaims, "I will build my church, and the gates of hell shall not prevail against it" (Matt. 16:18). Satan will oppose but be unable to stop the work of redemption. The death and resurrection of Christ enable those who have turned from their sin and set their gaze on him for pardon to crush that wily old serpent under their feet (Rom. 16:20) and return themselves to the task of glorifying their God in creation. The Holy Spirit is poured out on the church in abundance, ever empowering the proclamation of this message and the expansion of Christ's kingdom against all opposition.[104]

But this defeat of Satan and the forces of evil will not come easily. The progress of redemption is marked by a polarizing struggle between those whom God redeems and the systemic evils that oppose it. These evils stem both from within (the inner sinful corruption of the flesh) and from without (the world and the devil, Eph. 2:1–3; 4:17–27). But Christ will consistently magnify the glory of the Father by transforming recalcitrant sinners and expanding his kingdom to include "ransomed people for God from every tribe and language and people and nation" (Rev. 5:9).

Denouement: The Consummation of the Redeemer's Kingdom

The *denouement* of the story marks the consummation of Christ's kingdom when the Redeemer-King returns to earth to establish his rule forever and the work of redemption is completed.[105] "Then comes the end, when he

---

103. For a look at how this happened in the early centuries of the church, see Larry W. Hurtado, *Destroyer of the Gods: Early Christian Distinctiveness in the Roman World* (Waco, TX: Baylor University Press, 2016); Michael J. Kruger, *Christianity at the Crossroads: How the Second Century Shaped the Future of the Church* (Downers Grove, IL: InterVarsity Press, 2018).

104. See Acts 1:5, 8; 2:1–13; 4:31; 8:14–17; 10:44–48; 11:15–18; 13:1–4, 52; 19:1–7.

105. The early church fathers were consistently premillennial in their eschatology. Philip Schaff writes, "The most striking point in the eschatology of the ante-Nicene age is the prominent chiliasm, or millenarianism, that is the belief of a visible reign of Christ in glory on earth with the risen saints for a thousand years, before the general resurrection and judgment. It was

delivers the kingdom to God the Father after destroying every rule and every authority and power" (1 Cor. 15:24). At this point, several things will happen to fully untie every loosened knot in the plotline.

First, every follower of Christ will experience full restoration with resurrected bodies fit for life in a newly restored paradise. Satan and every one of his spiritual offspring (human and demonic) will resist God's rule and authority till the end, but they will be finally defeated by Christ and banished forever in "the lake that burns with fire and sulfur, which is the second death" (Rev. 21:8). The first death is the bodily death that all people must undergo. The "second death" is an eternally conscious torment of both body and soul for those who have rejected their Creator.

Second, the creation itself, which was "subjected to futility" by God as a result of the fall, will undergo its own bodily death (2 Peter 3:10–12) and then redemption (Rom. 8:20–21). Paradise will be restored, with a new heaven and a new earth emerging from the ashes of the old creation. Therein will reside a new Eden, filling the whole earth—a place where perfect "righteousness dwells" (2 Peter 3:13).

Craig Blaising makes this important point: "The new earth will not be an utterly new creation from nothing but a refinement and renovation of the present earth. God's plan for His creation is not to destroy it and start over from nothing but to redeem, cleanse, and renew it."[106] God's redeemed creatures will glorify him forever without fear that the kingdom's order, beauty, peace, or harmony will be disrupted ever again. It is the time when every sad thing comes untrue.[107] A truly beautiful and godly civilization will then unfold.

Furthermore, this new paradise outshines the old. Why? Because the crisis of evil ensured that opposition to its emergence would be fierce. Restoring the

indeed not the doctrine of the church embodied in any creed or form of devotion, but a widely current opinion of distinguished teachers, such as Barnabas, Papias, Justin Martyr, Irenaeus, Tertullian, Methodius, and Lactantius" (*History of the Christian Church*, vol. 2, *Ante-Nicene Christianity* [1858; repr., Peabody, MA: Hendrickson, 1996], 614). Origen (A.D. 184–253) and later Augustine (A.D. 354–430) opposed this view. In book 20 of the *City of God*, Augustine rejects premillennialism in favor of amillennialism. Augustine had a profound impact on the transition from premillennialism to amillennialism as the majority view of eschatology in subsequent church history. See Nathan Saunders, "Amillennialism," in *End of Days: An Encyclopedia of the Apocalypse in World Religions*, ed. Wendell G. Johnson (Santa Barbara, CA: ABC-CLIO, 2017), 5.

106. Craig Blaising, "A Critique of Gentry and Wellum's Kingdom through Covenant: A Hermeneutical-Theological Response," *MSJ* 26.1 (Spring 2015): 122. Blaising calls this eschatological outlook *New Creation Eschatology*. He says, "New Creation Eschatology envisions not a nonmaterial eternity nor an alternate material reality but the redemption of this earth and heavens fit for an everlasting glorious manifestation of the presence of God" (Blaising, "Critique," 122).

107. In chapter 4 of book 6 in Tolkien's *The Lord of the Rings*, Samwise Gamgee awakes after he helps his friend Frodo Baggins destroy the malevolent One Ring in the fires of Mount Doom. He sees the great wizard Gandalf and, realizing the success of their mission, asks, "Is everything sad going to come untrue?"

created order would not come easily. In fact, it would be impossible unless the transcendent Author himself intervened in dramatic and miraculous fashion. The steepest possible price had to be paid to restore the irrepressibly tattered and tainted world. Only a uniquely suited divine-human hero could pay the price, and he paid it joyfully (Heb. 12:2) on behalf of ill-deserving rebels who are subsequently showered with the riches of God's glorious grace (Eph. 1:7–8).

When we, the redeemed of God, circumspectly reflect on the depths to which the conflict has dragged us fallen creatures, then the glory of our redemption begins to emerge. We inflicted ourselves with this festering curse and can do nothing to suppress it, let alone reverse it. But when we realize that the divine hero was dragged even deeper through the conflict we created, and then rose up victorious—this is where glory is *supremely* magnified.

Christianity has taken the world by storm and transformed countless lives. But as J. Gresham Machen has pointed out: "The strange thing about Christianity was that it [has] . . . transformed the lives of men not by appealing to the human will, but by telling a story, not by exhortation, but by narration of an event"—the death and resurrection of a most unusual person. Such a story appeared "foolish" two thousand years ago, and it still does today (1 Cor. 1:18–25). "Where the most eloquent exhortation fails, the simple story of an event succeeds; the lives of men are transformed by a piece of news."[108]

Strange news indeed, but what we have here is the one and only true happily-ever-after because it is part of the One True Story. No other story will do. No other plan for history can suffice. "God freely chose to create a world with a more difficult and more beautiful story, in which there is both Adam and Christ, sin and redemption, Good Friday and Easter Sunday."[109]

A STORY WITHOUT EVIL?

But how can we be sure that this is the way it had to be? Is it not possible that God could have authored a better story that left evil out of the picture? Did he have to decree the fall? Why not remove the tree of the knowledge of good and evil from the garden? Why not prevent the wicked serpent from slithering into Eden to tempt the man and woman? Could he have suited his beloved creatures in such a way that sin was not possible for them? Or when they did sin, why not start all over with newly minted image-bearers who would *forever* get it *right* the next time around? The question is this: could his glory be so supremely manifested to his creatures in any other storyline?

108. J. Gresham Machen, *Christianity and Liberalism* (1923; repr., Grand Rapids: Eerdmans, 2009), 40.

109. Phillip Cary, "A Classic View," in *God and the Problem of Evil: Five Views*, ed. Chad Meister and James K. Dew Jr. (Downers Grove, IL: InterVarsity Press, 2017), 35.

No. We must contend otherwise.

So it is not enough for a mere *showing* of the story. There must be a fuller *telling* of its meaning to clarify its remarkable power. There must be an exposition of the central theme that drives the plot of this grandest of stories. There must be a theology of it. We turn now to that critical explanation and thus to introduce the theodicy that makes the best sense of its trajectory.

KEY TERMS

creation	fall
Freytag's Pyramid	incarnation
monomyth	myth
redemption	True Myth

STUDY QUESTIONS

1. How is the historical narrative of the Bible, which C. S. Lewis called the *True Myth*, distinguished from ancient pagan myths?
2. How is the biblical concept of history distinguished from all other ancient ways of looking at temporal events in the world?
3. What are the advantages and disadvantages of framing the storyline of Scripture by using Freytag's Pyramid?
4. What distinguishing features of the One True Story of the Bible make it stand out from every other lesser story ever told?
5. What is unique or unprecedented about the death and resurrection of Christ that makes it an especially climactic event in the history of redemption?
6. How has seeing the whole story of the Bible helped you to better understand the Christian faith?

FOR FURTHER READING

D. A. Carson, *The God Who Is There: Finding Your Place in God's Story* (Grand Rapids: Baker, 2010).

Abner Chou, ed., *What Happened in the Garden?* (Grand Rapids: Kregel, 2016).

James M. Hamilton Jr., *God's Glory in Salvation through Judgment: A Biblical Theology* (Wheaton, IL: Crossway, 2010).

John N. Oswalt, *The Bible among the Myths* (Grand Rapids: Zondervan, 2009).

Thomas R. Schreiner, *The King in His Beauty: A Biblical Theology of the Old and New Testaments* (Grand Rapids: Baker Academic, 2013).

12

THE FORTUNATE FALL AND GOD'S GREATEST GLORY

John Milton's epic poem *Paradise Lost* wrestles with the implications of an assault on God's divine integrity in light of evil's introduction into this world. Toward the end of his literary masterpiece, Milton peers into the *raison d'être* for Adam and Eve's sin, the fall of the human race:

> "With glory and power to judge both quick and dead,
> To judge th' unfaithful dead, but to reward
> His faithful, and receive them into bliss,
> Whether in Heav'n or Earth, for then the Earth
> Shall all be Paradise, far happier place
> Than this Eden, and far happier days."
>   So spake th' Archangel Michael, then paused,
> As at the world's great period; and our sire
> Replete with joy and wonder thus replied:
>   "O goodness infinite, goodness immense!
> That all this good of evil shall produce,
> And evil turn to good; more wonderful
> Than that which by creation first brought forth
> Light out of darkness! Full of doubt I stand,
> Whether I should repent me now of sin
> By me done and occasioned, or rejoice
> Much more, that much more good thereof shall spring,
> To God more glory, more good will to men,
> From God, and over wrath grace shall abound."[1]

---

1. John Milton, *Paradise Lost*, ed. William Kerrigan, John Rumrich, and Stephen M. Fallon (New York: Random House, 2007), 12.460–78 (408–9).

In this magnificent passage, Milton drew on a rare but early theological reflection on the purpose of the fall, known by the Latin phrase *O felix culpa*, which translates to "O fortunate fall."[2] The phrase can be traced back as far as a fourth-century liturgical hymn known as the *Exultet*, likely composed by Ambrose the bishop of Milan. A line in the hymn reads, "O assuredly necessary sin of Adam, which has been blotted out by the death of Christ! O fortunate fault [fall], which has merited such and so great a Redeemer!"[3]

But wasn't the fall an *unfortunate* occurrence? What was Milton trying to say? What is this seemingly contradictory notion of *felix culpa*?

In a few short lines, Milton captures the whole grand storyline of Scripture: creation, fall, and redemption. The first lines are spoken by the archangel Michael, who indicates that the final state of paradise will be "happier" than the initial bliss of Eden. Adam ("sire") responds to this declaration, "replete with joy and wonder." The "light" that shone "out of darkness" in the original creation was good, but not as good as the light of redemption that bursts out of the darkness of Adam's sin. For in this fortunate turn of evil events, God's glory is magnified. Indeed, his just wrath against sin is good, and God's glory is duly represented when he doth "judge th' unfaithful dead." But that glory pales when we see that "over wrath grace shall abound."[4]

Arthur Lovejoy clarifies Milton's thought:

> These sublime mysteries would have had no occasion and no meaning; and therefore the plenitude of the divine goodness and power could neither have been exercised nor have become known to men. No devout believer could hold that it would have been better if the moving drama of man's salvation had never taken place; and consequently, no such believer could consistently hold that the first act of that drama, the event from which all the rest of it sprang, was really to be regretted. . . . Thus Adam's sin—and also, indeed, the sins of his posterity which it "occasioned"—were the *conditio sine qua non* both of a greater manifestation of the glory of God and of immeasurably greater benefits for man than could conceivably have been otherwise obtained.[5]

2. Or "O happy fault." Milton was not alone. Other English poets before him also drew on the same tradition. See Arthur O. Lovejoy, "Milton and the Paradox of the Fortunate Fall," reprinted in *Essays in the History of Ideas* (New York: Capricorn Books, 1960), 277–84.

3. David Lyle Jeffrey, ed., *A Dictionary of Biblical Tradition in English Literature* (Grand Rapids: Eerdmans, 1992), 274.

4. An apparent allusion to Romans 5:20–21.

5. Lovejoy, "Fortunate Fall," 278–79. Lovejoy includes Ambrose (c. 340–97), Augustine (354–430), Gregory the Great (c. 540–604), and John Wycliffe (c. 1320–84) among those who embraced *felix culpa*. Most Milton scholars have regarded Milton as an Arminian, but Grant

We come to that paramount question: Why did God purpose the fall, sin, tragedy, adversity, catastrophe, pain, suffering—all natural and moral evils? The answer to this question can never be exhaustive. There will always remain certain mysteries: irresolvable conundrums and tensions. And there may be countless numbers of lesser reasons for specific instances of evil—some ascertainable, most not. Solomon observes, "Just as you do not know the path of the wind . . . , so you do not know the activity of God who makes all things" (Eccl. 11:5 NASB). It would be absurdly impertinent to suppose that we could ferret out all the answers to these problems.

Yet the overarching reason for the existence of evil itself, as witnessed in the panoramic flow of the scriptural storyline, is that God provided a foil by which he could magnify his glory through redemption. The stark contrast between the depths of evil from which Eden fell and the heights of God's beatific goodness as displayed in the redemptive work of his Son serves to magnify the glory of his goodness beyond any other measure if evil had never entered the story. Just as conflict propels the yearning for resolution in the telling of all great stories, even so the introduction of evil into the *rising action* of the plotline of history itself ignites a burning thirst for redemption that can be satiated only by the surprising *climax* of the cross and the empty tomb. These momentous events epitomize the grandest story of all, bringing the greatest glory of all to its incomparable divine Author.

I believe this is the theodicy of the Bible.

SHAPING THE ARGUMENT OF THE GREATER-GLORY THEODICY

As indicated earlier, this solution to the problem of evil represents a specific version of the *greater-good theodicy* that includes some modified elements of the *best-of-all-possible-worlds defense*. I call it the *greater-glory theodicy* because it seeks to demonstrate where God's glory is most magnified (maximized). The greatest good is what will bring God the greatest glory, and his greatest glory will always be tied to the greatest good. While this theodicy does not answer every question about various occurrences of evil, it provides a sufficient answer to the broad question of evil's existence in the first place.

Horner has persuasively argued that he was a typical Reformed Calvinist Puritan who would have had no reason to write his theodical poem if he were not. See Grant Horner, "The Heresy of John Milton, Calvinist: Reforming the Puritan Poet with Historical Theology" (unpublished manuscript, 2017).

The following argument (three premises and a conclusion) seeks to lay out the essence of this theodicy:

1. God's ultimate purpose in freely creating the world is to supremely magnify the riches of his glory to all his creatures, especially human beings, who alone bear his image.
2. God's glory is supremely magnified in the atoning work of Christ, which is the sole means of accomplishing redemption for human beings.
3. Redemption is unnecessary unless human beings have fallen into sin.
4. Therefore, the fall of humanity is necessary to God's ultimate purpose in creating the world.

Let's examine the argument.

1. God's Ultimate Purpose in Creation Is to Supremely Magnify His Glory

Did God create the world because he was lonely? Did he just need somebody to love? "People have vainly fancied that God needed to create the universe so that he might have other persons, however inferior, to love and be loved by: much as a lonely old woman might crowd her house with cats."[6] Such a notion is absurd. God was under no compulsion to create the world, being fully satisfied in his own Trinitarian being. The perfect love and satisfaction existing among the members of the Trinity can never be matched by creating anything less. God has nothing to gain by creating anything.

Instead, he made this world of his own free purpose, and he could have fashioned it in any way he wanted (Ps. 115:3). Thus, "For God a billion rational creatures are as dust in the balance; if a billon perish, God suffers no loss, who can create what he wills with no effort or cost by merely thinking of it."[7] God does all things for his own glory (Rom. 11:36). But even then, God is under no compulsion to magnify the riches of his eternal glory to us, his image-bearing creatures (Rom. 9:23). Rather, he does this *freely*, simply so that we might marvel at his glory.[8]

2a. God's Glory Is Supremely Magnified in the Atoning Work of Christ

The atoning work of Christ is centered on his crucifixion and resurrection. As Romans 4:25 tells us, Jesus our Lord "was delivered up for our trespasses

---

6. Peter Geach, *Providence and Evil: The Stanton Lectures 1971–2* (Cambridge: Cambridge University Press, 1977), 124.

7. Geach, *Providence and Evil*, 128.

8. God displays his glory to the angels as well (e.g., Luke 2:13–14), but the angels are not the central focus of his external works of creation and providence even though they have an important role to play (see chapter 16).

and raised for our justification." The crucifixion and the resurrection of Christ must be seen as a unified work that the triune God accomplishes for salvation.[9] Yet his atoning work is part of his larger redemptive work that presupposes his incarnation, foreshadows his exaltation, and will come to full consummation at his return.

Thus, we might say that God's glory is supremely magnified in the incarnation, death, resurrection, exaltation, and return of Christ to consummate his glorious kingdom. Nonetheless, the death and resurrection of Christ as an atonement for sin are the nucleus of his redemptive work, and it is here that the glory of God shines brightest. It is the greatest good. No other good can compare. Can we possibly conceive of a stage in this world (or any other) on which God's glory could shine more brightly? Or some stupendous realm conjured by our most fruitful imagination whereby some greater good exists? What would we otherwise know of a place called Golgotha and the tomb of an obscure member of the ancient Sanhedrin named Joseph of Arimathea? Nothing else exceeds the divine glory revealed in the seminal events that unfolded in these locales.

More specifically, God's glory shines supremely in the Son's supremely manifested weakness exemplified in the incarnation and his bloody death (Phil. 2:6–8). The resurrection, exaltation, and return of Christ, which all vindicate his work on the cross, find their glory in the risen Lamb that was slain—whose precious blood purchased a people for God (Rev. 5:6–14).

2b. The Atoning Work of Christ Is the Sole Means of Redemption

The primary focus of the atoning work of Christ is the redemption of human beings, God's image-bearing creatures. Neither golden trout in a mountain stream nor sparrows in the sky above bear his image. Neither ants in the sand nor elephants in the savannah come close. Not even angels residing near God's throne or demons consigned to the pits of hell are made in the image of God. Thus, none of these creatures, great or small, noble or lowly, good or ill, are objects of redemption whereby God seeks to reconcile to himself a peculiar people.

The human race estranged itself from its Creator by its rebellion, but God in his ill-deserving, surprising, and magnificent grace chose a remnant of rebels for reconciliation. Furthermore, *only* the atoning work of Christ is capable of redeeming these fallen and alienated ones (Acts 4:12; Heb. 9:11–14). Once God determined to redeem a people for himself, no other

---

9. See pages 357–60.

means was available to him. Thus, the atoning work of Christ is necessary to the work of redemption.[10]

Note, however, that there is a broader work of redemption that is cosmic in scope. The whole material creation was ruined by human sin and will undergo a grand renewal as part of Christ's work of rescuing this corrupted world (Rom. 8:18–23; 1 Cor. 15:27; Col. 1:19–20). God's eternal plan focuses on uniting "all things" in the Lord Jesus Christ: "things in heaven and things on earth" (Eph. 1:10). Though many creatures, human and angelic, will suffer eternal judgment, this serves to highlight the rest of creation, whose glory will be restored from the curse of sin. Christ will reverse that curse—undoing the damage that Adam did—and return the cosmos to paradise.

3. Redemption Is Unnecessary without the Fall

Redemption speaks to the restoration to some good state (e.g., Eden) that was ruined (e.g., the fall). Without a world wrecked by human evil, there could be no redemption. Thus, sin ruined humanity—along with Eden—and God seeks to restore a chosen people to an Edenic state. Yet the elect will be restored to a new and *better* state than the Edenic state that marked prefall humanity (i.e., Adam and Eve). This new and better realm finds its culmination in the kingdom of God in the future new heaven and new earth (1 Cor. 15:24–28; see chapter 6).

Creation:
Paradise

Redemption:
Paradise Restored

Fall: *Paradise Lost*

Fig. 12.1. Standard U-Shaped Storyline of Scripture and Monomythic Stories

---

10. John Murray, *Redemption Accomplished and Applied* (Grand Rapids: Eerdmans, 1955), 3–13.

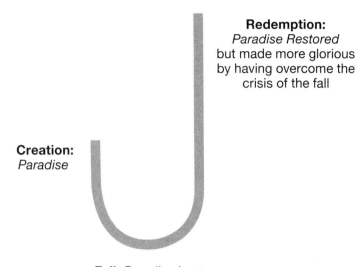

**Fig. 12.2. J-Shaped Storyline of the
Greater-Glory Theodicy**

Therefore, the storyline of Scripture is more accurately illustrated in the shape of a J. If it were merely conceived as a U-shaped storyline (as in common monomythic stories), then the restored paradise of the new creation emerging from the low point of the fall would appear to be no better than the paradise of the initial prefall creation, and we would wonder why the fall was necessary. But the greater-glory theodicy demonstrates that the paradise of the new creation will be far better—far more glorious—than the paradise of the unsullied initial creation, ironically, because the cosmos had to pass through the terrible crisis of the fall.

4. Therefore, the Fall Is Necessary to God's Ultimate Purpose in Creation

Why the fall? Why the entrance of evil into the good creation? Why a world full of corruption and unrest? Once God freely determined to create the world and to maximize his glory to his image-bearing creatures, there was no greater way to do so than through the redemption that comes via the atoning work of Christ. Therefore, this makes both the fall—with its deleterious effects on God's good creation—and God's redemptive work through Christ *alone* necessary aspects of his freely chosen, glory-maximizing plan. God ordained the fall to this end. This deliberate plan of creation, fall, and subsequent redemption culminating in a new (renewed) creation by an all-wise, all-good God is the greatest good conceivable. And the greatest good magnifies the glory of God supremely.

Note the tension between divine freedom and divine necessity.[11] God's freedom is expressed in (1) his desire to create the world, and (2) his desire to supremely magnify his extrinsic glory to his creatures in that world (see premise 1). He was not compelled to choose either. But once the triune God freely chose maximizing his extrinsic glory as the goal of creation, he necessarily chose the only means of achieving that goal: creating some possible world in which a fall took place and the subsequent redemptive work of the incarnate Son of God remedied the crisis of that fall via his atoning death and resurrection.

Incarnation, atoning death, and resurrection are necessary features of any plan to redeem a fallen world. These become necessary features of any plan to maximize God's glory. Without God's desire to maximize his glory, none of this would be a necessary part of his plan to create the world. In that sense, the desire to redeem would be strictly a free act of God. He could have created a world that did not need redemption or one that does. Or he could have chosen not to create at all.

Likewise, divine grace, the grounds on which God redeems fallen creatures, is a free act of God that is made necessary only once God determined to freely maximize his glory. Frame writes, "The very idea of grace is that God is not required to give it. If God is required, even by his own nature, to give grace to us, then we have a certain claim on him. But grace excludes such claims."[12] Grace becomes a necessity only given some prior goal of God, such as maximizing his glory. But even then, grace is still bestowed only on those whom God freely elects to redeem (Eph. 1:5). Grace and election are inextricably tied together at this point, and both are ultimately tied to God's freely chosen plan.

So the freedom of God in magnifying his glory is the driving force behind his plan of the gracious redeeming work of Christ. Not only is God's glory more magnified in a fallen-but-being-redeemed world than it would be in an unfallen-not-needing-redemption world, but his glory is most maximized in such a fallen-but-being-redeemed world—a world where the redeemed are exceedingly more benefited than in any other possible world. Therefore, this broken world is among *the* best possible worlds with no world that could possibly be better; that is, no world could produce a better possible set of goods.

---

11. For a fuller discussion of divine freedom and necessity, see John M. Frame, *The Doctrine of God* (Phillipsburg, NJ: P&R Publishing, 2002), 230–36.

12. Frame, *Doctrine of God*, 235.

This argument indicates that the greater-glory theodicy meets the two criteria that Greg Welty proposes for a faithful theodicy.[13] The first criterion says that the goods God pursues in the face of evil must be *dependent* on those evils. The goods cannot come about unless the evil in question is *necessary* for those goods to occur. The supreme glory that God receives through redemption and all it entails with regard to Christ's incarnation, atoning death and resurrection, exaltation, and return in glory to defeat the curse of sin, disaster, death, and the devil and to restore the fallen creation is clearly dependent on the fall of mankind and the manifold evils it produced.

Welty's second criterion says that the goods pursued in the face of evil must be *weighty* and *important* enough to justify the evils that produce those goods. I hope to show that even the most horrendous evils serve to magnify God's glorious grace in redemption even more than if those terrible evils had never occurred—all because of the utterly unique work of Christ that brings untold blessings to wretched sinners living in this desperately fallen-but-being-redeemed world. No other hero doing any other kind of work in an attempt to overcome the crisis of the fall could remotely magnify the glory of God as Christ has, nor do it so supremely. Without Christ, it is impossible that anything about God's story of cosmic redemption could be true.

Now let us consider in detail some of the key components of this argument.

GLORY IS GOD'S ULTIMATE END

Even though evil is an intrusion within God's good creation, it was not unexpected. It was not a risk that God took in order to preserve the libertarian free will of his creatures. It certainly did not catch God by surprise, as though God could be subject to such a thing as surprise. As we have already seen, it stands within the sovereign decree of God (see chapters 7, 8, and 9). This explains the *fact* of evil, but it does not explain the *why*. Furthermore, because its presence is so contrary to our moral sensibilities, which are derived from God himself, we are sorely inclined to think that evil somehow diminishes the good purposes of God. We would never say it aloud, but evil appears to make him inept, naive, or less than wise. We think he could have created a better world. Thus, to understand God's purpose in decreeing evil, we must step back and look at his ultimate objective.

---

13. Greg Welty, *Why Is There Evil in the World (and So Much of It)?* (Fearn, Ross-shire, Scotland: Christian Focus, 2018), 43–46.

God has manifold purposes in creation and providence, purposes whose wide regions can never be fully charted. But all such lesser goals are subordinate ends to God's ultimate end, which is to bring glory to himself in everything he does. The New England divine Jonathan Edwards (1703–58) has made this point as persuasively as anyone else in the history of the church: "The design of the Spirit of God is not to represent God's ultimate end as *manifold*, but as ONE. . . . For it appears, that all that is ever spoken of in the Scripture as an ultimate end of God's works, is included in that one phrase, *the glory of God.*"[14] The magnification of God's glory is his ultimate purpose in creating the world.[15]

Both the Westminster Larger and Shorter Catechisms affirm that God decrees "for his own glory . . . whatsoever comes to pass."[16] Paul says, "For from him and through him and to him are all things. To him be glory forever. Amen" (Rom. 11:36). God is the Creator ("from him"), Sustainer ("through him"), and goal ("to him") of "all things." Therefore, in all things "to him be glory forever."[17] The apostle emphasizes the same point

14. Jonathan Edwards, "The End for Which God Created the World," in *God's Passion for His Glory: Living the Vision of Jonathan Edwards*, ed. John Piper (Wheaton, IL: Crossway, 1998), 242. Edwards amasses an incredible amount of Scripture to make his case (183–241). For a defense of Edwards's thesis, see Daniel P. Fuller, *The Unity of the Bible: God's Unfolding Plan for Humanity* (Grand Rapids: Zondervan, 1992), esp. 99–138. For a response to various criticisms, see Walter Schultz, "Jonathan Edwards's End of Creation: An Exposition and Defense," *JETS* 49.2 (2006): 247–71. For a somewhat sympathetic but critical analysis, see Stephen R. Holmes, *God of Grace and God of Glory: An Account of the Theology of Jonathan Edwards* (Grand Rapids: Eerdmans, 2001). George M. Marsden writes that this seminal work was "the logical starting point for all of [Edwards's] thinking" (*Jonathan Edwards: A Life* [New Haven, CT: Yale University Press, 2003], 460).

15. Herman Bavinck has argued that this has been virtually the unanimous teaching of the church since the early fathers and especially in post-Reformation theology. See *Reformed Dogmatics*, ed. John Bolt, trans. John Vriend, 4 vols. (Grand Rapids: Baker Academic, 2003–8), 2:433–34; cf. Christopher W. Morgan, "Toward a Theology of the Glory of God," in *The Glory of God*, ed. Christopher W. Morgan and Robert A. Peterson (Wheaton, IL: Crossway, 2010), 175. Contemporary Reformed theology has reemphasized this historic belief. See James M. Hamilton Jr., *God's Glory in Salvation through Judgment: A Biblical Theology* (Wheaton, IL: Crossway, 2010), 53–56; Thomas R. Schreiner, *New Testament Theology: Magnifying God in Christ* (Grand Rapids: Baker Academic, 2008), 119–67; Robert L. Reymond, *A New Systematic Theology of the Christian Faith*, 2nd ed. (Grand Rapids: Zondervan Academic, 2001), 343–46. John Piper has done more to recover this emphasis than any other contemporary Christian. In addition to *God's Passion for His Glory*, see also *Desiring God*, rev. ed. (Sisters, OR: Multnomah Books, 2011); *The Pleasures of God: Meditations on God's Delight in Being God*, rev. ed. (Colorado Springs: Multnomah Books, 2012); *God Is the Gospel* (Wheaton, IL: Crossway, 2005); *Spectacular Sins* (Wheaton, IL: Crossway, 2008).

16. Questions 12 and 7, respectively. See also WCF 3.3; 3.5; 3.7. The first question of the Westminster Shorter Catechism is "What is the chief end of man?" The answer: "Man's chief end is to glorify God, and to enjoy Him for ever."

17. See also the doxological affirmations in Rom. 16:27; Gal. 1:5; Eph. 3:21; Phil. 4:20; 1 Tim. 1:17; 2 Tim. 4:18; Heb. 13:21; 1 Peter 4:11; 2 Peter 3:18; Jude 25; Rev. 1:6; cf. 1 Tim. 6:16; 1 Peter 5:11.

in Colossians with regard to Christ, who as deity shares the full glory of the Father (and the Spirit).[18] "For by him all things were created, in heaven and on earth, visible and invisible, whether thrones or dominions or rulers or authorities—all things were created through him and for him" (Col. 1:16; cf. 1 Cor. 8:6; Heb. 2:10). Everything—absolutely everything Christ made—is "for him," to magnify his glory.

Throughout Scripture, God's passion for his glory is paramount. As Bruce Ware puts it, "From the first verse of inspired Scripture to the last chapter of Revelation, God makes clear in ten thousand ways that the greatest value in the universe, and the final end of all of life, is the uncontested supremacy and unrivaled glory of God alone."[19] God is eternally self-existent and self-sufficient (his aseity) in the fullness of the unchanging perfections of his own Trinitarian being and therefore has no need to display his glory.[20]

God is devoid of need altogether. He did not need to create the world, as though he were lonely or lacking some happiness with which his creation could supply him. "He never receives any good" from anything "that is not already his."[21] Nor does he have any need to manifest his glory to us. His glory has been perfectly manifested between members of the Trinity from all eternity (John 17:5). Furthermore, none can magnify the glory of God as God himself magnifies his own glory. His triune being is none other than *the* "Majestic Glory" (2 Peter 1:17).

Nonetheless, the triune God so delights in his own glory, expressed in intra-Trinitarian relationships, that he desired in turn to express the overflow of that delight toward the creatures he freely made, especially those made in his image.[22] In Isaiah's magnificent vision of Yahweh in the temple, the seraphim "called to another and said: 'Holy, holy, holy is the LORD of hosts; the whole earth is full of his glory!'" (Isa. 6:3; cf. Num. 14:21). Yahweh shows forth his glory among his creatures *and* in his creation.[23] In all of God's actions toward Israel, he says, "For my own sake, for my own sake,

---

18. See Matt. 17:2; Luke 24:26; John 1:14; 17:5, 24; 1 Cor. 2:8; 2 Cor. 4:6; Eph. 1:20–23; Phil. 2:9–11; Col. 1:15–20; 1 Tim. 3:16; Heb. 1:3; 1 Peter 1:21; Rev. 1:12–16; 5:6–14. For a classic exposition of Christ's glory, see John Owen, *The Glory of Christ* (repr., Fearn, Ross-shire, Scotland: Christian Focus, 2004).

19. Bruce A. Ware, *God's Greater Glory: The Exalted God of Scripture and the Christian Faith* (Wheaton, IL: Crossway, 2004), 159.

20. Frame, *Doctrine of God*, 600–608; Bavinck, *Reformed Dogmatics*, 1:112–24.

21. Joel R. Beeke and Paul M. Smalley, *Reformed Systematic Theology*, vol. 1, *Revelation and God* (Wheaton, IL: Crossway, 2019), 847.

22. This point is essential to Edwards's argument in "The End for Which God Created the World," 152–61.

23. See Lev. 10:3; Pss. 19:1; 72:19; 97:6; Isa. 40:5; 60:1–3; 66:18–19; Ezek. 39:13, 21; Hab. 2:14.

I do it, for how should my name be profaned? My glory I will not give to another" (Isa. 48:11).

God shares none of his intrinsic glory with his creatures, nor does he share it with other so-called deities (42:8). Moses tells God's people, "For the LORD your God is God of gods and Lord of lords, the great, the mighty, and the awesome God" (Deut. 10:17; cf. Isa. 45:5). Yahweh's lordship is supreme. Scripture enjoins us to shout forth God's incomparable glory throughout the universe (Pss. 96:3; 145:11–12). "Be exalted, O God, above the heavens! Let your glory be over all the earth!" (108:5).

God's glory can be defined as that otherworldly divine transcendence that dwarfs our position as creatures before the Creator. It speaks to the weight and worth of God. It encompasses the full panorama of the supremacy and unity of his divine attributes.[24] It says that "he is preeminent in existence and that the whole universe is filled with evidence of his importance and sublimity."[25] The entire "universe is an explosion of God's glory."[26] The psalmist exclaims, "Bless the LORD, O my soul! O LORD my God, you are very great! You are clothed with splendor and majesty, covering yourself with light as with a garment" (Ps. 104:1–2).

Such glory is "sacred and dangerous" (cf. Ex. 24:17). It "combines awe and terror, and it simultaneously invites approach and distance."[27] It is not unlike standing on the precipice of the Grand Canyon. You wish to get close to the edge, but not too close. This tension between the repelling and attracting features of God's glory speaks of his transcendence and immanence.[28] The most spectacular analogy in God's creation, however,

---

24. This definition of glory refutes the contention that the Reformed focus on glory is merely about God's omnipotence. Gregory A. Boyd comments: "The common Reformed reply that God ordained all that comes to pass, including evil, 'for his glory' simply reveals that this model works with a power-centered criterion of greatness ('glory') rather than the criterion of other-oriented love that Jesus demonstrated when he gave his life on Calvary for those who were his enemies" ("God Limits His Control," in *Four Views on Divine Providence*, ed. Stanley N. Gundry and Dennis W. Jowers [Grand Rapids: Zondervan, 2011], 204). Divine glory emphasizes the unity of all the divine attributes as displayed in God's work of providence, not merely his omnipotence. It is Boyd and other free-will theists who have exalted the attribute of God's love above all other attributes and have thus presented a distorted picture of God. As will be seen in the theodicy I present, God's love (including his grace and mercy) cannot be understood apart from his righteousness, justice, wisdom, and power, to name but a few of God's attributes that are on display in the face of evil.

25. Allen P. Ross, *Recalling the Hope of Glory* (Grand Rapids: Kregel, 2006), 48.

26. Marsden, *Jonathan Edwards*, 463.

27. "Glory," in *Dictionary of Biblical Imagery*, ed. Leland Ryken, James C. Wilhoit, and Tremper Longman III (Downers Grove, IL: InterVarsity Press, 1998), 330.

28. Morgan, "Theology of the Glory of God," 165–67. God's transcendence speaks to his uniqueness as God (see chapter 7), especially as he is distinctly different from his creation (i.e., the Creator-creature distinction). God's immanence speaks of his closeness or relatedness to his creation, especially to humans as his image-bearing creatures. See Frame, *Doctrine of God*, 103–15.

is far too diminutive in scale to draw a comparison to the full weight of his incomprehensible being.

When the transfixed prophet Isaiah encounters a visionary glimpse of the refulgent glory of Yahweh, he cries out, "Woe is me! For I am undone" (Isa. 6:5 KJV). Isaiah is suddenly aware of becoming utterly disintegrated if he were to linger long in the piercing brightness of God's white-hot glory.[29] Calvin notes, "Men are never duly touched and impressed with a conviction of their insignificance until they have contrasted themselves with the majesty of God."[30]

God manifests the excellence of his being in spectacular actions, demanding awestruck gratitude from his creatures. From this humble vantage point, wonder and worship emerge. J. I. Packer writes, "The *emanation* (outflow) of divine glory in the form of creative and redemptive action results in a *remanation* (returning flow) of glory to God in the form of celebratory devotion."[31]

WE ARE NOT THE CENTER

God resides in an immutable state of unfathomable infinite worth that invariably elicits his delight in himself.[32] This directs us to a world that is radically God-centered. If God's ultimate end were merely to show love to his creatures or some other benefit to human beings—even our redemption—then the cosmos would be man-centered.[33] This is revolutionary, since many Christians firmly believe that God has them at the center of his purposes. And we certainly must not dismiss the importance we play in God's plan. But we are not the center. Not by a long shot.

God is the center.

"Not to us, O LORD, not to us, but to your name give glory" (Ps. 115:1).[34]

---

29. Edward J. Young, *The Book of Isaiah*, vol. 1, *Chapters 1–18* (Grand Rapids: Eerdmans, 1965), 247. See R.C. Sproul's exposition of the word *undone* in *The Holiness of God* (Carol Stream, IL: Tyndale House, 1998), 27–28.

30. John Calvin, *Institutes of the Christian Religion*, trans. Henry Beveridge (Edinburgh: T&T Clark, 1863), 1.1.3.

31. J. I. Packer, "The Glory of God and the Reviving of Religion: A Study in the Mind of Jonathan Edwards," in *A God Entranced Vision of All Things: The Legacy of Jonathan Edwards*, ed. John Piper and Justin Taylor (Wheaton, IL: Crossway, 2004), 92.

32. Edwards, "The End for Which God Created the World," 168–69; Owen, *Glory of Christ*, 160; Bavinck, *Reformed Dogmatics*, 1:324.

33. Richard A. Shenk, *The Wonder of the Cross: The God Who Uses Evil and Suffering to Destroy Evil and Suffering* (Eugene, OR: Pickwick Publications, 2013), 159.

34. Note passages that appear to have God's people at the center. The oft-appended phrase "for his name's sake" (in various forms) indicates that God's concern for his people is for the sake of bringing attention to his own person and glory (1 Sam. 12:22; Pss. 23:3; 25:11; 79:9; 106:8; Isa. 48:9, 11; Jer. 14:7, 21; Ezek. 20:9, 14, 22, 44; 36:22). Note also that the refrain indicating that

This is critical as we consider how evil comports with God's purposes. John Frame writes: "So many traditional treatments of the problem [of evil] assume that God's ultimate purpose is to provide happiness for man, and that is not so. God's ultimate purpose is to glorify himself."[35] We are wont to misconstrue the goodness of God. Instead of goodness being essential to the being of God, "through whom every contingent good exists and is good," we think of "God's goodness as essentially the power to provide and impart pleasurable and person-fulfilling states of affairs to his creatures."[36]

Our thoroughly self-absorbed mindset spouts out, "God is good insofar as he meets the criteria for the fulfillment of my dreams, my life goals, my never-ending bucket list." The theodicy I propose is partially a species of the *greater-good theodicy*.[37] Yet Frame states that even greater-good arguments "arrive at a doctrine hard to distinguish from pagan hedonism. . . . Instead of rejecting the greater-good defense we simply understand it theocentrically. That is, one good is greater than another when it is more conducive to the glory of God."[38]

Nonetheless, many are taken aback by the notion that God's greatest delight is in himself as the "blessed [eternally happy] God" (1 Tim. 1:11).[39] Does this not make him some cosmic egomaniac? Unfortunately, we tend to project our own condition as human beings on the unique self-satisfied intra-Trinitarian blessedness of the transcendent God. When humans are self-centered, it is rude, unloving, and marked by sinful pride. But why is this so? Because we are unworthy of such self-attention. We, simply put, are not God.

---

people will "know that I am the Lord [Yahweh]" when God acts occurs eighty-eight times in the Old Testament (seventy-two times in the book of Ezekiel).

35. John M. Frame, *Apologetics: A Justification of Christian Belief* (Phillipsburg, NJ: P&R Publishing, 2015), 184. This goes against a detracting aspect of Leibniz's best-of-all-possible-worlds theodicy, which holds that one of God's chief goals is to maximize humans' happiness. See Maria Rosa Antognazza, *Leibniz: A Very Short Introduction* (Oxford: Oxford University Press, 2016), 66. Alexander Pope's *Essay on Man* (1733–34) followed Leibniz on this point. It was in light of this popular sanguine view that Jonathan Edwards, during the mid-1750s, wrote "The End for Which God Created the World" (see Marsden, *Jonathan Edwards*, 460–62).

36. Paul Helm, "Discrimination: Aspects of God's Causal Activity," in *Calvinism and the Problem of Evil*, ed. David E. Alexander and Daniel M. Johnson (Eugene, OR: Pickwick Publications, 2016), 149.

37. Melville Y. Stewart, *The Greater-Good Defence: An Essay on the Rationality of Faith* (New York: Palgrave Macmillan, 1993), 144–45; Daniel M. Johnson, "Calvinism and the Problem of Evil: A Map of the Territory," in *Calvinism and the Problem of Evil*, ed. David E. Alexander and Daniel M. Johnson (Eugene, OR: Pickwick Publications, 2016), 43–48.

38. Frame, *Apologetics*, 184.

39. On the eternal blessedness of God, see also Rom. 1:25; 9:5; 2 Cor. 11:31; 1 Tim. 6:15–16 (cf. 1 Chron. 16:36; Pss. 41:13; 89:52; 106:48). See Piper, *Pleasures of God*.

Only the sun qualifies to be the center of our solar system. All other planets must orbit the sun in deference to its glory. They are too minuscule in weight to occupy the center of gravity. The solar system would fly apart without the sun at its center. Likewise, no other creature could possibly displace the majestic Creator as the center of all glory. His refulgent weightiness is unmatched. The absolute supremacy and perfection of his being indicate that he is the *summum bonum* (the "greatest good"), with not even the remotest contender for that position.[40]

Thus, God is the only legitimate self-centered being who exists, and everything else necessarily depends on him. There is no weakness or impertinence here. If God were to take greater pleasure in anything other than himself, then the object of that pleasure would have greater status and worth than he. This is unthinkable, rendering God inferior to something he created as well as making him an idolater.[41] "For human beings self-worship is the worst sin, for God it is the epitome of his righteousness."[42]

Job suffered at the hands of God in the face of Satan's arrogant challenge (Job 1:6–12; 2:1–6), but the suffering ultimately was neither about him nor about Satan. It was about exalting God's glory. Job wished to vindicate himself before God because he was dangerously tempted to place himself at the center (13:3, 18). God's response to him in Job 38–41 demonstrates how mistaken Job was. Strangely, God never directly addresses Job's pain and suffering in his grand monologue; instead, he recounts numerous instances of his own glorious acts in creation. Why? Because Job needed to see that there was something vastly larger than himself and the pain that circumscribed his own minuscule world. He needed to situate his pain within the larger realm of the "theater of God's glory."[43]

God's interaction with Job demonstrates how much he delights in sharing the abundance of his glory with his creatures.[44] But does this not appear at times to be at the expense of our pain and suffering? Could God be so cruel? Here is the answer: We are no more benefited than when we are given a taste of divine glory designed to be magnified in the face of evil. Only when Job could see and be absorbed within the magnificent enormousness of his God did his pain begin to pale in scale (Job 42:1–6). In the cosmic and

---

40. Matthew Barrett, *None Greater: The Undomesticated Attributes of God* (Grand Rapids: Baker, 2019), 241–42.

41. James M. Hamilton Jr., "The Glory of God," in *NIV Zondervan Study Bible*, ed. D. A. Carson (Grand Rapids: Zondervan, 2015), 2641.

42. Fuller, *Unity of the Bible*, 120.

43. John Calvin, *Institutes of the Christian Religion*, ed. John T. McNeill, trans. Ford Lewis Battles (Philadelphia: Westminster, 1960), 1.5.8.

44. Edwards, "The End for Which God Created the World," 170–71.

eternal scope of space and time, our suffering barely registers. But God's glory pervades and transcends all. And ironically, suffering for the believer is precisely designed to magnify this glory and to find our deepest joy in a supremely glorious God (James 1:2–4; cf. Ps. 16:11).

We must desperately find him and get lost in him.

Here is another glorious irony: When we take our eyes off our pain and focus them on God's enormous and splendid being, the magnitude of our pain shrinks exponentially. God is astronomically greater than even the most horrific evils that inflict seemingly intractable injury on our souls. To take refuge in him precisely when evil has appeared to overtake us is the place where hope is most amplified (Ps. 18:1–3). Hope is made meaningless without some seemingly futile adversity desperate to be overthrown. Hope is not to spurn the stubborn persistence of evil that threatens to overtake our lives, but to covet a Redeemer who promises to overtake evil (John 16:33).

When we see that God's glory *is* the center and we are able to immerse ourselves in that center no matter what we may encounter in this ever-dark world, we will find a deep well of joy and tranquility that transcends the adversity and sustains us in the midst of it. He alone is worthy of the joy of worship. Such happy worship is "triggered by our awareness" of his self-sufficient infinite worth in the face of our own finite and insufficient condition, wrecked by evil, sin, and misery.[45] Bruce Ware declares, "God's glory *is* our good. . . . When we turn from the deceptive emptiness of self-satisfaction and self-attainment to the fullness of God-given satisfaction and God-empowered attainment, we realize that by acknowledging our bankruptcy and God's endless riches, we now trade in our poverty for never-ending wealth."[46]

John Piper writes, "God's passion for his own glory and his passion for my joy in him are not at odds."[47] This reflects Piper's well-known dictum, tweaking the first question of the Westminster Shorter Catechism: "The chief end of man is to glorify God *BY* enjoying him forever."[48] Seeing and embracing the centrality of God's glory is crucial if we are ever to experience all-sufficient joy—and particularly if we are ever to make sense of the evil that otherwise steals the joy in him for which God made us (Ps. 16:11). The more that God's glory is seen and felt in the midst of evil's most painful thorns, the greater our good.

45. Morgan, "Theology of the Glory of God," 168.
46. Ware, *God's Greater Glory*, 160.
47. Piper, *God's Passion for His Glory*, 33.
48. Piper, *Desiring God*, 23.

GOD'S INTRINSIC AND EXTRINSIC GLORY

For our purposes, two important aspects of the divine majesty stand out: God's intrinsic and extrinsic glory.[49] God's intrinsic (*ad intra*) glory holds the place of preeminence. It speaks to the incomprehensible splendor and majesty of the perfections and excellence of all his attributes as they exist and are perceived within himself.[50] Such glory is immutable (James 1:17). It does not vary because it is essential to the eternal, infinite being of the Trinitarian God. Such glory is always on full display between the persons of the Trinity. Nor can any amount of our glorifying God by our actions add to or subtract from this intrinsic glory.

On the other hand, God's extrinsic (*ad extra*) glory refers to the external manifestation of this intrinsic glory as perceived by rational creatures.[51] God reveals different aspects of his character and attributes through his works in creation and providence. In this regard, the intensity of God's extrinsic glory can vary depending on the manner by which he seeks to display it and the degree to which his creatures perceive it. Morgan writes, "Since the infinite God does not exhaustively communicate himself to finite creatures, the extrinsic display is less than the intrinsic. As awe-inspiring as the extrinsic glory is, it never fully expresses the fullness of God's intrinsic glory that it communicates."[52]

Paul speaks of earthly bodies' lacking the glory of heavenly resurrected bodies in the same way that the moon has lesser glory than the sun (1 Cor. 15:40–41). This admits to degrees of divine glory reflected in created things. Likewise, when Moses sought to see the direct glory of God, he was not permitted to encounter its intrinsic fullness. God warned him, "You cannot see my face, for man shall not see me and live" (Ex. 33:20). Instead, God placed him in a cleft in a rock, covering his face until the glory passed by so that Moses glimpsed only the backside, as it were, of God's rare theophanic presence (vv. 21–23). The Israelites experienced a lesser manifestation of the divine glory via its reflection on the glowing face of Moses (34:29–35). Even this glory was so remarkable that it frightened them.

49. Jonathan Edwards, *Ethical Writings*, vol. 8 of *The Works of Jonathan Edwards*, ed. Paul Ramsey (New Haven, CT: Yale University Press, 1989), 518–21. Morgan's study "Theology of the Glory of God" is helpful with this distinction.

50. Owen, *Glory of Christ*, 148; Bavinck, *Reformed Dogmatics*, 2:252. See 1 Chron. 16:24–29; Pss. 29:1–11; 96:6–8; 104:1–2; 145:1–21.

51. Morgan, "Theology of the Glory of God," 161–65. Sometimes the external manifestation of God's glory comes in the form of a brilliant light (Ps. 104:1–2), such as the glory cloud in the Sinai wilderness or what Moses (Ex. 34) and others experienced (cf. Matt. 17:2; Luke 2:9; Rev. 1:14–16).

52. Morgan, "Theology of the Glory of God," 163–64.

If everything magnified God's glory equally, we wouldn't be able to appreciate its splendor. If the divine glory that Moses encountered (which was not revealed in its fullness) was equal to the reflection of that glory on his face that the Israelites experienced, then it would make no difference whether one saw the glory of God directly or not. If the water-carved desert arroyo equaled the grandeur of the Grand Canyon, then neither could be perceived as having any wonder at all. Glory is not nearly so magnified in that which is pedestrian. But we need both arroyos and Grand Canyons. What makes the rare wonder of the Grand Canyon appear so stupendous is that the lesser glory of a common arroyo pales in comparison.[53]

It is this contrast of the common and ordinary with the rare and extraordinary that makes the latter shine brighter. God accommodates our finite creaturely perception of his glory by supplying us with such contrasts.[54] Not everyone shares the privileges of Moses. There is only one Grand Canyon. Thus, God appears to limit the extent of his extrinsic glory in most instances precisely in order to highlight its magnificence to his creatures at other times.

SUPREME GLORY LOCATED IN CHRIST'S REDEMPTIVE WORK

God's glory is magnified not merely when greater glories are compared to lesser ones, but especially when it is seen against the polarizing backdrop of its opposite—moral and natural evil. Therefore, evil is in a unique position to magnify the glory of God. This leads us to our central question: Since God's ultimate end in creation is to magnify his extrinsic glory to his creatures, where is such glory *most* magnified? Christopher Morgan answers, "It could be argued that the entire biblical plotline of creation, fall, redemption and consummation is the story of God's glory."[55] Yet from this emerges a narrower claim. The movements of history's narrative specifically oriented toward redemption—both of God's fallen creatures and of the creation itself—magnify God's glory more than any other action he pursues.

Ephesians 1:3–14 is one of the seminal passages regarding God's eternal plan of redemption, further elaborated on in chapters 2 and 3. Paul writes:

> In love [God] predestined us for adoption to himself as sons through Jesus Christ, according to the purpose of his will, to the praise of his glorious grace, with which he has blessed us in the Beloved. In him we

53. Other passages that indicate degrees in the reception of divine glory include 2 Cor. 3:7–11, 18; 4:3–4, 17.

54. God in his infinite Trinitarian being does not need these contrasts; therefore, his maximal glory is always expressed to and within himself.

55. Morgan, "Theology of the Glory of God," 160.

have redemption through his blood, the forgiveness of our trespasses, according to the riches of his grace, which he lavished upon us, in all wisdom and insight. (Eph. 1:4–8)

Note that the electing work of God is accomplished as part of his sovereign (decretive) "purpose" (Eph. 1:5). But election is not the end purpose of God here. Election is simply the means by which God's "glorious grace" is to be praised (v. 6).[56] Two other times in the passage Paul indicates that the divine work of redemption is "to the praise of God's glory" (vv. 12, 14). Redemption reveals the majestic character of God supremely, and it does so in the face of human wickedness that demands divine justice, yet cries out for something more glorious—the grace of a redeeming God (v. 7). This grace is immeasurably rich (2:7) and flows from "the unsearchable riches of Christ" (3:8). In other words, such grace has no measurable equivalent. It has an infinitely glorious quality, having come from an unequaled source—the infinite and incomparable Christ.

So God's "eternal [redemptive] purpose" is fully "realized in Christ Jesus" (Eph. 3:11; cf. vv. 8–11), who alone brings restoration to all dislocated, disturbed things in heaven and earth (1:10). Christ is at the center of the redemptive purposes of the "eternal" and "only wise God" to whom "glory forevermore" belongs (Rom. 16:25–27). The incarnate God-man came that he might manifest the fullness of God to his image-bearing creatures and thereby reveal the untold riches of divine grace, and thus divine glory.

But the fullness of God's perfections came to a place of central, singular intensity at the cross at which Christ—the grand hero of history—purchased "redemption through his blood" (Eph. 1:7).[57] Christ's blood was spilled in order to "reconcile to himself all things" (Col. 1:20).[58] Redemption is the message of the gospel, and the gospel is "the glory of Christ" (2 Cor. 4:4). Jesus was "crowned with glory and honor"—alluding to his resurrection and exaltation—"because of the suffering of death" (Heb. 2:9). Thus, the crimson-stained cross—as the central focus of history and redemption—brings God the greatest glory (John 12:23; 13:31).[59]

56. The relevant phrase at the beginning of Ephesians 1:6 in the Greek literally reads "to the praise of the glory of his grace" (NASB). God's grace in the work of election (redemption) occasions the display of his glory.

57. See also Rom. 3:24; 1 Cor. 1:30; 2:2; Gal. 3:13; Heb. 9:12, 15.

58. That this is the end work of Christ is also seen in Acts 3:21; 1 Cor. 15:27–28; Eph. 1:10–11, 22; Phil. 3:21; Heb. 2:8–10; Rev. 21:5.

59. Welty, *Why Is There Evil?*, 134; Andreas J. Köstenberger, "The Glory of God in John's Gospel and Revelation," in *The Glory of God*, ed. Christopher W. Morgan and Robert A. Peterson (Wheaton, IL: Crossway, 2010), 119; Jeremy R. Treat, *The Crucified King: Atonement and*

None other than the venerable Puritan giant John Owen (1616–83) saw the ultimate end of the cross to be the supreme glory of God.[60] Furthermore, he embraced a rudimentary form of the redemptive greater-glory theodicy (*felix culpa*) presented here. After describing how God's pristine creation, and especially man, "was defaced by sin, and the whole creation rolled up in darkness, wrath, curses, confusion, and the great praise of God buried in the heaps of it,"
Owen goes on to write:

> Here, now, does the depth of the riches of the wisdom and knowledge of God open itself. A design in Christ shines out from his bosom, that was lodged there from eternity, to recover things to such an estate as shall be exceedingly to the advantage of his glory, infinitely above what at first appeared, and for the putting of sinners into inconceivably a better condition than they were in before the entrance of sin. He appears now glorious; he is known to be a God pardoning iniquity and sin [Ex. 33:18–19; 34:6–7], and *advances the riches of his grace*: which was his design (Eph. 1:6). He has infinitely vindicated his justice also, in the face of men, angels, and devils, in setting forth his Son for a propitiation (Rom. 3:24–25). It is also to our advantage; we are more fully established in his favor, and are carried toward a more exceeding weight of glory than formerly was revealed (2 Cor. 4:17). Hence was that ejaculation of one of the ancients, "*O felix culpa, quae talem meruit redemptorem!*"[61]

Milton and Owen agree on the fortunateness of the fall as meriting such a great Redeemer. Isaac Watts (1674–1748) also picks up the *felix culpa* theme in his hymn "Jesus Shall Reign Where'er the Sun" (1719), in which he writes:

> Where He displays His healing power,
> Death and the curse are known no more.
> In Him the tribes of Adam boast
> More blessings than their father lost.

Kingdom in Biblical and Systematic Theology (Grand Rapids: Zondervan, 2014), 160–62; cf. Piper, *Spectacular Sins*, 49. Note other references in John's Gospel to Christ's glory in the cross: John 12:16, 28; 13:32; 17:1, 4–5. See also Rev. 1:5–7; 5:12; 7:10–12, 14–15 (cf. 15:3–4). The "lifting up" of Christ on the cross (John 8:28; 12:32, 34) also speaks of his glory and points to his glorious ascension as well. See Thomas R. Schreiner, *The King in His Beauty: A Biblical Theology of the Old and New Testaments* (Grand Rapids: Baker Academic, 2013), 523, 525.

60. John Owen, *The Death of Death in the Death of Christ* (Carlisle, PA: Banner of Truth, 1959), 89–90.

61. John Owen, *Communion with the Triune God*, ed. Kelly M. Kapic and Justin Taylor (Wheaton, IL: Crossway, 2007), 195. Again, the Latin reads: "O fortunate fault [fall], which merits so great a redeemer!"

All three were likely drawing on the later but undeveloped thought of Augustine.[62] Owen, in more concrete fashion than Milton or Watts, gives us a sweeping view of the purposes of God embedded in the biblical storyline that is not merely U-shaped, but more precisely J-shaped. In other words, the threefold plot arc begins in a state of unsullied good (*creation*). Then it suddenly plummets into ruinous pits of darkness (*fall*). From there, it moves gloriously upward toward a state of renewed good (*redemption*). This final state of the good, however, is immeasurably greater than that initial state of good.

Why will the new creation be greater than Eden? Because the Redeemer himself descended into the depths of the impossible predicament that the fall brought about and emerged in unprecedented victory. The remarkable work of Christ in redeeming the good that seemed irreparably ruined gives that good a sweetness in the final paradisiacal state (i.e., the new creation) that would be unrealized if it had never been ruined in the first place. Without the force of evil tearing our hearts out and leaving us desperately screaming for redemption, the utterly unsullied state of restoration in the end would lose the luster of its victory.

Furthermore, without the astonishing and incomparable Redeemer sent to remedy the crisis of evil, again the victory would be less glorious. It would be hollow. What would the victory of redemption be without such a wonder-filled Redeemer as Christ? It is impossible to imagine a grander hero. And so we are indeed compelled to cry out: *O felix culpa!* that demanded such a magnificent Redeemer![63]

---

62. Jesse Couenhoven has argued that the theodicy of Augustine (A.D. 354–430) in his later years embraced something along the lines of the *felix culpa* theodicy. See "Augustine's Rejection of the Free-Will Defence: An Overview of the Late Augustine's Theodicy," *Religious Studies* 43.3 (2007): 279–98. Augustine's complex and sketchy theodicy encompasses the notion that evil contributes to the ultimate beauty of redemption in God's creation. Couenhoven writes, "Without the Fall, and negative consequences for it, Augustine believes that we would not be able to understand just how terrible sin is, and just how amazingly gracious God is" (292). Michael Peterson agrees with this assessment of Augustine in the "Introduction" of Peterson, in *The Problem of Evil: Selected Readings*, ed. Michael L. Peterson, 2nd ed. (Notre Dame, IN: University of Notre Dame Press, 2017), 6. The noted German philosopher Gottfried Leibniz (1646–1716), who champions the best-of-all-possible-worlds theodicy, also indicates an affinity for *felix culpa*. See *The Philosophical Works of Leibnitz*, ed. and trans. George Martin Duncan (New Haven, CT: Tuttle, Morehouse & Taylor, 1890), 195.

63. Alvin Plantinga, otherwise well known for championing the free-will defense, has more recently argued for *felix culpa*, drawing renewed attention among contemporary Christian thinkers to this older theodicy. See "Supralapsarianism, or 'O Felix Culpa,'" in *The Problem of Evil: Selected Readings*, ed. Michael L. Peterson, 2nd ed. (Notre Dame, IN: University of Notre Dame Press, 2017), 363–89, first published in *Christian Faith and the Problem of Evil*, ed. Peter Van Inwagen (Grand Rapids: Eerdmans, 2004), 1–25. Plantinga builds this positive theodicy on

There is a ringing paradox here. How could any good come from the fall? How could a hero purposed to defeat the grand conflict of the ages come from a dusty Galilean outpost called Nazareth (John 1:46)? "The great mystery" (Eph. 5:32 KJV), as Owen writes,

> is hid in Christ—the great and unspeakable riches of the wisdom of God, in *pardoning* sin, *saving* sinners, satisfying *justice*, fulfilling the *law*, repairing his own *honor*, and providing for us a more exceeding weight of glory; and all this out of such a condition as wherein it was impossible that it should enter into hearts of angels or men however the glory of God should be repaired, and one sinning creature delivered from everlasting ruin.[64]

his free-will defense, which seeks to employ God's knowledge of counterfactuals of (libertarian) freedom (i.e., middle knowledge) as affirmed by Molinism (see pages 103–8 for a critique of Molinism). I believe the *felix culpa* theodicy (especially as I have framed it) is much more coherent in a broadly Reformed (Calvinistic) understanding of theology (i.e., meticulous providence coupled with compatibilistic notions of human freedom and responsibility; see chapter 7). The fact that Plantinga associates this theodicy with supralapsarianism, a distinctively Reformed view of the order of divine decrees, indicates this (see Appendix: "Sullied by Supralapsarianism?"). Plantinga was raised as a Dutch Reformed Christian. See his essay "A Christian Life Partly Lived," in *Philosophers Who Believe*, ed. Kelly James Clark (Downers Grove, IL: InterVarsity Press, 1993), 45–82. Other philosophical defenses of *felix culpa* similar to Plantinga's may be found in Stewart, *Greater Good Defense*, 144–64; Nick Trakakis, "Does Hard Determinism Render the Problem of Evil Even Harder?," *Ars Disputandi* 6.1 (2006): 239–64. Critiques of Plantinga's version of *felix culpa* include: Hud Hudson, "The Argument from Evil: Felix Culpa!," in *Two Dozen (or So) Arguments for God: The Plantinga Project*, ed. Jerry L. Walls and Trent Dougherty (Oxford: Oxford University Press, 2018), 277–90; Kevin Diller, "Are Sin and Evil Necessary for a Really Good World?," in *The Problem of Evil: Selected Readings*, ed. Michael L. Peterson, 2nd ed. (Notre Dame, IN: University of Notre Dame Press, 2017), 390–409; Marilyn McCord Adams, "Plantinga on 'Felix Culpa': Analysis and Critique," *Faith and Philosophy* 25.2 (2008): 123–40. Others who endorse the *felix culpa* theodicy include Paul Helm, *The Providence of God* (Downers Grove, IL: InterVarsity Press, 1994), 193–216 (esp. 213–15); Phillip Cary, "A Classic View," in *God and the Problem of Evil: Five Views*, ed. Chad Meister and James K. Dew Jr. (Downers Grove, IL: InterVarsity Press, 2017), 33–36; and somewhat implicitly in Reymond, *New Systematic Theology*, 499–500. Others have suggested the value of this theodicy, including Johnson, "Calvinism and the Problem of Evil," 43–48; Timothy Keller, *Walking with God through Pain and Suffering* (New York: Dutton, 2013), 118; Randy Alcorn, *If God Is Good: Faith in the Midst of Suffering and Evil* (Colorado Springs: Multnomah Books, 2009), 196–98; Loraine Boettner, *The Reformed Doctrine of Predestination* (Philadelphia: Presbyterian and Reformed, 1932), 232. Similar theodicies to *felix culpa* are also found in P. T. Forsyth, *The Justification of God: Lectures for War-Time on a Christian Theodicy* (New York: Charles Scribner's Sons, 1917); Shenk, *Wonder of the Cross*; Piper, *Spectacular Sins*; Jay Adams, *The Grand Demonstration* (Santa Barbara, CA: EastGate Publishers, 1991); Henri Blocher, *Evil and the Cross* (Grand Rapids: Kregel, 1994). Other interesting treatments of the *felix culpa* position include Victor Yelverton Haines, "Drawing Evil with a Happy Face: The Iconography of the Felix Culpa," in *The Problem of Evil: An Intercultural Exploration*, ed. Sandra Ann Wawrytko (Amsterdam: Rodopi, 2000), 77–88; C. L. J. Culpepper, "'O Felix Culpa!' The Sacramental Meaning of Winnie-the-Pooh," in *The Pooh Perplex: A Student Casebook*, ed. Frederick C. Crews (1963; repr., Chicago: University of Chicago Press, 2003), 53–62.

64. Owen, *Communion with God*, 195–96.

It was an inconceivable plan, yet a grand stroke of divine genius. If the plotline were flat—good followed by good and then more of the same—there would be no occasion for God to display his unwavering justice and his holy wrath against the recalcitrant world, or his boundless compassion to the broken, and especially his unexpected mercy and forgiveness toward the wretched.[65] It is out of the depths of this latter condition where the divine glory via the glorious Christ especially pours forth like blinding light from a dungeon.

WAS THE FALL NECESSARY?

All this brings us to a stark, and to some an unpleasant, conclusion. Redemption is meaningless unless there is some state of dereliction that makes the notion of restoration meaningful.[66] The redemptive crux(!) of the crucifixion is meaningless unless a prior state of evil exists that cries out for the Redeemer's exclusive redress of its pandemic corruption.[67] Bavinck (like Owen) exposes the tension here: "Scarcely" had God introduced his good creation "before sin crept into it. . . . Almost at the same moment creatures came, pure and splendid, from the hand of their Maker, they were deprived of all their luster, and stood, corrupted and impure, before his holy face. Sin ruined the entire creation, converting its righteousness into guilt, its holiness into impurity, its glory into shame, its blessedness into misery, its harmony into disorder, and its light into darkness."[68] The emergence of evil appears to be a frustration of God's good plan for the creation. Yet on the other hand, it seems inevitable if we are to live in a world in which Christ the Redeemer supremely magnifies God's glory.

So does this mean that evil's existence is a necessary feature of the creation? Richard Shenk frames the question this way:

> Is evil avoidable? If evil is not avoidable, then evil is necessary in some sense. But if evil is avoidable and if there is, in fact, evil in the world, then the question naturally progresses to this: if evil is avoidable, why not start over? That is, why did God not destroy what he made, condemn the willful creatures who sinned, and start again to achieve a world without

---

65. Jonathan Edwards makes this point forcefully in Miscellany no. 348, *The "Miscellanies," a–500,* vol. 13 of *The Works of Jonathan Edwards,* ed. Thomas A. Schafer (New Haven, CT: Yale University Press, 1994), 419–20. See also Francis Turretin, *Institutes of Elenctic Theology,* ed. John T. Dennison Jr., trans. George Musgrave Giger, 3 vols. (Phillipsburg, NJ: P&R Publishing, 1992–97), 1:518; Helm, *Providence of God,* 215.

66. Helm, *Providence of God,* 96.

67. Plantinga, "Supralapsarianism, or 'O Felix Culpa,'" 372–73.

68. Bavinck, *Reformed Dogmatics,* 3:28–29.

evil? There is a biblical assertion that he did something like this in the days of Noah. And the biblical record attests that he was not effective, if avoiding a sinful world in the future was his goal.[69]

The fact is, God has never fully stamped out evil—not even when Satan first rebelled against him in the primordial halls of the Celestial City. But John Feinberg has pointed out that God is not obligated to act with a view toward accomplishing every morally good thing possible. Nonetheless, whatever he does do must necessarily have some good end. "If he fails to do something good which he apparently should do, he must have a morally sufficient reason for not doing it."[70] So we must conclude that he decreed the fall for some infinitely wise and morally satisfactory reason, "having purposed to order it to his own glory."[71] He purposely "subjected" creation "to futility" so that "in hope" it would "be set free from its bondage to corruption" (Rom. 8:20–21). As Paul Helm has said, "It is difficult to imagine that God could or would voluntarily surrender the superintendence of an act [the fall] with such cataclysmic consequences, knowing what those consequences would be."[72]

The Christian story has a clear, compelling, and logical trajectory: good creation, ruined by the fall, and redeemed by Christ. "No rebellion, no drama, no story. Without the high stakes of humanity's alienation from God, there can be no redemption."[73] And such a story means evil. Gregory Ganssle is correct:

> Christianity *requires* there to be evil. If no evil existed, we would know that Christianity is false. Furthermore, Christianity requires a great deal more than a superficial amount of evil. The evil has to be so significant that the highest sacrifice is warranted. Christianity is the story of God entering the world and paying the highest price to deal with the root of evil. It is the story of God becoming a human in Jesus and taking on himself the results of human sin. God went to incredible lengths to solve the root issue of evil in the world. If evil did not exist or if evil was only a minor part of reality, then this story would be false.[74]

69. Shenk, *Wonder of the Cross*, 99.
70. John S. Feinberg, *The Many Faces of Evil* (Wheaton, IL: Crossway, 2004), 229.
71. WCF, 6.1. See also Calvin, *Institutes*, 3.23.7; Johnson, *Calvinism and the Problem of Evil*, 43.
72. Helm, *Providence of God*, 101.
73. Alcorn, *If God Is Good*, 196.
74. Gregory E. Ganssle, "Evil as Evidence for Christianity," in *God and Evil: The Case for God in a World Filled with Pain*, ed. Chad Meister and James K. Dew Jr. (Downers Grove, IL: InterVarsity Press, 2013), 221.

But this still hasn't answered the question. It is one thing to say that God purposely decreed the fall of humanity and set the trajectory for redemption. But did Adam and Eve *have* to sin? Is evil a necessary result of God's plan to create the world?

If we are saying that God was absolutely compelled by his intrinsically moral and rational nature, then the answer is no. Nothing compels the supremely good God to fashion a world that contained evil. That would be absurd. The fact is, God's creation was conceived and fabricated in a cradle of goodness,[75] without any hint of evil. The goodness of the initial creation speaks to the uncorrupted perfection of the Creator's nature. Yet the incorruptible God reserves the right to fashion a world that *could* and *would* be corrupted.[76]

This means that the introduction of evil is a *consequence* of some other condition related to the *freedom* of God. Paul Helm clarifies this freedom as that which is self-determining: "God does not have to do what he does by any necessity of nature, nor is he 'free' in the sense that he has liberty of indifference to opt between alternatives [i.e., libertarian free will]. Rather he is free because he acts in accordance with his supremely excellent nature without coercion or hindrance."[77] As the first premise of my earlier argument stated, God freely conceived a plan for the creation in which he would maximize his glory to his creatures, but he was under no compulsion to create. Nonetheless, as we have seen, Scripture repeatedly indicates that this is what God has chosen to do.

Thus, given this freely exercised divine decision, evil suddenly becomes a necessary intrusion on God's good creation. While evil is not an *absolute*, *inherent*, or *intrinsic necessity*, we can say that it is a *conditional necessity*, conditioned on God's prior freedom to create a world intended to maximize his glory.[78] If God had not freely chosen to create, and thereby to maximize

---

75. Again, note that the Hebrew word for "good" (*tob*) is used seven times in the Genesis creation account (1:4, 10, 12, 18, 21, 25, 31).

76. Shenk, *Wonder of the Cross*, 198.

77. Paul Helm, *Eternal God: A Study of God without Time*, 2nd ed. (Oxford: Oxford University Press, 2010), 174.

78. Calvin distinguishes between "relative necessity" and "absolute necessity" (*Institutes*, 1.16.9). John Murray uses the phrase "consequent absolute necessity" to communicate the idea of conditional necessity in *Redemption Accomplished and Applied* (6). His idea is that certain things become *absolute necessities* as a consequence of God's prior freedom to decree that the world have certain outcomes. Yet I think that language is misleading. It is best to call this type of necessity *relative* (Calvin), *conditional*, *contingent*, or *hypothetical*, or even simply *consequent necessity*, leaving the word *absolute* out. *Absolute* describes something that is necessary no matter what, something that has an intrinsic or inherent necessity. See Paul Helm, "It Ain't Necessarily So: Calvin and the Will of God," *Credo Magazine* (December 2, 2011), found at

his glory, the introduction of evil would not have been necessary. But there is also an important chain of necessity here. Evil is not an end in itself.[79] The necessity of evil presupposes the prior necessity of redemption as the supreme means of maximizing God's glory, and furthermore, redemption requires the necessity that Christ become incarnated and offer himself as an atoning sacrifice for the sin of those he came to redeem.

In other words, if God had not specifically planned the redemptive work of Christ, which *alone* is capable of defeating evil so as to maximize God's glory, evil truly would be a disconcerting horror of the first order. And we would have reason to question the viability of God's existence. His goodness, power, wisdom, knowledge, righteousness, justice—indeed, his full nature—would be maligned. He would not resemble the God of the Bible whatsoever. The conclusion, then, is simple. Evil becomes necessary inasmuch as it brings about God's *greater* redemptive and glorious ends.[80] "Where sin increased, grace abounded all the more" (Rom. 5:20). And wherever grace abounds, the glory of God abounds (Eph. 1:6).

God's extrinsic glory could certainly be magnified in an unfallen-not-needing-redemption world, but such glory would be without the cross and empty tomb of the incarnate Son of God. It would be an acceptable world, but far closer to the lesser glories of a desert arroyo than we might imagine. His extrinsic glory is far more magnified in a fallen-but-being-redeemed world, and that is much more like the grandeur of the Grand Canyon. He is *supremely* glorified in such a world. God could have created many potential worlds to magnify his extrinsic glory, but no world seems poised to exalt him so supremely without the redemptive work of Christ.[81] The vicarious atoning sacrifice of the sinless Son of God is the *only* means by which God

---

: https://credomag.com/2011/12/it-aint-necessarily-so-calvin-and-the-will-of-god/. For example, in whatever God freely chooses to decree, there is an absolute, intrinsic, or inherent necessity that it have some good divine intention because it is impossible for God to will that for which he has evil intentions. Thus, if he chooses to will evil, it must of absolute necessity have a good intention. Furthermore, if God chooses to will evil, which he does, then it is necessary only given certain prior conditions that God sets forth in his decree, such as supremely magnifying his glory to his creatures. See further discussion of evil's necessity in Shenk, *Wonder of the Cross*, 63–67; Feinberg, *Many Faces of Evil*, 166–67.

79. Bavinck, *Reformed Dogmatics*, 2:391.

80. Helm, *Providence of God*, 197; cf. Calvin, *Institutes*, 3.23.7; WCF 6.1. Passages that explicitly teach that God brings good out of evil: Gen. 50:20; Rom. 5:20–21; 8:20–21, 28; 2 Cor. 4:17 (cf. Rom. 8:18).

81. Plantinga writes: "No matter how much evil, how much sin and suffering a [potential created] world contains, the aggregated badness would be outweighed by the goodness of incarnation and atonement, outweighed in such a way that the world in question is very good" ("Supralapsarianism, or 'O Felix Culpa,'" 371). See also Stewart, *Greater-Good Defence*, 147–48.

could have redeemed his image-bearing creatures (Rom. 3:21–26; Heb. 2:17; 9:11–28).[82]

It is important to understand the claim here. Leibniz's model says that the world God decreed and brought into existence is the best of *all* possible worlds.[83] In other words, of all the possible worlds (states of affairs) that God could have brought about, *only* this world (state of affairs) can qualify as *the* very best. But we have already shown that this is a problem.[84] It is more defensible to say that while there could be multiple worlds *equal* in optimal overall goodness to this world (with whatever balance between good and evil such a world might contain), there can be no possible worlds better than this world, including a world unsullied by the fall.

The contention of the greater-glory theodicy, however, also includes this point: Given God's freely chosen plan to maximize his extrinsic glory to his image-bearing creatures, which he is under no compulsion to do, then there can be no world that does not contain the *fall* and *redemption* as well as the *means of redemption*, which *must* include the incarnation, atoning death and resurrection, and exaltation of the Son of God. No world is poised to maximize God's glory without these features. Thus, we can say that there is a *contingent necessity* to this world. It necessarily contains fall and redemption together with the person and work of Christ only because, first of all, those features are contingent on God's freedom to create any world *at all*! And second, because of God's freedom to maximize his *extrinsic* glory.[85]

Furthermore, the position advocated here does not seek to explain why this world contains either the *extent* or the horrendous *degree* of evil that it does. Per the claims of skeptical theism ("*sensibly humble* theism"), there is no obligation to explain why God has chosen the precise mix of good and evil that this world contains.[86] It is not possible that anyone could give such reasons. But neither is it possible that one could explain why there *must*

---

82. Murray, *Redemption Accomplished and Applied*, 3–13; Turretin, *Institutes of Elenctic Theology*, 2:299–304; Stephen Wellum, *Christ Alone: The Uniqueness of Jesus as Savior* (Grand Rapids: Zondervan, 2017), 34–35, 107–23, 221–28; Donald Macleod, *Christ Crucified: Understanding the Atonement* (Downers Grove, IL: InterVarsity Press, 2014), 194–219.

83. See pages 132–38.

84. See pages 137–38. Paul Helm seeks to defend the claim that this world is the best of all possible worlds in *Eternal God*, 171–94.

85. Remember, God's *intrinsic glory* is an *absolute necessity* because it is who he is in himself and it is impossible for God to deny himself. God's *extrinsic* glory is that external manifestation of his glory that he chooses to reveal to his creation.

86. See pages 123–27. The designation "*sensibly humble* theism" comes from Stephen Wykstra, "The Skeptical Theist View," in *God and the Problem of Evil: Five Views*, ed. Chad Meister and James K. Dew Jr. (Downers Grove, IL: InterVarsity Press, 2017), 111.

not be the precise mix of good and evil that this world contains for God's glory to be maximized.

God has all-wise, inscrutable reasons for making this world as he has, with all its particular strengths, wonders, blessings, and graces along with all its particular weaknesses, heartaches, curses, and evils. This is a more defensible position than the classic best-of-all-possible-worlds defense provides, for it preserves God's freedom while maintaining his exalted attributes as a being "than-which-a-greater-cannot-be thought."[87] The freedom of the maximally great God to pursue maximal glory makes no other world better than this world, which contains the greatest possible goods. There is no greater good for ill-deserving sinners mired in the pit of their own miserable sin, situated within a world of miserable sin, than to be set on the rock of Christ's redemptive righteousness (Ps. 40:1–3).

THE HOPE OF THE GREATER-GLORY THEODICY

But what are these goods? How does this theodicy bring practical hope to humanity? How does it meet the mother who has lost her newborn child? The hardworking couple who has lost everything to an unexpected forest inferno? The father grieving over the suicide of his teenage daughter? Or the family torn apart by a soldier's battle with post-traumatic stress syndrome? The value of this theodicy above every other theodicy that Christians have devised is found in its direct connection to the gospel.

The gospel of a redeeming Christ is the first line of hope in the face of evil, and it is the primary reason for evil's existence. The gospel of redemption is humanity's greatest good in the face of the greatest evils that can assail us. Without this providentially orchestrated hope, no answer to the problem of evil makes any sense. Our life story has no choice but to trade in comedy for tragedy (see chapter 10) without God's gospel storyline. "The cross alone makes the suffering that disfigures human history understandable within God's providence."[88] Here are four important ways in which the greater-glory theodicy brings hope through the redemptive gospel that it is centered on.

Christ Bears Our Sins

The atoning death of Christ addresses evil as it is perpetrated by us and as it is perpetrated against us. When we consider the problem of evil,

---

87. Anselm, *Proslogion*, 2–3, in *Anselm of Canterbury: The Major Works*, ed. Brian Davies and G. R. Evans (Oxford: Oxford University Press, 1998), 87–88.

88. David Bebbington, *Patterns in History* (Downers Grove, IL: InterVarsity Press, 1979), 175.

we usually consider it from the perspective of evil that comes against us unjustly. But we must first consider it a problem as perpetrated by our own rebellion against a holy God. The grief we bear for evil should first point us to our own culpable actions. The first signs of real hope come only when we acknowledge our sin and turn to Christ, who offers pardon and restoration.

To the redeemed, Isaiah declares that the Suffering Servant "was pierced for our transgressions; he was crushed for our iniquities; upon him was the chastisement that brought us peace, and with his wounds we are healed" (Isa. 53:5). Our good and Christ's glory are supremely magnified in the incomprehensible gap of this divinely orchestrated dichotomy: when hopeless and wretched sinners steeped in dark thoughts and conduct repent of their sin, and then by faith emerge into the midst of the resplendent light of the crucified and risen Christ for their redemption. The only way that fallen human beings can benefit from God's glory in redemption is to turn to the Redeemer.

For the apostle Paul, nothing equaled the unexpected grace he received from Christ, knowing how ill-deserving he truly was. He tells Timothy:

> I thank him who has given me strength, Christ Jesus our Lord, because he judged me faithful, appointing me to his service, though formerly I was a blasphemer, persecutor, and insolent opponent. But I received mercy because I had acted ignorantly in unbelief, and the grace of our Lord overflowed for me with the faith and love that are in Christ Jesus. The saying is trustworthy and deserving of full acceptance, that Christ Jesus came into the world to save sinners, of whom I am the foremost. (1 Tim. 1:12–15)

Paul's appreciation for the grace of God is made more potent by the fact of his utter rebellion. What's more, after contemplating how remarkable it is that God would rescue him from a life steeped in wickedness, Paul can only conclude with this doxological reflection: "To the King of the ages, immortal, invisible, the only God, be honor and glory forever and ever. Amen" (1 Tim. 1:17). Paul sees that the end game of his own evil is the glory of God in redemption. Like Peter, all the redeemed may boldly "proclaim the excellencies of him who called [us] out of darkness into his marvelous light" (1 Peter 2:9). The more horrendous our evil, the more glorious is the dawning of our redemption.

Ironically and shockingly, the goods achieved by Christ's redemptive work are more glorious than if our sin had never ruined good in the first place.[89] The grace that was lost in Adam is a grace that is made far better in Christ.[90] Paul's testimony tells us that the more horrific our sin, the greater the rewards Christ's redemptive work supplies. Why so much seemingly gratuitous (senseless) evil in the world? One reason is that it highlights the magnificence of the grace that defeats it in those who once perpetuated it. Horrendous sin elicits more grace from Christ to the elect (Rom. 5:20–21), more joy for the elect sinner, and greater glory to God.[91]

Jesus highlights this truth with Simon the Pharisee who was appalled at the deplorable sinner of a woman who showered Jesus with tears, ointment, and deep affection (Luke 7:36–39):

> And Jesus answering said to him, "Simon, I have something to say to you." And he answered, "Say it, Teacher."
> "A certain moneylender had two debtors. One owed five hundred denarii, and the other fifty. When they could not pay, he cancelled the debt of both. Now which of them will love him more?" Simon answered, "The one, I suppose, for whom he cancelled the larger debt." And he said to him, "You have judged rightly." Then turning toward the woman he said to Simon, "Do you see this woman? I entered your house; you gave me no water for my feet, but she has wet my feet with her tears and wiped them with her hair. You gave me no kiss, but from the time I came in she has not ceased to kiss my feet. You did not anoint my head with oil, but she has anointed my feet with ointment. Therefore I tell you, her sins, which are many, are forgiven—for she loved much. But he who is forgiven little, loves little." (Luke 7:40–47)

The state of renewal for one who has drunk deeply at the well of wickedness is much more glorious than for one who has digested only small amounts of sin's deathly potion. The former brings fuller satisfaction, greater joy, more lasting peace, and larger displays of love and gratitude for the Redeemer.[92]

Jonathan Edwards remarks that no matter how much happiness God bestowed on Adam and Eve in their sinless state, "this goodness would be nothing near so much prized and admired, and the sense of it not near so great," as that experienced in their redemption. "We little consider how

89. Piper, *Spectacular Sins*, 54.
90. Owen, *Communion with God*, 195.
91. But this is not a justification to engage in greater acts of evil. That is to trivialize the high stakes involved in God's dispensing grace in the first place (Rom. 3:8; 6:1–2; Heb. 6:4–6).
92. Alcorn, *If God Is Good*, 197.

much the sense of good is heightened by the sense of evil, both moral and natural."[93]

This answers an important objection to this theodicy that God is "using" his creatures for his own ends.[94] Alvin Plantinga frames the objection: "Isn't it too much like a father who throws his children into the river so that he can then heroically rescue them, or a doctor who first spreads a horrifying disease so that he can then display enormous virtue in fighting it in heroic disregard of his own safety and fatigue?"[95] If this represents the substance of this theodicy, then perhaps we would have reason to doubt the value of God's decreeing the fall. But part of that which constitutes God's glory is "the flourishing of his people."[96] There is greater flourishing for a redeemed sinner than there is for a good (unfallen) person who needs no redemption (cf. Luke 5:31–32). The unmitigated effusions of divine love, grace, mercy, kindness, and compassion that God eagerly extends to prodigals are made all the more glorious by their having desperately wallowed in the mud, the filth, the stench of rebellion's pigpen (Luke 15:11–32).

Likewise, Michael Peterson objects that the *felix culpa* theodicy contradicts the classical doctrine of creation, whose original purpose (*telos*) is to facilitate intimacy between God and his image-bearing creatures. Thus, he thinks, "the highest good for creation is available without creation's descent into sin and evil."[97] But this misses the fact that such intimacy is intensified precisely because God's people have been redeemed from sin and evil, although deserving death and hell. Instead of incurring the crushing weight of divine wrath, amazingly they have been unexpectedly, graciously, and marvelously restored to this *telos* of creation. Sin and evil do not undermine the *telos* of creation; they enhance it via the introduction of redemption.

Christ's redemptive work establishes greater intimacy between God and purified sinners than if such creatures had never fallen into the deplorable conditions of evil in the first place. The deepest intimacy that can exist between God and his creatures occurs when his incomparably exalted

---

93. Edwards, Miscellany no. 348, *Miscellanies*, 420. Although Edwards neither articulated a precise theodicy nor referred explicitly to the *felix culpa*, nonetheless his careful musings on the fall indicate a sympathy for this position.

94. William Hasker, *The Triumph of God over Evil: Theodicy for a World of Suffering* (Downers Grove, IL: InterVarsity Press, 2008), 168–69.

95. Plantinga, "Supralapsarianism, or 'O Felix Culpa,'" 382.

96. Johnson, "Calvinism and the Problem of Evil," 48.

97. Michael L. Peterson, "Christian Theism and the Evidential Argument from Evil," in *The Problem of Evil: Selected Readings*, ed. Michael L. Peterson, 2nd ed. (Notre Dame, IN: University of Notre Dame Press, 2017), 179.

holiness shrouded in an untouchably "high and holy place" condescends to dwell "with him who is of a contrite and lowly spirit" (Isa. 57:15). The woefully broken sinner is God's closest creaturely companion. And all who experience deep-seated godly contrition before such a merciful God know this very well (e.g., the sinful woman of Luke 7; the prodigal son of Luke 15; cf. Pss. 32:3–7; 51:8, 12).

Christ Bears Our Sorrows

The atoning death of Christ not only bears our personal sins, but bears the sorrows that a sinful world brings on us. Again, Isaiah prophesies that the Messiah would be "a man of sorrows and acquainted with grief" (Isa. 53:3). But these sorrows and griefs are not his own; they are the property of those he redeems.[98] The prophet explains in verse 4: "Surely he has borne our griefs and carried our sorrows." Jesus has no reason by virtue of his own character to live a life of pain and sorrow. He is unassailably content as a member of the perfect blessedness of the Godhead.

So the pain and sorrow he experienced as a man was that which he voluntarily took on himself vicariously on behalf of those he delivers from sin and sorrow. He bore our pain that exists as a consequence not only of our personal sin, but of the sin that an evil world crushes us with. Motyer observes that the terms "griefs" and "sorrows" encompass "all that mars our lives. We wish for more than we are able to achieve, so that the good life is always eluding us; we long for a truly happy life but are constantly baulked by sorrow in whatever form it may come—disappointment, bereavement, tragedy, whatever. But he makes our burdens his."[99]

This is incredibly beautiful and reassuring. Christ humbly and eagerly comes to our aid when believers cry out to him, and he brings relief to our suffering because his atoning work has already borne its relentless weight. We can identify with the cry and simultaneous confidence of David:

> You have kept count of my tossings;
>   put my tears in your bottle.
>   Are they not in your book?
> Then my enemies will turn back
>   in the day when I call.
> This I know, that God is for me.

---

98. Edward J. Young, *The Book of Isaiah*, vol. 3, *Chapters 40–66* (Grand Rapids: Eerdmans, 1972), 345.

99. J. Alec Motyer, *The Prophecy of Isaiah: An Introduction & Commentary* (Downers Grove, IL: InterVarsity Press, 1993), 430. See also Matt. 8:17.

In God, whose word I praise,
in the LORD, whose word I praise,
in God I trust; I shall not be afraid.
What can man do to me? (Ps. 56:8–11)

There is no evil that anyone can do to disrupt the blessings of those who love God and are predestined to salvation and then effectually called by him to adoption as sons and daughters of his kingdom (Rom. 8:29–30; Eph. 1:4–6). All the ill-treatment, injustice, and cursed adversity that slam us on the cold, hard floor of this life have already been ordained by God so that his atoning grace in Christ will redeem them for our good (Rom. 8:28).

Our present redemption does not relieve all the burdens of the evils we suffer in this life. But it points to the consummation of redemption in Christ's glorious kingdom when our merciful Father "will wipe away every tear from" our weary eyes, "and death shall be no more, neither shall there be mourning, nor crying, nor pain anymore, for the former things have passed away" (Rev. 21:4). There is more than enough hope for us, in the present along with a down payment of hope for the future, contained in the riches of Christ's treasury of grace.

Focusing on Future Glory

The New Testament instructs believers to continually keep their focus oriented toward their future redemption at the return of Christ.[100] The redemptive glory that sustains believers in the now also points them to its greater magnification in its future consummation. "For this light momentary affliction is preparing for us an eternal weight of glory beyond all comparison" (2 Cor. 4:17). Edwards comments:

> This is one way whereby the future happiness of saints is increased: happiness receives all its relish from a sense of the contrary; if it were not for this, joy would be dull and flat. Now this sense is obtained by a reflection on the miseries of this life, and looking on the torments of the damned. Wherefore, the greater the afflictions of this life were, the more sweet . . . will the heavenly happiness be.[101]

Adding to Edwards's reflections on 2 Corinthians 4:17, Paul Helm speaks of the deep relationship between suffering and glory:

100. See, for example, John 14:1–3; Rom. 8:18–25; 1 Cor. 15:50–57; Phil. 3:17–21; Col. 3:1–4; 1 Thess. 4:13–18; Titus 2:13; 1 Peter 1:3–9; Rev. 22:20.
101. Edwards, Miscellany no. 122, *Miscellanies*, 286.

> Not only does suffering produce or work for glory, but the character of the glory, according to Paul, is such that it cannot be properly understood except in terms that presuppose sin and suffering. Sin and suffering, and glory, are not contingently or accidentally related, but internally related; there is a relationship of meaning between the two states. The character of glory can be understood only in terms of the suffering.[102]

Future glory would be muted, domesticated, stripped of its ever-refreshing wonder without being preceded by the persistent nagging, biting, agonizing pangs of affliction that mark our present sordid existence. Augustine saw how the hope of future glory far exceeds the bliss of humanity before the fall:

> The first man was more blessed in paradise than any righteous man in this state of mortal frailty, as far as concerns the enjoyment of present good. But as for the hope of the future, any man in the extreme of bodily suffering is happier than the first-created. For it has been revealed to man with the certainty of truth—it is no mere opinion—that, free from all distresses, he will share with the angels the endless enjoyment of God Most High, whereas that first man, in all that bliss of paradise, had no certainty about his future.[103]

John Newton (1725–1807), the pastor, hymnist, and former notorious slave trader, understood well the miseries of evil. He witnessed fellow human beings shoved into the hull of a slave ship like sardines: screaming, chained, beaten, bloodied, starving, suffocating, and many summarily perishing—all at Newton's command. Likewise, he cherished the amazing character of grace, knowing firsthand the nightmarish miseries of sin from which that divine grace rescued him (1 Peter 2:9).

Yet his memory was still haunted by his deeds of terror even while his slaves perpetually recoiled from being so terrorized. Though he inwardly burned, desperate to reverse the course of suffering to which he had subjected so many, he could not help them now. Years after the fact, he wrote, "I hope it will always be a subject of humiliating reflection to me that I was once an active instrument in a business at which my heart now shudders."[104] But whether misery comes from being the terrorist or

---

102. Helm, *Providence of God*, 203.

103. Augustine, *City of God*, trans. Henry Bettenson (New York: Penguin Books, 1984), 11.12.

104. From a pamphlet that Newton wrote in 1788 against the slave trade, entitled *Thoughts upon the African Slave Trade*, quoted in Jonathan Aitken, *John Newton: From Disgrace to Amazing Grace* (London: Continuum, 2007), 242.

the terrorized, if one is redeemed, the foulest miseries make the hope of heaven sweeter.

Note, however, that Edwards also mentions contemplation of the "torments of the damned." If there is no real threat of divine judgment and no actual judgment enacted on sinful human beings, then there is no appreciation of the danger from which the redeemed are delivered. Although universal redemption (universalism) is expressly denied in Scripture, it is certainly possible that God could have saved all people as part of his freely exercised plan for the creation.

Yet the glory of God in redemption would be severely diminished if universalism held true. If all were saved and none were damned, it would suggest not only that redemption is sheer banality but that it is a matter of divine obligation.[105] We might know the temporal miseries of sin, but we would mock its failure to elicit lasting retributive consequences. Fear of real and terrible judgment heightens the longing for redemption and the merciful relief it brings to the redeemed. We therefore ache for the grand consummation, the irreversible reversal of all that defaces and disturbs our present condition. Knowing that nothing but a merciful thread has kept the redeemed from descending, along with everyone else, into the frightful fires of judgment gives us ample reason to rejoice in our future glorious estate.[106]

Raising the Banner of Divine Grace

The greater-glory theodicy is centered on the wonder of God's grace as manifested in redemption from sin, evil, Satan, death, and hell. Kevin Diller raises another objection at this point: "Would the depths of God's love for creation have been any less if sin and evil had not entered the world? Surely not."[107] But where does God's deepest love for humanity reside? It resides in the unparalleled manifestation of his unmerited *grace* to humbled wretches—a feature of God's eternal immutable character that finds no occasion to be displayed apart from the fall of his creatures. The greater glory of God's supreme love in the grace of redemption, in both its present and future manifestation, is precisely what has moved the redeemed throughout history to raise the banner of grace, and to pour forth their greatest praises to God.[108]

105. Benjamin B. Warfield, *The Plan of Salvation* (repr., Boonton, NJ: Simpson Publishing, 1989), 72.

106. This underlies the force of Jonathan Edwards's famous sermon *Sinners in the Hands of an Angry God*. See *A Jonathan Edwards Reader*, ed. John E. Smith, Harry S. Stout, and Kenneth P. Minkema (New Haven, CT: Yale University Press, 1995), 89–105.

107. Diller, "Are Sin and Evil Necessary?," 397.

108. A survey of the most frequently printed hymns in American hymnals from 1737 to

In addition to all the great biblical odes to God's redemption,[109] nothing else could have possibly motivated John Newton, the former slave trader, to pen some of the most beloved words of Christian hymnody: "Amazing grace! How sweet the sound that saved a wretch like me!" Or Julia H. Johnston (1849–1919) to pen: "Marvelous grace of our loving Lord, grace that exceeds our sin and our guilt."[110] Without being rescued from the clutches of sin, Frederick Lehman (1868–1953) could never have put forth such magnificent lines:

> The love of God is greater far
> Than tongue or pen can ever tell;
> It goes beyond the highest star,
> And reaches to the lowest hell;
> The guilty pair bowed down with care,
> God gave His Son to win;
> His erring child He reconciled,
> And pardoned from his sin.[111]

There is something immensely humbling about contemplating the glory of God that he purposely reveals only in the face of evil's cold and disturbing grip on this weary world. God, in the mystery and wonder of his being and perfect purposes, ordained evil to lead us to a purer worship. John MacArthur has proclaimed:

> The whole reason God ordained evil to exist was for His own glory's sake, so that forever and ever, holy angels and redeemed saints would give Him glory in full comprehension of all His attributes.
>
>   Prior to sin, God was not worshiped fully for His righteousness against the background of unrighteousness. He was not worshiped, nor could be, fully for His love until He demonstrated the kind of love that loves enemy, rebel sinners. He was not worshiped fully for His holiness until His wrath

---

1960 reveals that celebrating the redemptive work of the cross is an overwhelming theme in the history of Christian hymnody. See "Appendix 1," in *Wonderful Words of Life: Hymns in American Protestant History and Theology*, ed. Richard J. Mouw and Mark A. Noll (Grand Rapids: Eerdmans, 2004), 251–64.

109. See, for example, Pss. 6:1–5; 16; 25; 32:1–7; 85; 86:1–13; 103:1–14; 130. First Corinthians 15:3–5, Philippians 2:6–11, and Colossians 1:15–20 are regarded by New Testament scholars to be early church hymns that were either sung or confessed in corporate gatherings. See Ralph P. Martin, *Worship in the Early Church* (Grand Rapids: Eerdmans, 1964), 49–63. See also the heavenly hymns of Revelation 5:9–10, 12; 7:10.

110. Julia H. Johnston, "Grace Greater than Our Sin" (1911).

111. Frederick M. Lehman, "The Love of God" (1917).

displayed how He hated sin. And He was not worshiped for His grace until He displayed forgiveness and mercy on the elect. In every case, there is this great disclosure of the nature of God. Why? To display His glory.[112]

KEY TERMS

creation
extrinsic glory (of God)
fall
felix culpa
greater-glory theodicy
incarnation
intrinsic glory (of God)
monomyth
redemption

STUDY QUESTIONS

1. What is the basic thesis (argument) of the greater-glory theodicy?
2. What is the difference between God's intrinsic glory and his extrinsic glory?
3. Why does the redemptive work of Christ, centered on his death and resurrection, bring greater (extrinsic) glory to God than anything else?
4. What is the difference between the standard way of thinking about monomythic stories, which are U-shaped, and the J-shaped storyline of Scripture as understood by the greater-glory theodicy?
5. When thinking about the problem of evil, why is it important to place God at the center of the issues it raises instead of ourselves?
6. Was it "necessary" that the fall of humanity in the garden of Eden take place? Why or why not? Make sure to define what you mean by the term *necessary.*
7. What are some of the benefits (greater goods) of the greater-glory theodicy that the author points to?
8. What do you think of the greater-glory theodicy so far? Is it helping you resolve the broader problem of evil? Why or why not?

112. From a sermon entitled "Why Does Evil Dominate the World?," delivered on March 4, 2007. See https://www.gty.org/library/sermons-library/90-333.

FOR FURTHER READING

Phillip Cary, "A Classic View," in *God and the Problem of Evil: Five Views*, ed. Chad Meister and James K. Dew Jr. (Downers Grove, IL: InterVarsity Press, 2017), 13–36.

Paul Helm, *The Providence of God* (Downers Grove, IL: InterVarsity Press, 1994).

Christopher W. Morgan and Robert A. Peterson, eds., *The Glory of God* (Wheaton, IL: Crossway, 2010).

John Piper, *Spectacular Sins* (Wheaton, IL: Crossway, 2008).

Advanced

David E. Alexander and Daniel M. Johnson, eds., *Calvinism and the Problem of Evil* (Eugene, OR: Pickwick Publications, 2016).

Jonathan Edwards, "The End for Which God Created the World," in *God's Passion for His Glory: Living the Vision of Jonathan Edwards*, ed. John Piper (Wheaton, IL: Crossway, 1998), 125–251.

Alvin Plantinga, "Supralapsarianism, or 'O Felix Culpa,'" in *The Problem of Evil: Selected Readings*, ed. Michael L. Peterson, 2nd ed. (Notre Dame, IN: University of Notre Dame Press, 2017), 363–89.

Richard A. Shenk, *The Wonder of the Cross: The God Who Uses Evil and Suffering to Destroy Evil and Suffering* (Eugene, OR: Pickwick Publications, 2013).

13

GOD'S REDEMPTIVE
GLORY IN SCRIPTURE

The Sony World Photography Awards is the largest and leading photography competition in the world. In 2017, Aksel Martin Larsen of Denmark entered a startling photograph under the "Street Photography" category. It is a stark image of a fair-haired, dirty, naked little boy taken in a cemetery in Manila, the Philippines. Among the towering tombs in the photograph resides a community of homeless people. The boy is surrounded by trash, discarded bones, and decaying bodies. But what makes the image so startling is that he is holding a big, bright-red balloon that shimmers against the gray desecration all around him.[1]

That which piques our wonder, our longing, our attraction to beauty in nature, art, poetry, or music is the presence of dissonance: the juxtaposition of discordant features that contrasts the unexpected with the expected, the mundane with the exceptional. Beauty is magnified when it collides with ugliness. A shiny red balloon against a dismal landscape captures our attention. Because the largest diameter of a tree trunk is usually no more than about thirty-six *inches*, it is astonishing to see a tree whose diameter is over thirty-six *feet*, as is the case with the giant sequoia "General Sherman" in Sequoia National Park.

You don't expect a boy born blind whose learning disabilities are so severe that he can't even recall his own age to be a musical wunderkind. Yet the autistic savant Derek Paravicini instantly recalls any piece of music he hears once and replays it perfectly on his piano. Furthermore, he can play the piece in any style asked—classical, jazz, ragtime, boogie-woogie, and so on.[2]

1. See http://www.dailymail.co.uk/travel/travel_news/article-4335654/Portraits-2017-Sony
-World-Photography-Awards.html.
2. See http://www.cbsnews.com/news/derek-paravicinis-extraordinary-gift-12–03–2010/.

Dissonance in the contemplation of beauty points to the longing for transcendence. Glimpses of unadulterated beauty in a fallen world direct us toward the world as it should be, a cosmic landscape transformed in which goodness, truth, and beauty are restored to perfection. These echoes of aesthetic reality in the midst of such tension between truth and error, beauty and ugliness, good and evil, highlight the reality that fallen man's fundamental longing can be truly met only by coming face to face with the goodness, truth, and beauty of God's unbridled glory (Ps. 50:2).[3]

The magnification of God's glory in redemption is demonstrated by a panoply of contrasts and dichotomies. Those antitheses can be a matter of *degree*, such as the difference between raising a mortal man from the dead (e.g., Lazarus), which is utterly stunning in itself, and the rising of the eternal, impassible, self-existing Son of God from the dead. Glory can be manifested in the contrast between *differing* displays of divine attributes. For example, God may magnify his glory in the judgment of evildoers, yet glory is more highly magnified when severe judgments are contrasted with the spectacular and merciful salvation of others (e.g., Egyptians and Israelites, respectively, in the exodus).

The contrasts may take the form of *ironies*, such as Christ's dying for his enemies instead of vanquishing them (Rom. 5:10). They can be manifested in *paradoxes*, such as the idea that the Son of God would display power via weakness (1 Cor. 1:25) and humiliation, submitting himself to a cruel death (Phil. 2:5–11). The most poignant contrast involves the *polarities* between the heinousness of evil itself and the pure goodness of God in redeeming that which has succumbed to the dark forces of rebellion.

All these contrasts involve a constellation of the expected and unexpected, the conventional and unconventional, the ordinary and extraordinary. In this and the following chapters, I will consider the juxtaposition of many such contrasting and unusual features of Christ and his work of redemption, which serves to cast a brighter light on the glory of God in the tenebrous face of evil.

One area where these dissimilarities are prominent is in the grand narrative of Scripture that unfolds the U-shaped (really J-shaped) plot arc, which moves from creation to fall to new creation (i.e., the new heaven and the new earth). But the redemptive motif of this larger narrative is recast over and over in condensed form in nearly every significant subnarrative we find in

---

3. For a Christian perspective on the paradox of beauty in the arts, see David Skeel, *True Paradox: How Christianity Makes Sense of Our Complex World* (Downers Grove, IL: InterVarsity Press, 2014), 63–88.

both the Old and New Testaments. These smaller historical episodes contain telltale signs of these contrasting realities unveiling fresh dimensions of God's redemptive glory. Each has its comic and tragic heroes, villains, and compelling conflicts that test the mettle of the heroes and point us toward the insatiable thirst for restoration with God, one another, and the creation itself. In this chapter, I will examine several of these relevant narratives in Genesis, Exodus, and the Gospel of John.[4]

REDEMPTIVE GLORY IN THE OLD TESTAMENT

The Fall and the First Family

Genesis 1–3 sets forth the historical ground for creation and fall. But already within this broader narrative resides a series of smaller episodes that echo the larger plot arc. The whole book of Genesis sets the tone for the broader U-shaped narrative that marks the rest of Scripture and is foreshadowed and repeated in subnarratives throughout the larger plotline of creation, fall, and redemption. In the immediate aftermath of the fall, Adam and Eve are expelled from the paradisiacal garden and removed from the intimate fellowship they enjoyed with God (Gen. 3:23–24).

The crisis brought about by the fall strikes its primary blow to the personal relationship between the Creator and his image-bearing creatures. Though naked, they are covered in shame, and physical garments cannot hide their ruin. We expect their banishment to be the end of their tragic disobedience, but in the midst of God's judgment we see his mercy emerge. God intervenes and supplies them with adequate skins, requiring the sacrifice of an innocent animal that bespeaks atonement and reconciliation with their God (v. 21). Their ruin is met with repair.

---

4. I am being extremely selective. I can canvass only a handful of these U-shaped narratives and their redemptive themes. Beyond what I cover in Genesis and Exodus, the Old Testament contains similar themes in the following hero stories: Joshua (and the conquest of Canaan), Gideon (and the Midianites), David (versus Goliath, Saul, and Absalom), Elijah (versus Ahab and Jezebel), Ruth (including Naomi and Boaz), Nehemiah, Esther (versus Haman), Job (versus his accusers), and Daniel, to name a few. In the New Testament, the U-shaped pattern is often followed in Jesus' parables, such as the good Samaritan (Luke 10), the prodigal son (Luke 15), the rich man and Lazarus (Luke 16), and the persistent widow (Luke 18). The historical narratives surrounding the birth of Jesus, Peter's denial and restoration, and Paul's conversion fit the same pattern. Obviously, the passion narratives in the four Gospels are exemplars of this pattern, as is the book of Revelation. For how these stories work, see Leland Ryken, *Words of Delight: A Literary Introduction to the Bible* (Grand Rapids: Baker, 1992), 1–156; Leland Ryken, *The Literature of the Bible* (Grand Rapids: Zondervan, 1974), 45–78; Robert Alter, *The Art of Biblical Narrative* (New York: HarperCollins, 1981); J. P. Fokkelman, *Reading Biblical Narrative: An Introductory Guide* (Louisville, KY: Westminster John Knox Press, 1999).

Such is not the case with their firstborn son. Eve thinks Cain might be the promised Deliverer (Gen. 3:15; 4:1) who would redress the disaster that she and Adam have brought on the world.[5] Contrary to all hope, he becomes the Bible's first tragic hero.[6] He is blessed with a bountiful harvest (4:3), but cannot escape making himself the center of his world even in the face of God's encouragement (vv. 6–7). Instead, he murders his brother (v. 8), is unpersuaded to repent, and is then consigned to a terrifying existence.

Tragic figures in Scripture such as Cain (and Judas) are not unambiguous villains. Rather, they are often embattled creatures fighting the metaphorical demons of their souls, like Gollum in Tolkien's *The Lord of the Rings*. Voices are calling them to moral clarity, but other dark regions within drown out those voices, and the tragic figures doom themselves to catastrophe. Every Cain and Judas should tear at our own souls and strike us with fear. They should serve to expose the darkness and misery that lurk beneath that fissure and evoke the longing for repair and the reversal of our alienation from God. When tragic examples thwart the trajectory of the expected U-shaped plotline, it ought to increase our own burden for redemption.

The Flood and God's Favor

It is not long before the unfortunate misdirection of Cain spreads across the broad and broken landscape of the entire earth. "The LORD saw that the wickedness of man was great in the earth, and that every intention of the thoughts of his heart was only evil continually" (Gen. 6:5). The enormity of God's fearsome judgment reaches catastrophic proportions, desecrating creation's goodness that has already been fractured by the fall. The earthly domain that God made for humanity to "have dominion over" (1:28) now swallows its inhabitants in a sudden watery abyss during the days of Noah.

This exposes how befouling evil truly is in the face of a holy God. We can blithely dismiss how much wrongdoing appears to slip away unnoticed in this world with no hint of divine displeasure. The ubiquitous mercy of God is so frequently taken for granted (or missed altogether) that when such mercy is removed to reveal the severity of divine judgment that sin rightfully deserves, then our numbness to evil gives way to taking umbrage

---

5. Thomas R. Schreiner, *The King in His Beauty: A Biblical Theology of the Old and New Testaments* (Grand Rapids: Baker Academic, 2013), 11.

6. Other tragic heroes in Scripture include Lot, Jephthah, Samson, Saul, Absalom, Solomon, Jonah, and Judas. See Ryken, *Words of Delight*, 145–56; Ryken, *Literature of the Bible*, 95–106.

at the Judge. How could God wipe out the entire creation? The plain reading of Genesis 6–8 thus seems to paint a God whose sense of righteous indignation is gravely disproportionate to the infractions of his creatures. This may partly explain why many interpreters relegate the Noahic flood to a local disturbance instead of a worldwide cataclysm.[7]

Such misreading of the text misses the real impact of God's purpose here. It is only against the ominous backdrop of apocalyptic destruction that God's undeserved "favor" (Gen. 6:8) toward Noah stands out. No one is free from culpability for evil (Rom. 3:10–20, 23), much less Noah, as the sordid incident of his drunken nakedness after the flood makes clear (see Gen. 9:20–23). Grace is not grace unless it is freely poured out to those who should justly perish. Noah was among the world's transgressors, and God was under no obligation to spare him. But in order to preserve his promise to Eve to provide a future Redeemer (3:15), God ordered the massive wooden vessel of mercy to lift up its inhabitants from the watery ruin and transport them all to a renewed world under the colorful and gracious bow of a new beginning (9:11–17). To minimize the historical magnitude of the flood and these attendant themes is to minimize God's glory in judgment and redemption.

God's Promise and the Testing of Abraham

The U-shaped (monomythic) themes that come next in the patriarchal narratives of Genesis stand out. The sacrifice of Isaac is particularly arresting for its array of unexpected turns. Abraham was divinely elected to receive remarkable promises. God ensured that he would father a great nation, receive great blessing, and forever maintain a great name (Gen. 12:2). So blessed was he that "all the families of the earth" would benefit from his privileged status (v. 3).

These promises foreshadowed the gospel of a crucified and resurrected Messiah (Gal. 3:8). God would provide the old and childless man with an heir (Isaac) through whom these promises would be fulfilled (Gen. 15:3–4). The seriousness of God's promise came when he executed a self-maledictory oath (a self-binding covenant) in which his presence passed through animals cut in two. This signified that the Almighty would submit himself to the same deadly fate of those animals if he did not make good on his promise

---

7. For a defense of the global flood and its biblical and theological implications, see the relevant essays in Terry Mortenson and Thane H. Ury, eds., *Coming to Grips with Genesis: Biblical Authority and the Age of the Earth* (Green Forest, AR: Master Books, 2008). For its geological implications, see Andrew A. Snelling, *Earth's Catastrophic Past: Geology, Creation & the Flood*, 2 vols. (Dallas: Institute for Creation Research, 2009).

(vv. 9–21).[8] Obviously, the infinite, immutable, eternally self-existent Creator of the universe could never suffer such a fate.

Therefore, this unassailable truth assures us that every promise God makes to his redeemed children will be fulfilled. As Abraham would come to know, God's "promises, though they be for a time seemingly delayed, cannot be finally frustrated. . . . The heart of God is not turned though His face be hid; and prayers are not flung back, though they be not instantly answered."[9]

Yet none of this prepared Abraham for one of the more poignant and painful tests we learn of in the annals of Old Testament history. After being filled with great joy at the arrival of the promised heir, the beaming father was instructed by his covenant-keeping God: "Take your son, your only son Isaac, whom you love, and go to the land of Moriah, and offer him there as a burnt offering on one of the mountains of which I shall tell you" (Gen. 22:2). It is too easy to casually read this command and lose its excruciating force—go slaughter your beloved son!

Wait a minute! Doesn't this violate the moral will of God? How could he command that which is repulsive to his nature?

Herein lies the central paradox of Genesis 22: was there a conflict between God's disturbing command and the unfailing nature of his promise? Where would Abraham place his hope—in the God of promise or the promised son? The boy bore the burden of his own impending death on his back (v. 6; cf. John 19:17). He carried the wood to "Mount Doom,"[10] the place of sacrifice, and then was "bound" to the wood (Gen. 22:9). While Isaac was rendered helpless and expressed no resistance, his father "reached out his hand and took the knife to slaughter his son" (v. 10).

At this point in the story, doubting readers are filled with horror at a malevolent father and his malevolent God—child abusers of the first order. But again, we must not miss how God has purposed to magnify his glory in boldly rectifying the crisis that stands before Abraham. For the believer, every crisis that God throws our way is not unlike the test he cast on the patriarch. Abraham proved to be unwavering in his trust, and so must we. He had already assured his son that God would "provide for himself the lamb" for the sacrifice (Gen. 22:8). Yahweh the Provider (v. 14) would spare

8. Paul R. Williamson, *Sealed with an Oath: Covenant in God's Unfolding Purpose* (Downers Grove, IL: InterVarsity Press, 2007), 86.

9. Timothy Cruso, quoted in I. D. E. Thomas, *A Puritan Golden Treasury* (Carlisle, PA: Banner of Truth, 1977), 226.

10. Stephen G. Dempster, *Dominion and Dynasty: A Theology of the Hebrew Bible* (Downers Grove, IL: InterVarsity Press, 2003), 84.

Isaac somehow. And if not, then he would resurrect his limp body from the bloody altar and ensure the fulfillment of the promise (Heb. 11:19).

God's self-maledictory oath gives full assurance of the end result. The sovereign God knew all along that Abraham would demonstrate how much he truly feared him (Gen. 22:12) and that a suitable substitute—an unsuspecting little ram—was already waiting in a nearby "thicket" (v. 13).

Without this deeply personal crisis, Abraham's faith would never be given an opportunity to shine, much less God's mercy. In the absence of such severe trials, not only is faith domesticated, but the glory of God's rescue and provision is muted. What makes the divine glory pour forth in this narrative, however, is that New Testament believers look back on the plight of these two and come to realize that the greater Father "did not spare his own Son but gave him up for us all" (Rom. 8:32). In the former case, divine mercy is extended to both father and son. In the latter case, the searing-hot knife of judgment slices through the innocent body of the willing Son in order that the Father may extend mercy to many sons, destining them for glory (Heb. 2:10).[11] Over and over, Scripture explodes with surprising (even shocking) narratives like this—mirroring the broader paradigmatic themes of divine grace and glory that the greater-glory theodicy seeks to highlight.

The Redemptive Paradigm of the Exodus

The second book of the Bible is perhaps the greatest paradigmatic foreshadowing of Scripture's broad U-shaped storyline. The unfolding plot of the exodus is *the* quintessence of redemption in the Old Testament.[12] As such, it became the central event in the life of Israel that has marked her identity ever since.[13] It colors every subsequent biblical narrative, pulling together the cosmic motifs of creation, sin, and bondage; of divine rulership, presence, glory, judgment, mercy, and deliverance; and of the covenant promises of paradise restored.[14]

The backstory for the exodus is found in the final patriarchal narrative of Genesis. The impertinent and mollycoddled young Joseph emerges as the unlikely hero whom God employs to bring restoration to the fledgling

---

11. Iain M. Duguid, *Living in the Gap between Promise and Reality: The Gospel according to Abraham* (Phillipsburg, NJ: P&R Publishing, 1999), 137–38.

12. Schreiner, *The King in His Beauty*, 30.

13. Paul Johnson, *A History of the Jews* (New York: Harper & Row, 1987), 23, 26.

14. See R. Michael Fox, ed., *Reverberations of the Exodus in Scripture* (Eugene, OR: Pickwick Publications, 2014); Alastair J. Roberts and Andrew Wilson, *Echoes of Exodus: Tracing Themes of Redemption through Scripture* (Wheaton, IL: Crossway, 2018); Bryan D. Estelle, *Echoes of Exodus: Tracing a Biblical Motif* (Downers Grove, IL: InterVarsity Press, 2018).

seed of Abraham. Joseph rises from the pit of slavery into which his jealous siblings have cast him to become the prime minister of Egypt. He then establishes the sons of Jacob and their families in the land of Goshen, where they grow prosperous (Gen. 47:27)—in fact, too prosperous for the new Pharaoh, who cuts off all favor to these foreigners (Ex. 1:8–10). Their lives are made "bitter with hard service" as their newly appointed taskmasters "ruthlessly made them work as slaves" (v. 14). Throughout the narrative, slavery becomes the principal conflict.

Enter Moses, the next unlikely hero of the Israelites. Miraculously preserved among the reeds of the Nile (Ex. 2:1–9), like Joseph he, too, comes into royal favor (v. 10). But he does not find favor with his fellow Israelites. They become suspicious of him after he seeks to avenge their desperate plight by killing one of their taskmasters (vv. 11–14). Moses flirts with Pharaoh's lethal anger and flees to Midian (v. 15), where God begins to prepare the roughhewn hero for his real work. After hearing the "groaning" of his people, Yahweh has begun preparations to deliver them, ironically, with the kinsman whom they have already rejected (v. 24).

The drama here is rich and complex, intertwining the personal conflicts facing Moses with those facing the Israelites.[15] This mirrors most of the conflicts we all face when multiple strands of people and problems become quickly entangled, and do not invite clear analysis or solutions for untying the knots. Adversity is always designed by God to humble us (consider Job), rendering our own understanding, wisdom, and strength inadequate. We are often perched on a precipice of desperation by divine appointment so that we find no one else to turn to except God alone. The waiting, the silence, the prolonged agony is but a foil for his eventual glory in the work of deliverance. For Moses, the waiting is forty years (Acts 7:23, 30). For Israel, it would be an excruciating four hundred years (Gen. 15:13).

After encountering a fiery theophany in a desert bush (Ex. 3:1–9), Moses is commissioned as an instrument of Yahweh's redemption from the iron furnace of a despotic nation (vv. 10–22). He returns to Egypt a changed man. Leaders often need their character crushed and refined before they can be used as agents of redemption. God's hand has forged Israel's archetypal hero. Historian Paul Johnson writes that the Bible presents

> Moses as a giant conduit through which the divine radiance and ideology poured into the hearts and minds of the people. But we must also see

---

15. Roberts and Wilson state, "Moses has an exodus journey at birth, he has another at age forty, then he leads Israel in a third at age eighty, and then he dies at one hundred and twenty, right after seeing the land to which his whole life had been pointing" (*Echoes of Exodus*, 35).

Moses as an intensely original person, becoming progressively, through experiences which were both horrific and ennobling, a fierce creative force, turning the world upside down. . . . He illustrates the fact, which great historians have always recognized, that mankind does not invariably progress by imperceptible steps but sometimes takes a giant leap, often under the dynamic propulsion of a solitary, outsize personality. That is why the contention of Wellhausen and his school that Moses was a later fiction and the Mosaic code a fabrication of the post-Exilic priests in the second half of the first millennium B.C. . . . is scepticism carried to the point of fanaticism, a vandalizing of the human record. Moses was beyond the power of the human mind to invent, and his power leaps out from the page of the Bible narrative, as it once imposed itself on a difficult and divided people, often little better than a frightened mob.[16]

Moses is a leader deftly fashioned by God. When he confronts the king of Egypt under orders from the great I AM (Ex. 3:15), he is no longer the brutish yet fearful neophyte who fled Egypt forty years earlier. His apprenticeship in the wilderness has weathered the shepherd, molding him for an intrepid encounter with the most powerful ruler in the world. God has replaced cowardice with confidence as Moses boldly declares the message of Yahweh to Pharaoh: "Let my people go" (5:1). But Pharaoh is intractable: "I do not know the LORD, and moreover, I will not let Israel go" (5:2). The man is a fool, having no idea that he will come "to know the LORD" in a manner that would strip him of all pride and pretense.

The self-inflated sovereign would come to know the glory of the true Sovereign in judgment (7:4–5), while Israel would come to know the glory of this same God—her God—in glorious deliverance (6:6–7; 14:13–14). Israel's spectacular salvation would come at the expense of Egypt's equally spectacular judgment.[17] God is emphatic: "I will harden Pharaoh's heart, and he will pursue [the sons of Israel], and I will get *glory* over Pharaoh and all his host, and the Egyptians shall know that I am the LORD" (14:4; cf. 14:17).

God's glory is magnified precisely in the juxtaposition of two utterly polarizing destinies. Egypt is poised to be the unsuspecting recipient of horrific and inexplicable (miraculous) plagues about to descend on her head, while Israel is about to experience an exodus from her dreaded slaveholders while riding on the wings of equally unprecedented supernatural power.

16. Roberts and Wilson, *Echoes of Exodus*, 27.
17. James M. Hamilton Jr., *God's Glory in Salvation through Judgment: A Biblical Theology* (Wheaton, IL: Crossway, 2010), 91, 93–94.

The crossing of the Red Sea set against the backdrop of Egypt's devastation has forever since been an indelible and paradigmatic image of deliverance and freedom for oppressed and dispirited people. Furthermore, God's repeated hardening of Pharaoh's heart affords the opportunity to prolong and increase the destruction that descends on the Egyptians.[18] In this way, Egyptians and Israelites alike will come to see what it means "to know that I am the LORD," so that God's extrinsic glory will be raised to heights hitherto unknown.

The antagonists here appear as "the mightiest nation on earth," while the lowly protagonists appear as "an intimidated, powerless community of slaves."[19] But behind the utter helplessness of this people lies an enormously powerful Redeemer, wielding in his hand his instrument of rescue—Moses the under-redeemer. Moses calls forth ten plagues that move in a crescendo of devastating intensity,[20] each mocking the Egyptians for their worship of false and impotent gods (Ex. 12:12).[21] They are a comprehensive divine assault on Egypt's fatuous conception of "creation, order, and harmony in the universe."[22]

After the first six devastating plagues, however, the stubbornness of Pharaoh's heart was not yet breached (7:13, 22; 8:15, 19, 32; 9:7, 12), whereupon God makes his purposes clear to the recalcitrant ruler:

> For this time I will send all my plagues on you yourself, and on your servants and your people, so that you may know that there is none like me in all the earth. For by now I could have put out my hand and struck you and your people with pestilence, and you would have been cut off from the earth. But for this purpose I have raised you up, to show you my power, so that my name may be proclaimed in all the earth. (Ex. 9:14–16)

God could have easily made quick work of the king and his people if he had so chosen. If that had been his design, then their demise likely would

18. Throughout the episode of the plagues, we read of Pharaoh's hardening his own heart eight times (Ex. 7:13, 22; 8:15, 19, 32; 9:7, 34–35), while God is said to be the source of hardening nine times (4:21; 7:3; 9:12; 10:1, 20, 27; 11:10; 14:4, 8). See also 7:14; 13:15; 14:17. See further G. K. Beale, "An Exegetical and Theological Consideration of the Hardening of Pharaoh's Heart in Exodus 4–14 and Romans 9," *Trinity Journal* 5.2 (1984): 129–54. For a nuanced discussion of the Hebrew syntax with regard to the hardening, see Duane A. Garrett, *A Commentary on Exodus* (Grand Rapids: Kregel Academic, 2014), 370–75 (see especially the chart on p. 371).

19. Eugene H. Merrill, *Everlasting Dominion: A Theology of the Old Testament* (Nashville: B&H Publishing Group, 2006), 260.

20. Garrett, *Commentary on Exodus*, 270.

21. John D. Currid, *Ancient Egypt and the Old Testament* (Grand Rapids: Baker, 1997), 108–13; John J. Davis, *Moses and the Gods of Egypt* (Grand Rapids: Baker, 1986), 87–160.

22. Currid, *Ancient Egypt*, 118.

have garnered a short piece on the lower left quadrant of the front page of the *Mesopotamian Times*. Instead, the Almighty prolongs their agony with four more protracted judgments in order that the terrible power of his majesty might bring all those who witness these events to their knees in fear and trembling. Every front page of the world's newspapers has plastered in big, bold, black font:

"YAHWEH DEVASTATES EGYPT!"

A holy God is not to be trifled with. R.C. Sproul captures the essence of such trenchant encounters with the holiness of God:

> The clearest sensation that human beings have when they experience the holy is an overpowering sense of creatureliness. That is, when we are aware of the presence of God, we become most aware of ourselves as creatures. When we meet the Absolute, we know immediately that we are not absolute. When we meet the Infinite, we become acutely conscious that we are finite. When we meet the Eternal, we know we are temporal. To meet God is a powerful study in contrasts.[23]

After the seventh plague of thunder, hail, fire (Ex. 9:23), and annihilation (vv. 20–21, 25), Pharaoh cries for God to relent (v. 27). But he and the Egyptians are still not sufficiently humbled. Moses responds, "I know that you do not yet fear the Lord God" (v. 30). Here is where the *reader* must be humbled. While Pharaoh acknowledges the culpability of his sin and continues to harden his heart in rebellion against God (vv. 27, 34–35), it is God's sovereign purposes that will prevail.

Only a few verses later, we read: "Then the Lord said to Moses, 'Go to Pharaoh, for I have hardened his heart and the heart of his servants, that I may perform these signs of Mine among them, and that you may tell in the hearing of your son, and of your grandson, how I made a mockery of the Egyptians and how I performed My signs among them, that you may know that I am the Lord'" (10:1–2 NASB). God is the one who has undeniably hardened Pharaoh, ensuring his sinful stubbornness, and has brought a host of natural evils as a result, and yet it is Pharaoh who is to blame for his evil intentions, while God seeks only his good intentions—namely, the magnification of his power and glory for generations to come.[24]

---

23. R.C. Sproul, *The Holiness of God* (Carol Stream, IL: Tyndale House, 1998), 43.

24. The inhabitants of Canaan were well aware of this awe-filled history (Josh. 2:9–10), even four hundred years later (1 Sam. 4:7–8; 6:6). See Eugene H. Merrill, *Kingdom of Priests: A History of Old Testament Israel*, 2nd ed. (Grand Rapids: Baker Academic, 2008), 149.

Human intentions for evil are always evil, whereas God's intentions for the same evil are always good (Gen. 50:20). This fact holds true even when we are unable to ascertain what precisely his immediate goals for evil might be. But in the case of Pharaoh, we know God's good purposes. The king of Egypt means his hardened heart for evil, but God, who superintends his hardened heart, means for it to deliver his people Israel from slavery attended with divine drama on full display. The transcendent Choreographer orchestrates every detail of the whole affair, while simultaneously holding Pharaoh blameworthy for his willful act of rebellion. "We should not deny God's power to bend and move the human heart, but neither should we imply that Pharaoh was coerced into doing something that he did not really want to do. God stiffened Pharaoh's resolve, but the will to oppress Israel and resist God was his own."[25]

After a plague of locusts (Ex. 10:12–15), Yahweh brings a fearful and eerie darkness on the land—a thick blackness that is acutely "felt" (vv. 21–22). This is not physical harm; it is psychological terror. But the final plague would sear the fear of God on the heart of every Egyptian. "At midnight the LORD struck down all the firstborn in the land of Egypt, from the firstborn of Pharaoh who sat on his throne to the firstborn of the captive who was in the dungeon, and all the firstborn of the livestock. And Pharaoh rose up in the night, he and all his servants and all the Egyptians. And there was a great cry in Egypt, for there was not a house where someone was not dead" (12:29–30).

During this time, the Israelites would be spared. God commands them to observe the first Passover (Ex. 12:1–13, 23–27, 42–49). It would commemorate this night in which Yahweh will pass over the homes of his people. Their firstborn would live. But in their place, lambs would be sacrificed whose blood is to mark their doors and thus shield them from the judgment of Yahweh. He diverts his wrath to the lambs. This mercy does not extend to their Egyptian neighbors. Their distraught cries can be heard as young and old fall limply into their quivering hands.

The hands of the Israelites quiver, too. This is the fear of the Lord—a fear by which they are compelled to circumspectly contemplate both Yahweh's unrelenting judgment and his overflowing mercy. His mercy awakens them from their slave-induced spiritual stupor, assuaging their bitterness, pain, and toil. They now have reason to take serious note of their God.

Thus, Passover is to be a crucial and perpetually practiced reminder of atonement indicating to the children of Israel that just as Noah was no more

---

25. Garrett, *Commentary on Exodus*, 374–75.

innocent than those who perished in the flood, so, too, they were no more innocent than the children of Egypt.[26] Furthermore, it is a pointer to the future Paschal Lamb (1 Cor. 5:7), who takes away the sin of the world (John 1:29). It is no mistake that God would providentially order Jesus' crucifixion to coincide with the slaughter of the paschal lambs in the temple during Passover.[27]

The solemn observance of Passover signals that while there is a deliverance from Israel's external enemies, the more important deliverance is that of being rescued from their own internal enemy—a sinful heart that also incurs the wrath of God. Pharaoh's stubborn heart incurs judgment. Israel's stubborn hearts are met with mercy. Like Noah, the Israelites are wondrously spared from the watery cataclysm that is about to cap God's outpouring of retribution on Egypt.

Romans 9 and God's Glory in the Exodus

At this point, it is important to locate the exodus in the broader panorama of redemptive history and God's purposes for it. In Romans 9, Paul unfolds some of these purposes while taking some cues from the exodus. What he says brings clarity to the greater-glory theodicy. God's sparing of the sons of Israel and their deliverance from slavery are not the main points of these seminal events. The exodus is about neither judgment nor salvation (as important as both are). God's hardening of one group while showing mercy to the other is ultimately about the magnification of his glory.

This is made clear in Romans 9. Paul indicates that God's sovereign purpose in election stands not because of the moral attractiveness of those whom he chooses to save (v. 11), but because he reserves the right to generously "call" some and not others. This is the unrestrained prerogative of God, and yet this effusive outpouring of his mercy is the principal means by which he magnifies his glory.

As John Piper observes:

> God's glory and his name consist fundamentally in his propensity to show mercy and his sovereign freedom in his distribution. Or to put it more precisely, *it is the glory of God and his essential nature mainly to dispense mercy (but also wrath, Ex 34:7) on whomever he pleases apart from any constraint originating outside his own will. This is the essence of what it means to be God. This is his name.*[28]

26. Schreiner, *The King in His Beauty*, 33–34.
27. Harold W. Hoehner, *Chronological Aspects of the Life of Christ* (Grand Rapids: Zondervan, 1977), 76–93.
28. John Piper, *The Justification of God: An Exegetical & Theological Study of Romans 9:1–23*, 2nd ed. (Grand Rapids: Baker, 1993), 88–89.

Paul asserts this divine prerogative by stating bluntly that God has "hated" (rejected) Esau and has "loved" (chosen) the scoundrel Jacob (Rom. 9:12–13). An immediate hue and cry are sounded forth in many quarters: "That's . . . not . . . fair!" (cf. v. 14). Paul anticipates this response to his robust doctrine of divine sovereignty. It is not remotely possible that "injustice" could be found in God (v. 14). Choosing Jacob over Esau is a matter neither of justice nor of injustice. It is purely an act of unprompted, unmitigated "mercy" exercised by the sovereign freedom of God (vv. 15–16). At this point, Paul recalls the events of the exodus: "For the Scripture says to Pharaoh, 'For this very purpose I have raised you up, that I might show my power in you, and that my name might be proclaimed in all the earth.' So then he has mercy on whomever he wills, and he hardens whomever he wills" (vv. 17–18).

Again, this fixed determination of human destinies ruffles more than a few feathers. Does it not imply divine coercion? How does God escape moral responsibility if he determines our future while we appear to have no choice in the matter? Paul's indignant interlocuter complains, "Why does he still find fault? For who can resist his will?" (Rom. 9:19). Paul could certainly have made an argument that defends God from the charge of being culpable for evil, but the apostle senses something deeper going on here.

Most people who chafe hard against the sovereignty of God do so because it impinges on their own sense of autonomy. What Paul says strikes deeply at our pride, our self-centeredness, our woeful lack of God-centeredness. Alluding to Jeremiah 18:1–11, he says, "But who are you, O man, to answer back to God? Will what is molded say to its molder, 'Why have you made me like this?' Has the potter no right over the clay, to make out of the same lump one vessel for honorable use and another for dishonorable use?" (Rom. 9:20–21).

This is not the smiling providence. It is the frowning providence. And both have their place in the economy of God's supreme lordship. He is God and we are not. Again, Piper observes:

> The only way Paul can even attempt to justify God's sovereign hardening is not to show that it accords with *normal* human values, nor that it follows from the ways humans *regularly* employ their reason, but rather that it follows necessarily from what it means to be God. It is precisely the incomprehensible distinction between the never-having-begun givenness of the infinite God and the utterly dependent brevity of human life that makes it so hard for us, especially with our incorrigible bent toward self-exaltation, to affirm the ways of God.[29]

29. Piper, *Justification of God*, 188.

Here we can only stand quietly with Job, laying our hands over our mouths (Job 40:4). After working himself weary to figure out why God's hand has rested so heavily on him, Job concludes, "I have uttered what I did not understand, things too wonderful for me, which I did not know" (42:3). When we cannot wrap our minds around God's ways, we must simply bow before the freedom he has to extend his inscrutable mercies. We are in no position to question his goodness, his righteousness, or his wisdom.

As Paul moves forward, he comes to the crux of the matter. Romans 9:22–23 has been a further source of controversy among those who debate the sovereignty of God in matters of election and reprobation.[30] But this misses Paul's important point, a point that has profound implications for a proper theodicy. He writes in these verses, "What if God, desiring to show his wrath and to make known his power, has endured with much patience vessels of wrath prepared for destruction, in order to make known the riches of his glory for vessels of mercy, which he has prepared beforehand for glory[?]"[31]

Schreiner concludes, "The awesomeness of the subject indicates that these verses are among the most important in all of Pauline literature."[32] They come as close to providing us with a propositional handle on a theodicy as the Bible offers us.[33] In verse 22, Paul is alluding to the wrath and power that God purposely put on display before Pharaoh and the Egyptians. It is another vivid reminder (like the Noahic flood) of how weighty and terrifying his judgment is.

The narrative of Exodus puts the primary accent on the prolonged and supernatural nature of the plagues. Plague after devastating plague continues until a crescendo of supernatural power seems to crack the earth under the trembling feet of Israel's oppressors. God's righteous power and holy wrath are demonstrated with such force that we are bowled over with a mightier vision of glory in judgment than if God had simply dispensed with these

30. For further discussion of this debate on Romans 9, see Appendix: "Sullied by Supralapsarianism?"

31. I understand the participle "desiring" (*thelon*) as causal instead of concessive. In other words, God purposely displays his "wrath" and "power" (Rom. 9:22) in order to make known "the riches of his glory" in "mercy" (v. 23). For the difficulties of translating these verses, see Douglas J. Moo, *The Epistle to the Romans*, New International Commentary on the New Testament (Grand Rapids: Eerdmans, 1996), 604–5.

32. Thomas R. Schreiner, *Romans*, Baker Exegetical Commentary on the New Testament, 2nd ed. (Grand Rapids: Baker, 2018), 507.

33. Piper points out that these two verses are "probably the closest that the Bible ever comes to offering us a justification of the mysterious ways of God with man"—in other words, a theodicy (*Justification of God*, 187).

enemies in short order. He could have employed forms of judgment that were far less spectacular.[34]

But this astonishing display of supernatural retributive power is only the setup for revealing where even greater glory for God resides. Paul's assertions indicate that the power and wrath contained in the plagues, and eventually the destruction of Pharaoh and his chariot forces in the Red Sea, are but a foil for the far more glorious deliverance of Israel.

Furthermore, the paradigm of judgment and mercy in the exodus is but illustrative of the broader purpose of divine redemption that Paul seeks to make clear throughout Romans 9.[35] The "riches of his glory" extended to "vessels of mercy" are magnified by their contrast to the awesome and unprecedented destruction of the "vessels of wrath."

Thomas Schreiner indicates the significance of Paul's argument:

> When the vessels of mercy perceive the fearsome wrath of God on the disobedient and reflect on the fact that they deserve the same, then in a deeper way they appreciate the riches of God's glory . . . and the grace lavished on them. . . . The mercy of God is set forth in clarity against the backdrop of his wrath. Thereby God displays the full range of his attributes: both his powerful wrath and the sunshine of his mercy. The mercy of God would not be impressed on the consciousness of human beings apart from the exercise of God's wrath, just as one delights more richly in the warmth, beauty, and tenderness of spring after one has experienced the cold blast of winter. . . . God's ultimate purpose is to display his glory to all people. His glory is exhibited through both wrath and mercy, but especially through mercy.[36]

The greater glory of God's mercy would be far less magnificent if God had not repeatedly hardened Pharaoh's heart, brought extensive and dramatic judgments on him and the mighty Egyptians, and simultaneously rescued an obscure tribe of people—sheepherders of no consequence—who apart from God's covenant promises wouldn't even exist in the first place. The very real threat of an assured eternity of alienation from the blessedness of the Creator (2 Thess. 1:9) is something to give all of God's objects of mercy

---

34. Schreiner argues that God's "endur[ing] with much patience vessels of wrath" in Romans 9:22 speaks not of his waiting for Pharaoh's repentance, but of his delaying of judgment in order to magnify his glory, as verse 17 indicates (*Romans*, 508).

35. Hamilton indicates that "the manifestation of God's glory in salvation through judgment is the central and controlling reality of the . . . inner logic" of the book of Romans (*God's Glory in Salvation*, 452).

36. Schreiner, *Romans*, 510–11; cf. Hamilton, *God's Glory in Salvation*, 455–56.

pause. The redeemed throughout the ages dare not take for granted the awesome hand that lifts us from the "pit of destruction, out of the miry bog" (Ps. 40:2), and sets our feet on a rock of "such a great salvation" (Heb. 2:3).

This is one of the compelling strengths of the greater-glory theodicy. It moves us to stand in awe of the incredible graciousness of a God who should decimate us the moment one errant thought should stray from our polluted minds. The pain we suffer under the hand of our own Egyptian overlords (oppressive enemies) certainly causes us to cry out for relief and justice. But we cannot afford to forget that we are never free from our own guilt no matter how much unwarranted evil is perpetrated against us. For unless we repent of our stubborn transgressions and cling to the mercy that God owes no one, we will likewise perish (Luke 13:1–5).

But herein is the substance of our rejoicing: "The blood of Jesus [God's] Son cleanses us from *all* sin" (1 John 1:7). John Newton comments, "What arithmetic can compute the whole that is included in the word *all*! One transgression would be sufficient to sink the soul into ruin. But the blood of Jesus Christ frees those who believe in him from the guilt of all."[37] The Father of abundant mercy has removed every vestige of "condemnation for those who are in Christ Jesus" (Rom. 8:1) and adopted us as his dearly beloved children (1 John 3:1). God ran breathlessly to the front line to meet his enemies and embraced us as friends (John 15:15).

The Red Sea of Redemptive Mercy

This leads us to the final scene of the exodus, which provides a polarizing image unprecedented in the history of storytelling and history itself (Ex. 14:21–22): Moses' raising his staff before the Red Sea as the waters split wide open before the quivering sons of Israel. They rush into the narrow exit path, with the Egyptian army in ferocious pursuit. Then massive walls of water come crashing down on the confused heads of horses, iron, and men. Less than a javelin's throw ahead, panicked men, women, and children escape unscathed on dusty, hot sand by the mighty hand of their God.

To be fully struck with the glory of their redemption, the Israelites simply needed to turn around and gaze on the terror in the faces of their oppressors. Then they must consider that were it not for the free mercy of God, the watery cataclysm would be crushing them as well (Deut. 15:15). Noah's ark had been made of wood and rode *on top* of the waves of wrath. Their ark was made of sand and cut a path *through* the waves of wrath.[38]

---

37. Quoted in Iain H. Murray, *Heroes* (Carlisle, PA: Banner of Truth, 2009), 115.
38. Hamilton, *God's Glory in Salvation*, 96.

This image typifies the supreme glory of redemption seen in the cross. It is through the diverting of God's judgment from sinners to a crucified Christ that salvation is achieved. The walls of water that should have been crashing down on the heads of elect "vessels of mercy" crushed Christ in their stead. He became, as it were, a "vessel of wrath" in our place. He paid the steep price necessary for us to escape the onrush of God's fierce judgment (1 Peter 1:18–19).

The cataclysmic image can be construed in multiple ways. Paul tells us in Ephesians 2 that the believer was once "dead in trespasses and sins" (v. 1). The deluge of wickedness that once engulfed the sinner in death cannot compare to "the immeasurable riches of [God's] grace in kindness toward us in Christ Jesus" (v. 7; cf. 1:14). "God, being rich in mercy" (2:4), is thereby rich in glory when he "made us alive together with Christ." He has rescued us from the watery grave of sin, death, and wrath by uniting us to the death and resurrection of Christ and all its benefits that accrue to us. Regeneration echoes the exodus. "Entering the waters, the sons of Israel die; emerging out of the waters, they are reborn."[39]

John Piper summarizes Paul's theodical focus: "God's chief end in creation and redemption is to display for the benefit of his elect the fullness of his glory, especially his mercy."[40] The brilliant diamond of divine mercy is magnified against the black backdrop of divine justice, and neither attribute would find occasion for display unless God ordered evil to overtake his creation.

Apart from creation and the subsequent fall of creation, God has no opportunity to display justice or mercy. There is certainly no need to display these attributes among members of the immanent (ontological) Trinity![41] In eternity past (from our perspective), such divine attributes lie dormant.[42] Nonetheless, every evil that exists in the created order is explained in one way or another in relation to God's justice or mercy. "A universe without evil would be a universe without divine justice or forgiveness."[43] Once God freely decided to magnify his glory in creation, he had to order the fall.

---

39. L. Michael Morales, *The Tabernacle Pre-figured: Cosmic Mountain Ideology in Genesis and Exodus*, Biblical Tools and Studies 15 (Leuven: Peeters, 2012), 203, quoted in Estelle, *Echoes of Exodus*, 106.

40. Piper, *Justification of God*, 214. Piper quotes at length (215–16) similar sentiments in Daniel Fuller, *The Unity of the Bible: Unfolding God's Plan for Humanity* (Grand Rapids: Zondervan, 1992), 445–48.

41. Oliver D. Crisp, "Francis Turretin on the Necessity of the Incarnation," in *Retrieving Doctrine: Essays in Reformed Theology* (Downers Grove, IL: InterVarsity Press, 2010), 89.

42. Crisp, "Francis Turretin on the Necessity of the Incarnation," 89.

43. Greg Welty, *Why Is There Evil in the World (and So Much of It)?* (Fearn, Ross-shire, Scotland: Christian Focus, 2018), 135.

This explains why Paul states later to the Romans: "For God has consigned all to disobedience, that he may have mercy on all" (Rom. 11:32).[44] In other words, God hardened national Israel (vv. 7, 25) in order to extend his mercy to the disobedient Gentiles. But in the end, he will return to disobedient Israel, that she might once again receive mercy (vv. 30–31). God purposely (and ironically) imprisons both groups in the misery of their own disobedience so that he might magnify the glory of his mercy to each.[45]

John MacArthur acknowledges that this sovereign action in ordering disobedience as the backdrop for the display of God's mercy is precisely where Paul's theodicy lies.[46] Elsewhere he says:

> God demonstrates His attributes for the sake of His own glory. Without sin, God's wrath would never be on display. Without sinners to redeem, God's grace would never be on display. Without evil to punish, God's justice would never be on display. And He has every right to put Himself everlastingly on display in all the glory of all His attributes.[47]

It is the work of redemption that uniquely encompasses the full display of divine attributes in a way that the singling out of God's wrath and justice in acts of judgment alone does not reveal. Even the attribute of mercy in redemption is but part of the harmonious display of *all* of God's attributes as they are seen in the atoning work of Christ, who reveals God's nature supremely.[48] Thomas Boston points out:

> The glory of one attribute is more seen in one work than in another: in some things there is more of His goodness, in other things more of His wisdom is seen, and in others more of his power. But in the work of redemption all His perfections and excellencies shine forth in their greatest glory.[49]

Thus, every disparate strand of good and evil, together with the unrestrained current of wrath and mercy, comes streaming into the cross with unparalleled force and resolution as God exercises the full gamut of his divine essence.

44. This passage is not teaching universal salvation. See Schreiner, *Romans*, 613.

45. Schreiner, *Romans*, 613.

46. John MacArthur, *Romans 9–16*, MacArthur New Testament Commentary (Chicago: Moody Publishers, 1994), 133.

47. John MacArthur, *No Other: Discovering the God of the Bible* (Sanford, FL: Reformation Trust, 2017), 63.

48. See John 14:7–11; Col. 1:15, 19; 2:9; Heb. 1:3.

49. Thomas Boston, *An Illustration of the Doctrines of the Christian Religion, with Respect to Faith and Practice*, in *The Whole Works of the Late Reverend Thomas Boston of Ettrick* (Aberdeen: George and Robert King, 1848), 1:158, quoted in Mark Jones, *God Is: A Devotional Guide to the Attributes of God* (Wheaton, IL: Crossway, 2017), 33. See also MacArthur, *No Other*, 64–65.

That blood-drenched instrument of torture followed by a deserted sepulchre is where the glory of God exceeds the unfathomable.

God's Maximal, Discriminating Love

Notice how God's love is both a maximizing and a discriminating love in this theodicy of redemption.[50] Many theologians and philosophers who wish to rescue God's omnibenevolence in the face of the problem of evil assume that if God is truly all-loving, then his love must extend to all equally. But this is clearly not the case (Rom. 9:13). Why? Well . . . because there is evil in the world.

So people suffer at the hands of those who perpetrate evil. And all people are perpetrators of like evil (3:23). Neighbor hates neighbor. Love has never been the norm in interpersonal human relations ever since Adam and Eve partook of the forbidden fruit. Presumably, an *all-loving* God would prevent the perpetration of such ubiquitous hatred and seek the unmitigated well-being of *all* his creatures, creating conditions in which only loving relationships occur. But God has not done so.

God did not prevent the Egyptians from enslaving and brutalizing even his own chosen people, the Israelites. God did not prevent Judas from betraying Christ, nor did he prevent the acts of any of the other participants who brought about Christ's death. He ordained their actions so that redemptive good would overflow to countless objects of God's mercy. But this unique display of divine love and goodness could, ironically, happen only *through* his enemies' acts of evil—their hatred, their despising of neighborly love (John 17:12; Acts 2:23; 4:27–28).

Furthermore, there is often the assumption that God should extend his love to all maximally. Again, the definition of love assumed here usually means altogether preventing evil from overcoming anyone while maximizing the person's well-being—his or her happiness and tranquility. There is nothing to suggest that a divine love minus the presence of evil is impossible. After all, it describes the conditions of Eden in the past and the restoration of paradise in the future new earth.

But can we say that the extension of this evil-less love *maximizes* God's love? If we are to speak of divine love's being maximized, is this the way it is done? And can it be done for *all* people? No, and this is why: without ordaining at least *some* significant evil, it is not possible for God to *maximize* his love to *any*. How so? The maximal display of God's love toward

50. See Paul Helm, "Discrimination: Aspects of God's Causal Activity," in *Calvinism and the Problem of Evil*, ed. David E. Alexander and Daniel M. Johnson (Eugene, OR: Pickwick Publications, 2016), 145–67.

his creatures is uniquely located in his mercy, and mercy as an act of divine love makes sense only when it comes in the face of evil.

Mercy comes in two ways. First, it comes to sinners who don't deserve it because they have been perpetrators of evil. Second, it comes to those who have been victims of evil—both natural and moral evil. The greater the evil, the greater the mercy that pardons its perpetrators and heals the wounds of its victims. In Luke 7, a nameless woman, notorious for her life of sin, came to Jesus, weeping, no doubt due to the depth of her transgressions and realizing the equal depth of Jesus' mercy. She wet Jesus' feet with her tears, wiping them with her hair, kissing them, and anointing them with perfume (vv. 37–38). This extraordinary display of love and worship could come only as a response to the extraordinary forgiveness she sought and received from Jesus (vv. 47–50). "Where sin increased, grace abounded all the more" (Rom. 5:20).

Earlier in Luke 7, Jesus showed a different kind of mercy—compassion for a woman who had lost her only son (v. 12). Death is a most grievous evil—not a moral evil, but a natural evil that unnaturally afflicts the world because of moral evil. Moved by her loss, Jesus said, "Do not weep" (v. 13), and then proceeded to raise her son from the dead (vv. 14–15). Imagine her elation! The unusual display of divine love conveyed in this act of mercy is demonstrated by the response of the crowd: "Fear seized them all, and they glorified God, saying, 'A great prophet has arisen among us!' and 'God has visited his people!'" (v. 16). Such striking mercy has no occasion to be displayed unless an equally striking set of dire circumstances precedes it.

For both these kinds of divine mercy to occur, people will have inevitably and necessarily suffered at the hands of wicked people or unfortunate calamities. This rules out any kind of maximal love that prevents at least some evil from taking place. So God's love cannot prevent evil from happening if he intends to maximize his love (via mercy) to others, whether it be perpetrators or victims. Furthermore, God can maximize his love in this way only to *some*, not *all*.

Nonetheless, some will still protest.

"Let us concede," they will say, "that maximizing God's love via mercy means permitting evil." So why doesn't God permit evil but then show mercy to all, especially to sinners in the face of their unbounded rebellion? What prevents him from showering everyone with a boundless grace in a feat of universal salvation? Couldn't the death of Christ atone for the sins of all so that all might be saved?

To respond, if God had chosen *not to maximize* his glory among his creatures, then perhaps there is reason to think that he could have chosen to save all. But wouldn't universal salvation maximize his grace? And as a result, wouldn't it maximize his glory? No—because Romans 9:22–23 indicates that God's wrath on some is precisely what magnifies the mercy he pours out on others.

Thus, the maximization of divine glory—and this is what the greater-glory theodicy argues—is connected to two important realities. First, maximal love to God's creatures is uniquely displayed in his mercy, which requires that evil be experienced by others. Second, this mercy is further maximized when contrasted with those who get what they deserve—divine wrath. And this contrast between wrath and mercy highlights and maximizes God's glory in ways that could not happen otherwise.

Part of this maximal love is experienced when sinners who have been pardoned by God's mercy contemplate the torments of the damned. When the redeemed solemnly realize that reprobates occupy the fiery pit where the lot of the redeemed would have resided if God had not plucked them from the fires of his judgment, a sobering relief rests on their pounding hearts.[51] The Judge allowed his Son to absorb those fires on a lonely cross of unspeakable brutality in their stead, and this produces a far-reaching awe, a quiet joy that dismisses all disquieting fears as we tremble with a deeper gratitude than any could muster on their own. Oh, what mercy he hath wrought!

> What language shall I borrow
> To thank Thee, dearest Friend,
> For this, Thy dying sorrow,
> Thy pity without end?
> O make me Thine forever;
> And should I fainting be,
> Lord, let me never, never
> Outlive my love to Thee.[52]

The fall and our hopeless captivity to the curse and to our own helpless wretchedness place us in a desperate context whereby mercy becomes an inconceivable and glorious gift. Thus, if all receive mercy, mercy becomes

---

51. Jonathan Edwards, Miscellany no. 122, in *The "Miscellanies," a–500*, vol. 13 of *The Works of Jonathan Edwards*, ed. Thomas A. Schafer (New Haven, CT: Yale University Press, 1994), 286.
52. Bernard of Clairvaux, "O Sacred Head, Now Wounded," trans. Paul Gerhardt (1656), trans. James W. Alexander (1830).

domesticated, banal, expected, even demanded. When a vile sinner sees the fierce wrath that he most certainly should have incurred from a just and holy God and was rescued from it instead, he joyously marvels at the mercy of this one who retains the right to put us on trial, this one who is Judge, Jury, and Executioner.

God's glory in Israel's deliverance was magnified precisely because of the unmitigated judgment that the Egyptians both incurred and deserved. God is under no obligation to extend his mercy; otherwise, it would not be mercy. Nor is God unjust to carry out the full weight of his wrath on willful, recalcitrant sinners. When God carries out his justice, it highlights those rare and precious moments when he chooses to show mercy. When hell's "gloomy pits of darkness" (2 Peter 2:4 NLT) are contrasted with Christ's elect basking under the luminescent beacon of the Creator of light (Rev. 22:5), only then will the full wonder of redemption become apparent. Thus, if God's love is to be maximized, it can be none other than a discriminating love. And this discriminating, this maximal love to some and not all is what supremely magnifies (maximizes) his glory.

REDEMPTIVE GLORY IN JOHN'S GOSPEL

U-shaped (monomythic) themes abound in the New Testament, but I will focus our attention on a few episodes in the Gospel of John. A succession of incidents in John's Gospel serves to highlight the redemptive glory of God by setting forth some illuminating contrasts. The apostle opens his narrative of Christ by funneling our attention to a critical statement: "And the Word became flesh and dwelt among us, and we have seen his glory, glory as of the only Son from the Father, full of grace and truth" (John 1:14). John is enthralled with the "glory" of the incarnate Word. One of the ways that he seeks to convince his readers to "believe that Jesus is the Christ, the Son of God" (20:31), is to see how God's glory is magnified in his Son.[53]

John recounts two miraculous episodes that fit within the Gospel's crescendo leading to the final episode—the climactic glory of Christ at Calvary.[54] Each of the three episodes highlights the fearful consequences of living in a fallen world: physical suffering and death. But in each episode,

53. See also John 2:11; 5:39–47; 7:14–18; 8:54–55; 12:23–24, 27–43; 13:31–32; 14:13; 17:1–5, 10, 22–26.

54. Andreas J. Köstenberger indicates that John's Gospel reveals Christ's glory first in messianic signs/miracles (chapters 1–12) and then in the cross (chapters 13–21). See "The Glory of God in John's Gospel and Revelation," in *The Glory of God*, ed. Christopher W. Morgan and Robert A. Peterson (Wheaton, IL: Crossway, 2010), 108.

God's providential power injects itself into these natural evils born of Adam's original moral evil. Furthermore, each episode indicates an increasing level of intensity of the suffering that such evil brings and thereby highlights God's glory in increasing degrees. The crescendo leads us to the greatest glory located in the cross.

Glory in Blindness

The first narrative occurs in John 9, where we read: "As [Jesus] passed by, he saw a man blind from birth. And his disciples asked him, 'Rabbi, who sinned, this man or his parents, that he was born blind?' Jesus answered, 'It was not that this man sinned, or his parents, but that the works of God might be displayed in him'" (vv. 1–3). The disciples' assertions about the sinful cause of the man's blindness are not accurate; yet their assumptions are not entirely unfounded either. They realize that blindness has no part in the good creation God made. It is one of the natural evils that befell a world cursed by Adam's sin.

The wonder and beauty of creation ought not to be hidden from anyone's eyes, but this poor beggar has experienced the unfortunate effects of the fall. Now when Jesus proceeds to explain the man's blindness, it is obvious that it entails a divinely orchestrated purpose. There is no insolence in saying that God ordained this natural evil to overtake a man even as his infant body was emerging into the world, and before he had an opportunity to do good or evil (cf. Rom. 9:11).

Does this not bring the glory of God into disrepute? Hardly.

Jesus indicates that the man's condition was decreed in order that "the works of God might be displayed in him." The "works of God" here refers to the miracle that Jesus is about to do in order to give the man his first view of the world. But this is merely the vehicle for God to display his glory in the face of the conflict he has written into this man's life story. Now, it would be one thing if the man had had an accident that temporarily blinded him and then he received his sight back. This would occasion rejoicing, to be sure, but the man has never had sight to begin with. He has never seen a coursing field of white lilies or the orange hues of a sunset streaking across an azure sky.

This bleaker state of the man's predicament provides the foil for God's extrinsic glory to be manifested to a greater degree. Dare we say that it was better for the man to be born blind? That there was a fortunateness to the fall? It appears that God thinks so.

> Judge not the Lord by feeble sense,
> But trust Him for His grace;

Behind a frowning providence
He hides a smiling face.[55]

The Almighty is glorified not so much in the *absence* of suffering, but in its *presence*.[56] *O felix culpa!*

This becomes clear in the aftermath when the man has to endure the preposterous indignation of the Jewish authorities for the miracle that has taken place. Ironically, they tell him: "Give glory to God. We know that this man [Jesus] is a sinner" (John 9:24). The man *has* given glory to God, precisely because the miracle testifies that Jesus *is* no sinner, but the Son of God. Then we read:

> Jesus heard that they had cast him out, and having found him he said, "Do you believe in the Son of Man?" He answered, "And who is he, sir, that I may believe in him?" Jesus said to him, "You have *seen* him, and it is he who is speaking to you." He said, "Lord, I believe," and he worshiped him. Jesus said, "For judgment I came into this world, that those who do not see may see, and those who see may become blind." (John 9:35–39)

Jesus points out that the former blind man has now "seen" him (John 9:37). He has seen the source of glory. The glory of Christ has been manifested in the reversing of blindness—both physically and then especially spiritually as the man believes and worships (v. 38). And this glory is heightened by the irony of Jesus' conferring spiritual blindness on those who, like the Pharisees, think they see (vv. 40–41).[57]

Some might suppose that this episode gives reason for Christians who suffer similar physical disabilities to expect divine healing and recovery within their lifetime. But this misinterprets the lessons to be learned. No doubt God brings about healing in the present to many whose bodies are racked with pain and debilitating injury, disease, or impairment.[58] But sometimes the prolonging of our pain, often for a lifetime, is simply intended to bring greater glory to God at the consummation of our future redemption.

Joni Eareckson Tada became paralyzed from her shoulders down in a diving accident in 1967. After working through a volatile mix of anger, depression, suicidal thoughts, and doubts about her faith, Joni began to

---

55. William Cowper, "God Moves in a Mysterious Way" (1774).
56. Köstenberger, "Glory of God," 110.
57. Hamilton, *God's Glory in Salvation*, 412.
58. See Richard Mayhue, *The Healing Promise* (Fearn, Ross-shire, Scotland: Mentor, 2009).

see God's hope in her debilitating condition.[59] Although she had recurring bouts with pain and many other difficulties, she was able to adjust to her quadriplegia and manage to accomplish great things with relative ease (if that can be said of her condition). She had long since come to terms with the fact that God might not offer her healing in this lifetime.

But after forty years of successfully cultivating spiritual contentment with her paralysis, she suddenly began to encounter new levels of excruciating pain hitherto unexperienced. It revived many of her old battles that she thought she had won.[60] Joni writes honestly yet encouragingly of her newly ramped-up struggles:

> Pain is a bruising of a blessing; but it *is* a blessing nevertheless. It's a strange, dark companion, but a companion—if only because it has passed through God's inspecting hand. It's an unwelcome guest, but still a guest. I know that it drives me to a nearer, more intimate place of fellowship with Jesus, and so I take pain as though I were taking the left hand of God. . . . These afflictions of mine—*this very season of multiplied pain*—is the background against which God has commanded me to show forth his praise. . . . God bids me that I not only seek to accept it, but to *embrace* it, knowing full well that somewhere way down deep—in a secret place I have yet to see—lies my highest good.[61]

Joni does not pretend to know all the reasons why God has purposed her suffering. There are tinges of uncertainty in her words. But she sees clearly that the pain must elicit praise for the good that he *will* accomplish, even if that good is not readily apparent. God does not prolong our pain unless it serves his glory and our good (Rom. 8:28).

Glory in Raising the Dead

In returning to John's Gospel, we encounter a scene a few pages later in chapter 11 that opens with an even greater tragedy. Lazarus, a young man in seemingly perfect health, suddenly falls ill and dies. He and his sisters are some of Jesus' closest friends and most devout followers. When Jesus hears that his beloved friend is sick (John 11:1–3), he deliberately waits to show up to Lazarus's home in Bethany (vv. 6–7) until he has already been dead for four days (v. 17).

---

59. See Joni Eareckson Tada, *Joni: An Unforgettable Story* (repr., Grand Rapids: Zondervan, 2001).

60. See Joni Eareckson Tada, *A Place of Healing: Wrestling with the Mysteries of Suffering, Pain, and God's Sovereignty* (Colorado Springs: David C. Cook, 2010).

61. Eareckson Tada, *Place of Healing*, 34–35.

Some would suppose this to be a callous, even scandalous, response given Jesus' foresight of the matter and requisite powers to heal Lazarus.[62] He could have easily prevented his death and all the grieving it was producing (v. 21). But Jesus has a good purpose that will emerge right from the core of the pain of death. He declares, "This illness does not lead to death" (v. 4). By "death" he means permanent separation from the present world. Instead, Lazarus's passing "is for the glory of God, so that the Son of God may be glorified through it" (v. 4). The apologetic for the gospel in John's narrative is always the glory of God, which Christ seeks to highlight.

When Jesus finally arrives in Bethany, the pain experienced by Lazarus's sisters Mary and Martha is palpable. Tears are staining every inch of ground across the village (John 11:33), and Jesus himself adds some of his own (v. 35). We should never suppose that Jesus is without compassion or that he is never "deeply moved" (vv. 33, 38) by our pain.[63] But once Jesus gives the unusual instruction to open the tomb where Lazarus is buried, Martha resists. Four days in the grave means bodily decay and a horrid stench—a malodor that she would never forget (v. 39). But Jesus responds: "Did I not tell you that if you believed you would see the glory of God?" (v. 40).

The healing of the blind man in John 9 was unexpected and remarkable, but death always appears irreversible. It erases all hope. So when Jesus calls Lazarus to return from the grave, it strains credibility. Who expects the coming reversal of this conflict? Who is this man, speaking as he does to a dead man? "Lazarus, come forth!" (v. 43 NASB). A dramatic shift of emotions among the dumbstruck witnesses occurs in the span of mere minutes, and in this compacted moment God's glory lights on them with unforgettable force. They go from utter despair to overwhelming joy, from shouldering the unbearable curse of death to beholding the wondrous blessing of life restored. The polarities serve as the magnifiers of God's extrinsic glory. No wonder so many come to faith in the Christ (v. 45).[64]

Glory in the Cross

These two episodes (John 9 and 11), though moving the reader to contemplate marvelous displays of divine majesty, pale once the final episode of

---

62. D. A. Carson, *Scandalous: The Cross and Resurrection of Jesus* (Wheaton, IL: Crossway, 2010), 117.

63. Rob Lister, *God Is Impassible and Impassioned: Toward a Theology of Divine Emotion* (Wheaton, IL: Crossway, 2013), 240–41, 261–62. The term "deeply moved" (*embrimaomai*) normally has the idea of outrage or severe indignation. Here, however, it has the idea of intense sorrow, a powerful groaning in Jesus' spirit (KJV).

64. Note that in both episodes (John 9 and 11), beholding divine glory precedes saving faith.

John's Gospel unfolds. They are precursors to the crucifixion of Christ, to which the grand conflict of the ages adheres itself. The Son of God will descend deep into the core of this conflict and through its resolution erect the crowning monument to his glory. John takes the whole second half of the Gospel to chronicle the Passion Week. Several times Jesus speaks of how the Father will glorify him in his death. He states, "The hour has come for the Son of Man to be glorified. Truly, truly, I say to you, unless a grain of wheat falls into the earth and dies, it remains alone; but if it dies, it bears much fruit" (John 12:23–24).[65]

Death for Jesus is like the germination of seed planted in the ground and given up for dead. There is a deep paradox here. Death becomes the source of fruitfulness. It results in life for untold legions of the spiritually dead. It is for the joy of seeing this fruit that Jesus "endured the cross, despising the shame" of it all (Heb. 12:2).

Ironically, the most shameful incident in history reaps God's greatest glory. We see here "an identity of the Glorious and the Crucified."[66] This is odd. How is glory found when the hero of the story finds himself massacred on a rough-hewn plank of wood? The crucifixion is no "accident at the end of an otherwise glorious career."[67] Rather, the cross represents the purposeful culmination of Jesus' long descent into ever-darker depths of humiliation. Yet paradoxically, the depths of his humiliation directly correspond to the heights of his glory.[68]

Jesus wades vulnerably into the heart of evil and succumbs to its inexorable consequence—death. Nonetheless, Jesus cannot remain a hostage to death. Thus, his glory is magnified in two stages. The first stage is the crucifixion. The second stage is the resurrection.

Redemption is achieved by a comprehensive display of unique powers that only the Son of God could wield. It is accomplished by the unconventional defeat of sin and death through his death, coupled with the more conventional, yet extraordinary, use of power in rising from the dead. The crucifixion of the incarnate Word has all the appearances of undermining the glory of God as nothing else possibly could. Yet the resurrection of Christ is the great reversal in the greatest plot that vin-

---

65. See also John 12:27–28; 13:31–32; 17:1.

66. Köstenberger, "Glory of God," 111.

67. Köstenberger, "Glory of God," 111.

68. This motif is prominent throughout the Gospel. See John 1:14; 2:11; 8:54; 12:23, 32; 17:22, 24. See also 1 Cor. 2:8; Heb. 1:3; 2 Peter 1:17. For an elaboration on this theme in John, see Jeremy R. Treat, *The Crucified King: Atonement and Kingdom in Biblical and Systematic Theology* (Grand Rapids: Zondervan, 2014), 160–62.

dicates the greatest climax (the cross) in the greatest story that history has ever told.[69]

If Lazarus's death and resuscitation to life strains the ability to measure the emotional polarities of Mary and Martha's before-and-after—miserable grief followed by rapturous joy—certainly when the eternally self-existent Son of God succumbs to a brutal death and then emerges from a stone-cold grave three days later, the meter calculating his followers' elation must burst to pieces.

Consider the tender exchange between the grieving Mary Magdalene and her resurrected Lord. She surveys the empty tomb, looking for him in vain (John 20:11–13). Tears flow through the narrative once again (vv. 11, 13, 15), clouding Mary's vision. His death is already unbearable. Now his disappearance from the grave is as unsettling as it is inexplicable. Cracks have formed in her previously solid confidences. Confusion and dismay now fill the voids, and the cracks do not hold. All messianic hopes are shattered.

But then her ears are arrested. She hears that voice, that peculiar calming, reassuring tone:

"Mary."

"She turned and said to him in Aramaic, 'Rabboni!'" (John 20:16). Suddenly, all is made well—somehow, her Lord is very much alive. She should have known better. But like all the other disciples, she is but a babe in understanding. She needs the Teacher. She clings to him for dear life. She could have clung to him for an eternity (v. 17). And one day she will. This is why no meter can measure the glory brought to the Father through the crucified and resurrected Son. Nothing can contain the torrent of joy that his restorative power brings to the sin-weary wretches of the world.

Isaac Watts captures the wonder of the bleeding Savior:

> Alas! and did my Savior bleed,
> And did my Sov'reign die?
> Would He devote that sacred head
> For sinners such as I?
>
> Was it for sins that I have done
> He suffered on the tree?
> Amazing pity! Grace unknown!
> And love beyond degree![70]

69. See G. K. Beale, *Redemptive Reversals and the Ironic Overturning of Human Wisdom* (Wheaton, IL: Crossway, 2019). See esp. pp. 79–114.

70. "Alas! and Did My Savior Bleed" (1707).

KEY TERMS

creation
fall
monomyth
redemption

STUDY QUESTIONS

1. Why is the story of the exodus such a pivotal and significant event in the history of redemption?
2. In what ways was God's glory magnified in the exodus?
3. Can you think of other stories in the Bible that fit the monomythic U-shaped pattern?
4. How does Romans 9:14–23 contribute to a biblical theodicy, especially verses 22–23?
5. How is God's love both a maximizing and a discriminating love, according to the greater-glory theodicy?
6. How do each of the three stories in John's Gospel highlighted by the author increasingly build on the glory that God seeks to display?
7. How have instances of adversity or tragedy in your own life helped you to see the glory of God?

FOR FURTHER READING

G. K. Beale, *Redemptive Reversals and the Ironic Overturning of Human Wisdom* (Wheaton, IL: Crossway, 2019).

James M. Hamilton Jr., *God's Glory in Salvation through Judgment: A Biblical Theology* (Wheaton, IL: Crossway, 2010).

Alastair J. Roberts and Andrew Wilson, *Echoes of Exodus: Tracing Themes of Redemption through Scripture* (Wheaton, IL: Crossway, 2018).

Advanced

G. K. Beale, "An Exegetical and Theological Consideration of the Hardening of Pharaoh's Heart in Exodus 4–14 and Romans 9," *Trinity Journal* 5.2 (1984): 129–54.

Bryan D. Estelle, *Echoes of Exodus: Tracing a Biblical Motif* (Downers Grove, IL: InterVarsity Press, 2018).

John Piper, *The Justification of God: An Exegetical & Theological Study of Romans 9:1–23*, 2nd ed. (Grand Rapids: Baker, 1993).

14

THE PEERLESS REDEEMER

This anxious world must have its grand protagonists, those marvels of both history and our literary imagination, whose feats of redemptive power overcome impossible obstacles and intractable forces of darkness and emerge out of the black crisis as beloved victors—heroes worthy of honor and emulation. We don't name our sons Judas or our daughters Jezebel. We parade names such as David and Daniel, shepherd boys who slay giants and innocent captives who defy the jaws of lions. We long for heroines such as Ruth and Esther, fearless damsels who overcome death, famine, and destruction. The most admirable heroes and heroines are forged in furnaces of weakness in order to be made strong. Frodo Baggins was an unlikely hero among his companions in *The Fellowship of the Ring*. He began his mission to destroy the One Ring in the fires of Mount Doom with fear and trepidation and ended it by summoning nether regions of courage that a lowly hobbit was not expected to possess.

But there is one hero, one grand protagonist, one cosmic Redeemer who stands peerless among the pretenders in the whole of our collective pantheon of redeemers. What makes Jesus Christ the supremely admirable hero of history defies all expectations. He did not enter the conflict of history as one who was weak and needed to be made strong. He was already the paragon of all strength. Rather, his rise to the task of facing the most critical crisis of history is fraught with strange irony. It really wasn't a rise at all, but a descent from unbridled strength into inexplicable ordinary weakness.

This is the mystery of the incarnation in which the infinite and transcendent qualities of the divine Being assume the finite realities of humanity. This meeting of such disparate natures is beautifully captured by F. W. Pitts:

The Maker of the universe
As Man, for man was made a curse.
The claims of law which He had made
Unto the uttermost He paid.

His holy fingers made the bough
Which grew the thorns that crowned His brow.
The nails that pierced His hands were mined
In secret places He designed.

He made the forest whence there sprung
The tree on which His body hung.
He died upon a cross of wood,
Yet made the hill on which it stood.

The sky that darkened o'er His head
By Him above the earth was spread.
The sun that hid from Him its face
By His decree was poised in space.

The spear which spilled His precious blood
Was tempered in the fires of God.
The grave in which His form was laid
Was hewn in rocks His hands had made.

The throne on which He now appears
Was His from everlasting years.
But a new glory crowns His brow
And every knee to Him shall bow.[1]

The poet beautifully captures the striking ambiguities and tensions of both the grand Redeemer and his unique work of redemption. When facing the conflict of the ages, the marring of all that is good by the fall, we expect our hero to courageously summon conventional modes of raw power to defeat evil. But the Son of God wouldn't have donned the humble robes of humanity if he had come to do nothing more than that. With the same simple word by which he had formed boughs and iron, vast

---

1. "This Is the True God" (a.k.a. "Maker of the Universe"), in *Songs of the Blessed Hope*, ed. J. H. Showalter (West Milton, OH: J. Henry Showalter, 1927), hymn 197. This hymn/poem was brought to light by the contemporary Christian music artist Phil Keaggy on his 1986 album *Way Back Home*.

forests and granite hills, even the sun poised in space, he could summarily decimate every realm of wicked rule and authority, dismantle every haunt of darkness, and destroy all vestiges of villainy. But in order to redeem what sin had disfigured, a different, unfamiliar mode of power had to be employed. This called for an unprecedented form of heroics achieved by an unparalleled hero.

We saw at the end of the previous chapter that there is something deeply ironic, surprising, and unconventional about the way in which the triune God addresses the problem of evil. Jesus Christ defeats evil in a comprehensive display of both conventional and unconventional power. Evil comes face to face not just with the usual and expected displays of divine retribution, but also with the unusual and unexpected display of his extraordinary mercy, and this required the incarnation of the Son of God. It required that God invest himself in weakness and vulnerability, and this is utterly confounding.

How can the Son of God be joined to the frailty that we associate with his finite creation? How does the God marked with supreme and immutable strength overpower evil with weakness? The mystery of the incarnation and crucifixion of the Son of God takes us to the nucleus of the divine solution to the problem of evil. In this paradoxical reality, all the resplendent rays of divine glory converge and shine forth at their brightest.[2]

THE BATTLE TO CLARIFY THE INCARNATION

The early church needed to bring clarity to the doctrine of God (theology proper), and this thrust Christians into debates about the Trinity. In truth, Trinitarian debates were directly linked to the church's coming to terms with who the second person of the Trinity is, as well as with the nature of the incarnation. The utter uniqueness of Christ is at the heart of the Christian faith and of its story of redemption. If we mistake his true identity, we mistake the gospel, and the whole faith runs aground on the deadly rocks of confusion and error. A clear path to defining the incarnation needed to be cut through the Christological mire that was developing, one that would irradiate the glorious truth concerning the Son of God.

Eventually, this resulted in the finely tuned definition of Christ's identity formulated at the Council of Chalcedon in A.D. 451. Years of seemingly insurmountable battles and earnest wrestling with the scriptural data finally yielded a confession of orthodox truth that the church could faithfully rest on:

2. Paul Helm, *The Providence of God* (Downers Grove, IL: InterVarsity Press, 1994), 224–27.

We all with one voice teach the confession of one and the same Son, our Lord Jesus Christ: the same perfect in divinity and perfect in humanity, the same truly God and truly man, of a rational soul and a body; consubstantial [of one substance] with the Father as regards his divinity, and the same consubstantial with us as regards his humanity; like us in all respects except for sin; begotten before the ages from the Father as regards his divinity, and in the last days the same for us and for our salvation from Mary . . . one and the same Christ, Son, Lord, only-begotten, acknowledged in two natures which undergo no confusion, no change, no division, no separation; at no point was the difference between the natures taken away through the union, but rather the property of both natures is preserved and comes together into a single person and a single subsistent being; he is not parted or divided into two persons, but is one and the same only-begotten Son, God, Word, Lord Jesus Christ.[3]

These words form the standard by which all subsequent historical reflections about the identity of Christ have been measured.

Chalcedonian Christology has warded off subtle and not-so-subtle heresies, such as Docetism, Adoptionism, Arianism, Apollinarianism, Nestorianism, and Eutychianism (Monophysitism). Each of these heresies denies something essential about the identity of Christ and the proper relationship between his divine and human natures.[4] While many claim that this battle to identify the Redeemer of the world involves unnecessary hairsplitting, the fact is, pinning down the precise nature of the supreme protagonist makes all the difference between a winsome figure parading across the stage of history and the *one* Victor standing apart from *all* other victors who has the unique and unprecedented qualities that are indispensable to defeat the crisis of a wrecked creation. Only one who is truly and perfectly God and at the same time truly and perfectly man can undo the malevolent forces wreaking havoc on our planet and the ruin of creatures who bear a shattered *imago Dei*.

THE MYSTERY OF THE INCARNATION

We have seen in chapter 13 that the magnification of God's glory in the work of redemption is enhanced through various contrasts, dichotomies, polarities, ironies, and paradoxes that are integral to the flow of the redemptive

---

3. Norman Tanner, ed., *Decrees of the Ecumenical Councils*, vol. 1, *Nicaea I to Lateran V* (Washington, DC: Georgetown University Press, 1990), 86.

4. One of the best assessments of these heresies is found in Gerald Bray, *God Has Spoken: A History of Christian Theology* (Wheaton, IL: Crossway, 2014), 211–402.

storyline. Everything about the story defies the ordinary, the expected, and the conventional, thus pointing to its divine origin. Likewise, even though Chalcedon brought us clarity concerning the identity of Christ, it has not removed all the mystery surrounding the incarnation. Cyril of Alexandria (A.D. 378–444) writes, "We see in Christ the strange and rare paradox of Lordship in servant's form and divine glory in human abasement."[5] John of Damascus (c. A.D. 675–749) speaks further of this paradox: "He who was of the Father, yet without mother, was born of woman without a father's co-operation."[6]

What confounds us is not that the eternal transcendent God condescended to his creation, but that he, in his immanence, condescended to *us*. God the Son situated his newly acquired identity squarely among the very creatures who had purposely poised themselves from the beginning as rebels against his own being. Without forfeiting anything of his infinite divine essence, the Son of God suddenly assumed within his person a finite human nature that would appear to be incongruous with his preexisting divine nature.

The messianic expectations of the Old Testament did not fully anticipate this strange turn of events.[7] God "manifested in the flesh" is the greatest of all mysteries (1 Tim. 3:16), and yet somehow it is profoundly appropriate. "It is precisely because God transcends the whole created order of time and history that his immanent actions within time and history acquire singular significance."[8]

Theologians describe the hypostatic union as the person of the Word (Son) assuming a human nature to himself. This involves the joining or assumption of a human *nature* to the eternally preexisting divine *person* of the Word (John 1:1, 14). The Son of God is the person (and thus one acting subject) in this new mode of existence, but now subsisting with two distinct natures, who is unlike any other person. There is no commingling of the natures. Each retains its own inherent characteristics such that the Creator-creature distinction is maintained.[9] Jesus is not to be "dissolved by

5. Cyril of Alexandria, *On the Unity of Christ*, trans. John McGuckin (Crestwood, NY: St. Vladimir's Seminary Press, 1995), 101.

6. John of Damascus, "The Orthodox Faith," in *Fathers of the Church: St. John of Damascus, Writings*, trans. Fredric H. Chase Jr. (Washington, DC: Catholic University of America Press, 1958), 4.14.

7. Passages strongly pointing to the divine identity of the Messiah, however, include Pss. 16; 45; 110; Isa. 7:14; 9:6–7.

8. Thomas G. Weinandy, "Human Suffering and the Impassibility of God," *Testamentum Imperium* 2 (2009): 7.

9. Stephen J. Wellum, *God the Son Incarnate: The Doctrine of Christ* (Wheaton, IL: Crossway, 2016), 437.

a reductionism" in his divinity or humanity, whereby he is either divine and shorn of his humanity or human and shorn of his divinity.[10]

But does this not create a contradiction? How can the uncreated Creator and the created be united in one person?[11] This seems like asking fire to coexist with ice. There is no formal contradiction here, but there is a deep paradox (mystery), one that is essential to our understanding of how the crisis of the fall not only is solved, but supremely magnifies the glory of the transcendent Author of history.[12]

There is no escaping the tension between God's transcendence and immanence—loftiness embracing lowliness.

The second person of the Trinity assumes a human nature without ever ceasing to be the eternal Son of God. The uncreated Creator (John 1:3) assumes a created nature without ceasing to be the Creator (v. 14). The infinite bears the finite. The Son who is independent, in need of nothing and no one (Isa. 40:13–14), now adds a dependent nature, relying in his humanity on the Spirit (John 3:34). The one who "upholds the universe by the word of his power" (Heb. 1:3) becomes subject to its divinely directed laws. The immutable God yields to the mutable conditions of his fragile, vacillating creatures. The invisible is suddenly made visible; incorporeal spirit (John 4:24) acquires a corporal body (1:14).

The omnipresent Being (Ps. 139:7–8) is now spatially located (John 16:28). The timelessly eternal One (1 Tim. 1:17) comes to live in a temporal realm. Unfettered omnipotence coexists with weakness (Mark 4:38–39). The Son who knows all mysteries and is the source of all knowledge (Col. 2:3) must now, with human mind, grow and learn (Luke 2:40, 52). The Holy One who is utterly untemptable (James 1:13) must persevere under every possible temptation (Heb. 4:15). The impassible God who cannot suffer became a passible man, "a man of sorrows and acquainted with grief" (Isa. 53:3). The Immortal One "who lives forever and ever" (Rev. 4:9) becomes mortal, dying a brutal, pitiable death.

This is the matchless theanthropic Savior of the world.

THE REASON FOR THE INCARNATION

Why all the fuss to maintain these precisely calibrated tensions? Why does the hypostatic union matter? Because the precise and unparalleled dynamics that

---

10. Wellum, *God the Son Incarnate*, 156.

11. John S. Feinberg, "The Incarnation of Jesus Christ," in *In Defense of Miracles: A Comprehensive Case for God's Action in History*, ed. R. Douglas Geivett and Gary R. Habermas (Downers Grove, IL: InterVarsity Press, 1997), 226–27.

12. Again, note Joshua Rasmussen's helpful distinction: "A paradox is something we do not see how to put together, whereas a contradiction is something we do see cannot go together" (*How Reason Can Lead to God: A Philosopher's Bridge to Faith* [Downers Grove, IL: InterVarsity Press, 2019], 15).

encompass the *identity* of Christ are critical to the *work* of Christ. Redeeming a wrecked world requires a special Redeemer—one that our creaturely imaginations would never be inclined to conceive. God must condescend to and enter our lowly habitat as one of us in order to rescue us from the plight of evil. Calvin observes, "We must understand that as long as Christ remains outside of us, and we separated from him, all that he has suffered and done for the salvation of the human race remains useless and of no value for us."[13]

This means, as Peter Berger points out, that "*the* essential Christian solution" to theodicy is "posited in Christology," the incarnation of the Son of God.[14] For without the incarnation, redemption is not possible. Even the nihilist Albert Camus, who saw the world as steeped in irredeemable hopelessness, understood that the incarnate God of Christianity might provide the only ray of light:

> In that Christ had suffered, and had suffered voluntarily, suffering was no longer unjust and all pain was necessary. In one sense, Christianity's bitter intuition and legitimate pessimism concerning human behavior is based on the assumption that over-all injustice is as satisfying to man as total justice. Only the sacrifice of an innocent god could justify the endless and universal torture of innocence. Only the most abject suffering by God could assuage man's agony. If everything, without exception, in heaven and earth is doomed to pain and suffering, then a strange form of happiness is possible.[15]

Who would orchestrate such a counterintuitive plan?

Building on Anselm's thesis in the important eleventh-century work *Why God Became Man* (*Cur Deus Homo*), the seventeenth-century Reformed theologian Francis Turretin argues that if (1) humans had not fallen into sin, and (2) God had not decided in his sovereign grace and freedom to make their redemption possible, then the incarnation of the God-man would be unnecessary.[16] Furthermore, *only* such an unprecedented divine-human Mediator (1 Tim. 2:5) as clarified by Chalcedon's Christology could offer salvation to fallen human beings.[17]

13. John Calvin, *Institutes of the Christian Religion*, ed. John T. McNeill, trans. Ford Lewis Battles (Philadelphia: Westminster, 1960), 3.1.1.

14. Peter L. Berger, *The Sacred Canopy* (New York: Anchor Books, 1969), 76.

15. Albert Camus, *The Rebel* (New York: Vintage Books, 1956), 34.

16. Anselm himself was building on a central thesis in Athanasius' fourth-century work *On the Incarnation* (*De Incarnatione*).

17. Francis Turretin, *Institutes of Elenctic Theology*, ed. John T. Dennison Jr., trans. George Musgrave Giger, 3 vols. (Phillipsburg, NJ: P&R Publishing, 1992–97): 2:299–304. In what follows

To accomplish redemption, we needed a

> man to suffer, God to overcome; man to receive punishment we deserved, God to endure and drink it to the dregs; man to acquire salvation for us by dying, God to apply it to us by overcoming; man to become ours by the assumption of flesh, God to make us like himself by the bestowal of the Spirit. This neither a mere man nor God alone could do. For neither could God alone be subject to death, nor could man alone conquer it. Man alone could die for men; God alone could vanquish death. Both natures, therefore, should be associated that in both conjoined, both the weakness of humanity might exert itself for suffering and the highest power and majesty of the divinity might exert itself for the victory.[18]

Such a unique Redeemer would need to be free from the stain of sin that affects every other human creature in order to offer himself to God as an acceptable propitiation (atoning sacrifice) for sin (Heb. 2:17; 1 Peter 1:18–19). God's response to humanity's sin must act in accordance with his immutable justice, which demands that he execute punishment against all instances of sin. God cannot deny himself. To allow sin to go unpunished would forfeit God's righteousness (Deut. 32:3–4). Ordinarily, this means punishing each individual sinner who is guilty of sin (Ezek. 18:4).

Thus, all mankind without exception falls under divine retributive condemnation (Rom. 3:9, 19). But God in his unexpected, extraordinary grace and electing freedom may choose to pardon some ill-deserving sinners (Eph. 1:4–7) by diverting their just punishment to the uniquely suited God-man, whose penal substitutionary death effectively secures the expiation (removal) of their guilt (Rom. 5:8–10; Heb. 9:27) while meeting his own righteous demands.[19] If that substitute were himself stained by sin, however, then his death would fail as an atonement. It would be nothing more than the just recompense for his own rebellion.

Thus, the reconciliation of sinners to a holy God could happen no other way except through both the humble incarnation of the Son of God and the

---

I am dependent on the treatment of Turretin's views by Oliver D. Crisp, "Francis Turretin on the Necessity of the Incarnation," in *Retrieving Doctrine: Essays in Reformed Theology* (Downers Grove, IL: InterVarsity Press, 2010), 69–91.

18. Turretin, *Institutes of Elenctic Theology*, 2:302–3.

19. On the significance of the terms *propitiation* and *expiation* in making sense of the atonement, see Leon Morris, *The Atonement: Its Meaning and Significance* (Downers Grove, IL: InterVarsity Press, 1983), 151–76; Donald Macleod, *Christ Crucified: Understanding the Atonement* (Downers Grove, IL: InterVarsity Press, 2014), 101–50; Graham A. Cole, *God the Peacemaker: How Atonement Brings Shalom* (Downers Grove, IL: InterVarsity Press, 2009), 143–48.

high cost involved in his bloody atonement (John 14:6; Acts 4:12). Incarnation and atonement are inseparably linked. "Just as there can be no incarnation without atonement so also there can be no atonement without incarnation."[20] The human blood of the incarnate second person of the Trinity had to be spilled. God, in his immaterial being, "has no circulatory system: no heart, no arteries, no veins, and no blood. For God to shed blood, He had to become man."[21]

THE KENOSIS OF CHRIST

The Gospel narratives give ample evidence that Jesus possesses two natures. Sometimes the evidence of these natures is juxtaposed in dramatic fashion. For example, Mark 4 indicates that after a long day of preaching and teaching (vv. 1, 35), Jesus succumbed to the divinely orchestrated laws that govern our weak bodies. He retired to the back of a fishing boat, suffering from utter exhaustion, and immediately fell fast asleep (v. 38). He was so tired that even a fierce storm that rocked the boat (v. 37) could not wake him. The disciples had to forcibly rouse him from his slumber. Yet at a moment's notice, he calmly spoke to the same forces of nature to which his body had been subject, and they instantly ceased from exerting their power over the wind and waves (v. 39).

Showcasing both divine and human natures in such proximity was not the norm for Jesus during his earthly ministry. The Gospels primarily picture Christ as operating as a man, and only when the occasion warrants do we see evidences of his deity, even though he is always acting as the eternal Son of God. It was in the context of messy interpersonal relationships in a fallen world that Jesus

> lived his incarnate life, experiencing pain, poverty and temptation; witnessing squalor and brutality; hearing obscenities and profanities and the hopeless cry of the oppressed. He lived not in sublime detachment or in ascetic isolation, but "with us," as "the fellowman of all men," crowded, busy, harassed, stressed and molested. No large estate gave him space, no financial capital guaranteed his daily bread, no personal staff protected him from interruptions and no power or influence protected him from injustice. He saved us from alongside us.[22]

20. Robert Letham, *The Work of Christ* (Downers Grove, IL: InterVarsity Press, 1993), 29.
21. Robert Gromacki, *The Virgin Birth: A Biblical Study of the Deity of Jesus Christ* (Grand Rapids: Kregel, 2002), 160.
22. Donald Macleod, *The Person of Christ* (Downers Grove, IL: InterVarsity Press, 1998), 180.

This points us to the doctrine of kenosis—the self-emptying of Christ spelled out in Philippians 2:5–11. Paul declares that Christ Jesus, "who, though he was in the form of God, did not count equality with God a thing to be grasped, . . . emptied himself, by taking the form of a servant, being born in the likeness of men" (vv. 6–7). Erroneous interpretations of this passage suggest that the divine Son divested himself of his divine attributes in the incarnation, or at least during his earthly ministry. This is known as *kenoticism*.[23] But the emptying here is not an abnegation of divinity, which would be impossible, but a veiling (hiding) of divine glory.[24] The description of Jesus as being "in the form [*morphe*] of God" (v. 6) refers to an outward manifestation of an inward essence.

In other words, the Son is fully God and reveals the glory of the Godhead in his preincarnate mode of existence (John 17:5; Heb. 1:3).[25] The incarnation veiled this glory in accordance with his earthly mission. So Jesus did not seek to take undue advantage of his "equality with God."[26] This qualifies what the term "emptied" (*ekenosen*) means in Philippians 2:7. Jesus did not empty himself of divinity. Rather, he assumed a new "form" (*morphe*, the same term used in verse 6): that of a "servant." In other words, Paul says that Jesus was "born in the likeness [*homoiama*] of men," taking on "full identity with the human race."[27]

Thus, the kenosis of Christ ironically occurred not by removing something (the divine essence and attributes), but by adding something (the humble realities of humanity). Jesus' divinity was not readily apparent to the ordinary observer. Isaiah 53:2 states that the Messiah "had no form or majesty that we should look at him, and no beauty that we should desire him." Macleod notes, "There was nothing in his appearance to distinguish him from anyone else. There was no halo, no glow, probably not even anything that made him particularly handsome or striking. Not a head would have turned as he walked. He looked utterly ordinary."[28]

The humility of Christ is exemplified in his refusal to take advantage of his divine prerogatives. Macleod explains:

23. For an assessment of various versions of kenoticism, including those of evangelical theologians, see Wellum, *God the Son Incarnate*, 355–419.

24. Wellum, *God the Son Incarnate*, 414; Macleod, *Person of Christ*, 218.

25. Peter T. O'Brien, *Commentary on Philippians*, New International Greek Testament Commentary (Grand Rapids: Eerdmans, 1991), 210–11.

26. The NIV translates this portion of Philippians 2:6: "[Christ] did not consider equality with God something to be used to his own advantage." The NRSV translates it: "as something to be exploited."

27. O'Brien, *Philippians*, 225.

28. Macleod, *Person of Christ*, 216.

Never once does he in his own interest or in his own defence break beyond the parameters of humanity. He had no place to lay his head; but he never built himself a house. He was thirsty; but he provided for himself no drink. He was assaulted by the powers of hell; but he did not call on his legions of angels. Even when he saw the full cost of kenosis, he asked for no rewriting of the script. He bore the sin in his own body, endured the sorrow in his human soul and redeemed the church with his human blood. The power which carried the world, stilled the tempest and raised the dead was never used to make his own conditions of service easier. Neither was the prestige he enjoyed in heaven exploited to relax the rules of engagement. Deploying no resources beyond those of his Spirit-filled humanness, he faced the foe as flesh and triumphed as man.[29]

CHRIST'S EARTHLY MINISTRY AND TRINITARIAN RELATIONS

In order to fulfill his mission as the last Adam, Christ came to undo the damage done by the first Adam. To succeed where Adam had failed, Jesus needed to live fully under the same conditions of humanity that our first representative did. This explains why the incarnation is necessary to Christ's mission. Thomas Weinandy makes a point that we should not miss: "Within the Incarnation the Son of God" never acts or wills "as God *in a man*. . . . All that Jesus did as the Son of God was done *as a man*."[30] Wellum adds, "If he cannot choose *as a man* then he cannot stand in our place as the last Adam and obey as our covenant head."[31]

This requires some explanation so as not to misconstrue what the kenosis of Christ means. It does not mean that the Son never exercised divine powers during his earthly ministry. He acted with a dual agency through both natures, doing things appropriate to the attributes of each nature. Thus, supernatural acts (e.g., miracles and healings) were done through his divine nature.

Furthermore, even as a babe in the manger, he was continuously upholding the universe through his divine nature (Col. 1:17; Heb. 1:3), operating, as it were, "outside" his human nature.[32] The transcendent reality of divine omnipotence, omniscience, omnipresence, and so forth in relation to the

29. Macleod, *Person of Christ*, 220.
30. Thomas G. Weinandy, *Does God Suffer?* (Notre Dame, IN: University of Notre Dame Press, 2000), 205.
31. Wellum, *God the Son Incarnate*, 348.
32. Wellum, *God the Son Incarnate*, 333. This is known as the *extra Calvinisticum*. See Richard A. Muller, *Dictionary of Latin and Greek Theological Terms*, 2nd ed. (Grand Rapids: Baker Academic, 2017), 116–17.

universe at large cannot suddenly cease to operate just because the eternal Word chooses to simultaneously submit himself to the limitations of finite humanity.

But in his role as our representative and Mediator, the whole earthly life and ministry of God the Son, as it was lived *in the creation* and *as a man*, was exercised in filial obedience to the Father and his redemptive plan (John 4:34) through the power of the Holy Spirit (3:34).[33] The entire work of salvation is a Trinitarian affair in which each person of the Godhead plays a necessary part and receives glory.[34] Without these Trinitarian roles, there is no salvation.[35]

For Jesus, that meant submitting his human will to the will of the Father (which is also the one triune divine will), who had sent him on this remarkable mission (5:30; 6:38).[36] As Maximus the Confessor (A.D. 580–662) has said, "As God, [the Son] approved that salvation along with the Father and the Holy Spirit; as man, he *became* for the sake of that salvation *obedient to his Father unto death.*"[37] Christ acting through his human will never departed from the divine will even when he was tempted to (Luke 22:42).

Furthermore, the Holy Spirit uniquely prepared Christ for his public ministry (Luke 3:22; 4:18–19; cf. Mark 1:10; John 1:32–33). All Jesus did was done "in company with the Holy Spirit."[38] He was given the Spirit without measure (John 3:34). He was filled and led by the Spirit (Luke 4:1), marked by "power" (v. 14).[39] His entrance into the world was conceived by the Spirit (Matt. 1:20), who was instrumental in the "forming and setting apart of Christ's human nature."[40]

---

33. Wellum, *God the Son Incarnate*, 409–11. See Andreas J. Köstenberger and Scott R. Swain, *Father, Son and Spirit: The Trinity in John's Gospel* (Downers Grove, IL: InterVarsity Press, 2008).

34. See the full discussion of this matter in Fred Sanders, *The Deep Things of God*, 2nd ed. (Wheaton, IL: Crossway, 2017), 131–53. Note especially how the Father plans and sends the Son and the Spirit on the redemptive mission, the Son accomplished the work of redemption for the believer, and the Spirit applies that work in the life of the believer. See also the classic treatment of this theme in John Murray, *Redemption Accomplished and Applied* (Grand Rapids: Eerdmans, 1955).

35. Sanders, *Deep Things of God*, 147.

36. Orthodox Christology embraces dyothelitism (two wills in Christ, one divine and one human) and rejects monothelitism (one will in Christ). See Wellum, *God the Son Incarnate*, 338–48.

37. Maximus the Confessor, *Opusculum* 6.4, quoted in Robert Letham, *The Holy Trinity: In Scripture, History, Theology, and Worship*, rev. ed. (Phillipsburg, NJ: P&R Publishing, 2019), 479.

38. Sanders, *Deep Things of God*, 138.

39. The Old Testament anticipated that the Messiah would be filled by the Spirit. See Isa. 11:2; 42:1; 61:1.

40. Sanders, *Deep Things of God*, 138.

Therefore, Jesus was endowed with all the "gifts, powers, and faculties" inherent in human nature, "not *from the Son* by communication from the divine nature, but from the *Holy Ghost* by communication to the human nature."[41] The Father "anointed" him "with the Holy Spirit and with power" (Acts 10:38; cf. Heb. 9:14). This Spirit-empowered life enabled him as a man to increase "in wisdom and in stature and in favor with God and man" (Luke 2:52; cf. Heb. 5:8). It was not the divine nature that "increased in wisdom and in stature" because the divine nature is already perfect. It was not the divine nature that benefited from the Spirit's filling because the divine nature needs nothing.[42] This explains many of Jesus' temporary, self-imposed limitations that marked his earthly humiliation.[43]

Thus, Jesus the Son acted in ways appropriate to the attributes of his *human nature* through the agency of the Spirit. But anytime the Father's purposes for the redemptive mission of the Son would be adequately served, then Jesus acted in ways appropriate to his *divine nature*. In such cases, the Spirit pulled back the veil obscuring Christ's glory to an appropriate degree so as to facilitate a limited exercise of his divine attributes at particular moments of his earthly mission even though simultaneously his cosmic, divine functions were never interrupted (nor could they be).[44]

In these unique moments of supernatural activity, Jesus' divine nature shone forth more fully, while his human nature became more obscured. This is what happened in Mark 4:35–39 when Jesus expressed his humanity while sleeping on the boat, but then suddenly and supernaturally overcame—via his divine nature—the same earthly forces that had exhausted his human nature.

Even when Jesus acted through his divine nature supernaturally during his earthly mission, the Spirit was not absent. Many of his miraculous deeds in the Gospels are said to be accomplished through the Spirit.[45] His resurrection was facilitated by the power of the Spirit (Rom. 1:4; 8:11).[46] The Spirit's involvement in Jesus' divine powers can be illustrated by comparing

---

41. Abraham Kuyper, *The Work of the Holy Spirit*, trans. Henri De Vries (Grand Rapids: Eerdmans, 1975), 94–95.

42. Kuyper, *Work of the Holy Spirit*, 95.

43. See, for example, Matt. 26:53; Mark 13:32; John 8:28.

44. Wellum, *God the Son Incarnate*, 414.

45. See, for example, Matt. 12:28; Luke 11:20; Acts 2:22; 10:38.

46. Note that the Father is said to have raised Jesus from the dead as well. See, for example, Acts 2:24, 32; 4:10; 10:40; Rom. 10:9; 1 Cor. 15:15; Eph. 1:20; 1 Thess. 1:10. In John 10:17–18, Jesus says that he lays down his life voluntarily and also has the power and authority to raise it up again, which was granted to him by the Father.

two other interesting incidents. In Mark 5:30, Jesus is immediately aware that divine power has proceeded from him to heal an infirm woman, but he has no idea that she has touched him, activating that power. This makes sense if the Son's primary mode of operation here is confined to his human nature while the Spirit conceals his divine glory at the behest of the Father. In this case, we would expect the Son's human mind to know only humanly and thus to be unaware of such things.

In John 1:47–48, however, Jesus is fully aware of the precise identity and secret thoughts of Nathanael the moment he first lays eyes on him. Thus, whenever it serves the Father's purposes, the Spirit openly and unashamedly pulls back the veil while the Son freely acts though his divine mind and powers. Of course, we come crashing back into mystery here, since Jesus acts fully in and through both divine and human natures. The beauty and mystery of Christ, like the beauty and mystery of the Trinity, speak of the incomprehensibility of this magnificent God!

THE UNIQUE WORK OF THE UNIQUE REDEEMER

The uniqueness of Christ the Redeemer qualifies him to achieve the unique work that is involved in solving the crisis of the fall and its devastating impact on humanity and the world. Christ is the second Adam. As the new representative of humanity, he needed to succeed where Adam had failed. Adam is a tragic hero. Even though God was gracious to him in the aftermath of his sad disobedience, nonetheless the consequences of his sin left his universal progeny in a cosmic quandary. Ever since the warm luster of Eden turned to a cold, dark, wintry wasteland, creation has cried out for someone capable of doing what neither Adam nor anyone else could possibly do—reverse the curse.

The Obedience and Sacrifice of Christ

God created humans to be submitted to his benevolent lordship in the bonds of holiness and covenant loyalty. Because God is supremely holy and the standard of all holiness, then we must be holy as he is (Lev. 11:44–45; Matt. 5:48; 1 Peter 1:15–16). Sadly, Adam failed as our covenant representative before our Creator and Lord; therefore, Christ came as our new representative. He needed to meet every demand of the moral law of God *as a man* in order to provide what is necessary for fallen men to be made right before their Creator, Possessor, and Judge.

Restored communion with God must be based on our conformity to his righteous character as expressed in his righteous law. Humanity's rebellion against God and the violation of his law have brought about a cosmic breach between Creator and creature (Rom. 5:10) that cannot be repaired by those who have fallen, namely, all of Adam's progeny (3:23). This divine-human (Creator-creature) breach is *the* central crisis of humanity occasioned by the fall and its curse. And it points us to the doctrine of justification that is facilitated by the active and passive obedience of the grand Mediator (1 Tim. 2:5).[47]

Christ's active obedience is the positive fulfillment of God's demand for perfect righteousness (Matt. 3:15) that he accomplished for the benefit of all who are justified by God's grace through faith in Christ (Eph. 2:8–9). He vicariously lays (imputes) his righteousness on them for their redemption, a righteousness that they could never gain by their own efforts (Gal. 2:16).

This alien righteousness enables believers to be accepted by the Father, who establishes *shalom* (peace) with them, restores the shattered *imago Dei*, and renews the sacred communion between Creator and creature (Rom. 5:1; 1 John 1:3), which is the true end of redemption. As Thomas Traherne notes: "The fellowship of the mystery that hath been hid in God since the creation is not only the contemplation of the work of His Love in the redemption, tho' that is wonderful, but the end for which we are redeemed; a communion with Him in all His Glory."[48]

Additionally, Jesus' passive obedience is the work of suffering whereby he voluntarily submits to humiliation, scorn, and violent death on the cross on behalf of the believer. His suffering and death pay the price they owed, demanded by the negative sanctions of having violated God's righteous standards.[49] The just and fierce wrath of God rightly rests on all sinners (Rom. 1:18; 2:5) because "all have sinned and fall short of the glory of God" (3:23). Therefore, God sent the unblemished Lamb of God (1 Peter 1:19), who diverts divine wrath from guilty and repentant sinners to himself and absorbs it squarely in his own person, shedding his precious blood to free them from

---

47. For recent defenses of the doctrine of justification, see Thomas Schreiner, *Faith Alone: The Doctrine of Justification* (Grand Rapids: Zondervan, 2015); Matthew Barrett, ed., *The Doctrine on Which the Church Stands or Falls: Justification in Biblical, Theological, Historical, and Pastoral Perspective* (Wheaton, IL: Crossway, 2019). For a defense of the active and passive obedience of Christ, see chapter 14 in the aforementioned volume: Brandon Crowe, "The Passive and Active Obedience of Christ: Retrieving a Biblical Distinction," 441–68; Brandon Crowe, *The Last Adam: A Theology of the Obedient Life of Jesus in the Gospels* (Grand Rapids: Baker Academic, 2017).

48. Thomas Traherne, *Centuries of Meditations*, 1.5, quoted in William Witt, "Creation and Cross in the Anglican Spirituality of Thomas Traherne," *Pro Ecclesia* 25.4 (2016): 418.

49. It is interesting to note the etymology of the English word *passive*, which is derived from Greek and Latin terms that mean "suffering."

their bondage to sin and the devil. He has paid the price of justice. He cancels (remits) the believer's debt.

This is an unexpected move. Justice is expected—demanded. Mercy is a surprise. God must maintain his justice to remain God. But mercy is a matter of his freedom, and no sinner who has been the object of his free mercy can take that surprising move for granted. And it is mercy indeed, because it came at an unimaginably high price that God himself was willing to pay on behalf of those on whom he graciously sets his affections.

The venerable "Rabbi" Duncan—with tears streaming down his cheeks—captures the sober force of what Jesus embraced: "D'ye know what Calvary was? what? what? what? . . . It was *damnation*; and he took it *lovingly*."[50] The mortal wounds sustained by Christ heal the festering wound of sin that diseased our souls and corrupted our communion with the living God (Isa. 53:5). The whole rotten repository of our sins is utterly destroyed (expiated), and God's holy justice against our wickedness and rebellion is completely satisfied (propitiated).[51] This means that penal substitutionary atonement is essential to the work of justification and redemption.[52]

So, then, all believers are justified not only by the *active* righteousness of Christ imputed to their account but also by his *passive* reception of the penalty they have incurred by their crimes against God. Justification is gloriously praised as *The Great Exchange*! The guilty sinner's unrighteousness is imputed to Christ, while the rich righteousness of Christ is imputed to the impoverished sinner (Rom. 5:12–19; 9:30–10:4; 1 Cor. 1:30).[53] Christ is reckoned as guilty for the sinner's sin even though he is innocent, while the sinner is reckoned as a faithful keeper of the law even though he is guilty (2 Cor. 5:21; Phil. 3:8–9).

As Luther famously declared, the believer is "simultaneously just (righteous) and sinner" (*simul justus et peccator*). None of this liberation from

---

50. Quoted in J. I. Packer, "What Did the Cross Achieve? The Logic of Penal Substitution," in *In My Place Condemned He Stood: Celebrating the Glory of the Atonement*, ed. J. I. Packer and Mark Dever (Wheaton, IL: Crossway, 2007), 95.

51. Again, for a defense of expiation and propitiation, see Morris, *Atonement*, 151–76; Macleod, *Christ Crucified*, 101–50, Cole, *God the Peacemaker*, 143–48.

52. See Rom. 3:24–26; 5:6–11; Gal. 3:13; 1 Peter 2:24; 3:18. For a thorough defense of penal substitutionary atonement, see Packer, "What Did the Cross Achieve?," 53–100; Steve Jeffery, Michael Ovey, and Andrew Sach, *Pierced for Our Transgressions: Rediscovering the Glory of Penal Substitution* (Wheaton, IL: Crossway, 2007).

53. For a defense of the doctrine of imputation, see Brian Vickers, *Jesus' Blood and Righteousness: Paul's Theology of Imputation* (Wheaton, IL: Crossway, 2006); J. V. Fesko, *Death in Adam, Life in Christ: The Doctrine of Imputation* (Fearn, Ross-shire, Scotland: Mentor, 2016); John Piper, *Counted Righteous in Christ: Should We Abandon the Imputation of Christ's Righteousness?* (Wheaton, IL: Crossway, 2002).

sin, guilt, shame, divine alienation, death, and damnation is possible apart from the person and work of the unparalleled God-man (Heb. 2:17). He alone is uniquely suited to achieve everything necessary for the believer's redemption and reconciliation to God.

Divine Righteousness Vindicated by Christ

When translating his famous Bible into German, Martin Luther scribbled a conspicuous note in the margin next to Romans 3:21–26. It reads: "This is the chief point, and the very central place of the Epistle, and of the whole Bible." Other commentators agree.[54] The passage succinctly and powerfully presents the gospel of justification by grace alone (v. 24) in Christ alone (vv. 22, 24) though faith alone (vv. 22, 25) to the glory of God alone (vv. 23, 26).

> But now the righteousness of God has been manifested apart from the law, although the Law and the Prophets bear witness to it—the righteousness of God through faith in Jesus Christ for all who believe. For there is no distinction: for all have sinned and fall short of the glory of God, and are justified by his grace as a gift, through the redemption that is in Christ Jesus, whom God put forward as a propitiation by his blood, to be received by faith. This was to show God's righteousness, because in his divine forbearance he had passed over former sins. It was to show his righteousness at the present time, so that he might be just and the justifier of the one who has faith in Jesus. (Rom. 3:21–26)

Not only does Paul present the *what* of the cross (Rom. 3:21–25a), but nowhere does Scripture present the *why* of the cross more explicitly than here (vv. 25b–26).[55]

We are quickly drawn to the notion that the cross is the central source and demonstration of God's mercy—and surely it is. But before the cross is about divine mercy, it is first of all the quintessential demonstration of God's

---

54. See D. A. Carson, *Scandalous: The Cross and Resurrection of Jesus* (Wheaton, IL: Crossway, 2010), 36–72. Most commentators believe it is at least the center of Paul's letter. See Douglas J. Moo, *The Epistle to the Romans*, New International Commentary on the New Testament (Grand Rapids: Eerdmans, 1996), 218; C. E. B. Cranfield, *Romans 1–8*, International Critical Commentary (repr., New York: T & T Clark, 2010), 199; Thomas R. Schreiner, *Romans*, 2nd ed., Baker Exegetical Commentary on the New Testament (Grand Rapids: Baker, 2018), 187; John Piper, *The Justification of God: An Exegetical & Theological Study of Romans 9:1–23*, 2nd ed. (Grand Rapids: Baker, 1993), 135.

55. Peter J. Gentry and Stephen J. Wellum, *Kingdom through Covenant: A Biblical-Theological Understanding of the Covenants*, 2nd ed. (Wheaton, IL: Crossway, 2018), 727.

righteousness.[56] In Romans 3:21–22, "the righteousness of God" refers to his "saving righteousness"[57]—that righteousness whereby God justifies sinners "through the redemption that is in Christ Jesus, whom God put forward as a propitiation by his blood" (vv. 24–25a). But God's "righteousness" in verses 25 and 26 refers to his "judging righteousness" (cf. 2:5; 3:5).[58]

The context here is the very character of God. The saving actions of God—that is, his saving or justifying righteousness imputed to the believing sinner—must be rooted in the broader scope of his eternal, perfect goodness and moral uprightness, out of which flows his unwavering justice. Thus, Paul's broader concern in this passage is to show not only that the propitiatory sacrifice of Christ is the sole means of justifying sinners, and thereby redeeming them, but also that it preeminently demonstrates the goodness, righteousness, and justice of God.

The arresting phrase "But now . . ." (Rom. 3:21) that introduces this passage represents a monumental shift in Paul's flow of thought in Romans, which coincides with the redemptive-historical shift he is highlighting between the old covenant and the inauguration of the new covenant. He is boldly proclaiming the unashamed power of the gospel (1:16) as the only answer to the desperate and hopeless crisis of universal sin that he has outlined in 1:18–3:20. This derelict condition of humanity is summarized in 3:23: "For all have sinned and fall short of the glory of God."

This is a unique way of describing sin, which Anselm (1033–1109) perceptively pointed out. God is all-consuming and all-glorious in the fullness of his perfections, and therefore worthy of all worship, honor, and praise, which in turn demands from our wills a total allegiance to him. Thus, "to sin is nothing other than not to give to God what is owed to him. . . . Someone who does not render to God this honor due to him is taking away from God what is his, and dishonoring God."[59] The refusal to "repent" of one's sins before God is a refusal to "give him glory" (Rev. 16:9). John Piper, building from Anselm's insight, puts it this way: "All sins are an expression of dishonor to God, stemming as they do from the evil inclination of man's heart to value anything above the glory of God."[60]

Thus, when Paul is speaking about how the cross demonstrates—and thereby vindicates—the righteousness of God (Rom. 3:25–26), he is speaking

---

56. Carson, *Scandalous*, 66–67.

57. Schreiner, *Romans*, 186.

58. Schreiner, *Romans*, 187. On how Paul uses the phrase "righteousness of God" in Romans, see Moo, *Romans*, 79–89.

59. Anselm, *Why God Became Man* [*Cur Deus Homo*], in *Anselm of Canterbury: The Major Works*, ed. Brian Davies and G. R. Evans (Oxford: Oxford University Press, 1998), 283.

60. Piper, *Justification of God*, 148.

to a whole constellation of God's fundamental moral attributes standing behind this righteousness, including his unbridled holiness (otherness), goodness, love, and, in particular, righteous display of justice. Together, these all point to his glory. God desires to manifest and uphold the infinite dignity of his glory to his creatures, and this in turn "undergirds his desire to demonstrate" the sort of "judging righteousness" spoken of in verses 25 and 26.[61]

Piper explains the implications that Paul has in mind:

> For God to condone or ignore the dishonor heaped upon him by the sins of men would be tantamount to giving credence to the value judgment men have made in esteeming God more lowly than his creation. It is not so much that he would be saying sins do not matter or justice does not matter; more basically, he would be saying that *he* does not matter. But for God thus to deny the infinite value of his glory, to act persistently as if the disgrace of his holy name were a matter of indifference to him—this is the heart of unrighteousness. Thus if God is to be righteous he must repair the dishonor done to his name by the sins of those whom he blesses. He must magnify the divine glory man thought to deny him.[62]

As Romans 3:21–26 unfolds the gospel of justification by means of Christ's bloody sacrificial death, Paul has in the back of his mind the objection that some have undoubtedly raised concerning the sins of Old Testament saints. He has indicated that no one could ever be justified by the law of Moses (v. 20). Furthermore, the sacrificial system could not make up for the deficiencies of the law.

So the question arises: how could God pardon the "former sins" (v. 25) of those who lived before the sacrifice of Christ? It would seem that the old covenant pardon of sins was based on a fiction. The sacred grounds of the tabernacle-temple were flowing with animal blood, which had zero efficacy to atone for sins (Heb. 10:1–4). It appears that God brushed the sins of Old Testament believers under the rug, offering forgiveness without genuine atonement, never adequately dealing with the punishment that their sins deserved. This would not be merely a travesty of justice; it would impugn the very character of God himself. Would not God be disregarding—dishonoring, as it were—his own honor as a good, holy, righteous, and just God?

The fact is, "God would not *be* righteous in Himself, if He failed to show Himself to be righteous: it is essential to His *being* the righteous, the loving,

---

61. Schreiner, *Romans*, 207.
62. Piper, *Justification of God*, 148.

the merciful, God, that He prove His righteousness."[63] The prophet Habak-kuk notes that Yahweh is "of purer eyes than to see evil and cannot look at wrong" (Hab. 1:13). God reigns as Judge over the earth (Pss. 96:13; 98:9). The psalmist says of him, "Righteousness and justice are the foundation of your throne" (97:2; cf. 89:14). God is bound by his nature to address the scourge of sin. And if he is to extend mercy, then all the more so.

Gentry and Wellum frame the problem like this:

> Whereas *sin* is an *internal* moral problem for humanity, *forgiveness* is an *intrinsic* moral problem of God. It is an *intrinsic* problem for God in the sense that it arises due to tensions in God's own moral nature. As holy, righteous, and just, God, in order to forgive us, cannot deny himself; he cannot arbitrarily forgive without full satisfaction of his own moral char-acter and nature, for he himself is the moral standard of the universe.[64]

How can God justify rebellious sinners and at the same time satisfy the demands of his own righteous and just character? "How can God express his holiness without consuming us and his love without condoning our sins? How can he satisfy his holy love?" The answer is that "*God himself must solve the problem.*"[65] And he has done so through the propitiatory sacrifice of his Son.

Yes, God in "his divine forbearance . . . passed over former sins" (Rom. 3:25). He forgave sins, but he did not "exact a *full* and *complete* punishment for sin" by means of a genuine atonement.[66] But the Righteous and Holy One could never dispense with his justice, putting his honor in jeopardy. He postponed atonement "to show his righteousness at the present time, so that he might be just and the justifier of the one who has faith in Jesus" (v. 26).

Paul is making two points. First, the work of "redemption that is in Christ" (v. 24) through his propitiatory sacrifice provides the only ade-quate atonement that justifies sinners—for both those who lived before and those who live after he made atonement through his blood. Second, what Christ did to justify sinners also vindicates the righteousness of the justifying God.[67] The death of Jesus Christ is the most remarkable display of God's mercy, and it is the most remarkable display of his justice—his "judging righteousness."

63. C. E. B. Cranfield, *Romans: A Shorter Commentary* (Grand Rapids: Eerdmans, 1992), 74.
64. Gentry and Wellum, *Kingdom through Covenant*, 682.
65. Gentry and Wellum, *Kingdom through Covenant*, 682.
66. Schreiner, *Romans*, 206.
67. John Murray, *The Epistle to the Romans*, New International Commentary on the New Testament (Grand Rapids: Eerdmans, 1968), 118–19.

C. E. B. Cranfield puts Paul's point in this critical passage in perspective:

> The words afford an insight into the innermost meaning of the Cross as Paul understands it. For God to have forgiven men's sin lightly—a cheap forgiveness which would have implied that moral evil does not matter very much—would have been altogether unrighteous, a violation of His truth, and profoundly unmerciful and unloving toward men, since it would have annihilated their dignity as persons morally accountable. But God does not insult His creature man by any suggestion that that, which man himself at his most human knows full well . . . is desperately serious, is of little consequence. The forgiveness accomplished through the Cross is the costly forgiveness, worthy of God, which, so far from condoning man's evil, is, since it involves nothing less than God's bearing the intolerable burden of that evil Himself in the person of His own dear Son, the disclosure of the fulness of God's hatred of man's evil at the same time as it is its real and complete forgiveness.[68]

This demonstrates just how monumental, how earth-rattling, how heaven-shaking the death of Christ truly is. Surely the Puritan divine John Owen (1616–83) accurately conveys the reality, though perhaps no words could overstate the truth:

> To see him who is the wisdom of God, and the power of God (1 Cor. 1:30), always beloved of the Father (Matt. 3:17); to see him, I say, fear, and tremble, and bow, and sweat, and pray, and die; to see him lifted up upon the cross, the earth trembling under him, as if unable to bear his weight; and the heavens darkened over him, as if shut against his cry; and himself hanging between both, as if refused by both; and all this because our sins did meet upon him—this of all things does most abundantly manifest the severity of God's vindictive justice.[69]

Jesus Christ, the Son of God, is the fullest revelation of the triune God; and as such, he has brought about the fullest manifestation of divine glory (John 1:14; 14:9; Heb. 1:1–4). That glory is centered on the bloody death of Jesus and his formidable power over death and sin through his rising on the third day. The fullness of divine mercy, justice, power, wisdom, wonder, and glory comes streaming in at light speed on these stupendous events in the person of Christ.

---

68. Cranfield, *Romans*, 75.
69. John Owen, *Communion with the Triune God*, ed. Kelly M. Kapic and Justin Taylor (Wheaton, IL: Crossway, 2007), 190.

The perfections of God are most clearly seen here, and that means that this is where his glory is bursting forth at its greatest. Reconciliation and peace with God are firmly established for redeemed sinners. As William Gurnall (1617–79) proclaims to the believer, "God will not make war between his own attributes to make peace with you."[70] And this extends not only to the redemption of sinners, but to the redemption of all creation (Rom. 8:18–23). If the God of heaven and earth is to provide any hope for a restored universe supremely enriched by his glory, then he must not fail to act in accordance with who he is. He has done so through the grand Redeemer at Calvary.

But there is more to see here.

The Temptation of Christ

When Christ set his mind toward obeying the Father's will and the mission of rescuing impoverished sinners (John 6:38–39), this was no walk in the park. First, his obedience was achieved *as a man*, not by automatic recourse to his divine nature. Second, in order to succeed as the second Adam, Jesus needed to be tested with temptation, placed in the same condition as our first representative. This is made clear by the preface to Jesus' temptation at the beginning of his ministry: "Jesus was led up by the *Spirit* into the wilderness to be tempted by the devil" (Matt. 4:1).

But if Christ were constituted as nothing more than a man, no different from Adam, then what prevented him from succumbing to the serpent's craftiness in the way that Adam did? Jesus, in his humanity, was able to be tempted (Heb. 4:15). Yet because his humanity was united to his deity, there was every assurance that he would not fail, since his divine nature, being wholly righteous and immutable (Heb. 13:8), meant that Christ in reliance on the Spirit could not be moved to temptation and therefore could not sin (James 1:13). Thus, while Jesus was tempted, he was incapable of sin. This is known as the *doctrine of impeccability.*[71]

---

70. William Gurnall, *The Christian in Complete Armour*, vol. 1 (Carlisle, PA: Banner of Truth, 1964), 512.

71. While there is no debate among orthodox theologians about the fact that Jesus did not sin, nonetheless there is debate about whether he assumed the prefall or the fallen nature of Adam and whether he could have sinned. For the contours of this debate, see Kelly M. Kapic, "The Son's Assumption of a Human Nature: A Call for Clarity," *IJST* 3.2 (2001): 154–66. Stephen Wellum argues decisively against the assumption of a fallen nature. See *God the Son Incarnate*, 232–36. He states that a corrupt nature is the direct result of the curse of original sin to which Jesus is not subject: "A corrupt nature is the result of sin against God that places us in a metaphysical and judicial state of sinfulness under God's curse and judgment" (234).

S. Lewis Johnson provides a memorable illustration of what transpires in the temptations of Christ that assures us of his impeccability.[72] Jesus, acting through his human nature, can be likened to a piece of wire. By itself, the wire can be bent (i.e., tempted) this way and that. We can imagine that if it were bent long and vigorously enough, it would break—that is, it would give in to temptation and sin as Adam did. God constituted humanity in the garden to be both temptable and peccable (able to sin).[73] Jesus, however, acting through his divine nature, can be likened to a steel beam. Such a beam cannot be tempted (i.e., bent) by any tempter, and therefore it cannot break. It is untemptable and impeccable (unable to sin).

Thus, given that Jesus was temptable and potentially breakable through his human nature, yet being inseparably wrapped around (conjoined to) his untemptable and unbreakable divine nature, he could not sin. The actions of Jesus are the actions of his *person*, not of his *human nature* isolated from his person.[74] Since the person of the Son eternally subsists along with the Father and the Spirit in the divine nature, if the incarnate Son, now subsisting in two natures, were to sin, then the triune God would be implicated in the action of sinning. The hypostatic union is crucial here. In order to serve as our suitable *representative*, Christ needed to be tested and tempted as Adam was. But in order to be a suitable *Redeemer* who rescues us from Adam's curse, he needed to pass all testing with flying colors.

This truth, however, should not minimize the gravity of Jesus' temptations. While living his life in the flesh through his human nature, Christ did not take undue advantage of the powers of his divine nature that he had at his disposal (Phil. 2:6). This is what Paul means when he says that Christ was sent by God in the "likeness of sinful flesh" (Rom. 8:3). The term "likeness" means not that Jesus' assumption of "sinful flesh" is to be interpreted as though he inherited our sin nature, but that he assumed all the effects that fallen creatures have with regard to their vulnerability to Satan's devices of temptation.[75] "The human experiences of the Son were

72. Found at: http://sljinstitute.net/the-life-of-christ/the-temptation-of-christ/. Johnson borrows this illustration from W. G. T. Shedd's *Dogmatic Theology*, ed. Alan W. Gomes, 3rd ed. (Phillipsburg, NJ: P&R Publishing, 2003).

73. In the eternal state, glorified saints will be constituted such that they are unable to be tempted or to sin. According to Augustine's taxonomy, prefall humans are "able to sin" (*posse peccare*) as well as "able not to sin" (*posse non peccare*). Unregenerate postfall humans are "not able not to sin" (*non posse non peccare*). Present regenerate postfall humans (saints) are still "able to sin" (*posse peccare*), but also "able not to sin" (*posse non peccare*). But glorified regenerate humans (saints) will be in a positive state whereby they are "not able to sin" (*non posse peccare*).

74. Wellum, *God the Son Incarnate*, 460.

75. Wellum, *God the Son Incarnate*, 233. This point should be qualified. Because Jesus did

neither anaesthetized by his divinity nor desensitized by some generic or pedigreed humanity which differed from our own."[76]

The force of his temptations was no less than that which we experience. In fact, it was greater. Wellum writes, "Jesus's sinless nature ensured that his temptations far surpassed anything we will encounter in our sinful natures."[77] Macleod argues that Jesus had an unparalleled protracted battle with temptation that we do not because we easily give in to the slightest provocations of the tempter. By contrast, the devil tirelessly worked Jesus over with every last bit of energy he could muster, trying to press the Son of God to fall away from obedience to the Father done on our behalf as the last Adam and our faithful Mediator. The result is a battle much greater than ours could ever be.[78]

If Jesus had lived with his divine nature unobscured by his kenosis—that is, living in the full humiliation of his humanity—there would have been no battle at all. Why? Because trying to throw temptation at the divine nature of Christ is like trying to stand on the edge of the earth to fire a peashooter at the sun. Even if by some miracle the shots had the momentum to come near their target, they would disintegrate long before reaching it. Given this reality, some suggest that Jesus' temptations lose their force, since he ultimately had his divine nature to rely on (via the Holy Spirit). But this objection fails.

First, it fails because Jesus' temptations were directed not at his divine nature but fully at his human nature. Furthermore, his temptations strained all conceivable limits in terms of their force and duration to bring Jesus to the breaking point. He didn't break because he relied till the end on the Spirit and in obedience to the Father to resist every effort to bring him down.

Yes, Jesus' divine nature ultimately prevented him from succumbing, but this is beside the point. Jesus needed to learn obedience through his human nature to serve as our adequate representative (Heb. 5:8), so he never took advantage of the divine nature to resist because acting through the divine nature wouldn't have required him to resist temptation at all. This is why we must maintain that it was only Jesus as he acted voluntarily through his human nature who

---

not possess a sinful nature, he did not possess the disordered desires inherent in a sinful nature. Therefore, the source of all of Jesus' temptations was strictly external and not from any internal impulses arising from a corrupt nature, as is the case for fallen human beings (James 1:14–15). Denny Burk writes, "Temptation had no landing pad in Jesus' heart nor did it have a launching pad from Jesus' heart" ("Is Homosexual Orientation Sinful?," *JETS* 58.1 [2015]: 105). See also Denny Burk and Heath Lambert, *Transforming Homosexuality: What the Bible Says about Sexual Orientation and Change* (Phillipsburg, NJ: P&R Publishing, 2015), 52–53.

76. Weinandy, *Does God Suffer?*, 212.

77. Wellum, *God the Son Incarnate*, 234.

78. Macleod, *Person of Christ*, 227–28.

was subject to temptation and all the powers of hell that stood behind it. This was necessary for the fulfillment of all righteousness (Matt. 3:15).

OUR SYMPATHETIC SAVIOR

Charles Taylor argues that the modern world has come to despise the idea of an incarnate and crucified God. To do so has perilous consequences for a world reeling under the weight of sin and suffering. The brutality of the cross must be at the center of any hopeful response to this planet's futile condition. Jesus did not come as a kindhearted sage who was sadly arrested and unjustly murdered. Taylor writes, "The Crucifixion" of Christ "cannot be sidelined as merely a regrettable by-product of a valuable career of teaching."[79]

Any theodicy of substance must contend that the fall was no accident. It has a profound reason for occurring—to glorify a peerless Redeemer who conquers its dark designs. Nothing satisfies the human soul more than to walk through the black valley of deadly terrors and to come out the backside into resplendent light and hope. But this light of hope would never envelop the soul so gloriously without the seemingly impenetrable blackness of creation's curse.

Furthermore, this hope is found only in a matchless hero who deftly enters that black valley as well, enduring the full weight of its curse, sympathizing with us cursed ones, and then summarily obliterating it. Taylor says, "The ultimate meaning of the Fall was the Incarnation that was God's response to it (hence its paradoxical description as a '*felix culpa*')."[80]

The uniqueness of Christ's person and work is what gives hope to this sorely tempted and suffering world. Only the theanthropic Savior is able to sympathize with our weaknesses and temptations when the evil one would seek to undo us (Heb. 2:14–18). Christ overcame the forces of darkness so that we do not have to fear their sinister threats.

Kelly Kapic encourages the believer with these truths:

> Even as our hearts can be prone to question, filled with dread and doubt, let us take confidence that our God personally understands us, not hypothetically but concretely in Christ. Jesus wept tears, for in and through his incarnate life he had fully entered the drama of fallen human experience. His ache and struggle give new meaning to our tears and suffering. God cares about our sin and distress so much that he enters into it himself.[81]

79. Charles Taylor, *A Secular Age* (Cambridge, MA: Belknap Press, 2007), 651.
80. Taylor, *Secular Age*, 654.
81. Kelly M. Kapic, *Embodied Hope: A Theological Meditation on Pain and Suffering* (Downers Grove, IL: InterVarsity Press, 2017), 91–92.

This is astounding. God is not an austere and uncaring deity standing aloof in a distant throne room, disconnected from the rank and file of his kingdom. He knows, through Christ, what it means to be mistreated, misunderstood, maligned. He understands our weaknesses, our fears, our struggles. Our battles with temptation and with the tempter were his battles as well. Kapic continues:

> Jesus identifies with us, not only in our beauty, not only in our grandeur, but especially in our vulnerability and temptation. At our worst, he knows us best. He knows what it is like to face questions, doubt, and loneliness when he was physically weak, exhausted, and exposed. So often when we find ourselves in vulnerable situations we easily give ourselves over to sinful desires, whether in the form of cultivating bitterness and envy or through fits of harmful self-indulgence. Jesus was tempted as we are—fully, consistently, truly—and those temptations took place in the flesh, in real time, under real pressures. Jesus, however, remained faithful during those temptations even amid physical weakness and the jeers meant to cause him to doubt the Father's goodness and love.[82]

Jesus conquers temptation where we inevitably fail. He faced suffering with perfect resolve. Thus, as Hebrews 2 tells us, "he is able to help those who are being tempted" (v. 18). Furthermore, we do not need to be afraid. Because of his human suffering and death, he destroyed "the one who has the power of death, that is, the devil" (v. 14). Consequently, he delivers "all those who through fear of death were subject to lifelong slavery" (v. 15). Fear falls to the ground. The devil takes a dive. Death is a foe defanged and dismembered. We cling to Christ, and he never releases his grip on us. He is our strong Deliverer, an all-encompassing Savior who conquers our pain by his own pain. The transcendent Lord of the universe is our closest friend (Prov. 18:24; John 15:15). This makes him supremely captivating to our guilty and wounded souls and worthy of our humble, yet unflinching confidence.

Yet questions remain. The otherworldly wonder of Christ moves us to ponder precisely how the eternal, immortal, unchanging, transcendent God enters our suffering and pain, and how deeply he penetrates its dark portals. If God takes on weakness, humiliation, suffering, temptation, and even death, does this not contradict the fundamental essence of what it means to be God? We turn to those questions next.

KEY TERMS

active obedience (of Christ)   atonement

expiation   hypostatic union

---

82. Kapic, *Embodied Hope*, 92.

immanence (of God)
kenosis (of Christ)
penal substitution
transcendence (of God)

incarnation
passive obedience (of Christ)
propitiation

STUDY QUESTIONS

1. What seminal creedal statement helped the early church clarify its understanding of the person of Christ? What aspects of the person of Christ was the statement seeking to clarify?
2. What are some of the tensions that exist between Christ's divine and human natures?
3. Why did the Son of God become a man? In other words, why did the incarnation take place? Give as many reasons as you can, including the most important reason.
4. What does the doctrine of kenosis teach? How is this distinguished from what it does not teach?
5. What is the active obedience of Christ, and how is it distinguished from his passive obedience?
6. How does Romans 3:21–26 show that Christ vindicates the righteousness of God?
7. What illustration did S. Lewis Johnson draw on to explain the impeccability of Christ (i.e., his inability to sin)?
8. How does Christ offer unique sympathy for lowly and sinful human beings? Can you explain what this has meant for you during difficult times in your life?

FOR FURTHER READING

Donald Macleod, *Christ Crucified: Understanding the Atonement* (Downers Grove, IL: InterVarsity Press, 2014).
———, *The Person of Christ* (Downers Grove, IL: InterVarsity Press, 1998).
Fred Sanders, *The Deep Things of God*, 2nd ed. (Wheaton, IL: Crossway, 2017).

Advanced

Steve Jeffery, Michael Ovey, and Andrew Sach, *Pierced for Our Transgressions: Rediscovering the Glory of Penal Substitution* (Wheaton, IL: Crossway, 2007).
Stephen J. Wellum, *God the Son Incarnate: The Doctrine of Christ* (Wheaton, IL: Crossway, 2016).

15

THE SUFFERING REDEEMER

The model for the quintessential hero is the tough, fearless, gritty paragon of virtue who either has abundant strength, talent, and wisdom or has sufficient courage to somehow summon enough of these qualities to face whatever conflict threatens disaster. In Tolkien's *The Lord of the Rings* trilogy, Aragorn fits the former category, while Frodo Baggins fits the latter. What makes Tolkien's epic unusual, however, is that its heroes never actually defeat the evil contained in the One Ring *directly*. While Frodo and his faithful companion Samwise Gamgee summon the courage and strength to bring the malicious Ring to the fiery Cracks of Mount Doom where it can be properly destroyed, in the end they fail.

Like everyone else who has tried for thousands of years before, they are overcome by the powers of temptation emanating from the Ring. Frodo lingers dangerously before the fiery pit under the Ring's sinister spell. This leaves him unprepared to fend off the one last violent attack of Gollum, who has himself long been transfixed by the evil lure of the Ring. In the ensuing struggle, Gollum accidentally falls into the lava, where he and the Ring are destroyed. Ironically, evil is destroyed by itself, not by the good of the protagonists.[1]

Tolkien's astute theology of sin is profoundly expressed in this turn of events. No mortal creature (whether human or hobbit) can defeat evil by any possible strength, courage, or wisdom he might muster. Evil is too powerful in Tolkien's world and in ours. Therefore, a hero like none other is necessary if evil is to be defeated.

---

1. This insight has been pointed out by Steve Hays. See http://triablogue.blogspot.com/2019/08 /when-evil-loses-by-winning.html.

Jesus stands alone as such a hero. But Jesus' defeat of evil is far more unusual than any storyline that we could imagine on our own. Most heroes use conventional brute force to overcome evil, and certainly Jesus will use such retributive force in the future to defeat an entire world arrayed against the God of the universe. But in order to *redeem* the elect in the present, otherwise impossibly tainted by evil, and to *fully restore* the world to Edenic conditions in the future, Jesus could not employ merely conventional methods of heroics. He had to succumb to death to gain victory over a fallen world.

This is something that his enemies could not anticipate. The early church father Athanasius (A.D. 296–373) explains: "A marvelous and mighty paradox has . . . occurred, for the death which they thought to inflict on Him as dishonor and disgrace has become the glorious monument to death's defeat."[2] All of Jesus' enemies, including Satan, thought death would defeat Jesus. They failed to see the irony of their actions. By killing the Son of God, they helped ensure that his death would result in their defeat, not his. His pain, his anguish, his torture, his forsakenness, his bloody murder were in fact his glorious victory.

This leads us to consider one of the most important issues that any theodicy faces. One cannot speak to the problem of evil without speaking to the matter of divine suffering. This is especially true with the *felix culpa* theodicy advocated here. In order to penetrate what transpires at the heart of the unique work of redemption achieved by the incarnate God, we must take a deeper look into the inner life of suffering that he had to endure. The Redeemer revealed in the pages of Scripture is shaped by the picture of the Suffering Servant so powerfully brought to light in Isaiah 52:13–53:12. That enigmatic portrait of the coming Messiah as one who underwent incomprehensible terrors on behalf of the redeemed is essential to the greater-glory theodicy.

DID GOD DIE?

There is nothing unusual about heroic figures' dying in the process of defeating evil. We regularly venerate those such as Scotland's William Wallace (1270–1305), who was hanged, drawn, and quartered by the king of England (Edward I) in his valiant efforts to free his native countrymen from English rule. But in most such cases, death and martyrdom are simply an incidental risk that one takes in the course of seeking to overcome wicked forces. It is always a possibility that these heroes will succeed while facing such risks and emerge on the other side of victory unscathed.

2. Athanasius, *On the Incarnation* (Crestwood, NY: St. Vladimir's Seminary Press, 2000), § 24.

But in the case of Jesus, his brutal death on the cross wasn't an incidental risk. It was wholly necessary to achieve victory over evil for the sake of redeeming the world. The Son of God *had* to embrace the cup of suffering, ironically, filled to the brim with his Father's divine wrath. He had to drink it to the dregs. Redemption for those in the grip of sin has no other course. Jesus faced evil not with divine power but with human weakness—deliberate, humiliating weakness, abject suffering, and a scandalous, bloody undoing of his life. The King establishes his kingdom by way of a brutal cross.[3]

The crucifixion of Christ has unfortunately been domesticated through centuries of its being the center of the Christian faith. Its shame has been shorn. We wear crosses—implements of torture—as cute little decorations around our necks and on our ears.[4] This was unheard of early on. The notion of a crucified Savior was so scandalous in the imperial Roman milieu of the early church that Christians did not even start to depict it in their art until the beginning of the fifth century.[5]

And yet, as we have already seen, this unusual course of Christ's human heroics was also necessarily tethered to the perfections of his divine identity. Jesus did not cease being God in his incarnation or his work of redemption on the cross. His divine nature is inextricably joined to a human nature in one person. The ineffable deity condescends to life on the earthly plane, to know and experience the lowly conditions of humanity, including our suffering. To save us from suffering, he had to suffer. To rescue us from death, the second person of the Trinity had to die.

And so we are led to a profound and shocking affirmation that we must share with the early church fathers:

> "God has been murdered" (Melito of Sardis, d. A.D. 180).
> "The Lord of majesty is said to have been crucified" (Ambrose, c. A.D. 340–97).
> "The God of glory was crucified" (John of Damascus, c. A.D. 675–749).[6]

How can this be? Does God suffer? Surely the divine Being cannot die!

---

3. Jeremy R. Treat, *The Crucified King: Atonement and Kingdom in Biblical and Systematic Theology* (Grand Rapids: Zondervan, 2014).

4. D. A. Carson likens the decorative display of a cross as jewelry to that of displaying "an image of the mushroom cloud of the atomic bomb dropped over Hiroshima." *The Cross and Christian Ministry* (Grand Rapids: Baker, 2004), 12.

5. Tom Holland, *Dominion: How the Christian Revolution Remade the World* (New York: Basic Books, 2019), 7.

6. Quotes found in Paul Gondreau, "St. Thomas Aquinas, the Communication of Idioms, and the Suffering of Christ in the Garden of Gethsemane," in *Divine Impassibility and the Mystery of Human Suffering*, ed. James F. Keating and Thomas Joseph White (Grand Rapids: Eerdmans, 2009), 217.

DIVINE IMPASSIBILITY

The early church fathers were not trying to be unnecessarily provocative with these kinds of statements. No one held that the immortal God could suffer, let alone die. The orthodox position of the early church uniformly held to the impassibility of God—the belief that God as God does not experience suffering. But if God does not suffer, does he not experience emotion either? If not, how can he even sympathize with our suffering? Contemporary discussions on this matter have generated a great deal of confusion and controversy, with many Christians' rejecting impassibility for a passible God.[7]

It is now widely believed that any theodicy that does not espouse a suffering God is cold, dark, and monstrous.[8] Many agree with the process theologian A. N. Whitehead that God in his essence as God is a "fellow-sufferer who understands."[9] And as Dietrich Bonhoeffer states, "Only the suffering God can help."[10] Jürgen Moltmann has made the boldest claims: "Were God incapable of suffering in any respect, and therefore in an absolute sense, then he would also be incapable of love."[11] Many already think the God of Calvinism is cold and indifferent to the plight of humanity. If we add impassibility to our picture of God, is that going too far?

7. In addition to the aforementioned volume, the best treatments of the doctrine of impassibility and the issues surrounding it are found in Thomas G. Weinandy, *Does God Suffer?* (Notre Dame, IN: University of Notre Dame Press, 2000); Paul L. Gavrilyuk, *The Suffering of the Impassible God: The Dialectics of Patristic Thought* (Oxford: Oxford University Press, 2004). See also perspectives in Ronald S. Baines et al., eds., *Confessing the Impassible God: The Biblical, Classical, & Confessional Doctrine of Divine Impassibility* (Palmdale, CA: Reformed Baptist Academic Press, 2015); Robert J. Matz and A. Chadwick Thornhill, eds., *Divine Impassibility: Four Views of God's Emotions and Suffering* (Downers Grove, IL: InterVarsity Press, 2019). Good insights are also found in Rob Lister, *God Is Impassible and Impassioned: Toward a Theology of Divine Emotion* (Wheaton, IL: Crossway, 2013). But see James E. Dolezal's review of Lister's book in "Appendix 2," in *Confessing the Impassible God: The Biblical, Classical, & Confessional Doctrine of Divine Impassibility*, ed. Ronald S. Baines et al. (Palmdale, CA: Reformed Baptist Academic Press, 2015), 409–14. The best succinct and accessible treatment of impassibility can be found in Joel R. Beeke and Paul M. Smalley, *Reformed Systematic Theology*, vol. 1, *Revelation and God* (Wheaton, IL: Crossway, 2019), 829–51; Matthew Barrett, *None Greater: The Undomesticated Attributes of God* (Grand Rapids: Baker, 2019), 111–37; and the articles in the online journal *Credo Magazine*, "The Impassibility of God," *Credo Magazine* 9.1 (2019), found at: https://credomag.com/magazine_issue/the-impassibility-of-god/.

8. See, for example, Richard Bauckham, "'Only the Suffering God Can Help': Divine Passibility in Modern Theology," *Themelios* 9.3 (1984): 12.

9. A. N. Whitehead, *Process and Reality* (Cambridge: Cambridge University Press, 1923), 532. Process theology has led to the rise of modern passibilism. Other notable contemporary passibilists include Karl Barth (Barth's position is disputed), Wolfgang Pannenberg, T. F. Torrance, Clark Pinnock, Greg Boyd, Nicholas Wolterstorff, and Richard Swinburne.

10. Dietrich Bonhoeffer, *Letters and Papers from Prison* (London: SCM Press, 1967), 361.

11. Jürgen Moltmann, *The Crucified God: The Cross of Christ as the Foundation and Criticism of Christian Theology*, trans. R. A. Wilson and J. Bowden (New York: Harper & Row, 1974), 230.

The rejection of impassibility is based on significant misunderstandings of what the doctrine teaches.[12] The view espoused by classic orthodox theism says that God does not suffer but that this does not mean that he is apathetic, without feelings or compassion for others who suffer. "God is not a metaphysical iceberg."[13] The patristic writers, however, made a strong distinction between two terms to describe mental states that have taken on entirely different meanings today: *affections* and *passions*. Classical theism holds that God experiences affections but not passions.[14]

Passions in the older theology are confined to human experience and indicate disordered, unruly, and often sinful mental states (emotions).[15] They are involuntary (passive) disturbances caused by outside forces that overpower the mind and thus tend toward the irrational, unstable, and unpredictable.[16] Passions reflect the mutable conditions of creatures under the power of both finite and sinful natures. Thus, in this sense, God is "without . . . passions."[17]

12. For example, our modern therapeutic culture has clouded the issues. Others believe that impassibility was too heavily influenced by Greek thought. This is known as the *Hellenization thesis* and was first propagated by Adolf von Harnack in the *History of Dogma* (1902). For refutations of this position, see Michael S. Horton, "Hellenistic or Hebrew? Open Theism and Reformed Theological Method," in *Beyond the Bounds: Open Theism and the Undermining of Biblical Christianity*, ed. John Piper, Justin Taylor, and Paul Kjoss Helseth (Wheaton, IL: Crossway, 2003), 201–34; Gerald L. Bray, "Has the Christian Doctrine of God Been Corrupted by Greek Philosophy?," in *God under Fire: Modern Scholarship Reinvents God*, ed. Douglas S. Huffman and Eric L. Johnson (Grand Rapids: Zondervan, 2002), 105–17. See also Ronald H. Nash, *The Gospel and the Greeks: Did the New Testament Borrow from Pagan Thought?*, 2nd ed. (Phillipsburg, NJ: P&R Publishing, 2003).

13. Phil Johnson, "God without Mood Swings," in *Bound Only Once: The Failure of Open Theism*, ed. Douglas Wilson (Moscow, ID: Canon Press, 2001), 121. Passibilists who have charged that impassibilism teaches that God is without feelings (emotions) include Nicholas Wolterstorff, "Suffering Love," in *Philosophy and the Christian Faith*, ed. Thomas V. Morris (Notre Dame, IN: University of Notre Dame Press, 1988), 196–237; John C. Clark and Marcus Peter Johnson, *The Incarnation of God: The Mystery of the Gospel as the Foundation of Evangelical Theology* (Wheaton, IL: Crossway, 2015), 97–98. Unfortunately, some medieval and Protestant scholastics tended to see the impassible God as without feeling, eclipsing the view of the patristic writers. Gavrilyuk indicates that not a single patristic author suggested that God is apathetic or without feelings (Paul L. Gavrilyuk, "God's Impassible Suffering in the Flesh: The Promise of Paradoxical Christology," in *Divine Impassibility and the Mystery of Human Suffering*, ed. James F. Keating and Thomas Joseph White [Grand Rapids: Eerdmans, 2009], 136–37).

14. Beeke and Smalley, *Revelation and God*, 839.

15. The word *emotions* is also used frequently in the debate, but this is a modern term fraught with all kinds of difficulties, adding confusion to the discussion. See Thomas Dixon, *From Passions to Emotions: The Creation of a Secular Psychological Category* (Cambridge: Cambridge University Press, 2003). See also Andrea Scarantino and Ronald de Sousa, "Emotion," in *The Stanford Encyclopedia of Philosophy*, ed. Edward N. Zalta (Winter 2018), found at: https://plato.stanford.edu/archives/win2018/entries/emotion/.

16. See Richard A. Muller, *Dictionary of Latin and Greek Theological Terms*, 2nd ed. (Grand Rapids: Baker Academic, 2017), 255.

17. WCF 2.1.

On the other hand, God does have affections. In classical orthodoxy, *affections* refers to voluntary (self-controlled), rational, stable, predictable dispositions of the soul. Conversely, *passions* represents alterations to the soul, but God cannot be moved either negatively or positively by people, things, and events in the sense that his self-sufficient dispositions are not dependent on the actions of others. He is not surprised by what he already knows and has decreed from all eternity. He is timelessly eternal, and so his actions are not dependent on time-bound events or persons. Furthermore, divine impassibility is a natural consequence of divine immutability.[18] He is "the Father of lights, with whom there is no variation or shadow due to change" (James 1:17).[19]

This does not mean that God is a stoic—an impersonal, aloof, unfeeling, stodgy sort of deity.[20] Rather, it means that the mental states of God *ad intra* (intrinsic to the internal Trinitarian being) are perfect and perfectly poised. Thus, God's *ad extra* (external) temporal responses to our actions are appropriately and precisely measured and known from all eternity, having proceeded from his eternal nature and decree. When Scripture speaks of God's responses of love or hate, compassion or anger, joy or grief, and so forth, these reflect his eternal, incorruptible, righteous character.

Kevin DeYoung writes:

> To be impassible is not to be passionless. To be immutable is not to be motionless. God is always active, always dynamic, always relational. In fact, it is because God is so completely full of action that he cannot change. He is love to the maximum at every moment. He cannot change because he cannot possibly be any more loving, or any more just, or any more good. God cares for us, but it is not a care subject to spasms or fluctuations of intensity. His kindness is not capable of being diminished or augmented.[21]

God is not a malleable being, shaped and molded by things external to himself. He is not tossed to and fro by the unexpected winds of change encountered in his creation or creatures. There is not a give-and-take

18. Weinandy, *Does God Suffer?*, 123–27.

19. See Richard C. Barcellos and James P. Butler, "The New Testament on the Doctrine of Divine Impassibility," in *Confessing the Impassible God: The Biblical, Classical, & Confessional Doctrine of Divine Impassibility*, ed. Ronald S. Baines et al. (Palmdale, CA: Reformed Baptist Academic Press, 2015), 197–98. See also Num. 23:19; 1 Sam. 15:29; Mal. 3:6; Heb. 13:8.

20. Beeke and Smalley, *Revelation and God*, 843.

21. Kevin DeYoung, "'Tis Mystery All, the Immortal Dies: Why the Gospel of Christ's Suffering Is More Glorious because God Does Not Suffer," unpublished paper presented at T4G Conference, Louisville, KY, April 2010, 9.

interaction between God and humans, as though we could affect unpredictable fluctuations in his emotional state.[22] Again, DeYoung writes:

> We do not move God to tears in the strict sense of the word—move. He is not *overcome* with rage; he does not *fall* in love; he does not *get* frustrated. Emotions do not just happen to him, such that he is forced to act in a certain way in order to make himself happier or change his mood from bad to good. God is completely free. He makes decisions based on his own immutable will and unchangeable purposes not on changing emotional states.[23]

Furthermore, God's affections are unique in relation to human beings. In other words, they are not related to our affections univocally (i.e., exactly like ours). Nor are they equivocally related (i.e., completely unlike ours). Rather, they are analogically related (i.e., similar but dissimilar to ours).[24] Thus, scriptural depictions of God's affections are indeed analogical, but they are not mere anthropomorphisms.[25] They are not mere accommodations to human understanding. God has real feelings. He is "*perfectly* vibrant in his affections."[26]

Some important distinctions will bring clarity here. Unlike humans, God can never have sinful emotions, such as bitterness, greed, anxiety, lust, unjust anger (e.g., temper tantrums), or petty forms of jealousy.[27] Nor can he be characterized by weak (finite) and debilitating emotions, such as pain, sorrow (due to some loss to himself), depression, fear, or disappointment, although there is a real and important sense in which he can be displeased by sin or grieved over the pain of others.[28]

This is where the principal meaning of *impassibility* must direct us. To speak of God as impassible means that he is unable to suffer as humans do. He suffers no loss or threat to his intrinsic perfections as God.[29] It is also in this sense that God is "without passions."[30] God does not suffer physical

---

22. Lister, *God Is Impassible and Impassioned*, 36.

23. DeYoung, "'Tis Mystery All," 10.

24. Beeke and Smalley, *Revelation and God*, 833.

25. Divine affections are often called *anthropopathisms*, a subcategory of anthropomorphisms. Both are analogical to one degree or another. Lister makes a helpful distinction: "Divine incorporeality leads us to the conclusion that *anthropomorphisms* are *analogical and nonliteral* (though nevertheless truth bearing), whereas *anthropopathisms* are *analogical and literal*" (*God Is Impassible and Impassioned*, 187). He concludes, "We should affirm that the emotional predications of God in Scripture refer literally and truthfully to him" (187).

26. Lister, *God Is Impassible and Impassioned*, 36.

27. Gavrilyuk, *Suffering of the Impassible God*, 6.

28. See, for example, Gen. 6:6; Judg. 10:16; Isa. 63:9–10.

29. Weinandy, *Does God Suffer?*, 157–58; Lister, *God Is Impassible and Impassioned*, 256.

30. WCF 2.1.

pain because he is an incorporeal being. He does not suffer mental pain (anguish), for this would indicate a weakness whereby some outside force could alter his mental disposition in a debilitating manner.

"Evil is contained within and confined to the created order."[31] Both sinful and debilitating emotions are tied to a fallen world. Therefore, due to the ontological Creator-creature distinction, God cannot be touched by evil.[32] Nothing can alter the supreme tranquility, blessedness, and fullness of God's perfect affections. Thus, when God expresses his wrath, grief, or displeasure, it is not due to some loss to his tranquility or blessedness; rather, it is the proper response of his love, righteousness, and justice that uniformly expresses his perfect blessedness.

DIVINE COMPASSION AND THE ERADICATION OF SUFFERING

With this in mind, we must see the importance of properly construing God's love. It is simply not true that for God to love and sympathize with his creatures, he must necessarily suffer as they do.[33] Suffering "is not a constitutive element of love."[34] Weinandy notes:

> Sorrow and grief are attributed to God not by way of predicating a passible emotional change within him, but rather by way of denoting that he is all-loving and good. Because he is perfectly loving and good, he finds sin and evil repugnant, and so he can be said to sorrow and grieve in the light of their presence. God does not grieve or sorrow because he himself experiences some injury or the loss of some good, nor that he has been affected, within his inner being, by some evil outside cause, rather he grieves or sorrows only in the sense that he knows that human persons experience some injury or the loss of some good, and so embraces them in love.[35]

Thus, God may express deep compassion for those who suffer without suffering hurt himself.[36] This is a great source of comfort. "The sick do not need another sick person, but a powerful and loving healer."[37] We need a rock, a fortress, a refuge and stronghold in the midst of the raging storm and the enemies who would overtake us.[38] We need a God who rises above

31. Weinandy, *Does God Suffer?*, 153.
32. Weinandy, *Does God Suffer?*, 153–54.
33. Gavrilyuk, *Suffering of the Impassible God*, 7–8.
34. Weinandy, *Does God Suffer?*, 160.
35. Weinandy, *Does God Suffer?*, 169.
36. Beeke and Smalley, *Revelation and God*, 863.
37. Beeke and Smalley, *Revelation and God*, 864.
38. See, for example, Pss. 27; 46; 59; 91.

the din of destructive forces wreaking havoc on the world and our weary souls. "If God were of such a nature that he suffered when his creatures suffered, then he would be the most to be pitied. His omniscience and love would taste the bitter poison of every tragedy in history. The majestic God would be dethroned in misery."[39]

THE IMPASSIBLE GOD TAKES ON A PASSIBLE NATURE

Nonetheless, we must not dismiss the reality that the New Testament emphasizes the suffering of the God-man in fulfillment of Isaiah's picture of the Messiah as the Suffering Servant.[40] Thus, the impassible God takes on a passible nature. He always remains what he is (the eternal Son of God) and became what he was not (a human like you and me). Jesus is subject to suffering in his human nature, and this serves two functions in relation to theodicy. First, it is necessary for the defeat of sin and evil. Second, it complements the sympathetic care that the impassible God extends to those who suffer. In this regard, the incarnation of the eternal Word as a passible (suffering) human tells us that God knows our suffering not just intellectually but experientially.

Weinandy explains at length:

> This is the marvelous truth of the Incarnation. God from all eternity may have known, within his divine knowledge, what it is like for human beings to suffer and die, and he may have known this perfectly and comprehensively. But until the Son of God actually became man and existed as a man, God, who is impassible in himself, never experienced and knew suffering and death as a man *in a human manner*. In an unqualified manner one can say that, as man, the Son of God had experiences he never had before because he never existed as man before—not the least of which are suffering and death. This is what humankind is crying out to hear, not that God experiences, in a divine manner, our anguish and suffering in the midst of a sinful and depraved world, but that he actually experienced and knew first hand, as one of us—as a man—human anguish and suffering within a sinful and depraved world. . . . The eternal, almighty, all-perfect, unchangeable, and impassible divine Son, he who is equal to the Father in all ways, actually experienced, as a weak human being, the full reality of human suffering and death.[41]

This is where divine compassion must be located and where our hope lies. Christ came to be like us in order to sympathize with our weaknesses (Heb.

---

39. Beeke and Smalley, *Revelation and God*, 864–65.

40. See Darrell L. Bock and Mitch Glaser, eds., *The Gospel according to Isaiah 53: Encountering the Suffering Servant in Jewish and Christian Theology* (Grand Rapids: Kregel, 2012).

41. Weinandy, *Does God Suffer?*, 206.

4:15), but more importantly to achieve salvation through human suffering (2:10, 14–18). So while we have a Savior who knows intimately the depths of suffering that afflict us—even a suffering beyond what any human could bear—this is not primarily why we find hope and comfort in his sufferings. Rather, "we hope because in Christ, God has taken on human suffering and death so that they are emptied of their ultimate sting."[42]

As the apostle Paul declares:

> "O death, where is your victory?
>   O death, where is your sting?"

> The sting of death is sin, and the power of sin is the law. But thanks be to God, who gives us the victory through our Lord Jesus Christ. (1 Cor. 15:55–57)

The greatest comfort that God could offer those who suffer is to promise them the eradication of every vestige of suffering, which culminates in death itself.[43] Divine compassion cannot be reduced to "sentimental commiseration,"[44] and especially if God himself is marked by eternal suffering in his very nature, as passibilists such as Moltmann would have us believe.[45] If passibilism were true, then pain and suffering could never be defeated because God would be eternally affected by it.[46]

To the contrary, Scripture indicates that the God-man suffered once and for all to defeat evil, pain, and suffering. He rose again to vindicate his victory, and then he returned to his place of glory beside the Father, where no suffering can coexist (Heb. 10:12–14; cf. 9:23–28). Thus, suffering and death have no hold on the believer. We are promised victory over death. We are promised that we will overcome death by the same power invested in the resurrection of Christ (Rom. 6:5). Ultimately, we are promised the same pain-free, perfect immortal bliss of our glorified Lord, for whom we wait to bring us all to glory.

Jesus condescended to our station, suffered as no man ever did, participated in the curse of death, and then returned to his glorious throne. This

---

42. J. Todd Billings, *Rejoicing in Lament* (Grand Rapids: Brazos Press, 2015), 161; cf. Lister, *God Is Impassible and Impassioned*, 47–48.

43. Gavrilyuk, "God's Impassible Suffering," 144.

44. Gavrilyuk, "God's Impassible Suffering," 145.

45. Moltmann, *Crucified God*, 205. This view is also promoted by Eberhard Jüngel and Hans Urs von Balthasar. See Bruce D. Marshall, "The Dereliction of Christ and the Impassibility of God," in *Divine Impassibility and the Mystery of Human Suffering*, ed. James F. Keating and Thomas Joseph White (Grand Rapids: Eerdmans, 2009), 248–53.

46. Lister, *God Is Impassible and Impassioned*, 248.

he did so that the children of God might follow his path to glory, where every last vestige of suffering is finally eradicated:

> But we see him who for a little while was made lower than the angels, namely Jesus, crowned with glory and honor because of the suffering of death, so that by the grace of God he might taste death for everyone. For it was fitting that he, for whom and by whom all things exist, in bringing many sons to glory, should make the founder of their salvation perfect through suffering. (Heb. 2:9–10)

The point is clear: "If God suffers for all eternity, then there is nothing uniquely redemptive about Christ's suffering on the cross. Incarnation becomes a pale copy of what God has been enduring for all eternity."[47] Thus, the true power of divine compassion is inextricably tied to the cross, where the Suffering Servant defeats the sources that first introduced suffering to the world. Original sin and the original tempter are the enemies that Christ conquered by bearing an unfathomable weight of suffering on his shoulders (Rom. 5:19; Col. 2:15). When the holy seed of the woman was promised to victoriously crush the head of the serpent (Gen. 3:15), humanity had every reason to rejoice because the reversal of the cosmic curse is what every suffering soul longs for. If compassion has no power to eradicate the source of suffering, then it is of little consolation to those who are trying to escape suffering's sinister grip. Just ask any Holocaust survivor.

THE DEPTHS OF CHRIST'S SUFFERING

This leads us to consider the unfathomable depths of Christ's suffering and death. Some of the greatest mysteries of the gospel and of the Christian faith lie in the unprecedented nature of the suffering that Christ endured and of the Father-Son breach it entailed. What exactly happened that led Jesus to utter the cry of God-forsakenness from the cross (Matt. 27:46)? Ironically, the soul-rattling spasms of pain to which the Lord of the universe was subject speak of the greatest glories to which the greater-glory theodicy points. The ignominy that Christ suffered at the hands of evil men is simply a mirror of the just wrath of the Father poured out on his beloved Son (Acts 2:22–23), the severest wrath ever put on display. Yet it also happens to be the greatest display of his mercy poured out on debased

---

47. Gavrilyuk, "God's Impassible Suffering," 147. Gavrilyuk further points out that if Christ suffers in his divine nature, then the human nature becomes superfluous. The human nature is only duplicating what the divine nature has already experienced forever (147).

sinners deserving wrath instead (Rom. 5:8–11). The cross is a paradigm of paradoxical wonder—the preeminent meeting place of wrath and mercy, the supreme display of divine glory.

Jesus entered suffering the moment he was born and laid in a lowly manger. His whole life was marked by afflictions, but it is in the garden of Gethsemane where it begins to take on uniquely redemptive features with a distressing sharpness.[48] As he prayed for what he was about to endure, "he began to be sorrowful and troubled" (Matt. 26:37). The term "sorrowful" (*perilypos*) indicates deep sadness. The second term, "troubled" (*ademonein*), means "bewilderment, anxiety and near-panic."[49] Mark's account (Mark 14:33) uses an even stronger term, "greatly distressed" (*ekthambeomai*). Raymond Brown informs us that this term connotes "a profound disarray, expressed physically before a terrifying event: a shuddering horror."[50]

Macleod's description is even more vivid: "the feeling we experience in the presence of the unearthly, the uncanny and the utterly eerie. In Gethsemane Jesus knew that he was face to face with the unconditionally holy, that absolutely overwhelming might that condones nothing, cannot look on impurity and cannot be diverted from its purpose."[51] To enter this unmitigated realm of pure holiness is incomprehensible to us. "What would it do to him?"[52] Jesus did not fear soldiers, councils, priests, or magistrates. Rather, he was reluctant to face a preternatural force that no human could wield—that of his Father in heaven. His person did not face God as God, but *as a man*. In this regard, the Spirit directed his human mind and will to face impending doom all alone.[53] Jesus accomplished the work of redemption as the messianic Son of the living God, but he needed to bear the brunt of that work *as a man*.[54]

The agonies of Gethsemane reveal the wrestling of the human soul of the Son with the Father. This is why he prays, "Not my will, but yours, be done" (Luke 22:42). The human will is tempted to abandon the will of the Father (which, of course, is the one divine will of the Trinity).[55] The "cup" that he is tempted to have "removed" is the cup of unmitigated divine wrath.[56] What

---

48. Donald Macleod, *Christ Crucified: Understanding the Atonement* (Downers Grove, IL: InterVarsity Press, 2014), 16–17.

49. Macleod, *Christ Crucified*, 27.

50. Raymond E. Brown, *The Death of the Messiah*, 2 vols (Garden City, NY: Doubleday, 1994), 1:153.

51. Macleod, *Christ Crucified*, 28.

52. Macleod, *Christ Crucified*, 28.

53. Lister, *God Is Impassible and Impassioned*, 276–77.

54. Wellum, *God the Son Incarnate*, 339.

55. Gondreau, "St. Thomas Aquinas," 222.

56. See Isa. 51:17, 22; Jer. 25:15; Rev. 14:10; 16:19.

a daunting prospect! Jesus stands on a precipice. "For a moment the whole salvation of the world, the whole of God's determinate counsel, hangs in the balance, suspended on the free, unconstrained decision of this man. There is dread here and bewilderment and awe and self-doubt, and fear."[57]

The writer of Hebrews paints a vivid image: "In the days of his flesh, Jesus offered up prayers and supplications, with loud cries and tears, to him who was able to save him from death, and he was heard because of his reverence" (Heb. 5:7). God secretly sustains the Son's human obedience as he faces his most severe test. Like Moses facing Yahweh on the fiery pinnacle of Sinai, Jesus faces the same "revelation of God as an absolute overwhelming might, the Wholly Other who brooks no disobedience and no familiarity. And here was the ultimate in 'creature-felling': a sense of the infinite qualitative divide between humanity and deity, a sense of total vulnerability, a sense of nothingness and of defenceless fragility."[58] Unlike Moses, Jesus is not here "to receive the Law, but to suffer its curse."[59]

Yet Jesus meets with decisive resolve in the garden, and this is difficult for us to comprehend.

> It is clear from all accounts that Jesus' experience of turmoil and anguish was both real and profound. His sorrow was as great as a man could bear, his fear convulsive, his astonishment well-nigh paralyzing. He came within a hairsbreadth of break-down. He faced the will of God as raw holiness, the *mysterium tremendum* in its most acute form: and it terrified him.[60]

Luke gives us a glimpse of how far this trauma extended as "his sweat became like great drops of blood falling down to the ground" (Luke 22:44).

This bloody sweat is likely a rare instance of a condition called *hematidrosis*.[61] It occurs in circumstances "associated with a severe anxiety reaction triggered by *fear*."[62] Other symptoms include shortness of breath, sensations of choking, strong heart palpitations, muscular tension, weakness, tightening of the chest, and trembling.[63] Jesus emerges from the garden deeply shaken but intent on his mission. Having passed the first test of redemptive suffering, he moves through his arrest and trial like a silent sheep before

57. Macleod, *Christ Crucified*, 29.
58. Macleod, *Christ Crucified*, 29.
59. Macleod, *Christ Crucified*, 30.
60. Donald Macleod, *The Person of Christ* (Downers Grove, IL: InterVarsity Press, 1998), 174.
61. Brown, *Death of the Messiah*, 1:185; Frederick T. Zugibe, *The Crucifixion of Jesus: A Forensic Inquiry* (New York: M. Evans and Company, 2005), 8–15.
62. Zugibe, *Crucifixion of Jesus*, 9.
63. Zugibe, *Crucifixion of Jesus*, 11–12.

the shearer and the lamb led to slaughter (Isa. 53:7). There is nothing but unresisting meekness as he descends deeper into the abyss.

Note Christ's humiliations. His treatment by the Praetorian guard during his interrogation and death sentence bespeaks ironies utterly foreign to us (Matt. 27:27–31). Here is the King of cosmic glory and unrivaled power regarded as a pathetic pauper. These unruly brutes have no idea who they are savagely mocking while cramming a crown of thorns on his kingly skull. They are giddy as the blood streaks down his face. They wrap his unclothed body in a royal robe and shove a spindly stick into his hand—his "golden scepter." Bowing before the one they imagine to be a great imperial pretender, they can barely contain their laughter while blurting out, "Hail, king of the Jews!" To honor this great king, they hawk up a few loogies on him and then proceed to slap him senseless (John 19:3). Then they rip the "royal scepter" out of his hand to bash his already-bloodied head. It's a jovial good time.

This lighthearted locker-room banter by the guard, together with the brutal beating that Jesus receives across his backside (Matt. 27:26), is only the beginning—preparation before his soft hands and feet are pierced through with iron spikes to the rough-hewn planks of wood. No representatives from the local branch of the Association for the Humane Treatment of Roman Criminals are present to look after him.

But these tortures cannot compare to the affliction that the Lord is about to encounter. As Jesus is hoisted up on the cross, his mental anguish soon converges on a singularly dense point of unfathomable duress while menacing blackness hovers over his crucified form and an unearthly silence pours over his blood-red head. His redemptive suffering has reached its apex on the lonely beams on which his battered body is nailed. But then comes the very darkest moment when his "agony was so compacted—so infinite—as to be well-nigh unsustainable.... The whole entail of sin (pains and agonies it would have taken the world eternity to endure) were all poured out on him in one horrific moment."[64]

Suddenly he pierces the silence with an equally unearthly cry of abandonment, of God-forsakenness—the cry of dereliction. Jesus echoes the forlorn words of David:

"My God, my God, why have you forsaken me?" (Ps. 22:1; cf. Matt. 27:46)

No longer is the Father's face shining on Jesus. He finds no paternal sustenance. No mercy. No words of commendation. No expressions of

---

64. Macleod, *Person of Christ*, 176.

comfort. Instead, he feels the heat of the Father's hot displeasure. There would be no rescue. Jesus no longer sees himself as the beloved Son, but the Cursed One for sin: "vile, foul and repulsive."[65] R.C. Sproul explains the abandonment: "To be forsaken by God is the ultimate penalty for sin. The pit of hell is the abode of the utterly forsaken."[66] This is what Jesus meant by "outer darkness" (Matt. 8:12; 22:13; 25:30). "It is to receive the fury of the curse of God."[67]

As darkness descends on Calvary at noon, it becomes a nightmarish image of the absence of God in hell. Jesus is cast into this outer darkness—the scapegoat taken "beyond the cosmos, the realm of order and beauty, sinking instead into a black hole which no light could penetrate and from which, in itself, nothing benign or meaningful could ever emanate."[68] And there he bears the unbearable in its completeness, satisfying every last demand of God's just wrath against those for whom the Son died.

And yet herein lies the nucleus of divine glory in salvation—the strange hour in which the Son of Man would be glorified (John 12:23). How can one experience *glory* and the ignobility of a God-forsaken *cross* at the same time? "Is that like being enthroned on an electric chair? Is it like being honored by a firing squad?"[69] Yet it is out of this black hole that an ineffable light eventually pours forth, defying the life- and light-sucking power of sin and death. The darkness shrouding the cross represents the penultimate point in the redemptive drama. Here "the Light was almost exhausted in its struggle with the Darkness."[70] The Light seems poised for certain defeat. Satan's plan is veering toward success.

Yet what nobody knows except God (the Son's knowledge through his human mind at this moment appears to be in eclipse) is that the darker the sky grows, the more certain it is that the darkness would be defeated.[71] Ironically, unexpectedly, the darkness has to temporarily crush the Light in order for the Light to crush the darkness forever (Gen. 3:15). Jesus bravely enters the blackest of blackness, the darkest darkness—the very darkness itself. And there he absorbs its feral wickedness and then . . . summarily

---

65. Macleod, *Person of Christ*, 176.

66. R.C. Sproul, *The Glory of Christ* (Phillipsburg, NJ: Presbyterian and Reformed, 1990), 158.

67. Sproul, *Glory of Christ*, 158. The forsakenness of the Father can be none other than a manifestation of his wrath. See Peter G. Bolt, *The Cross from a Distance: Atonement in Mark's Gospel* (Downers Grove, IL: InterVarsity Press, 2004), 133–34.

68. Macleod, *Person of Christ*, 177.

69. Cornelius Plantinga Jr., "Deep Wisdom," in *God the Holy Trinity: Reflections on Christian Faith and Practice*, ed. Timothy George (Grand Rapids: Baker Academic, 2006), 151.

70. Macleod, *Person of Christ*, 218.

71. On the limitations of Christ's knowledge on the cross, see Macleod, *Person of Christ*, 166–69.

pulverizes its power. And out of the darkness comes pouring forth an ineffable brightness. Never has God's pure grace penetrated this filthy world so deeply. Never has his glory shone forth so brilliantly. Never has the sinner's benefit emerged so spectacularly.

Supreme glory is preceded—and thus enhanced—by the foulest scene that this ugly realm could conjure. "At the moment when Christ took on Himself the sin of the world, His figure on the cross was the most grotesque, most obscene mass of concentrated sin in the history of the world."[72] Luther put the matter memorably: "Christ was to become the greatest thief, murderer, adulterer, robber, desecrator, blasphemer, etc., there has ever been anywhere in the world. He is not acting in His own person now [i.e., through the divine nature]. Now He is not the Son of God, born of the Virgin. But He is a sinner, who has and bears the sin of Paul . . . ; of Peter . . . ; of David."[73] He bears our sins in "His body—not in the sense that He has committed them but in the sense that He took these sins, committed by us, upon His own body, in order to make satisfaction for them with His own blood."[74]

The Son *as man* was abandoned by the Father so that those of us who trust in him for pardon will never be abandoned. God should have turned his face from us, leaving us to suffer endlessly in the darkness. Instead, he turned his offended visage away from the Son so that the Light would shine on us forever.

THE MYSTERY OF CHRIST'S SUFFERING

This leads us to looming questions about the nature of the Father-Son breach expressed by the cry of dereliction. Was there a rupture in the Trinity on the cross? Did the Father experience a momentary loss of abandonment in the same way the Son did? Did he suffer? Did he undergo a brief lapse in his impassible nature during the cry of the Son? Did God himself somehow participate in death? After all, Acts 20:28 says that God purchased the church "with his own blood."

The orthodox patristic tradition concurred with Melito of Sardis, who declares: "He who hung the earth is hanging; he who fixed the heavens has been fixed; he who fastened the universe has been fastened to a tree; the Sovereign has been insulted; God has been murdered."[75] The Judge of the universe has been judged![76] There is undeniable mystery here, and the early

---

72. R.C. Sproul, *The Truth of the Cross* (Orlando, FL: Reformation Trust, 2007), 134.

73. Martin Luther, *Luther's Works*, vol. 26, *Lectures on Galatians 1535, Chapters 1–4*, trans. and ed. Jaroslav Pelikan (St. Louis: Concordia Publishing House, 1963), 277.

74. Luther, *Lectures on Galatians*, 277.

75. Peri Pascha, 96.711–15, quoted in Gavrilyuk, "God's Impassible Suffering," 128–29.

76. Bolt, *Cross from a Distance*, 141.

church did not shy away from the tension it presented. In order to grasp something of the mystery, however, we must clear away some misconceptions.

Orthodoxy rejects patripassianism, the idea that God the Father suffers as did the Son in the work of redemption. Patripassianism is historically connected to the heresy of Sabellianism (modalism), which says that the Father morphs into the Son incarnate and thereby suffered as the Son. The Father did not suffer in any direct manner. Only the Son underwent the palpable pain of redemption. Furthermore, *only* the human nature of Christ suffered loss. The divine nature cannot suffer loss and cannot die. This would be an absurdity of the highest order. Likewise, there was no rupture, or even the threat of rupture, in the Trinity on the cross or during the cry of dereliction. There was no breach in the same divine essence shared by Father and Son (and Spirit).

So what exactly happened on the cross?

The orthodox position of the early church is that God remains impassible and yet mysteriously participates via the incarnation in human suffering.[77] Gavrilyuk calls this a "qualified divine impassibility" or "paradoxical Christology."[78] He notes that the question whether God experiences suffering as part of the inner life (*ad intra*) of the *immanent* (ontological) Trinity—that is, the three persons of the triune God as they eternally are in their shared essence—is different from the question whether God somehow participates in the redemptive suffering of the incarnate Son as part of the *economic* Trinity—that is, the temporal function of each person of the Trinity acting in the works of creation and redemption.

The triune God does not and cannot suffer in any way as part of the divine essence. But the Father does participate in the suffering of the Son in ways that are difficult for us to comprehend.[79] Gavrilyuk writes that the paradox of suffering in the impassible God

> captures the vital tension between God's transcendence and undiminished divinity on the one hand and God's intimate involvement in human suffering on the other hand. God is impassible inasmuch as he is able to conquer sin, suffering, and death; and God is also passible (in a carefully qualified sense) inasmuch as in the incarnation God has chosen to enter the human condition in order to transform it. God suffers in and through human nature, by taking human grief and sorrow into his life and making these experiences his own.[80]

77. Gavrilyuk, "God's Impassible Suffering," 131.
78. Gavrilyuk, "God's Impassible Suffering," 131.
79. Gavrilyuk, "God's Impassible Suffering," 133.
80. Gavrilyuk, "God's Impassible Suffering," 146–47. Elsewhere, Gavrilyuk says that the divine Logos "was involved in human sufferings without being overwhelmed by them and without copying the suffering of the flesh" (*Suffering of the Impassible God*, 134).

In order to understand the tension, it is important to note another doctrine worked out in the Christology of the early church called the "communication of properties" (*communicatio idiomatum*).[81] The idea is that the divine nature has unique properties (attributes) that are distinct from the properties (attributes) of human nature. The divine is impassible, the human is passible; the divine is immortal, the human is mortal; the divine is all-powerful, the human is weak; the divine is immutable, the human is mutable; the divine is untemptable, the human is temptable; and so forth. The unique attributes that belong only to the divine nature cannot be shared by the human nature, and vice versa.

Yet all these attributes, human and divine, belong to the *person* of Christ. Furthermore, it is the *person* of Christ (consisting of the hypostatic union of his two natures) that suffers and dies (as the acting subject), even though it is the *human nature alone* that directly undergoes the suffering. In other words, Jesus the *person* experienced suffering and death *humanly*.[82]

So this leads to the doctrine stating that the properties (attributes) of the theanthropic person's two natures cannot be communicated to one another at the level of *nature* but that some properties can be communicated at the level of *person*.[83] The divine *nature* of Jesus participates in the suffering of the human *nature*—not directly, but rather because the two natures are joined together in the *person* of the Son. This prevents both the "person-nature distinction" and the "Creator-creature distinction" from being violated.[84]

Furthermore, since there is an interpersonal unity or mutual indwelling (*perichoresis*) between the persons of the Father and Son (and Spirit; cf. John 14:10–11), then the Father also participates in the suffering of the Son, though not directly.[85] There is a strange and incomprehensible sense in which it both pleased and grieved the Father to crush his beloved Son (Isa. 53:10). And so we can affirm that God via the incarnation came to mysteriously know "human pain and anguish first hand and in the same human manner that we experience it."[86]

---

81. See Muller, *Dictionary of Latin and Greek*, 69–71.

82. Lister, *God Is Impassible and Impassioned*, 274. Note how Kevin DeYoung applies the "communication of properties" to the question of God's suffering on the cross. See "Divine Impassibility and the Passion of Christ in the Book of Hebrews," *WTJ* 68.1 (2006): 41–50.

83. Gondreau, "St. Thomas Aquinas," 218; Weinandy, *Does God Suffer?*, 200. WCF 8.7 says, "Christ, in the work of mediation, acts according to both natures, by each nature doing that which is proper to itself. But by reason of the unity of the person, that which is proper to one nature is sometimes in Scripture attributed to the person referred to by the other nature."

84. Wellum, *God the Son Incarnate*, 324–26.

85. Macleod, *Person of Christ*, 140–42.

86. DeYoung, "Divine Impassibility and the Passion of Christ," 46.

IT IS FINISHED!

Charles Taylor, in his monumental work *A Secular Age,* draws attention to the devastating effects of secularism in the modern world. He notes why the Christian faith is uniquely positioned to speak to the problems of our age as nothing else can because no other worldview understands the central problem of humanity and how it must be addressed. "There are at least two key mysteries that the Christian faith turns on: one is why we are in the grip of evil, why we were/are somehow incapable of helping ourselves to overcome this condition, and become the kind of creatures which we know we were made to be; the other is how the sacrifice of Christ broke through this helplessness, and opened a way out."[87] Taylor acknowledges that the first question has been answered historically by the doctrine of original sin and the second by the doctrine of penal substitution. He essentially sets forth the conditions for a faithful theodicy.

The crisis facing humanity is not a run-of-the-mill sort of problem. It has insurmountable forces propelled by an intractable enemy (Satan), who has unparalleled hatred for both God and humanity. Thus, the solution to the conflict cannot be an ordinary one. The only theodicy that can satisfy the demands posed by the conflict of evil must be something extraordinary. A theodicy must not merely address how to make sense of humanity's plight under the frightful pale of suffering and evil; it must understand how God intersects this fallen world via the incarnation and how he fares under the devastating condition of a cursed creation.

The strength of the greater-glory theodicy is revealed in the unusual glory that God receives as a result of the paradoxical uniqueness of the plan of redemption he engineered to defeat evil. This plan employs something unheard of—divine infirmity (1 Cor. 1:25), an ironic and mysterious form of strength completely unfamiliar to our way of thinking. Paul Helm notes, "It is tempting to think of God as a Herculean figure, able to outlift and out-throw and outrun all his opponents. Such a theology would be one of physical and metaphysical power; whatever his enemies can do God can do it better or more efficiently than they."[88]

Of course, God has reserves of power in one finger to devastate the whole cosmos, but this is not the only kind of power he employs. He employs the strange, subversive, and counterintuitive power of frailty as well. The infinite God enters the lowly habitat of his finite creatures. He becomes one of them in order to save them. The all-powerful, impassible God condescends

---

87. Charles Taylor, *A Secular Age* (Cambridge, MA: Belknap Press, 2007), 651.
88. Paul Helm, *The Providence of God* (Downers Grove, IL: InterVarsity Press, 1994), 224.

to weakness, to incomprehensible pain and suffering, in order to eradicate it. Jesus had to "taste" death (Heb. 2:9). He had to experience the long, excruciating power of it "unanesthetized" in order to disarm it completely.[89] "He had to walk . . . through the valley of the shadow of death, tasting the fear of it and the encroachments of it and the power of it, and then yielding himself to it consciously and deliberately."[90]

In 1 Corinthians 1, Paul tells us that the world scoffs at an incarnate and crucified God and regards it as folly (v. 23). This is not how the story should go. Embracing shame, weakness, and abject suffering is not the expected path of victory over evil. The evidence for this perception is vividly portrayed in the Alexamenos graffito, a vile depiction of Jesus dated to the late second century A.D. discovered in the Palatine Hill in Rome. The crude drawing scrawled on a plaster wall was intended to mock a Christian named Alexamenos. It shows a boy bowed before a crucified figure with an ass's head. An inscription reads, "Alexamenos worshipping his god." But the true God is never vexed by such blasphemous scorn. "Has not God made foolish the wisdom of the world?" (v. 20). Divine weakness is, strangely enough, divine power, and it imbibes a divine brand of wisdom that the world can never know (vv. 24–25).

Yes, Jesus died an ignominious death. "His life did not ebb away, slowly and peacefully, ending with a pathetic death-rattle."[91] Rather, it was bloody. It was brutal. It was shameful. Scandalous. Grotesque. But this should not evoke our horror and dismay. In the irony of all ironies, ignominy begets triumph. The cross is where three monumental forces clash in the most momentous battle in history.[92] On the one side you have the *"sheer and utter evilness of evil,"* whose pall of death seems to spell defeat for the anointed hero. But this is met on the other side by the *"complete sovereignty of God"* in all its transformative power together with the *"unadulterated goodness of God"* emanating from the blood and sweat streaming down the battered body of Christ.[93]

No wicked stratagems can match such unearthly power and goodness exhibited on the cross as it twists and turns the foul wreckage of the fall until it has been transformed into a gift of exquisite beauty and grace for those ravaged by sin. The evidence of Christ's unusual and unexpected victory over the cosmic crisis of evil came when he uttered that singular

---

89. Macleod, *Christ Crucified*, 35.
90. Macleod, *Christ Crucified*, 35.
91. Macleod, *Christ Crucified*, 35.
92. See Henri Blocher, *Evil and the Cross* (Grand Rapids: Kregel, 1994), 203–4.
93. Blocher, *Evil and the Cross*, 204.

commanding word, *Tetelestai* ("It is finished") (John 19:30). Only this unequaled theanthropic figure—battered and bleeding—could make such a declaration that results in blessedness for undeserving sinners, destruction of all evil forces, and unprecedented glory for the Architect of this amazing plan of redemption.

And this is where the trilemma of evil is solved. Since evil exists, it is assumed that the existence of either God's goodness or his power must go. Either he is good but sadly not powerful enough to defeat evil, or he is all-powerful but disconcertingly not good enough and therefore wishes for evil to prevail. But this misses the confluence of the incongruities of God and evil altogether. The solution is simple.

God purposed evil to exist so that his power and goodness would be supremely demonstrated in the strange and ironic wonder of the cross and empty tomb that crush evil in such dramatic fashion as to produce supreme goods outstripping any good that could come about without the prevalence of evil. This is not how any human intellect would devise the world. But then again, we cannot pretend to match the otherworldly goodness and wisdom of God's sovereign plan.

If the crisis facing the world is to be dismantled, there can be only one Redeemer, one Savior (Acts 4:12), one Mediator between Creator and creature (1 Tim. 2:5). He must be truly God and truly man. He needs the power and perfection of Almighty God to rescue us because the enemies that he must defeat are no ordinary foes. He needs the weakness of a man to be our adequate substitute, to enter our worst suffering, and to bear our horrid sin. If he is not these things, then we are "left with a hollow Saviour and a God aloof and detached from us at the point of our greatest need."[94] Paul Gavrilyuk is surely correct when he states, "God is neither eternally indifferent to suffering, nor eternally overcome by it. Rather, there is eternal victory over suffering in God, manifest most fully through the cross and resurrection."[95]

This has been the testimony of the church for two thousand years, and it never ceases to confound the sensibilities of the watching world. The self-professed wise men of the world call this *crucicentric* plan foolishness (1 Cor. 1:18–21). But they are shrouded by ignorance, not knowing that "the foolishness of God is wiser than men, and the weakness of God is stronger than men" (v. 25). Tertullian (A.D. 155–220) expresses the strange and paradoxical wonder of our redemption and of the grand Redeemer who secured it for us:

94. Robert Letham, *The Work of Christ* (Downers Grove, IL: InterVarsity Press, 1993), 29.
95. Gavrilyuk, "God's Impassible Suffering," 131.

Today He who hung the earth upon the waters is hung upon the Cross.
He who is King of the angels is arrayed in a crown of thorns.
He who wraps the heaven in clouds is wrapped in the purple of mockery.
He who in Jordan set Adam free receives blows upon His face.
The Bridegroom of the Church is transfixed with nails.[96]

Those nails drove a deathblow through sin, suffering, and death as the Savior cried out, "It is finished!" This bloody cry is the locus of God's extrinsic glory and explains why the heavenly chorus shouts out: "Worthy is the Lamb who was slain, to receive power and wealth and wisdom and might and honor and glory and blessing!" (Rev. 5:12). Christ's supreme glory is forever connected with his identity as "the Lamb who was slain."

KEY TERMS

affections
immutability (of God)
impassibility (of God)
passibility (of Christ)
passions

STUDY QUESTIONS

1. What shocking statements were made by early church fathers about God?
2. What is the difference between affections and passions in classical theism?
3. How should one summarize the orthodox position of classical theism on the impassibility of God?
4. Is it better to have a suffering God or a God who does not suffer when he sympathizes with his suffering creatures? Explain your answer.
5. Why can we find hope and comfort in Christ's sufferings?
6. How do the depths of Christ's suffering magnify the glory of God?
7. In what sense does the triune God participate in Christ's sufferings?
8. Why is the incarnation of the Son of God so important to a faithful theodicy?

FOR FURTHER READING

Matthew Barrett, *None Greater: The Undomesticated Attributes of God* (Grand Rapids: Baker, 2019).

96. Tertullian, *The Lenten Triodion*, trans. Mother Mary and Kallistos Ware (London: Faber & Faber, 1984), 587, quoted in Gavrilyuk, *Suffering of the Impassible God*, 135.

Rob Lister, *God Is Impassible and Impassioned: Toward a Theology of Divine Emotion* (Wheaton, IL: Crossway, 2013).

Donald Macleod, *Christ Crucified: Understanding the Atonement* (Downers Grove, IL: InterVarsity Press, 2014).

———, *The Person of Christ* (Downers Grove, IL: InterVarsity Press, 1998).

Advanced

Paul L. Gavrilyuk, *The Suffering of the Impassible God: The Dialectics of Patristic Thought* (Oxford: Oxford University Press, 2004).

James F. Keating and Thomas Joseph White, eds., *Divine Impassibility and the Mystery of Human Suffering* (Grand Rapids: Eerdmans, 2009).

Thomas G. Weinandy, *Does God Suffer?* (Notre Dame, IN: University of Notre Dame Press, 2000).

16

THE COSMIC REDEEMER

One of the dominant Christian strands of Western art from the Middle Ages to the nineteenth century emphasized the lordship of Christ over the whole of creation. This theme has been carried out particularly in the long ecclesiastical tradition of depicting scenes of Christ presiding over judgment and hell. The apocalyptic imagery in the apostle John's Revelation has always lent itself easily to graphic representations, with aesthetic imaginations often going far beyond the biblical text.[1] Lurid hellscapes became popular, complete with leaping rivers of fire, sinners mercilessly tortured in highly inventive ways, and darkly painted demons that rule the fiery abyss with diabolical glee. Dante Alighieri's enduring and vivid poetic descriptions of hell in the *Inferno* (c. 1308–20) established a kind of canonical benchmark for all subsequent artistic renditions of hell.

Coming toward the end of this artistic tradition is a massive triptych of oil paintings that emerged from the hand of the nineteenth-century English Romantic painter John Martin (1789–1854). Few have captured the force of Christ's cosmic reign over the end of this-earthly life as Martin has. The centerpiece of the collection is *The Last Judgement*, which draws on different motifs from the book of Revelation, namely, chapters 4 and 5, in which the twenty-four elders and myriads of angels surround the throne of God and of the Lamb in anticipation of the Godhead's sweeping judgments on the world.

The luminescent scene presides over two fates of mankind. On the bottom left, we see the redeemed saints preparing to enter the new Jerusalem,

---

1. Artistic depictions of divine judgment and hell reached their peak during the Renaissance. Painters drew not only from biblical descriptions but also from Greek and Roman mythology.

which is emerging out of the landscape just above their heads. This New World is more fully depicted in all its bright serenity in the painting to the left entitled *The Plains of Heaven*. On the bottom right are the damned souls awaiting the Lamb's wrath. They are separated from the redeemed by a great chasm—a hell-descending pit, which is their destiny.

This latter image is but a glimpse of the fullness of wrath depicted in the painting to the right, *The Great Day of His Wrath*. Here Martin was specifically influenced by the imagery of the opening of the sixth seal in Revelation 6:12–14. There is a visceral force to Martin's rendering of apocalyptic judgment here. The scene is now completely dominated by the vast black chasm that is only hinted at in the center painting. In the foreground, we are directly confronted with the sea of the damned, both clothed and naked, clinging hopelessly for their lives as they are slipping inexorably down the edges of the abyss into oblivion.

In the background, a whole city with its crashing pillars and edifices is being consumed as well. Above the bottomless pit looms a blood-red moon presiding over an emerging conflagration from a fiery sea of lava working its way through the already-scorched landscape. Its massive plumes of smoke billow upward to the bright heavens while being overcome by the blackness of the pit below. Searing bolts of lightning assault the upturned cityscape to the right as it hurtles into the abyss. To the left, colossal boulders come flying out of nowhere like primordial beasts ready to crush their helpless prey. The whole scene epitomizes sublime forces of destruction and leaves the viewer quite unsettled.

Taken as a whole, Martin's triptych encompasses the full gamut of divine mercy and benevolence on the one hand and divine wrath and justice on the other. At the center of this vision of God sits the Lamb on his heavenly throne. Martin provides a glimpse of what the apostle Paul describes as the divine "plan for the fullness of time, to unite all things in [Christ], things in heaven and things on earth" (Eph. 1:10). Paul gives testimony to an all-inclusive domain on which Christ makes his indelible mark. The grand storyline of biblical redemption is not confined to the rescue and reconciliation of a handful of desperate souls. It encompasses the restoration of "all things" (cf. Acts 3:21).

Evil is met by Christ in two ways. It is met by the humbled and crucified Lamb at the cross (Rev. 5:12). But it is also met by the resurrected One glorified as a Lion (v. 5), who will return to earth in a colossal display of far-reaching power. When the day of the Lord bursts forth on the horizon, the Messiah will wield his fearsome sword (19:15) to dispense with myriads of fallen creatures (human and angelic) who have aligned themselves against him. Likewise, he will establish the fullness of his kingdom, culminating in the sudden dissolution and renewal of the entire cosmos (2 Peter 3:10–13).

We cannot escape either vision of Christ if we are to understand the fullness of his person and work. The stark tension drawn ever so taut between these two visions—Christ as the humble, merciful Redeemer and Christ as the commanding, unyielding Judge—brings further magnification to the greater of the two visions: that of Christ the Redeemer. Without Christ as Judge (the Lion), the glory he receives as the Redeemer (the Lamb) would be severely muted. What enhances the glory of Christ lies in the juxtaposition of his inglorious path to the cross with his undiminished status as the risen Lord and King of the universe. Let us consider this cosmic scope of redemption and its implications for the greater-glory theodicy.

CHRIST AS LION AND LAMB

Scripture situates the person and work of Christ within a strange heterogeneous atmosphere. On the one hand, there are those conventional, though supremely exalted, attributes and actions that we expect of one who lays claim to deity. Christ is the eternal (John 1:1–2), immutable (Heb. 13:8), omnipotent, authoritative God of the universe (Eph. 1:20–22). He is the Creator of all (John 1:3) and possesses the title deed to all that he has made (Rev. 5:1–5). He sustains and governs every molecule in the universe (Col. 1:16–17). He is the supreme Judge (John 5:22) and Ruler of every creature, and none can impede the progress of his cosmic kingdom (Rev. 5:6–10).

On the other hand, given the priority of Christ's deity, we must never cease to be astounded when we encounter the attributes and actions attributed to him in the lowly state of his humanity (Phil. 2:5–8). We expect to encounter Christ, as Lord of heaven and earth, in exaltation, not humiliation, and invincibility, not vulnerability. We have every reason to anticipate the uninterrupted exercise of divine authority and power, not one who stands bound in silence, subjecting himself to human authorities and powers (e.g., Matt. 26:59–63).

We expect Christ, as the Judge of all humanity, to mete out justice. We have no warrant to assume his mercy. A sin-filled world ought to be prepared to face his unrelenting wrath and retribution, not the offer of his pardon. What *should* confound us is that the Son of God would himself meet up with the same wrath that he ordinarily and rightfully imposes on the guilty, yet gladly heaves the severe weight of it on his own innocent shoulders (1 Peter 2:22–24)—all because he is eager to pour out his mercy on many unworthy vessels of wrath (Rom. 9:23).

The proximity of these seemingly incongruous features of the Messiah contributes to his utter uniqueness. And we must not miss God's redemptive plan for history as it encompasses both dimensions of the Son of God. Redemption is not confined to the cross. It also embraces a crown—a cosmic crown. It is a comprehensive work that involves a comprehensive Savior—one whose identity and activity entail the conventional *and* unconventional, the unsurprising *and* surprising. Extraordinary power combines with ordinary weakness in an all-encompassing plan to conquer evil.

The incongruities are indeed peculiar. When people first learned that Jesus was no mere man, but God incarnate performing deeds of deity, they were amazed (e.g., Matt. 7:28–29; Mark 4:41; Luke 7:49). But after they reckoned with this fact, nothing could prepare them to witness the incarnate God's being swallowed up by blood, brutality, and unjustified death. At this they were utterly dumbfounded (Matt. 16:21–23). A crucified God? Who could imagine such a subversive turn of events?

If Jesus were merely a man, then succumbing to an ignominious death would be largely unremarkable. What raises eyebrows is to watch the Lord of the universe embracing utter condescension and eagerly submitting to crucifixion—perhaps the cruelest form of torture and death ever devised.[2] We would expect a divine Messiah to summarily dispense with his wicked captors with Herculean bravado. The expectant Jews of his day certainly thought so (John 6:15; cf. Luke 24:21). He wouldn't even need to bear a weapon. A miraculous wave of the hand or a simple word from his mouth would suffice.

Christ displayed this preternatural power in his resurrection. One day he will employ it with even greater force (Rev. 19:11–21). We get a foretaste of it in the garden of Gethsemane when Jesus' enemies fell backward before the peculiar gust that erupted from a simple utterance by which he identified himself as the venerable I AM (John 18:6).[3] "John pictures a scene in the gloom of the garden, imperfectly lit by the torches carried by the arresting posse. But instead of the terrified fugitive they expected would be hiding in the shadowy recesses of the garden, the soldiers find themselves confronted by a majestic figure who advances to meet them and addresses them in the language of deity."[4]

2. See Martin Hengel, *Crucifixion* (Philadelphia: Fortress Press, 1977).
3. Jesus' statement in reference to the query about his identity as "Jesus the Nazarene" (John 18:4–5 NLT) uses the emphatic form of "I am" in the Greek—*ego eimi*. This is a direct claim to deity (cf. Ex. 3:14) and in this case appears to have carried with it a supernatural force that literally knocked the party off its feet. See Leon Morris, *Jesus Is the Christ: Studies in the Theology of John* (Grand Rapids: Eerdmans, 1989), 107–25.
4. Morris, *Jesus Is the Christ*, 125.

The power of the resurrection and the subsequent glory that Christ exhibits in his ascension and return tell us that more than just incarnation and kenosis (self-emptying) are involved in the work of redemption. The defeat of evil employs both unconventional power through weakness and abject suffering displayed in Christ's death, and also conventional power via blunt and traumatic force during the resurrection and Christ's second coming.

When we consider where the roots of redemption lie, however, we are inevitably drawn to Christ's atoning death. And the primary metaphors used in Scripture to portray the atonement conjure images of defeat and weakness. For example, Isaiah 53 describes the Messiah as the Suffering Servant: a "man of sorrows" (v. 3), "despised" (v. 3), "stricken, smitten by God, and afflicted" (v. 4), "pierced" (v. 5), "crushed" (v. 5), "oppressed" (v. 7), and the "lamb that is led to the slaughter" (v. 7). But we should not allow these humiliating descriptors to eclipse other imagery in Scripture that pictures Christ in his atonement as a warrior-king triumphing in battle, not as a vanquished sacrificial lamb.

CHRISTUS VICTOR

This triumphant aspect of Christ's atoning death is known as *Christus Victor*, a term that Gustaf Aulén revived with his important work of that title in 1931.[5] This metaphor serves as a bridge between Christ's humiliation and exaltation. While death marks the work of redemption that Christ accomplished during his first coming, *Christus Victor* as a descriptor of that atoning work begins to hint more directly at the raw power that Christ's broader (cosmic) work of redemption employs in his resurrection and second coming.

This is how Aulén defines the motif: "Christ—Christus Victor—fights against and triumphs over the evil powers of the world, the 'tyrants' under which mankind is in bondage and suffering, and in Him God reconciles the world to Himself."[6] *Christus Victor* speaks primarily of the victory over evil that Christ's death secured, but it also encompasses the triumph over death that Christ's resurrection secured (Eph. 1:19–21), the establishment of Christ's lordship in his exaltation (Phil. 2:9–11), and the final triumph over evil forces that will occur at his second coming (1 Cor. 15:24–26).

Metaphors of the Atonement

While Aulén has drawn necessary attention to this important perspective on the atonement, it needs to be seen in context with other ways in which

---

5. Gustaf Aulén, *Christus Victor: An Historical Study of the Three Main Types of the Idea of Atonement*, trans. A. G. Herbert (New York: Macmillan, 1969).

6. Aulén, *Christus Victor*, 4.

Scripture envisions Christ's atoning work, especially penal substitution.[7] Henri Blocher has identified five key metaphors used in Scripture to circumscribe the atonement:[8]

(1) "It was a *sacrifice* of *atoning*... value and efficacy." The extensive Old Testament paradigm of sacrificial shedding of blood in Israel's worship is the background here.

(2) "It was a *judicial execution*, and infliction of penalty (capital punishment)." This emphasizes that the atonement is essentially a judicial or forensic act satisfying the demands against sin set forth by God as Lawgiver and Judge. This stands behind the sacrificial metaphor.

(3) "It was a payment of a *ransom* that *redeems* beneficiaries 'unto freedom.'" Here the seminal exodus event in the Old Testament is the background. It speaks to what was necessary to free slaves from oppressive conditions and wicked overlords and to reconcile them to their rightful Lord, Yahweh.

(4) "Consequently, it was the *victory* won by the Lion-Lamb over the Enemy, the whole power of evil." Here God is seen as a warrior who wages warfare against various dark forces to secure victory for his people.[9] This is where we get the *Christus Victor* motif.

(5) Finally, "synthetically, it was the true *Passover*." The Passover metaphor pulls all the images together. The paschal lamb employs sacrificial and judicial aspects of the atonement (#1 and #2) together with the ransom/redemptive aspects (#3). Passover celebrates the exodus and reminded Israel of how Yahweh went before her as a victorious Deliverer (#4), rescuing her from oppression (Ex. 14:13–14).[10]

Each facet of atonement enhances our understanding of the whole. Taken together, Scripture envisions the atoning work of Christ as a kingly victory over evil (i.e., sin, Satan, the world, the creational curse, and death) by *means of* (through) his bloody death. "The motifs of conquest and victory

---

7. For an assessment of Aulén's work and its significant shortcomings, see Michael J. Ovey, "Appropriating Aulén? Employing *Christus Victor* Models of the Atonement," *Churchman* 124.4 (2010): 297–330.

8. Henri Blocher, "Biblical Metaphors and the Doctrine of the Atonement," *JETS* 47.4 (2004): 629–30.

9. Passages that picture God as a warrior include Ex. 14:13–14; 15:3; Judg. 5:4–5; 1 Sam. 17:45–47; Pss. 2:1–12; 89:8–10; 110:1–7; Isa. 42:13; 63:1–4; Dan. 7:13–14; Zech. 14:3; Rev. 19:11. See Tremper Longman III and Daniel G. Reid, *God Is a Warrior* (Grand Rapids: Zondervan, 1995).

10. Robert A. Peterson, *Salvation Accomplished by the Son* (Wheaton, IL: Crossway, 2012), 416. Blocher points out that Romans 3:24–26 makes use of the first four images and that Colossians 2:14–15 connects the judicial metaphor (#2) with "the vision of the Conqueror's triumph" ("Biblical Metaphors," 640). Furthermore, Hebrews 2:14–17 combines sacrificial language (#1) and traces of judicial language (#2) with the defeat of Satan (#4) ("Biblical Metaphors," 640). Thus, the various metaphors inform and complement one another.

are not alternatives to expiation, propitiation, reconciliation, satisfaction and redemption. None of these can stand alone." Nonetheless, "the cross secures its victory precisely because it expiates sin, propitiates God and ransoms the sinner."[11] Thus, penal substitution becomes the controlling metaphor of the atonement—the means by which the King secures victory.[12] All other images and metaphors lose their significance without penal substitution at the center.[13] Michael Horton emphasizes the *Christus Victor* theme this way:

> Sacrificial, judicial, and economic images of Christ's atoning work combine with those of the battlefield. Christ's cross is a *military conquest*. Christ is King not only in his resurrection and ascension but already at the cross—precisely at the place where Satan and his principalities and powers of death thought that they had triumphed. The event that in the eyes of the world appears to display God's weakness and the failure of Jesus to establish his kingdom is actually God's mightiest deed in all of history.[14]

The grand protagonist of history surrendered himself to death, marking the climax of the U-shaped storyline of Scripture—creation, fall, and redemption. Christ's death and resurrection are the heroic acts by which he overcomes the principal crisis of history. Disobedience in the primordial garden needed to be overcome. The ancient serpent needed to be crushed for good. Thus, the *Christus Victor* metaphor (#4) frames Christ's atoning work in terms of the *narrative* dimension of Scripture—its overall redemptive plotline. But the *theological* significance of Christ's atoning work is carried by the sacrificial and judicial metaphors (#1, #2, and #5), which tells us that Christ's death is primarily an atoning sacrifice that satisfies God's holy and righteous demands against the sin that violated his character, justice, and design for humankind and secures a people for himself. That atoning sacrifice ransoms sinners (metaphor #3) from sin and death. It frees them from God's wrath and from languishing under Satan's grip.[15]

11. Donald Macleod, *Christ Crucified: Understanding the Atonement* (Downers Grove, IL: InterVarsity Press, 2014), 239–40.

12. Jeremy R. Treat, *The Crucified King: Atonement and Kingdom in Biblical and Systematic Theology* (Grand Rapids: Zondervan, 2014), 193; Sinclair R. Ferguson, "Christus Victor et Propitiator: The Death of Christ, Substitute and Conqueror," in *For the Fame of God's Name: Essays in Honor of John Piper*, ed. Sam Storms and Justin Taylor (Wheaton, IL: Crossway, 2010), 185.

13. Treat, *Crucified King*, 189.

14. Michael Horton, *The Christian Faith: A Systematic Theology for Pilgrims on the Way* (Grand Rapids: Zondervan Academic, 2011), 500.

15. In this sense, the ransom metaphor (#3) serves as a kind of bridge between the narrative focus of the victory metaphor (#4) (*Christus Victor*) and the theological focus of the sacrificial-judicial metaphor (#1 and #2).

From Crisis to Victory

The crisis of disobedience in Eden resulted in humanity's enslavement to sin (John 8:34). Furthermore, "the whole world" now "lies in the power of the evil one" (1 John 5:19). Yet the anticipation of victory over evil was already declared in Eden before the infestation started spreading across the cursed landscape. The Seed of Eve was prophesied to crush the head of the serpent (Gen. 3:15). The critical movement toward victory occurred in another garden—the garden of Gethsemane, where Christ began to ingest the cup of divine wrath and suffering.

The conflict of the ages started at one tree—the Tree of the Knowledge of Good and Evil (Gen. 2:9)—and was resolved on the cursed tree (Gal. 3:13) to which the Seed of Eve was nailed. Christ's heel was crushed by those nails, which ironically proved to be the decisive blow to Satan's head. Death begot victory. Thus, every believer can confidently declare that God "has delivered us from the domain of darkness and transferred us to the kingdom of his beloved Son, in whom we have redemption, the forgiveness of sins" (Col. 1:13–14; cf. Acts 26:18).

Colossians 2:13–15 demonstrates how victory was achieved for this vast host of sinners trapped by sin and Satan but rescued by God and grace:

> And you, who were dead in your trespasses and the uncircumcision of your flesh, God made alive together with him, having forgiven us all our trespasses, by canceling the record of debt that stood against us with its legal demands. This he set aside, nailing it to the cross. He disarmed the rulers and authorities and put them to open shame, by triumphing over them in him.

The means by which satanic "rulers and authorities" are "disarmed" is through Christ's "canceling the debt" incurred by sinners against the "legal demands" of God.[16] That debt was paid by "nailing it to the cross."

Paul indicates two conflicts in the drama of redemption. There is conflict between humanity and Satan, but that conflict is preceded by the more serious conflict between humanity and God. Being severed from the blessedness of God results in being joined to the power of Satan. Jeremy Treat states, "If the God-human problem is the root of the Satan-human problem, then resolving the former must be the means of dealing with the latter. How is Satan defeated? Christ defeats Satan (*Christus Victor*) by removing the

---

16. On the identity of "rulers and authorities" as evil angelic hosts, see Clinton E. Arnold, *The Colossian Syncretism* (Grand Rapids: Baker, 1996), 158–94.

ground of Satan's accusation, which Jesus does by paying the penalty for sin (penal substitution)."[17]

The Triumph of Substitutionary Atonement

So, then, *Christus Victor* ceases to be victory without penal substitutionary atonement.[18] The New Testament consistently links Christ's triumph over evil and satanic powers by means of his atoning sacrifice on the cross. Paul gives a clear expression of this when he says that Christ "gave himself for our sins to deliver us from the present evil age" (Gal. 1:4). In John 12:31, Jesus indicates that "the ruler of this world [will] be cast out." How? By Christ's being "lifted up from the earth" on a cross (vv. 32–33).

But there is more here. Jesus' being "lifted up" has a double sense. It speaks of being lifted up on the cross, but also of being lifted to the place of victory through his resurrection and ascension. D. A. Carson explains, "When Jesus was glorified, 'lifted up' to heaven by means of the cross, enthroned, then too was Satan dethroned."[19] Thus, Christ established his reign as King while being nailed to the cursed tree.[20]

In Colossians 1, our rescue from "the domain of darkness" is connected to our "redemption, the forgiveness of sins" (vv. 13–14). This redemptive work is later said to be part of God's plan "through" Christ "to reconcile to himself all things." Reconciliation means being at peace with God; *shalom* is the goal of our rescue. Jesus makes this "peace by the blood of his cross" (v. 20; cf. vv. 21–22).

In 1 John 3:8, the apostle explains, "The reason the Son of God appeared was to destroy the works of the devil" (cf. John 12:31; 16:11). This is linked to another reason why the Son of God "appeared" in 1 John 3:5—so that he would "take away sins." Thus, John connects expiation of sin (cf. 1 John 4:10) with destroying (judging) the works of the devil, both occurring by the appearance of Christ as he makes his way to Mount Doom, where he allows himself to be fastened to those dreaded beams of deadly torture.[21] In short order, Satan is conquered "by the blood of the Lamb" (Rev. 12:11).[22]

---

17. Treat, *Crucified King*, 204. See also Peterson, *Salvation Accomplished by the Son*, 445–46.

18. Treat, *Crucified King*, 204–5.

19. D. A. Carson, *The Gospel according to John* (Grand Rapids: Eerdmans, 1991), 443.

20. Psalm 96:10 declares, "The LORD [Yahweh] reigns." Early Latin versions of the psalm added: "from the cross" (Allan Harman, *Psalms*, vol. 2, *Psalms 73–150* [Fearn, Ross-shire, Scotland: Mentor, 2011], 702).

21. Richard A. Shenk, *The Wonder of the Cross: The God Who Uses Evil and Suffering to Destroy Evil and Suffering* (Eugene, OR: Pickwick Publications, 2013), 203.

22. Ferguson, "Christus Victor et Propitiator," 181.

Hebrews 2:14–15 indicates that Christ's death defeats not only Satan but also the power that he holds sway over—death: "Since therefore the children share in flesh and blood, [Jesus] himself likewise partook of the same things, that through death he might destroy the one who has the power of death, that is, the devil, and deliver all those who through fear of death were subject to lifelong slavery." Sinclair Ferguson points to the wonderful implications for the believer:

> Our deepest fear, the fear of death, is a mother phobia which gives birth to all the phobias of life. . . . The angst of man, and many of the spiritual neuroses of our day, must therefore be analyzed in these terms as aspects and symptoms of bondage to Satan, or as aspects of his malevolent efforts to hinder Christian believers and to rob them of their joy in Christ. . . . Christ is not offered to us in the gospel as a panacea for our fears. But he is a deliverer from that bondage to Satan which engenders the fear of death and gives rise to all manner of other fears.[23]

Putting Sin and Satan in Perspective

The sacrificial-judicial orientation in which Scripture situates the atonement places Christ's victory over the forces of evil in perspective. We dare not emphasize the defeat of *satanic powers* at the expense of Christ's defeat of *human sin*. Bondage to Satan has resulted from rebellion against God.[24] Sin is not primarily the result of Satan's assault on our parents, Adam and Eve. Scripture lays the primary emphasis on Adam's disobedience to God (Rom. 5:12). He is not an innocent victim of Satan's evil, but a willing participant in a plot to overthrow God's authority. Satan is certainly an accessory to Adam's crimes. He is the supervillain in a multifaceted story and must be defeated.

But he only draws attention to the real problem—the problem of sin that has ruined humankind's relationship with its Creator, Possessor, and Lord. Pain, suffering, guilt, and shame together with universal physical and spiritual corruption and death in the cosmos have resulted from the crisis of *human* rebellion. This is the problem that Christ is uniquely suited to remedy as the theanthropic Mediator between God and man (1 Tim. 2:5).

Jeremy Treat writes:

> A fractured relationship between God and humanity results in the shattered *shalom* of creation. The movement of corruption is not from cosmos to community, but from community to cosmos. . . . People are victims *and*

---

23. Ferguson, "Christus Victor et Propitiator," 187.
24. Treat, *Crucified King*, 198.

violators. . . . [They] are in bondage to Satan *because* they have rejected God as king; they are in the kingdom of Satan *because* they have been banished from the kingdom of God. . . . Bondage to Satan *is a result* of enmity with God.[25]

Satan and his demonic hordes are never redeemed from their rebellion. Their fall from the pristine conditions of their initial creation has never engendered the gracious response that God extended to humans created in his image. Adam and Eve are the principal focus of the creation narratives in Genesis 1–3. Mankind (Heb. *adam*) and his relationship to the Creator are always the central focus of Scripture's plotline. Angels and demons always occupy the periphery. They are always accessories to a larger story. Satan is consigned throughout history to play nothing more than the role of adversary. There is no redemption in his future. He is afforded no possibility of repenting of his own rebellion. No grace. No mercy. Only judgment (Matt. 25:41).

Satan occupies the periphery in another way as well. Amazingly, Scripture always points to God as the one who pays the price demanded by redemption (Acts 20:28). This accords with the broader theocentric focus of reality. Humans are not the center of the story either. They are not the protagonists. Ultimately, we belong not to ourselves, to the world, or to Satan . . . but to God (1 Cor. 6:19–20).[26] Sin separates us from God and locks us up in a dungeon claimed by the world and Satan.

Yet the price for release is paid *to* God and *by* God. The blood of Christ is offered as a ransom, not to Satan, but to God (Heb. 9:14). Macleod notes:

> This immediately creates a paradox, particularly if we view the atonement as exclusively a divine act: God pays the price of redemption, and God pays it to himself. But a similar paradox applies to every aspect of the atonement. In expiation, God covers ours sins from himself; in propitiation, God appeases himself; in reconciliation, God makes peace with himself. Now, in redemption, God himself meets the cost of liberating moral and spiritual debtors, and he pays it to himself, because it is to himself the debt is owed.[27]

Our rescue from sin and Satan cost the Son of God dearly, but it offered no benefit to Satan. Rather, Christ's death ensured the devil's full and final demise, which only increases the glory that God receives in this costly act of redemption.

25. Treat, *Crucified King*, 198–99.
26. Macleod, *Christ Crucified*, 232.
27. Macleod, *Christ Crucified*, 235.

CHRIST THE RESURRECTED KING

The Christian hope of Christ's defeat over sin, death, cosmic corruption, and the devil would be a complete fiction if the bloody figure of Christ's crucified body had remained on the cross. The symbol of the Christian faith can by no means be a crucifix.[28] It must be an empty cross. But it cannot merely be an empty cross. Christ's victory at the cross would ring hollow if his body had undergone uninterrupted decay as it lay lifelessly on the cold stone platform of his tomb.

As John MacArthur proclaimed, without the resurrection Jesus' "death becomes the heroic death of a noble martyr, the pathetic death of a madman, or the execution of a fraud."[29] Thus, the symbol of Christianity and its hope-giving proclamation must be an *empty cross* accompanied by an *empty sepulchre* with light bursting forth from its bowels. "Only the resurrection transforms the cross from a symbol of despair to a symbol of hope."[30]

The Historical and Theological Significance of the Resurrection

This explains why Paul is at great pains to say, "If Christ has not been raised, then our preaching is in vain and your faith is in vain" (1 Cor. 15:14). He tells the Corinthian believers that if they have such empty faith in a nonempty tomb, then such faith "is futile and you are still in your sins. Then those also who have fallen asleep in Christ have perished. If in Christ we have hope in this life only, we are of all people most to be pitied" (vv. 17–19). George Ladd explains the significance of Paul's claims:

> If Christ is not risen from the dead, the long course of God's redemptive acts to save his people ends in a dead-end street, in a tomb. If the resurrection of Christ is not reality, then we have no assurance that God is the living God, for death has the last word. Faith is futile because the object of that faith has not vindicated himself as the Lord of life. Christian faith is then incarcerated in the tomb along with the final and highest self-revelation of God in Christ—if Christ is indeed dead.[31]

Ladd acknowledges that the truth claims of the Christian faith are *historical* claims. The truth about salvation is not merely about what Jesus *taught*,

---

28. Adrian Warnock, *Raised with Christ: How the Resurrection Changes Everything* (Wheaton, IL: Crossway, 2010), 29.

29. John MacArthur, *Acts 1–12*, MacArthur New Testament Commentary (Chicago: Moody Press, 1994), 64.

30. MacArthur, *Acts 1–12*, 64.

31. George Eldon Ladd, *A Theology of the New Testament*, rev. ed. (Grand Rapids: Eerdmans, 1993), 354.

but about who he *is* and what he came to *do*. Redemption is embodied in a dramatic narrative centered on Christ as the grand protagonist who descends to the grave and rises again.

Ladd writes, "God did not make himself known through a system of teaching nor a theology nor a book, but through a series of events recorded in the Bible. The coming of Jesus of Nazareth was the climax of this series of redemptive events; and his resurrection is the event that validates all that came before."[32] Thus, the resurrection must be a literal, bodily, and historically verifiable fact in real time and space or there is no redemption.[33]

The resurrection, however, is more than a historical fact. The interpretation of its facticity is of vital importance. When God raised Jesus from the dead, he placed his stamp of approval on the meritorious work of the cross. The resurrection vindicates every atoning deed that Christ accomplished on the cross to satisfy God's demands necessary for the reconciliation of sinners to himself and their redemption from the curse of sin and death and the devil and the whole panoply of corruptions that have marred this present existence in the cosmos.

Thus, the cross and the resurrection are inseparable components of the gospel, as Paul makes clear in 1 Corinthians 15:1–8. "Now I would remind you, brothers, of the gospel . . . that Christ died for our sins . . . , that he was buried, [and] that he was raised on the third day" (vv. 1, 3, 4). Whenever the New Testament speaks of the cross, the empty tomb is in the background. When it speaks of the resurrection, the cross is in the foreground.[34]

> The perfect life, obedient death, and life-giving resurrection of Jesus should be thought of as one saving work—a combined and inseparable act of God. It is only through the life, death, and resurrection of Jesus that salvation is possible. There is a single complete arc of movement down through incarnation, death, and burial and then up through resurrection, ascension, and enthronement.[35]

32. Ladd, *Theology of the New Testament*, 354.

33. For a historical defense of Christ's resurrection, see Gary R. Habermas and Michael R. Licona, *The Case for the Resurrection of Jesus* (Grand Rapids: Kregel, 2004). For a more rigorous defense, see N. T. Wright, *The Resurrection of the Son of God* (Minneapolis: Fortress Press, 2003).

34. Warnock, *Raised with Christ*, 73–78.

35. Warnock, *Raised with Christ*, 77. When Paul says, "I decided to know nothing among you except Jesus Christ and him crucified" (1 Cor. 2:2), this cannot be isolated from his focus on "preaching Jesus and the resurrection" (Acts 17:18). John Calvin saw the cross and resurrection as synecdoche. One is always implied in the use of the other. See *Institutes of the Christian Religion*, ed. John T. McNeill, trans. Ford Lewis Battles (Philadelphia: Westminster, 1960), 2.16.13.

Christ's resurrection is an integral component of the salvific work of Christ. It is pivotal in terms of understanding the whole panorama of God's saving actions via the themes of the believer's adoption (Rom. 1:3; 8:23), justification (4:25; 8:33–34), progressive sanctification (6:1–14), and glorification (1 Cor. 15:42–43, 49; Phil. 3:20–21).[36]

Note also Paul's emphasis on the burial of Jesus as part of the gospel message (1 Cor. 15:4). His burial implies a descent to the grave (Heb. *sheol*; Gr. *hades*), as the Apostles' Creed declares. Jesus descended to the nether regions of spiritual darkness in order that he might declare victory to his enemies and crush the head of Satan such that the wily old serpent is rendered powerless over those whom Christ forever redeems (1 Peter 3:18–22; cf. Gen. 3:15; Heb. 2:14–15).[37] Charles Hill indicates the significance of Jesus' descent for the believer:

> Christ descended into Hades so that you and I would not have to. Christ descended to Hades so that we might ascend to heaven. Christ entered the realm of death, the realm of the strong enemy, and came away with his keys. The keys of Death and Hades are now in our Savior's hands.[38]

The Contrasting Powers of the Cross and Resurrection

All the heroic actions of Christ to resolve the conflict of the ages involve a constellation of disparate—even polarizing—powers and effects exemplified in the contrasting achievements of his death and resurrection. The cross represents the darkest, most brooding moment in history hanging over the cosmos wherein the eternal Son of God entered abject human humiliation and displayed extraordinary weakness, especially when we consider that this is a person possessing the divine nature.

36. See Richard B. Gaffin Jr., *Resurrection and Redemption: A Study in Paul's Soteriology* (Phillipsburg, NJ: Presbyterian and Reformed, 1987), esp. 117–27.

37. See Charles E. Hill, "He Descended into Hell," *Reformed Faith & Practice* 1.2 (September 2016): 3–10, found at: https://journal.rts.edu/article/he-descended-into-hell/; Matthew Y. Emerson, "Christ's Descent to the Dead," found at: https://www.thegospelcoalition.org/essay/christs-descend-dead/; Matthew Y. Emerson, "'He Descended to the Dead': The Burial of Christ and the Eschatological Character of the Atonement," *SBJT* 19.1 (2015): 115–31, found at: https://equip.sbts.edu/publications/journals/journal-of-theology/he-descended-to-the-dead-the-burial-of-christ-and-the-eschatological-character-of-the-atonement/; Matthew Y. Emerson, *"He Descended to the Dead": An Evangelical Theology of Holy Saturday* (Downers Grove, IL: InterVarsity Press, 2019). Other passages that relate to Jesus' descent into hell include Rom. 10:7; Eph. 4:9–10; Rev. 1:18.

38. Hill, "He Descended into Hell," 10. The reference to the keys of death and Hades comes from Revelation 1:18. Jesus' "descent to hell," as the Apostles' Creed puts it, doesn't mean that he suffered the flames of hell, or that suffering souls in hell were given a second chance. See Emerson, *He Descended to the Dead*, 16, 91–97.

Three days later, the bare tomb represents the brightest, most breathtaking moment in history filling the cosmos wherein the Son of God discarded all weakness and displayed extraordinary supernatural powers over death and hell. The cross was an unexpected response to evil for the Sovereign of the universe. Defeating sin and death by one who has an immortal nature and "no sin," and who then suddenly becomes "sin" (2 Cor. 5:21) and dies, is an ironic, unexpected, unconventional, and, dare we say, subversive expression of divine wisdom and power. Foolishness is wisdom; weakness is power (1 Cor. 1:18–25).

On the other hand, the power exemplified in the resurrection is the sort of conventional show of force that we'd expect to emanate from the divine Being (Eph. 1:19–21; Phil. 3:10). The Son of God dead? Strange and unsettling. The Son of God dead forever? Not possible: "God raised him up, loosing the pangs of death, because it was not possible for him to be held by it" (Acts 2:24).

Furthermore, in the cross we see the greatest concentration of divine wrath, ironically resting on the one person in history who is truly innocent. The unmitigated wrath of the divine Father crushes his only Son (Isa. 53:5, 10). The one who was "stricken, smitten by God, and afflicted" (Isa. 53:4) is the one who is forever the object of the Father's greatest love (John 5:20). The Father orchestrates the plan of redemption, and the Son executes it through the fullness of the Spirit's power (Luke 4:1). The whole terrible and costly price of it is gladly embraced in order to shower the fullness of divine mercy on innumerable loathsome sinners.

Yet the dark, humiliating, and miserable God-forsakenness resting on the Son quickly morphs into the Father's declaration of the Son's supreme exaltation (Phil. 2:6–11) exemplified in the untold splendor pouring forth from the empty tomb. The resurrection of the Son of God is the greatest display of God's extrinsic (*ad extra*) glory (Phil. 3:21).

The peculiar glory of the cross is entirely muted without the resurrection to which the achievement of the cross is inextricably linked. Without the paradoxically conjoined glory of the shameful crucifixion and stupendous resurrection (John 12:23; 13:31), there would be no hope of future glory for the redeemed in the consummation of their redemption at the resurrection of their own bodies.

The Holistic Benefits of the Resurrection

The burden of the Edenic curse was lifted from God's elect and absorbed by Christ on the cross. "Surely he has borne our griefs and carried our sorrows" (Isa. 53:4). The curse was then heaved by the Son of God into everlasting oblivion, which became clear the moment he lifted his restored body from the shelf of the tomb. Moreover, this dissipation of the curse is no legal fiction. The resurrection has direct bearing on the lives of all saints—redeemed sinners burdened with sin, guilt, death, and decay. It has holistic benefits.

The resurrection is essential for the saints' justification (Rom. 4:24). Gaffin notes that "the eradication of death in [Christ's] resurrection is nothing less than the removal of the verdict of condemnation and the effective affirmation of his (Adamic) righteousness."[39] Consequently, "Jesus' death establishes our relationship with God by bringing about the forgiveness of sins, while his resurrection guarantees that this forgiveness is real, sufficient, and permanent."[40] Martyn Lloyd-Jones writes, "It is only in the light of the Resurrection that I ultimately know that I stand in the presence of God absolved from guilt and shame and every condemnation."[41]

Furthermore, the resurrection is essential for believers' sanctification and glorification. Paul enjoins believers to consider their union with Christ, particularly in his death, burial, and resurrection.[42] These seminal events in the life of Christ intersect the life of the believer at three focal points in redemptive history.[43]

First, somehow in the mysterious and timeless (transtemporal) providential actions of God, every person chosen "in [Christ] before the foundation of the world" (Eph. 1:4) also was located with (participated with) Christ in the spatiotemporal events of his death, burial, and resurrection wherein every single transgression that the person committed in thought, word, or deed was nailed to the cross and summarily taken away (Col. 2:13–14).[44] Commenting on Romans 6:1–14, Robert Tannehill writes, "If the believer dies and rises with Christ, as Paul claims, Christ's death and resurrection are not merely events which produce benefits for the believer, but also are events in which the believer partakes. The believer's new life is based upon his personal participation in these saving events."[45]

---

39. Gaffin, *Resurrection and Redemption*, 122.

40. Scott J. Hafemann, *The God of Promise and the Life of Faith: Understanding the Heart of the Bible* (Wheaton, IL: Crossway, 2001), 119.

41. Martyn Lloyd-Jones, *Sanctified through the Truth: The Assurance of Our Salvation* (Wheaton, IL: Crossway, 1989), 144.

42. See, for example, Rom. 6:1–14; Gal. 2:20; Eph. 2:4–7; Col. 2:12–15; 3:1–4. See also Constantine R. Campbell, *Paul and Union with Christ: An Exegetical and Theological Study* (Grand Rapids: Zondervan, 2012).

43. Gaffin, *Resurrection and Redemption*, 60. Gaffin builds on John Murray's seminal article "Definitive Sanctification," *CTJ* 2.1 (1967): 5–21, reprinted in *Collected Writings of John Murray* (Carlisle, PA: Banner of Truth, 1976), 2:277–84.

44. Campbell, *Paul and Union with Christ*, 333–43.

45. Robert C. Tannehill, *Dying and Rising with Christ: A Study in Pauline Theology* (repr., Eugene, OR: Wipf and Stock, 2006), 1. See also Gaffin, *Resurrection and Redemption*, 50.

Second, the reality of these events has an experiential and transformative impact on the believer's life at the moment the Spirit immerses the believer into the life of Christ via regeneration and conversion (Rom. 6:3–4; cf. 1 Cor. 12:13).[46] Consequently, the believer's new (resurrected) life means that he "must consider" himself "dead to sin and alive to God in Christ Jesus" (Rom. 6:11; cf. Col. 3:3). Sin is no longer our master (Rom. 6:14); rather, we must say with Paul, "I have been crucified with Christ. It is no longer I who live, but Christ who lives in me. And the life I now live in the flesh I live by faith in the Son of God, who loved me and gave himself for me" (Gal. 2:20). We are under the power of grace and righteousness (Rom. 6:12–22; cf. Eph. 4:20–24).

The resurrection of Christ is the ground and source of ongoing spiritual power. This provides the believer with hope not only for this life, but for the life to come. The temporal spiritual anguish we suffer in this present world (Rom. 7:24) is giving way to supremely *weighty* goods in the glorious world to come. Paul encourages us:

> So we do not lose heart. Though our outer self is wasting away, our inner self is being renewed day by day. For this light momentary affliction is preparing for us an eternal weight of glory beyond all comparison, as we look not to the things that are seen but to the things that are unseen. For the things that are seen are transient, but the things that are unseen are eternal. (2 Cor. 4:16–18)

Third, the resurrection of Christ in particular is a guarantee of the believer's future bodily resurrection and glorification. This present mortal pain is not the believer's destiny. Because Christ, the "firstfruits" of the resurrection (1 Cor. 15:20), conquered death, we look forward to our final victory and habitation in our *real* home in our *real* bodies: "But our citizenship is in heaven, and from it we await a Savior, the Lord Jesus Christ, who will transform our lowly body to be like his glorious body, by the power that enables him even to subject all things to himself" (Phil. 3:20–21; cf. 2 Cor. 4:14). Our redemption draws nigh. "For in this tent we groan, longing to put on our heavenly dwelling" (2 Cor. 5:2). Paul believed that

---

46. Baptism in Romans 6:3–4 is to be taken not as the literal baptismal rite, but metaphorically. It is the work of the Spirit uniting believers to Christ's death and resurrection as part of his work of regenerating the believers, resulting in their conversion and new life. See Campbell, *Paul and Union with Christ*, 335–37; C. E. B. Cranfield, "Romans 6:1–14 Revisited," *Expository Times* 106 (1994): 40–41. See also discussion in G. R. Beasley-Murray, *Baptism in the New Testament* (Grand Rapids: Eerdmans, 1962), 130–38.

"the present body is corruptible, decaying and subject to death; but death, which spits in the face of the good creator God, cannot have the last word."[47]

The Cross	The Resurrection
The darkest (most brooding) moment of history that has hung over the cosmos.	The brightest (most breathtaking) moment of history that has filled the cosmos.
The display of extraordinary human weakness and death is an unexpected and unconventional means of defeating evil.	The display of extraordinary supernatural divine power is an expected and conventional (by divine standards) means of defeating evil.
The greatest concentration of God's wrath. There is no hope of future glory without the satisfaction of God's just wrath.	The greatest display of God's external (*ad extra*) glory. No glory is derived from the cross without the resurrection.
The heirs of God have died "in [with] Christ" and suffer now with him (Rom. 8:11, 16–18; cf. 6:1–14).	The heirs of God have been raised up "in [with] Christ" and will be glorified with him (Rom. 8:11, 16–18; cf. 6:1–14).

Fig. 16.1. Contrasting the Cross and Resurrection of Christ

Our Glorious Resurrection Bodies

In 1 Corinthians 15:42–44, Paul teaches that our present body is "perishable," that is, mortal. But our new body will be "imperishable," never subject to the Edenic curse ever again (v. 42; cf. Rom. 8:11). Our present body is marked by "dishonor" and "weakness"; the new body "is raised in glory" and "power" (1 Cor. 15:43). Our present body is "natural," meaning that which is common to our present corrupted world. Our new body "is raised up a spiritual body" (v. 44). In other words, it will be animated by the power of the Holy Spirit, enabling it to be "adapted for existence in the new redeemed order of the Age to Come."[48]

---

47. Wright, *Resurrection of the Son of God*, 372.

48. George Eldon Ladd, *I Believe in the Resurrection of Jesus* (Grand Rapids: Eerdmans, 1975), 117.

This is marvelous! For our "earthly, historical experience knows nothing and has no analogy for what the New Testament says about the resurrection body."[49] The New Testament gives us every evidence that our bodies will in some ways defy and in other ways transcend any known laws of physics that mark our present world—ways that we cannot fully comprehend.[50]

Joni Eareckson Tada, a quadriplegic bound to her wheelchair most of her life, knows all too well the hope that our future bodily resurrection brings:

> I can scarcely believe it. I with shriveled, bent fingers, atrophied muscles, gnarled knees, and no feeling from the shoulders down, will one day have a new body, light, bright, and clothed in righteousness—powerful and dazzling. Can you imagine the hope this gives someone spinal cord-injured like me? Or someone who is cerebral palsied, brain-injured, or who has multiple sclerosis? Imagine the hope this gives someone who is manic depressive. No other religion, no other philosophy promises new bodies, hearts and minds. Only in the Gospel of Christ do hurting people find such incredible hope.[51]

Joni understands that we live with tragic suffering in this world and that the believer is not immune to it. The wounds that mark our souls are matched by pain that racks our bodies. Physical pain is the most tangible manifestation of the inglorious curse. The resurrection of Jesus Christ remedies this problem. Paul addresses this hope in Romans 8: "If the Spirit of him who raised Jesus from the dead dwells in you, he who raised Christ Jesus from the dead will also give life to your mortal bodies through his Spirit who dwells in you" (v. 11). Suffering gives way to future glory, and the Spirit will not rest until he takes us there.

> The Spirit himself bears witness with our spirit that we are children of God, and if children, then heirs—heirs of God and fellow heirs with Christ, provided we suffer with him in order that we may also be glorified with him. For I consider that the sufferings of this present time are not worth comparing with the glory that is to be revealed to us. (Rom. 8:16–18)

Everything groans until that day comes (Rom. 8:22).

49. Ladd, *I Believe in the Resurrection of Jesus*, 123.
50. For more on what Paul means by a "spiritual body," see Wright, *Resurrection of the Son of God*, 347–56; Murray J. Harris, *From Grave to Glory: Resurrection in the New Testament* (Grand Rapids: Zondervan, 1990), 401–25. "Spiritual" does not mean "nonphysical," but rather describes a body that in some senses will be hyperphysical in the same way that Jesus' resurrected body appeared to be. See Luke 24:30–31, 43; John 20:17, 19–20, 26–27 (cf. Matt. 28:9); Acts 1:9–11. Also note the dazzling appearance of the exalted Christ depicted in Revelation 1:12–16.
51. Joni Eareckson Tada, *Heaven: Your Real Home* (Grand Rapids: Zondervan, 1995), 53.

The *Christus Victor* theme concerns not just the victory of the cross, but the victory of the resurrection over death and the curse. "The resurrection of Christ demonstrates that God can and will transform even the severest suffering into a glorious triumph."[52] Martyn Lloyd-Jones summarizes the conquering and resurrected Christ's triumph over the entrance of evil into this world:

> The Resurrection proved that he has conquered every enemy that was opposed to him, to God, and to us. He has not only satisfied the law and conquered death and the grave, he has vanquished the devil and all his forces, and hell and all the principalities and powers of evil. He has triumphed over them all, and he proves it in the Resurrection. The devil cannot hold him; death and hell cannot hold him. He has mastered them all; he has emerged on the other side. He is the Son of God, and he has completed the work which the Father had sent him to do.[53]

And so we see how the polarities and peculiarities of the cross and resurrection and the stupendous achievement of redemption they secure are uniquely designed and situated in this theo-drama so as to magnify the glory of God supremely.

CHRIST THE COMING KING

The *Christus Victor* theme also prefigures Christ's larger role as the triumphant King who is poised to return to this earth with commanding authority and power to complete his work of redemption. This is what Paul meant in Ephesians 1:10 when he spoke of the divine "plan for the fullness of time, to unite *all things* in [Christ], things in heaven and things on earth." Peter calls this the "period of restoration of *all things*" (Acts 3:21 NASB); it comes at the end of the ages, when "the former things have passed away" and the divine King commences "making *all things* new" (Rev. 21:4–5; cf. Matt. 19:28). There will be no more curse that debases our present cruel world (Rev. 22:3). Evil will forever cease to be.

Cosmic Redemption

Again, take note of how Paul envisions this comprehensive blueprint for redemption in the Christ-hymn of Colossians 1:13–20. He frames the historical-redemptive plot for the ages within the divine lordship of Christ, who

---

52. Hafemann, *God of Promise*, 120.
53. Lloyd-Jones, *Sanctified through the Truth*, 143–44.

is the "image of the invisible God" (v. 15).[54] This explains why redemption must have a cosmic scope, as indicated by Paul's repeated use of "all things" throughout the hymn.[55] If Christ is the Lord of all creation, then he must be an all-encompassing Redeemer. Paul affirms Christ as the Creator of *all things*," which includes all things "in heaven and on earth, visible and invisible, whether thrones or dominions or rulers or authorities" (v. 16).

This means that the "domain of darkness" (v. 13) has no independent power or authority apart from Christ. Believers are easily "transferred" from Satan's kingdom to "the kingdom of [God's] beloved Son, in whom we have redemption" (vv. 13–14). To emphasize Christ's lordship, Paul reiterates that *all things* were created through him and for him" (v. 16).

Christ is the beginning of all things coming into existence and the end for which they were created (cf. John 1:1–3; Heb. 1:2; 2:10). As if his point were not already clear, Paul continues, "And he is before *all things*, and in him *all things* hold together" (Col. 1:17). Christ as a member of the eternally existent Godhead is the precondition for all created reality, and in him, as the fundamental source of all power, this reality (all things) is continually sustained (cf. Heb. 1:3).

In Colossians 1:18, Paul emphasizes Christ's preeminence in the church and then goes on to demonstrate the same point he made in Ephesians 1:10. Colossians 1:19–20 declares: "For in him all the fullness of God was pleased to dwell, and through him to reconcile to himself *all things*, whether on earth or in heaven, making peace by the blood of his cross." When Adam fell, the creation fell with him and experienced alienation from the Creator. The Son of God would not be the eternal Lord, Creator, Possessor, and Sustainer of all things (at the pleasure of the Father) if, when all things fell, he did not restore them to their rightful place. Christ is the Creator of everything and therefore the Restorer of everything once it succumbed to futility (cf. Rom. 8:20).

It is clear that "the blood of his cross" is the ground of this work of reconciling all things to the Father and restoring *shalom* (peace) to a chaotic cosmos.[56] This peace pacifies demonic forces and renews what the curse ruined.[57] The work of Christ as the Lamb grounds his crowning achievement of redemption at the cross in his later work as the risen and conquering Lion. The incongruous combination of cross and crown cannot but coexist in this all-encompassing kingdom of Christ.

---

54. See Arnold, *Colossian Syncretism*, 246–70.

55. "All things" (*ta panta*) is used six times in Colossians 1:15–20.

56. Graham A. Cole, *God the Peacemaker: How Atonement Brings Shalom* (Downers Grove, IL: InterVarsity Press, 2009), 20–21.

57. F. F. Bruce, "Christ as Conqueror and Reconciler," *Bibliotheca Sacra* 141.4 (1984): 293.

Cosmic Judgment

Salvation in Scripture always comes in the context of judgment.[58] God graciously rescues Noah through a cataclysmic flood that destroys the world. God rescues Lot while raining fire on Sodom and Gomorrah. He rescues his people Israel by a watery escape while drowning their captors in the Red Sea. This typifies the broader judgment of Egypt via the plagues and set up the exodus paradigm for subsequent motifs of salvation in Scripture.[59] Yahweh brings judgment on the wicked Canaanites in order to bring his people into the promised land.

These motifs of judgment ultimately typify the judgment found in the cross. There, God's judgment rightly reserved for sinners falls on Christ so that an elect people may be saved through his bearing their condemnation in their stead. Likewise, his reception of divine wrath ironically serves as judgment on satanic principalities and powers that hold sinners in their power.

But salvation through judgment does not terminate on the cross. The cross frees elect sinners from their bondage to sin, the world, and Satan, but the cross does not eliminate every last vestige of evil. In fact, it brings salvation to only a few. Jesus urges, "Enter by the narrow gate. For the gate is wide and the way is easy that leads to destruction, and those who enter by it are many. For the gate is narrow and the way is hard that leads to life, and those who find it are few" (Matt. 7:13–14).

The world is sadly populated with a vast number of people—some religious and moralistic, others blasphemous and openly immoral, and a great many others who are indifferent and self-satisfied. All of them have spurned the mercies of God and rejected the narrow gate. They have heeded the ill-conceived counsels of their demonic enablers, knowingly or not. A dreadful end awaits both categories of debased creatures. The satanic host will meet their final destruction in the eternal hellfire that has been their destiny from the beginning (25:41). Then the unbelieving world of humanity will descend after them into the same harrowing destination of misery and torment.

Paul speaks of these final acts of judgment in 1 Corinthians 15:24–26 in epic kingdom language: "Then comes the end, when [Christ] delivers the kingdom to God the Father after destroying every rule and every authority and power. For he must reign until he has put all his enemies under his feet.

58. See James M. Hamilton Jr., *God's Glory in Salvation through Judgment: A Biblical Theology* (Wheaton, IL: Crossway, 2010).

59. See R. Michael Fox, ed., *Reverberations of the Exodus in Scripture* (Eugene, OR: Pickwick Publications, 2014); Alastair J. Roberts and Andrew Wilson, *Echoes of Exodus: Tracing Themes of Redemption through Scripture* (Wheaton, IL: Crossway, 2018); Bryan D. Estelle, *Echoes of Exodus: Tracing a Biblical Motif* (Downers Grove, IL: InterVarsity Press, 2018).

The last enemy to be destroyed is death." *Christus Victor* is not confined to the work of the cross but extends to the royal reign of Christ in the advent of his earthly kingdom whereby every human and angelic creature arrayed against the King of kings is put in subjection to his authority and justice.[60] Finally, Christ will abolish death itself, that enemy who has no friend.

When the Messiah steps foot on the earth again at the end of the age, its inhabitants will not find a lowly babe who was laid in a manger. Those who refuse to repent of their corruption, wallowing in a stew of angry rebellion, will not encounter a meek and mild Lamb. Rather, they will gaze up into the sky and "the sun will be darkened, and the moon will not give its light, and the stars will fall from heaven, and the powers of the heavens will be shaken. Then will appear in heaven the sign of the Son of Man, and then all the tribes of the earth will mourn, and they will see the Son of Man coming on the clouds of heaven with power and great glory" (Matt. 24:29–30; cf. Rev. 6:12–13).

The apostle John presents a similar vision during the opening of the sixth seal:

> The sky vanished like a scroll that is being rolled up, and every mountain and island was removed from its place. Then the kings of the earth and the great ones and the generals and the rich and the powerful, and everyone, slave and free, hid themselves in the caves and among the rocks of the mountains, calling to the mountains and rocks, "Fall on us and hide us from the face of him who is seated on the throne, and from the wrath of the Lamb, for the great day of their wrath has come, and who can stand?" (Rev. 6:14–17)

The Lamb of God sacrificed his life to absorb his Father's wrath against sin at his first coming. But at his second coming, the Lamb will launch his own wrath—a divine fury hitherto unknown to mankind and the principalities

---

60. I subscribe to a premillennial eschatology (doctrine of last things), which believes that Christ will return after the present evil age and establish a literal thousand-year reign of peace on earth. See John MacArthur and Richard Mayhue, eds., *Christ's Prophetic Plans: A Futuristic Premillennial Primer* (Chicago: Moody Publishers, 2012); Michael J. Vlach, *He Will Reign Forever: A Biblical Theology of the Kingdom of God* (Silverton, OR: Lampion Press, 2016). This eschatological perspective, however, is not essential to the greater-glory theodicy. The two other major eschatological views are amillennialism (i.e., we are in the millennial reign of Christ now, at the end of which he will return for the church) and postmillennialism (i.e., the present age will end with a thoroughly Christianized time of peace and gospel prosperity, after which Christ will return for the church). For a defense of amillennialism, see Sam Storms, *Kingdom Come: The Amillennial Alternative* (Fearn, Ross-shire, Scotland: Christian Focus, 2013); Kim Riddlebarger, *A Case for Amillennialism: Understanding the End Times*, expanded ed. (Grand Rapids: Baker, 2013). For a defense of postmillennialism, see Keith A. Mathison, *Postmillennialism: An Eschatology of Hope* (Phillipsburg, NJ: P&R Publishing, 1999).

and powers of this present darkness. It is not the diluted anger of God expressed in previous ages. It is "the wine of God's wrath, poured full strength into the cup of his anger" (Rev. 14:10). The image here comes from the fact that wine in biblical days was largely diluted with water, reducing its alcoholic potency. This wine is full strength.[61] It will cause everyone who drinks it to stagger wildly like psychotic brutes (cf. Isa. 51:17, 21–22).

The judgment of Satan and his host of wicked minions comes in stages. In Revelation 20, at the beginning of Christ's millennial reign, the apostle John explains what will transpire:

> Then I saw an angel coming down from heaven, holding in his hand the key to the bottomless pit and a great chain. And he seized the dragon, that ancient serpent, who is the devil and Satan, and bound him for a thousand years, and threw him into the pit, and shut it and sealed it over him, so that he might not deceive the nations any longer, until the thousand years were ended. (Rev. 20:1–3)[62]

At the end of the millennial kingdom, "Satan will be released from his prison . . . to deceive the nations" once again (Rev. 20:7–8). But his short-lived rebellion will be futile. As John relates, "Fire came down from heaven and consumed" his rebel force, "and the devil who had deceived them was thrown into the lake of fire and sulfur where the beast and the false prophet were, and they will be tormented day and night forever and ever" (vv. 9–10). The nastiest villains of history—antagonists of divine goodness and truth—who conjure the most revolting and terrifying examples of fear, deception, manipulation, tyranny, cruelty, hate, and violence—these will have absolutely no power to resist their fatal demise.

And neither will the rest of those whose names are "not found written in the book of life" (Rev. 20:15). The whole of unredeemed humanity will stand before the "great white throne" in a scene that evokes panic. No more mercy will issue forth from the One seated on the throne. Rather, "From his presence earth and sky fled away, and no place was found for them" (v. 11). Every last unrepentant sinner, "great and small," will be judged and "thrown into the lake of fire" (vv. 12, 15). Then "Death and Hades" themselves will

---

61. See D. A. Carson, *The God Who Is There: Finding Your Place in God's Story* (Grand Rapids: Baker, 2010), 206–7.

62. For a defense of a premillennial understanding of Revelation 20, see Matthew Waymeyer, *Revelation 20 and the Millennial Debate* (The Woodlands, TX: Kress Christian Publications, 2004). For an amillennial interpretation, see Storms, *Kingdom Come*, 423–74. For a postmillennial interpretation, see Mathison, *Postmillennialism*, 139–62. See also Darrell L. Bock, ed., *Three Views on the Millennium and Beyond* (Grand Rapids: Zondervan, 1999).

be consumed in the everlasting abode of doom (v. 14). Nothing will ever escape this black hole of torment and misery.

Cosmic Glory in Judgment

Many find this stark picture of eternal judgment preceded by Christ's returning as a fearsome sword-wielding warrior disconcerting, to say the least. The apostle John casts a radically different light on the apocalyptic Lamb in the book of Revelation than the sacrificial Lamb he portrays in his Gospel (e.g., John 1:29, 36). "Lamb" is used twenty-eight times, and yet the image is decidedly not that of a docile animal (e.g., Rev. 6:16; 7:17; 14:10).[63] Ironically, Revelation presents Christ and his acts as "awesomely powerful," but he "executes these acts of justice, power and authority *as the Lamb slain*. If a symbol of power were wanted, the more 'fitting' Lion of the tribe of Judah lay close at hand [Rev. 5:5] . . . . But strikingly, this title does not reappear in the book!"[64]

Christ is the Lion-Lamb, and the incongruity presented in this strange identity raises the question: how can the familiar image of our tender, suffering Savior morph into one "clothed in a robe dipped in blood"—and that not of his own (Rev. 19:13)? Rather, as one who "judges and makes war . . . , he will tread the winepress of the fury of the wrath of God the Almighty" (vv. 11, 15). The blood of the Lamb's terrible suffering will give way to immaculate garments that he will stain with the blood of his enemies so that the birds of the air can feast on their flesh (vv. 17–18; cf. 14:20).[65]

There is no question that the warrior-king archetype (more commensurate with lion imagery) presents a glorious, albeit conventional, image of a victor; and no one exceeds the glory of the apocalyptic Lamb (Lion) unveiled in the Revelation of John. But given the thesis of the greater-glory theodicy, how does this final act of the Messiah enhance the glory of the Lamb crucified? Does it not present us with a radically conflicting image that in the end diminishes the grace and glory of the cross?

Kevin Diller raises a difficult question for any theodicy embracing *felix culpa* (the fortunateness of the fall): in a world where the fall and its disastrous

---

63. Charles E. Hill, "Atonement in the Apocalypse of John," in *The Glory of the Atonement*, ed. Charles E. Hill and Frank A. James III (Downers Grove, IL: InterVarsity Press, 2004), 196–97.

64. Hill, "Atonement in the Apocalypse of John," 199.

65. Note other contrasts in Scripture between Christ as Lion and Lamb. He will not break a bruised reed (Isa. 42:3), yet he will break (rule) the nations with a rod of iron (Ps. 2:9; cf. Rev. 19:15). He is killed by the wicked (Isa. 53:8), but then the wicked will be killed by him (11:4). He did not open his mouth when judged (53:7), yet he strikes the earth with the sword of his mouth (11:4; cf. Rev. 19:15).

aftermath become necessary for greater redemptive goods, to whom do these goods accrue? Obviously, only to those who are redeemed, not to those who are eternally condemned.[66] Many suppose that if the greater mass of humanity is committed to eternal perdition, then it propels us not toward the beatific vision, but to what Lewis's Screwtape calls the "Miserific Vision."[67] Diller argues that *felix culpa* would make sense only if universal salvation (universalism) held true.[68]

Walls and Dongell agree: "If God chooses not to save many, perhaps even most, persons who are born into sin and thereby consigns them to eternal misery, how can this be a greater good than determining everyone freely to do right from the beginning?"[69] It would appear to make better sense if there had never been sin and the fall in the first place. They continue: "If many are far worse off, indeed infinitely worse off, as a result of the Fall—it is difficult to see how the Fall can be seen as a fortunate crime. Moreover, it is most difficult to see how God could be good in any ordinary sense of the term if he ordained or allowed the Fall knowing that it would have such consequences."[70]

In framing a response, first, it pays to reconsider John Frame's important insight: "So many traditional treatments of the problem [of evil] assume that God's ultimate purpose is to provide happiness for man, and that is not so. God's ultimate purpose is to glorify himself."[71] God would not be God if he placed man's happiness above his own glory. The only theodicy worthy of the name is one in which God's glory is supremely magnified.

Those who raise these objections to *felix culpa* (the greater-glory theodicy) assume that maximizing the degree of happiness for the maximum number of humans must be at the center of God's theodical goals. We have already argued that God cannot maximize his love if it means that all are loved equally and that such love comes in the absence of evil—in other words, a love that implies, at the very least, some sort of universalism.[72] Furthermore, we have argued that God's glory is magnified in both judgment and mercy. And the glory of mercy is enhanced in the face of judgment.[73]

---

66. Kevin Diller, "Are Sin and Evil Necessary for a Really Good World?," in *The Problem of Evil: Selected Readings*, ed. Michael L. Peterson, 2nd ed. (Notre Dame, IN: University of Notre Dame Press, 2017), 399.

67. C. S. Lewis, *Screwtape Letters* (New York: Macmillan, 1961), 101.

68. Diller, "Are Sin and Evil Necessary?," 399.

69. Jerry L. Walls and Joseph R. Dongell, *Why I Am Not a Calvinist* (Downers Grove, IL: InterVarsity Press, 2004), 212–13.

70. Walls and Dongell, *Why I Am Not a Calvinist*, 213. Walls and Dongell refer to *felix culpa* as a "fortunate crime," caricaturing its meaning.

71. John M. Frame, *Apologetics: A Justification of Christian Belief* (Phillipsburg, NJ: P&R Publishing, 2015), 184.

72. See chapter 13, pages 336–39.

73. See chapter 13, pages 331–36.

The severer the judgment, the sweeter the mercy. The sweeter the mercy, the greater the glory—glory certainly for the believer, but preeminently the glory magnifying the supremacy of our mighty God. Every child of God needs to be struck with this hope: the tenderness of the Messiah's grace toward us ill-deserving wretches marked by his vicarious unearthly suffering is unimaginably amplified when we ponder the alternative: that what we deserved was to stand naked before a rushing inferno of his fury. Furthermore, we must humbly consider the rare and precious value of this gift of salvation. Although God is establishing an extensive kingdom consisting of a "ransomed people . . . from every tribe and language and people and nation" (Rev. 5:9), comparatively speaking, the children of the kingdom are few in number (Matt. 7:13–14).

Pearls are highly prized because they are so rare and require extraordinary forces to fashion their exquisite beauty. We possess a "pearl of great value" (Matt. 13:46)—an inestimable treasure that came at a cost that no one but the Son of God could pay. Pardoned sinners must soberly cherish his grace, realizing that they form an uncommon company snatched from the vast throng of souls entering the wide gate to perdition. Those gates represent every sinner's justly warranted destiny. Yet here we stand, firm on the Rock of our Deliverer, having escaped "the wrath to come" (1 Thess. 1:10).

If the gate to destruction were narrow (or nonexistent) and the gate to life were wide, then the grace that saves would not be nearly so prized. It would be domesticated, expected. It would barely be recognized as grace at all. Consequently, the glory of the Savior would be diminished. If Pharaoh died of old age and Israel's taskmasters grew weary of their tormenting ways, letting their whips drop by the wayside, who would notice the escape of God's people? If the Israelites took the short and comfortable path to the promised land while the Egyptians bade them a hearty farewell, where would the glory be in their deliverance?

Suppose their slavery meant soft reprimands for resistance and frequent retreats at royal resorts on the beaches of the Nile; would they garner our sympathies? If they endured four hundred minutes of discomfort instead of four hundred long years of backbreaking toil, not even their sons and daughters would remember the exodus. This would be especially true if Yahweh had not invaded the land of Egypt with terrifying plagues of supernatural power over and over again while holding Pharaoh in the unrelenting stubbornness of his heart. God's mercy toward his people would not be nearly as exalted nor as dearly cherished.

No human being can justify the Holocaust. Its atrocities are too great to bear. And the Holocaust is only a sad reminder that throughout history, the Jews have repeatedly suffered at the hands of those who, for reasons we cannot explain, have imbibed a virulent form of hatred. Anti-Semitism is threaded throughout Jewish history.[74] The bondage of Israel typified by her four hundred years in Egypt seems to be part of the Jewish DNA. She has been marked for suffering, as many Christians have as well. During the reign of the Antichrist's terror, many followers of the Lamb will be slain for the testimony of their faith (Rev. 6:9). Their cries are similar to all the ageless cries of those who claim the God of Abraham, Isaac, and Jacob: "O Sovereign Lord, holy and true, how long before you will judge and avenge our blood on those who dwell on the earth?" (Rev. 6:10).

Yet the magnitude of suffering that the Jews have borne through the ages directly corresponds to the magnitude of the rejoicing that will erupt when the Messiah finally comes and fulfills his promises to Israel, the chosen nation of God. That day when "all Israel will be saved" and her "Deliverer" banishes "all ungodliness from Jacob" (Rom. 11:26) and judges all her oppressors will be a day of unprecedented dancing and happy tears and glory. The corporate salvation of Israel would never engender such rapturous celebration, however, if God had not allowed her to endure such prolonged pain and suffering in her history.

The national salvation of the beaten, broken, and hardened descendants of the patriarchs typifies the glory that will mark the final redemption of *all* the saints of history. Paul gives testimony to this facet of glory when he tells the believers at Thessalonica that the persecutions they have borne for their faith are not in vain. Their vindication will come soon enough:

> This is evidence of the righteous judgment of God, that you may be considered worthy of the kingdom of God, for which you are also suffering—since indeed God considers it just to repay with affliction those who afflict you, and to grant relief to you who are afflicted as well as to us,

---

74. On the general history of anti-Semitism, see Léon Poliakov, *The History of Anti-Semitism*, 4 vols. (Philadelphia: University of Pennsylvania Press, 2003); Phyllis Goldstein, *A Convenient Hatred: The History of Antisemitism* (Brookline, MA: Facing History and Ourselves, 2012). On the history of Christianity's anti-Semitism, see Michael L. Brown, *Our Hands Are Stained with Blood: The Tragic Story of the Church and the Jewish People*, rev. and expanded ed. (Shippensburg, PA: Destiny Image Publishers, 2019). For a Roman Catholic perspective, see James Carroll, *Constantine's Sword: The Church and the Jews, A History* (New York: Houghton Mifflin, 2001). For a biblical perspective on anti-Semitism, see Barry E. Horner, *Future Israel: Why Christian Anti-Judaism Must Be Challenged* (Nashville: B&H Publishing Group, 2007). See also Carl F. H. Henry's thoughts on Israel's contemporary plight and future in *God, Revelation and Authority*, vol. 6, *God Who Stands and Stays*, pt. 2 (Wheaton, IL: Crossway, 1999), 485–91.

when the Lord Jesus is revealed from heaven with his mighty angels in flaming fire, inflicting vengeance on those who do not know God and on those who do not obey the gospel of our Lord Jesus. They will suffer the punishment of eternal destruction, away from the presence of the Lord and from the glory of his might, when he comes on that day to be glorified in his saints, and to be marveled at among all who have believed, because our testimony to you was believed. (2 Thess. 1:5–10)

It is no opprobrium for beleaguered believers to anticipate their relief from suffering, especially for the cause of Christ, and to rejoice over the future justice that their persecutors will rightly bear. We *will* get our vindication from our enemies, and Christ *will* get his glory through the punishment that these enemies will receive. Christ was judged for our sin against him, and our enemies will be judged by Christ for their sin against us. Salvation is all-encompassing and comes through judgment, and Christ gets all the glory.[75]

God is glorified through judgment in a further way. We see this in Romans 5:20, where Paul paints a counterintuitive purpose for God's law: "The law came in to increase the trespass" of sinners. The law of Moses was no savior to the Jews. Likewise, God's moral law written on the heart of Gentiles (Rom. 2:14–15) is no savior to those who try to keep it. Rather, it only provokes more sin, more violation of God's holy commands, more reviling of the holy Lawgiver. Sin becomes more serious, more focused, more intent on shattering the restraints of the law.

Why would God set up conditions for this to happen? So that "grace" would abound "all the more." The moral imperatives of God provoke greater quantities and graver acts of rebellion, and this should provoke greater condemnation on the part of the Judge—and for most, it does. Yet for some, it is merely the black backdrop by which the diamonds of his grace can shine more brilliantly. God purposes to demonstrate that grace is greater than sin.

> Marvelous grace of our loving Lord,
> Grace that exceeds our sin and our guilt![76]

Sin and judgment increase so that grace superincreases. Sin can never outstrip grace. As deep as sin dives into the darkness, grace dives deeper still, rescuing recalcitrant rebels. Meth addiction, alcoholic abuse, child pornography, slavery, sex trafficking, adultery, spousal violence, torture, abortion, serial murder, genocide—nothing is beyond the reach of his deep and magnificent mercy!

75. Hamilton, *God's Glory in Salvation*, 497–98.
76. Julia H. Johnston, "Grace Greater than Our Sin" (1911).

This increasing and prolonging of transgressions and abject rebellion for the sake of magnifying the glory of grace also explains why God did not immediately destroy the devil. Just as he did not immediately wipe out Pharaoh, he allows the old serpent's slithering and wicked scheming to persist. John Piper writes, "It is strange that God, with total sovereign rights over Satan, his archenemy, would allow him to do so much harm."[77] The devil hates God and his people with a godless and incorrigible hatred. This is why history is always marked by anti-Semitic and anti-Christian sentiments.

Since there is no possibility of repentance or redemption for Satan, why not end his reign of terror before it even starts? Piper quotes 2 Corinthians 4:4: "the god of this world has blinded the minds of the unbelievers, to keep them from seeing the light of the gospel of the glory of Christ, who is the image of God." The prolonged veiling of Christ's glory by satanic deception ironically serves to magnify that glory in the end.

Piper explains:

> God's purpose is to defeat Satan in a way that glorifies not only Christ's raw power, but also his superior beauty and worth and desirability. Christ could simply exert sovereign power and snuff Satan out. That would indeed glorify Christ's power. But it would not display so clearly the superior worth of Jesus over Satan. It would not display the transforming beauty and power of Christ's meekness and humility and lowliness and self-emptying love. The aim of the gospel is to put the glory of the crucified Christ on display and to shame Satan by millions of people who "turn from darkness to light and from the power of Satan to God" (Acts 26:18) and forsake Satan's lies in preference for the beauty of Christ in the gospel.[78]

This *requires* Satan and the scourge of evil to persist throughout the ages so that grace may have a long black stage to shine that much brighter. When Christ finally consigns Satan and his fiendish hordes to the lake of fire, it will come with all the drama so powerfully typified in the long-awaited exodus of Israel. When the archvillain finally exits the stage, it will produce uproarious cheers in heaven and earth, and all will say that it was none too soon. And that is precisely how the Playwright intended everyone to respond to his script.

Martin Luther (1483–1546) understood the rejoicing that is anticipated in the devil's demise:

---

77. John Piper, *God Is the Gospel* (Wheaton, IL: Crossway, 2005), 113.
78. Piper, *God Is the Gospel*, 113–14.

And though this world, with devils filled,
Should threaten to undo us,
We will not fear, for God hath willed
His truth to triumph through us;
The Prince of Darkness grim,
We tremble not for him;
His rage we can endure,
For lo! his doom is sure;
One little word shall fell him.[79]

On that day when the messianic Conqueror utters that fatal word, felling the dark lord, then his retributive justice will be forever praised and his kingly glory supremely adored.

Cosmic Renewal

With judgment comes renewal, not just for the redeemed and vindicated children of God, but for their eternal habitation as well. The creation was made for the creature. When the creature fell, the creation fell with it (Gen. 3:17–19), making it an unsuitable place for glorified children of God to live and carry out their renewed purpose as fully restored human beings. Thus, there is a parallel work of redemption in both creature and creation. The apostle Paul explains:

> For I consider that the sufferings of this present time are not worth comparing with the glory that is to be revealed to us. For the creation waits with eager longing for the revealing of the sons of God. For the creation was subjected to futility, not willingly, but because of him who subjected it, in hope that the creation itself will be set free from its bondage to corruption and obtain the freedom of the glory of the children of God. For we know that the whole creation has been groaning together in the pains of childbirth until now. (Rom. 8:18–22)

When Adam fell, a curse descended on the created order. The cosmos was purposely "subjected to futility" (Rom. 8:20) by the sovereign Lord. The laws that governed pre-fall Eden were somehow altered, made less hospitable, lending themselves to death and decay—the "bondage to corruption" (v. 21). The world suddenly became a hostile environment, no longer the paradisiacal wonderland that God initially intended it to be. Its ground became unyielding to the plow. It produced thorns and thistles. The creature was made much

79. Martin Luther, "A Mighty Fortress Is Our God" (c. 1527–29).

weaker, more vulnerable. His body would have to sweat and toil and writhe with pain until his muscles and organs gave out. Pathogens would invade his system, and he would become diseased. His defenses against the hostile forces of nature would be compromised. The landscape would be broken by earthquakes, torched by fire, flooded with tsunamis, and blown away by tornadoes. Death would leave its mark on everything, with the whole world reduced to tears.

Shalom (peace) would be shattered.

Yet the story of redemption cannot properly end in celebration of the happily-ever-after without a happy *place* for the happily-ever-after to live and thrive. The world that produces death must itself die and be reborn, gloriously resurrected. Peter describes this death and rebirth of the cosmos at the culmination of Christ's return:

> But the day of the Lord will come like a thief, and then the heavens will pass away with a roar, and the heavenly bodies will be burned up and dissolved, and the earth and the works that are done on it will be exposed.
>
> Since all these things are thus to be dissolved, what sort of people ought you to be in lives of holiness and godliness, waiting for and hastening the coming of the day of God, because of which the heavens will be set on fire and dissolved, and the heavenly bodies will melt as they burn! But according to his promise we are waiting for new heavens and a new earth in which righteousness dwells. (2 Peter 3:10–13)

Peter does not speak of annihilation here, but rather speaks of a dissolution of the present universe—a death by fire, just as the earth experienced a death by flood in the days of Noah.[80]

Nor is Peter envisioning a story that involves absolute discontinuity between the original creation and the new creation, a completely new start from nothing. Michael Vlach illustrates how such a disjointed plotline would go:

---

80. "Pass away" (*pareleusontai*) in 2 Peter 3:10 "does not assert annihilation but rather suggests the passing of the heavens from one state of existence to another, in that their form and structure will change radically" (D. Edmond Hiebert, *Second Peter and Jude: An Expositional Commentary* [Greenville, SC: Unusual Publications, 1989], 159). Likewise, "dissolved" (*luthesetai*) indicates that the "elements" are "loosened and broken up into their component parts, like a building being torn down" (Hiebert, *Second Peter and Jude*, 159). For a fuller defense of the dissolution-and-restoration view of creation, see Michael J. Svigel, "Extreme Makeover: Heaven and Earth Edition—Will God Annihilate the World and Re-create It Ex Nihilo?," *Bibliotheca Sacra* 171. 684 (2014): 401–17; J. Richard Middleton, *A New Heaven and a New Earth: Reclaiming Biblical Eschatology* (Grand Rapids: Baker Academic, 2014), 189–200.

Creation (out of nothing) > Fall > Annihilation > Creation (out of nothing)

Rather, the apostle envisions a restoration of what was lost:

Creation > Fall > Restoration[81]

There is both continuity and discontinuity between old and new. At the resurrection, believers' bodies do not face extinction only to receive entirely new bodies created *ex nihilo* (out of nothing). Rather, their previous bodies will be restored in a glorified (perfected and immortalized) condition devoid of the corruption of the curse (1 Cor. 15:42–44, 50–54).[82] Likewise, the creation neither faces extinction nor longs for such a dire end; rather, it, too, will be renewed and glorified, a fit habitation for glorified saints (cf. Rom. 8:19).[83] The longing of creation is personified in passages such as Psalm 96:11–13 and Romans 8:22, which make no sense if extinction is anticipated.

The hope that creature and creation alike so desperately long for is a metamorphic glory—like ugly caterpillars' being transformed into beautiful butterflies.[84] Again, Vlach illustrates the parallels:

Fall of Man > Fall of Creation
Glorification of Man > Glorification of Creation[85]

The fall of the creature brings about the fall of the creation. Likewise, the glorification of the creature brings about a glorification of the creation. The created order will undergo a massive conflagration, purging it from the corruptions and miseries resulting from the fall. Then out of the molten fires of its purification, a glory will arise hitherto unseen by postfall eyes.[86]

Thus, at no point along the U-shaped (and again in this case, J-shaped) trajectory of the biblical story is the plotline severed; otherwise, Satan could claim victory and nihilism would reign.[87] There is no hope in extinction. Jesus succumbed to death, but he was not cut off forever. Rather, he defeated all the powers of death, Satan, and hell by rising again to glory. He is the firstfruits of the resurrection for the redeemed, who also face death but not

81. Vlach, *He Will Reign Forever*, 510.
82. Anthony A. Hoekema, *The Bible and the Future* (Grand Rapids: Eerdmans, 1979), 280.
83. Vlach, *He Will Reign Forever*, 510.
84. Vlach, *He Will Reign Forever*, 514–15. Compare the passing of "the old" person and the coming of "the new" in 2 Corinthians 5:17 with the passing of the old heaven and earth and the coming of the "new" in Revelation 21:1.
85. Vlach, *He Will Reign Forever*, 510.
86. Svigel, "Extreme Makeover," 413.
87. Hoekema, *The Bible and the Future*, 281.

annihilation. Rather, their bodies will rise again in victory, sharing in the power of their resurrected Lord (1 Cor. 15:20–23). The material universe faces its own death and victorious resurrection as well. In each case, death brings a palpable silence that seems to spell the end . . . but then gives way to renewed life.

According to Romans 8:20–21, true "hope" for the cosmos lies in God's *J-shaped plan* (!) to move the creation from prefall perfection to "subjection" unto "futility" and then to share in "the freedom of the glory of the children of God." This future state of glory is made immeasurably more glorious than it otherwise could be *only* because of the divine plan to subject creation to futility. The ubiquitous groaning of the world is not a gratuitous exercise in hopelessness. It is designed to catapult believers to greater glory. This is why Paul assures us, "The sufferings of this present time are not worth comparing with the glory that is to be revealed" (Rom. 8:18). The depth of our present pain results in greater longing, and greater longing produces the hope for future glory, which is made more glorious by the terrible pain that preceded it.

This future glory does not entail annihilation of the created order, but rather annihilation of all the pain, misery, hatred, violence, injustice, tears, disease, deformities, catastrophes, and pandemics that have wreaked havoc on the present condition of our world. It is death and evil that will be annihilated. These will be altogether missing from the new heaven and earth (Rev. 21:4; 22:3). This picture of creation's future redemption is in keeping with the cosmic renewal of "all things" (Eph. 1:10).[88] And it is precisely in this *renewal* of *shalom* that we must see the theodical glory of God.

But one last set of questions remains: How are the distinctive contours of the greater-glory theodicy best expressed in the life of the believer now? How does the believer live out the implication of this theodicy? Is it possible to see how the problem of evil is resolved simply by observing the way in which Christians are called to carry on in this broken world? How do followers of the theanthropic hero, Jesus Christ, contribute to the magnification of God's glory in the face of adversity, injustice, pain, and suffering? Let us turn to explore these final questions.

KEY TERMS

Christus Victor
penal substitution

---

88. See also Acts 3:21; Col. 1:20 (cf. Matt. 19:28). Note the language of renewal, restoration, reconciliation, and regeneration in these passages.

STUDY QUESTIONS

1. What does *Christus Victor* refer to?
2. What five key metaphors has Henri Blocher identified that describe the atonement of Christ? What is the central metaphor for the atonement?
3. How precisely does Christ defeat satanic powers? How can Christ's victory give you confidence?
4. Why must the cross and the resurrection of Christ be thought of as one saving work?
5. How would you describe the resurrected body of glorified saints? If you are a Christian, what do you most look forward to with your future resurrected body?
6. How far beyond the redemption of sinners does Christ's work of redemption extend? Why is this important for understanding what the greater-glory theodicy teaches?
7. How is God glorified in the judgment that Christ will mete out to a cursed and evil world when he returns to the earth?
8. Why does it make no sense for the heavens and the earth to be annihilated (taken out of existence) at the end of history as we know it?

FOR FURTHER READING

Donald Macleod, *Christ Crucified: Understanding the Atonement* (Downers Grove, IL: InterVarsity Press, 2014).

Jeremy R. Treat, *The Crucified King: Atonement and Kingdom in Biblical and Systematic Theology* (Grand Rapids: Zondervan, 2014).

Michael J. Vlach, *He Will Reign Forever: A Biblical Theology of the Kingdom of God* (Silverton, OR: Lampion Press, 2016).

Adrian Warnock, *Raised with Christ: How the Resurrection Changes Everything* (Wheaton, IL: Crossway, 2010).

Advanced

Henri Blocher, "Biblical Metaphors and the Doctrine of the Atonement," *JETS* 47.4 (2004): 629–45.

Constantine R. Campbell, *Paul and Union with Christ: An Exegetical and Theological Study* (Grand Rapids: Zondervan, 2012).

17

THE GRACE-AND-GLORY EFFECT

Pain is an inescapable part of our world. But as the inexorable forces of our post-Christian zeitgeist seek to expel God from our collective conscience, the story that the world tries to tell us becomes hollow and hopeless, leaving us lost and unable to cope with the obstinate reality of pain. We can make no sense of it in a Godless worldview, and so we do everything we can to push the ugly reality out of sight. Glen Scrivener captures the pablum that passes for the wisdom of the muddled charade under which so many seek refuge:

> We are the flotsam of a cosmic explosion and biological survival machines—wet robots—clinging to an insignificant rock, hurtling through a meaningless universe towards eternal extinction. Still, all that being said, the new flavored latte from Starbucks is *incredible*. And have you tried hot yoga? We're renovating the kitchen too. So, you know, that's nice . . . . As the annihilating tsunami of time bears down on us we obsess over our sandcastles—the promotion, the holiday, the new gadget—and we dare not look up.
>
> Life is a tragedy and this dismal tale is sold to us in every magazine and paperback: "The thousand books you must read before you die"; "The ten must-see destinations for your bucket list." The shape of the story is *up* then *down* and the advertisers are primed to sell you the *uppiest up* that money can buy because the *down* really is a downer. The photographs are glossy, but they mask an unutterable tragedy. Life, according to the wisdom of the age, is about enjoying our brief "moment in the sun." We clamber upwards, grab for ourselves all the achievements, experiences and pleasures that we can and then, so soon, we are "over the hill" and the grave awaits. It's up then down. The frowny face. The tragedy.[1]

1. Glen Scrivener, *Divine Comedy: Human Tragedy* (Leyland, UK: 10Publishing, 2018), 11–12.

432

And so the fragile edifice comes crashing down. The whole story that we so eagerly embraced turns out to be an elaborate fraud. Yet we cannot bear to face the consequences of the tragedy, and so we prop up the fluffy fake narrative at all costs. "All the while though we are marching, inevitably, towards a 'miserable ever after.'" The charade ends up only exacerbating the problem of evil that everyone, not just religious types, must come to grips with. But for those who are paying close attention, "against all the odds and in distinction to all its competitors—the Bible comes along and dares to tell a different story."[2] That story doesn't ignore the pain, the tragedy, but rather transforms it into a brilliant comedy of indomitable quality. And those who embrace this remarkable story find their own lives radically transformed.

The greater-glory theodicy turns on a handful of points pregnant with applications to everyone living in this better unerring narrative. God. Glory. Good and evil. Grace. Redemption. And the Redeemer—Jesus Christ.

The story of *felix culpa* (the fortunate fall) turns on that which supremely magnifies the glory of God. This glory is centered on the grace of redemption. The grace of redemption presupposes massive tensions between good and evil as they intersect creature and creation. But most importantly, redemptive grace turns on an utterly unique Redeemer whose goodness penetrates the dense black nucleus of evil and blows it to smithereens. The Redeemer himself—Christ—encompasses wide-ranging dimensions and tensions within his person and work that serve to further highlight the glory and grace of the redemptive storyline.

All this we have seen. What remains is to canvass the implications of God's theodical glory for those who are the recipients of his redemptive work. The redeemed are called to live a very different kind of life marked by grit and grace—the grace through which they have been rescued. This is not a lighthearted venue for the latte crowd. It is taking the indomitable spirit of the story and casting it with indomitable characters who can face the darkness with confidence because they have taken sure refuge in a Savior who has already won the victory. The transformation wrought by Christ that especially marks the lives of beleaguered believers living in the trenches of this tragic world proves to be one of the greatest, though unexpected, apologetics for Christianity. It involves a display of weakness, humility, unearthly love, compassion, perseverance under trial, and forgiveness of vile offenders. It is what Larry Taunton calls "the grace effect."[3]

2. Scrivener, *Divine Comedy*, 13.
3. Larry Alex Taunton, *The Grace Effect: How the Power of One Life Can Reverse the Corruption of Unbelief* (Nashville: Thomas Nelson, 2011).

TRANSFORMING GRACE

All of heaven and earth will bow before the name of Christ as he brings glory to the Father (Phil. 2:9–11) by his comprehensive work of judgment and salvation, of both destruction and renewal. Yet Christ's theodical glory rests the strongest on the elect—those cracked and stained by the fall but transformed by the grand reversal, trading black rags for the golden robes of redemption. They have a direct and unique experience of God's grace that no other creature, angelic or human, has. Not even the inanimate creation knows the wonders of his grace as the children of God do. Only the souls of the redeemed can sing:

> O the deep, deep love of Jesus,
> Vast, unmeasured, boundless, free!
> Rolling as a mighty ocean
> In its fullness over me.[4]

The boundless love of Christ invests the redeemed with an unearthly power and disposition. We are distinctly set apart from the rest of the world. Once we were sinners bound for judgment. Now we have been enveloped in the mighty ocean of grace that has washed our sin away, absolving our guilt and shame and purifying our conscience from rebellion against our rightful Lord. Suddenly, we have been constituted by the Holy Spirit as purveyors of the same grace by which we have been redeemed (Titus 2:11–14; 3:4–6). The distinguishing measure of Christianity's claims to truth lies in the unprecedented, unexpected, undeserved, and transformative power of the gospel in the lives of lowly sinners.

This is especially true when believers face what seems like insurmountable pain, adversity, and diabolical opposition to their new life in Christ. This is where the proverbial rubber of this *felix culpa* theodicy meets the road. The supreme glory that marks God's full response to evil in redemption finds its most tangible manifestation in the transforming grace that he extends to his children when they encounter otherwise insufferable evil.

To understand how this transforming grace works, we need to see how God conditioned our sin-weary souls to operate in a broken world. Eleonore Stump describes how prolonged evil and suffering produce a longing for goodness and redemption that only such desperate conditions can evoke:

---

4. Samuel Trevor Francis, "O the Deep, Deep Love of Jesus" (1875).

We discern true goodness, sometimes, with tears. Why tears, do you suppose? A woman imprisoned for life without parole for killing her husband had her sentence unexpectedly commuted by the governor, and she wept when she heard the news. Why did she cry? Because the news was good, and she had been so used to hearing only bad. But why cry at good news? Perhaps because if most of your news is bad, you need to harden your heart to it. So you become accustomed to bad news, and to one extent or another, you learn to protect yourself against it, maybe by not minding so much. And then good news cracks your heart. It makes it feel keenly again all the evils to which it had become dull. It also opens it up to longing and hope, and hope is painful because what is hoped for is not yet here.[5]

When people are enslaved to sin and bitterness, when they are used to pain and disillusionment, and then unexpectedly the resplendent beams of blessing and redemption invade their cold, gray hovel, it sends shock waves through every room. It arrests them, chokes them, and then releases all the tension that holds back the pain. It forces all the pent-up emotions that lay dormant to rise to the surface and come alive. Darkness gives birth to hope.

Stump argues that tears of joy are always connected to suffering.[6] I would add that such tearful joy is always connected to some manner of redemption from evil and suffering that our souls are hardwired by our Designer to long for. Stump writes, "We sometimes weep when we are surprised by true goodness. The latest tales of horror in the newspaper distress us but don't surprise us. We have all heard so many stories of the same sort already. But true goodness is unexpected and lovely, and its loveliness can be heartbreaking."[7]

The most arresting form of goodness is mercy when all we expect is more awful tales of horror. In this perennially corrupt world, the sword that silences the vile lawbreaker may surprise us and satisfy our thirst for justice. But even justice doesn't awaken us from our stupor as does the cool breeze of mercy—both the mercy of compassion for defenseless victims and the gracious pardon that is extended to vile victimizers. Mercy is particularly strong when we become vividly aware that we ourselves are not only victims, but victimizers.

Stump provides a good framework to make sense of how grace and goodness can commingle with evil: "Start with a view of evil and a deep taste of

---

5. Eleonore Stump, "The Mirror of Evil," in *God and the Philosophers*, ed. Thomas V. Morris (Oxford: Oxford University Press, 1996), 240.

6. Stump, "Mirror of Evil," 246n8.

7. Stump, "Mirror of Evil," 240.

the goodness of God, and you will know that there must be a morally sufficient reason for God to allow evil—. . . a reason in which true goodness is manifest."[8] But this all seems unreasonable. The natural bent of humans broken by sin from within and without is to think that God has betrayed us, forever consigning us to this bottomless pit without hope of escape. We operate from hearts incurably hardened by sin and hate and in turn find ourselves battered by others of the same disposition. It becomes a vicious cycle of sinners against sinners trapped in an endless orbit of enmity against God. We see enmity all around with no remedy. And ultimately, we suppose that God is to blame.

The believer, however, is given a brilliant vision of hope along with a necessary faith that sees beyond the fog clouding our fallen condition. In the midst of our plight with evil, we encounter a divine face suffused with a commanding love that erases any thought of betrayal and removes the enmity first between us and God and then between us and the cold, hard world arrayed against us. Instead, grace comes alive, and we inhabit this present darkness with a confidence in Christ and a resolve to live by means of a hope-filled power that no devil, no murderer, no cancer, no vile fires in the heart can overcome.

Our Lord's smiling providences are always sweeter when preceded by the foul conditions that conceal his frowning providences. Buried within the morass of devilry, murder, cancer, and all manner of evil machinations lies a mysterious and ineffable love that distinguishes the Christian faith from all pretenders. It melts even the most hardened sinners and those hardened by the ruthless transgressions of others.

GRACE OVERCOMING EVIL

The apostle Paul issues a simple but extraordinary command in Romans 12:14: "Bless those who persecute you; bless and do not curse." He draws on Jesus' teaching during the Sermon on the Mount in Matthew 5, where the Lord notes that our natural inclination as humans, and what we are often taught to do, is to lash out at those who threaten us, to "hate your enemy" (v. 43). "But I say to you, love your enemies and pray for those who persecute you" (v. 45; cf. Luke 6:27–28). Douglas Moo indicates that Jesus' teaching, on which Romans 12:14 is based, was unprecedented in both the Jewish and Greek worlds.[9]

---

8. Stump, "Mirror of Evil," 242.

9. Douglas J. Moo, *The Epistle to the Romans*, New International Commentary on the New Testament (Grand Rapids: Eerdmans, 1996), 781. Moo cites Michael B. Thompson, *Clothed with Christ: The Example and Teaching of Jesus in Romans 12.1–15.13* (Sheffield, UK: Sheffield Academic Press, 1991), 97–98.

Likewise, Thomas Schreiner calls this "one of the most revolutionary statements" in the New Testament.[10] Its ubiquitous deployment in the lives of the early Christians helps explain why Christianity forever changed the world we live in. Yet how have Christians been consistently enabled to live this way? The only explanation is found in grace. The transforming grace that saves sinners is the same grace that sanctifies them (Titus 2:11–14). Grace is invested with a preternatural—indeed, an otherworldly—divine power that enables believers to endure suffering and to conquer any evil set before them.

The grace that we are talking about is but a reflection of the grace that Christ displayed when he humbly faced down evil among the trees of Gethsemane and then finally overcame it on the tree of Golgotha. From the dawn of the church, Christians have been consistently motivated and empowered by Christ's example of conquering the colossal mass of suffering by painfully enduring the weight of it.[11] Like Christ, we conquer suffering by suffering, and we are enabled to do so by his grace.

This is the grace that first softens our heart, pardons us, and comforts our weary soul. It is the grace that sustains our steps through dangerous valleys and empowers our weakness. It comes to our aid when loving others is hard, when loving our enemies is otherwise impossible. This is the grace that seasons our speech (Col. 4:6) and circumscribes our actions in the midst of adversity (2 Cor. 8:7). The life of the believer must be saturated with this grace, especially when dark powers threaten us the most.

There is no shortage of examples to demonstrate how the transforming grace of God is manifested in the lives of the saints and in the history of redemption. Paul was completely unperturbed when he spoke of his impending demise under the heavy hand of Roman power: "For I am already being poured out as a drink offering, and the time of my departure has come. I have fought the good fight, I have finished the race, I have kept the faith" (2 Tim. 4:6–7). The confidence expressed here is not Paul speaking; it is Christ in him, "the hope of glory" (Col. 1:27).

Paul knew that the life of the Christian is no cakewalk: "Indeed, all who desire to live a godly life in Christ Jesus will be persecuted" (2 Tim. 3:12). Jesus said it first: "If the world hates you, know that it has hated me before it hated you. . . . 'A servant is not greater than his master.' If they persecuted me, they will also persecute you" (John 15:18, 20).

10. Thomas R. Schreiner, *Romans*, 2nd ed., Baker Exegetical Commentary on the New Testament (Grand Rapids: Baker, 1998), 648.

11. See Paul L. Gavrilyuk, *The Suffering of the Impassible God: The Dialectics of Patristic Thought* (Oxford: Oxford University Press, 2004), 69–75.

Anyone who has come to Christ under the promise that life will be all peaches and cream has been sold a bill of goods. Once we come to Christ, the battle has only just begun. But we are already assured victory even before the landing craft spills us out onto the beachhead. The superior power of the Holy Spirit present with us on D-Day enables us to press forward off the beaches toward the final destination, where the V-Day banners will wave proudly.

Peter's empty braggadocio during Jesus' hour of testing (cf. Matt. 26:35, 69–75) gave way to a humble confidence—the same kind that Paul inherited from the persecuted Lord. Peter instructs believers to endure "sorrows while suffering unjustly. . . . This is a gracious thing in the sight of God. For to this you have been called, because Christ also suffered for you, leaving you an example, so that you might follow in his steps" (1 Peter 2:19–21). Then Peter admits something very counterintuitive about Christian suffering: "But even if you should suffer for righteousness' sake, you will be blessed" (3:14). No adversity that accrues for our greater good will be wasted (cf. Rom. 8:28). And later he exhorts, "Therefore let those who suffer according to God's will entrust their souls to a faithful Creator while doing good" (1 Peter 4:19). The "Father of mercies and God of all comfort" (2 Cor. 1:3) will never abandon his children during their hour of testing.

These were not empty charges. Peter, as well as Paul, was likely martyred by the Emperor Nero in the Roman ruler's efforts to discredit and malign the early Christians. The evidence suggests that Peter was crucified, something that Jesus seems to be alluding to in John 21:18–19 as he predicts the kind of death that Peter would suffer. It is even possible that Peter was crucified upside down, submitting to this willingly. Witnesses said that he wanted to disavow himself of the honor of being crucified upright as his Lord had been.[12]

Peter and Paul are but paradigmatic examples of the long history of Christian suffering. Among extrabiblical works having the greatest influence on the Christian self-understanding, particularly in the English-speaking world where Christianity has had its greatest impact, one thinks of two important books, both of which emphasize suffering at the center of the Christian life.

The first is the allegorical tale *The Pilgrim's Progress*, written by John Bunyan (1628–88), which details the hard-fought plight of young Christian as he faces multiple obstacles and hardships while making his way to the Celestial City. The second book, written by the Puritan John Foxe (1517–87),

---

12. See discussion of the evidence for this in Bryan M. Litfin, *After Acts: Exploring the Lives and Legends of the Apostles* (Chicago: Moody Publishers, 2015), 143–60.

is *Acts and Monuments*, more popularly known as *Foxe's Book of Martyrs*. In its ever-expanding editions, Foxe demonstrated through a long series of biographical sketches of suffering heroes of the faith that persecution is very much the story of the church.

Bunyan himself had been imprisoned for preaching the gospel when he wrote *The Pilgrim's Progress*, and he had Foxe's book at his side all the while.[13] John Newton (1725–1807), the repentant slave trader, picks up Bunyan and Foxe's theme in Christianity's most beloved hymn, "Amazing Grace." The believer's path must run "through many dangers, toils, and snares" in order for grace to lead him to his eternal home. Suffering runs deep in all these accounts of the Christian life, and this explains why they universally resonate with afflicted believers. But grace runs through them even deeper, and this really explains their enduring value.

GRACE IN THE HOLOCAUST

The twentieth century was the bloodiest in history. The Holocaust, which nearly wiped out Europe's Jewish population, serves as a testament to the depths of depravity to which humanity has stooped. Consider the horrors: unsuspecting souls crammed into railcars so tightly that they can't breathe; the sounds of small children having their bones broken without anesthesia for the sake of "medical" studies; or perhaps the stench and black smoke of human flesh wafting into the air from massive brick stacks. People have responded to these vile acts of cruel malice in a number of ways.

Elie Wiesel's response was to say that Auschwitz was the place where the life of God was extinguished as he hung in the gallows vicariously via a small boy placed there by cruel prison masters.[14] American soldiers encountering the carnage for the first time were moved to deep anger. Their natural impulse was to take violent revenge, an eye for an eye. This is the response of most people who spend any amount of time examining what took place at the death camps. It was certainly how many Jews who suffered under the brutality of the SS guards felt.[15]

There is nothing inherently immoral or even un-Christian about this latter impulse. Neither the Bible nor the Christian faith in general commits the Christian to a principled form of pacifism in all circumstances.[16] But it

---

13. Christopher Hill, *A Turbulent, Seditious, and Factious People* (repr., London: Verso, 2016), 157–58.

14. Elie Wiesel, *Night* (New York: Hill and Wang, 2006), 64–65.

15. Simon Wiesenthal, *The Sunflower: On the Possibilities and Limits of Forgiveness* (New York: Schocken Books, 1998), 64.

16. See J. Daryl Charles and Timothy J. Demy, *War, Peace, and Christianity: Questions and Answers from a Just-War Perspective* (Wheaton, IL: Crossway, 2010).

is not a distinctly Christian response either. *Everyone* is hardwired to see justice carried out. It doesn't take unique courage or any special virtues to demand retribution for unspeakable crimes.

Yet some distinctive Christian responses to those heart-wrenching atrocities typified by the Nazis do not involve shows of force or retribution. Rather, believers obtain an exceptional brand of strength through weakness and humble dependence on the transforming grace of Christ's gospel. It requires a steely resolve, imitating Christ's own example of a lamb bound while deliberately entering hostile Jewish and Roman territory and knowing that they were ready to hand him over to slaughter.

The extraordinary, indeed subversive, way in which many Christians have responded to various kinds of injustice, oppression, and violence points to the transformative power that only God's grace can carry out.[17] Only a special measure of divine grace could enable the courage of William Tyndale (1494–1536) as he cried, "Lord, open the king of England's eyes" as he meekly submitted to being strangled and burned at the stake for translating the Bible into English. We fight evil with grace and goodness, with self-sacrificial resolve, and with a desire to see others come to Christ for the same pardon we received by his sacrifice. This uncommon power is what Larry Taunton means by "the grace effect." Let us consider three ways in which this distinctive brand of grace was exemplified during the Holocaust.

Showing Mercy to Victims

First, transforming grace was exemplified by showing mercy to victims of Nazi terror. Philip Hallie was a philosopher, ethicist, and researcher of Holocaust atrocities. He was also a Jew and no stranger to anti-Semitism. But after investigating the sheer volume of Nazi atrocities, his research became monotonous and numbing. Hallie writes, "For years I had been studying cruelty, the slow crushing and grinding of a human being by other human beings." Soon he was getting bored with it all. His initial reaction to Nazi evil was the normal indignation it evokes in most people. He thought that the best way to combat people such as Hitler and his henchmen was the use of deadly force.

Then he came across something that happened in a forgotten village in France named Le Chambon.[18] It was populated by Huguenots, Reformed

---

17. See the insights of Miroslav Volf, *Exclusion and Embrace: A Theological Exploration of Identity, Otherness, and Reconciliation* (Nashville: Abingdon Press, 1996); Miroslav Volf, *Free of Charge: Giving and Forgiving in a Culture Stripped of Grace* (Grand Rapids: Zondervan, 2005).

18. Philip Hallie, *Lest Innocent Blood Be Shed: The Story of the Village of Le Chambon and How Goodness Happened There* (New York: HarperCollins, 1994), 2.

Protestant Christians tracing their roots to the sixteenth-century Reformation. The villagers were led by their pastor, André Trocmé, who organized a rescue operation to hide and save thousands of Jewish children and adults. They did this while eluding the watchful eyes of the local Nazi SS and their collaborators in the Vichy government. The whole village risked annihilation if their plot were discovered.

As Hallie researched the story, he was merely trying to consider the facts as an objective investigator. But then he says during a moment of reflection, "I reached up to my cheek to wipe away a bit of dust, and I felt tears upon my fingertips. Not one or two drops; my whole cheek was wet."[19] Hallie was not religious, but when he traveled to Le Chambon to investigate the story in 1976, he knew that some unusual kind of "goodness had happened" there that had to be a product of the villagers' Christian convictions.[20] As an ethics professor, he needed to understand the strange moral impulse to save lives at the risk of losing one's own.

He came to discover "that there is a mystery to goodness that is even deeper than the mystery of evil."[21] Le Chambon gave powerful substance to James's simple maxim: "Religion that is pure and undefiled before God the Father is this: to visit orphans and widows in their affliction, and to keep oneself unstained from the world" (James 1:27). The gospel rescues those afflicted by their own sin and rebellion. It also rescues us from the affliction we experience by the sin and rebellion of others.

A-theistic societies give no heed to the value of life. When the *imago Dei* in the human identity is discarded, a process of dehumanization takes place, and it is not long before mistreatment and violent oppression of others becomes normalized and even trivialized. The weakest members of society are among the first to be crushed. Taunton perceptively instructs and warns us:

> Proponents of a society free from religious influence can point to no nation or civilization that was founded upon atheistic principles that we might call even remotely good. The story of those regimes is well documented and may be summarized in a word—*murderous*. What those proponents can point to are secular societies that are still running off of their accumulated Christian capital. But beware. When the fumes in that tank are spent, tyranny cannot be far away. How many dictatorships, genocides,

19. Hallie, *Lest Innocent Blood Be Shed*, 3.
20. Hallie, *Lest Innocent Blood Be Shed*, 7.
21. Os Guinness, *Unspeakable: Facing Up to Evil in an Age of Genocide and Terror* (San Francisco: HarperSanFrancisco, 2005), 226.

purges, wars, famines, gulags, economic disasters, morally bankrupt leaders, and impoverished nations must the world suffer before its people realize that belief in God is necessary for the stability of civilization?[22]

Some may suggest that Germany was a Christian nation at the time of World War II. In reality, Germany was at the forefront of European nations already imbibing the poison of higher criticism in biblical studies along with its antisupernaturalism and replacing the Christian worldview with Nietzsche's godless nihilism. Nazism is Nietzschean through and through. Germany was trying to produce a society of Nietzschean "Supermen" (*Übermensch*)—a master race of pure Aryan stock—and the dirty Jews were threatening to contaminate their unspoiled DNA and needed to be purged.[23]

Victims Bearing Up under God's Mercy

There is a second, more excruciating way in which transforming grace was exemplified during the Holocaust. It involved the reception of divine mercy while bearing up under unearthly suffering. It produced that same distinctive brand of transforming grace. The Huguenots in Le Chambon would have found kindred spirits among the ten Boom family of Haarlem, a principal city in the Netherlands. They, too, were devout believers risking their lives during the war to hide Jews in their home. Unfortunately, they got caught, were arrested, and were sent to various Nazi concentration camps, where most of the family members died.

The story is told by Corrie ten Boom in her gripping memoir *The Hiding Place*.[24] It is one thing to extend mercy to the helpless and the afflicted. It is quite another when you are afflicted—severely, with no one to offer help of any kind. No compassion. No sympathy. No understanding. Sometimes Christians are driven into the spiritual wildernesses where they are alone, battered by hot winds of despair and deprived of any means of sustenance. Sometimes they are driven into the hands of literal devils, where they are enslaved, beaten, starved, and exposed to undiluted evil. Such was the case for Corrie and her sister Betsie when they came to Ravensbrück, the notorious concentration camp for women.

22. Taunton, *Grace Effect*, 216.
23. Steven E. Aschheim, "Nietzsche, Anti-Semitism and the Holocaust," in *Nietzsche and Jewish Culture*, ed. Jacob Golomb (New York: Routledge, 1997), 3–20; Richard Weikart, *Hitler's Religion: The Twisted Beliefs That Drove the Third Reich* (Washington, DC: Regnery Publishing, 2016).
24. Corrie ten Boom, *The Hiding Place*, 35th anniversary ed. (Grand Rapids: Chosen Books, 2006).

When they came to the camp, one of the first things they had to endure was to be stripped naked before SS men and sent to showers before putting on their drab prison clothes. Showering seemed a waste of time, since they lived in filthy barracks that had the stench of urine and feces. They were allowed no toilet paper. Their beds were made of straw and rife with squirming lice. Each prisoner bore the daily insults and beatings of the pitiless female guards.

One guard was known as The Snake for reasons that need no further explanation. The subfreezing days were numbing, and many women simply froze to death. The sisters' barracks was next to the punishment barracks. "From there, all day long and often into the night, came the sounds of hell itself. They were not the sounds of anger, or of any human emotion, but of a cruelty altogether detached: blows landing in regular rhythm, screams keeping pace."[25]

This was not a place where goodness dwelt. It was not a place you'd expect to find mercy. Yet God did something miraculous there. Corrie was able to smuggle a Bible into the compound without detection. When she first arrived outside the prison barracks, she found a place to hide it: behind old wooden benches "slimy with mildew, crawling with cockroaches, but to me they seemed the furniture of heaven itself."[26]

Then she managed to slip past the guards with the precious book and bring it into the barracks, where it was never found. The sovereign Lord had prepared Corrie and her sister for this moment, and it is reflected in the distinctive God-centered, God-dependent perspective that Corrie began to cultivate. She recalls that having that Bible meant that "we were not poor, but rich. Rich in this new evidence of the care of Him who was God even of Ravensbrück."[27]

Barracks 8 became a haven for all the women languishing in this hell:

> From morning until lights-out, whenever we were not in ranks for roll call, our Bible was the center of an ever-widening circle of help and hope. Like waifs clustered around a blazing fire, we gathered about it, holding out our hearts to its warmth and light. The blacker the night around us grew, the brighter and truer and more beautiful burned the word of God. "Who shall separate us from the love of Christ? Shall tribulation, or distress, or persecution, or famine, or nakedness, or peril, or sword? . . . Nay, in all these things we are more than conquerors though him that loved us."[28]

25. Ten Boom, *Hiding Place*, 205–6.
26. Ten Boom, *Hiding Place*, 204.
27. Ten Boom, *Hiding Place*, 204.
28. Ten Boom, *Hiding Place*, 206.

Most Holocaust survivors were so traumatized by the horrid things they saw and endured in those camps of death that life was unbearable after the war for many years. For some, there was no recovery. But to see divine favor and blessing in those dark days? How could that be? "Life in Ravensbrück took place on two separate levels, mutually impossible. One, the observable, external life, grew every day more horrible. The other, the life we lived with God, grew daily better, truth upon truth, glory upon glory."[29] This can be none other than the precious Light shining out of an impossible darkness. "I am the light of the world," Jesus proclaims. "Whoever follows me will not walk in darkness, but will have the light of life" (John 8:12).

But we should not suppose that all struggles somehow disappeared or that temptation lost its force. Soon afterward, the sisters came to their permanent barracks. It was more unlivable than the first barracks and infested with biting fleas. It didn't seem possible that one could endure such a place for more than an hour. Corrie was tempted to doubt and to fall into despair. But Betsie was ready to shine as she prayed for an answer. It was revealed in their Scripture reading that morning: 1 Thessalonians 5:14–18. Verse 18 really struck her: "Give thanks in all circumstances." Betsie thanked God for every horrible thing about the barracks, and so she urged her sister.

Corrie was flabbergasted. But finally, she said, "Oh, all right. Thank You for the jammed, crammed, stuffed, packed, suffocating crowds."[30] But she wouldn't give thanks for the fleas. That was going too far. Betsie responded, "'Give thanks in all circumstances,' . . . it doesn't say, 'in pleasant circumstances.' Fleas are part of this place where God has put us."[31] Some days later it occurred to them why they were able to read the Bible freely in the barracks. The infestation of fleas kept the guards out. The fleas allowed the Bible to be read without detection.[32]

Give thanks in all circumstances.

Though Betsie was the stronger of the two spiritually, she was weaker physically. Soon she grew even weaker till she was unable to work as hard as the others. She was mocked mercilessly for her helpless condition and then whipped in the face by one of the guards for not picking up the pace. This provoked the rise of a "murderous anger" in Corrie. She picked up a shovel to rush at the guard, but Betsie stopped her before she could act. Corrie tried to examine Betsie's injury, but her sister "laid a bird-thin hand over

---

29. Ten Boom, *Hiding Place*, 206.
30. Ten Boom, *Hiding Place*, 210.
31. Ten Boom, *Hiding Place*, 210.
32. Ten Boom, *Hiding Place*, 220.

the whip mark" and said, "Don't look at it, Corrie. Look at Jesus only."[33] For Betsie, every disheartening place throughout the encampment was "simply a setting in which to talk about Jesus." She evangelized everyone she could talk to. "As her body grew weaker, her faith seemed to grow bolder."[34]

Betsie was teaching her sister deeper levels of dependence on Christ than Corrie ever thought possible. Thinking only of yourself takes on remarkable power when your life is at stake. At Ravensbrück, it was every woman for herself even if it meant the death of the one you were competing with. Shoving others aside in order to grasp for a scrap of food—and for your life—was the constant temptation. But Corrie started to realize that "the real sin lay in thinking that any power to help and transform came from me. Of course it was not *my* wholeness, but Christ's that made the difference."[35] Betsie taught this to her even as her life was being sucked out of her. She was dying with an exceptional level of dignity that belied her outward shame.

Medical help didn't come soon enough. As she was laid on a stretcher headed to the hospital, freezing, unable to move, no strength left, at death's doorstep, she achingly whispered to Corrie: ". . . must tell people what we have learned here. We must tell them that there is no pit so deep that He is not deeper still. They will listen to us, Corrie, because we have been here."[36] Betsie was taken away, and moments later her spirit departed from her battered body. Not long afterward, Corrie managed to see her sister.

> For there lay Betsie, her eyes closed as if in sleep, her face full and young. The care lines, the grief lines, the deep hollows of hunger and disease were simply gone. In front of me was the Betsie of Haarlem, happy and at peace. Stronger! Freer! This was the Betsie of heaven, bursting with joy and health.[37]

Betsie appears as the near-equal to the apostle Paul when he penned these words in 2 Corinthians 6: "we appeal to you not to receive the grace of God in vain" (v. 1). Betsie knew all the inner contours of this transformative grace, and she passed on its lessons to her sister. Paul describes how it manifests itself when the darkness overtakes us:

> As servants of God we commend ourselves in every way: by great endurance, in afflictions, hardships, calamities, beatings, imprisonments, riots,

33. Ten Boom, *Hiding Place*, 215.
34. Ten Boom, *Hiding Place*, 215.
35. Ten Boom, *Hiding Place*, 225.
36. Ten Boom, *Hiding Place*, 227.
37. Ten Boom, *Hiding Place*, 229.

labors, sleepless nights, hunger; by purity, knowledge, patience, kindness, the Holy Spirit, genuine love; by truthful speech, and the power of God; with the weapons of righteousness for the right hand and for the left; through honor and dishonor, through slander and praise. We are treated as impostors, and yet are true; as unknown, and yet well known; as dying, and behold, we live; as punished, and yet not killed; as sorrowful, yet always rejoicing; as poor, yet making many rich; as having nothing, yet possessing everything. (2 Cor. 6:4–10)

The perseverance of the saints under the worst of conditions is Christianity's greatest living proof, where its apologetic mettle—via its faithful adherents—is tested by fire and found to be "more precious than gold." This tenacious life of suffering will eventually "result in praise and glory and honor at the revelation of Jesus Christ" (1 Peter 1:7). Yet it is not the Christian as he is in himself, but "Christ in you, the hope of glory" (Col. 1:27). When people see the followers of Christ live this way, can they deny the living God? Can they deny the wealthy Sovereign as the source of the riches of this unearthly grace? Can they deny that such grace incarnated in the lives of battered saints supremely magnifies his glory in the face of evil as nothing else can?

Showing Mercy to Victimizers

But we are not through. It is one thing to show mercy to victims while risking one's own personal well-being, as many did while hiding Jews from the Nazis during the days of the Final Solution. It is quite another to suffer as a victim and bear the pain of having no one to show you mercy, especially when your life is on the line, as Corrie's and Betsie's were. Christians find themselves without human help and hope all the time, and this must drive us to seek refuge in our Lord, who has not abandoned us or refused to offer us his care and transcendent mercy. Both circumstances test the genuine character of our faith.

But a third test that battered believers must face may be the most difficult of all: whether as victims they are willing to show mercy to their victimizers, offering forgiveness toward their oppressors and tormentors. Can you forgive your father who abused you as a child? Can you forgive the teenager whose drunken midnight caper down the freeway took the life of your young and beautiful wife? Can you forgive the cutthroat who partnered with you in business and embezzled all your profits?

Nowhere is the human heart tested more severely than at this point. If you want to know the moral fortitude of any system of thought, ask what price it is willing to pay in order to offer forgiveness to the vilest offender. Christianity is explicitly built on the principle that God forgives the most foul and incorrigible sinner whose crimes surpass the reprehensible. God is fundamentally revealed as the one who "forgives iniquity, transgression and sin" (Ex. 34:7 NASB; cf. Num. 14:18). The psalmist declares, "If you, O LORD, should mark iniquities, O Lord, who could stand? But with you there is forgiveness, that you may be feared" (Ps. 130:3–4). God is an utterly merciful God to those who stand guilty before his fiery bar of justice, yet fall fearfully to their knees in repentance.

The foundation of the kingdom of heaven rests on the eternal pardon of godless rebels who previously lived in unbroken violation of God's holy law. This is the testimony of Paul: "Formerly I was a blasphemer, persecutor, and insolent opponent. But I received mercy because I had acted ignorantly in unbelief, and the grace of our Lord overflowed for me with the faith and love that are in Christ Jesus" (1 Tim. 1:13–14). The people of God are the trophies of Christ's defeat of suffering, death, and evil through the cross and the empty tomb. This is the gospel, and it is opened deep and wide with love excelling, love divine. "For as high as the heavens are above the earth, so great is his steadfast love toward those who fear him; as far as the east is from the west, so far does he remove our transgressions from us" (Ps. 103:11–12).

The vastness of the universe cannot contain his love for his forgiven children.

> The love of God is greater far
> Than tongue or pen can ever tell;
> It goes beyond the highest star,
> And reaches to the lowest hell . . . .
>
> Could we with ink the ocean fill,
> And were the skies of parchment made;
> Were ev'ry stalk on earth a quill,
> And ev'ry man a scribe by trade;
> To write the love of God above
> Would drain the ocean dry;
> Nor could the scroll contain the whole,
> Though stretched from sky to sky.[38]

What does this mean for the ranks of the pardoned?

---

38. Frederick M. Lehman, "The Love of God" (1917).

The forgiveness of sin by a righteous and merciful God results in humbled servants who are called to extend this same forgiveness to others who have sinned against them (Eph. 4:32; Col. 3:13). Jesus draws this connection in the fourth petition of the Lord's Prayer that he taught his disciples: "And forgive us our sins, for we ourselves forgive everyone who is indebted to us" (Luke 11:4). If a professing believer is never inclined to extend grace, then it is a sure sign that God has refused that person his grace. In the parable of the unforgiving servant (Matt. 18:23–35), Jesus castigates those who receive mercy from their Lord and Master and yet are unwilling to extend it to others: "Should not you have had mercy on your fellow servant, as I had mercy on you?" (v. 33).

To be a Christian is to be forgiven *and* to forgive. This is the essence of grace in action—the grace effect—which is a distinguishing feature of Christianity and is what sets it apart from all other religions and ethical ideologies. Christianity eschews all merit-based approaches to resolving our human predicament and the problem of evil in a world rife with wickedness. The gift of salvation didn't come to believers because we met the proper moral and religious requirements. We were not released from our sentence because we impressed the parole board with our good behavior. We were rebels. The teacher gave us the prize even though we were the worst hellions in the classroom. But once we received the prize, we were surprised and humbled and transformed.[39]

We were forgiven by a divine effusion of grace and grace alone, and this engenders the impulse to forgive others. But forgiveness is not an end in itself. It is the means by which reconciliation is achieved. The fall resulted in severed relationships and the loss of *shalom* (peace) in the world. Adam and Eve were severed from God, from each other, and from the creation. In order for paradise to be restored, for *shalom* to reign once again in the new creation, peace must be made within the fractured community of Eden.[40]

The most marvelous stories in the world are stories of divine grace. And the most marvelous stories of grace are stories of forgiveness. Scripture sets forth the paradigm. After Adam and Eve thrust the world into darkness and despair, God fashions garments of skin to cover their nakedness and signify

---

39. This illustration is drawn from Adrian Warnock, *Raised with Christ: How the Resurrection Changes Everything* (Wheaton, IL: Crossway, 2010), 145.

40. On the nature and importance of biblical forgiveness, see Chris Brauns, *Unpacking Forgiveness: Biblical Answers for Complex Questions and Deep Wounds* (Wheaton, IL: Crossway, 2008); John MacArthur, *The Freedom and Power of Forgiveness* (repr., Wheaton, IL: Crossway, 2009); Jay Adams, *From Forgiven to Forgiving: Learning to Forgive One Another God's Way* (Amityville, NY: Calvary Press, 1994).

forgiveness and reconciliation (Gen. 3:21). With trembling and copious tears, Joseph forgives his brothers who sold him into slavery (45:1–8; 50:15–21). David abuses his power, murdering Uriah and taking the man's wife, and then the prophet Nathan announces God's pardon to the insensible and obstinate king (2 Sam. 12:1–15).

The expectant father who was radically shamed by his prodigal son runs to embrace the returning wretch with kisses and the fatted calf (Luke 15:11–32). A woman caught in adultery stands trembling before an itching crowd ready to stone her to death before Jesus intervenes and refuses to condemn her (John 8:1–11). A pathetic thief casts insults on the crucified Lord while hanging on his own cross (Matt. 27:44), and then humbly realizes his grave error and receives the promise of paradise from the offended One (Luke 23:39–43).

Stories of sin, shame, brokenness, and restoration grip our hearts, but forgiveness does not come easily for the human race. Even the Christian has reservations. We must not underestimate the burden that rests on a person who has been mistreated, maligned, and in some cases horribly crushed by perpetrators of abject cruelty. It is never easy to refrain from spewing forth venom toward one's enemy or to tear yourself away from craving delicious morsels of vengeance.

Simon Wiesenthal was a Jew suffering as a prisoner in a concentration camp during the Holocaust. While on a work detail in the town of Dnepropetrovsk, he was compelled by a nurse to visit a dying German soldier in a makeshift hospital. The soldier was a Hitler Youth fervent in his devotion for the "Fatherland" (*Vaterland*) and now languishing on his deathbed. He had participated in murdering a group of Jewish families crammed into a house and then set aflame by gasoline and hand grenades. The conscience of the soldier had tortured him ever since. With only hours to live, he sought for the only Jew available to confess his crime and seek forgiveness.

The nurse presented Wiesenthal to the Nazi, and Wiesenthal was dumbstruck by his request for forgiveness. He could not answer him. He left in silence, and the soldier died in short order. For years afterward, Wiesenthal had no answer, and wrote the book *The Sunflower* to detail the struggle. Fifty-three well-known political and religious leaders, human-rights activists, and survivors of genocide also took up Wiesenthal's question: Should he have offered the soldier forgiveness? What are the limits of forgiveness? Most respondents struggled to answer that question.[41] The tension between

---

41. See Wiesenthal, *The Sunflower*. Many, including Wiesenthal himself, came back to the idea that he was in no position to offer forgiveness on behalf of the victims of Nazi murders.

justice and mercy—of craving vengeance and knowing the power of pardon—is palpable in the human soul.

Corrie ten Boom understood the unyielding lure of bitterness, hate, and thoughts of vicious reprisals that can light a normally cool head on fire when the severity of an offense appears unbearable. Shortly after the war (1947), Corrie began to speak at churches, telling her and Betsie's story. Many in Germany eagerly received her message. At one of these engagements in Munich, a man made a beeline to her after she spoke. He was "beaming and bowing" before her. "'How grateful I am for your message, *Fraulein*,' he said. 'To think that, as you say, He has washed my sins away!'"[42]

One would expect a hearty *Amen*. The man, however, introduced himself as one of the SS men who had worked at Ravensbrück. He happened to be one of the guards who had leered lustfully at the women as they walked unclothed into the shower room. Corrie remembered him well. He told her that he had become a Christian and expressed confidence that God had forgiven him of all the cruel deeds he had done.

He reached out to shake her hand, but she froze. "Vengeful thoughts boiled through me . . . . *Lord Jesus*, I prayed, *forgive me and help me to forgive him*." Still nothing. Awkward silence. Just like Simon Wiesenthal. "I tried to smile, I struggled to raise my hand. I could not. I felt nothing, not the slightest spark of warmth or charity."[43] Her pained thoughts wondered how forgiving him could possibly erase what had happened to her sister. He had certainly not been the worst perpetrator of evil at Ravensbrück, but he served as a kind of surrogate for every despicable Nazi who had worked there, and for the whole complex of Hitlerian evil that had overtaken Europe. She had never imagined having to do something this difficult, yet she knew that harboring bitterness would eat her alive and that her sudden failure to forgive after coming this far would haunt her more than all the harm that had befallen her in the death camp.

Only the victims themselves could legitimately face that question. Can a man offer forgiveness on behalf of others with whom he may identify? Without venturing into the complexities of the question and others like it, one cannot miss the undercurrent of difficulty with the whole notion of forgiveness. If Wiesenthal had been a more direct victim of this man's crime, would he have had a different response? What if one of his own family members had been burned alive in that house? A distinctly Christian perspective on this issue can be found in Volf, *Exclusion and Embrace*; Volf, *Free of Charge*.

42. Ten Boom, *Hiding Place*, 247. The recollection of this incident is given fuller details in a *Guideposts* article that Corrie wrote in 1972. See "Guideposts Classics: Corrie ten Boom on Forgiveness," https://www.guideposts.org/better-living/positive-living /guideposts-classics-corrie-ten-boom-on-forgiveness.

43. "Corrie ten Boom on Forgiveness."

Corrie knew that her Christian faith would risk the danger of never thriving again. "And so I breathed again a silent prayer. *Jesus, I cannot forgive him. Give Your forgiveness.*" It seemed like a rather halfhearted prayer, but the grace of Christ did its miraculous work. "As I took his hand the most incredible thing happened. From my shoulder along my arm and through my hand, a current seemed to pass from me to him, while into my heart sprang a love for this stranger that almost overwhelmed me."[44] They held hands a long time, the former tormentor and the one tormented joined in the unbreakable bonds of Christ-centered unity.

This is the grace effect.

This is Spirit-wrought power forged in the crucible of our weakness. Just as Christ demonstrated power in his humiliation and weakness, so do his followers. When we are weak, then we are strong (2 Cor. 12:10). Corrie concludes, "So I discovered that it is not on our forgiveness any more than on our goodness that the world's healing hinges, but on His. When He tells us to love our enemies, He gives, along with the command, the love itself."[45]

Just as the Spirit empowered the Lord Jesus in his humanity to embrace and bear our burdens as the second Adam, so the Spirit enables us to do what we otherwise could not. We have no reason to expect a Simon Wiesenthal to pardon a dying soldier who murdered his people. But the Spirit of the living God imparts to those who have experienced *his* pardon the undeniable power of grace-saturated Christian forgiveness. Such forgiveness can defuse something as simple as a harsh word, and it can bring peace between mortal enemies.

But the surprising power of forgiveness serves a greater function. By mirroring what Christ did on the cross to pardon incorrigible rebels against the living God, we become instruments to exalt the riches of divine glory and grace. We become living analogies of the gospel by pointing to what happened on the cross. The cross is the apex of the story of Scripture—the story of the gospel, of the serpent-crushing Seed of the woman bringing forth beauty out of the hard and foul ground where the serpent slithers. The suffering of the incarnate Son of God brings to life the essence of grace as he suffers judgment for those of us who once hated him. Instead of crushing the onslaught of us rebels as we deserved, he pours out tender mercy on us instead. Christ's example enables every Christian who is faced with adversity and affliction to live out this grace-saturated, glory-magnifying gospel that defuses the worst kinds of evil and melts the hearts of stone-cold malefactors.

44. "Corrie ten Boom on Forgiveness."
45. "Corrie ten Boom on Forgiveness."

452   *The Grace-and-Glory Effect*

THE GLORY EFFECT

This brings us full circle to the theodicy that I have tried to spell out in detail throughout these pages. It seems appropriate to end this book by summarizing what the greater-glory theodicy is all about.

As humans created in the image of God, we recognize that there is something very wrong with the world. Everybody knows it. This is not news. We have always known this. The cosmos is overrun with a malignant tumor festering not only within the broader scope of creation but within our own souls.

First, this disease results in the material world's being consumed by *natural evil*. If it's not out-of-control forest fires, then it's overwhelming floods. If it's not tornadoes blowing everything to bits from above the ground, then it's earthquakes rocking everything out of place from below the ground. If it's not cancer wreaking havoc with our fragile cells, then it's some contagious and deadly virus spreading through the populace and putting everyone at risk. A thousand and one catastrophes at any moment can turn this world into a very dangerous and inhospitable place to live.

But that is not the worst of it. *Natural evil* is merely the product of *moral evil*. Life is precious. This we also know. We cherish our existence as human beings. We were designed to have a purpose, to pursue worthy goals, and to live in a world that has meaning—important and transcendent meaning. Yet something has gone terribly wrong.

From the cradle to the grave, humans have all the makings of moral monsters within them, waiting to prey on all that is pure and innocent. We chafe against what is good and right and true. We fight and bicker with one another. We tell lies. We steal what rightfully belongs to others. We scratch and claw and hate and lust and kill until there is no peace, no joy, no community. Instead, we have become infected with loneliness, dissatisfaction, pain, and misery, subsisting in a darkened vale of tears. We are haunted with tragedy all around. Life is full of an inescapable poison, and we are infected with death. But we hate to admit this.

Certainly, the tragic world we live in is punctuated with plenty of goodness, with blessings and graces common to us all. There are significant moments of peace, wonderful instances of camaraderie, laughter, tenderness, and even tears of gladness. We get to witness acts of extraordinary courage, deep compassion, and surprising generosity. Our natural but fallen world is full of beautiful fields of bluebonnets, bright orange and purple sunsets over placid waters, majestic granite peaks soaring into the clouds, bugling elk echoing across grand canyons, and songbirds filling the canopies of the forest.

Common grace extends to every man, woman, and child. We can listen to the concertos of Bach or the crooning of Johnny Mathis. We can ponder the weighty lines of Shakespeare or relax with the wisecracking duo of Calvin and Hobbes. Our eyes are enamored of the delicate strokes of Leonardo da Vinci and the architectural genius of Frank Lloyd Wright. We celebrate Olympic athletes and doctors without borders. We have figured out how to harness electricity, running water, and the Internet. We have developed sophisticated means of travel on land, through the water, and in the air. We live in a world of ever-expanding talent, skill, and imagination forming an aesthetic, entertaining, and technological wonderland. Yes, we live with a shattered visage, but the *imago Dei* has been far from eradicated.

But what does all this signify?

It means that there are deep incongruities in our world. There is certainly good—much of it. And yet there is evil—many times overshadowing any semblance of good. But the universally favorable experience of good drives the core of our human identity—our soulish DNA. We long and strive for goodness, all the more so when the fearsome hydra of evil rears its many ugly heads and disrupts the hope of any thoroughly abiding goodness. Oh! how we crave this dream of utopia—a heaven of pure and unfading delight, free of tragedy, pain, and suffering. And we endlessly imagine how it can come to fruition, but we also wonder why our imagination of a better world always seems to meet failure. Anytime we are entertained with hope, it gets crushed by another disheartening tragedy.

Yet this leads us inevitably to ponder deeper matters. We know that good and evil do not exist in isolation. We know this because we know that there is a God—not just any god, but the eternal, infinite, all-wise, all-powerful, omnibenevolent Creator and Sustainer of the universe. Some wish to deny this at their peril, but everybody everywhere knows that *he is there and he is not silent.*[46] This is not news. We have always known this.

We know that if there is anything that proves to be true, honorable, just, pure, lovely, or commendable, anything of excellence and worthy of praise (Phil. 4:8), then it must come from the hand of God. What confounds us is evil—natural and moral degradation: tsunamis in the Indian Ocean, earthquakes along the San Andreas Fault, AIDS in Africa, worldwide wars decimating Europe and Asia, Communist genocide in Russia and China. Why would this supremely virtuous, wise, and powerful God whom we know to be alive and active in the world and in our lives permit this endless parade of catastrophe, hate, corruption, lies, theft, rape, murder, and mayhem?

46. See Francis A. Schaeffer, *He Is There and He Is Not Silent*, rev. ed. (Carol Stream, IL: Tyndale House, 2001).

We know that he has the requisite power to have prevented the fall. He could have banned the dreaded serpent from entering Eden. He could have made Adam and Eve incapable of sin just as every saint in heaven will be. He could have limited the consequences and effects of their act of disobedience. The crisis could have stopped with them. Later on, the Almighty could have halted the spread of evil and annihilated the wicked world at the time of Noah's flood and started *completely* from scratch, making a new world out of nothing—Genesis 1:1 all over again—with entirely new creatures constituted so as to choose nothing but good this time, just like God himself. But he did none of these things.

Furthermore, suggesting that all this tragedy and misery is the unfortunate side effect of granting humankind libertarian free will is no escape hatch from this troubled earth. God was not cautiously cringing, teeth clenched, eyes squinting, head slightly cocked sideways, slowly shaking it back and forth as he wondered what a huge risk he was taking. No . . . God *wanted* all this to happen. He planned it. If he is the holy and sovereign God that he has revealed himself to be in the pages of Scripture, then it could be no other way. By extension, this means that God intended every horrendous evil, like the Holocaust, to transpire.

But why?

Well, consider first of all: God is radically free. Without violating anything of his character, he could have done whatever he pleased. He didn't have to create the world. He certainly didn't have a *need* to do so. Nor was he required to make unique and wonderful creatures fashioned in his image. And there is no question that he didn't need to set up a world with the possibility of sin and evil corrupting its original goodness. In fact, we'd expect him *not* to constitute the conditions for such a world!

So why did he do so?

God, in his freedom, desired to put himself on display before the material and immaterial cosmos—before all creatures and all creation—to be marveled at, to be worshiped and praised. But the greatest display of his glory is directed toward us, his image-bearing creatures. We were designed and designated to elicit the most important praise. This is not cosmic egomania. It is right that the Sovereign of the universe should be exalted—because he is worthy; he is *absolutely, supremely* worthy, and it would be utterly wrongheaded for anything else to displace his worth and glory.

Furthermore, he designed us for communion with him, an all-life-giving, all-joy-filling, all-soul-satisfying relationship between Creator and creature, Father and child, Master and servant. This tranquil communion is to be forged in holiness because he is perfectly and eternally holy. This is how it all began, God and man walking in the unsullied luster of Eden. No cares, no concerns. Goodness. Peace. Joy. Excitement. Adventure.

Then the serpent came in. Lies. Deception. Temptation. Questioning of the divine character and purposes. Then disillusionment and disobedience. Shame and misery followed. Curses. Toil. Decay. Corruption. Peace destroyed. Excitement crushed. Fellowship broken. Community disbanded. Joy forgotten. Sin and curses spread and expanded. Nothing has ever been the same again. It has been a long march through tragedy after tragedy, with a modest number of special but fleeting glimpses of how it *could* be, of how it *ought* to be, of how we desperately *ache* for it to be once again.

And this is precisely where God wants us. This is the story that he purposely scripted. He wanted us to see the weight of evil, the horror of every Holocaust, the misery, the numbing, bitter pain of it all. But he also wanted us to see glimpses of goodness, peace, and joy.

Why?

Because only through such a bitter and tragic story with hope held out before us could his glory be so remarkably magnified—*supremely* magnified. When the conditions get so bad, the miseries piling up and stretching our exasperation to the limits; when Satan makes his relentless and resistless attacks; when the immediate intentions for chaos escape us and the inscrutable designs of the divine Architect are past finding out—then . . . the incomprehensible and wondrous God intervenes and interjects hope. He supernaturally calms the raging storm with a simple command, and suddenly a transworldly peace permeates our fragile hearts and minds, surpassing any ability to make sense of the miracle that he has just performed (Phil. 4:7).

Yet the aching for this hope of *shalom* would not exist without the tragic loss of paradise devolving into hell. Furthermore, the prolonging of the hellish nightmare only intensifies our longing for the brighter hope that shines only dimly now. God delays fully redressing the crisis in order to test and expand our faith in him, and so that our hope in his trustworthy promises is thereby increased. Again, this is by design. "For you, O Lord, are my hope, my trust, O LORD, from my youth" (Ps. 71:5).

The promise-keeping God provides hope by introducing an unprecedented hero, the only suitable Savior, one who exceeds all our expectations and shatters others. He bursts through the fearsome blackness to save the day, to grapple mightily with the damnable crisis and restore the world as it ought to be.

In preparation for the coming Messiah, God in his grace and from all eternity elects an undeserving and rebellious people for salvation: to forgive their sin and deliver them from his wrath and judgment, promising them eternal freedom from pain, suffering, and death. He then in time reconciles these estranged people, tenderly drawing them to communion with himself and then setting them apart to be recipients of a restored paradise, bright and beautiful.

And Jesus Christ, the promised Savior, accomplishes all this work of restoration, reconciliation, redemption, and renewal. This One, the same eternal, infinite, all-wise, all-powerful, omnibenevolent God, unexpectedly, surprisingly takes on human flesh. The unsuffering God defeats suffering in the world by coming into the world as one who suffers. The messianic Seed of ancient prediction defeats sin by becoming sin on behalf of the elect. He defeats death by dying an ignoble death in their place, satisfying God's righteous demands against their guilt. He destroys evil by entering the heart of it and dismantling its feral strength. He exerts curse-destroying power by imbibing powerlessness. The weakness of the cross is his weapon. The grave is the signal of his success.

But the grave can never be his end. He rises out of the stench of a cold, black tomb as the resurrected Lord of glory, ascending back to his throne of old, awaiting the day when he will complete his work of redemption, restoration, and renewal of all things in heaven and earth, removing every semblance of the curse, judging all remaining evil and evildoers, and establishing his imperishable, undefiled, unfading kingdom of the redeemed. The redemption of the cosmos came at a severe price that no human could fathom, a price that God himself paid.

This is such a stupendous story. No one would have thought of it except the transcendent Author of history. Yet it is the story that we all long for, whether we realize it or not. But none of it would make any sense unless God purposed evil to enter the portals of his good and perfect paradise, corrupting it and taking it down to the pits of such hellish misery. The pristine wonder of creation is thrust to the horrid depths of depravity and then rescued by the phenomenal Lord of glory, and he restores the lost paradise to its original condition.

The restored cosmos, however, will shine far brighter *only* because it had to endure such a terrible crisis and required such a severe price to redeem. If there were no crisis to solve, the whole story would fall flat. We'd have no reference point by which to judge the magnificence of the Lord's power and wisdom and holiness and justice and love as seen through the lens of judgment and salvation, of retribution and redemption. Grace would be eliminated. There would be no need for it. And though God is eternally glorious, we would not see and experience the full wonder of it.

God's purpose in creating the world and us, his image-bearing creatures, was not simply to display his glory, but to magnify it *supremely*. There was no other way he could do that without, first, the deadly fall of mankind, and then the lowly incarnation, the bloody cross, the powerful resurrection, the magnificent ascension, and the Savior's all-glorious return.

This is the work of his freedom, power, righteousness, and especially grace. It is the grand grace effect. And this leads to glory, the *grand glory effect*. It is why we call this the *greater-glory theodicy*: the surprisingly hope-inspiring reality of *felix culpa*, the fortunateness of the fall. As strange as it seems, we thank God for the fall of our human parents. We do not praise their arrogance and rebellion. We praise God for wisely structuring their fall to bring about the glory of redemption. I assure you that we would want it no other way!

And he is not finished.

One day the thunderous and eardrum-crushing sound of the Redeemer's return rattling the foundations of the earth will indicate that his coming kingdom far outweighs the puny kingdom of darkness and all the pain it brings. "For this light momentary affliction is preparing for us an eternal weight of glory beyond all comparison" (2 Cor. 4:17). No Holocaust of pain and madness can match his grace and glory. If you know Christ, your suffering is never wasted. Your deepest pain is not in vain. Your sin cannot condemn you. Your fear of death need not worry you, for your redemption draweth nigh!

Theodore Cuyler was the little-known, unassuming pastor of Lafayette Avenue Presbyterian Church in Brooklyn, New York, in the late nineteenth century. Like all of us, he was no stranger to suffering the effects of the fall. In his autobiography he writes, "In the autumn of 1881, 'the four corners of my house were smitten' again with a heart-breaking bereavement in the death, by typhoid fever, of our second daughter, Louise Ledyard Cuyler, at the age of twenty-two."[47]

Cuyler and his wife had already experienced the loss of two children when they were but little babes. Cuyler tells us more of his loss: "[Louise] possessed a most inexpressible beauty of person and character. Her playful humour, her fascinating charm of manner, and her many noble qualities drew to her the admiration of a large circle of friends, as well as the pride

---

47. Theodore L. Cuyler, *God's Light on Dark Clouds* (repr., Carlisle, PA: Banner of Truth, 2008), viii.

of our parental hearts." Cuyler sounds like any parent who loves his or her children. Like all who grieve, he wants to remember with fondness the loved one lost.

He adds:

> After her departure I wrote, through many tears, a small volume entitled God's Light on Dark Clouds, with the hope that it might bring some rays of comfort into those homes that were shadowed in grief. Judging from the numberless letters that have come to me I cannot but believe that, of all the volumes which I have written, this one has been the most honoured of God as a messenger-bearer to that largest of all households—the household of the sorrowing.[48]

This is a clue that Cuyler has something of significance to say to the bereaved Christian mother or father—indeed, to all the suffering saints of God.

Among his wise words are these gems of encouragement:

> So, to all my fellow-sufferers who are treading their way through the tunnels of trial, I would say: "Tighten your loins with the promises, and keep the strong staff of faith well in hand. Trust God in the dark. We are safer with him in the dark than without him in the sunshine. He will not suffer your foot to stumble. His rod and his staff never break. Why he brought us here we know not now, but we shall know hereafter. At the end of the gloomy passage beams the heavenly light. Then comes the exceeding and eternal weight of glory!"[49]

Let this evil and pain-filled world be as it may. We will worry not what afflictions come our way. Rather, "we rejoice in our sufferings, knowing that suffering produces endurance, and endurance produces character, and character produces hope, and hope does not put us to shame, because God's love has been poured into our hearts through the Holy Spirit who has been given to us" (Rom. 5:3–5). We hope in his salvation, and in a glorious Savior. Our glory is to bask in his glory.

His glory is made infinitely more comforting and satisfying for us when we have trod long and hard through dark, mucky, filthy trenches and come out the backside into crisp fresh air and resplendent sunshine. Paul declares: "For God, who said, 'Let light shine out of darkness,' has shone in our hearts to give the light of the knowledge of the glory of God in the face of Jesus Christ" (2 Cor. 4:6). The darkness cannot overcome the One whose face shines on us so brightly.

48. Cuyler, *God's Light on Dark Clouds*, viii.
49. Cuyler, *God's Light on Dark Clouds*, 31–32.

John the Revelator saw it all so clearly:

> And I heard every creature in heaven and on earth and under the earth and in the sea, and all that is in them, saying,

> "To him who sits on the throne and to the Lamb
> be blessing and honor and glory and might forever and ever!"
> (Rev. 5:13)

Amen and amen! To God be the glory!

KEY TERMS

felix culpa
greater-glory theodicy
redemption

STUDY QUESTIONS

1. Why do good things often bring tears of joy instead of smiles or laughter?
2. What is it about the concept of grace that makes Christianity stand apart from every other religion or philosophy?
3. Why is suffering a necessary part of the Christian life?
4. According to the author, what are three ways in which biblical grace was displayed during the Holocaust? Elaborate on each way.
5. What sustained Corrie and Betsie ten Boom during their harrowing experience at Ravensbrück, the notorious concentration camp for women? What can be learned from their example of bearing up under severe trials?
6. Why is it so important for the Christian to forgive others? List as many reasons as you can think of.
7. How has this book impacted your thinking about God and the problem of evil?

FOR FURTHER READING

Chris Brauns, *Unpacking Forgiveness: Biblical Answers for Complex Questions and Deep Wounds* (Wheaton, IL: Crossway, 2008).

Philip Hallie, *Lest Innocent Blood Be Shed: The Story of the Village of Le Chambon and How Goodness Happened There* (New York: HarperCollins, 1994).

Eleonore Stump, "The Mirror of Evil," in *God and the Philosophers,* ed. Thomas V. Morris (Oxford: Oxford University Press, 1996), 235–47.

Larry Alex Taunton, *The Grace Effect: How the Power of One Life Can Reverse the Corruption of Unbelief* (Nashville: Thomas Nelson, 2011).

Corrie ten Boom, *The Hiding Place*, 35th anniversary ed. (Grand Rapids: Chosen Books, 2006).

Miroslav Volf, *Free of Charge: Giving and Forgiving in a Culture Stripped of Grace* (Grand Rapids: Zondervan, 2005).

Simon Wiesenthal, *The Sunflower: On the Possibilities and Limits of Forgiveness* (New York: Schocken Books, 1998).

Advanced

Miroslav Volf, *Exclusion and Embrace: A Theological Exploration of Identity, Otherness, and Reconciliation* (Nashville: Abingdon Press, 1996).

APPENDIX:
SULLIED BY SUPRALAPSARIANISM?

The greater-glory theodicy (*felix culpa*) that I am advocating is commonly associated with the tongue-twisting term *supralapsarianism*, which is found only in the deepest bowels of theology textbooks.[1] And it is here that we enter arcane debates about the order of God's decrees. The Westminster Confession of Faith says, "God, from all eternity, did, by the most wise and holy counsel of his own will, freely, and unchangeably ordain whatsoever comes to pass."[2] But how did God order his decrees? What has he prioritized? Reformed theologians in the sixteenth and seventeenth centuries fiercely debated where God's eternal decree of election (to salvation) and reprobation (condemnation) stood logically in relation to his decree of the fall.[3]

The majority of Reformed theologians have taken the position of infralapsarianism, which states that God decreed the election of some to salvation and the reprobation of others to judgment *after* (*infra*) he decreed humanity's *lapse* (*lapsum*) into sin. A minority of Reformed theologians have held

1. Alvin Plantinga, "Supralapsarianism, or 'O Felix Culpa,'" in *The Problem of Evil: Selected Readings*, ed. Michael L. Peterson, 2nd ed. (Notre Dame, IN: University of Notre Dame Press, 2017), 363–89; Robert L. Reymond, *A New Systematic Theology of the Christian Faith*, 2nd ed. (Grand Rapids: Zondervan Academic, 2001), 499–500; Edwin Chr. van Driel, *Incarnation Anyway: Arguments for Supralapsarian Christology* (New York: Oxford University Press, 2008), 126–32; Melville Y. Stewart, *The Greater-Good Defence: An Essay on the Rationality of Faith* (New York: Palgrave Macmillan, 1993), 150–52.

2. WCF 3.1. See especially Eph. 1:9–11; cf. Ps. 33:11; Prov. 19:21; Isa. 46:10; Acts 20:28; Rom. 8:28; Eph. 3:11; 2 Tim. 1:9; Heb. 6:11.

3. For the history of this debate, see Richard A. Muller, *Christ and the Decree* (Grand Rapids: Baker Academic, 2008); J. V. Fesko, *Diversity within the Reformed Tradition: Supra- and Infralapsarianism in Calvin, Dort, and Westminster* (Greenville, SC: Reformed Academic Press, 2001). For a history of the doctrine of reprobation, see Peter Sammons, *Reprobation: From Augustine to the Synod of Dort: The Historical Development of the Reformed Doctrine of Reprobation*, Reformed Historical Theology 63 (Oakville, CT: Vandenhoeck & Ruprecht, 2020).

461

to supralapsarianism, which says that God made the decree of election and condemnation *prior* (*supra*) to this lapse into sin.[4] While infralapsarianism is the majority report and has been implicitly endorsed in some Reformed confessions, supralapsarianism has always been regarded as being within the pale of Reformed orthodoxy.[5]

Infralapsarianism	Supralapsarianism
1. Decree to create humans	1. Decree to elect some humans to salvation and condemn others to judgment
2. Decree to permit all humans to fall	2. Decree to create both kinds of humans
3. Decree to elect some fallen humans to salvation and condemn the rest to judgment	3. Decree that all humans would fall
4. Decree to redeem the elect by the work of Christ	4. Decree to redeem the elect by the work of Christ

Fig. A.1. The Order of God's Decrees

Supralapsarians believe that God first conceived of human beings as creations capable of falling into sin. Subsequently, the fall is the means by which God would manifest his glory either in his mercy toward the elect in salvation or in his justice toward reprobates in judgment.[6] Infralapsarians believe that God conceived of humans as already created and fallen before

---

4. It is important to note that God's decrees are not made in time (i.e., in chronological succession), even though their outworking occurs in time as part of the created order. Strictly speaking, God's decrees (plural) are all of one piece (i.e., his *decree*, singular) made by a timeless, eternal, infinite deity. But in order for us to make sense of it, we speak in terms of a logical order and employ chronological terminology (i.e., *infra-* and *supra-*).

5. Benjamin B. Warfield, "Predestination in the Reformed Confessions," in *Studies in Theology*, in *The Works of Benjamin B. Warfield*, vol. 9 (repr., Grand Rapids: Baker, 2000), 228–29; Herman Bavinck, *Reformed Dogmatics*, ed. John Bolt, trans. John Vriend, 4 vols. (Grand Rapids: Baker Academic, 2003–8), 2:384. Although the Westminster Confession leans toward an infralapsarian position, the head of the Westminster Assembly, William Twisse, was a strong advocate for supralapsarianism.

6. Richard A. Muller, *Dictionary of Latin and Greek Theological Terms*, 2nd ed. (Grand Rapids: Baker Academic, 2017), 348–49.

he considered his election of some to salvation and the condemnation of others to judgment.[7]

While both positions claim that the order of the decrees is strictly logical and atemporal, for infralapsarians, the actual chronological occurrence of the decrees in history happens to follow the logical order. Supralapsarianism is often framed by its opponents as an austere manifestation of double predestination. In other words, God saw the unfallen "lump" of humanity from Romans 9:21 and indiscriminately fashioned one group as "vessels of mercy" (v. 23) and the other group as "vessels of wrath" (v. 22). Infralapsarians see the "lump" of humanity as already fallen from out of which two actions occur.

First, some are positively elected to receive the mercy of salvation. Second, the others are passed over (called *preterition*) and yet are also actively precondemned based on their foreseen willful rebellion against God.[8] It is often thought that supralapsarians place the accent of God's decree of election on his sovereignty, whereas for infralapsarians it is placed on his mercy.[9] But this is a false dichotomy. Both would agree that election is a sovereign mercy as well as a merciful sovereignty. In the same way, reprobation is a sovereign justice as well as a just sovereignty. One must not impugn the simplicity of God here by elevating one divine attribute over another.[10] We must see God's character revealed in his decree as a symphony whereby every instrument contributes to one beautifully crafted score.

---

7. Muller, *Dictionary of Latin and Greek*, 349–50.

8. Romans 9:22–23 supports the idea that election is a positive (active) decree and reprobation is a negative (passive) decree. (As noted, however, reprobation includes active precondemnation based on foreseen sin. Therefore, it may be best to say that election and reprobation are a matter of unequal ultimacy.) Verse 23, which speaks of God's election of "vessels of mercy" who are "prepared beforehand," uses an aorist active verb (*prohetoimazo*). On the other hand, the term "prepared" (*katartizo*) regarding the "vessels of wrath" in verse 22 is a passive participle. Furthermore, the use of the prepositional prefix *pro-* in *prohetoimazo* (v. 23) gives the term a temporal reference ("beforehand"), whereas *katartizo* (v. 22) has no temporal reference. This would suggest that more specific attention is given to the elect in God's pretemporal decree, as passages such as Romans 8:29–30 and Ephesians 1:4 attest. Thomas R. Schreiner writes that "the use of the passive voice [of *katartizo*] in contrast to the active for [*prohetoimazo*] signals that the plan to destroy the wicked is asymmetrical with the plan to save the vessels of mercy. In any case, one cannot by exegetical means rescue God from willing the fate of the vessels of wrath" (*Romans*, Baker Exegetical Commentary on the New Testament, 2nd ed. [Grand Rapids: Baker, 2018], 509–10).

9. J. V. Fesko, "Lapsarian Controversy at the Synod of Dort," in *Drawn into Controversie: Reformed Theological Diversity and Debates within Seventeenth-Century British Puritanism*, ed. Michael A. G. Haykin and Mark Jones (Oakville, CT: Vandenhoeck & Ruprecht, 2011), 112.

10. John M. Frame, *The Doctrine of God* (Phillipsburg, NJ: P&R Publishing, 2002), 600–608; Bavinck, *Reformed Dogmatics*, 1:112–24.

LAPSARIAN LIMITATIONS

Why all the fuss? Well, the debate has much to do with the problem of evil.[11] Infralapsarians have often charged that supralapsarians (and thus the *felix culpa* theodicy) make God culpable for sin given that he decrees the reprobation of humans without regard for their fallen state.[12] The idea is that as God creates faith in the hearts of the elect, so he also creates unbelief in the hearts of the reprobate in a game of equal ultimacy.[13]

Furthermore, God seems to craft some humans for no other reason than to torture them in hell. God is conceived of as a cosmic Sid, the sociopathic neighbor in the Pixar film *Toy Story*, who disassembles perfectly good toys and converts them into grotesque contraptions for sinister and destructive purposes. Supralapsarians, however, have vigorously denied God's culpability for sin. And they would deny that God is morally capricious.

On the other hand, supralapsarians have accused infralapsarians of positing a God who has no purpose in permitting the fall except to say that it was his own "good pleasure."[14] It appears to be a frustration of his original plan. Responding to postlapsarian creatures in salvation and judgment suggests that God had to suddenly come up with plan B. Infralapsarians deny that God alters his one plan for creation, and the fall was certainly part of that plan.

Nevertheless, many infralapsarians doubt whether a positive theodicy can be formulated. Only a strict defense of God's sovereign and moral integrity can be offered in the face of evil. For example, the infralapsarian R.C. Sproul states, "I do not know the solution to the problem of evil. Nor do I know of anyone else who does. I have never been satisfied by any of the theodicies I've ever seen. This does not mean the problem is insoluble or that the question is unanswerable."[15] For us humans, the matter is relegated largely to mystery.

Many contemporary Reformed theologians have questioned the value of this intramural debate. While some matters may be deduced from a synthesis of the relevant data, Scripture is not explicit about the order of divine decrees; therefore, we must be careful about trying to read too much where divine revelation is silent.[16] John Frame has argued that trying to ascertain

---

11. Frame, *Doctrine of God*, 339.

12. Gerald Bray, *The Doctrine of God* (Downers Grove, IL: InterVarsity Press, 1993), 90–91.

13. While hyper-Calvinists hold to this view (see discussion in R.C. Sproul, *Chosen by God* [Wheaton, IL: Tyndale House, 1986], 142–43), the majority of supralapsarians do not. Therefore, the charge is spurious.

14. Bavinck, *Reformed Dogmatics*, 2:385; Reymond, *New Systematic Theology*, 499–500.

15. R.C. Sproul, *The Invisible Hand* (Phillipsburg, NJ: P&R Publishing, 1996), 167. Yet he does go on to say, "Ultimately it must be good that there is evil or evil would not exist" (167).

16. Frame, *Doctrine of God*, 337.

what precisely is meant by the logical relationship between the decrees is fraught with all sorts of problems.[17]

Likewise, Herman Bavinck points out that God's multifaceted, multi-perspectival decrees form an "interconnected pattern" that is "enormously rich and complex" and cannot be reduced to the overly simple formulations that each side has put forward. "Preceding components impact subsequent components, but even future events already condition the past and the present. The whole picture is marked by immensely varied omnilateral interaction."[18] In other words, both positions make important points but are hampered by their limited perspectives.

Nonetheless, the matter of moral culpability is an important issue. Infralapsarians are correct in stating that God's condemnation of reprobates finds little biblical justification apart from first contemplating their willful actions as a violation of his moral will. Furthermore, God does not actively, directly, coercively harden human hearts. In other words, he does not infuse evil into the hearts of the reprobate. He is never the immediate, efficient cause of human sin. Rather, he hardens hearts, like that of Pharaoh (Rom. 9:17–18), by various secondary causes, including the removal of his restraints, abandoning his common grace, and giving people over to their sin (1:24–31). In this regard, hardening is a form of divine judgment.[19]

God is still the ultimate Author of the destinies of all men, however, irrespective of their actions (Rom. 9:11–13, 21). Frame addresses this tension by noting that election and reprobation cannot be conceived of as being "parallel in every respect. They are equally ultimate in the sense that both decrees of God are ultimately efficacious. Yet there is an asymmetry between them. The blessings ordained by God's eternal election are received entirely by God's grace, apart from human works. But the curses ordained by God's eternal reprobation are fully deserved, because of the sins of the reprobate."[20] God stands directly (proximately) behind good and only indirectly (remotely) behind evil. The latter is always attributed to proximate secondary causes—in other words, willful creatures who rebel against God's moral will.[21]

17. John M. Frame, *The Doctrine of the Knowledge of God* (Phillipsburg, NJ: P&R Publishing, 1987), 261–63. See also John S. Feinberg, *No One like Him: The Doctrine of God* (Wheaton, IL: Crossway, 2001), 533–36.

18. Bavinck, *Reformed Dogmatics*, 2:392; cf. Frame, *Doctrine of the Knowledge of God*, 265–66.

19. Sproul, *Chosen by God*, 144–48. I deal more fully with the charge that God is the author of evil in chapter 9.

20. Frame, *Doctrine of God*, 334.

21. D. A. Carson, *How Long, O Lord? Reflections on Suffering and Evil*, 2nd ed. (Grand

Frame summarizes the problematic polarities of this debate with specific regard for the problem of evil. Supralapsarianism appears guilty of domesticating evil "as a mere step upward toward the glorification of the elect." But while infralapsarians have a proper revulsion for "the horrible, inexplicable character of evil, . . . they find it more difficult to understand evil as part of a harmonious plan."[22] I believe the way both sides have framed the order of the decrees has obscured these as well as the other important points that Frame, Bavinck, and others have made.

VIEWING GOD'S DECREES FROM ANOTHER ANGLE

I offer another way of viewing God's decrees oriented around three controlling and indisputable propositions, and a subsequent question.[23]

> Proposition 1: God's ultimate end is delighting in the magnificence of his own glory.
>
> Proposition 2: God is in no way required to display his glory outside the intra-Trinitarian self-delight it elicits.
>
> Proposition 3: God freely chose to create the world in order that he might have a theater to display and thus share the delight of his own glory with his intelligent creatures, especially human beings.

The subsequent question, then, is this: how did God deem it best to magnify his glory to those creatures? The following argument regarding God's decree (purposes) seeks to take into consideration these three propositions and the question they pose.

I am not offering here anything like the traditional order of decrees; I am simply drawing inferences from these statements. My points take into account the controlling motif of the biblical storyline of creation, fall, and redemption (see chapter 11). In this regard, there is some consideration of the infralapsarian focus on the chronological outworking of God's decree. The flow of each point, however, takes the teleological concerns of

---

Rapids: Baker Academic, 2006), 189; Paul Helm, *The Providence of God* (Downers Grove, IL: InterVarsity Press, 1994), 190–91; Sproul, *Chosen by God*, 142–43. Like infralapsarians, many supralapsarians posit both a negative and a positive reprobation. Negative reprobation occurs before the fall and involves the passing over (preterition) of some humans for salvation. Positive reprobation (precondemnation) occurs after the fall and is rooted in God's justice and the willful culpability of the fallen (Bavinck, *Reformed Dogmatics*, 2:363–64). Robert Reymond, a supralapsarian, has recognized the moral-culpability problem. He proposes a revised and nuanced supralapsarian order to account for it. See *New Systematic Theology*, 389, 394–96.

22. Frame, *Doctrine of God*, 339.

23. I have provided the details of this argument in chapter 12.

supralapsarianism for establishing an actual biblical theodicy seriously.[24] Thus, the order here follows neither the traditional infralapsarian nor the supralapsarian scheme.

1. The Supreme Magnification of God's Glory

God freely decided to supremely magnify his glory to his intelligent creatures (especially his image-bearing creatures—human beings) as an overflow of his own delight in his glory.

2. Creation as the Theater for God's Glory

In order to do this, God decided to create the universe, and our world in particular, as a theater for his extrinsic glory and placed his creatures within it to enjoy that glory. The unfallen world gives a glimpse of divine glory in its perfections, beauty, harmony, and order as somewhat ideally intended. I say "somewhat" because the final state of creation is better than its initial state. The movement from creation's fall to its ultimate redemption (consummation) magnifies the glory of its final state in a way that would be unrealized and unappreciated without the fall.

3. Redemption as the Vehicle for God's Supreme Glory

God determined, however, that his glory be supremely magnified in the redemption of his creation and his particular image-bearing creatures— human beings. Thus, election finds its grounding in the broader scriptural motif of redemption.

4. The Fall as Necessary for Redemption

Redemption is not necessary unless God has decreed humanity's fall and that of creation as a whole. Paradise restored from its lost estate is better than paradise that was never lost in the first place—thus, *felix culpa*: the fortunateness of the fall. In the nature of the case, this is precisely where the glory of redemption is manifested. Robert Reymond is correct: "The Fall has significance as a real event of history only as it is allowed to stand in the redemptive history of Scripture as a means to an end in relation to God's one eternal plan of redemption, on the ground . . . that the state of *the elect as children of God in Christ by divine grace* is ultimately a higher, more

---

24. Robert Reymond sees the importance of supralapsarianism's teleological focus and thus offers an improved order of decrees from older attempts. But he seems unwilling to concede important points about infralapsarianism. See his extended discussion in *New Systematic Theology*, 479–502.

glorious, and more praiseworthy end than the state of *all men as children of God in unfallen Adam by divine justice.*"[25]

Thus, God's glory is best magnified in the juxtaposition of creation, fall, and redemption. Note that the accent never rests on evil (the fall), but always on redemption's triumph over it. The whole complex of salvific terms that use the *re-* prefix in Scripture, such as *redemption, reconciliation (reunion), restoration, regeneration (rebirth), resurrection,* and *repentance,* speak of returning from an unsatisfactory state of affairs to a previous satisfactory or ideal state.[26] There is a distinct U-shaped—or, better yet, J-shaped—flow to redemptive history. While redemption is the controlling motif of this theodicy, it is simply the foil whereby God supremely magnifies his glory. Consequently, I call this the *greater-glory theodicy.*

5. Reprobation as a Magnification of Glory vis-à-vis Redemption

God could have chosen to redeem all his image-bearing creatures, but he determined that redemption magnifies his glory more greatly when some are damned (reprobated) and others redeemed (elected). God's mercy and grace (and thus his glory) are magnified more fully against the backdrop of his justice being executed against vessels of wrath rightly deserving judgment (Rom. 9:22–23). Without the display of justice against a vast host of sinners, God's mercy and grace toward the elect are viewed as normal and expected, thereby domesticating God's extrinsic glory.

6. The Cross as the Center of Redemption and Therefore God's Supreme Glory

This merciful and gracious work of redemption is accomplished only through the incarnated Son of God so that he exists as the center of God's glory, thus highlighting "the riches of his grace" (Eph. 1:7, 14; 2:7). This is the apex of the broad purpose of God. Christ is the center of God's glory as manifest to his creatures. Furthermore, the nucleus of that center is focused on the redemptive work he achieved through a set of events suffused with such otherworldly and efficacious grace that it is otherwise inconceivable to human minds. The crucifixion of the Son of God and his subsequent resurrection and exaltation are not what we would expect from conventional

---

25. Reymond, *New Systematic Theology,* 500.

26. This tends to support the temporal order of the decrees present in infralapsarianism (i.e., creation, fall, redemption) while still suggesting the teleological focus of supralapsarianism.

heroes. But Jesus is no conventional hero. The cross is scandalous, and for this reason it is glorious beyond compare.

In explicating this order, at first it appears that redemption is the primary focus. But we are not talking about ordinary conceptions of redemption like those expressed in common monomythic storytelling (see chapter 10). Biblical redemption is unprecedented, for at its center we find the atoning work of the utterly incomparable Christ. While the cross is the *means* to redemptive *ends*, the uniqueness of the cross stands out supremely above every other kind of redemption (see chapters 14 through 16).

In other words, biblical redemption finds its glory specifically and uniquely in Christ. Christ is the center of redemptive glory. Redemption loses its luster without Christ. Nothing exalts the glory of God more highly. Furthermore, the elect find all their redemptive good in Christ. The eternal glory of the saints will always be centered on how "the Lamb who was slain" achieved it (Rev. 5:6–14). When the story of our rescue from sin and ruin is replayed in our minds, the cross and empty tomb at the climax of the story will always be remembered and celebrated as that which brings God greatest glory and our greatest good—reconciliation with our magnificent God (1 Peter 3:18).

Thus, the incarnation of Christ is the more proper focus of the traditional order of the divine decree, not the election of saints per se. This is a departure from the way that older supralapsarians have conceived of the decree, in which it appears that the accent is on election while the broader motif of redemption, and especially the cross and resurrection, appears as a secondary concern. Even when Scripture pictures the elect as redeemed in the eternal decree, they are viewed only through the all-encompassing lens of their union "in Christ" (Eph. 1:4).

Therefore, God's glory is most magnified in the atoning work of Christ, which brought about the redemption of the elect. From here, the ancillary means to redemption come into view, such as the fall, which otherwise makes redemption unnecessary. Furthermore, if none are damned, the glory of redemption is domesticated, being blunted by its ubiquity, its commonality. The contrast between the rare and undeserving objects of redemption against the backdrop of the common and deserved judgment of reprobates amplifies the glory of redemption. Just like pearls of great price (Matt. 13:45–46), redemption is made more precious and glorious by the rare privilege afforded the grace-drenched minority who benefit from it (7:13–14).

The core argument for the greater-glory theodicy of *felix culpa* can be summarized another way via the following premises and conclusion:[27]

1. God's ultimate purpose in freely creating the world is to supremely magnify the riches of his glory to all his creatures, especially human beings, who alone bear his image.
2. God's glory is supremely magnified in the atoning work of Christ, which is the sole means of accomplishing redemption for human beings.
3. Redemption is unnecessary unless human beings have fallen into sin.
4. Therefore, the fall of humanity is necessary to God's ultimate purpose in creating the world.

So is this cross-centered theodicy of redemptive glory sullied by supralapsarianism? I do not believe so. I believe it seeks to assimilate the primary concerns of both supra- and infralapsarianism while discarding each of their inherent limitations. Technically, my proposal cannot be categorized as either, since election and reprobation are secondary considerations. Ironically, the fall (*lapse*) figures prominently in the lapsarian debate even though its purpose is not always made clear. While the fall along with all its attendant evils is not a first-order concern of God's decree, neither is it a mysterious accident. It is, as it were, *a necessary evil* (!) purposed toward the greater end of magnifying God's glory in the redemptive work of Christ whereby he brings about our rescue from evil's dark domain (Col. 1:13–14). While evil figures prominently in our experience, it is overshadowed by the blood-soaked tree on which Christ hung, and the empty tomb from which he gloriously emerged three days later.

KEY TERMS

greater-glory theodicy
infralapsarianism
supralapsarianism

STUDY QUESTIONS

1. What is the difference between infralapsarianism and supralapsarianism? What are the strengths and weaknesses of each position?

---

27. See chapter 12 for a detailed explanation of each of these points.

2. What does the author offer as a better way to frame the order of God's decrees? Do you think this is a helpful way forward concerning the lapsarian debate? Why or why not?

FOR FURTHER READING

John M. Frame, *The Doctrine of God* (Phillipsburg, NJ: P&R Publishing, 2002).

Robert L. Reymond, *A New Systematic Theology of the Christian Faith*, 2nd ed. (Grand Rapids: Zondervan Academic, 2001).

R.C. Sproul, *Chosen by God* (Wheaton, IL: Tyndale House, 1986).

Advanced

Herman Bavinck, *Reformed Dogmatics*, ed. John Bolt, trans. John Vriend, 4 vols. (Grand Rapids: Baker Academic, 2003–8).

J. V. Fesko, *Diversity within the Reformed Tradition: Supra- and Infralapsarianism in Calvin, Dort, and Westminster* (Greenville, SC: Reformed Academic Press, 2001).

Richard A. Muller, *Christ and the Decree* (Grand Rapids: Baker Academic, 2008).

GLOSSARY

active obedience (of Christ). A doctrine stating that Christ's deliberate obedience in fulfilling the positive demands of the law of God is imputed to the believer as one of the means whereby the believer is justified (declared or counted righteous) before God. See **passive obedience** (of Christ); **penal substitution**.

affections. As maintained in **classical theism**, God's mental (emotional) states (i.e., his expressions of love, compassion, joy, patience, anger, etc.) whereby he is marked by voluntary (self-controlled), rational, stable, predictable dispositions of the soul. This is distinguished from **passions**, which classical theism claims that God does not have.

Age of Reason. See **Enlightenment**.

archetypal. See **archetypes**.

archetypes. Universal themes, patterns, images, plot motifs, and characters (protagonists and antagonists) in storytelling that universally resonate with audiences because they mirror our common experiences. **archetypal**, adj. See **Freytag's Pyramid; monomyth**.

Arminianism. A theological orientation associated with the teachings of Jacob Arminius (1560–1609). Arminianism teaches five basic ideas. First, God has predestined to save those who he foreknows (via **simple foreknowledge**) will exercise faith in Christ. Second, Christ's death was an **atonement** for all humanity regardless of who believes on Christ for salvation. Third, humans in their natural state do not have **free will** or the capacity for saving faith. But, fourth, God has supplied **prevenient grace** to all humans so that they can recover free will (in the libertarian sense) and exercise saving faith. This prevenient grace enables them to either cooperate with God's saving grace or resist it if they choose. Fifth, the grace of God assists the believer throughout his life, but this grace can be neglected. Consequently, the believer can incur the loss of salvation. Arminianism's belief in **libertarian free will** puts it in the category of **free-will theism**, and Arminianism usually embraces some form of the **free-will defense** in response to the **problem of evil**.

aseity (of God). The attribute of God affirmed by **classical theism** that indicates his self-existence, self-sufficiency, and independence. God alone is the eternal, uncreated, and ever-active uncaused cause of all. He has life within himself and is in no way dependent on anything outside himself.

atonement. The satisfaction of a holy God's righteous demands against the violation of his character and laws (see **propitiation**) so that the **sin** and guilt of the violator (sinner) may be removed (see **expiation**) and the sinner reconciled to God. Only the bloody death and resurrection of Christ can serve as an acceptable atoning sacrifice to God for the reconciliation of sinners. **atoning,** adj. See **penal substitution.**

atoning death. See **atonement.**

atoning sacrifice. See **atonement.**

Augustinianism. A theological orientation that embraces a broad spectrum of ideas associated with the teachings of Augustine (A.D. 354–430), especially as he opposed the heretical ideas of **Pelagianism.** Augustine emphasized God's all-encompassing sovereignty and **meticulous providence,** the depravity of man, and the bondage of the human will apart from the grace of God. Augustinian theology had a major impact on the Protestant Reformation, including the views of Martin Luther (1483–1546) and John Calvin (1509–64). These distinctive views of Augustinianism are broadly associated today with **Reformed theology,** which in turn is associated with **Calvinism.**

beatific vision. The experience of fully redeemed and glorified saints whereby upon death they come face to face with the unveiled **glory** of God and thus enter a state of perfect blessedness, joy, peace (*shalom*), and satisfaction. Such saints will exist forever in a restored *imago Dei*.

best-of-all-possible-worlds defense. A way of addressing the **problem of evil** that claims that a perfect God (see **classical theism**) would create only the best **possible world** that could exist even though such a world contains **evil.** Ironically, various evils are necessary in order for God to bring about the unique goods that make this the best possible world. See **greater-glory theodicy.**

Calvinism. A theological orientation that embraces a broad spectrum of ideas associated with the teachings of the Protestant Reformer John Calvin (1509–64). Calvinism, however, is often identified by the five points of Calvinism, traditionally represented by the acronym *TULIP.* The *T* stands for *total depravity,* which indicates that humanity is in bondage to **sin.** The *U* stands for *unconditional election,* which indicates that

God chooses people for salvation wholly apart from anything they do. The *L* stands for *limited atonement*, which indicates that Christ's death secured **atonement** only for the elect. The *I* stands for *irresistible grace*, which indicates that God draws chosen sinners to Christ for salvation irresistibly. The *P* stands for *perseverance of the saints*, which indicates that the elect will certainly persevere in their salvation until the end. *Calvinism* is broadly synonymous with **Reformed theology** and has its antecedents in **Augustinianism**. See **Arminianism; free-will theism**.

Christus Victor. A term revived by Gustaf Aulén (1879–1977) that speaks to the victorious aspect of Christ's work of **atonement** and **redemption** whereby he defeats all the forces of **evil**, including **sin**, Satan and his demonic host, death, and all other Edenic curses that came as a result of the **fall** that afflict the **creation**. See **penal substitution**.

classical theism. The orthodox doctrine of God that dates back to theological reflection on the nature of God developed in the patristic era and beyond. It maintains, as Anselm (1033–1109) taught, that the triune God is a being "than-which-a-greater-cannot-be thought." His essence includes such things as perfection, absoluteness, infinity, **timeless eternality**, **aseity**, **simplicity**, **transcendence** and **immanence**, **immutability**, **impassibility**, **omnipotence**, omniscience, and omnipresence. Classical theism is also called *perfect-being theology* and has been associated with theologians such as Irenaeus (c. A.D. 130–202), Clement of Alexandria (A.D. 150–215), Augustine (A.D. 354–430), Boethius (A.D. 447–524), and Aquinas (A.D. 1225–74).

climax. The third movement of the plot structure in **Freytag's Pyramid**, which is the critical point, the moment of crisis when the conflict reaches its apex and there appears to be no reasonable way to resolve matters. The climax marks the turning point of the plot. In the case of a **tragedy**, the turning point goes from bad to worse and, in a **comedy**, from bad to good.

comedy. A plot type in classical literature in which a story has a good, happy, or satisfying ending. According to the great medieval poet Dante (c. 1265–1321), a comedy begins in pain and ends with joy. Comedy is contrasted with **tragedy**. See **Freytag's Pyramid**.

compatibilism. The view of **free agency** held by most proponents of **Calvinism** that claims that **divine determinism** is compatible with human freedom and **moral responsibility**. There is a dual explanation for every choice that humans make. God determines human choices, yet every person freely makes his or her own choices. God's causal power is exercised so that he never coerces people to choose as they do, yet they always choose according to his sovereign plan (see **decretive will** [of God]). People are free when they voluntarily choose according to their most compelling desires and as long as their choices are made in an unhindered way. While God never hinders one's choices, other factors can hinder people's freedom and thus their moral responsibility. Furthermore, moral and spiritual choices are conditioned on one's base nature, whether good or **evil** (i.e., unregenerate or regenerate). In this sense, one is either in bondage to his or her **sin** (unregenerate) nature or freed by a new spiritual (regenerate) nature. The compatibilist view of free agency is contrasted with **libertarianism**. **compatibilist, compatibilistic,** adj.

compatibilist. See **compatibilism.**

compatibilistic free will. See **compatibilism.**

contrary choice. See **Principle of Alternative Possibilities.**

creation. With respect to the metanarrative of Scripture, the "very good" (pristine) conditions of the world as God ideally intended it before the **fall** of Adam and Eve into **sin.** The prefall world represented by the garden of Eden was a paradise in which peace (*shalom*) and harmony existed between Creator and creatures (especially God's image-bearing creatures), between image-bearing creatures and themselves (i.e., Adam and Eve), and between God's creatures and the rest of the created order. See **redemption.**

decree(s) (of God). See **decretive will** (of God).

decretive will (of God). God's sovereign will, especially as it is understood in **Calvinism,** whereby he decrees (ordains) all events that transpire in space, time, and history, including all human actions. God's **providence** ensures that everything he has decreed will certainly come to pass. The Westminster Confession of Faith states, "God, from all eternity, did, by the most wise and holy counsel of his own will, freely, and unchangeably ordain whatsoever comes to pass" (WCF 3.1). Sometimes God's decretive will is known as his *secret will* because he rarely reveals beforehand what he has ordained to take place. See **preceptive will** (of God).

defense. A way of addressing the **problem of evil** that indicates *possible* reasons why God might permit (i.e., not prevent) **evil** to transpire in the world, but that, unlike a **theodicy,** does not seek to give a *definite* solution to the problem. A defense is more modest; it merely seeks to show that, broadly speaking, there is no logical inconsistency between the existence of God and the existence of evil. It claims that the one who has raised charges against God based on evil has not made his case. Thus, a defense carries a lighter burden than a theodicy. In this book, the terms *defense* and *theodicy* are generally used synonymously.

deism. A view of God that rose to prominence during the **Enlightenment** that says that he created the world and set it in motion using natural laws but does not otherwise interact within the world. Deism holds that God is **transcendent** but not **immanent**, thus denying or downplaying many of the personal and communicable attributes of God traditionally associated with Christian **theism. deistic,** adj.

deistic. See **deism.**

denouement. The last movement of the plot structure in **Freytag's Pyramid** in which the final unraveling of the action takes place and the conflict is fully resolved—the knot finally untied. In the case of a **comedy**, all is made well; the happily-ever-after can begin. In the case of a **tragedy**, it is the final catastrophe that unfolds, but always with a moral lesson to be learned.

divine determinism. The idea, usually promoted by **Calvinism**, claiming that God sovereignly stands behind and in some way causally determines every event and human choice in history. **Free-will theism** denies that God's sovereignty is deterministic, but rather holds that he respects the **libertarian free will** of his moral creatures, a freedom that is indeterministic (see **indeterminism**). Calvinism argues that divine determinism is not **fatalism**. Rather, to achieve his ends, God generally uses secondary causes (means), such as the compatibilistically free choices of human beings (see **compatibilism**) for which they bear **moral responsibility**.

divine-judgment defense. A way of addressing the **problem of evil** that claims that pain and suffering are the result of God's retributive punishment of evildoers, including the everlasting judgment of hell. Good comes out of judgment in the form of rehabilitation, deterrence, societal protection, and retribution. The hope of ultimate divine justice for evildoers redresses the suffering of the innocent. See **greater-good theodicy.**

divine providence. See **general providence; meticulous providence.**

divine transcendence. See **transcendence** (of God).

emotional problem of evil. See **existential problem of evil.**

Enlightenment. The intellectual movement that swept the Western world in the seventeenth and eighteenth centuries. Sometimes known as the *Age of Reason*, the Enlightenment introduced new ways of thinking about reality (see **epistemology**) that radically impacted science, religion, theology, ethics, aesthetics, and so forth. It rejected divine revelation as a source of truth and emphasized antisupernaturalism, humanism, rationalism, and empiricism, shifting Western thinking from a largely theocentric (God-centered) to an autonomous anthropocentric (man-centered) worldview. See **postmodernism; secularism.**

epistemology. An account (or theory) about knowledge; how we know what we know. It speaks to the sources and conditions that are necessary for rational thought, understanding, and cognitive processes as well as the limitations we have as intelligent creatures in making sense of the world around us. Epistemology tries to provide justification and rationality for truth claims, the things that we can or cannot know, and for the beliefs we hold.

eucatastrophe. J. R. R. Tolkien's term, meaning "good catastrophe," for "the sudden happy turn in a story" in which matters otherwise appeared hopeless. Tolkien believed that the highest purpose in a great story comes in the reversal of bad fortunes that then "pierces you with a joy that brings tears." Tolkien's use of the term fits within the framework of how the **monomyth** in the history of storytelling works. See **True Myth.**

evidential problem of evil. An argument that moves beyond the **logical problem of evil**, conceding that that argument has been successfully answered, and instead suggests that God's existence is improbable because of (1) the tremendous *quantity* of **evil** in the world or (2) the **horrendous evil** (often interpreted to be **gratuitous evil**) that exists in the world.

evil. See **moral evil; natural evil.** See also **gratuitous evil; horrendous evil.**

existential problem of evil. The deeply personal and religious aspect of the **problem of evil** that speaks to the soul-wrenching pain and bewilderment that occurs when God appears to be silent and no forthcoming answers can be ascertained as to why **evil** afflicts us. The problem is especially acute when suffering comes from **horrendous evil**, evil that appears unjustified, or evil that appears to be **gratuitous evil**. In such cases, pastoral care is needed when rational answers are often unsatisfying. Also called the *personal, religious,* or *emotional problem of evil.*

expiation. The removal of a sinner's **sin** and guilt by the **atoning sacrifice** of Christ, wiping the sinner's slate clean (i.e., purifying his heart) so that he is made acceptable before a just and holy God. See **penal substitution; propitiation.**

exposition. The first movement of the plot structure in **Freytag's Pyramid** in which the story is set up, introducing the characters and themes that lead to the emerging conflict.

extrinsic glory (of God). The external manifestation of the **intrinsic glory** of God as perceived by intelligent creatures. God reveals different aspects of his character and attributes through his works in creation and **providence**. Such extrinsic glory can vary depending on the manner in which God seeks to display it and the degree to which his creatures perceive it.

fall. With respect to the metanarrative of Scripture, the cataclysmic devastation of the "very good" **creation** resulting from the disobedience of God's image-bearing creatures Adam and Eve as they rebelled against their God and Creator. Adam's primordial **sin** brought about a universal curse on subsequent humanity and the rest of creation, which resulted in the perpetuation of **moral evil** and **natural evil** that now plagues the present world with pain and suffering and causes it to long for **redemption**.

falling action. The fourth movement of the plot structure in **Freytag's Pyramid** in which the conflict moves toward resolution, whether satisfying (**comedy**) or unsatisfying (**tragedy**). In Aristotle's language, it is the "reversal" whereby the knot ("entanglement") starts to be untied.

fatalism. A form of determinism denied by Christian **theism**, especially **Calvinism** (see **divine determinism**), that states that future events are fixed in such a way that human choices are irrelevant. It claims that what will be will be, and that there is nothing that anyone can do about it.

felix culpa. Latin for "fortunate fall" (or "fortunate fault"). The phrase can be traced back as far as a fourth-century liturgical hymn known as the *Exultet*, likely composed by Ambrose (c. A.D. 340–97), the bishop of Milan. It is connected to a **theodicy** claiming that it was better (fortunate) that Adam's **fall** occurred because this occasioned the coming of a great Redeemer—Jesus Christ—who would graciously redeem the world from the curse brought about by the fall. See **greater-glory theodicy.**

foreknowledge (of God). The attribute of God affirmed by **classical theism** whereby he knows exhaustively and infallibly all past, present, and future events that transpire in history. This presents problems for **free-will theism**, which embraces **libertarianism**. According to libertarianism, one could always choose differently than he did under exactly the same circumstances, so then how can God know what his creatures will choose? Most free-will theists have answered this problem in one of three ways: (1) **Arminianism** embraces **simple foreknowledge** as a solution. (2) **Open theism** denies exhaustive foreknowledge altogether. (3) **Molinism** embraces **middle knowledge** as a solution.

free agency. See **free will.**

free will. The idea that humans, as free moral agents, are designed by God with the capacity for freely making choices, which undergirds their **moral responsibility.** Most proponents of **Calvinism** and varieties of **free-will theism** agree that some kind of free agency is necessary for moral responsibility. But each branch of theology defines *free agency* differently. Free-will theists embrace a libertarian notion of free agency (see **libertarianism**). Many Calvinists embrace a **compatibilist** notion of free agency.

free-will defense. A way of addressing the **problem of evil** that claims that God risks the occurrence of **evil** by preserving the extremely valuable good of **libertarian free will,** which he bestows on his intelligent free moral agents (including humans and angels). The valuable freedom that such free agents possess, and that permits them to choose good, comes with the risk of also choosing evil. Thus, the free-will defense seeks to shift **moral responsibility** for evil from God to such free moral agents. This **defense** (or **theodicy**) is often coupled to the **natural-law defense.**

free-will theism. A theological orientation whose proponents emphasize the importance of God's granting humans significant freedom via **libertarian free will** and who also champion some version of the **free-will defense** in response to the **problem of evil.** Among those free-will theists who espouse these positions are proponents of **Arminianism, open theism,** and **Molinism.**

Freytag's Pyramid. The elements that frame a ubiquitous plot structure, using various **archetypes,** found in almost all literature (and, later, filmmaking), as observed by the nineteenth-century German novelist and playwright Gustav Freytag. The plot structure of stories in Freytag's Pyramid is marked by five movements: (1) the **exposition;** (2) the **rising action;** (3) the **climax;** (4) the **falling action;** and (5) the **denouement** of the story. See **monomyth.**

general providence. A view of divine providence, usually associated with **Arminianism** and **open theism,** whereby God has a general plan for history that respects the **libertarian free will** of his moral creatures and therefore does not meticulously ensure every detail of his plan. This view of providence is distinguished from **meticulous providence**.

general revelation. God's revelation of himself through the created order (creation) and the human conscience given to all people in all times and places. God has revealed a general but limited knowledge of his **providential**, **transcendent**, and moral attributes to all humanity. This knowledge is not sufficient for salvation, but it is sufficient for condemnation, leaving human beings who are created in God's image (see *imago Dei*) without excuse, bearing **moral responsibility** for their rebellion against God. Also called *natural revelation*.

glory (of God). See **extrinsic glory; intrinsic glory**.

gratuitous evil. Instances of **moral evil** or **natural evil**, which is also usually categorized as **horrendous evil** and which appears to be senseless, that is, without meaning, purpose, or sound reasons for occurring. Such **evil** appears to undermine God's goodness, making him an uncaring and capricious deity. See **skeptical-theism defense**.

greater-glory theodicy. A way of addressing the **problem of evil** that claims that God freely chose to create a world that included the crisis of **evil** initiated by the **fall** so that he might supremely magnify his **glory** through the **redemption** that is achieved by his **incarnate** Son, Jesus Christ. This **theodicy** is historically known as *felix culpa*, a phrase that speaks to the fortunateness of the fall. The greater-glory theodicy claims that a fallen-but-being-redeemed world is far better than an unfallen-not-needing-redemption world because such a world brings far greater glory to God. The greater-glory theodicy is a specific version of the **greater-good theodicy** with qualified aspects of the **best-of-all-possible-worlds defense**. No better world seems possible than one in which God's gracious work of redemption through Christ brings him such supreme glory.

greater good(s). See **greater-good theodicy**.

greater-good theodicy. A way of addressing the **problem of evil** that claims that God brings about greater goods via **evil** that could not otherwise come about without the evils connected to the emergence of those goods. These goods significantly outweigh the evils that they are connected to. Some of God's good and wise reasons for the occurrence of these greater goods can be ascertained, and other reasons cannot. The fact that some reasons remain hidden from us does not soundly argue against their existence (see **skeptical-theism defense**).

horrendous evil. Moral evil or **natural evil** that is especially horrific, shocking, violent, devastating, or the like, and that causes an unusual amount of pain and suffering. See **gratuitous evil; skeptical-theism defense.**

hypostatic union. The union of the fully divine nature to a fully human nature in the one person of the **incarnate** Son of God in which the two natures, according to Chalcedonian orthodoxy, undergo no confusion, no change, no division, and no separation.

imago Dei. Latin for "image of God"—the doctrine stating that human beings are unique among God's personal intelligent creatures in that they are created in his image, particularly as they reflect his communicable, personal, and relational attributes, such as intellect, volition, moral understanding, love, joy, wisdom, and exercising dominion. The **fall** of Adam into **sin** resulted in a shattered *imago Dei* in subsequent humanity but did not erase it. God's work of **redemption** through Christ begins the process of restoring the *imago Dei* in those whom he redeems. See **beatific vision; general revelation.**

immanence (of God). The attribute of God, related to his omnipresence, whereby he acts within and draws near to his creation. He especially expresses his immanence in a personal way in relating to his image-bearing creatures, human beings. In contrast to his **transcendence,** God condescends to creaturely understanding and experience so that he may make himself known to us in powerful ways. God's greatest act of immanent condescension came in the **incarnation** of the Son of God. **immanent,** adj.

immanent. See **immanence** (of God).

immutability (of God). The attribute of God affirmed by **classical theism** indicating that the perfections of his essential nature (i.e., who he is in himself—*ad intra*) cannot undergo change or alteration. Even though God does not change in his essence and character, he is always acting (i.e., he is not static). **immutable,** adj. See **impassibility** (of God).

immutable. See **immutability** (of God).

impassibility (of God). One of the attributes of deity affirmed by **classical theism** (and connected to God's **immutability**) whereby he does not suffer pain or loss and does not experience change in his intrinsic **affections** (mental or emotional state) as a result of outside influences. **impassible,** adj.

impassible. See **impassibility.**

incarnate. See **incarnation.**

incarnation. The doctrine stating that the second person of the Trinity, God the Son, assumed a human nature in addition to his eternally preexisting divine nature so that he might fully reveal the Godhead to his image-bearing creatures and accomplish the work of **redemption** that God the Father sent him to do. Without the incarnation, the redemption of fallen human beings is not possible. **incarnate,** adj. See **hypostatic union; kenosis** (of Christ).

indeterminism. The idea that is embraced by proponents of **free-will theism,** and that is an essential component of **libertarian free will,** that denies that all events and human choices are necessarily and causally determined by prior conditions, including the causal determinations of God. This is in contrast to most proponents of **Calvinism,** who embrace some form of **divine determinism.**

infralapsarianism. A view of God's **decrees** as understood by **Calvinism** that claims that God's decree of the **fall** logically precedes his decree of election. In this view, the order of decrees is as follows: God (1) creates humans; (2) permits all humans to fall; (3) elects some humans to salvation and condemns the rest; and (4) redeems the elect by the work of Christ. This view is distinguished from **supralapsarianism.**

intrinsic glory (of God). The incomprehensible, eternal, immutable, and invariable splendor and majesty of the perfections and excellence of all of God's attributes as they subsist and are perceived within himself. This is distinguished from God's **extrinsic glory.** See **classical theism.**

kenosis (of Christ). From the Greek *ekenōsen* ("emptied") in Philippians 2:7, the condescension of God the Son in his **incarnation** whereby he assumed all the weaknesses of humanity and veiled his divine **glory,** making use of his divine attributes in his earthly first-century ministry only as the Father willed, and in conjunction with the power of the Holy Spirit. See **hypostatic union.**

libertarian free will. See **libertarianism.**

libertarianism. The view held by varieties of **free-will theism** claiming that **free will** is incompatible with **divine determinism** because this would undermine human freedom and **moral responsibility.** God's sovereignty is exercised so that he does not causally determine human actions. Freedom of choice comes about when one has the ability to choose contrary (see **Principle of Alternative Possibilities**) to any prior factors that influence the choice, including external circumstances, one's motives, desires, character, and nature, and, of course, God himself. If these prior influences are sufficient to determine choices, then the freedom and responsibility of those choices are undermined. The libertarian view of free will is contrasted with **compatibilism. libertarian,** adj.

liberty of indifference. See **Principle of Alternative Possibilities.**

logical problem of evil. The classic trilemma formulating the basic **problem of evil** that suggests that the presence of **evil** in the world places God's all-encompassing power or goodness, and therefore his existence, in question. The trilemma can be stated with the following three premises and a conclusion: (1) God is omnipotent (all-powerful—see **omnipotence** [of God]); (2) God is omnibenevolent (all-good); (3) evil exists; (4) therefore, God does not exist. The assumption is that God *can* prevent evil because he is all-powerful (premise 1) and that he would *want* to prevent evil because he is all-good (premise 2). But since there is evil (premise 3), then either premise 1 or 2 is thought to be false, leading to the conclusion (4) that God does not exist. The problem was first raised by Epicurus (341–270 B.C.) and famously restated by David Hume (1711–76). In recent times, the problem was posed again by J. L. Mackie in a seminal article entitled "Evil and Omnipotence" (1955) and famously responded to by Alvin Plantinga's **free-will defense** (1967).

meticulous providence. A view of divine providence, usually associated with **Augustinianism** and **Calvinism** (but also **Molinism**), whereby God ensures that everything he decrees (which is all events in space, time, and history, including the choices of his intelligent creatures) comes to pass in meticulous detail (see **decretive will** [of God]). This view of providence (also called *meticulous sovereignty*) is distinguished from **general providence.**

meticulous sovereignty. See **meticulous providence.**

middle knowledge. A view of divine **foreknowledge** embraced by **Molinism** that claims that God has knowledge of *counterfactuals of creaturely freedom*—what people *would* freely choose (in a libertarian sense—see **libertarianism**) under any possible scenario in any **possible world** that might exist.

Molinism. A form of **free-will theism** derived from the teaching of Luis de Molina (1535–1600) that seeks to reconcile exhaustive **foreknowledge** and **meticulous providence** with **libertarian free will** by introducing God's **middle knowledge.** Middle knowledge indicates God's knowledge of *counterfactuals of creaturely freedom*—what people *would* freely choose (in a libertarian sense) under any possible scenario in any **possible world**

that might exist. God then sovereignly selects (decrees—see **decretive will** [of God]) from among the possible and feasible worlds that lie before him the one that best serves his purposes. Molinists say that their view preserves God's sovereignty while excusing him from **moral responsibility** for humans' misuse of their freedom to choose **evil**.

monomyth. In literary criticism, the "one story." The monomyth speaks to a ubiquitous pattern in storytelling (literature, filmmaking, etc.) in which the plot of such stories is U-shaped: good followed by a crisis of adversity (or **evil**) followed by some restoration to good. The term is commonly associated with Joseph Campbell's study of mythic stories in his book *The Hero with a Thousand Faces*, in which he connects it more narrowly to the "Hero's Journey," one of many **archetypes** in storytelling. The term as it is used in this book, however, fits its broader use in literary criticism, especially in the work of Northrop Frye and the Christian literary scholar Leland Ryken. **monomythic**, adj. See **Freytag's Pyramid; True Myth.**

monomythic. See **monomyth.**

moral culpability. See **moral responsibility.**

moral evil. Evil that is objectively unrighteous in nature (i.e., **sin**, sinful), violating the moral character and standards of God, and that is committed by personal, intelligent, and responsible moral creatures (see **moral responsibility**), and that also causes pain and suffering in the world. Adam's disobedience in the garden of Eden brought about the curse of the **fall** in which **original sin** passed on a corrupt sin nature to all of Adam's progeny, who are enslaved to moral evil. In addressing the **problem of evil**, moral evil is contrasted with **natural evil**. See **gratuitous evil; horrendous evil.**

moral nihilism. A form of **moral relativism** that leads to the notion that because there are no objective moral standards, then there can be no objective meaning to life, leaving humanity in a state of perpetual hopelessness. See **moral realism; nihilism.**

moral realism. The idea that moral judgments are grounded in objective truth values or standards that are independent of the person making such value judgments, and thus place all humans under moral obligations to those standards. Such objective moral standards must be transcendent: timeless, invariant, and universal. In Christian **theism**, moral realism is grounded in the personal moral perfections of the triune God and the universal commands that flow from his character. Moral realism is contrasted with **moral relativism** and **moral nihilism**.

moral relativism. The denial of objective moral standards by which moral judgments can be grounded and to which intelligent moral agents are obligated (see **moral responsibility**). Moral relativism is contrasted with **moral realism** and often leads to **moral nihilism.**

moral responsibility. The culpability that one bears for moral choices to which he or she is obligated. One who does good deserves praise or reward. One who does **evil** deserves blame or punishment. Most proponents of **Calvinism** and varieties of **free-will theism** believe that some kind of **free agency** is necessary for moral responsibility. Virtually all proponents of Christian **theism** believe that God bears no moral responsibility for evil that occurs in the world.

moral will (of God). See **preceptive will** (of God).

myth. A broad term with many disparate (and sometimes conflicting or confusing) meanings. The three following definitions are employed in this book: (1) A falsehood, a distorted reality, or a fictitious narrative. (2) A deeply foundational story (or set of stories), whether factual and historical, or fictitious (or a combination of fact and fiction), employed by a particular people to help frame their cultural and communal identity, which in turn forges a sense of meaning and purpose for themselves. Such stories, which are forged through a mythmaking process, convey worldviews that include important rituals, corporate identity markers, values, and ethics, as well as familiar heroes and villains identified with that particular culture. (3) Loosely connected to the **monomyth** in the broader history of storytelling and how the mythmaking impulse of human beings indistinctly mirrors what C. S. Lewis calls the **True Myth** when speaking of *the* **archetypal** (paradigmatic) source of truth found in the grand historical-redemptive narrative of Christianity.

natural evil. **Evil** that consists of some adverse condition in the world that does not necessarily proceed from specific moral choices of intelligent creatures but causes pain and suffering nonetheless. Natural evil came about in the cosmos as a result of the curse of the **fall**. It generally falls into different categories, such as: (1) natural disasters; (2) accidents; (3) illness and disease; (4) physical and mental handicaps; and (5) physical toil. In addressing the **problem of evil**, natural evil is contrasted with **moral evil**. See **gratuitous evil; horrendous evil.**

natural-law defense. A way of addressing the **problem of evil** that includes God's design of orderly, repeatable, predictable laws to govern the world whereby good and bad consequences can result from the proper or improper use of these laws. These laws can be utilized in constructive (helpful) ways or destructive (unhelpful) ways. Therefore, God bears no **moral responsibility** when his intelligent free moral agents (especially human beings) misuse such laws. The natural-law defense is often coupled to the **free-will defense.**

natural revelation. See **general revelation.**

nihilism. A worldview that came into prominence especially as a result of the influence of the thinking (see **epistemology**) of Friedrich Nietzsche (1844–1900). Nihilism claims that life has no objective meaning, leaving humanity in a state of perpetual hopelessness. **nihilistic,** adj. See **moral nihilism.**

nihilistic. See **nihilism.**

noumenal. In the thinking (see **epistemology**) of Immanuel Kant (1724–1804), descriptive of things as they are in themselves apart from our experience and that therefore cannot be known. The noumenal world is contrasted with the **phenomenal** world consisting of our experience, which can be known via empirical and rational means. Kant believed that religious faith resides in the realm of the noumenal, which leaves us with uncertainty about its truth. Science and reason reside in the realm of the phenomenal, which gives us reliable sources of truth.

omnipotence (of God). The attribute of God affirmed by **classical theism** whereby he possesses all the requisite power to do anything unless it (1) is logically impossible (e.g., God cannot make square circles) and (2) contradicts his other attributes (e.g., God does not act capriciously or tell lies). **Calvinism** claims that God has unrestricted use of his power, whereas varieties of **free-will theism** claim that God restricts the use of his power in order to respect the **libertarian free will** of his moral creatures.

One True Story. See **True Myth.**

open theism. A radical form of **Arminianism** developed in the late twentieth and early twenty-first centuries that embraces **libertarianism.** This places it among the varieties of **free-will theism,** which usually embraces some form of the **free-will defense** in response to the **problem of evil.** Open theism, however, denies orthodox doctrines that **classical theism** embraces, namely, that God is timelessly eternal (see **timeless eternality** [of God]) and has exhaustive **foreknowledge** of the future. According to open theists, the future is "open"; God acts and reacts in response to what humans do in time and thus changes his plans accordingly.

original sin. The biblical doctrine that teaches that all humans have inherited a corrupted sin nature from Adam that predisposes them to willingly (voluntarily) act in accordance with their corrupted nature. Unregenerate human beings suffer from total depravity (see **Calvinism**), under which they are willing slaves to their sinful natures and inclinations.

ought **implies** *can.* The idea, often promoted by proponents of **free-will theism**, claiming that if we *ought* to obey the moral commands of God, then it is only fair that we be constituted so that we *can* obey them. This idea assumes that **libertarian free will** to obey or disobey God's commands is necessary for **moral responsibility**.

PAP. See **Principle of Alternative Possibilities.**

passibility (of Christ). An attribute of the human nature of the **incarnate** Son of God whereby he suffered pain and loss during his earthly ministry, which culminated in his crucifixion and death. **passible,** adj.

passible. See **passibility** (of Christ).

passions. As maintained in **classical theism,** involuntary (passive) emotional disturbances caused by outside forces that overpower the human mind and thus tend toward the irrational, unstable, and unpredictable. Passions reflect the mutable conditions of human beings under the power of both finite and sinful natures. Thus, this is one sense in which God is said to be "without passions" (i.e., he is **impassible**). Compare **affections.**

passive obedience (of Christ). A doctrine stating that the believer's **sin,** whereby he or she has transgressed the law of God, is imputed to Christ and that he passively bore its penalty on the cross in obedience to God as part of the means whereby the believer is justified (declared or counted righteous) before God. See **active obedience** (of Christ); **penal substitution.**

Pelagianism. A theological orientation derived from the teachings of the British monk Pelagius (c. 354–415). Pelagius denied **original sin** and taught that divine grace was not necessary for humans to achieve salvation. Rather, people are born morally neutral, and through their **free will** (defined in a libertarian sense—see **libertarianism**) they are able to choose equally between sinful and righteous actions. Historically, Pelagianism has been regarded as heretical by both **Calvinism** and **Arminianism** and was countered in its day by **Augustinianism.**

penal substitution. The primary saving motif of Christ's suffering and death whereby his bloody crucifixion served as a voluntary, vicarious

atoning sacrifice made on behalf of guilty sinners in order to pay the penalty incurred by their **sin**, which in turn satisfies the demands of God's retributive justice and wrath against those sinners. See **active obedience** (of Christ); *Christus Victor*; **expiation; passive obedience** (of Christ); **propitiation.**

perfect-being theology. See **classical theism.**

permission (divine). See **permissive will** (of God).

permissive will (of God). That aspect of God's **decretive will** whereby he permits **sin** and **evil** to transpire in the world. **Arminianism** embraces a *general* permission whereby God leaves it up to the **libertarian free will** of his moral creatures as to whether they will choose good or evil. **Calvinism** embraces a *specific* (or willing, efficacious) permission whereby God specifically permits his moral creatures to choose evil he has ordained by not preventing it and by ensuring the circumstances in which the evil comes about (see **meticulous providence**), but in such a way that he does not bear **moral responsibility** for their choices.

personal problem of evil. See **existential problem of evil.**

phenomenal. In the thinking (see **epistemology**) of Immanuel Kant (1724–1804), descriptive of things in our experience that can be known via empirical and rational means. The phenomenal world is contrasted with the **noumenal** world, which consists of things as they are in themselves apart from our experience and therefore cannot be known. Kant believed that science and reason reside in the realm of the phenomenal, which gives us reliable sources of truth. Religious faith resides in the realm of the noumenal, which leaves us with uncertainty about its truth.

possible world. Any state of affairs that fits the realm of logical possibility for God to bring it about. This could include a state of affairs whereby God creates something, or a state of affairs whereby he chooses not to create anything (i.e., a state of affairs whereby he alone exists). It includes God's creation of the present universe (i.e., "the heavens and the earth") or any similar universe that is in the realm of logical possibility for God to create it. See **best-of-all-possible-worlds defense; Molinism.**

postmodern. See **postmodernism.**

postmodernism. An intellectual and cultural movement that emerged in the late twentieth century that rejects (or questions) the validity of modernism as espoused by the **Enlightenment.** Postmodernism has a skeptical **epistemology**, questioning whether we can know with certainty any claims to objective truth, morals, aesthetics, and so on. **postmodern,** adj.

preceptive will (of God). God's revealed, moral, or instructive will that is rooted in Scripture whereby he establishes, declares, or commands all that is good, right, wise, and true. See **decretive will** (of God).

prevenient grace. A doctrine promoted in **Arminianism** that teaches that mankind is morally depraved as the result of our sin nature inherited from Adam, thus placing our wills in bondage to **sin**, but that God bestows a unique grace on unbelievers that restores their **free will** (i.e., defined as **libertarianism**), thus allowing them to cooperate with or resist further effusions of God's grace, especially his saving grace.

Principle of Alternative Possibilities. One of the defining features of **libertarian free will** indicating that moral agents have the ability to freely choose between alternative possibilities. Sometimes it is called *contrary choice* or the *liberty of indifference*. The idea is that if a person chooses one course of action (*A*), her freedom of will gives her the power to equally choose a contrary (alternative) course of action (*not A*) in exactly the same set of circumstances. Abbr. *PAP*.

problem of evil. The idea that **evil** poses a problem for belief in the existence of God or in many of the traditional attributes associated with the God of **theism**, especially the **classical theism** associated with orthodox Christianity. The problem of evil is usually expressed in the following trilemma: (1) God is all-powerful; (2) God is all-good; (3) yet evil exists. Since most people believe that premise 3 is a given, then premise 1 or 2 seems to be questionable. The problem of evil has also been expressed in three distinct kinds of problems: (a) the **logical problem of evil**; (b) the **evidential problem of evil**; and (c) the **existential problem of evil**.

propitiation. The satisfaction of God's just (retributive) wrath against **sin**, necessary in order for **atonement** to be made on behalf of sinners. Only Christ's bloody death on the cross truly satisfies God's wrath against sinners to whom God extends mercy and whom he reconciles to himself. See **expiation; penal substitution**.

providence (of God). **providential,** adj. See **general providence; meticulous providence**.

providential. See **general providence; meticulous providence**.

redemption. With respect to the metanarrative of Scripture, the movement within history, as orchestrated by the Creator, that brings about the restoration of **creation** due to the universal curse brought about by the **fall**. Only God in his sovereign wisdom, power, and grace is able to redeem the fallen creatures he has chosen as well as the created order they inhabit. Furthermore, this remarkable work of redemption can be achieved only by the **incarnation** of the Son of God through his **atoning death** and resurrection. **redemptive,** adj.

redemptive. See **redemption.**

Reformed theology. A theological orientation that is commonly associated with the Reformer John Calvin (1509–64) but that finds its roots in **Augustinianism**—the theology of Augustine (A.D. 354–430). It has had a rich tradition since the sixteenth-century Protestant Reformation and later Puritanism emerging in the late sixteenth and early seventeenth centuries. *Reformed theology* is broadly synonymous with **Calvinism.**

religious problem of evil. See **existential problem of evil.**

rising action. The second movement of the plot structure in **Freytag's Pyramid** in which the conflict builds and the plot thickens. Aristotle saw this as an "entanglement" or the tying of a knot.

secret will (of God). See **decretive will** (of God).

secularism. A broad-ranging worldview that has grown out of the **Enlightenment** whereby belief in God has been marginalized or discarded altogether in favor of naturalistic science and a self-sufficient humanism. Secularism has been largely embraced by the Western world and places a premium on human autonomy instead of God as the measure of meaning, morals, and purpose. See **secularization.**

secularization. Charles Taylor's term in his book *A Secular Age* that indicates the conditions and processes whereby belief in God as the fundamental grid by which the world is viewed in Western thinking (see **epistemology**) has been largely replaced by natural science and a self-sufficient humanism. **Theism** has been displaced by human autonomy as the measure of meaning, morals, and purpose. See **secularism.**

simple foreknowledge. The view of divine **foreknowledge** embraced by **Arminianism** that claims that after God chooses to create a particular kind of world (i.e., one with creatures containing **libertarian free will**), then the knowledge he gains from what will happen in that world affords him an exhaustive prevision of the choices that people will definitely make in that world.

simplicity (of God). The attribute of God affirmed by **classical theism** whereby he is not composed of parts to form a composite being. There is a unity to God's being (essence) and attributes (including his simplicity) such that all that is predicated of God is God. Thus, one attribute of God cannot be pitted against another. For example, God's love is neither greater nor lesser than his justice, and vice versa.

sin. See **moral evil.**

skeptical-theism defense. A way of addressing the **problem of evil**, usually connected to the **greater-good theodicy**, that claims that we do not know enough to make definite pronouncements about the greater goods that God may have in permitting particular **evils**, especially **horrendous evil.** Skeptical theism claims that the charge that horrendous evil is **gratuitous evil** cannot be a defeat for the greater-good theodicy. While there may be uncertainty about what greater goods a particular evil might produce, neither can there be certainty that absolutely *no* greater goods can be justified by the evils that might produce them. Humans are too limited in their knowledge and wisdom to make that case.

soul-making theodicy. A way of addressing the **problem of evil** that claims that humans are born in a state of immaturity and must experience pain and adversity in order to mature. God permits humans to suffer as the result of various **evil** circumstances because it is a way to build character that could not otherwise be built. Just as a fiery furnace purifies gold, likewise evil and suffering purify and strengthen the human soul. See **greater-good theodicy.**

sovereign will (of God). See **decretive will** (of God).

state of affairs. See **possible world.**

substitutionary atonement. See **penal substitution.**

supralapsarianism. A view of God's **decrees** as understood by **Calvinism** claiming that God's decree of election logically precedes his decree of the **fall.** In this view, the order of decrees is as follows: God (1) elects some humans to salvation and condemns the rest; (2) creates both kinds of humans; (3) permits all humans to fall; and (4) redeems the elect by the work of Christ. This view is distinguished from **infralapsarianism.** The **theodicy** known as *felix culpa* as well as what is termed the **greater-glory theodicy** in this book has often been associated with supralapsarianism.

theism. The belief that God exists and is active in the world. Theism is generally associated with the Judeo-Christian tradition of monotheism (one God) and Trinitarianism (one God subsisting as three persons) and is contrasted with **deism. theistic,** adj. See **classical theism.**

theistic. See **theism.**

theodicist. Someone who develops a **theodicy** or **defense** when addressing the **problem of evil.**

theodicy. A term coined by Gottfried Wilhelm Leibniz (1646–1716) that combines the Greek words for "God" (*theós*) and "justice" (*dikē*). A theodicy seeks to provide an explanation of how an all-good and all-powerful God relates to the **problem of evil** in the world. A **theodicist** attempts to justify the ways of God, including how God is exonerated of **moral responsibility** in light of the existence of **evil**. In a more technical sense, a theodicy is an attempt to provide a definite reason for (or solution to) why God permits (i.e., does not prevent) or decrees (see **decretive will** [of God]) evil in the world as opposed to the more modest aims of a **defense**. In this book, the terms *defense* and *theodicy* are generally used synonymously.

timeless eternality (of God). The attribute of God affirmed by **classical theism** stating that he has no beginning and no end and does not subsist in a succession of moments, but rather subsists outside (or transcends) time as the eternal, infinite God. See **transcendence** (of God).

tragedy. A plot type in classical literature in which a story has a bad, unhappy, or unsatisfying ending. According to the great medieval poet Dante (c. 1265–1321), a tragedy begins with joy and ends in pain. Tragedy is contrasted with **comedy**. See **Freytag's Pyramid.**

transcendence (general). In Charles Taylor's book *A Secular Age*, the state of a world before the onset of **Enlightenment** thinking (see **epistemology**) that was marked by a pervasive sense that the present temporal, material realm was not all there is; rather, people believed in some notion of eternal and supernatural realities, such as disembodied spirits, heaven and hell, and particularly God's ubiquitous and weighty presence presiding over everything. Instead, we now live in what Taylor calls the "immanent frame," which is a world consisting of nothing more than what can be ascertained in the temporal and material realm. Compare **transcendence** (of God).

transcendence (of God). The attribute of God affirmed by **classical theism** that indicates his incomprehensible uniqueness as the independent, self-sufficient, exalted Lord of all whereby he is distinctly different from all else. He is utterly holy, meaning that he dwells in unapproachable light (i.e., **glory**), possessing unique attributes that establish an unbridgeable Creator-creature distinction. God's transcendence is not absolute in the sense that it denies his **immanence. transcendent**, adj. See **transcendent Author** (God as).

transcendent. See **transcendence** (general); **transcendence** (of God).

transcendent Author (God as). A model of **divine providence** that is based on God's attribute of **transcendence** embraced by some proponents of **Calvinism** whereby God's providential actions in the world are likened to that of an author of a virtuous story, though it contains both good and **evil**. Since God is transcendent and therefore distinct from his creation (e.g., the Creator-creature distinction) and history, then his ordaining of the events of history means that he bears no **moral responsibility** for the evil they contain, especially since that evil contributes to the overall **greater goods** and virtuous goals that he intends for history.

True Myth. C. S. Lewis's term to describe the true and historically factual yet mythopoetic character of Christianity. For Lewis, Christianity's broad scriptural storyline (metanarrative) of **creation, fall,** and **redemption** as the *One True Story* is *the* **archetypal** (paradigmatic) source of truth that has been indistinctly and imperfectly mirrored by the **myths** and the mythmaking (storytelling) impulse of human cultures and—we might add—by the universal **monomyth** in the broader history of storytelling (e.g., literature and filmmaking). Lewis says that Christianity is where "myth becomes fact." As the True Myth, Christianity stands alone as that which is able to fulfill and satisfy the deeply embedded redemptive longing that fallen human beings possess. See **eucatastrophe.**

TULIP. See **Calvinism.**

universalism. The heretical doctrine that claims that at some point in the future, all human beings will be saved from their **sins** and from divine condemnation.

SELECT BIBLIOGRAPHY

Adams, Jay. *The Grand Demonstration*. Santa Barbara, CA: Eastgate Publishers, 1991.

Adams, Marilyn McCord. *Horrendous Evils and the Goodness of God*. Ithaca, NY: Cornell University Press, 1999.

———. "Plantinga on 'Felix Culpa': Analysis and Critique." *Faith and Philosophy* 25.2 (2008): 123–40.

Alcorn, Randy. *If God Is Good: Faith in the Midst of Suffering and Evil*. Colorado Springs: Multnomah Books, 2009.

Alexander, David E. "Orthodoxy, Theological Determinism, and the Problem of Evil." In *Calvinism and the Problem of Evil*, edited by David E. Alexander and Daniel M. Johnson, 123–44. Eugene, OR: Pickwick Publications, 2016.

Alexander, David E., and Daniel M. Johnson, eds. *Calvinism and the Problem of Evil*. Eugene, OR: Pickwick Publications, 2016.

Alexander, D. T. Desmond. *From Eden to the New Jerusalem*. Downers Grove, IL: InterVarsity Press, 2008.

Anderson, James N. "Calvinism and the First Sin." In *Calvinism and the Problem of Evil*, edited by David E. Alexander and Daniel M. Johnson, 200–232. Eugene, OR: Pickwick Publications, 2016.

———. "How Biblical Is Molinism? (Parts 1–5)." Found at: http://www.proginosko.com/.

Anselm. *Proslogion*. In *Anselm of Canterbury: The Major Works*, edited by Brian Davies and G. R. Evans, 82–104. Oxford: Oxford University Press, 1998.

———. *Why God Became Man* [*Cur Deus Homo*]. In *Anselm of Canterbury: The Major Works*, edited by Brian Davies and G. R. Evans, 260–356. Oxford: Oxford University Press, 1998.

Antognazza, Maria Rosa. *Leibniz: A Very Short Introduction*. Oxford: Oxford University Press, 2016.

Aristotle. *Poetics*. Translated by Anthony Kenny. Oxford: Oxford University Press, 2013.

Athanasius. *On the Incarnation*. Crestwood, NY: St. Vladimir's Seminary Press, 2000.

Augustine. *City of God*. Translated by Henry Bettenson. New York: Penguin Books, 1984.

———. *Enchiridion*. Edited and translated by Albert C. Outler. Philadelphia: Westminster Press, 1955.

———. *On the Free Choice of the Will, On Grace and Free Choice, and Other Writings*. Edited and translated by Peter King. Cambridge: Cambridge University Press, 2010.

Aulén, Gustaf. *Christus Victor: An Historical Study of the Three Main Types of the Idea of Atonement*. Translated by A. G. Herbert. New York: Macmillan, 1969.

Baines, Ronald S., et al., eds. *Confessing the Impassible God: The Biblical, Classical, & Confessional Doctrine of Divine Impassibility*. Palmdale, CA: Reformed Baptist Academic Press, 2015.

Barrett, Matthew. *None Greater: The Undomesticated Attributes of God*. Grand Rapids: Baker, 2019.

———, ed. "The Impassibility of God." *Credo* 9.1 (2019). Found at: https://credomag.com/magazine_issue/the-impassibility-of-god/.

Barrs, Jerram. *Echoes of Eden*. Wheaton, IL: Crossway, 2013.

Bartholomew, Craig G., and Michael W. Goheen. *The Drama of Scripture: Finding Our Place in the Biblical Story*. Grand Rapids: Baker Academic, 2014.

Bauckham, Richard. "'Only the Suffering God Can Help': Divine Passibility in Modern Theology." *Themelios* 9.3 (1984): 6–12.

Bavinck, Herman. *Reformed Dogmatics*. Edited by John Bolt. Translated by John Vriend. 4 vols. Grand Rapids: Baker Academic, 2003–8.

Beale, G. K. "An Exegetical and Theological Consideration of the Hardening of Pharaoh's Heart in Exodus 4–14 and Romans 9." *Trinity Journal* 5.2 (1984): 129–54.

———. *Redemptive Reversals and the Ironic Overturning of Human Wisdom*. Wheaton, IL: Crossway, 2019.

Beale, G. K., and Mitchell Kim. *God Dwells among Us: Expanding Eden to the Ends of the Earth*. Downers Grove, IL: InterVarsity Press, 2014.

Beasley-Murray, Paul. *The Message of the Resurrection*. Downers Grove, IL: InterVarsity Press, 2000.

Bebbington, David. *Patterns in History*. Downers Grove, IL: InterVarsity Press, 1979.

Beeke, Joel R., and Paul M. Smalley. *Reformed Systematic Theology*. Vol. 1, *Revelation and God*. Wheaton, IL: Crossway, 2019.

Berkouwer, G. C. *The Providence of God*. Grand Rapids: Eerdmans, 1952.

———. *Sin*. Grand Rapids: Eerdmans, 1971.

Bignon, Guillaume. *Excusing Sinners and Blaming God: A Calvinist Assessment of Determinism, Moral Responsibility, and Divine Involvement in Evil*. Eugene, OR: Pickwick Publications, 2018.

———. "'Lord Willing and God Forbid': Divine Permission, Asymmetry, and Counterfactuals." In *Calvinism and Middle Knowledge*, edited by John D. Laing, Kirk R. MacGregor, and Greg Welty, 221–40. Eugene, OR: Pickwick Publications, 2019.

Billings, J. Todd. *Rejoicing in Lament*. Grand Rapids: Brazos Press, 2015.

Blocher, Henri. "Biblical Metaphors and the Doctrine of the Atonement." *JETS* 47.4 (2004): 629–45.

———. *Evil and the Cross*. Grand Rapids: Kregel, 1994.

Bock, Darrell L., and Mitch Glaser, eds. *The Gospel according to Isaiah 53: Encountering the Suffering Servant in Jewish and Christian Theology*. Grand Rapids: Kregel, 2012.

Boettner, Loraine. *The Reformed Doctrine of Predestination*. Philadelphia: Presbyterian and Reformed, 1932.

Boyd, Gregory A. "God Limits His Control." In *Four Views on Divine Providence*, edited by Stanley N. Gundry and Dennis W. Jowers, 183–208. Grand Rapids: Zondervan, 2011.

———. *God of the Possible*. Grand Rapids: Baker, 2000.

———. *Satan and the Problem of Evil*. Downers Grove, IL: InterVarsity Press, 2001.

Brauns, Chris. *Unpacking Forgiveness: Biblical Answers for Complex Questions and Deep Wounds*. Wheaton, IL: Crossway, 2008.

Bruce, F. F. "Christ as Conqueror and Reconciler." *Bibliotheca Sacra* 141.4 (1984): 291–302.

Bruce, James E. "Not the Author of Evil: A Question of Providence, Not a Problem for Calvinism." In *Calvinism and the Problem of Evil*, edited by David E. Alexander and Daniel M. Johnson, 96–122. Eugene, OR: Pickwick Publications, 2016.

Burk, Denny. "Eternal Conscious Torment." In *Four Views on Hell*, edited by Preston Sprinkle, 17–60. 2nd ed. Grand Rapids: Zondervan, 2016.

Calvin, John. *Institutes of the Christian Religion*. Edited by John T. McNeill. Translated by Ford Lewis Battles. Philadelphia: Westminster, 1960.

———. *The Secret Providence of God*. Edited by Paul Helm. Translated by Keith Goad. Wheaton, IL: Crossway, 2010.

Campbell, Constantine R. *Paul and Union with Christ: An Exegetical and Theological Study.* Grand Rapids: Zondervan, 2012.

Camus, Albert. *The Myth of Sisyphus and Other Essays.* New York: Vintage Books, 1991.

———. *The Rebel.* New York: Vintage Books, 1956.

Carpenter, Humphrey. *J. R. R. Tolkien: A Biography.* London: George Allen & Unwin, 1977.

Carson, D. A. *The God Who Is There: Finding Your Place in God's Story.* Grand Rapids: Baker, 2010.

———. *How Long, O Lord? Reflections on Suffering and Evil.* 2nd ed. Grand Rapids: Baker Academic, 2006.

———. *Scandalous: The Cross and Resurrection of Jesus.* Wheaton, IL: Crossway, 2010.

Cary, Phillip. "A Classic View." In *God and the Problem of Evil: Five Views,* edited by Chad Meister and James K. Dew Jr., 13–36. Downers Grove, IL: InterVarsity Press, 2017.

Chisholm, Roderick M. "Human Freedom and the Self." In *The Elements of Philosophy: Readings from Past and Present,* edited by Tamar Szabo Gendler et al., 480–88. New York: Oxford University Press, 2008.

Chou, Abner, ed. *What Happened in the Garden?* Grand Rapids: Kregel, 2016.

Christensen, Scott. *What about Free Will? Reconciling Our Choices with God's Sovereignty.* Phillipsburg, NJ: P&R Publishing, 2016.

Clifford, Ross, and Philip Johnson. *The Cross Is Not Enough: Living as Witnesses to the Resurrection.* Grand Rapids: Baker, 2012.

Cole, Graham A. *God the Peacemaker: How Atonement Brings Shalom.* Downers Grove, IL: InterVarsity Press, 2009.

———. *The God Who Became Human: A Biblical Theology of Incarnation.* Downers Grove, IL: InterVarsity Press, 2013.

Copan, Paul. "Evil and Primeval Sin." In *God and Evil: The Case for God in a World Filled with Pain,* edited by Chad Meister and James K. Dew Jr., 109–23. Downers Grove, IL: InterVarsity Press, 2013.

Couenhoven, Jesse. "Augustine's Rejection of the Free-Will Defence: An Overview of the Late Augustine's Theodicy." *Religious Studies* 43.3 (2007): 279–98.

Cowan, Steven B., and James S. Spiegel. *The Love of Wisdom: A Christian Introduction to Philosophy.* Nashville: B&H Academic, 2009.

Coyne, Jerry A. *Why Evolution Is True.* New York: Penguin Books, 2009.

Crabtree, J. A. *The Most Real Being: A Biblical and Philosophical Defense of Divine Determinism.* Eugene, OR: Gutenberg College Press, 2004.

Craig, William Lane. "God Directs All Things." In *Four Views on Divine Providence*, edited by Stanley N. Gundry and Dennis W. Jowers, 79–100. Grand Rapids: Zondervan, 2011.

———. *The Only Wise God*. Grand Rapids: Baker, 1987.

Cranfield, C. E. B. *Romans: A Shorter Commentary*. Grand Rapids: Eerdmans, 1992.

Crisp, Oliver D. "Francis Turretin on the Necessity of the Incarnation." In *Retrieving Doctrine: Essays in Reformed Theology*, 69–91. Downers Grove, IL: InterVarsity Press, 2010.

Cuyler, Theodore L. *God's Light on Dark Clouds*. Reprint, Carlisle, PA: Banner of Truth, 2008.

Cyril of Alexandria. *On the Unity of Christ*. Translated by John McGuckin. Crestwood, NY: St. Vladimir's Seminary Press, 1995.

Dawkins, Richard. *The God Delusion*. New York: Houghton Mifflin Company, 2008.

Delbanco, Andrew. *The Death of Satan: How Americans Have Lost the Sense of Evil*. New York: Farrar, Straus and Giroux, 1995.

Dembski, William A. *The End of Christianity: Finding a Good God in an Evil World*. Nashville: B&H Academic, 2009.

DeYoung, Kevin. "Divine Impassibility and the Passion of Christ in the Book of Hebrews." *WTJ* 68.1 (2006): 41–50.

———. "'Tis Mystery All, the Immortal Dies: Why the Gospel of Christ's Suffering Is More Glorious because God Does Not Suffer." Unpublished paper presented at T4G Conference, Louisville, KY, April 2010.

Diller, Kevin. "Are Sin and Evil Necessary for a Really Good World?" In *The Problem of Evil: Selected Readings*, edited by Michael L. Peterson, 390–409. 2nd ed. Notre Dame, IN: University of Notre Dame Press, 2017.

Dostoevsky, Fyodor. *The Brothers Karamazov*. Translated by Richard Pevear and Larissa Volokhonsky. New York: Farrar, Straus and Giroux, 1990.

Edwards, Jonathan. "The End for Which God Created the World." In *God's Passion for His Glory: Living the Vision of Jonathan Edwards*, edited by John Piper, 125–251. Wheaton, IL: Crossway, 1998.

———. *The Freedom of the Will*. Vol. 1 of *The Works of Jonathan Edwards*. Edited by Paul Ramsey. New Haven, CT: Yale University Press, 1957.

———. *The "Miscellanies," a–500*. Vol. 13 of *The Works of Jonathan Edwards*. Edited by Thomas A. Schafer. New Haven, CT: Yale University Press, 1994.

Elliot, Elisabeth. *A Path through Suffering.* Grand Rapids: Revell, 1990.

Epstein, Greg M. *Good without God.* New York: HarperCollins, 2009.

Estelle, Bryan D. *Echoes of Exodus: Tracing a Biblical Motif.* Downers Grove, IL: InterVarsity Press, 2018.

Evans, Jeremy A. *The Problem of Evil: The Challenge to Essential Christian Beliefs.* Nashville: B&H Academic, 2013.

Fant, Gene C., Jr. *God as Author: A Biblical Approach to Narrative.* Nashville: B&H Publishing Group, 2010.

Feinberg, John S. *The Many Faces of Evil.* Wheaton, IL: Crossway, 2004.

——. *No One like Him: The Doctrine of God.* Wheaton, IL: Crossway, 2001.

Ferguson, Sinclair B. "Christus Victor et Propitiator: The Death of Christ, Substitute and Conqueror." In *For the Fame of God's Name: Essays in Honor of John Piper*, edited by Sam Storms and Justin Taylor, 171–89. Wheaton, IL: Crossway, 2010.

——. *Deserted by God?* Carlisle, PA: Banner of Truth, 1993.

——. *The Holy Spirit.* Downers Grove, IL: InterVarsity Press, 1996.

Fesko, J. V. *Diversity within the Reformed Tradition: Supra- and Infralapsarianism in Calvin, Dort, and Westminster.* Greenville, SC: Reformed Academic Press, 2001.

Forsyth, P. T. *The Justification of God: Lectures for War-Time on a Christian Theodicy.* New York: Charles Scribner's Sons, 1917.

Fox, R. Michael, ed. *Reverberations of the Exodus in Scripture.* Eugene, OR: Pickwick Publications, 2014.

Frame, John M. *Apologetics: A Justification of Christian Belief.* Phillipsburg, NJ: P&R Publishing, 2015.

——. *The Doctrine of God.* Phillipsburg, NJ: P&R Publishing, 2002.

——. *Systematic Theology: An Introduction to Christian Belief.* Phillipsburg, NJ: P&R Publishing, 2013.

Frye, Northrop. *Anatomy of Criticism.* Princeton, NJ: Princeton University Press, 1957.

——. *The Educated Imagination.* Bloomington, IN: Indiana University Press, 1964.

——. *The Great Code: The Bible and Literature.* New York: Harcourt Books, 1982.

Fudge, Edward William, and Robert A. Peterson. *Two Views of Hell: A Biblical & Theological Dialogue.* Downers Grove, IL: InterVarsity Press, 2000.

Fuller, Daniel P. *The Unity of the Bible: God's Unfolding Plan for Humanity.* Grand Rapids: Zondervan, 1992.

Furman, Dave. *Kiss the Wave: Embracing God in Your Trials.* Wheaton, IL: Crossway, 2018.

Gaffin, Richard B., Jr. *Resurrection and Redemption: A Study in Paul's Soteriology.* Phillipsburg, NJ: Presbyterian and Reformed, 1987.

Ganssle, Gregory E. "Evil as Evidence for Christianity." In *God and Evil: The Case for God in a World Filled with Pain,* edited by Chad Meister and James K. Dew Jr., 214–23. Downers Grove, IL: InterVarsity Press, 2013.

Garrett, Duane A. *A Commentary on Exodus.* Grand Rapids: Kregel Academic, 2014.

Gavrilyuk, Paul L. "God's Impassible Suffering in the Flesh: The Promise of Paradoxical Christology." In *Divine Impassibility and the Mystery of Human Suffering,* edited by James F. Keating and Thomas Joseph White, 127–49. Grand Rapids: Eerdmans, 2009.

———. *The Suffering of the Impassible God: The Dialectics of Patristic Thought.* Oxford: Oxford University Press, 2004.

Geach, Peter. *Providence and Evil: The Stanton Lectures 1971–2.* Cambridge: Cambridge University Press, 1977.

Geisler, Norman L. *If God, Why Evil?* Bloomington, MN: Bethany House, 2011.

Gentry, Peter J., and Stephen J. Wellum. *Kingdom through Covenant: A Biblical-Theological Understanding of the Covenants.* 2nd ed. Wheaton, IL: Crossway, 2018.

Godawa, Brian. *Hollywood Worldviews.* Downers Grove, IL: InterVarsity Press, 2009.

Gondreau, Paul. "St. Thomas Aquinas, the Communication of Idioms, and the Suffering of Christ in the Garden of Gethsemane." In *Divine Impassibility and the Mystery of Human Suffering,* edited by James F. Keating and Thomas Joseph White, 214–45. Grand Rapids: Eerdmans, 2009.

Gruenler, Royce Gordon. "Jesus as Author of the Evangelium: J. R. R. Tolkien and the Spell of the Great Story." In *New Approaches to Jesus and the Gospels: A Phenomenological and Exegetical Study of Synoptic Christology,* 204–20. Grand Rapids: Baker, 1982.

Guinness, Os. *Unspeakable: Facing Up to Evil in an Age of Genocide and Terror.* New York: HarperCollins, 2005.

Hafemann, Scott J. *The God of Promise and the Life of Faith: Understanding the Heart of the Bible.* Wheaton, IL: Crossway, 2001.

Hallie, Philip. *Lest Innocent Blood Be Shed: The Story of the Village of Le Chambon and How Goodness Happened There.* New York: HarperCollins, 1994.

Hamilton, James M., Jr. *God's Glory in Salvation through Judgment: A Biblical Theology*. Wheaton, IL: Crossway, 2010.

———. "The Skull Crushing Seed of the Woman: Inner-Biblical Interpretation of Genesis 3:15." *SBJT* 10.2 (2006): 30–54.

Hansen, Colin, ed. *Our Secular Age: Ten Years of Reading and Applying Charles Taylor*. Deerfield, IL: Gospel Coalition, 2017.

Hart, David Bentley. *The Doors of the Sea: Where Was God in the Tsunami?* Grand Rapids: Eerdmans, 2005.

———. *The Experience of God: Being, Consciousness, Bliss*. New Haven, CT: Yale University Press, 2013.

Hart, Matthew J. "Calvinism and the Problem of Hell." In *Calvinism and the Problem of Evil*, edited by David E. Alexander and Daniel M. Johnson, 248–72. Eugene, OR: Pickwick Publications, 2016.

Hasker, William. "The Open Theist View." In *God and the Problem of Evil: Five Views*, edited by Chad Meister and James K. Dew Jr., 57–76. Downers Grove, IL: InterVarsity Press, 2017.

———. *The Triumph of God over Evil: Theodicy for a World of Suffering*. Downers Grove, IL: InterVarsity Press, 2008.

Hawthorne, Gerald F. *The Presence and the Power: The Significance of the Holy Spirit in the Life and Ministry of Jesus*. Eugene, OR: Wipf and Stock, 2003.

Helm, Paul. "Discrimination: Aspects of God's Causal Activity." In *Calvinism and the Problem of Evil*, edited by David E. Alexander and Daniel M. Johnson, 145–67. Eugene, OR: Pickwick Publications, 2016.

———. *Eternal God: A Study of God without Time*. 2nd ed. Oxford: Oxford University Press, 2010.

———. *The Providence of God*. Downers Grove, IL: InterVarsity Press, 1994.

———. Review of *Molinism: The Contemporary Debate*, edited by Ken Perszyk. *Themelios* 37.3 (2012): 567–70.

Helm, Paul, and William Lane Craig. "Calvinism vs. Molinism." In *Calvinism and Middle Knowledge*, edited by John D. Laing, Kirk R. MacGregor, and Greg Welty, 241–61. Eugene, OR: Pickwick Publications, 2019.

Helm, Paul, and Terrance L. Tiessen. "Does Calvinism Have Room for Middle Knowledge? A Conversation." *WTJ* 71.2 (2009): 95–117.

Helseth, Paul Kjoss. "God Causes All Things." In *Four Views on Divine Providence*, edited by Stanley N. Gundry and Dennis W. Jowers, 25–52. Grand Rapids: Zondervan, 2011.

Hernandez, Jill. "Leibniz and the Best of All Possible Worlds." In *God and Evil: The Case for God in a World Filled with Pain*, edited by Chad

Meister and James K. Dew Jr., 94–105. Downers Grove, IL: InterVarsity Press, 2013.

Hick, John. *Evil and the Love of God*. New York: Harper and Row, 1975.

———. "Soul-Making and Suffering." In *The Problem of Evil*, edited by Marilyn McCord Adams and Robert Merrihew Adams, 168–88. Oxford: Oxford University Press, 1990.

Hoekema, Anthony A. *The Bible and the Future*. Grand Rapids: Eerdmans, 1979.

Hoffecker, W. Andrew, ed. *Revolutions in Worldview*. Phillipsburg, NJ: P&R Publishing, 2007.

Holmes, Stephen R. *God of Grace and God of Glory: An Account of the Theology of Jonathan Edwards*. Grand Rapids: Eerdmans, 2001.

Horner, Grant. "Genesis 3—A Map of Misreadings." In *What Happened in the Garden?*, edited by Abner Chou, 101–18. Grand Rapids: Kregel, 2016.

Howard-Synder, Daniel, ed. *The Evidential Argument from Evil*. Bloomington, IN: Indiana University Press, 1996.

Hudson, Hud. "The Argument from Evil: Felix Culpa!" In *Two Dozen (or So) Arguments for God: The Plantinga Project*, edited by Jerry L. Walls and Trent Dougherty, 277–89. Oxford: Oxford University Press, 2018.

Hume, David. *Dialogues concerning Natural Religion*. Edited by Richard H. Popkin. Indianapolis: Hackett Publishing, 1980.

Jacobs, Alan. *Original Sin: A Cultural History*. New York: HarperCollins, 2008.

Jeffery, Steve, Michael Ovey, and Andrew Sach. *Pierced for Our Transgressions: Rediscovering the Glory of Penal Substitution*. Wheaton, IL: Crossway, 2007.

Jenkins, Eric L. *Free to Say No? Free Will and Augustine's Evolving Doctrine of Grace and Election*. Eugene, OR: Wipf and Stock, 2012.

Johnson, Daniel M. "Calvinism and the Problem of Evil: A Map of the Territory." In *Calvinism and the Problem of Evil*, edited by David E. Alexander and Daniel M. Johnson, 19–55. Eugene, OR: Pickwick Publications, 2016.

Jones, Mark. *God Is: A Devotional Guide to the Attributes of God*. Wheaton, IL: Crossway, 2017.

Kaiser, Walter C., Jr. *The Messiah in the Old Testament*. Grand Rapids: Zondervan, 1995.

Kapic, Kelly M. *Embodied Hope: A Theological Meditation on Pain and Suffering*. Downers Grove, IL: InterVarsity Press, 2017.

Keating, James F., and Thomas Joseph White, eds. *Divine Impassibility and the Mystery of Human Suffering*. Grand Rapids: Eerdmans, 2009.

Keller, Timothy. *Walking with God through Pain and Suffering*. New York: Dutton, 2013.

Kendrick, T. D. *The Lisbon Earthquake*. Philadelphia: J. B. Lippincott, 1955.

Kinman, Brent. *History, Design and the End of Time: God's Plan for the World*. Nashville: Broadman & Holman, 2000.

Klemke, E. D., ed. *The Meaning of Life*. 2nd ed. New York: Oxford University Press, 2000.

Köstenberger, Andreas J. "The Glory of God in John's Gospel and Revelation." In *The Glory of God*, edited by Christopher W. Morgan and Robert A. Peterson, 107–26. Wheaton, IL: Crossway, 2010.

Kushner, Harold S. *When Bad Things Happen to Good People*. New York: HarperCollins, 1989.

Ladd, George Eldon. *I Believe in the Resurrection of Jesus*. Grand Rapids: Eerdmans, 1975.

Leibniz, Gottfried W. *The Philosophical Works of Leibnitz*. Edited and translated by George Martin Duncan. New Haven, CT: Tuttle, Morehouse & Taylor, 1890.

———. *Theodicy*. Edited by Austin M. Farrar. Translated by E. M. Huggard. New York: Cosimo Classics, 2009.

Letham, Robert. *The Holy Trinity: In Scripture, History, Theology, and Worship*. Rev. ed. Phillipsburg, NJ: P&R Publishing, 2019.

———. *The Work of Christ*. Downers Grove, IL: InterVarsity Press, 1993.

Lewis, C. S. *The Collected Letters of C. S. Lewis*. Vol. 1, *Family Letters 1905–1931*. Edited by Walter Hooper. New York: HarperCollins, 2004.

———. *Miracles*. New York: Macmillan, 1960.

———. "Myth Became Fact." In *God in the Dock*, edited by Walter Hooper, 63–67. Grand Rapids: Eerdmans, 1970.

———. *The Problem of Pain*. New York: Macmillan, 1962.

Lister, Rob. *God Is Impassible and Impassioned: Toward a Theology of Divine Emotion*. Wheaton, IL: Crossway, 2013.

Lovejoy, Arthur O. "Milton and the Paradox of the Fortunate Fall." Reprinted in *Essays in the History of Ideas*, 277–95. New York: Capricorn Books, 1960.

Luther, Martin. *The Bondage of the Will*. Translated by J. I. Packer and O. R. Johnston. Grand Rapids: Fleming H. Revell, 1957.

MacArthur, John. *No Other: Discovering the God of the Bible*. Sanford, FL: Reformation Trust, 2017.

Mackie, J. L. "Evil and Omnipotence." *Mind*, n.s., 64.254 (1955): 200–212.

Macleod, Donald. *Christ Crucified: Understanding the Atonement.* Downers Grove, IL: InterVarsity Press, 2014.

———. "Original Sin in Reformed Theology." In *Adam, the Fall, and Original Sin: Theological, Biblical, and Scientific Perspectives*, edited by Hans Madueme and Michael Reeves, 129–46. Grand Rapids: Baker Academic, 2014.

———. *The Person of Christ.* Downers Grove, IL: InterVarsity Press, 1998.

Madueme, Hans, and Michael Reeves, eds. *Adam, the Fall, and Original Sin: Theological, Biblical, and Scientific Perspectives.* Grand Rapids: Baker Academic, 2014.

Magee, Bryan. *Confessions of a Philosopher.* New York: Random House, 1997.

Marsden, George M. *Jonathan Edwards: A Life.* New Haven, CT: Yale University Press, 2003.

Matz, Robert J., and A. Chadwick Thornhill, eds. *Divine Impassibility: Four Views of God's Emotions and Suffering.* Downers Grove, IL: InterVarsity Press, 2019.

McGrath, Alister. *C. S. Lewis: A Life.* Carol Stream, IL: Tyndale House, 2013.

Meister, Chad, and James K. Dew Jr., eds. *God and Evil: The Case for God in a World Filled with Pain.* Downers Grove, IL: InterVarsity Press, 2013.

Menzies, James W. *True Myth: C. S. Lewis and Joseph Campbell on the Veracity of Christianity.* Eugene, OR: Pickwick Publications, 2014.

Merrill, Eugene H. *Everlasting Dominion: A Theology of the Old Testament.* Nashville: B&H Publishing Group, 2006.

———. *Kingdom of Priests: A History of Old Testament Israel.* 2nd ed. Grand Rapids: Baker Academic, 2008.

Middleton, J. Richard. *A New Heaven and a New Earth: Reclaiming Biblical Eschatology.* Grand Rapids: Baker Academic, 2014.

———. "Why the 'Greater Good' Isn't a Defense: Classical Theodicy in Light of the Biblical Genre of Lament." *Koinonia* 9.1, 2 (1997): 81–113.

Milton, John. *Paradise Lost.* Edited by William Kerrigan, John Rumrich, and Stephen M. Fallon. New York: Random House, 2007.

Mohler, R. Albert, Jr. "Modern Theology: The Disappearance of Hell." In *Hell under Fire*, edited by Christopher W. Morgan and Robert A. Peterson, 15–41. Grand Rapids: Zondervan, 2004.

Molesky, Mark. *This Gulf of Fire.* New York: Alfred A. Knopf, 2015.

Moltmann, Jürgen. *The Crucified God: The Cross of Christ as the Foundation and Criticism of Christian Theology.* Translated by R. A. Wilson and J. Bowden. New York: Harper & Row, 1974.

Morgan, Christopher W. "Toward a Theology of the Glory of God." In *The Glory of God*, edited by Christopher W. Morgan and Robert A. Peterson, 153–88. Wheaton, IL: Crossway, 2010.

Morris, Leon. *The Atonement: Its Meaning and Significance*. Downers Grove, IL: InterVarsity Press, 1983.

Morris, Thomas V. *Our Idea of God*. Downers Grove, IL: InterVarsity Press, 1991.

Morrow, Lance. *Evil: An Investigation*. New York: Basic Books, 2003.

Mortenson, Terry, and Thane H. Ury, eds. *Coming to Grips with Genesis: Biblical Authority and the Age of the Earth*. Green Forest, AR: Master Books, 2008.

Motyer, J. Alec. *The Prophecy of Isaiah: An Introduction & Commentary*. Downers Grove, IL: InterVarsity Press, 1993.

Muller, Richard A. *Christ and the Decree*. Grand Rapids: Baker Academic, 2008.

——.*Dictionary of Latin and Greek Theological Terms*. 2nd ed. Grand Rapids: Baker Academic, 2017.

Murray, John. *Redemption Accomplished and Applied*. Grand Rapids: Eerdmans, 1955.

Nadler, Steven. *The Best of All Possible Worlds: A Story of Philosophers, God, and Evil*. New York: Farrar, Straus and Giroux, 2008.

Nash, Ronald H. *Faith and Reason: Searching for a Rational Faith*. Grand Rapids: Zondervan, 1988.

Neiman, Susan. *Evil in Modern Thought: An Alternative History of Philosophy*. Princeton, NJ: Princeton University Press, 2002.

Nietzsche, Friedrich. *The Gay Science*. Edited by Bernard Williams. Translated by Josefine Nauckhoff. New York: Cambridge University Press, 2001.

——. *Twilight of the Idols*. In *The Portable Nietzsche*, edited and translated by Walter Kaufman, 463–563. New York: Penguin Books, 1982.

O'Connor, Flannery. *Mystery and Manners: Occasional Prose*. New York: Farrar, Straus and Giroux, 1969.

Oliphint, K. Scott. *Covenantal Apologetics*. Wheaton, IL: Crossway, 2013.

Olson, Roger E. *Against Calvinism*. Grand Rapids: Zondervan, 2011.

——. *Arminian Theology: Myths and Realities*. Downers Grove, IL: InterVarsity Press, 2006.

——. "The Classical Free Will Theist Model of God." In *Perspectives on the Doctrine of God: 4 Views*, edited by Bruce A. Ware, 148–72. Nashville: B&H Academic, 2008.

Oord, Thomas Jay. "An Essential Kenosis View." In *God and the Problem of Evil: Five Views*, edited by Chad Meister and James K. Dew Jr., 77–98. Downers Grove, IL: InterVarsity Press, 2017.

——. *The Uncontrolling Love of God: An Open and Relational Account of Providence*. Downers Grove, IL: InterVarsity Press, 2015.

Oswalt, John N. *The Bible among the Myths*. Grand Rapids: Zondervan, 2009.

Ovey, Michael J. "Appropriating Aulén? Employing *Christus Victor* Models of the Atonement." *Churchman* 124.4 (2010): 297–330.

Owen, John. *Communion with the Triune God*. Edited by Kelly M. Kapic and Justin Taylor. Wheaton, IL: Crossway, 2007.

——. *The Glory of Christ*. Reprint, Fearn, Ross-shire, Scotland: Christian Focus, 2004.

Packer, J. I. "The Glory of God and the Reviving of Religion: A Study in the Mind of Jonathan Edwards." In *A God Entranced Vision of All Things: The Legacy of Jonathan Edwards*, edited by John Piper and Justin Taylor, 81–108. Wheaton, IL: Crossway, 2004.

——. "Universalism: Will Everyone Be Ultimately Saved?" In *Hell under Fire*, edited by Christopher W. Morgan and Robert A. Peterson, 169–94. Grand Rapids: Zondervan, 2004.

——. "What Did the Cross Achieve? The Logic of Penal Substitution." In *In My Place Condemned He Stood: Celebrating the Glory of the Atonement*, edited by J. I. Packer and Mark Dever, 53–100. Wheaton, IL: Crossway, 2007.

Pascal, Blaise. *Pascal's Pensées*. Translated by W. F. Trotter. New York: E. P. Dutton, 1958.

Pearcey, Nancy R., and Charles B. Thaxton. *The Soul of Science: Christian Faith and Natural Philosophy*. Wheaton, IL: Crossway, 1994.

Peterson, Michael L. "Christian Theism and the Evidential Argument from Evil." In *The Problem of Evil: Selected Readings*, edited by Michael L. Peterson, 166–92. 2nd ed. Notre Dame, IN: University of Notre Dame Press, 2017.

——. *Evil and the Christian God*. Grand Rapids: Baker, 1982.

——. *God and Evil: An Introduction to the Issues*. Boulder, CO: Westview Press, 1998.

Peterson, Robert A. *Hell on Trial: The Case for Eternal Punishment*. Phillipsburg, NJ: P&R Publishing, 1995.

——. *Salvation Accomplished by the Son*. Wheaton, IL: Crossway, 2012.

Pinker, Steven. "The Moral Instinct." *New York Times Magazine*, January 13, 2008.

Piper, John. *Desiring God*. Rev. ed. Sisters, OR: Multnomah Books, 2011.

———. *God Is the Gospel*. Wheaton, IL: Crossway, 2005.

———. *The Justification of God: An Exegetical & Theological Study of Romans 9:1–23*. 2nd ed. Grand Rapids: Baker, 1993.

———. *The Pleasures of God: Meditations on God's Delight in Being God*. Rev. ed. Colorado Springs: Multnomah Books, 2012.

———. *Spectacular Sins*. Wheaton, IL: Crossway, 2008.

Piper, John, and Justin Taylor, eds. *Suffering and the Sovereignty of God*. Wheaton, IL: Crossway, 2006.

Placher, William C. *The Domestication of Transcendence: How Modern Thinking about God Went Wrong*. Louisville, KY: Westminster John Knox Press, 1996.

Plantinga, Alvin. *God, Freedom, and Evil*. Grand Rapids: Eerdmans, 1977.

———. *God and Other Minds*. Ithaca, NY: Cornell University Press, 1967.

———. *The Nature of Necessity*. New York: Oxford University Press, 1974.

———. "Supralapsarianism, or 'O Felix Culpa.'" In *Christian Faith and the Problem of Evil*, edited by Peter Van Inwagen, 1–25. Grand Rapids: Eerdmans, 2004. Republished in *The Problem of Evil: Selected Readings*, edited by Michael L. Peterson, 363–89. 2nd ed. Notre Dame, IN: University of Notre Dame Press, 2017.

———. *Warranted Christian Belief*. New York: Oxford University Press, 2000.

Plantinga, Cornelius, Jr. *Not the Way It's Supposed to Be: A Breviary of Sin*. Grand Rapids: Eerdmans, 1995.

Postman, Neil. "Learning by Stories." *Atlantic Monthly*, December 1989.

Powlison, David. *God's Grace in Your Suffering*. Wheaton, IL: Crossway, 2018.

Pugh, T. Maurice. "Dispensationalism and Views of Redemption History." In *Dispensationalism and the History of Redemption: A Developing and Diverse Tradition*, edited by D. Jeffrey Bingham and Glenn R. Kreider, 219–48. Chicago: Moody Press, 2015.

Quinn, Philip L. "God, Moral Perfection, and Possible Worlds." In *The Problem of Evil: Selected Readings*, edited by Michael L. Peterson, 428–43. 2nd ed. Notre Dame, IN: University of Notre Dame Press, 2017.

Reinke, Tony. *Lit! A Christian Guide to Reading Books*. Wheaton, IL: Crossway, 2011.

Reymond, Robert L. *A New Systematic Theology of the Christian Faith*. 2nd ed. (Grand Rapids: Zondervan Academic, 2001).

Roberts, Alastair J., and Andrew Wilson. *Echoes of Exodus: Tracing Themes of Redemption through Scripture*. Wheaton, IL: Crossway, 2018.

Rosenberg, Alex. *The Atheist's Guide to Reality: Enjoying Life without Illusions.* New York: W. W. Norton, 2011.

Rowe, William L., ed. *God and the Problem of Evil.* Malden, MA: Blackwell Publishing, 2001.

Ruse, Michael. "Evolutionary Theory and Christian Ethics." In *The Darwinian Paradigm*, 251–72. London: Routledge, 1989.

Russell, Jeffrey Burton. *The Devil: Perceptions of Evil from Antiquity to Primitive Christianity.* Ithaca, NY: Cornell University Press, 1977.

———. *The Prince of Darkness: Radical Evil and the Power of Good in History.* Ithaca, NY: Cornell University Press, 1988.

Ryken, Leland. *Triumphs of the Imagination: Literature in Christian Perspective.* Downers Grove, IL: InterVarsity Press, 1979.

———. *Words of Delight: A Literary Introduction to the Bible.* Grand Rapids: Baker, 1992.

Saint, Stephen F. "Sovereignty, Suffering, and the Work of Missions." In *Suffering and the Sovereignty of God*, edited by John Piper and Justin Taylor, 111–22. Wheaton, IL: Crossway, 2006.

Sanders, Fred. *The Deep Things of God.* 2nd ed. Wheaton, IL: Crossway, 2017.

Sanders, John. "God, Evil, and Relational Risk." In *The Problem of Evil: Selected Readings*, edited by Michael L. Peterson, 327–43. 2nd ed. Notre Dame, IN: University of Notre Dame Press, 2017.

———. *The God Who Risks: A Theology of Providence.* Downers Grove, IL: InterVarsity Press, 1999.

Sayers, Dorothy L. "The Greatest Drama Ever Staged." In *The Whimsical Christian*, 11–16. New York: Macmillan, 1978.

Schreiner, Thomas R. *The King in His Beauty: A Biblical Theology of the Old and New Testaments.* Grand Rapids: Baker Academic, 2013.

———. *New Testament Theology: Magnifying God in Christ.* Grand Rapids: Baker Academic, 2008.

———. *Romans.* 2nd ed. Baker Exegetical Commentary on the New Testament. Grand Rapids: Baker Academic, 2018.

Schultz, Walter J. "'No-Risk' Libertarian Freedom: A Refutation of the Free-Will Defense." *Philosophia Christi* 10.1 (2008): 183–99.

Segal, Robert A. *Myth: A Very Short Introduction.* New York: Oxford University Press, 2004.

Shedd, W. G. T. *The Doctrine of Endless Punishment.* 1885. Reprint, Carlisle, PA: Banner of Truth, 1986.

Shenk, Richard A. *The Wonder of the Cross: The God Who Uses Evil and Suffering to Destroy Evil and Suffering*. Eugene, OR: Pickwick Publications, 2013.

Shippey, Tom. *J. R. R. Tolkien: Author of the Century*. New York: Houghton Mifflin Harcourt, 2002.

Shrady, Nicholas. *The Last Day: Wrath, Ruin, and Reason in the Great Lisbon Earthquake of 1755*. New York: Viking, 2008.

Smith, James K. A. *How (Not) to Be Secular: Reading Charles Taylor*. Grand Rapids: Eerdmans, 2014.

Spiegel, James S. *The Benefits of Providence: A New Look at Divine Sovereignty*. Wheaton, IL: Crossway, 2005.

Sproul, R.C. *Chosen by God*. Wheaton, IL: Tyndale House, 1986.

———. *The Holiness of God*. Carol Stream, IL: Tyndale House, 1998.

———. *The Invisible Hand*. Phillipsburg, NJ: P&R Publishing, 1996.

Stambaugh, James. "Whence Cometh Death? A Biblical Theology of Physical Death and Natural Evil." In *Coming to Grips with Genesis: Biblical Authority and the Age of the Earth*, edited by Terry Mortenson and Thane H. Ury, 373–97. Green Forest, AR: Master Books, 2008.

Stewart, Matthew. *The Courtier and the Heretic: Leibniz, Spinoza, and the Fate of God in the Modern World*. New York: W. W. Norton, 2006.

Stewart, Melville Y. *The Greater-Good Defence: An Essay on the Rationality of Faith*. New York: Palgrave Macmillan, 1993.

Stokes, Mitch. *How to Be an Atheist: Why Many Skeptics Aren't Skeptical Enough*. Wheaton, IL: Crossway, 2016.

Stump, Eleonore. "The Mirror of Evil." In *God and the Philosophers*, edited by Thomas V. Morris, 235–47. Oxford: Oxford University Press, 1996.

———. *Wandering in Darkness: Narrative and the Problem of Suffering*. Oxford: Oxford University Press, 2010.

Surin, Kenneth. *Theology and the Problem of Evil*. Reprint, Eugene, OR: Wipf and Stock, 2004.

Svigel, Michael J. "Extreme Makeover: Heaven and Earth Edition—Will God Annihilate the World and Re-create It Ex Nihilo?" *Bibliotheca Sacra* 171.684 (2014): 401–17.

Swinburne, Richard. *Providence and the Problem of Evil*. Oxford: Oxford University Press, 1998.

Tada, Joni Eareckson. *A Place of Healing: Wrestling with the Mysteries of Suffering, Pain, and God's Sovereignty*. Colorado Springs: David C. Cook, 2010.

Taunton, Larry Alex. *The Grace Effect: How the Power of One Life Can Reverse the Corruption of Unbelief*. Nashville: Thomas Nelson, 2011.

Taylor, Charles. *A Secular Age.* Cambridge, MA: Belknap Press, 2007.

Taylor, Daniel. "In Praise of Stories." In *The Christian Imagination,* edited by Leland Ryken, 407–26. Colorado Springs: Shaw Books, 2002.

ten Boom, Corrie. *The Hiding Place.* 35th anniversary ed. Grand Rapids: Chosen Books, 2006.

Tolkien, J. R. R. *The Lord of the Rings.* 50th anniversary one-vol. ed. New York: Houghton Mifflin, 2004.

———. "On Fairy-Stories." In *The Monsters and the Critics and Other Essays,* edited by Christopher Tolkien, 109–61. London: George Allen and Unwin, 1983.

Trakakis, Nick. "Does Hard Determinism Render the Problem of Evil Even Harder?" *Ars Disputandi* 6.1 (2006): 239–64.

Treat, Jeremy R. *The Crucified King: Atonement and Kingdom in Biblical and Systematic Theology.* Grand Rapids: Zondervan, 2014.

Tripp, Paul David. *Suffering: Gospel Hope When Life Doesn't Make Sense.* Wheaton, IL: Crossway, 2018.

Turner, James. *Without God, Without Creed: The Origins of Unbelief in America.* Baltimore: Johns Hopkins University Press, 1985.

Turretin, Francis. *Institutes of Elenctic Theology.* Edited by John T. Dennison Jr. Translated by George Musgrave Giger. 3 vols. Phillipsburg, NJ: P&R Publishing, 1992–97.

Varner, William. "The Seed and Schaeffer." In *What Happened in the Garden?,* edited by Abner Chou, 153–72. Grand Rapids: Kregel, 2016.

Vlach, Michael J. *He Will Reign Forever: A Biblical Theology of the Kingdom of God.* Silverton, OR: Lampion Press, 2016.

Volf, Miroslav. *Exclusion and Embrace: A Theological Exploration of Identity, Otherness, and Reconciliation.* Nashville: Abingdon Press, 1996.

———. *Free of Charge: Giving and Forgiving in a Culture Stripped of Grace.* Grand Rapids: Zondervan, 2005.

Walls, Jerry L., and Joseph R. Dongell. *Why I Am Not a Calvinist.* Downers Grove, IL: InterVarsity Press, 2004.

Ware, Bruce A. *God's Greater Glory: The Exalted God of Scripture and the Christian Faith.* Wheaton, IL: Crossway, 2004.

———. "A Modified Calvinist Doctrine of God." In *Perspectives on the Doctrine of God: 4 Views,* edited by Bruce A. Ware, 76–120. Nashville: B&H Academic, 2008.

Warnock, Adrian. *Raised with Christ: How the Resurrection Changes Everything.* Wheaton, IL: Crossway, 2010.

Weinandy, Thomas G. *Does God Suffer?* Notre Dame, IN: University of Notre Dame Press, 2000.

——. "Human Suffering and the Impassibility of God." *Testamentum Imperium* 2 (2009): 1–18.

Wells, David F. *Above All Earthly Pow'rs: Christ in a Postmodern World.* Grand Rapids: Eerdmans, 2005.

——. *God in the Wasteland: The Reality of Truth in a World of Fading Dreams.* Grand Rapids: Eerdmans, 1994.

Wellum, Stephen J. *God the Son Incarnate: The Doctrine of Christ.* Wheaton, IL: Crossway, 2016.

Welty, Greg. "Molinist Gun Control: A Flawed Proposal? A Reply to Kenneth Keathley's 'Friendly Reply.'" In *Calvinism and Middle Knowledge*, edited by John D. Laing, Kirk R. MacGregor, and Greg Welty, 80–92. Eugene, OR: Pickwick Publications, 2019.

——. *Why Is There Evil in the World (and So Much of It)?* Fearn, Ross-shire, Scotland: Christian Focus, 2018.

Wiesel, Elie. *Night.* New York: Hill and Wang, 2006.

Wiesenthal, Simon. *The Sunflower: On the Possibilities and Limits of Forgiveness.* New York: Schocken Books, 1998.

Wolterstorff, Nicholas. *Lament for a Son.* Grand Rapids: Eerdmans, 1987.

Wright, N. T. *Evil and the Justice of God.* Downers Grove, IL: InterVarsity Press, 2006.

——. *The Resurrection of the Son of God.* Minneapolis: Fortress Press, 2003.

Wykstra, Stephen. "The Skeptical Theist Response." In *God and the Problem of Evil: Five Views*, edited by Chad Meister and James K. Dew Jr., 173–84. Downers Grove, IL: InterVarsity Press, 2017.

Young, Edward J. *The Book of Isaiah.* 3 vols. Grand Rapids: Eerdmans, 1965–72.

INDEX OF SCRIPTURE

INDEX OF SUBJECTS AND NAMES

climax (in Freytag's Pyramid), 237–39,
    259, 261, 270–74, 403
Cogniet, Léon, 92
comedy (in storytelling), 235–36,
    238, 240–42
communication of properties
    (*communicatio idi-
    omatum*), 391
compatibilism. *See* free
    will, compatibilistic
Conrad, Joseph (author), 12
conscience, 55–56, 58, 66–67,
    206–7, 242
contrary choice. *See* Principle of
    Alternative Possibilities
Copan, Paul, 192–93, 209
Cottrell, Jack, 100
Couenhoven, Jesse, 299
Council of Chalcedon, 349
counterfactuals of creaturely free-
    dom, 103–7, 300. *See
    also* Molinism
covenants in Scripture, 269–70,
    321–23, 332, 364–65
Cowper, William, 13–14, 341
Coyne, Jerry, 64–66
Crabtree, J. A., 160, 178, 261
Craig, William Lane, 87, 104, 107, 199
Cranfield, C. E. B., 367
creation
    annihilation theory of, 428–30
    corrupted by fall, 303
    God's purpose in, 282, 285
    as part of biblical storyline,
        262, 267, 299
    renewal of, 11, 113, 136, 260, 276,
        284–85, 318, 427–30
creation *ex nihilo*, 3, 91, 158,
    160, 262, 429
Creator-creature distinction, 101,
    107, 160, 189, 213, 262,
    290, 351, 381, 391

Crime and Punishment (novel), 232
critical theory, 47–48
CSI: Crime Scene Investigation (tele-
    vision show), 238
Cuyler, Theodore, 457–58
Cyril of Alexandria, 351

da Vinci, Leonardo, 18, 209
Dante. *See* Alighieri, Dante
Darwin, Charles, 20, 52, 62
Darwinism, 20, 43–44, 48,
    52, 62, 64, 72
David, 78, 132, 152–54, 190, 197,
    270–71, 347, 387, 389, 449
David (Michelangelo), 18
Dawkins, Richard, 44, 64
de Molina, Luis, 103
de Sade, Marquis, 63
death
    of cosmos, 428–30
    defeat of by Christ, 261, 273–77,
        343–45, 367, 372, 375–76,
        382–95, 401–6,
        408–16, 429–30, 456
    and the fall, 54, 114, 267,
        273, 406, 428
    fear of, 31–32, 244, 372,
        393, 406, 457
    meaning of, 267, 276, 343
    as natural evil, 337
decree(s) of God. *See* God, decree of;
    God, will of, decretive will
decretive will. *See* God, will of,
    decretive will.
defense (vs. theodicy). *See also* evil,
    problem of; theodicy
    definition of, 5, 81–82, 119
deism, 17–18, 25, 28, 113, 262
deistic. *See* deism
Delbanco, Andrew, 33, 50, 70
Dembski, William A., 131

Scott Christensen (MDiv, The Masters Seminary) is the author of the highly acclaimed *What about Free Will?*, foreword by D. A. Carson (P&R, 2016). Scott worked for nine years at the award-winning CCY Architects in Aspen, Colorado; several of his home designs were featured in *Architectural Digest* magazine. Called out of this work to the ministry, he graduated with honors from seminary. He pastored Summit Lake Community Church in southwest Colorado for sixteen years and now serves as the associate pastor of Kerrville Bible Church in Kerrville, Texas.

ALSO BY SCOTT CHRISTENSEN

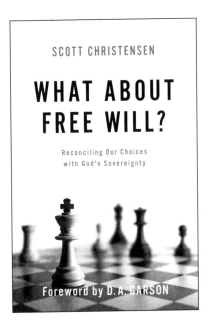

SCOTT CHRISTENSEN

WHAT ABOUT FREE WILL?

Reconciling Our Choices
with God's Sovereignty

Foreword by D. A. CARSON

Free will is a complex topic, but the Bible is clear: God's absolute sovereignty exists alongside our free, responsible choices. Only one view, *compatibilism*, fully embraces this truth.

Making a fresh, scriptural case for compatibilism, Scott Christensen explains the issues involved and addresses arguments on both sides. His absorbing pastoral analysis will help you to develop a new appreciation for the role your choices play in God's sovereign plans and to better understand the Bible's views on evil and suffering, prayer, evangelism, sanctification, and more.

"A clear, intelligent, immensely helpful overview of one of the most confusing conundrums in all of theology. . . . Scott Christensen doesn't sidestep the hard questions. The answers he gives are thoughtful, biblical, satisfying, and refreshingly coherent. Lay readers and seasoned theologians alike will treasure this work."
—**John F. MacArthur**, Grace Community Church

ALSO FROM P&R ON SIN AND EVIL

This book takes dead aim at the heart of ongoing sin. Drawing from two masterful works by John Owen, Kris Lundgaard offers insight, encouragement, and hope for overcoming the enemy within.

"A solid reminder that apart from the grace of God we are far weaker than we can imagine—but greater is he that is in us than he that is in the world."
   —**Bryan Chapell**, Author of *Holiness by Grace: Delighting in the Joy That Is Our Strength*

"Fresh, contemporary, highly readable. Every Christian who is serious about holiness should read this book."
   —**Jerry Bridges**, Author of *Respectable Sins: Confronting the Sins We Tolerate*

Did you find this book helpful?
Consider leaving a review online.
The author appreciates your feedback!

Or write to P&R at editorial@prpbooks.com
with your comments. We'd love to hear from you.